LITIGATION LIBRARY

EXPERT EVIDENCE:
LAW AND PRACTICE

AUSTRALIA
The Law Book Company Ltd.
Sydney : Melbourne : Perth

CANADA
The Carswell Company Ltd.
Agincourt, Ontario

INDIA
N. M. Tripathi Private Ltd.
Bombay
and
Eastern Law House Private Ltd.
Calcutta and Delhi
M.P.P. House
Bangalore

ISRAEL
Steimatzky's Agency Ltd.
Jerusalem : Tel Aviv : Haifa

PAKISTAN
Pakistan Law House
Karachi

Litigation Library

EXPERT EVIDENCE: LAW AND PRACTICE

by

Tristram Hodgkinson, LL.B., LL.M.,
of the Middle Temple, Barrister

WITH A FOREWORD BY
The Right Hon. The Lord Scarman O.B.E

LONDON
SWEET & MAXWELL
1990

Published in 1990 by
Sweet & Maxwell Limited of
183 Marsh Wall, London E14
Computerset in Great Britain by
Promenade Graphics Ltd, Cheltenham
Printed and bound in Great Britain by
BPCC Hazell Books, Aylesbury, Bucks.
Members of BPCC Ltd.

British Library Cataloguing in Publication Data

Hodgkinson, Tristram
   Expert Evidence.
   1. England. Law courts. Expert evidence
   I. Title
   344.20767

ISBN 0–421–37860–3

All rights reserved.
No part of this publication may be
reproduced or transmitted, in any form
or by any means, electronic, mechanical, photocopying,
recording or otherwise, or stored in any retrieval
system of any nature, without the
written permission of the copyright
holder and the publisher, application
for which shall be made to
the publisher.

©
Tristram Hodgkinson
1990

To Frantzianna

FOREWORD

This is a book for the practitioner and the scholar. It is a comprehensive survey of the law and practice governing the admission of expert evidence in the courts, tribunals, official enquiries and other proceedings (including arbitration) where issues arise upon which it is submitted that expert evidence can throw light. Essentially, it is a book of reference, and a very valuable one. If its sheer size is at first sight intimidating, its writing is not. The author has a straightforward clear English style.

Now that our court tribunal systems are being decentralised so as to become more accessible to the public, the publication of this work is timely. Lawyers, and others, who represent litigants and disputants in a great variety of legal proceedings, will be comforted by the presence of the work on their bookshelves. Statute and case law is set out clearly and is accompanied by comment and explanation for which practitioners country-wide will be grateful.

The increasing use in our courts, civil and criminal, of expert evidence is an interesting development. Expert evidence is opinion evidence and often includes hearsay (for example the witness who refers to the findings and opinions of other experts in the same field). Traditional legal principle is that opinion and hearsay evidence is inadmissible. Expert evidence is an exception. One can trace by a study of this work how the courts have, albeit with a certain reluctance and some hesitation, allowed themselves to recognise and develop expert evidence as an exception, an alternative, and an addition, to direct evidence. This development has now reached a stage at which it can be truly said that expert evidence has become a widely used and potent agent for discovering the truth in a great variety of cases.

I congratulate the author on a book whose value will prove as great as the effort that has gone into its preparation. It is a publication which the student, the research scholar, and the practitioner will find offers real assistance. It is an aid to all who one way or another are concerned to get at the truth in legal proceedings where without expert evidence the truth might well lie concealed.

October 1990   Scarman

PREFACE

There is an obvious popular interest in the activities of expert witnesses. It arises in part no doubt out of a fascination with the more macabre aspects of the work of professionals such as pathologists in the investigation of crime, but also perhaps from a natural curiosity about the ways in which scientific or other technical methods can be employed in order to suggest how a particular state of affairs came about. The prodigious number of titles reflecting this interest, to be observed on any station bookstall, has though not been mirrored in the legal sphere. Despite its clear significance in almost all areas of modern litigation, no text has hitherto attempted to describe the legal aspects of expert evidence with any degree of comprehensiveness. Most authors in the field have been non-lawyers, writing guides for those who find themselves called as expert witnesses but who are unfamiliar with the legal process, and require instruction upon how to prepare for trial or to field particular lines of cross-examination once in court. This book is intended primarily for the lawyer whose practice involves the pre-trial preparation of expert evidence or the presentation and questioning of it in court. It may also be of use to other professionals who have a substantial involvement with such evidence, and Chapter 4 provides guidance as to the duties of the expert witness and the practical aspects of writing the report. It is however principally a law book, and assumes some familiarity with legal, particularly evidential legal, concepts.

Expert evidence raises a number of questions of legal principle, arising particularly out of the bisection between the general evidential rules and the fact that the expert is the only witness who is permitted as a matter of course to give evidence of opinion. Those of a theoretical cast of mind will find such issues addressed mainly in the introductory chapter and in Chapters 5 to 10. They will also find, however, that the purpose of such discussion is with the exception perhaps of the first chapter that it has seemed to be a necessary preliminary to the exposition of principles and procedures described for the practitioner. Despite the many issues of principle which expert evidence raises, these prior conceptual questions have not been extensively investigated by others, certainly on this side of the Atlantic.

The first three parts of the book are concerned with the rules according to which, pre-trial and at trial, in civil and criminal proceedings, expert evidence is generally adduced. It is perhaps obvious to state, but nonetheless important to recognise when referring to these parts of the book, that the discussion concerns expert evidence alone, and that much may seem misleading if this is not borne firmly in mind. Chapter 2, thus, is not a comprehensive guide to all pre-trial procedure, and Chapter 8 is not a description of the rule against hearsay as it is applied to witnesses who are not experts. The corollary of this is that rules as to witnesses generally apply to experts where they are not in conflict with specifically expert evidential rules, and the former have not been exhaustively set out here: they are well described in works such as *Phipson* and *Cross*. Principles in civil and criminal cases can be assumed to be the same, with appropriate adjustments for the particular form of the proceedings in question, save where otherwise stated in the text or obviously precluded by the circumstances.

The fourth and fifth parts of the book describe the application of the general rules in specific contexts, and exceptions to those general rules. Part D focuses on particular expert disciplines which are commonly employed in the courts. The discussion does not extend to the scientific or other technical content of those disciplines, however, save where this is necessary for the elucidation of legal principles. The trainee forensic scientist requiring guidance about how to analyse a swab sample must seek it elsewhere. Part E consists of a number or areas of legal practice which are deserving of specific treatment, whether because of their importance in the litigation context, or because they have given rise to unique procedures and rules which are substantially at variance with, or additional to, the general law set out in the first three parts of the book. Readers will doubtless not unanimously agree with the basis upon which the inevitably selective process of inclusion has been executed, particularly if their own special concern has been largely or wholly omitted. Proposals as to areas of legal practice which could profitably be included or given fuller treatment in a future edition would be welcomed. The reader using parts D and E will find some of their contents incomplete without reference to the general rules in parts A, B and C, and must bear with patience the numerous cross-references for this purpose. It has furthermore been impossible to avoid all repetition in parts D and E of the material which precedes them, though this has been obviated by cross-references where practicable.

All the important statutory provisions and rules of court have been quoted in full, and fairly lengthy passages from the cases have been extracted where substantial assistance can be derived from them. It must be appreciated that judicial guidance in the reported decisions frequently appears within a judgment or speech the *ratio decidendi* of which is principally concerned with a question of substantive law, rather than evidential or procedural questions relating to experts. Whether, therefore, a particular decision is authority for the proposition advanced, or merely an indication of good practice, can sometimes be established only by reference to the actual report.

PREFACE

I would like to thank a number of people for their assistance in the preparation of this book. Lord Scarman generously agreed to write the foreword, and the following individuals kindly read particular chapters and made helpful comments upon them: Master Robert Turner (Chapters 2 and 3), Paul Darling (Chapter 20), and Amanda Meusz (Chapter 22). Any errors from which they have not saved me are of course my responsibility alone. The staff at Sweet & Maxwell have been most helpful, and have tolerated with good humour the competing demands of my practice. My greatest debt is though to my wife Frantzianna, whose contributions, both direct and indirect, to the book's completion, in spite of pressing professional commitments, could not be overestimated.

I have endeavoured to state the law as on September 1, 1990.

The Temple, September 13, 1990. Tristram Hodgkinson

CONTENTS

Foreword vii
Preface ix
Table of Cases xxiii
Table of Statutes lv

PART A. INTRODUCTION

1. Introduction 3
   A. The Law Of Evidence 3
      1. A Positive Body Of Rules 3
      2. Relevance And Probative Value 4
   B. The Development Of Expert Evidence 6
      1. Expert Knowledge In The Medieval Courts 6
    2. The Growth Of Witness Evidence: Fact And Opinion 7
      3. The Foundations Of The Modern Law Of Expert Evidence 8
   C. The Nature Of Expert Evidence 9
      1. The Categories Of Expert Evidence 9
      2. Admissibility 10
      3. What Is An Expert? 10
      4. The Contradiction Within Expert Evidence 14
      5. Legal Method And Scientific Method 15
   D. The Limits Of Expert Evidence 16
      1. Fact And Opinion 16
      2. Non Expert Evidence 17
      3. Judicial Notice 22
   E. Specialist Or Personal Knowledge Possesses By The Tribunal 26
      1. Lay Tribunals 26
      2. Special Tribunals 27
      3. The Judge As Specialist Tribunal 28

PART B. PRE-TRIAL PRACTICE AND PROCEDURE

2. Pre-Trial Procedure 31
   I Civil Proceedings 31

CONTENTS

		A.	General	31
			1. County Court	31
			2. Rationale	32
			3. Rules Constitute A Complete Code	33
			4. Methods Of Adducing Expert Evidence Under R.S.C. Order 38 Rule 36	34
		B.	Seeking Pre-Trial Directions	35
			1. General	35
			2. Procedure	36
		C.	Disclosure Of Expert's Report	37
			1. Privilege And Disclosure	39
			2. The Principle Of Disclosure	40
			3. The Extent Of Disclosure	44
			4. Time for disclosure	46
			5. Non-Mutual Disclosure	48
			6. Revocation, Variation And Enforcement	49
		D.	Agreement Not To Seek Directions As To Disclosure	49
		E.	Other Directions	50
			1. Number Of Experts	50
			2. Meeting Of Experts Without Prejudice	51
		F.	Other Methods Of Adducing Expert Evidence	52
			1. Oral Evidence	53
			2. Written Evidence	53
			3. Court Expert	55
		G.	No Property In Expert Evidence	55
			1. Adducing The Expert's Report Of Another Party	55
			2. No Property In An Expert Witness	56
		II.	Criminal Proceedings	56
3.		Court Appointed Experts		60
		A.	The Court Expert	60
			1. Power To Appoint A Court Expert	61
			2. Procedure	62
			3. County Court	64
			4. Use Of Order 40	64
		B.	Power Of The Court To Call Expert Witnesses	65
			1. The General Rule And Its Exceptions	66
			2. Expert Witnesses	67
		C.	Assessors	68
			1. The Power To Appoint Assessors	68
			2. The Nature And Function Of Assessors	70
			3. Expert Evidence Where Assessors Sit	72
			4. Assessors Advise But Do Not Decide	72
			5. Court Of Appeal	73
		D.	Referees	73

		E. Hearings In Chancery Chambers	73
		F. Experts Regularly Appointed By The Courts For Specific Purposes	74
		1. Interpreters	74
		2. Shorthand Writers	76
4.	Preparation And Presentation Of Expert Evidence		79
	A.	Preservation, Inspection, Tests Etc. In Relation To The Subject Matter Of Proceedings	79
		1. Civil Proceedings	79
		2. Criminal Proceedings	82
	B.	Experts' Reports	84
		1. Drafting The Report	85
		2. Agreeing Reports	88
	C.	Duties Of The Expert Witness	89
		1. Evidence Contrary To The Case	90
	D.	Contact With Counsel	92
	E.	Without Prejudice Meetings Of Experts	92
		1. Before Or After Exchange	93
		2. Meeting During A Trial	93
		3. Pre-Trial Without Prejudice Meeting	94
		4. Joint Written Statement	95
		5. The Experts Evidence In Court	97
		6. Conduct Of The Without Prejudice Meeting	98

PART C.   EVIDENCE AT TRIAL

5.	Expert Witness At Trial		103
	A.	Pre-Trial Disclosure And Leave To Adduce Expert Evidence	103
	B.	Competence And Compellability	104
		1. Competence	104
		2. Compellability	104
	C.	The Calling Of Expert Witnesses	106
	D.	Examination In Chief	108
		1. Establishing The Expert's Qualifications	108
		2. Adducing The Expert's Report	109
		3. Refreshing Memory	110
		4. Hostile Witness	111
	E.	Cross Examination	112
		1. Disputed Evidence Must Be Challenged	112
		2. The Tribunal's Role	112
		3. Credit	113
	F.	Evidence After Close Of Case	114
		1. Civil	114

		2. Criminal	115
	G.	Evidence After Trial	116
		1. Civil	116
		2. Criminal	117
6.	The Nature And Admissibility Of Expert Evidence		119
	A.	Nature And Admissibility	119
		1. The Nautre Of Expert Evidence	119
		2. Admissibility	121
	B.	Fields Of Expertise	124
		1. Admissible Fields Of Expertise	125
		2. Appropriate Expertise	127
		3. Novel Sciences: The "Twilight Zone"	131
7.	The Form And Content Of Expert Evidence		135
	A.	Opinion And Fact	136
		1. Facts In Issue	136
		2. Formation And Use Of The Opinion	138
	B.	Opinion And Standards	141
		1. Standards Of Professional Conduct	141
		2. Opinion Concerning Group Reactions	145
		3. Non-Professional Standards	146
	C.	Hypothetical Questions	147
	D.	Questions On An Ultimate Issue	150
		1. Civil Proceedings: Statute	150
		2. Criminal Proceedings	151
		3. Application Of The Rule	153
	E.	The Meaning Of Words	155
		1. Statute	155
		2. Legal Documents	156
		3. Non-Legal Statements	158
	F.	Contract	158
		1. Custom	159
		2. Factual Matrix	160
8.	Hearsay		162
	A.	Hearsay Evidence Of Fact	163
		1. Facts In Issue	163
		2. Fact Extrinsic To The Proceedings: Comparison	169
	B.	Extrinsic Materials And The Expert's Opinion	172
		1. Extrinsic Materials As General Influence Upon Expert's Opinion	173
		2. Extrinsic Materials Specifically Cited	176
	C.	Hearsay Materials Admissible Without Expert Evidence	181
		1. British Pharmacopoeia	181
		2. Dictionaries	181
		3. Others	182

	D.	Admissibility By Statute	182
		1. General	182
		2. Civil Proceedings Involving Children	183
		3. Criminal Proceedings	183
	E.	Adducing Hearsay Evidence Of An Expert At Common Law	183
9.	Privilege And Confidentiality		186
	A.	The Law Of Privilege	186
		1. Communications Between Party And Legal Adviser	188
		2. Privileged Communications With Third Parties	188
		3. Expert Evidence Not Attracting Privilege	193
		4. Party-Party Communications	194
	B.	Professional Confidences Of Expert Witnesses	195
		1. The Principal Rule	195
		2. The Exceptions	196
		3. Public Interest As A Matter Of Law	199
10.	The Evidential Value Of Expert Evidence		203
	A.	Burden And Standard Of Proof	203
		1. Burden Of Proof	203
		2. Standard Of Proof	204
	B.	Weight	205
		1. Admissibility And Weight	205
		2. Conflicting Expert Evidence	206
		3. Opinion Of Fact	207
		4. Weight On Appeal	211
	C.	Bias	213
		1. Perjury	214
11.	Costs And Fees		216
	A.	Civil Proceedings	216
		1. The Necessity For Expert Evidence	216
		2. Costs And Damages	218
		3. Pre-trial Considerations	221
		4. Considerations At Trial	222
		5. The Expert's Fees	223
		6. Assessors And Court Experts	224
		7. Arbitration And Tribunals	224
	B.	Criminal Proceedings	225

PART D.   METHODS OF PROOF

12.	Psychiatric And Psychological Evidence		229
	A.	Criminal Proceedings: Expert Evidence As To The State Of Mind Of The Accused	229
		1. The Abnormality Rule	229

		2. Admissible Psychiatric Evidence	232
		3. Necessity For Expert Evidence	236
		4. Assessment Of The Evidence	236
		5. Evidence Of Disposition: Co-Defendants	238
	B.	Criminal Proceedings: Witness Reliability	240
		1. Psychiatric Evidence As To Witness's Mental Abnormality	240
		2. Normal Witnesses: Psychology	242
		3. Ancillary Scientific Techniques	242
	C.	Civil Proceedings: Sanity	245
13.	Valuation Of Land And Buildings		247
	A.	Admissibility	248
		1. Relevant Considerations	248
		2. Comparables	249
	B.	Weight	252
		1. Method Of Valuation	252
		2. The Tribunal's Own Expertise	254
	C.	Lands Tribunal	256
		1. Pre-Hearing Procedure	256
		2. Admissibility And Weight Of Evidence	258
14.	Forensic Science And Techniques		260
	A.	Criminal Investigation And Proof	260
		1. Fingerprints	261
		2. Tracking Dogs	262
		3. Other Admissible Forensic Scientific Evidence	263
		4. New Forensic Sciences	264
		5. Visual Images Of Suspects	265
	B.	Handwriting	266
		1. Criminal Proceedings	266
		2. Civil Proceedings	269
	C.	Scientific Tests Of Parentage In Civil Proceedings	270
		1. Ordering Scientific Tests	270
		2. The Court's Discretion	274
		3. Standard Of Proof	276
15.	Mathematical, Statistical And Financial Calculations		279
	A.	Actuarial Evidence	279
		1. Actuarial Calculations	279
		2. Admissibility Of Actuarial Evidence	280
		3. Will Acturial Evidence Be More Extensively Received In The Future?	283
	B.	Accountancy	286
	C.	Market Research Surveys	289
16.	Proof Of Foreign Law		294
	A.	General	294

B.	The Exceptions	294
	1. Miscellaneous Statutes	294
	2. Previous Decisions Of The English Courts	294
C.	Proving Foreign Law By Expert Evidence	298
	1. Competence Of Expert Witnesses	298
	2. Form Of Expert Evidence Of Foreign Law	303
	3. Evidence Experts May Give As To Questions Of Foreign Law	304

PART E. SPECIFIC TRIBUNALS

17. Tribunals Not Governed By The Strict Rules Of Evidence — 310
    A. Statutory Tribunals And Inquiries — 310
    B. Industrial Tribunals — 311
    C. Planning Inquiries — 313
       1. Pre-Inquiry Procedure — 314
       2. Procedure At The Inquiry — 315
       3. Admissibility — 317
       4. Weight — 319
    D. Cororner's Report — 320
       1. Admissible Expert Evidence — 320
       2. Procedure And Practice — 321
    E. Arbitrations — 322

18. Specific Commercial Jurisdictions — 325
    A. The Restrictive Practices Court — 325
       1. Adducting Expert Evidence — 325
       2. Trade Witnesses — 327
    B. Admiralty Proceedings — 328
    C. The Commercial Court — 329

PART F. FIELDS OF LITIGATION

19. Medical Reports In Personal Injury Cases — 333
    A. Disclosure Of Reports — 333
       1. Service Of Medical Report By The Plaintiff — 333
       2. Automatic Directions In Personal Injury Actions — 336
       3. Medical Negligence Actions — 338
    B. Preparation Of Medical Reports — 339
       1. Enforcing The Co-operation Of The Party To Be Medically Examined — 339
       2. Conditional Agreement To Examination: Ousting Rules Of Court — 340

		3. Conditional Agreement To Examination: Own Doctor To Be Present	341
		4. Conditional Agreement To Examination: Different Doctor	343
		5. Medical Tests During Examination	344
		6. Joint Examinations	347
		7. Ethical Duty Of The Examining Doctor	347
	C.	Contents Of Medical Reports	347
	D.	Agreeing Medical Reports	348
		1. Procedure	348
		2. Agreed Reports Must Agree	349
		3. Oral Evidence By The Expert	349
		4. Oral Evidence By The Plaintiff	350
		5. Plaintiff's Condition Or Prognosis Changes Before Trail	351
		6. Judge Departs From Agreed Medical Reports	352
		7. Number Of Agreed Reports	352
		8. Adducing The Other Party's Expert's Report In Evidence	353
	E.	Disclosure Of Medical Records	353
	F.	Lodging Of Reports	353
20.	Construction Claims		354
	A.	Official Referees Business	354
		1. Directions As To Disclosure Of Reports	355
		2. Without Prejudice Meetings Of Experts	358
		3. Further Procedural Considerations	358
	B.	Arbitration	258
	C.	Costs And Expert's Fees	360
	D.	Admissibility And Weight	362
		1. Admissibility	362
		2. Weight	364
		3. Expert Evidence As To Negligence	364
		4. Expert Evidence As To Contractual Obligations	367
	E.	Quantum Of Damages	368
21.	Patents		370
	A.	Pre-Trial Procedure	370
		1. Inspection	370
		2. Experiments	372
		3. Directions As To Expert Evidence	373
		4. Court Experts	374
	B.	Admissibility	375
		1. Meaning Of The Specification	376
		2. Obviousness And The Question Of Common General Knowledge	379

		3. Scientific Background Material	380
22.		Matrimonial And Other Proceedings Involving Children	381
	A.	Welfare Reports	381
		1. Ordering The Report	381
		2. Prepatation Of The Report	382
		3. Welfare Officer Attending The Hearing To Give Evidence	386
		4. Departing From The Welfare Officer's Recommendation	387
		5. Independent Social Workers	387
	B.	Other Experts' Reports	390
	C.	Guardian Ad Litem	391
		1. Introduction	391
		2. Role In The Proceedings	392
		3. Official Solicitor	393
		4. Confidentiality Of The Guardian Ad Litem's Report	395
	D.	Other Evidential Considerations	396
		1. Hearsay	396
		2. Privilege And Confidentiality	399
		3. Weight	401
	E.	Child Sexual Abuse	402
		1. Interviews: Forensic Utility	404
		2. Conduct Of Interviews	407
		3. Weight	408
	F.	Blood And Other Scientific Tests Of Paternity	411
23.		Criminal Sentencing	412
	A.	Probation Officers	412
		1. Obtaining A Social Inquiry Report	412
		2. Content Of The Social Inquiry Report	413
		3. Use Of The Report	415
	B.	Medical Reports	416
		1. The Mental Health Act 1983	417
		2. Discretionary Life Imprisonment	418
24.		Drink/Driving Offences	420
	A.	Expert Evidence	420
		1. The Need For Expert Evidence And Its Admissibility	421
		2. Analysis Of Bodily Samples	422
		3. Weight	423
	B.	Blood Samples	424
	C.	Back-Calculation	426
		1. Admissibility	427
		2. Limits To Reliance Upon Back Calculation	429

25.	Obscenity	431
	A. General	431
	B. Admissibility	432
	1. Expert Evidence Inadmissible As To Obscenity	432
	2. Expert Evidence On Factual Issues Prior To Issue Of Obscenity	432
	3. Expert Evidence On The "Public Good" Defence	434

Index   437

Table of Cases

A. (A Minor), *Re* (1979) 10 Fam.Law 114 383
A. *v.* Berkshire County Council [1989] 1 F.L.R. 273; [1989] F.C.R. 184 392
A.A.A.S. *v.* London Aluminium Co. (1920) 37 R.P.C. 153 379
A.A.A.S. fur A.A.S. *v.* London Aluminium Co. Ltd. (1922) 39 R.P.C. 296 376
A., B., C. and D. (Minors) (Wardship: Guardian *ad litem*), *Re* [1988] 2 F.L.R. 500;
    (1988) 18 Fam.Law 385 393
A/S Rendel *v.* Arcos [1937] 3 All E.R. 577; [1936] 1 All E.R. 623; 106 L.J.K.B. 756;
    157 LT. 485; 53 T.L.R. 953; 81 Sol.Jo. 733; 43 Com.Cas. 1; 58 Lloyd L.R.
    287, H.L. 24, 26
A.-W. (Minors), *Re* (1974) 5 Fam.Law 95 .... 390, 402
Abbey *v.* Lill (1829) 5 Bing. 299; 2 Moo. & P. 534; 7 L.J.O.S.C.P. 96; 130 E.R. 1076 .. 130
Abbot *v.* Abbott and Godoy, 4 S.W. & T.R. 254; 29 L.J.P.M. & A. 57; 164 E.R.
    1513 300
Aberdeen Steak Houses Group plc *v.* Ibrahim [1988] I.C.R. 550; [1988] I.R.L.R. 420;
    (1988) 138 New L.J. 151 .... 310, 312
Abinger *v.* Ashton (1873) L.R. 17 Eq. 358; 22 W.R. 582 .... 207, 214
Accountancy Tuition Centre, The *v.* Secretary of State for the Enviroment and
    London Borough of Hackney [1977] J.P.L. 792 317
Adam Steamship Co. Ltd. *v.* London Assurance Co. [1914] 3 K.B. 1256; 83 L.J.K.B.
    1361; 20 Com.Cas. 37; 59 S.J. 42 190
Adams *v.* Canon (1621) 1 Dyer 53b; Ley 68; 73 E.R. 117 214
—— *v.* Peters (1849) 2 Car. 2 Kir. 723, N.P. 159
Adoption Application, *Re* [1990] 1 F.L.R. 412 401
Aegis Blaze, The [1986] 1 Lloyd's Rep. 203; (1986) 130 S.J. 15 190
Agnew *v.* Jobson (1877) 13 Cox C.C. 625; 47 L.J.M.C. 67; 42 J.P. 424 .... 81, 84
Ajami *v.* Comptroller of Customs [1954] 1 W.L.R. 1405; 98 S.J. 803 .... 300, 301
Ainley *v.* Secretary of State for the Environment and Fylde Borough Council [1987]
    J.P.L. 33 319
Aitchison *v.* Lohre (1879) 4 App.Cas. 755; 49 L.J.Q.B. 123; 41 L.T. 323; 28 W.R. 1; 4
    Asp.M.L.C. 168 25
Aitken *v.* McMeckan [1895] A.C. 310 .... 209, 212
Aktieselskabet de Danske Sukkerfabrikker *v.* Bajamar Compania Naviera S.A.;
    Torenia, The [1983] 2 Lloyd's Rep. 210 .... 9, 119, 120, 121, 138, 216, 356
Alcock *v.* Royal Exchange Assurance (1849) 13 Q.B. 292; 18 L.J.Q.B. 121; 12
    L.T.O.S. 473; 13 Jur. 445; 116 E.R. 1275 114
Aldwych Club *v.* Copthall (1862) 185 E.G. 219 .... 249, 250
Alsop *v.* Bowtrell (1619) Cro.Jac. 541; 79 E.R. 464 .... 7, 60
Aluma Systems Inc. *v.* Hunnebeck GmbH [1982] F.S.R. 239 379
American Cyanamid Co. *v.* Ethicon Ltd. [1977] F.S.R. 593; [1978] R.P.C. 667 373,
    378
Amys *v.* Barton [1912] 1 K.B. 40; 81 L.J.K.B. 65; 105 L.T. 619; 28 T.L.R. 29; 5
    B.W.C.C. 117, C.A. 165
Ancrum *v.* Cooperative Wholesale Society (1945) 172 L.T. 248 72
Anderson *v.* The Queen [1972] A.C. 100; [1971] 3 W.L.R. 718; *sub nom.* Anderson
    v. R., 115 S.J. 791; *sub nom.* Anderson *v.* Reginam [1971] 3 All E.R.
    768 .... 210, 211
—— *v.* Wallace (1835) 3 Cl. & F. 26 .... 323, 324
Ann and Mary, The (1843) 2 Wm.Rob. 189; 2 L.T.O.S. 107; 7 Jur. 999; 166 E.R.
    725 72
Arbon *v.* Fussell (1862) 3 F. & F. 152 269

TABLE OF CASES

Arenson v. Arenson. *See* Arenson v. Casson, Beckman Rutley & Co.
—— v. Casson, Beckman Rutley & Co. [1975] 3 W.L.R. 815; 119 S.J. 810; [1975] 3 All E.R. 901; [1976] 1 Lloyd's Rep. 179, H.L.; reversing *sub nom.* Arenson v. Arenson [1973] Ch. 346 .... 323, 359
Armvent Ltd., *Re* [1975] 1 W.L.R. 1679; 119 S.J. 845; [1975] 3 All E.R. 441 169
Arton, *Re* [1896] 1 Q.B. 509; 65 L.J.M.C. 50; 60 J.P. 132; 74 L.T. 249; 44 W.R. 351; 18 Cox 277 .... 53, 303
Aspinall v. Sterling Mansell [1981] 3 All E.R. 866 .... 344, 345, 346
Associated Shipping Services Ltd. v. Department of Private Affairs of the Ruler of Abu Dhabi, *The Independent*, August 14, 1990 301
Assyrian, The (1890) 63 L.T. 91; 6 Asp.M.L.C. 525, C.A. 72
Att.-Gen. v. Birmingham Drainage Board (1908) S.J. 855 217
—— v. Birmingham, Tame and Rea District Draining Board [1912] A.C. 788 67
—— v. Hitchcock (1847) 1 Exch. 91 114
—— v. Horner (No. 2) [1913] 2 Ch. 140; 82 L.J.Ch. 339; 108 L.T. 609; 77 J.P. 257; 29 T.L.R. 451; 57 Sol.Jo. 498; 11 L.G.R. 784, C.A. 182
—— v. Kenny (1959) 94 I.L.T.R. 185 21
—— v. Mulholland; Att.-Gen. v. Foster [1963] 2 Q.B. 477; [1963] 2 W.L.R. 658; 107 S.J. 154; [1963] 1 All E.R. 767, C.A. Petition for leave to appeal to H.L. dismissed *sub nom.* Mulholland v. Att.-Gen.; Foster v. Att.-Gen., *The Times*, March 7, 1963, H.L. 196
—— v. Ringwood Rural District Council (1928) 92 J.P. 65; 26 L.G.R. 174 90
Att.-Gen. (South Australia) v. Brown [1960] A.C. 432; [1960] 2 W.L.R. 588; 104 S.J. 268; [1960] 1 All E.R. 734; 44 Cr.App.R. 100, P.C.; reversing (1959) 33 A.L.J.R. 89 .... 203, 236
Att.-Gen.'s Reference (No. 3 of 1977) [1978] 1 W.L.R. 1123; 122 S.J. 641; [1978] 3 All E.R. 1166; (1978) 67 Cr.App.R. 393 .... 432, 435
Atwell v. Ministry of Public Building and Works [1969] 1 W.L.R. 1074; 113 S.J. 488; [1969] 3 All E.R. 196 .... 51, 218
Australia, The [1927] A.C. 145; 95 L.J.P. 145; 135 L.T. 576; 42 T.L.R. 614; 32 Com.Cas. 82; 17 Asp.M.C. 86 72
Automatic Coil Winder Co. Ltd. v. Taylor Electrical Instruments Ltd. (1943) 60 R.P.C. 111 379
Auty v. National Coal Board [1985] 1 W.L.R. 784; 129 S.J. 249; [1985] 1 All E.R. 930; (1985) 82 L.S.Gaz. 1782 .... 134, 281, 282, 283, 285
Aveling Barford, *Re* [1989] 1 W.L.R. 360; 133 S.J. 512; [1988] 3 All E.R. 1019; (1988) 4 BCC 548; [1989] BCLC 122; 1989 PCC 240 188
Aveson v. Kinnaird (1806) 6 East. 188; 2 Smith. 286 165

B. (A Minor), *Re* [1980] 1 F.L.R. 300 387
——, *Re*, *The Times*, October 21, 1983 392
—— (Adoption by Parent), *Re* [1975] Fam. 127; [1975] 2 W.L.R. 569; *sub nom.* B. (A Minor), *Re* (1974) 119 S.J. 133; (1974) 5 Fam.Law 153; *sub nom.* B. (A Minor) (Adoption: Jurisdiction), *Re* [1975] 2 All E.R. 449 392
B. v. B. and E. [1969] 1 W.L.R. 1800; 113 S.J. 625; *sub nom.* B. v. B. and E. (B. Intervening) [1969] 3 All E.R. 1106 278
—— v. W. (Wardship: Appeal) [1979] 1 W.L.R. 1041; 123 S.J. 536; [1979] 3 All E.R. 83 402
B. (B.R.) v. B. (J.) [1968] P. 466; [1968] 3 W.L.R. 566; *sub nom.* B. v. B. (1968) 112 S.J. 689; *sub nom.* B.R.B. v. J.B. [1968] 2 All E.R. 1023 275
B. (M.) v. B. (R.) (Note) [1968] 1 W.L.R. 1182; 112 S.J. 504; [1968] 3 All E.R. 170 .... 390, 402
Badische v. Levinstein (1887) 12 App.Cas. 710; 52 L.J.Ch. 704; 48 L.T. 822; 31 W.R. 913; reversing (1883) 24 Ch.D. 156 377
Badische Anilin und Soda Fabrik v. Levinstein (1883) 24 Ch.D. 156; 52 L.J.Ch. 704; 48 L.T. 822; 31 W.R. 913 .... 67, 77, 197
Bagnall v. Baker (1972) 17 R.R.C. 387 259
Bainbrigge v. Bainbrigge (1850) 4 Cox 454; 16 L.T.O.S. 245 245

TABLE OF CASES

Baker v. London & South Western Railway Co. (1867) L.R. 3 Q.B. 91; 8 B. & S. 645; 37 L.J.Q.B. 53; 32 J.P. 246; 16 W.R. 126 194
Baldwin and Francis v. Patents Appeal Tribunal [1959] A.C. 663; [1959] 2 W.L.R. 826; 103 S.J. 451; [1959] 2 All E.R. 433; [1959] R.P.C. 221, H.L.; affirming sub nom. R. v. Patents Appeal Tribunal, ex p. Baldwin & Francis [1959] 1 Q.B. 105 .... 24, 70
Ballantine (George) and Son Ltd. v. Ballantyne, Stewart and Co. Ltd. (No. 2) [1959] R.P.C. 273 .... 146, 290
Banque des Marchands de Moscou (Koupetschesky), Re, Moscow Merchants' Trading Co., Re [1958] Ch. 182; [1957] 3 W.L.R. 637; 101 S.J. 798; [1957] 3 All E.R. 182 .... 302, 307
Barnes v. B.P.C. (Business Forms) Ltd. [1975] I.C.R. 390; [1975] 1 W.L.R. 1565; 119 S.J. 776; [1976] 1 All E.R. 237; [1975] I.T.R. 110; [1975] I.R.L.R. 313 106
Baron de Bode's Case (1845) 8 Q.B. 208 .... 304, 306
Barnett v. Cohen [1921] 2 K.B. 461; 96 L.J.K.B. 1307; 125 L.T. 733; 37 T.L.R. 629 322
Barratt v. Harrison (1956) 167 E.G. 761 255
Barton (W.J.) v. Long Acre Securities Ltd. [1982] 1 W.L.R. 398; [1982] 1 All E.R. 465; (1982) 263 E.G. 877 248
Bater v. Bater [1907] P. 333 297
—— v. —— [1951] P. 35; 66 T.L.R. (Pt. 2) 589; 114 J.P. 416; 94 S.J. 533; [1950] 2 All E.R. 458; 48 L.G.R. 466 205
Baugh v. Delta Water Fittings [1971] 1 W.L.R.1 295; 115 S.J. 485; [1971] 3 All E.R. 258 340
Bayerrische Ruckversicherung Aktiengesellschaft v. Clarkson Puckle Overseas Limited, The Times, January 29, 1989 107
Beckwith v. Sydebotham (1807) 1 Comp. 116 .... 8, 131, 137, 148
Benham v. Gambling [1941] A.C. 157; 110 L.J.K.B. 49; 164 L.T. 290; 57 T.L.R. 177; [1941] 1 All E.R. 7; 84 S.J. 703 280
Benmax v. Austin Motor Co. [1955] A.C. 370; [1955] 2 W.L.R. 418; 99 S.J. 129; [1955] 1 All E.R. 326; 72 R.P.C. 39, H.L.; affirming (1953) 70 R.P.C. 284, C.A.; reversing (1953) 70 R.P.C. 143 212
Bennett v. Griffiths (1861) 3 E. & E. 467; 30 L.J.Q.B. 98; 3 L.T. 745; 7 Jur.N.S. 284; 9 W.R. 332; 121 E.R. 517 81
Bent v. Allot (1850) Cary 94 187
Berd v. Lovelace (1577) Cary 62; 21 E.R. 33 188
Berthon v. Logham (1817) 2 Stark. 258 .... 143, 146, 149
Bett v. Menzies (1862) 10 H.L.C. 117; 31 L.J.Q.B. 233; 9 Jur.(N.S.) 29; 7 L.T. 110; 11 W.R. 1 378
Betts, Re (1887) 19 Q.B.D. 39; affirmed by (1888) 13 A.C. 570; 58 L.J.Q.B. 113; 59 L.T. 734; 53 J.P. 164; 37 W.R. 259; 4 T.L.R. 770, H.L. 81
Bevan Investments Ltd. v. Blackhall and Struthers [1973] 2 N.Z.L.R. 45 .... 145, 366
—— v. —— (No. 2) [1978] 2 N.Z.L.R. 97 368
Bigsby v. Dickinson (1876) 4 Ch.D. 24; 46 L.J.Ch. 280; 35 L.T. 679; 25 W.R. 89, C.A. 79
Bird v. Adams [1972] Crim.L.R. 174 203
—— v. Keep [1918] 2 K B 692; 87 L.J.K.B. 1199; 118 L.T. 633; 34 T.L.R. 513; 62 S.J. 666; 11 B.W.C.C. 133, C.A. 182, 322
Birrell v. Dryer (1884) 9 App.Cas. 345; 51 L.T. 130; 5 Asp.M.L.C. 267, H.L. 137, 144
Bishop v. Wiltshire County Council (1984) 14 Fam.Law 118 390
Blakemore, Re (1845) 14 L.J.Ch. 336 81
Blunt v. Park Lane Hotel Ltd. [1942] 2 K.B. 253; 111 L.J.K.B. 706; 167 L.T. 359; 58 T.L.R. 356; [1942] 2 All E.R. 187 187
Blyth v. Blyth (No. 2) [1966] A.C. 643; [1966] 2 W.L.R. 634; 110 S.J. 148; [1966] 1 All E.R. 524, H.L.; reversing sub nom. Blyth v. Blyth and Pugh [1965] P. 411 266
Bolam v. Friern Hospital Management Committee [1957] 1 W.L.R. 582; 101 S.J. 357; [1957] 2 All E.R. 118 .... 15, 141
Bolton v. Mahadeva [1972] 1 W.L.R. 1009; 116 S.J. 564; [1972] 2 All E.R. 1322 .... 219, 220, 361

xxv

Bond v. Barrow [1902] 1 Ch. 353; 71 L.J.Ch. 246; 86 L.T. 10; 50 W.R. 295; 9 Manson 69
Bone v. Bone (Practice Note) [1953] 1 W.L.R. 1310; 97 S.J. 746; [1953] 2 All E.R. 879 391
xrBoots v. Cowling (1903) 88 L.T. 539; 67 J.P. 195; 1 L.G.R. 884; 20 Cox 420; 19 T.L.R. 370 181
Borowski v. Quayle [1966] V.R. 382 124
Borthwick v. Vickers [1973] R.T.R. 390; [1973] Crim.L.R. 317 26
Bottomley v. Ambler (1877) 38 L.T.(N.S.) 545; 26 W.R. 566, C.A. 324
Bourne v. Swan & Edgar Ltd. [1903] 1 Ch. 211; 72 L.J.Ch. 168; 51 W.R. 213; 19 T.L.R. 59; 47 S.J. 92; 20 R.P.C. 105 153
Bowden v. Bowden (1917) 62 S.J. 105; 42 L.J. 402 210
Bradford City Metropolitan Council v. K. (Minors) [1989] F.C.R. 738; (1989) 153 J.P.N. 787; [1989] 2 F.L.R. 507 .... 397, 398, 399
Braid Investments Ltd. v. East Lothian District Council (1981) 259 E.G. 1088 255
Brailey v. Rhodesia Consolidated Ltd. [1910] 2 Ch.D. 95; 79 L.J.Ch. 494; 102 L.T. 805; 54 S.J. 475 .... 298, 299
Brandao v. Barnett (1846) 12 Cl. & Fin. 787; 3 C.B. 519 .... 22, 25
Bratty v. Att.-Gen. (Northern Ireland) [1963] A.C. 386; [1961] 3 W.L.R. 965; 105 S.J. 865; [1961] 3 All E.R. 523; 46 Cr.App.R. 1 236
Bremer v. Freeman (1857) 1 Deane Ecc.Rep. 192 307
Bremer Handelsgesellschaft mbH v. Toepfer [1980] 2 Lloyd's Rep. 643 27
Bright's Trustee v. Sellar [1904] 1 Ch. 369 77
Brisbane City Council v. Att.-Gen. for Queensland [1979] A.C. 411; [1978] 3 W.L.R. 299; 122 S.J. 506; [1978] 3 All E.R. 30 157
Bristol Corporation v. Aird [1913] A.C. 241; [1911–13] All E.R.Rep. 1076; 108 L.T. 434; 77 J.P. 209; 29 T.L.R. 360, H.L. 256
Bristow v. Sequeville (1850) 5 Exch. 275; 19 L.J.Ex. 289; 14 Jur. 674 .... 298, 299
British Celanese v. Courtaulds (1933) 50 R.P.C. 63 .... 81, 370, 372, 373, 377
British Hartford Fairmont Syndicate Ltd. v. Jackson (1932) 49 R.P.C. 495; affirmed (1934) 51 R.P.C. 254 114
British Ore Concentration Syndicate Ltd. v. Minerals Separation Ltd. (1909) 26 R.P.C. 124 380
British Syphon Co. Ltd. v. Homewood (No. 2) [1956] 1 W.L.R. 1190; 100 S.J. 633; [1956] 2 All E.R. 897; [1956] R.P.C. 225, 330 371
British Thompson-Houston v. Duram (1920) 37 R.P.C. 121 371
British Thomson-Houston Co. Ltd. v. Tungstalite Ltd. (1938) 55 R.P.C. 280; 4 All E.R. 177; 82 S.J. 909 .... 373, 379
British Xylonite Co. Ltd. v. Fibrenyle Ltd. [1959] R.P.C. 252, C.A.; reversing [1959] R.P.C. 90 .... 370, 372
Brock v. Kellock (1861) 43 Griff. 38; 30 L.J.Ch. 498; 4 L.T. 572; 25 J.P. 595; 7 Jur.N.S. 789; 9 W.R. 939, L.J.J. 207, 210
Broder v. Saillard (1876) 24 W.R. 456 73
Brooks v. Steele and Currie (1897) 14 R.P.C. 46 376
Broughton v. Whittaker [1944] 1 K.B. 269; 113 L.J.K.B. 248; 170 L.T. 298; 60 T.L.R. 247; 108 J.P. 75; [1944] 2 All E.R. 544 154
Brown v. Houston [1901] 2 K.B. 855; 70 L.J.K.B. 902; 85 L.T.1 60; 17 T.L.R. 683, C.A. 222
—— v. Matthews [1990] 2 W.L.R. 879 399
—— v. Merton, Sutton and Wandsworth Area Health Authority (Teaching) [1982] 1 All E.R. 650 50
Brunswick (Duke) v. King of Hanover (1844) 6 Beav. 1; 13 L.J.Ch. 107; 2 H.L.Cas. 1; 8 J.R. 253 309
Bryant v. Foot (1867) L.R. 2 Q.B. 161; 7 B. & S. 725; 36 L.J.Q.B. 65; 16 L.T. 55; 31 J.P. 229; 15 W.R. 421; affirmed (1868) L.R. 3 Q.B. 497 24
Buccleuch (Duke) (1889) 15 P.D. 86 328
—— v. Metropolitan Board of Works (1872) L.R. 5 H.L. 418; 41 L.J.Ex. 137; 27 L.T. 1 324

Buckingham v. Daily News Ltd. [1956] 2 Q.B. 534; [1956] 3 W.L.R. 375; 100 S.J. 528; [1956] 2 All E.R. 904 364
Buckley v. Rice Thomas (1554) 1 Plowd. 118; 75 E.R. 182 .... 7, 10, 15, 122, 151
Buerger v. New York, 96 L.J.K.B. 930; 137 L.T. 431; 43 T.L.R. 601 306
Burditt v. Roberts (Note) [1986] R.T.R. 391; (1986) 150 J.P. 344; [1986] Crim.L.R. 636 423
Burgess v. Purchase & Sons (Farms) [1983] Ch. 216; [1983] 2 W.L.R. 361; [1983] 2 All E.R. 4 247
Burk v. Wooley (unreported), 1980 C.A. 774 351
Burmah Oil v. Governor & Co. of the Bank of England [1980] A.C. 1090; [1979] 3 W.L.R. 722; 123 S.J. 786; *sub nom.* Burmah Oil Co. v. Bank of England and Att.-Gen. [1979] 3 All E.R. 700, H.L.; affirming [1979] 1 W.L.R. 473; [1989] 2 All E.R. 461 .... 197, 199, 200
Bushell v. Secretary of State for the Environment [1981] A.C. 75; [1980] 3 W.L.R. 22; 125 S.J. 168; [1980] 2 All E.R. 608; (1980) 40 P. & C.R. 51; (1980) 78 L.G.R. 269; [1980] J.P.L. 458, H.L. 315, 317, 318
Bushell's Case (1670) Vaug. 135; Freem.K.B. 1; 1 Mod.Rep. 119; 124 E.R. 1006 .... 7, 8
Bustros v. White (1876) 1 Q.B.D. 423; 45 L.J.Q.B. 642; 34 L.T. 865; 24 W.R. 721 189
Bute (Marquis) v. James (1886) 33 Ch.D. 157; 55 L.J.Ch. 658; 55 L.T. 133; 34 W.R. 754 74
Buttes Gas and Oil Co. v. Hammer (No. 3); Occidental Petroleum Corp. v. Buttes Gas and Oil Co. (No. 2) [1982] A.C. 888; [1981] 3 W.L.R. 787; 125 S.J. 776; [1981] 3 All E.R. 616; [1981] Com.L.R. 257, H.L.; reversing [1980] 3 W.L.R. 668; *sub nom.* Buttes Gas and Oil Co. v. Hammer and Occidental Petroleum Co. [1981] Q.B. 223 .... 189, 199, 200, 309

C., *Re* (1982) 3 F.L.R. 95 396
C. (A Minor), *Re* [1984] 5 F.L.R. 419 .... 388, 389, 393
C. (An Infant), *Re, The Times,* November 10, 1986 .... 390, 394
C. (Wardship: Independent Social Worker), *Re* (1985) 15 Fam.Law 56; *sub nom.* C. (Minors), *Re* (1984) 81 L.S.Gaz. 2464 .... 389, 390
C. v. C. (1982) 126 S.J. 243 386
—— v. —— (Child Abuse: Access) [1988] 1 F.L.R. 462; [1988] F.C.R. 458; (1988) 18 Fam.Law 254 .... 403, 408
—— v. —— (Child Abuse: Evidence) [1988] F.C.R. 147; (1988) 152 J.P.N. 446; [1987] 1 F.L.R. 321; [1987] 151 J.P.N. 734 .... 403, 405, 408, 409
—— v. C. and C. (Legitimacy: Photographic Evidence) [1972] 1 W.L.R. 1335; 116 S.J. 663; [1972] 3 All E.R. 577 21
Cable v. Dallaturca (1977) 121 J.P. 795 .... 49, 103, 222
Cadman v. Cadman (1981) 125 S.J. 791; (1982) 3 F.L.R. 275; (1982) 12 Fam.Law 82 .... 386, 389
Cafell v. Cafell [1984] F.L.R. 169; (1984) 14 Fam.Law 83 385
Calcraft v. Guest [1898] 1 Q.B. 759; [1895–99] All E.R.Rep. 346; 67 LJ.Q.B. 505; 78 L.T. 283; 46 W.R. 420; 42 S.J. 343, C.A. 186
Calder (John) (Publications) v. Powell [1965] 1 Q.B. 509; [1965] 2 W.L.R. 138; 129 J.P. 136; 109 S.J. 71; [1965] 1 All E.R. 159 .... 432, 435
Callis v. Gunn [1964] 1 Q.B. 495; [1963] 3 W.L.R. 931; 128 J.P. 41; 107 S.J. 831; [1963] 3 All E.R. 677; 48 Cr.App.R. 36 261
Callwood v. Callwood [1960] A.C. 659; [1960] 2 W.L.R. 705; 104 S.J. 327; [1960] 2 All E.R. 1 304
Camden v. I.R.C. [1914] 1 K.B. 641; [1914] W.N. 5; 83 L.J.K.B. 509; 110 L.T. 173; 30 T.L.R. 225; 58 S.J. 219, C.A. 155, 157
Campbell v. Hopkins (1933) 50 R.P.C. 213 380
—— v. Rickards (1883) 5 B. & Ad. 840; 2 L.J.K.B. 204; 2 N. & M. 542 146
—— v. Tameside Metropolitan Borough Council [1982] Q.B. 1065; [1982] 3 W.L.R. 74; 126 S.J. 361; [1982] 2 All E.R. 791; (1982) 80 L.G.R. 700 199
Canadian Pacific Railway v. Jackson (1915) 52 S.C.R. 281 (Can.) 180
Capitaine Le Goff, The [1981] 1 Lloyd's Rep. 322 110

TABLE OF CASES

Carl Zeiss Stiftung v. Rayner and Keeler Ltd.; Rayner & Keeler v. Courts [1967] 1
  A.C. 853; sub nom. Carl Zeiss Stiftung v. Rayner & Keeler [1966] 3 W.L.R.
  125; 110 S.J. 425; [1966] 2 All E.R. 536; [1967] R.P.C. 497, H.L.; reversing
  [1965] Ch. 596, C.A.; reversing [1964] R.P.C. 299 26
Carnell Computer Technology Ltd. v. Unipart Group Ltd. (1988) 45 B.L.R. 100 .... 95, 96
Carreras Ltd. v. Levy (D.E. & J.) (1970) 215 E.G. 707 254
Carter v. Boehm (1766) 1 W.Bl. 593; (1766) 3 Burr. 1905 .... 3, 8, 140
Cartwright v. Cartwright and Anderson (1878) 26 W.R. 684 .... 298, 299
—— v. Sculcoates Union [1900] A.C. 150; 69 L.J.Q.B. 403; 82 L.T. 157; 48 W.R.
  394; 64 J.P. 229; 16 T.L.R. 238 250
Castle v. Cross [1984] 1 W.L.R. 1372; 128 S.J. 855; [1985] 1 All E.R. 87; [1985]
  R.T.R. 62; [1984] Crim.L.R. 682; (1984) 81 L.S.Gaz. 3596 423
Catnic Components Ltd. v. Hill and Smith Ltd. [1981] F.S.R. 60; [1982] R.P.C. 237,
  H.L.; reversing [1979] F.S.R. 405 378
Causton v. Mann Egerton (Johnsons) [1974] 1 W.L.R. 162; 117 S.J. 877; [1974] 1 All
  E.R. 453; [1974] 1 Lloyd's Rep. 197 .... 39, 187
Cement Makers' Federation Agreement, Re [1961] 1 W.L.R. 581; 105 S.J. 284;
  [1961] 2 All E.R. 75; [1961] L.R. 2 R.P. 241 326
Cementation Construction v. Keaveney (1988) 138 New L.J. 242 216
Chamberlain v. Stoneham (1889) 24 Q.B.D. 113; 59 L.J.Q.B. 95; 61 L.T. 560; 38
  W.R. 107; 6 T.L.R. 21, D.C. 217
Chantrey Martin (a Firm) v. Martin [1953] 2 Q.B. 286; [1953] 3 W.L.R. 459; 97 S.J.
  539; [1953] 2 All E.R. 691; 46 R. & I.T. 516 196
Chapman v. Walton (1833) 10 Bing. 57; 3 Moo. & S. 389; [1824–34] All E.R.Rep.
  384; 2 L.J.C.P. 210; 131 E.R. 826 .... 143, 144
Chatenay v. Brazilian Submarine Telegraph Co. [1891] 1 Q.B. 79; 60 L.J.Q.B. 295;
  63 L.T. 739; 39 W.R. 65 158
Chaurand v. Angerstein (1791) Peake 43 158
Chenowith, Re, Ward v. Donelly [1902] 2 Ch. 488; 71 L.J.Ch. 739; 86 L.T. 890; 50
  W.R. 633; 18 T.L.R. 702 25
Chin Keow v. Government of Malaysia [1967] 1 W.L.R. 813; 111 S.J. 333 144
Chinnery v. Basildon Development Corporation [1970] R.V.R. 530 258
Chocolate and Sugar Confectionery Reference, Re (1967) L.R. 6 R.P. 338; [1967] 1
  W.L.R. 1175; 111 S.J. 617; sub nom. Chocolate and Sugar Confectionery
  Resale Price Reference, Re [1967] 3 All E.R. 261 .... 326, 327
City Equitable Fire Insurance Co. Ltd., Re [1925] 1 Ch. 407; 94 L.J.Ch. 407; 94
  L.J.Ch. 445; 133 L.T. 520; 40 T.L.R. 853; 17 Ll.L.Rep. 225 288
City of Berlin, The [1908] P. 110; 77 L.J.P. 76; 98 L.T. 298; 11 Asp.M.L.C. 4,
  C.A. 72, 329
Clarence, Re, 54 S.J. 117 269
Clark v. Adie (1877) 2 App.Cas. 423; 46 L.J.Ch. 598; 37 L.T. 1; 26 W.R. 45 380
—— v. Clark [1939] P. 228; 108 L.J.P. 92; 161 L.T. 46; 55 T.L.R. 550; 83 S.J. 280;
  [1939] 2 All E.R. 59 209
—— v. —— (1970) 114 S.J. 318 387
—— v. Gill (1854) 1 K. & J. 19; 2 Eq.Rep. 1108; 23 L.J.Ch. 711; 2 W.R. 652; 69 E.R.
  351 223
—— v. Ryan (1960) 103 C.L.R. 486 .... 12, 129, 131, 137, 138, 140
Clarke v. Martlew [1973] 1 Q.B. 58; [1972] 3 W.L.R. 653; 116 S.J. 618; [1972] 3 All
  E.R. 764 341
Clarkson v. Winkley (1987) 151 J.P.N. 526; (1987) 1 F.L.R. 33 .... 383, 384
Clay Cross (Quarry Services) Ltd. v. Fletcher [1979] I.C.R. 1; [1978] 1 W.L.R. 1429;
  122 S.J. 776; [1979] 1 All E.R. 474; sub nom. Fletcher v. Clay Cross (Quarry
  Services) Ltd. [1978] 3 C.M.L.R. 1, C.A.; reversing [1977] I.C.R. 868 313
Clayton v. Hardwick Colliery Co. (1915) 32 T.L.R. 159; 85 L.J.K.B. 292; W.C. &
  Ins.Rep. 33; 114 L.T. 241; 60 S.J. 138 24
Cliff's Trusts, Re [1892] 2 Ch. 229; 61 L.J.Ch. 220; 106 L.T. 14; 56 S.J. 91; 28 T.L.R.
  57 158
Clode v. Clode; sub nom. C. v. C. (1982) 12 Fam.Law 175; (1982) 3 F.L.R. 360 386
Cluer v. Chiltern Works (Engineering) (1975) 119 S.J. 85 341

Clyde, The (1856) Sw. 23; L.T. 121 210
Coca-Cola Company of Canada Ltd. *v.* Pepsi-Cola Company of Canada Ltd. (1942) 59 R.P.C. 127 181
Cockburn *v.* Edwards (1881) 18 Ch.D. 449; 51 L.J.Ch. 46; 45 L.T. 500; 30 W.R. 446, C.A. 219, 361
Coles *v.* Coles (1866) L.R. 1 P. & D. 70; 35 L.J.P. 40; 13 L.T. 608; 14 W.R. 290 111
Collier *v.* Simpson (1831) 5 C. & P. 73 175
Collins *v.* Barking Corporation [1943] K.B. 419; 112 L.J.K.B. 406; 107 J.P. 117; 169 L.T. 12; 59 T.L.R. 257; [1943] 2 All E.R. 249 154
Colls *v.* Home & Colonial Stores Ltd. [1904] A.C. 179; 73 L.J.Ch. 484; 90 L.T. 687; 53 W.R. 30; 20 T.L.R. 475 67
Coloured Asphalte Co. Ltd. *v.* British Asphalt and Bitumen Ltd. (1935) 53 R.P.C. 89 371
Compton Group Ltd. *v.* Estates Gazette Ltd. (1977) 36 P. & C.R. 148; (1977) 244 E.G. 799 247
Concentrated Foods *v.* Champ [1944] 1 K.B. 342; 113 L.J.K.B. 417; 170 L.T. 302; 60 T.L.R. 194; 108 J.P. 271; [1944] 1 All E.R. 272 154
Concha *v.* Murrietta (1889) 40 Ch.D. 543; 60 L.T. 798 .... 294, 307
Consolidated Pneumatic Tool Co. *v.* Ingersoll Sergeant Drill Co. (1908) 25 R.P.C. 574 222
Conway *v.* Rimmer [1968] A.C. 910; [1968] 2 W.L.R. 998; 112 S.J. 191; [1968] 1 All E.R. 874; reversing [1967] 1 W.L.R. 1031 200
Cooper-King *v.* Cooper-King [1900] P. 65; 69 L.J.P. 33 302
Corbett *v.* Corbett (Orse. Ashley) [1971] P. 83; (1969) 113 S.J. 982 105
Corisand Developments *v.* Druce & Co. (1978) 248 E.G. 315, 407, 504 248
Cosgrove *v.* Baker (unreported), 1979 C.A., No. 744 340
Countrywide Properties *v.* Moore, *The Times*, January 30, 1987 222
Courtenay-Evans *v.* Passey & Associates [1986] 1 All E.R. 932; (1985) 1 Const.L.J. 285; (1985) 135 New L.J. 603 .... 37, 355
Cracknell *v.* Willis [1988] A.C. 450; [1987] 3 W.L.R. 1082; 131 S.J. 1514; [1987] 3 All E.R. 801; [1988] R.T.R. 1; (1988) 86 Cr.App.R. 196; (1987) 137 New L.J. 1062 422
Crocour *v.* Salter (1881) 18 Ch.D. 30 25
Crofts *v.* Marshall (1836) 7 C. & P. 597 156
Crofton Investment Trust Ltd. *v.* Greater London Rent Assessment Committee [1967] 2 Q.B. 955; [1967] 3 W.L.R. 256; 111 S.J. 334; [1967] 2 All E.R. 1103; *sub nom.* Crofton Investment Trust *v.* Rent Assessment Committee for Greater London [1967] R.V.R. 284 311
Crompton (Alfred) Amusement Machines Ltd. *v.* Customs and Excise Commissioners (No. 2) [1974] A.C. 405; [1973] 3 W.L.R. 268; 117 S.J. 602; [1973] 2 All E.R. 1169, H.L.; affirming on different grounds [1972] 2 Q.B. 102, C.A.; reversing (1971) 115 S.J. 587 188
Cronkshaw *v.* Rydeheard (1969) 113 S.J. 673; [1969] Crim.L.R. 493 425
Crosfield *v.* Techno-Chemical Laboratories (1913) 30 R.P.C. 297; (1913) 29 T.L.R. 378 .... 157, 377
Culver *v.* Sekulich (1959) 80 Wyoming 437 148
Curtis *v.* March (1858) 3 H. & N. 866; 28 L.J.Ex. 36; 32 L.T.O.S. 149; 23 J.P. 663; 4 Jur.N.S. 1112; 157 E.R. 719 24
—— *v.* Peek (1864) 29 J.P. 70; 13 W.R. 230 Ex.Ch. 156
Curtler *v.* London Tramway Company Ltd., *The Times*, February 13, 1891 204
Customglass Boats Ltd. *v.* Salthouse Brothers Ltd. [1976] R.P.C. 589 .... 166, 177, 289, 291, 292, 293

D. (A Minor) (Wardship: Sterilisation), *Re* [1976] F. 185; [1976] 2 W.L.R. 279; 119 S.J. 696; [1976] 1 All E.R. 326 394
D. (Infants), *Re* [1970] 1 W.L.R. 599; 114 S.J. 188; [1970] 1 All E.R. 1088; 68 L.G.R. 183 .... 202, 401

TABLE OF CASES

D. v. National Society for the Prevention of Cruelty to Children [1978] A.C. 171; [1977] 2 W.L.R. 201; 121 S.J. 119; [1977] 1 All E.R. 589; 76 L.G.R. 5 .... 195, 198, 199, 200, 201, 401
Darby v. Ouseley (1856) 1 H. & N. 1; 25 L.J.Ex. 227; 2 Jur.N.S. 497; 156 E.R. 1093 .. 175
Dass v. Masih [1968] 1 W.L.R. 756; 112 S.J. 295; *sub nom.* Dass (An Infant) v. Masih [1968] 2 All E.R. 226 .... 183, 399
Davey v. Harrow Corporation [1958] 1 Q.B. 60; [1957] 2 W.L.R. 941; 101 S.J. 405; [1957] 2 All E.R. 305 24
Davidson v. Davidson (1860) 22 S.C. 749 213
Davie v. Edinburgh Corporation, 1953 S.C. 34; 1953 S.L.T. 54 ...... 6, 113, 136, 181, 208
Davy-Chiesman v. Davy-Chiesman [1984] Fam. 48; [1984] 2 W.L.R. 291; 127 S.J. 805; [1984] 1 All E.R. 321; (1984) 81 L.S.Gaz. 44 221
Dawson v. Lunn [1986] R.T.R. 234; (1985) 149 J.P. 491 .... 427, 428
—— v. Murex [1942] 1 All E.R. 483 208
Dear v. D.P.P. [1988] R.T.R. 148; (1988) 87 Cr.App.R. 181; [1988] Crim.L.R. 316 ... 425
De Beéche v. South American Stores (Gath and Chaves) Ltd. [1935] A.C. 148; [1934] All E.R.Rep. 284 306
Debenham v. King's College Cambridge (1884) Cab. & El. 438; 1 T.L.R. 170 N.P. 223
Dellow's Will Trusts, *Re*, Lloyds Bank v. Institute of Cancer Research [1964] 1 W.L.R. 451; 108 S.J. 156; [1964] 1 All E.R. 771 205
Demuth Ltd.'s Application, *Re* (1948) 65 R.P.C. 342 181
Dennis v. Codrington (1580) Cary 100 188
Devonald v. Rosser & Sons [1906] 2 K.B. 728; 75 L.J.K.B. 688; 95 L.T. 232; 22 T.L.R. 682 159
Dickenson v. Dickenson (1982) 13 Fam.Law 174; (1983) 133 New L.J. 233 387
Dickie v. Saari (1973) 43 D.L.R. (3d) 207 131
Dickins v. Randerson [1901] 1 K.B. 437; 70 L.J.K.B. 344; 84 L.T. 204; 65 J.P. 262; 19 Cox. 643; 17 T.L.R. 224 181
D.P.P. v. A. & B.C. Chewing Gum [1968] 1 Q.B. 159; [1967] 3 W.L.R. 493; 131 J.P. 373; 111 S.J. 331; [1967] 2 All E.R. 504 .... 133, 146, 152, 154, 433, 434
—— v. Frost [1989] R.T.R. 11; [1989] Crim.L.R. 154; (1989) 153 J.P. 405; (1989) 153 J.P.N. 371 421
—— v. Jordan [1976] 3 W.L.R. 887; [1976] 3 All E.R. 775; (1976) 64 Cr.App.R. 33; [1977] Crim.L.R. 109; *sub nom.* R. v. Staniforth; R. v. Jordan [1977] A.C. 699 .... 432, 434
—— v. Kilbourne [1973] A.C. 729; [1973] 2 W.L.R. 254; 117 S.J. 144; [1973] 1 All E.R. 440; 57 Cr.App.R. 381; [1973] Crim.L.R. 235, H.L.; reversing *sub nom.* R. v. Kilbourne [1972] 1 W.L.R. 1365 4
—— v. Parkin [1989] Crim.L.R. 379 423
—— v. Whyte [1972] A.C. 849; [1972] 3 W.L.R. 410; 116 S.J. 583; [1972] 3 All E.R. 12; 57 Cr.App.R. 74; [1972] Crim.L.R. 556, H.L.; reversing *sub nom.* Corbin v. Whyte [1972] Crim.L.R. 234 432
Distillers Co. (Biochemicals) Ltd. v. Times Newspapers Ltd.; Same v. Phillips [1975] Q.B. 613; [1974] 3 W.L.R. 728; 118 S.J. 864; [1975] 1 All E.R. 41 198
Divan Estates Ltd. v. Rossette Sunshine Savouries Ltd. (1982) 261 E.G. 364 249
Doe v. Bower (1851) 16 Q.B. 805 115
Doncaster and Retford Co-operative Societies' Agreement, *Re* (Practice Note) (1960) L.R. 2 R.P. 129 327
Dost Aly Khan (*In the Goods of*) (1880) 6 P.D. 6; 49 L.J.P. 78; 29 W.R. 80 .... 301, 302
Dove v. Banham's Patent Locks [1983] 1 W.L.R. 1436; 127 S.J. 748; [1983] 2 All E.R. 833; (1983) 133 New L.J. 538 14
Douglas Packing Co. v. Evans (W.) & Co. Ltd. (1929) 46 R.P.C. 493 379
Dowling v. Pontypool Co. (1874) L.R. 18 Eq. 714; 43 L.J.Ch. 761 156
Drew v. Josolyne (1888) 4 T.L.R. 717 223
Dreyfus (Camille and Henry) Foundation Inc. v. I.R.C. [1956] A.C. 39; [1955] 3 W.L.R. 451; 99 S.J. 560; [1955] 3 All E.R. 97; [1955] T.R. 229; 48 R. & I.T. 551; 34 A.T.C. 208; 36 T.C. 126; 1955 S.L.T. 335, H.L.; affirming [1954] Ch. 672, C.A.; affirming [1954] T.R. 69 305
Dryden v. Johnson [1961] Crim.L.R. 551 421

Du Barrié v. Livette (1791) Peake 77 .... 75, 190
Dubai Bank Ltd. v. Galadari, *The Independent*, June 20, 1990 309
Duchess Di Sora v. Phillips (1863) 10 H.L.C. 624 158
Duff Development Corporation v. Republic of Kelantan Government [1924] A.C.
    797; [1924] All E.R.Rep. 1; 93 L.J.Ch. 343; 131 L.T. 676; 40 T.L.R. 566; 68
    S.J. 559, H.L. 26
Dugdale v. Kraft Foods Ltd. [1977] I.R.L.R. 160; Industrial Tribunal rehearing
    following [1977] I.C.R. 48; [1977] 1 W.L.R.1288; (1979) 11 I.T.R. 309;
    [1977] 1 All E.R. 454 .... 27, 311, 312
Duncan v. Cammell Laird [1942] A.C. 624; 111 L.J.K.B. 406; 166 L.T. 366; 58
    T.L.R. 242; 86 S.J. 287; [1942] 1 All E.R. 587; 73 Ll.L.Rep. 109 200
Durrell v. Bederley (1816) Holt N.P. 283 8

E., Re, *The Times*, April 2, 1990 408
E. (A Minor) (Child Abuse: Evidence), Re [1987] 1 F.L.R. 269; [1987] F.L.R. 169;
    (1987) 151 J.P.N. 590 .... 403, 405, 407, 409
Eachus v. Leonard (1968) 106 S.J. 918 .... 88, 351, 352
Eads v. Williams (1854) L.J.Ch. 531 323
Earwicker v. London Graving Dock Company Ltd. [1916] 1 K.B. 970; 85 L.J.K.B.
    905; W.C. & Ins.Rep. 137; 114 L.T. 821; 32 T.L.R. 377 .... 70, 71
East London Rail Company v. Conservators of the River Thames (1904) 90 L.T. 347;
    68 J.P. 302; 20 T.L.R. 378 168
Eastern Counties Railway Co., Re (1863) 2 New Rep. 441 324
Eastern Counties Railway Company v. Eastern Union Railway (1863) 3 De G.J. & S.
    610; 2 New Rep. 538; 46 E.R. 773 67
Edelstein v. Schuler & Co. [1902] 2 K.B. 144; 71 L.J.K.B. 572; 87 L.T. 204; 50 W.R.
    493; 7 Com.Cas. 172; 18 T.L.R. 507 25
Edgington v. Fitzmaurice (1886) 29 Ch.D. 459; 55 L.J.Ch. 650; 53 L.T.3 69; 33 W.R.
    911; 50 J.P. 52 215
Edmeades v. Thames Board Mills [1969] 2 Q.B. 67; [1969] 2 W.L.R. 668; 113 S.J. 88;
    [1969] 2 All E.R. 127; [1969] 1 Lloyd's Rep. 221 .... 276, 340
Edler v. Victoria Press Manufacturing Co. (1910) 27 R.P.C. 114 .... 371, 372
Edwards v. Edwards (1986) 1 F.L.R. 187 .... 383, 386
El-G. v. El-G. (Minors: Adoption) (1982) 12 Fam.Law 251; (1983) 4 F.L.R. 421 389
Ellis-Don v. Parking Authority of Toronto (1978) 21 Build.L.R. 98 368
Emery v. Ware 5 Ves. 846 324
English Exporters (London) Ltd. v. Eldonwall Ltd.; Same v. Same [1973] Ch. 415;
    [1973] 2 W.L.R. 435; 117 S.J. 224; [1973] 1 All E.R. 726; (1972) 25 P. & C.R.
    379 .... 139, 163, 164, 169, 172, 174, 180, 251, 252
Enoch and Zaretsky, Bock and Co., Re [1910] 1 K.B. 327; [1908–10] All E.R.Rep.
    625; 79 L.J.K.B. 363; 101 L.T. 801 .... 66, 323, 324
Esso Petroleum v. Southport Corporation [1956] A.C. 218; [1956] 2 W.L.R. 81; 120
    J.P. 54; 100 S.J. 32; [1955] 3 All E.R. 864; 54 L.G.R. 91; *sub nom.* Southport
    Corporation v. Esso Petroleum Co. [1955] 2 Lloyd's Rep. 655, H.L. 70
Evans v. London Hospital Medical College (University of London) [1981] 1 W.L.R.
    184; 125 S.J. 48; [1981] 1 All E.R. 715 214

F. (Minors) (Sexual Abuse: Discretionary Jurisdiction in Wardship), Re; *sub nom.*
    Cleveland County Council v. A.; Same v. B. [1988] 2 F.L.R. 123; (1988) 18
    Fam.Law 255; [1988] F.C.R. 679; (1988) 152 J.P.N. 636 410
F. v. F. (No. 2) [1968] P. 506; [1968] 2 W.L.R. 190; 112 S.J. 214; [1968] 1 All E.R.
    242 276
Fairmount Investments v. Secretary of State for the Environment (1976) 120 S.J. 801;
    [1976] 2 All E.R. 865; *sub nom.* Fairmount Investments and Southwark
    London Borough Council v. Secretary of State for the Environment [1976] 1
    W.L.R. 1255, H.L.; affirming (1975) 119 S.J. 866 319
Faraday v. Tamworth Union (1919) 86 L.J.Ch. 436; 15 L.G.R. 258; 81 J.P. 81 223
Fennell v. Jerome Property Maintenance Ltd., *The Times*, November 26,
    1986 .... 165, 242, 243, 244

TABLE OF CASES

Fenwick v. Bell (1844) 1 C. & K. 312	154
Ferrers' Case (1760) 19 How.St.Tr. 885; Fost 138; 19 State Tr. 885, 946, H.L.	147
Ffinch v. Combe [1894] P. 191	270
52, 54 and 56 Osnaburgh Street, Re [1957] C.L.Y. 1947	250
Finnegan (J.F.) Ltd. v. Sheffield City Council (1988) 43 B.L.R. 124	368
Fisher v. Wellfair (P.G.); Fox v. Wellfair (P.G.) (1981) 125 S.J. 413; [1981] 2 Lloyd's Rep. 514; [1981] Com.L.R. 140; (1982) 19 Build.L.R. 52; (1982) 263 E.G. 589, 657, C.A.; [1979] I.C.R. 834	323, 359, 363
Fitzwalter Peerage, The (1842–44) 10 Cl. & Fin. 193; 8 E.R. 716, 997, H.L.	269
Fleet v. Murton (1871) L.R. 7 Q.B. 126; 41 L.J.Q.B. 49; 26 L.T. 181; 20 W.R. 97	144
Fletcher v. Autocar and Transporters [1968] 2 Q.B. 322; [1968] 2 W.L.R. 743; 112 S.J. 96; [1968] 1 All E.R. 726; [1968] 1 Lloyd's Rep. 317	281, 282, 284, 285
—— v. Clay Cross (Quarry Services) Ltd. See Clay Cross Quarry Services v. Fletcher.	
—— v. Winter (1862) 3 F. & F. 138	142
Florida Hotels Pty. Ltd. v. Mayo (1965) 113 C.L.R. 588	367
Flower v. Lloyd [1876] W.N. 230	371
Folkes v. Chadd (1782) 3 Doug. 157; 99 E.R. 589	3, 8, 10, 12, 122, 129, 139, 214, 229
Fomento Ltd. v. Selsdon Fountain Pen Co. Ltd. [1958] 1 W.L.R. 45; 102 S.J. 51; [1958] 1 All E.R. 11; [1958] R.P.C. 8, H.L.; reversing in part [1956] R.P.C. 344, C.A.; restoring [1956] R.P.C. 260	288
Footwear Reference (No. 2), Re (1968) L.R. 6 R.P. 398; [1968] 1 W.L.R. 1355; 112 S.J. 638; sub nom. Footwear Resale Price Reference, Re [1968] 3 All E.R. 129	327
Ford v. Tynte (1864) De G.J. & S. 127; 3 New Rep. 676; 10 L.T. 209; 10 Jur.(N.S.) 429; 12 W.R. 613; 46 E.R. 323	73
Ford Motor Co. Ltd. v. Nawaz [1987] I.C.R. 434; [1987] I.R.L.R. 163; (1987) 84 L.S.Gaz. 741	313
Forte and Co. v. General Accident Life Assurance Ltd. (1987) 54 P. & C.R. 9; [1986] 2 E.G.L.R. 115; (1986) 279 E.G. 1227	247
Foster v. Globe Venture Syndicate Ltd. [1900] 1 Ch. 811; 69 L.J.Ch. 375; 82 L.T. 353; 44 S.J. 314	26
Fox v. Chief Constable of Gwent. See R. v. Fox.	
—— v. Wellfair (P.G.). See Fisher v. Wellfair (P.G.); Fox v. Wellfair (P.G.).	
Foxon v. Foxon [1981] C.L.Y. 1778	387
Frankenburg v. Famous Lasky Film Service [1931] 1 Ch. 428	218
Freeman v. Chester Rural District Council [1911] 1 K.B. 783	256
French Kier Developments v. Secretary of State for the Environment [1977] 1 All E.R. 296; (1977) 244 E.G. 967	318
Friend v. London, Chatham & Dover Railway Co. (1877) 2 Ex.D. 437; 46 L.J.Ex. 696; 36 L.T. 729; 25 W.R. 735	190
Frith v. Frith and Paice [1896] P. 74; 65 L.J.P. 53	21
Frye v. United States (1923) 293 F. 1013	132
Fryer v. Bunney (1982) 263 E.G. 158	368
—— v. Gathercole (1849) 4 Exch. 262	22
Fuld, In the Estate of, Hartley v. Fuld (Fuld intervening) [1965] 1 W.L.R. 1336; 109 S.J. 335; [1965] 2 All E.R. 653	74
G., Re [1963] 2 Q.B. 73; [1963] 2 W.L.R. 69; 106 S.J. 958; sub nom. G. (T.J.) (An Infant), Re, 127 J.P. 144; [1963] 1 All E.R. 20; 61 L.G.R. 139	396
G. (A Minor), Re, The Times, July 20, 1987	205
—— (Child Abuse: Standard of Proof), Re [1987] 1 W.L.R. 1461; 131 S.J. 1550; (1988) 18 Fam.Law 129; [1988] 1 F.L.R. 314; (1987) 84 L.S.Gaz. 3415	411
G. (Minors) (Child Abuse: Evidence), Re [1988] F.C.R. 81; [1987] 1 F.L.R. 310; (1987) 151 J.P.N. 702	403, 404
Gadd v. Manchester (Mayor) (1892) 67 L.T. 569	377
Gaimster v. Marlow [1984] Q.B. 218; [1984] 2 W.L.R. 16; 127 S.J. 842; [1985] 1 All E.R. 82; [1984] R.T.R. 49; (1984) 78 Cr.App.R. 156; [1984] Crim.L.R. 176; (1984) 81 L.S.Gaz. 360	423
Gallagher Estates v. Walker (1973) 28 P. & C.R. 113	254, 259
Gannet, The [1900] A.C. 234; 69 L.J..P. 49; 82 L.T. 329; 9 Asp.M.L.C. 43, H.L.	72

Garton v. Hunter [1969] 2 Q.B. 37; [1968] 2 W.L.R. 86; 133 J.P. 162; (1968) S.J. 924; [1969] 1 All E.R. 451; 67 L.G.R. 229; 15 R.R.C. 145, C.A.; reversing 13 R.R.C. 375 248
Gaskin v. Liverpool City Council [1980] 1 W.L.R. 1549; 124 S.J. 498 401
Gaze v. Holden (1983) 266 E.G. 998 249
Gazelle, The (1842) 1 W.Rob. 471 329
George v. Davies [1911] 2 K.B. 445; 80 L.J.K.B. 924; 104 L.T. 648; 27 T.L.R. 415; 55 S.J. 481 25
General Accident Fire and Life Assurance Co. v. Tanter; Zephyr, The [1985] 2 Lloyd's Rep. 529, C.A.; reversing [1984] 1 W.L.R. 100; 127 S.J. 733; [1984] 1 All E.R. 35; [1984] 1 Lloyd's Rep. 58; [1984] L.M.C.L.Q. 376; (1984) 134 New L.J. 35 .... 187, 194
General Electric Co. (of U.S.A.) v. General Electric Co. [1972] 1 W.L.R. 729; 116 S.J. 412; [1972] 2 All E.R. 507; [1973] R.P.C. 297, H.L.; reversing sub nom. G E Trade Mark, Re [1970] F.S.R. 113 .... 166, 289
General Electric Trade Mark [1969] R.P.C. 418 .... 126, 290
General Tire and Rubber Co. Ltd. v. Firestone Tyre and Rubber Co. Ltd. [1975] 1 W.L.R. 819; 119 S.J. 389; [1975] 2 All E.R. 173; [1975] F.S.R. 273; [1976] R.P.C. 197, H.L.; varying [1974] F.S.R. 122, C.A.; affirming [1973] F.S.R. 79; after appeal to C.A. on preliminary point [1972] R.P.C. 457 375
Getty (Sarah C.) Trust, Re; Getty v. Getty and Treves [1985] Q.B. 956; [1985] 3 W.L.R. 302; 129 S.J. 523; [1985] 2 All E.R. 809; (1985) 135 New L.J. 532; (1985) 82 L.S.Gaz. 2823 188
Gibbs v. Bartlett, *The Times*, April 20, 1989 116
Gilson v. Howe (unreported), 1970 C.A. No. 46 .... 88, 350, 352
Glenister v. Glenister [1945] P. 30; [1945] 1 All E.R. 513; 114 L.J.P. 69; 172 L.T. 250; 109 J.P. 194; 43 L.G.R. 250, D.C. 27
Goblet v. Beechey (1829) 3 Sim. 24 156
Gold v. Patman and Fotheringham [1958] 1 W.L.R. 697; 102 S.J. 470; [1958] 2 All E.R. 497; [1958] 1 Lloyd's Rep. 587, C.A.; reversing [1957] 2 Lloyd's Rep. 319 157
Goods of Bonelli, The, Re (1875) 1 P.D. 69 298
Gordon v. Thorpe [1986] R.T.R. 358; [1986] Crim.L.R. 61 .... 209, 424
Gosford v. Alexander]1902] 1 I.R. 139 .... 113, 139, 172
Gossage v. Gossage and Heaton, 78 S.J. 551 301
Graigola Merthyr v. Swansea Corporation [1928] 1 Ch. 31; [1927] W.N. 30 .... 52, 90, 218
Grant v. Downs (1976) 135 C.L.R. 674 191
Graphic Arts Co. v. Hunters Ltd. (1910) 27 R.P.C. 677 150
Gray v. Wilson (1865) 35 L.J.C.P. 123 324
Great Western Railway Co. v. Carpalla [1909] 2 Ch. 471 223
Greaves and Co. Ltd. v. Baynham Meikle and Partners [1975] 1 W.L.R. 1095; 119 S.J. 372; [1975] 3 All E.R. 99; [1975] 2 Lloyd's Rep. 325, C.A.; affirming [1974] 1 W.L.R. 1261 .... 145, 366
Gredley (Investment Developments) Co. v. London Borough of Newham (1973) 26 P. & C.R. 400 259
Greville v. Chapman (1844) 5 Q.B. 731; 1 Dav. & Mer. 553; 13 L.J.Q.B. 172; 2 L.T.O.S. 419; 8 Jur. 189; 114 E.R. 1425 147
Guaranty Trust of New York v. Hannay & Co., 87 L.J.K.B. 1223 306
Gumbley v. Cunningham [1989] A.C. 281; [1989] 2 W.L.R. 1; 133 S.J. 84; [1989] R.T.R. 49; (1989) 88 Cr.App.R. 273; [1989] 1 All E.R. 5; [1989] Crim.L.R. 297; (1988) 138 New L.J. 356, H.L.; affirming [1988] Q.B. 170 .... 134, 426, 427, 428, 429
Guppys (Bridport) Ltd. v. Sandoe; Same v. Moyle; Same v. Radcliffe; Same v. Spencer (1975) 30 P. & C.R. 69; 235 E.G. 689 256
Guppys Properties Ltd. v. Knott; Guppys Properties Ltd. v. Strutt (1977) 245 E.G. 1023 252
Gurney v. Langlands (1822) 5 B. & Ald. 330; 106 E.R. 1212 269

H., Re (1987) 17 Fam.Law 155	410
H. (A Minor), Re; K. v. K. (1990) 134 S.J. 21; (1989) 153 J.P. 498; [1989] F.C.R. 356; (1989) 153 J.P.N. 803; [1989] 2 F.L.R. 313	398
H. (Conciliation: Welfare Reports), Re (1986) 130 S.J. 128; [1986] 1 F.L.R. 476; (1986) 16 Fam.Law 193; (1986) 83 L.S.Gaz. 525	383, 384
H. (Minors) (Child Abuse: Evidence), Re [1987] 1 F.L.R. 332; (1987) 151 J.P.N. 718	403, 409
—— (Welfare Reports), Re [1980] 2 F.L.R. 172	385
H. v. H. (Child Custody) (1983) 127 S.J. 578; (1984) 14 Fam.Law 112	383
—— v. —— (Welfare Officer) (1982) 126 S.J. 310; (1982) 12 Fam.Law 178; [1983] 4 F.L.R. 119	387
—— v. Schering Chemicals Ltd. [1983] 1 W.L.R. 143; 127 S.J. 88; [1983] 1 All E.R. 849	143, 163, 182
Hall v. Avon Area Health Authority (Teaching) [1980] 1 W.L.R. 481; 124 S.J. 293; [1980] 1 All E.R. 516	341, 342, 347
Halvanon Insurance v. Jewett Duchesne (International) [1987] 1 FTLR 503; [1987] 4 C.L. 245	217
Hambridge v. Harrison (1973) 117 S.J. 343; sub nom. Hambridge v. Harrison [1973] 1 Lloyd's Rep. 572	349, 352
Hammington v. Berker Sportcraft Ltd. [1980] I.C.R. 248	311, 312
Hammond v. Bradstreet (1854) 10 Ex. 390; 2 C.L.R. 1195; 23 L.J.Ex. 332; 23 L.T.O.S. 271; 2 W.R. 625; 156 E.R. 496	182
Harbinger, The (1852) 8 L.T. 612; 16 Jur. 729	67
Harding v. Hayes (1874) 118 S.J. 736; [1974] Crim.L.R. 713	156
Harewood Hotels v. Harris [1958] 1 W.L.R. 108; 102 S.J. 67; [1958] 1 All E.R. 104	248
Hargreaves v. Bretherton [1959] 1 Q.B. 45; [1958] 3 W.L.R. 463; 102 S.J. 637; [1958] 3 All E.R. 122	213
Hasman v. Secretary of State for the Home Office [1983] A.C. 280	198
Harmonides, The [1903] P. 1	210
Harmony Shipping Co. S.A. v. Saudi Europe Line; Same v. Orri (Trading as Saudi Europe Line); Same v. Davies [1981] 1 Lloyd's Rep. 377, C.A.; reversing [1979] 1 W.L.R. 1380; 123 S.J. 691; [1980] 1 Lloyd's Rep. 44; sub nom. Harmony Shipping Co. S.A. v. Davis [1979] 3 All E.R. 177	56, 105, 106, 193
Harrison v. Liverpool Corporation [1948] 2 All E.R. 449	352
Hatch v. Lewis (1861) 2 F. & F. 467; 7 H. & N. 367; 30 L.J.Ex. 26; 7 Jur.(N.S.) 1085; 5 L.T. 254; 10 W.R. 58	149
Hattersley v. Hodgson (1905) 21 T.L.R. 178; 22 R.P.C. 229	73
Hawkes, Re [1898] 2 Ch. 1; 67 L.J.Ch. 284; 78 L.T. 336; 46 W.R. 445	188
Haynes v. Doman [1899] 2 Ch. 13; 68 L.J.Ch. 419; 80 L.T. 569	154
Heather v. P.E. Consulting Group [1973] Ch. 189; [1972] 3 W.L.R. 833; 116 S.J. 824; [1973] 1 All E.R. 8; [1972] T.R. 237; 48 T.C. 293, C.A.; affirming [1972] 2 W.L.R. 918	287
Henaff v. Henaff [1966] 1 W.L.R. 598; 110 S.J. 269	309
Henthorn v. Fisk (unreported), 1980, C.A. No. 776	348, 351
Herald of Free Enterprise: appeal by Captain Lewry, The Independent, December 18, 1987	145
Hickmott v. Dorset County Council (1977) 35 P. & C.R. 195; [1977] J.P.L. 715; 243 E.G. 671	255, 259
Hill v. Baxter [1958] 1 Q.B. 277; [1958] 2 W.L.R. 76; 122 J.P. 134; 102 S.J. 53; [1958] 1 All E.R. 193; 56 L.G.R. 117; 42 Cr.App.R. 51	89, 236, 238
—— v. Clifford [1907] 2 Ch. 236; 76 L.J.Ch. 627; 97 L.T. 266; 23 T.L.R. 601, C.A.; on appeal [1908] A.C. 12; 77 L.J.Ch. 91; 98 L.T. 64, H.L.	169
Hilleary and Taylor, Re (1887) 36 Ch.D. 262; 56 L.J.Ch. 758; 56 L.T. 867; 35 W.R. 705; 3 T.L.R. 642, C.A.	77
Hindmarch, Re (1867) L.R. 1 P. & D. 307; 36 L.J.P. 24; 15 L.T. 391	269
Hinds v. London Transport Executive [1979] R.T.R. 103	36, 124, 140, 348
Hindson v. Ashby [1896] 2 Ch. 1; 65 L.J.Ch. 515; 74 L.T. 327; 45 W.R. 252, C.A.; 60 J.P. 484	67

TABLE OF CASES

Hodgkiss v. Hodgkiss & Walker (1984) 128 S.J. 332; [1984] J.P.N. 283; [1984] F.L.R. 563; (1985) Fam.Law 87; (1984) 81 L.S.Gaz. 658 275
Hodgson v. Trapp [1988] 3 W.L.R. 1281; 132 S.J. 1672; [1988] 3 All E.R. 870; (1988) 38 New L.J. 327, H.L.; reversing (1988) 18 Fam.Law 60 281
Hogg v. Belfast Corporation [1919] 2 Ir.R. 305 256
Holland Dredging (U.K.) v. Dredging and Construction Co. and Imperial Chemical Industries (Third Party) (1987) 37 Build.L.R. 1 367
Holmes v. Holmes (Holmes, by his Guardian, intervening) [1966] 1 W.L.R. 187; 110 S.J. 309; sub nom. H. v. H. (H, by his Guardian, intervening) [1966] 1 All E.R. 356n. 275
Hope and Ward v. Hope (unreported), 1981, C.A. No. 415 351
Hopes and Lavery v. Advocate (H.M.) [1960] Crim.L.R. 566; 1960 S.C.(J.) 104; 1960 S.L.T. 264 83
Hornal v. Neuberger Products [1957] 1 Q.B. 247; [1956] 3 W.L.R. 1034; 100 S.J. 915; [1956] 3 All E.R. 970 205
Horne v. Poland [1922] 2 K.B. 364 144
—— v. Mackenzie (1839) 6 Cl. & F. 682; Macl. & Rob. 977; 7 E.R. 834, H.L. 111
Horsford, Re (1874) L.R. 3 P. & D. 211; 44 L.J.P. 9; 31 L.T. 553; 23 W.R. 211 270
Hough v. London Express Newspaper Ltd. [1940] 2 K.B. 507; 109 L.J.K.B. 524; 163 L.T. 162; 56 T.L.R. 758; [1940] 3 All E.R. 31 19
Huddleston v. Control Risks Information Services Ltd. [1987] 1 W.L.R. 701; 131 S.J. 776; [1987] 2 All E.R. 1035; (1987) 84 L.S.Gaz. 1494 81
Hudson v. Bridge (1903) 88 L.T. 550; 67 J.P. 186; 1 L.G.R. 400; 19 T.L.R. 369 181
Hughes v. Ingersoll-Rand Co. Ltd. [1977] F.S.R. 406 374
Hunter v. Mann [1974] Q.B. 767; [1974] 2 W.L.R. 742; 118 S.J. 171; [1974] 2 All E.R. 414; [1974] R.T.R. 338; 59 Cr.App.R. 37; [1974] Crim.L.R. 260 . 194, 196, 199
Hutchinson v. Harris (1978) 10 Build.L.R. 19 .... 219, 220, 361
—— v. Hutchinson (1981) 2 F.L.R. 167 387
Hyundai Shipbuilding & Heavy Industries Co. Ltd. v. Pournaras; Same v. Bouboulina Shipping S.A. [1978] 2 Lloyd's Rep. 502 161

Imperial Group plc v. Morris (Philip) & Co. Ltd. [1984] R.P.C. 293 .... 134, 290, 291, 292
Independent Broadcasting Authority v. E.M.I. Electronics and B.I.C.C. Construction (1980) 14 Build.L.R. 1, H.L.; affirming (1978) 11 Build.L.R. 29 .... 145, 366
Ingram v. Percival [1969] 1 Q.B. 548; [1968] 3 W.L.R. 663; (1968) 133 J.P. 1; 112 S.J. 722; [1968] 3 All E.R. 657 26
Insurance Company of Pennsylvania v. Grand Union Ins. Co., Lloyd's List, November 3, 1989 .... 160, 161
International de Lavaud v. Stanton Ironworks Co. Ltd. (1941) 58 R.P.C. 177 373
Investors in Industry Commercial Properties Ltd. v. South Bedfordshire District Council; Ellison & Partners and Hamilton Associates (Third Parties) [1986] Q.B. 1034; [1986] 2 W.L.R. 937; [1986] 1 All E.R. 787; (1985) 5 Con.L.R. 1 .... 364, 365
Ireland v. Taylor [1949] 1 K.B. 300; [1949] L.J.R. 305; 65 T.L.R. 3; 92 S.J. 408; [1948] 2 All E.R. 450 136
Iron Master, The (1859) Sw. 441; 166 E.R. 1206 .... 207, 210
Itter (decd.), Re, Dedman v. Godfrey [1950] P. 130; 66 T.L.R. (Pt. 1) 45; 93 S.J. 805; [1950] 1 All E.R. 68 270

J. (A Minor) (Expert Evidence), Re, The Times, July 1990 390
—— (Wardship), Re (1988) 18 Fam.Law 91; [1988] 1 F.L.R. 65 276
J.D. (Wardship), Re [1984] 5 F.L.R. 359 .... 393, 394
J.S. (A Minor), Re [1981] Fam. 22; [1980] 3 W.L.R. 984; 124 S.J. 881; [1980] 1 All E.R. 1061; (1980) 10 Fam.Law 121 .... 204, 205, 275, 277
—— (An Infant), Re [1959] 1 W.L.R. 1218; 124 J.P. 89; 104 S.J. 15; [1959] 3 All E.R. 856 .... 395, 396

TABLE OF CASES

J. v. C. [1970] A.C. 668; [1969] 2 W.L.R. 540; [1969] 1 All E.R. 788; sub nom. C. (An Infant), Re (1969) 113 S.J. 164 211
—— v. J. (1978) 9 Fam.Law 91 387
Jabbour (F. & K.) v. Custodian of Israeli Absentee Property [1954] 1 W.L.R. 139; 98 S.J. 45; [1954] 1 All E.R. 145; [1953] 2 Lloyd's Rep. 760 309
Jackson v. Minister of Pensions [1946] 2 All E.R. 500 310
James v. James, ex rel., May 21, 1919 76
Jeffereys v. Hutton (1956) 168 E.G. 203 249
Johns-Manville Corporation's Patent [1967] F.S.R. 327; [1967] R.P.C. 479 376
Johnson v. Agnew [1980] A.C. 367; [1979] 2 W.L.R. 487; 123 S.J. 217; [1979] 1 All E.R. 883; (1979) 38 P. & C.R. 424; (1979) 251 E.G. 1167, H.L.; affirming [1978] Ch. 176 175
—— v. Kershaw (1847) 1 De G. & Sm. 260; 9 L.T.O.S. 216; 11 Jur. 553; 63 E.R. 1059 .... 163, 287
Johnston v. Cheape (1817) 5 Dow. 247 323
Jones v. Davies [1914] 3 K.B. 549 219
—— v. Griffith [1969] 1 W.L.R. 795; 113 S.J. 309; [1969] 2 All E.R. 1015; 6 K.I.R. 472 .... 87, 350
—— v. National Coal Board [1957] 2 Q.B. 55; [1957] 2 W.L.R. 760; 101 S.J. 319; [1957] 2 All E.R. 155 113
Joyce v. Yoemans [1981] 1 W.L.R. 549; 125 S.J. 34; [1981] 2 All E.R. 21 212
Jozwiak v. Sadek [1954] 1 W.L.R. 275; 98 S.J. 94; [1954] 1 All E.R. 3 19

K. (Infants), Re. See Official Solicitor v. K.
K.S.M. v. C.G. and M.C.C. (1988) 18 Fam.Law 173 390
Kaiser (An Infant) v. Carlswood Glassworks Ltd. (1965) 109 S.J. 537 351
Kaliszewska v. Clague (J.) and Partners (1984) C.I.L.L. 131; (1984) Const.L.J. 137; (1984) 5 Con.L.R. 62 364
Kashich v. Kashich [1951] W.N. 557; sub nom. Kashick v. Kashick, 116 J.P. 6 75
Keane v. Mount Vernon Colliery Co. Ltd. [1933] A.C. 309 28
Kelly v. London Transport Executive [1982] 1 W.L.R. 1055; 126 S.J. 262; [1982] 2 All E.R. 842 .... 87, 348
Kender v. St. John Mildmay [1938] A.C. 1 201
Kennard v. Ashman (1894) 10 T.L.R. 213 67
Kenning v. Eve Construction Ltd. [1989] 1 W.L.R. 1189 .... 41, 91, 187, 188
Kentucky Fried Chicken (G.B.) Ltd. v. Secretary of State for the Environment and Borough of Lambeth [1977] J.P.L. 727; (1977) 245 E.G. 839 319
Kidd (Archie) v. Sellick (1977) 20 R.R.C. 250; (1977) 243 E.G. 135 259
Kierman v. Willcock [1972] R.T.R. 270; [1972] Crim.L.R. 248 426
Kingston Cotton Mill Co. (No. 2), Re [1896] 2 Ch. 279 288
Kirby Hall, The (1883) 8 P.D. 71 72
Kirkham-Woodcraft v. Kirkham-Woodcraft (1984) Fam.Law 57 384
Kirkup v. British Railways Engineering; Priestly v. Same; Painter v. Same [1983] 1 W.L.R. 1165; [1983] 3 All E.R. 147, C.A.; affirming [1983] 1 W.L.R. 190; 126 S.J. 730; [1983] 1 All E.R. 855 .... 33, 42, 44, 46, 47, 48
Kleinwort Benson v. Barbrak; Same v. Choithram (T.) & Sons (London); Same v. Chemical Importation and Distribution State Enterprises; Same v. Shell Markets (M.E.); Myrto, The (No. 3) [1987] A.C. 597; [1987] 2 W.L.R. 1053; 131 S.J. 594; [1987] 2 All E.R. 289; [1987] 1 FTLR 43; [1987] 2 Lloyd's Rep. 1, H.L. 355
Klingemann, in the Goods of, Re (1862) 3 S. & T. 18; 32 L.J.P. 16; 8 L.T. 712; 27 J.P. 263; 11 W.R. 218 304
Knight's Motors v. Secretary of State for the Environment and Leicester City Council [1984] J.P.L. 584 318
Koning Willem II, The [1908] P. 125 .... 70, 72
Krajina v. Tass Agency (of Moscow) [1949] W.N. 309; 93 S.J. 539; [1949] 2 All E.R. 274 304

TABLE OF CASES

L. (An Infant), Re [1968] P. 119; [1967] 3 W.L.R. 1645; 111 S.J. 908; sub nom. L., Re [1968] 1 All E.R. 20, C.A.; affirming [1968] P. 119; [1967] 3 W.L.R. 1149; 111 S.J. 717 .... 275, 278, 394
L. v. L. (1968) 112 S.J. 840, C.A.; reversing (1968) 112 S.J. 294; The Times, March 5, 1968 275
Lach v. Williamson (1957) 108 L.J. 60; 2 R.R.C. 347; 171 E.G. 275 259
Lacon v. Higgins (1822) Stark. 178; Dow. & Ry.N.P. 38 304
Ladd v. Marshall [1954] 1 W.L.R. 1489; 98 S.J. 870; [1954] 3 All E.R. 745 116
Lane v. Willis (1971) 116 S.J. 102; [1972] 1 All E.R. 430 .... 340, 343
Lazard v. Midland Bank [1933] A.C. 289; [1932] All E.R.Rep. 571; 102 L.J.K.B. 191; 148 L.T. 242; 49 T.L.R. 94; 76 S.J. 888, H.L. 303, 308
Lee v. South West Thames Regional Health Authority [1985] 1 W.L.R. 845; 128 S.J. 333; [1985] 2 All E.R. 385; (1985) 135 New L.J. 438 .... 192, 193
Leete v. Leete and Stevens [1984] Fam.Law 21 387
Lego System Aktieselskab v. Lego M. Lemelstrich Ltd. [1983] F.S.R. 155 .... 166, 289
Lewis v. Port of London Authority (1914) 111 L.T. 776; 58 S.J. 686; 7 B.W.C.C. 577, C.A. 136
—— v. R. (1987) 88 F.L.R. 104 264
Lively v. City of Munich [1976] 1 W.L.R. 1004; 120 S.J. 719; [1976] 3 All E.R. 851 105
Lloyd v. Guibert (1865) L.R. 1 Q.B. 115; 6 B. & S. 100; 35 L.J.Q.B. 74; 13 L.T. 602; 2 Mar.L.C. 283; 122 E.R. 1134, Exch. 305
Lloyd Cheynham & Co. Ltd. v. Littlejohn & Co., 1986 PCC 389; [1987] BCLC 303 .... 287, 288
Lloyd's Bank v. Fox [1989] I.C.R. 80; [1989] I.R.L.R. 103; [1989] L.S.Gaz. February 1, 41 313
Locker and Woolf Ltd. v. Western Australian Insurance Co. Ltd. (1935) 153 L.T. 334 159
London and General Bank (No. 2), Re [1895] 2 Ch. 673 289
London and North-East Railway v. Berriman [1946] A.C. 278 155
London County Council v. Tobin [1959] 1 W.L.R. 354; 123 J.P. 250; 103 S.J. 272; [1959] 1 All E.R. 649; 57 L.G.R. 113; 10 P. & C.R. 79, C.A.; affirming sub nom. Tobin v. London County Council (1957) 8 P. & C.R. 453 258
Longley (James) & Co. v. South West Thames Regional Health Authority (1983) 127 S.J. 597; (1984) 25 Build.L.R. 56; (1983) 80 L.S.Gaz. 2362 .... 217, 222, 224, 324, 359, 361, 363
Lovatt v. Tribe (1862) 3 F. & F. 9 246
Lovell and Christmas v. Wall (1911) 104 L.T. 85 .... 155, 156
Lowery (Christopher Russell) v. Queen, The [1974] A.C. 85; [1973] 3 W.L.R. 235; [1973] 3 W.L.R. 235; sub nom. Lowery v. R., 117 S.J. 583; 58 Cr.App.R. 35; [1973] Crim.L.R. 523; sub nom. Lowery v. Queen, The [1973] 3 All E.R. 662, P.C.; affirming sub nom. R. v. Lowery [1972] V.R. 939 239
Lucas v. Williams & Sons [1892] 2 Q.B. 113; 61 L.J.Q.B. 595; 66 L.T. 706 .... 21, 22

M. Re, The Independent, January 11, 1990 202
——, Re [1990] 2 F.L.R. 36 401
M. (A Minor) (Child Abuse: Evidence), Re (Note) [1988] F.C.R. 47; [1987] 1 F.L.R. 293; (1987) 151 J.P.N. 654 .... 403, 406
—— (An Infant) (Adoption: Parental Consent), Re [1973] 1 Q.B. 108; [1972] 3 W.L.R. 531; 116 S.J. 373; [1972] 3 All E.R. 321 .... 39, 196, 197, 395, 396
—— (Minors) (Confidential Documents), Re [1987] 1 F.L.R. 46; (1986) 16 Fam.Law 336 .... 400, 401
M. v. M. (1989) Fam.Law 393 382
M. (D.K.) v. M. (S.V.) and G. (M. Intervening) [1969] 1 W.L.R. 843; sub nom. M. (D.) v. M. (S.) and G. (M. (D.A.) Intervening) [1969] 2 All E.R. 243 275
McCafferty v. Metropolitan Police District Receiver [1977] 1 W.L.R. 1073; [1977] I.C.R. 799; 12221 S.J. 678; [1977] 2 All E.R. 756 27
McCormick v. Garnett (1854) 5 De G.M. & G. 278; 23 L.J.Ch. 777; 18 Jur. 412; 2 W.R. 403; 23 L.T.1 36; 2 Eq.R. 136 297
McCreagh v. Frearson (1921) 91 L.J.K.B. 365 64

TABLE OF CASES

McDonald v. Bestway (1972) 27 D.L.R. (3d) 253	106
M'Donald v. M'Donald (1880) 5 App.Cas. 519	280, 283
McDougall v. Partington (1890) 7 R.P.C. 351	372
M'Fadden v. Murdock (1867) Ir.R. 1 C.L. 211	135, 138, 140
McGinley v. Burke [1973] 1 W.L.R. 990; 117 S.J. 488; [1973] 2 All E.R. 1010; [1973] 2 Lloyd's Rep. 508	341
McGuinness v. Fairbairn Lawson (1966) 110 S.J. 870	187
McLaren Maycroft v. Fletcher [1973] 2 N.Z.L.R. 100	143, 145, 367
McLean v. Weir, Goff and Royal Inland Hospital (1977) 5 W.W.R. 609; (1977) 3 C.C.L.T. 87	207, 210, 211, 352
McLoughlin v. O'Brien [1983] A.C. 410; [1982] 2 W.L.R. 982; 126 S.J. 347; [1982] 2 All E.R. 298; [1982] R.T.R. 209; (1982) 79 L.S.Gaz. 922, H.L.; reversing [1981] 1 Q.B. 599	210
McQuaker v. Goddard [1940] 1 K.B. 687; 109 L.J.K.B. 673; 162 L.T. 232; [1970] 1 All E.R. 471; 84 S.J. 203	23
McVeigh v. Beattie [1988] Fam. 69; [1988] 2 W.L.R. 992; 132 S.J. 125; [1988] 2 All E.R. 500; (1988) 18 Fam.Law 290; [1988] 2 F.L.R. 67; (1988) 152 J.P.N. 447; [1988] F.L.R. 516	278
Mahood v. Department of the Environment for Northern Ireland [1986] 1 E.G.L.R. 207; (1985) 277 E.G. 585	258
Mallick v. Allied Schools Agency Limited, *The Times*, March 4, 1980	56
Malsom v. Malsom (1982) 12 Fam.Law 91	398
Malton v. Nesbit (1824) 1 C. & P. 70	143
Manakee v. Brattle [1970] 1 W.L.R. 1607; [1971] 1 All E.R. 464n.	220, 361
Marathon, The (1879) 4 Asp. 75	328
Marchi-Stevenson Ltd. v. Edwards (1958) 51 R. & I.T. 553; 172 E.G. 195; (1958) 3 R.R.C. 289	257
Marconi v. Helsby Wireless Telegraph Co. Ltd. (1914) 31 R.P.C. 121	375
Maria Das Dores, The (1863) Brown and Lush. 27; 32 L.J.P.N. & A. 163; 7 L.T. 838; 11 W.R. 500; 1 Mar.L.C. 309; 167 E.R. 282	328
Marinegra, The [1960] 2 Lloyd's Rep. 1, H.L.; affirming [1959] 2 Lloyd's Rep. 65; [1959] C.L.Y. 3053, C.A.; affirming 2 Lloyd's Rep. 385	72
Marrinan v. Vibart [1963] 1 Q.B. 528; [1962] 3 W.L.R. 912; 106 S.J. 649; [1962] 3 All E.R. 380, C.A.; affirming [1963] 1 Q.B. 234	213
Martin v. Johnstone (1858) 1 F. & F. 122	129, 137, 245
Mason v. Secretary of State for the Environment and Bromsgrove District Council [1984] J.P.L. 332	319
Maxim v. Godson [1916] 1 Ch. 21	218
Maynard v. West Midlands Regional Health Authority [1984] 1 W.L.R. 634; 128 S.J.3 17; [1985] 1 All E.R. 635; (1983) 133 New L.J. 641; (1984) 81 L.S.Gaz. 1926, H.L.	15
Mediterranean and Eastern Export Co. Ltd. v. Fortress Fabrics (Manchester) Ltd. [1948] W.N. 244; [1948] L.J.R. 1536; 64 T.L.R. 337; 92 S.J. 362; [1948] 2 All E.R. 186; 81 Ll.L.Rep. 401	323
Meek v. Fleming [1961] 2 Q.B. 366; [1961] 3 W.L.R. 532; 105 S.J. 588; [1961] 3 All E.R. 148, C.A.; setting aside *The Times*, October 21, 1960	114
Megarity v. Ryan (D.J.) & Sons [1980] 1 W.L.R. 1237; 124 S.J. 498; [1980] 2 All E.R. 832	341, 347
Melanie SS. (Owners of) v. San Onofre SS. (Owners of) [1919] W.N. 151	70
Melik & Co. v. Norwich Union Fire Insurance Society and Kemp [1980] 1 Lloyd's Rep. 523	192
Mellin v. Monaco (1877) 3 C.P.D. 142	67
Mercer v. Denne [1905] 2 Ch. 538; 74 L.J.Ch. 71, 723; 93 L.T. 412; 3 L.G.R. 1293; 21 T.L.R. 760	71
Merriman v. Hardy (1987) 151 J.P.N. 526; (1987) 1 F.L.R. 44	383, 384
Metropolitan Asylum District v. Hill (1882) 47 L.t. 29; 47 J.P. 148, H.L.	139, 206
Metropolitan Properties Co. (F.G.C.) v. Lannon; R. v. London Rent Assessment Panel Committee, ex p. Metropolitan Properties Co. (F.G.C.) [1969] 1 Q.B. 577; [1968] 3 W.L.R. 694; *sub nom.* R. v. London Rent Assessment Panel	

Metropolitan Properties Co. (F.G.C.) v. Lannon—cont.
  Committee, ex p. Metropolitan Properties Co. (F.G.C.), 112 S.J. 585; sub
  nom. Metropolitan Properties Co. (F.G.C.) v. Lannon [1968] 3 All E.R. 304;
  19 P. & C.R. 858 27
Metropolitan Property Holdings v. Laufer (1974) 29 P. & C.R. 172 256
Midonbury Properties Ltd. v. Houghton T. Clark and Son (1981) 259 E.G. 565 .. 253,
                                                                                                                254, 256
Middleton v. Rowlett [1954] 1 W.L.R. 831; 98 S.J. 373; [1954] 2 All E.R. 277; 52
  L.G.R. 334; sub nom. Middleton v. Rowlatt, 118 J.P. 362 115
Midland Bank Trust Co. v. Hett, Stubbs and Kemp (a Firm) [1979] Ch. 384; [1978] 3
  W.L.R. 167; 121 S.J. 830; [1978] 3 All E.R. 571 141
Milirrpum v. Nobalco Pty. Ltd. (1971) 17 F.L.R. 141 .... 167, 206
Miller (T.A.) Ltd. v. Minister of Housing and Local Government [1968] 1 W.L.R.
  992; 112 S.J. 522; [1968] 2 All E.R. 633; (1968) 19 P. & C.R. 263; 66 L.G.R.
  39; [1969] R.P.C. 91, C.A.; affirming 19 P. & C.R. 263 318
Mitchell v. Mulholland (1973) 117 S.J. 307; The Times, April 12, 1973 217
—— v. —— (No. 2) [1972] 1 Q.B. 65; [1971] 2 W.L.R. 1271; 115 S.J. 227; [1971] 2
  All E.R. 1205; sub nom. Mitchell v. Mulholland and Mulholland [1971] 1
  Lloyd's Rep. 462 .... 134, 281, 282, 283, 284, 285
—— v. Stephens (1894) 63 L.J. 389 81
Mobil Oil Corporation v. Register of Trade Marks (1983) 51 A.L.R. 735 .... 166, 289
Moore v. Fox (R.) and Sons [1956] 1 Q.B. 596; [1956] 2 W.L.R. 342; [1956] 1 All
  E.R. 182; [1956] 1 Lloyd's Rep. 129 208
—— v. Lambeth County Court Registrar [1969] 1 W.L.R. 141; [1969] 1 All E.R.
  782, C.A. Petition for leave to appeal to the House of Lords refused [1969] 1
  W.L.R. 338 107
Morgan v. Bishop's Stores [1963] R.V.R. 585; [1963] J.P.L. 675; 187 E.G. 463;
  [1963] R.A. 305 259
Motor Vehicles Distribution Scheme Agreement, Re [1961] 1 W.L.R. 92; 105 S.J. 90;
  [1961] 1 All E.R. 161; L.R. 2 R.P. 173 .... 326, 328
Moult v. Halliday [1898] 1 Q.B. 125; 67 L.J.Q.B. 151; 77 L.T. 794; 46 W.R. 318;
  62 J.P. 8 25
Moxon v. Minister of Pensions [1945] K.B. 490; 115 L.J.K.B. 53; 173 L.T. 56; 61
  T.L.R. 458; [1945] 2 All E.R. 124 311
Mulholland v. Mitchell [1971] A.C. 666; [1971] 2 W.L.R. 93; 115 S.J. 15; sub nom.
  Mulholland v. Mitchell (by his next friend Hazel Doreen Mitchell) [1971] 1 All
  E.R. 307, H.L. 116
Mullard v. Ben Line Steamers [1970] 1 W.L.R. 1414; 114 S.J. 570; 9 K.I.R. 111;
  [1971] 2 All E.R. 424; [1970] 2 Lloyd's Rep. 121, C.A.; reversing [1969] 2
  Lloyd's Rep. 631 349
—— v. Philco (1935) 52 R.P.C. 261 375
Mulliner v. Florence (1878) 3 Q.B.D. 484; 47 L.J.Q.B. 700; 38 L.T. 167; 26 W.R.
  385 25
Murphy v. Ford Motor Co. (1970) 114 S.J. 886 344
—— v. Queen, The (1989) 63 A.L.J. 422 .... 122, 123, 232
—— v. Stone-Wallwork (Charlton) Ltd. [1969] 1 W.L.R. 1023; 113 S.J. 546; [1969]
  2 All E.R. 949; 7 K.I.R. 203, H.L. 116
Murray v. Muir (1940) S.C.(J.) 127 421
Murray Pipework Ltd. v. UIE Scotland Ltd. (1990) Const.L.J. 56 .... 50, 96, 97
Myers v. Director of Public Prosecutions [1965] A.C. 1001; [1964] 3 W.L.R. 145; 128
  J.P. 481; 108 S.J. 519; [1964] 2 All E.R. 881; 48 Cr.App.R. 348, H.L.;
  affirming sub nom. R. v. Myers [1964] 1 All E.R. 877 .... 179, 180, 184
—— v. Sarl (1860) 3 E. & E. 306; 30 L.J.Q.B. 9; 9 W.R. 96; 7 Jur. 97 157

N. (Minors) (Child Abuse: Evidence), Re [1987] 1 F.L.R. 280; [1987] F.C.R. 184;
  (1987) 151 J.P.N. 590 .... 403, 408
—— (Wardship: Evidence), Re [1987] 1 F.L.R. 65; (1987) 17 Fam.Law 87 397,
                                                                                                                        398

TABLE OF CASES

Naylor v. Preston Area Health Authority; Foster v. Merton and Sutton Health Authority; Thomas v. North West Surrey Health Authority; Ikumelo v. Newham Health Authority [1987] 1 W.L.R. 958; 131 S.J. 596; [1987] 2 All E.R. 353; (1987) 137 New L.J. 474; (1987) 84 L.S.Gaz. 1494 .... 42, 43, 45, 47, 89, 339, 357
Nelme v. Newton (1819) 2 W. & J. 186 188
Nelson v. Bridport (1845) 8 Beav. 527; [1843–60] All E.R.Rep. 1032; 8 L.T.O.S. 18; 10 Jur. 871; 50 E.R. 207 308
Nelson Guarantee Corporation Ltd. v. Hodgson [1958] N.Z.L.R. 609 288
Net Book Agreement, 1957, Re (1962) L.R. 3 R.P. 246; [1962] 1 W.L.R. 1347; 106 S.J. 902; [1962] 3 All E.R. 751 .... 326, 327
Newbold v. R. [1983] 2 A.C. 705; [1983] 3 W.L.R. 375; 127 S.J. 537; [1983] Crim.L.R. 676 182
Newton v. Ricketts (1861) 9 H.L.C. 262; 31 L.J.Ch. 247; 5 L.T. 62; 7 Jur.N.S. 953; 10 W.R. 1; 11 E.R. 731, H.L. 210
—— v. Woods (1987) 151 J.P. 436; [1987] R.T.R. 41 .... 209, 424
Nicholson v. Secretary of State for Energy (1977) 76 L.G.R. 693; [1978] J.P.L. 39; (1977) 245 E.G. 139 316
—— v. Watts [1973] R.T.R. 208; [1973] Crim.L.R. 246 426
Nickisson v. R. [1963] W.A.R. 114 13
Nightingale v. Biffen (1925) 18 B.W.C.C. 358; [1926] W.C. & I.Rep. 40 129
No, The (1853) 1 Sp.Ecc. 2 Ad. 184; 164 E.R. 107 72
Noble v. Thompson (Robert) & Partners (1979) 76 L.S.Gaz. 1060 348
Nokes v. Davies (unreported), May 5, 1970 347
Non-Drip Measure Co. Ltd. v. Strangers Ltd. (1941) 59 R.P.C. 1 375
Nossen's Letter Patent, Re [1969] 1 W.L.R. 638; 113 S.J. 445; sub nom. Nossen's Patent, Re [1969] 1 All E.R. 775; [1968] F.S.R. 617 .... 220, 373
Nugent v. Hobday [1973] R.T.R. 41; [1972] Crim.L.R. 569 426
Nuttall v. Nuttall and Twyman (Practice Note) (1964) 108 S.J. 605 196

Oak Manufacturing Co. v. Plessey Co. Ltd. (1950) 67 R.P.C. 71 372
Oakes v. Uzzell [1932] P. 19; 100 L.J.P. 99; 146 L.T. 95; 47 T.L.R. 573; 75 S.J. 543 111
O'Callaghan v. O'Sullivan [1925] 1 I.R. 90 308
Ockley v. Whitlesbye (1622) Palm. 294 215
Odeon Associated Cinemas v. Jones [1973] Ch. 288; [1972] 2 W.L.R. 331; 115 S.J. 850; [1971] T.R. 373; [1972] 1 All E.R. 681; (1971) 48 T.C. 257, C.A.; affirming [1971] 1 W.L.R. 442 287
Official Custodian for Charities v. Goldridge (1973) 26 P. & C.R. 191; (1973) 227 E.G. 1467 253
Official Solicitor v. K. [1965] A.C. 201; [1963] 3 W.L.R. 408; 107 S.J. 616; [1963] 3 All E.R. 191, H.L.; reversing sub nom. K. (Infants), Re [1963] Ch. 381, C.A.; restoring [1962] 3 W.L.R. 752 .... 196, 197, 202, 395, 396, 397, 400, 410
Oldenburg, in the Goods of (1884) 9 P.D. 234; 53 L.J.P. 46; 32 W.R. 724; 49 J.P. 104 304
Olin Mathieson Chemical Corporation v. Biorex Laboratories Ltd. [1970] R.P.C. 157 374
Ollett v. Bristol Aerojet Ltd. (Practice Note) [1979] 1 W.L.R. 1197; 123 S.J. 705; [1979] 3 All E.R. 544 .... 32, 40, 41, 44, 47, 91
Orford v. Orford (1979) 10 Fam.Law 114 384
Originating Summons in an Adoption Application, Exp., The Times, November 1989 400

P. (A Minor) (Independent Welfare Officer), Re [1989] 2 F.L.R. 43; (1989) 19 Fam.Law 312; [1989] F.C.R. 689; (1990) 154 J.P.N. 89 388
—— (Wardship), Re; sub nom. P. (A Minor) (Child Abuse), Re (1987) 151 J.P. 635; [1987] 2 F.C.R. 467; [1987] F.L.R. 123; (1987) 151 J.P.N. 333 402
P. (Minors) (Child Abuse: Medical Evidence), Re [1988] 1 F.L.R. 328; (1988) 18 Fam.Law 211 400

TABLE OF CASES

P. (Minors) (Wardship: Surrogacy), Re [1988] F.C.R. 140; [1987] 2 F.L.R. 421; (1987) 17 Fam.Law 414; (1987) 151 J.P.N. 334	398
P. v. P. (No. 2) (1969) 113 S.J. 343, C.A.	275
P.A. (An Infant), Re [1971] 1 W.L.R. 1530; 115 S.J. 586; [1971] 3 All E.R. 522	395
Pacific Acceptance Corporation Ltd. v. Forsyth (1970) W.N. (N.S.W.) 29	288
Paley Olga (Princess) v. Weisz [19239] 1 K.B. 718	305
Paric v. John Holland Constructions Pty. Ltd. [1984] 2 N.S.W.L.R. 505	148
Partington and Son (Builders) v. Tameside Metropolitan Borough Council (1985) 2 Const.L.J. 67; (1985) 5 Con.L.R. 99; [1985] C.I.L.L. 213; (1985) 32 Build.L.R. 150	64
Patterson v. Nixon [1960] Crim.L.R. 634; 1960 S.C.(J.) 42; 1960 S.L.T. 220	262
Payton v. Snelling [1901] A.C. 308; 70 L.J.Ch. 644; 85 L.T. 287; 17 R.P.C. 628, H.L.	153
Peak Construction (Liverpool) Ltd. v. Mckinney Foundations (1970) 69 L.G.R. 1, C.A.	219, 361
Pearson v. North Western Gas Board [1968] 1 All E.R. 669	208
Peart v. Bokkow, Vaughan and Co. Ltd. [1925] 1 K.B. 399; 94 L.J.K.B. 497; 132 L.T. 267; 69 S.J. 123; 17 B.W.C.C. 221, C.A.	28
People v. King [1969] A.T.L.A. Newsletter 16 (California)	264
Perlak Petroleum Maatschappij v. Deen [1924] 1 K.B. 111; 68 S.J. 81, C.A.	304
Perry v. Phillips (Sidney) & Son (A Firm) [1982] 1 W.L.R.1297; 126 S.J. 626; [1982] 3 All E.R. 705; (1983) 22 Build.L.R. 120; (1982) 263 E.G. 888; (1982) 79 L.S.Gaz. 1175, C.A.; reversing [1982] 1 All E.R. 1005	368
Perth Peerage, The (1848) 2 H.L.C. 865; 9 E.R. 1322, H.L.	304
Peters v. Harding (1963) 107 S.J. 852	169
Phenol Producers' Agreement, Re (Practice Note) (1960) L.R. 2 R.P. 49	327
Philips v. Ward [1956] 1 W.L.R. 471; 100 S.J. 317; [1956] 1 All E.R. 874	368
Phillion v. R. (1977) 74 D.L.R. (2d) 136	245
Pickering v. Barkley (1648) Sty. 132; 82 E.R. 587	67
—— v. Sogex Services (U.K.) Ltd. (1982) 263 E.G. 770; (1982) 20 Build.L.R. 66	224
Piggott v. Sims [1973] R.T.R. 15; [1972] Crim.L.R. 595	115
Piller, (Anton) K.G. v. Manufacturing Processes ltd. [1976] Ch. 55; [1976] 2 W.L.R. 162; 120 S.J. 63; [1976] 1 All E.R. 779; [1976] F.S.R. 129; [1976] R.P.C. 719	81
Pinion, Re, Westminster Bank v. Pinion [1965] Ch. 85; [1964] 2 W.L.R. 919; 108 S.J. 296; [1964] 1 All E.R. 890, C.A.; reversing [1963] 3 W.L.R. 778	126, 147
Pipe v. Fulcher (1958) 1 E. & E. 111; 28 L.J.Q.B. 12; 32 L.T.O.S. 105; 5 Jur.N.S. 146; 7 W.R. 19; 120 E.R. 850	182
Pivot Properties v. Secretary of State for the Environment (1980) 41 P. & C.R. 248; (1980) 256 E.G. 1176, C.A.; affirming (1979) 39 P. & C.R. 386; (1979) 253 E.G. 373	249
Plant v. Plant (1982) 12 Fam.Law 179; (1983) 4 F.L.R. 305	385
Planter, The; The Brixton (Owners) v. The Planter (Owners) [1955] 1 W.L.R. 898; 99 S.J. 526; [1955] 2 All E.R. 751n.; [1955] 1 Lloyd's Rep. 279	45, 328, 357
Pointer v. Norwich Assessment Committee [1922] 2 K.B. 471; 91 L.J.K.B. 891; 86 J.P. 149; 20 L.G.R. 673; 67 S.J. 98; 128 L.T. 48	250
Port Sudan Cotton Co. v. Govindaswamy Chettiar & Sons [1977] 2 Lloyd's Rep. 5, C.A.; reversing [1977] 1 Lloyd's Rep. 166	27
Porter v. Bell [1955] 1 D.L.R. 62	209
Portico Housing Association Ltd. v. Moorehead (Brian) and Partners (1985) 1 Const.L.J. 226; [1985] C.I.L.L. 155; (1985) 6 Con.L.R. 1, C.A.	355
Powell, Exp., Re Matthews (1875) 1 Ch.D. 501; 45 L.J.Bk. 100; 34 L.T. 224; 24 W.R. 378	25
Practice Direction [1965] 1 W.L.R. 853	329
—— (Crime: Antecedents) [1966] 1 W.L.R. 1184; 110 S.J. 508; [1966] 2 All E.R. 929; 50 Cr.App.R. 271	78
—— (Admiralty: Evidence of Expert Witnesses) [1968] 1 W.L.R. 312	328
—— [1968] 1 W.L.R. 1425	356
—— [1972] 3 All E.R. 912	303

TABLE OF CASES

Practice Direction [1973] 1 W.L.R. 1425	374
—— [1974] 1 W.L.R. 904	358
—— [1980] 1 W.L.R. 334	383
—— [1981] 1 W.L.R. 1162	383, 386
—— [1983] 1 W.L.R. 1420	384
—— [1984] 1 W.L.R. 34	394
—— [1984] 1 W.L.R. 446	386
—— [1985] 1 W.L.R. 360	390
—— [1987] 2 Lloyd's Rep. 563	224
—— (Q.B.D.) (Expert Evidence—Lodgement of Reports in Personal Injury Actions), November 29, 1989	353
Practice Note (Evidence: Ship's Log) [1953] 1 W.L.R.262; 97 S.J. 81; [1952] 2 Lloyd's Rep. 543	328
—— (1958) L.R. 1 R.P. 114	327
—— (1961) L.R. 2 R.P. 168	327
—— [1972] 1 W.L.R. 353	274
—— (1973) 117 S.J. 88	385
—— [1975] 1 W.L.R. 81	274
—— [1990] 1 F.L.R. 414	401
Preece v. H.M. Advocate [1981] Crim.L.R. 783	213
Preeper v. R. (1888) 15 S.C.R. 401	128, 175, 176
Prenn v. Simmonds [1971] 1 W.L.R. 1381; 115 S.J. 654; [1971] 3 All E.R. 237, H.L.	160
Prescott v. Bulldog Tools Ltd. [1981] 3 All E.R. 869	344, 345, 346, 347
Prest v. West Cumbria Health Authority [1990] 3 C.L.Y. 339	353
Preston-Jones v. Preston-Jones [1951] A.C. 391; [1951] 1 T.L.R. 8; 95 S.J. 13; [1951] 1 All E.R. 124; 49 L.G.R. 417, H.L.; reversing [1949] W.N. 339	23
Proctor v. Peebles [1941] 2 All E.R. 80	88, 349
Produce Brokers Co. Ltd. v. Ollympic Oil & Cane Co. Ltd. [1916] 1 A.C. 314; 85 L.J.K.B. 160; 114 L.T. 94; 32 T.L.R. 115; 21 Com.Cas. 320; 60 S.J. 74	159
Provincial Theatres Ltd. v. Holyoak (1969) 15 R.R.C. 198	258
Pugsley v. Hunter [1973] 1 W.L.R. 578; 117 S.J. 206; [1973] 2 All E.R. 10; [1973] R.T.R. 284; [1973] Crim.L.R. 247	420, 427, 428
Pursell v. Railway Executive [1951] 1 All E.R. 536, C.A.	89, 350
Queen Mary, The (1947) 80 Lloyd's Rep. 609	70
R. v. Aberdare Justices, ex p. Jones [1973] Crim.L.R. 545	416
—— v. Abadom [1983] 1 W.L.R. 126; 126 S.J. 562; [1983] 1 All E.R. 364; (1983) 76 Cr.App.R. 48; [1983] Crim.L.R. 254; (1983) 133 New L.J. 132	163, 164, 171, 177, 179, 180, 262, 285, 428, 429
—— v. Abbey (1982) 138 D.L.R. 202	164, 233
—— v. Adams [1970] Crim.L.R. 693	413
—— v. Ahmed Din [1962] 1 W.L.R. 680; 106 S.J. 329; [1962] 2 All E.R. 123; (1962) 46 Cr.App.R. 269	136, 238
—— v. Anderson; R. v. Neville; R. v. Dennis; R. v. Oz Publications Ink [1972] 1 Q.B. 304; [1971] 3 W.L.R. 939; 115 S.J. 847; sub nom. R. v. Anderson [1971] 3 All E.R. 1152; 56 Cr.App.R. 115; [1972] Crim.L.R. 40	432, 433
—— v. Angeli [1979] 1 W.L.R. 26; 122 S.J. 591; [1978] 3 All E.R. 950; (1978) 68 Cr.App.R. 32; [1979] Crim.L.R. 388	266
—— v. Antrim [1895] 2 I.R. 603	112
—— v. Attard (1958) 43 Cr.App.R. 90	75
—— v. Bacon (1915) 11 Cr.App.R. 90	262
—— v. Bailey [1961] Crim.L.R. 828; 112 L.J. 11	237
—— v. Bardoe [1969] Crim.L.R. 185	108, 110
—— v. Barker (unreported), 1954 ([1954]Crim.L.R. 423)	244
—— v. Beckett (1913) 8 Cr.App.R. 204; 29 T.L.R. 332	21
—— v. Bexley Justices, ex p. King [1980] R.T.R. 49	107

R. v. Birmingham Juvenile Court, *ex p.* G. and R. [1988] 1 W.L.R. 950; 132 S.J. 1117; [1988] 3 All E.R. 726; [1988] 2 F.L.R. 423; (1988) 18 Fam.Law 469; (1988) 152 J.P.N. 802; (1988) 138 New L.J. 143 393
—— v. Blowers [1977] Crim.L.R. 51 .... 414, 415
—— v. Bournemouth Justices, *ex p.* Grey; Same v. Same, *ex p.* Rodd (1986) 150 J.P. 392; [1987] 1 F.L.R. 36; (1986) 16 Fam.Law 337; (1986) 150 J.P.N. 588 401
—— v. Bracewell (1978) 68 Cr.App.R. 44; [1979] Crim.L.R. 111 204
—— v. Bradshaw (1985) 82 Cr.App.R. 79; [1985] Crim.L.R. 733 .... 164, 165, 233
—— v. Brampton, 10 East 282 300
—— v. Bryant and Dickson (1946) 31 Cr.App.R. 146 108
—— v. Byrne [1960] 2 Q.B. 396; [1960] 3 W.L.R. 440; 104 S.J. 645; [1960] 1 All E.R. 1; 44 Cr.App.R. 246 .... 153, 203, 210, 235, 237, 238
—— v. Calder and Boyars [1969] 1 Q.B. 151; [1968] 3 W.L.R. 974; 133 J.P. 20; 112 S.J. 688; [1968] 3 All E.R. 644; 52 Cr.App.R. 706 .... 433, 434
—— v. Camplin [1978] A.C. 705; [1978] 2 W.L.R. 679; 122 S.J. 280; (1978) 67 Cr.App.R. 14; [1978] Crim.L.R. 432; *sub nom.* D.P.P. v. Camplin [1978] 2 All E.R. 168, H.L.; affirming [1978] Q.B. 254 230
—— v. Castleton (1910) 3 Cr.App.R. 74 262
—— v. Cator (1802) 4 Esp. 117 269
—— v. Chapman (1838) 8 C. & P. 558 .... 112, 241
—— v. Chard (Peter John) (1971) 56 Cr.App.R. 268 .... 122, 229
—— v. Chatwood [1980] 1 W.L.R. 874; 124 S.J. 396; [1980] 1 All E.R. 467; [1980] Crim.L.R. 46; *sub nom.* R. v. Chatwood; R. v. Egan; R. v. Flaherty; R. v. Proctor; R. v. Walker (1979) 70 Cr.App.R. 39 203
—— v. Cleghorn [1967] 2 Q.B. 584; [1967] 2 W.L.R. 1421; 131 J.P. 320; 111 S.J. 175; [1967] 1 All E.R. 996; 51 Cr.App.R. 291 115
—— v. Constantinou [1989] Crim.L.R. 571 265
—— v. Cook (1907) 147 C.C.C.Sess.Pap. 466 111
—— v. —— [1982] Crim.L.R. 670 .... 124, 140
—— v. Cook (Christopher) [1987] Q.B. 417; [1987] 2 W.L.R. 775; 131 S.J. 21; [1987] 1 All E.R. 1049; (1987) 84 Cr.App.R. 370; [1987] Crim.L.R. 402 .... 21, 182, 265
—— v. Coroner for Inner London North District, *ex p.* Linnaie, *The Independent*, July 31, 1990 322
—— v. Court (1960) 44 Cr.App.R. 242 262
—— v. Cox [1898] 1 Q.B. 179; 67 L.J.Q.B. 293; 77 L.T. 534; 14 T.L.R. 122; 42 S.J. 135; 18 Cox 672 20
—— v. Crayden [1978] 1 W.L.R. 604; 122 S.J. 145; [1978] 2 All E.R. 700; (1978) 67 Cr.App.R. 1 182
—— v. Crespigny (1795) 1 Esp. 280 214
—— v. Crouch (1844) 1 Cox 94 175
—— v. —— (1850) 4 Cox 163 131
—— v. Crozier, *The Independent*, May 11, 1990 196
—— v. Crush [1978] Crim.L.R. 357 24
—— v. Davies (No. 2) [1962] 1 W.L.R. 111; 126 J.P. 455; 106 S.J. 393; [1962] 3 All E.R. 97; 46 Cr.App.R. 292 .... 12, 21, 421
—— v. Davis [1979] Crim.L.R. 167 232
—— v. Dawson [1976] R.T.R. 533; [1976] Crim.L.R. 692 209
—— v. Day [1940] 1 All E.R. 402; (1940) 27 Cr.App.R. 168; 162 L.T. 407; 104 J.P. 181; 38 L.G.R. 155 .... 115, 269
—— v. De Havilland (1983) 5 Cr.App.R.(S.) 109, C.A.; affirming [1983] Crim.L.R. 489 418
—— v. Deputy Industrial Injuries Commissioner, *ex p.* Moore [1965] 1 Q.B. 456; [1965] 2 W.L.R. 89; 108 S.J. 1030; [1965] 1 All E.R. 81, C.A.; affirming 108 S.J. 380 169
—— v. Derrick (1910) 5 Cr.App.R. 162 266
—— v. Divine, *ex p.* Walton [1930] 2 K.B. 29 322
—— v. Dix (1982) 74 Cr.App.R. 306; [1982] Crim.L.R. 302 .... 203, 235, 236
—— v. Eades [1972] Crim.L.R. 99 .... 149, 240

xliii

TABLE OF CASES

R. v. Elliot [1976] R.T.R. 308	424
—— v. Elliott (1909) 2 Cr.App.R. 171	78
—— v. Epsom Juvenile Court, *ex p.* G. [1988] 1 W.L.R. 145; 132 S.J. 54; [1988] 1 All E.R. 329; [1988] F.C.R. 32; [1988] 2 F.L.R. 36; (1988) 18 Fam.Law 208; (1988) 85 L.S.Gaz. 35	395
—— v. Ewing [1983] 1 W.L.R. 1212, H.L.; reversing in part [1983] Q.B. 1039; [1983] 3 W.L.R. 1; 127 S.J. 390; [1983] 2 All E.R. 645; [1988] E.C.C. 234; [1983] Crim.L.R. 472	266
—— v. Fisher [1961] O.W.N. 94	150
—— v. Fox [1985] 1 W.L.R. 1126; (1985) 150 J.P. 97; 129 S.J. 752; [1985] 3 All E.R. 392; (1985) 82 Cr.App.R. 105; [1985] R.T.R. 337; [1986] Crim.L.R. 59; (1985) 149 J.P.N. 223; (1985) 135 New L.J. 1058; *sub nom.* Fox v. Chief Constable of Gwent [1986] A.C. 281, H.L.; affirming [1985] 1 W.L.R. 33	420
—— v. Frances (1849) 4 Cox 57	234
—— v. Frankum (1983) 5 Cr.App.R.(S.) 259; [1984] Crim.L.R. 434	118
—— v. Gallagher [1983] Crim.L.R. 335	108
—— v. Gilmore [1977] 2 N.S.W.L.R. 935	132
—— v. Gordon [1954] Crim.L.R. 482	244
—— v. Greater Manchester Coroner, *ex p.* Tal [1985] Q.B. 67; [1984] 3 W.L.R. 643; 128 S.J. 500; [1984] 3 All E.R. 240; [1984] Crim.L.R. 557	322
—— v. Greenwich Juvenile Court, *ex p.* Greenwich London Borough (1977) 7 Fam.Law 171; (1977) 74 L.G.R. 99	400, 401
—— v. Grossman (Beth Susan). *See* R. v. Skirving; R. v. Grossman.	
—— v. Haas (1962) 35 D.L.R. 172	263
—— v. Hall (John Hamilton) (1988) 86 Cr.App.R. 159	238
—— v. Hampshire County Council, *ex p.* K. [1990] 1 F.L.R. 330	401
—— v. Harding (1936) 25 Cr.App.R. 190	118
—— v. Harrington (John) (1984) 6 Cr.App.R.(S.) 182; [1984] Crim.L.R. 487	115
—— v. Harris [1927] 2 K.B. 587; 96 L.J.K.B. 1069; 91 J.P. 152; 137 L.T. 535; 43 T.L.R. 774; 20 Cr.App.R. 86; 28 Cox 432	66, 115, 238
—— v. Hart (1932) 23 Cr.App.R. 202	112
—— v. Harvey (1869) 11 Cox 546	267, 268
—— v. Heaton (1832) 1 Lew.C.C. 116	264
—— v. Hendy (1850) 4 Cox C.C. 243	158
—— v. Heseltine (1873) 12 Cox C.C. 404	79, 137
—— v. Higginson (1843) 1 C. & K. 129	234
—— v. Hipson (1968) 112 S.J. 945; [1969] Crim.L.R. 85	206, 211
—— v. Holden (1838) 8 Car. & P. 606	66, 108, 236
—— v. Holmes [1953] 1 W.L.R. 686; 117 J.P. 346; 97 S.J. 355; [1953] 2 All E.R. 324; 37 Cr.App.R. 61	153, 203, 234, 235
—— v. Home Secretary, *ex p.* Lewes Justices [1973] A.C. 388	200, 201, 202
—— v. Hope (1955) 39 Cr.App.R. 33	268
—— v. Hove Juvenile Court, *ex p.* W. [1989] 2 F.L.R. 145	405, 410
—— v. Howard (1957) 42 Cr.App.R. 23	230
—— v. Income Tax Commissioners [1911] 2 K.B. 434; 80 L.J.K.B. 1035; 27 T.L.R. 353; 104 L.T. 764	310
—— v. Imrie (1917) 12 Cr.App.R. 282	75
—— v. James (1981) 3 Cr.App.R.(S.) 233	414
—— v. Jennion [1962] 1 W.L.R. 317; 106 S.J. 224; [1962] 1 All E.R. 689; 46 Cr.App.R. 212	237
—— v. Kershberg [1976] R.T.R. 526; [1977] I.C.L. 196	79, 164, 171, 252, 422, 423, 424
—— v. Kilner [1977] Crim.L.R. 740	232
—— v. King [1897] 1 Q.B. 214; 66 L.J.Q.B. 87; 75 L.T. 392; 18 Cox 447; 61 J.P. 329	19
—— v. —— [1983] 1 W.L.R. 411; (1983) 147 J.P. 65; 127 S.J. 88; [1983] 1 All E.R. 929; (1983) 77 Cr.App.R. 1; [1983] Crim.L.R. 326	105, 193
—— v. —— [1990] 1 All E.R. 835	193

TABLE OF CASES

R. v. Kirkham, February 9, 1968, reported in Thomas, *Current Sentencing Practice*, at L.5.4(b) 415
—— v. Kiszko (1978) 68 Cr.App.R. 62; [1979] Crim.L.R. 465 .... 209, 237
—— v. Kluczynski; R. v. Stefanowicz (Note) [1973] 1 W.L.R. 1230; [1973] 3 All E.R.401; *sub nom.* R. v. Kluczynski (Tadeusz); R. v. Stefanowicz (Jan), 57 Cr.App.R. 836 78
—— v. Kooken (1982) 74 Cr.App.R. 30 .... 236, 238
—— v. Lanfear [1968] 2 Q.B. 77; [1968] 2 W.L.R. 623; 132 J.P. 193; 112 S.J. 132; [1968] 1 All E.R. 683; 52 Cr.App.R. 176 .... 211, 425
—— v. Lattimore (Colin George); R. v. Salih (Ahmet); R. v. Leighton (Ronald William) (1975) 62 Cr.App.R. 53; *sub nom.* R. v. Lattimore (1975) 119 S.J. 863; [1976] Crim.L.R. 45 118
—— v. Layton (1849) 4 Cox 149 236
—— v. Lee Kun [1916] 1 K.B. 337; 85 L.J.K.B. 515; 114 L.T. 421; (1916) 11 Cr.App.R. 293; 32 T.L.R. 225; 80 J.P. 166; 25 Cox 304; 60 S.J. 158 75
—— v. Le-Caer (1972) 116 S.J. 680; 56 Cr.App.R. 727; [1972] Crim.L.R. 546 78
—— v. Levy and Tait (1966) 50 Cr.App.R. 198; 116 New L.J. 921; [1966] Crim.L.R. 454 115
—— v. Liddle (1930) 21 Cr.App.R. 3 115
—— v. Lindsay [1970] N.Z.L.R. 1002 263
—— v. Lloyd [1967] 1 Q.B. 175; [1966] 2 W.L.R. 13; 130 J.P. 118; 109 S.J. 955; [1966] 1 All E.R. 107n.; 50 Cr.App.R. 61; [1965] C.L.Y. 857 238
—— v. Lomas [1969] 1 W.L.R. 306; 133 J.P. 285; 113 S.J. 124; [1969] 1 All E.R. 920; *sub nom.* R. v. Lomas (Arthur James) 53 Cr.App.R. 256 .... 117, 118
—— v. Luffe (1807) 8 East 193 23
—— v. Lupien [1970] S.C.R. 263 231
—— v. Lurie [1951] W.N. 493; [1951] 2 T.L.R. 686; 115 J.P. 551; 95 S.J. 580; [1951] 2 All E.R. 704; 35 Cr.App.R. 113; 49 L.G.R. 752 77
—— v. Lushington, *ex p.* Otto [1894] 1 Q.B. 420; 10 R. 418; 70 L.T. 412; 42 W.R. 411; 17 Cox 754; 58 J.P. 282 82
—— v. McCartney [1976] 1 N.Z.L.R. 472 263
—— v. McGrath and Mckevitt (1881) 14 Cox 598 140
—— v. McGuire (1985) 81 Cr.App.R. 323; [1985] Crim.L.R. 663 .... 59, 184, 185
—— v. Mackay [1967] N.Z.L.R. 139 .... 243, 244
—— v. MacKenny (1981) 76 Cr.App.R. 271 .... 129, 241
—— v. Marr [1977] R.T.R. 168 424
—— v. Masih [1986] Crim.L.R. 395 231
—— v. Mason (1912) 76 J.P. 184; 7 Cr.App.R. 67; 28 T.L.R. 120 .... 137, 261
—— v. Massheder (1983) Cr.App.R.(S.) 442; [1984] Crim.L.R. 185 413
—— v. Matheson [1958] 1 W.L.R. 474; 102 S.J. 309; [1958] 2 All E.R. 87; 42 Cr.App.R. 145 .... 211, 237
—— v. Mawbey (1796) 6 Term.Rep. 619; 101 E.R. 736 215
—— v. McNaghten (1844) 10 Cl. & F. 200; 1 C. & K. 130n.; 8 Scott.N.R. 595 .... 234, 235
—— v. Meehan (1970) J.C. 11 244
—— v. Melville [1976] 1 W.L.R. 181; 120 S.J. 27; [1976] 1 All E.R. 395; [1976] Crim.L.R. 247; *sub nom.* R. v. Melville (Alan Brain) (1975) 62 Cr.App.R. 100 .... 117, 118
—— v. Menzies [1982] 1 N.Z.L.R. 40 83
—— v. Mitchell [1970] Crim.L.R. 153 75
—— v. Montgomery [1966] N.I. 120 .... 262, 263
—— v. Morgan [1978] 1 W.L.R. 735; 122 S.J. 366; [1978] 3 All E.R. 13; (1978) 67 Cr.App.R. 369 118
—— v. Morrison (1911) 6 Cr.App.R. 159 107
—— v. Mulcahy, March 29, 1977, C.A. reported in Thomas, *Current Sentencing Practice* at LS 3(a) 414
—— v. Murphy [1980] Q.B. 434; [1980] 2 W.L.R. 743; 124 S.J. 189; [1980] 2 All E.R. 325; (1980) 71 Cr.App.R. 33; [1980] R.T.R. 145; [1980] Crim.L.R. 309 13

TABLE OF CASES

R. v. Naguib [1917] 1 K.B. 359; 86 L.J.K.B. 709; 116 L.T. 640; 81 J.P. 116 299
—— v. Neale (1977) 65 Cr.App.R. 304 239
—— v. Newton (1849) 13 Q.B.D. 716 107
—— v. Nixon (John) [1969] 1 W.L.R. 1055; *sub nom.* R. v. Nixon (John Hawkins), 53 Cr.App.R. 432 425
—— v. North Yorkshire County Council, *ex p.* M. [1988] 3 W.L.R. 1344; 132 S.J. 1731 392
—— v. Nowell [1948] W.N. 154; [1948] 1 W.L.R. 830; 64 T.L.R. 277; 112 J.P. 255; 92 S.J. 351; [1948] 1 All E.R. 794; 32 Cr.App.R. 173; 46 L.G.R. 336 .. 114, 425
—— v. Oakley (1979) 1 Cr.App.R.(S.) 366; (1979) 70 Cr.App.R. 7; [1979] R.T.R. 417; [1979] Crim.L.R. 657 .... 13, 131, 423
—— v. O'Callaghan [1976] V.R. 676 262
—— v. O'Connell (1844) Arm. & Tr. 165 76
—— v. Oliva [1965] 1 W.L.R. 1028; 129 J.P. 500; 109 S.J. 453; [1965] 3 All E.R. 116; 49 Cr.App.R. 298 108
—— v. O'Sullivan [1969] 1 W.L.R. 497; 133 J.P. 338; 113 S.J. 161; [1969] 2 All E.R. 237; *sub nom.* R. v. O'Sullivan (John David) (1969) 53 Cr.App.R. 274 . 267, 268
—— v. Payne [1963] 1 W.L.R. 637; 127 J.P. 230; 107 S.J. 97; [1963] 1 All E.R. 848; 47 Cr.App.R. 122 .... 124, 425
—— v. Payne and Spillane [1971] 1 W.L.R. 1779; [1971] 3 All E.R. 1146; 56 Cr.App.R. 9; [1972] Crim.L.R. 61; *sub nom.* R. v. Spillane, 115 S.J. 847; [1972] J.C.L. 98 78
—— v. Pedley (1784) 1 Leach 325 215
—— v. Pembroke (1678) 6 How.St.Tr. 1337 8
—— v. Penguin Books [1961] Crim.L.R. 176 .... 140, 434
—— v. Penman (James) (1985) 82 Cr.App.R. 44 208
—— v. Peters (1886) 16 Q.B.D. 636; 55 L.J.M.C. 173; 54 L.T. 545; 34 W.R. 399; 16 Cox 36; 50 J.P. 631 181
—— v. Picton (1804) 30 How.St.Tr. 226 203
—— v. Pitt (1968) D.L.R. (2d) 513 243
—— v. Platt [1981] Crim.L.R. 332 .... 211, 430
—— v. Plymouth Juvenile Court, *ex p.* (1987) 151 J.P. 355; [1987] 1 F.L.R. 169; (1987) 17 Fam.Law 18; (1987) 151 J.P.N. 270 391
—— v. Powar (1984) Taxation Compendium 522 225
—— v. Powell [1980] Crim.L.R. 39 232
—— v. Pestano [1981] Crim.L.R. 397 111
—— v. R. (Blood Test: Jurisdiction) [1973] 1 W.L.R. 1115; 117 S.J. 394; [1973] 3 All E.R. 933 274
—— v. Reiter [1954] 2 Q.B. 16; [1954] 2 W.L.R. 638; 118 J.P. 262; 98 S.J. 235; [1954] 1 All E.R. 741; 38 Cr.App.R. 62 .... 140, 434
—— v. Reynolds [1950] 1 K.B. 606; 66 T.L.R. (Pt. 1) 333; 114 J.P. 155; 94 S.J. 165; [1950] 1 All E.R. 335; 34 Cr.App.R. 60; 48 L.G.R. 239 208
—— v. Richards (1858) 1 F. & F. 87 235
—— v. Rickard (1919) 13 Cr.App.R. 140; 88 L.J.K.B. 720; 119 L.T. 192; 82 J.P. 256; 26 Cox 318 .... 267, 268
—— v. Riley [1967] Crim.L.R. 656 231
—— v. Rimmer and Beech [1983] Crim.L.R. 250 240
—— v. Rivett (1950) 34 Cr.App.R. 87 .... 210, 237
—— v. Rutter [1977] R.T.R. 105 422
—— v. Schlesinger (1847) 10 Q.B. 670 215
—— v. Scott (1984) 148 J.P. 731; (1984) 79 Cr.App.R. 49; [1984] Crim.L.R. 235; (1984) 81 L.S.Gaz. 586 115
—— v. Searle (1831) 1 Moo. & Rob. 75 233
—— v. Secretary of State for India [1941] 2 K.B. 169; 111 L.J.K.B. 237; [1941] 2 All E.R. 546 302
—— v. Shaw (1830) 1 Lew.C.C. 116 264
—— v. Silcott [1987] Crim.L.R. 765 231
—— v. Silverlock [1894] 2 Q.B. 766; 63 L.J.M.C. 233; 58 J.P. 788; 10 R. 431; 72 L.T. 298; 43 W.R. 14; 18 Cox 104 .... 10, 11, 12, 130, 266, 268

TABLE OF CASES

R. v. Skirving; R. v. Grossman [1985] Q.B. 819; [1985] 2 W.L.R. 1001; 129 S.J. 299; (1985) 81 Cr.App.R. 9; [1985] Crim.L.R. 317	434
—— v. Smith (1909) 3 Cr.App.R. 87	268
—— v. —— (1915) 84 L.J.K.B. 2153; 59 S.J. 704; 31 T.L.R. 617; 11 Cr.App.R. 229; 114 L.T. 239; 25 Cox 271	149, 261
—— v. ——, October 23, 1967, reported in Thomas, *Current Sentencing Practice*, at I.S.4(a)	415
—— v. —— [1979] 1 W.L.R. 1445; 123 S.J. 602; [1979] 3 All E.R. 605; (1979) 69 Cr.App.R. 378; [1979] Crim.L.R. 592	165, 196, 230
—— v. —— [1987] V.R. 907	242
—— v. —— (John) [1973] 1 W.L.R. 1510; 117 S.J. 774; [1974] 1 All E.R. 376; [1973] Crim.L.R. 700; *sub nom.* R. v. Smith (John Anthony James) (1973) 58 Cr.App.R. 106	114
—— v. —— (Michael Graham) (1968) 112 S.J. 783; 52 Cr.App.R. 648; [1968] Crim.L.R. 674	268
—— v. Smith and Woolard (1978) 67 Cr.App.R. 211; [1978] Crim.L.R. 758	414
—— v. Sodo [1975] R.T.R. 357; [1975] Crim.L.R. 462; *sub nom.* R. v. Sodo (Frederick George), 61 Cr.App.R. 131	205, 423
—— v. Somers [1963] 1 W.L.R. 1306; 128 J.P. 20; 107 S.J. 813; [1963] 3 All E.R. 808; 48 Cr.App.R. 11; 61 L.G.R. 598	14, 128, 180, 428
—— v. Spencer, *The Times*, January 21, 1960	244
—— v. Stamford [1972] 2 Q.B. 391; [1972] 2 W.L.R. 1055; 116 S.J. 3123; [1972] 2 All E.R. 430; [1972] Crim.L.R. 374; *sub nom.* R. v. Stamford (John David), 56 Cr.App.R. 398	433
—— v. Stannard; R. v. Cope; R. v. Brown [1965] 2 Q.B. 1; [1964] 2 W.L.R. 461; 128 J.P. 224; [1964] 1 All E.R. 34; 48 Cr.App.R. 81	267
—— v. Statutory Visitors to St. Lawrence's Hospital, Caterham, *ex p.* Pritchard [1953] 1 W.L.R. 1158; 117 J.P. 458; 97 S.J. 590; [1953] 2 All E.R. 766	39, 44, 197
—— v. Sumner [1977] Crim.L.R. 362	432, 434
—— v. Sunderland Juvenile Court, *ex p.* G. (A Minor) [1988] 1 W.L.R. 398; 132 S.J. 372; [1988] 2 All E.R. 34; [1988] 2 F.L.R. 40; [1988] F.C.R. 193, C.A.; affirming [1988] 2 F.L.R. 40	388, 389, 390, 396
—— v. Sweet-Escott (1971) 55 Cr.App.R. 316	113
—— v. Tate [1977] R.T.R. 17	79, 115, 164
—— v. Taylor (1874) 13 Cox 77	175
—— v. Tilley [1961] 1 W.L.R. 1309; 125 J.P. 611; 105 S.J. 685; [1961] 3 All E.R. 406; 45 Cr.App.R. 360	267
—— v. —— [1985] V.R. 505	264
—— v. Tiverton Justices, *ex p.* Smith [1981] R.T.R. 280	203
—— v. Tolson (1864) 4 F. & F. 103	265
—— v. Treacey [1944] 2 All E.R. 228; 30 Cr.App.R. 93; 60 T.L.R. 544; 88 S.J. 367	114
—— v. Tupedo [1960] A.C. 58	263
—— v. Turnbull [1977] Q.B. 224; [1976] 3 All E.R. 549; [1976] Crim.L.R. 565; *sub nom.* R. v. Turnbull; R. v. Whitby; R. v. Roberts [1976] 3 W.L.R. 445; 120 S.J. 486; *sub nom.* R. v. Turnbull; R. v. Camelo; R. v. Whitby; R. v. Roberts (1976) 63 Cr.App.R. 132	242
—— v. Turner (Terence) [1975] Q.B. 834; [1975] 2 W.L.R. 56; 118 S.J. 848; 60 Cr.App.R. 80; *sub nom.* R. v. Turner [1975] 1 All E.R. 70; [1975] Crim.L.R. 98	109, 122, 123, 133, 136, 138, 147, 163, 164, 180, 229, 230, 231, 233, 239, 245, 264, 336, 348, 402
—— v. Uxbridge Justices, *ex p.* Sofaer (1987) 85 Cr.App.R. 367	82
—— v. Veltheim (1908) 148 C.C.C.Sess.Pap. 583	76
—— v. Vernege [1982] 1 W.L.R. 293; 126 S.J. 117; (1982) 74 Cr.App.R. 232; [1982] Crim.L.R. 598	235
—— v. Virgo (1988) 10 Cr.App.R.(S.) 427	418
—— v. Wagstaff [1983] Crim.L.R. 152	243
—— v. Waltham Forest London Borough, *ex p.* G. [1989] 2 F.L.R. 138; [1989] F.C.R. 509; (1989) 19 Fam.Law 429; (1989) 153 J.P.N. 644	392

TABLE OF CASES

R. v. Ward (1982) 4 Cr.App.R.(S.) 103 ... 415
—— v. Webb [1954] Crim.L.R. 49 ... 262
—— v. Wells [1976] Crim.L.R. 518 ... 209
—— v. West Malling Juvenile Court, Re K. (1986) 150 J.P. 367; 130 S.J. 650; [1986] 2 F.L.R. 405; (1986) 16 Fam.Law 328; (1986) 150 J.P.N. 542 ... 392
—— v. Whitehead (1848) 3 C. & K. 202 ... 144
—— v. —— (1866) 10 Cox C.C. 234; (1866) L.R. 1 C.C.R. 33; 35 L.J.M.C. 186; 14 L.T.4 89; 14 W.R. 677 ... 74, 241
—— v. Williams (1838) 8 C. & P. 434 ... 129
—— v. Wright (John) [1975] R.T.R. 193; sub nom. R. v. Wright (John Skirrow) (1974) 60 Cr.App.R. 114 ... 426
—— v. Wong [1977] 1 W.W.R. 1 ... 245
—— v. Wood Green Crown Court, ex p. P. [1982] 4 F.L.R. 206 ... 183, 399
—— v. Wright (1821) Russ. & Ry. 456 ... 152, 233, 234
R. (P.M.) (An Infant), Re [1968] 1 All E.R. 691n. ... 66, 394
Rabin v. Gerson Berger Association [1986] 1 W.L.R. 526; 130 S.J. 15; [1986] 1 All E.R. 374; (1986) 136 New L.J. 17, C.A.; affirming [1985] 1 W.L.R. 595 ... 168
—— v. Mendoza & Co. [1954] 1 W.L.R. 271; 98 S.J. 92; [1954] 1 All E.R. 247 ... 189
—— v. Kirklees Area Health Authority (Practice Note) [1980] 1 W.L.R. 1244; 124 S.J. 726; [1980] 3 All E.R. 610 ... 47, 338
Ramadge v. Ryan (1832) 9 Bing. 333; 2 L.J.C.P. 7; 2 M. & S. 421 ... 123, 124, 125
Ramsay v. Watson (1961) 108 C.L.R. 642 ... 164
Ramsdale v. Ramsdale (1945) 173 L.T. 393; 109 J.P. 239; 89 S.J. 447; 43 L.G.R. 301 ... 168
Randel v. Arcos [1937] 3 All E.R. 577 ... 294
Rasool v. West Midlands Passenger Transport Executive [1974] 3 All E.R. 638 ... 20
Reardon Smith Line Ltd. v. Yngvar Hansen-Tangen; Yangvar Hansen-Tangen v. Sanko Steamship Co. [1976] 1 W.L.R. 989; 120 S.J. 719; sub nom. Reardon Smith Line v. Hansen-Tangen; Hansen-Tangen v. Sanko Steamship Co. [1976] 3 All E.R. 570, H.L. ... 160, 367
Reckitt and Coleman Products v. Borden (No. 2) [1987] F.S.R. 407 . 119, 120, 121, 126, 289, 292
Reed Packaging v. Boozer [1988] I.C.R. 391; [1988] I.R.L.R. 333 ... 313
Reeve Bros. v. Lewis Reed & Co. [1968] R.P.C. 452 ... 372
Renshaw v. Dixon [1911] W.N. 40; 46 L.J. 92 ... 76
Reynolds v. Llanelly Associated Tin Plate Co. [1948] 1 All E.R. 140 ... 28
—— v. Meston (unreported), February 24, 1986, Q.B.D. ... 223
Rice v. Civil Service Commission [1977] I.R.L.R. 291 ... 313
—— v. Connolly [1966] 2 Q.B. 414; [1966] 3 W.L.R. 17; 130 J.P. 322; 110 S.J. 371; [1966] 2 All E.R. 649 ... 195
Richard Roberts Holdings Ltd. v. Douglas Smith Stimson (1989) 47 Build.L.R. 113 ... 92, 94, 95, 96, 98
Richardson v. Redpath Brown [1944] A.C. 62; 113 L.J.K.B. 81; 170 L.T. 93; 60 T.L.R. 117; 88 S.J. 34; [1944] 1 All E.R. 110; 36 B.W.C.C. 259 ... 71
Richmond v. Richmond (914) 111 L.T. 273; 58 S.J. 784 ... 246
Riddick v. Thames Board Mills [1977] 1 Q.B. 881; [1977] 3 W.L.R. 63; 121 S.J. 274; [1977] 3 All E.R. 677 ... 198
Rigolli v. London Borough of Lambeth (unreported), December 5, 1977 ... 224
Robertson v. Jackson (1845) 2 C.B. 412; 15 L.J.C.P. 28; 10 Jur. 98 ... 157
Robinson v. Shaw (1956) 167 E.G. 192 ... 249
—— v. Smith (W.H.) (1901) 17 T.L.R. 235 ... 24
Roe v. McGregor (Robert) and Sons Ltd.; Bills v. Roe [1968] 1 W.L.R. 925; 112 S.J. 235; [1968] 2 All E.R. 636 ... 116
Rofe v. Kevonkian [1936] 2 All E.R. 1334; 80 S.J. 719 ... 162
Rogers v. Rosedimond Investments (Blakes Market) Ltd. (1978) 247 E.G. 467 . 250, 251
Rose v. Ford [1937] A.C. 826; 106 L.J.K.B. 576; 157 L.T. 174; 53 T.L.R. 873; 58 Lloyd's Rep. 213; [1937] 3 All E.R. 359; 81 S.J. 688 ... 280
Rose-Troup v. Sleeping Car Co., The Times, January 31, 1911 ... 299
Rosedale Mouldings Ltd. v. Sibley [1980] I.C.R. 816; [1980] I.R.L.R. 387 ... 312

Rosen v. Dowley [1943] 2 All E.R. 172 224
Rosher, Re; Rosher v. Rosher (1884) 26 Ch.D. 801; 53 L.J.Ch. 722; 51 L.T. 785; 32
  W.R. 825 24
Ross v. Caunters [1980] Ch. 297; [1979] 3 W.L.R. 605; 123 S.J. 605; [1979] 3 All
  E.R. 580 .... 219, 361
Rossano v. Manufacturers Life Insurance Co. [1963] 2 Q.B. 352; [1962] 3 W.L.R.
  157; 106 S.J. 452; [1962] 2 All E.R. 214; [1962] 1 Lloyd's Rep. 187 307
Roussel Uclaf v. I.C.I. [1989] R.P.C. 59 371
Routh (J.M.) (Trustees of the Estate of) v. Central Land Board; E.J.D. Routh v. Same;
  R.A. Routh v. Same (1957) 8 P. & C.R. 290 258
Rouyer Guillet et Compagnie v. Rouyer Guillet and Co.; Rouyer Guillet v. Jackson
  Knowland & Co., 92 S.J. 731; [1949] 1 All E.R. 244n. 158
Rover International v. Cannon Film Sales [1987] 1 W.L.R. 1597; 131 S.J. 1591;
  [1987] 3 All E.R. 986; (1987) 3 BCC 369; [1987] BCLC 540; (1987) 84
  L.S.Gaz. 3658 .... 31, 33, 55, 341
Rowley v. London and North Western Railway Company (1873) L.R. 8 Ex.
  221; [1861–73] All E.R.Rep. 823; 42 L.J.Ex. 153; 29 L.T. 180; 21 W.R.
  869 .... 180, 280, 284
Royal Warrant Holders Association v. Edward Deane and Beal Ltd. [1912] 1 Ch. 10;
  81 L.J.Ch. 67; 105 L.T. 623; 28 T.L.R. 6; 28 R.P.C. 721; 56 S.J. 12 153
Rushton v. Higgins (1972) 116 S.J. 469; [1972] R.T.R. 456; [1972] Crim.L.R. 440 425

S. (An Infant), Re (Practice Note) [1959] 1 W.L.R. 921; 103 S.J. 545; [1959] 2 All E.R.
  675n. 391
S. (Infants), Re [1967] 1 W.L.R. 396; 110 S.J. 944; [1967] 1 All E.R. 202; 65 L.G.R.
  158; [1966] C.L.Y. 6308 .... 66, 394
S. and B. (Minors), Re, The Independent, June 1, 1990 .... 147, 154, 241, 242
S. and W., Re (1982) 12 Fam.Law 151 400
S.L. (A Minor) (Wardship: Mechanical Evidence), Re [1987] 2 F.L.R. 412 400
S. v. B. (1905) 21 T.L.R. 219 81
——— v. Distillers Co. (Biochemicals; J. v. Same [1970] 1 W.L.R. 114; 113 S.J. 672;
  [1969] 3 All E.R. 1412 282
——— v. W. (1980) 11 Fam.Law 81 402
S. (An Infant, by her guardian ad litem The Official Solicitor to the Supreme Court) v.
  S.; W. v. Official Solicitor (acting as guardian ad litem for a male infant named
  P.H.W.) [1972] A.C. 24; [1970] 3 W.L.R. 366; sub nom. S. v. S.; W. v. W., 114
  S.J. 635; sub nom. S. v. S.; W. v. Official Solicitor [1970] 3 All E.R. 107,
  H.L. 274, 275, 276
St.Chad, The, 109 S.J. 392; [1965] 2 Lloyd's Rep. 1, C.A.; affirming [1965] 1 Lloyd's
  Rep. 107 329
St. Pierre v. South American Stores [1937] 3 All E.R. 349 305
St. Piran, Re [1981] 1 W.L.R. 1300; 125 S.J. 586; [1981] 3 All E.R. 270 169
Salvin v. North Brancepeth Coal Company (1874) 31 L.T. 154; 9 Ch.App. 705; 44
  L.J.Ch. 149; 22 W.R. 904 .... 146, 148
Samuels v. Flavel [1970] S.A.S.R. 256 136
Sapporo Maru (Owners) v. Statue of Liberty (Owners); The Statue of Liberty [1968] 1
  W.L.R. 739; sub nom. Sapporo Maru (Owners) v. Statue of Liberty; The
  Statue of Liberty (1968) 112 S.J. 380 423
Sarah C. Getty Trust, Re. See Getty (Sarah C.) Trust, Re.
Savings & Investment Bank v. Gasco Investments (Netherlands) B.V. [1984] 1 W.L.R.
  271; 128 S.J. 115; [1984] 1 All E.R. 296; (1984) 81 L.S.Gaz. 657 .... 54, 169, 182
Saxby v. Fulton [1909] 2 K.B. 208; 101 L.T. 179; 78 L.J.K.B. 781; 25 T.L.R. 446; 53
  S.J. 397 294
Saxton, Re, Johnson v. Saxton [1962] 1 W.L.R. 968; 106 S.J. 668; [1962] 3 All E.R.
  92, C.A.; varying [1962] 1 W.L.R. 859 .... 65, 81, 187, 222
Schneider v. Leigh [1955] 2 Q.B. 195; [1955] 2 W.L.R. 904; 99 S.J. 276; [1955] 2 All
  E.R. 173 .... 186, 192, 200
Schultz v. R. [1981] W.A.R. 171 231

TABLE OF CASES

Science Research Council v. Nassé; Leyland Cars v. Vyas [1980] A.C. 1028; [1979] I.C.R. 921; [1979] 3 W.L.R. 762; 123 S.J. 768; [1979] 3 All E.R. 673; *sub nom.* Nassé v. Science Research Council; Vyas v. Leyland Cars [1979] I.R.L.R. 465, H.L.; affirming [1979] Q.B. 144 .... 39, 197, 199
Scott v. Scott [1913] A.C. 417; 82 L.J.P. 74; 109 L.T. 1; 29 T.L.R. 520; 57 S.J. 498 197
—— v. Scott [1982] 2 F.L.R. 320 .... 383, 384
—— v. Thompson [1958] 3 R.R.C. 261 259
Scott Ltd. v. Nice-Pak Products Ltd. [1988] F.S.R. 125 .... 134, 291, 292, 293
Scottish Shire Line Ltd. v. London and Provincial Marine and General Insurance Co. Ltd. [1912] 3 K.B. 51; 81 L.J.K.B. 1066; 107 L.T. 46; 17 Com.Cas. 240; 12 Asp.M.C. 253; 56 S.J. 551 144
Segama N.V. v. Penny Le Roy Ltd. (1984) 269 E.G. 322 249
Seneviratne v. R. [1936] 3 All E.R. 36 108
Serio v. Serio (1983) 4 F.L.R. 756; (1983) 13 Fam.Law 255 276
Seyfang v. Searle (G.D.) & Co. (1972) 117 S.J. 16, C.A.; affirming [1973] 1 Q.B. 148; [1973] 2 W.L.R. 17; [1973] 1 All E.R. 290 .... 104, 105, 106
Shaw v. Director of Public Prosecutions [1962] A.C. 220; [1961] 2 W.L.R. 897; 125 J.P. 437; 105 S.J. 421; [1961] 2 All E.R. 446; 45 Cr.App.R. 113, H.L.; affirming *sub nom.* R. v. Shaw [1961] 1 All E.R. 330 .... 130, 433
Sherrard v. Jacob [1965] N.I. 151 .... 17, 21, 421
Shawinigan v. Naud [1929] 4 D.L.R. 57 209
Sheffield City Council v. Siberry [1989] IC.R. 208; [1989] L.S.Gaz. March 8, 41 313
Shell Pensions Trust v. Pell Frischmann & Partners [1986] 2 All E.R. 911; (1987) 3 Const.L.J. 57; (1986) 6 ConLR 117; (1986) 136 New L.J. 238 .... 35, 41, 51, 216, 221, 356
Shield Properties and Investments Ltd. v. Anglo-Overseas Transport Co. Ltd. (1924) 273 E.G. 169 251
Shortt v. Robinson (1899) 63 J.P. 295; 68 L.J.Q.B. 352; 80 L.T. 261; 139 Cox C.C. 243 113
Shrewsbury (Earl) v. Trappas (1862) 31 L.J.Ch. 680 217
Sidaway v. Board of Governors of the Bethlem Royal Hospital and the Maudsley Hospital [1985] A.C. 871; [1985] 2 W.L.R. 480; 129 S.J. 154; [1985] 1 All E.R. 643; (1985) 135 New L.J. 203, H.L.; affirming [1984] Q.B. 498 .... 145, 193
Singer & Friedlander v. Wood (John D.) & Co. (1977) 243 E.G. 212 365
Skrzypkowski v. Silvan Investments [1963] 1 W.L.R. 525; [1963] 1 All E.R. 886; *sub nom.* Skrzypkowski v. Silvan Investments, 107 S.J. 134 249
Sleet v. Holman (1966) 12 R.R.C. 329; [1966] R.A. 589 259
Slingsby v. Att.-Gen. (1916) 33 T.L.R. 120; affirming (1916) 32 T.L.R. 364 .... 21, 67
Smith v. Buller (1875) L.R. 19 Eq. 473 224
—— v. Cole (1970) 114 S.J. 887; [1971] 1 All E.R. 200n.; [1970] R.T.R. 459 425
—— v. Cook (1876) 1 Q.B.D. 79; 45 L.J.Q.B. 122; 33 L.T. 722; 24 W.R. 206 .... 126, 130
—— v. Geraghty [1986] R.T.R. 222 .... 134, 428, 429
Snowball v. Gardner Merchant [1987] I.C.R. 719; [1987] I.R.L.R. 397; (1987) 84 L.S.Gaz. 1572 312
Société Anonyme Pêcheries Ostendaises v. Merchants' Marine Insurance Co. [1928] 1 K.B. 750 .... 217, 219, 361
Sodastream Ltd. v. Thorn Cascade Co. Ltd. [1982] R.P.C. 459; [1982] Com.L.R. 64 .... 145, 290
Sofaer v. Sofaer [1960] 1 W.L.R. 1173; 104 S.J. 892; [1960] 3 All E.R. 468 207
Sound Fisher, The (1937) 58 Lloyd's Rep. 135 328
Southgate v. Southgate (1978) 8 Fam.Law 246 382
Southwark London Borough v. Secretary of State for the Environment and Waterhouse [1987] J.P.L. 36 319
Spokes v. Grosvenor Hotel Co.]1897] 2 Q.B. 124; 66 L.J.Q.B. 598; 76 L.T. 677; 13 T.L.R. 426; 45 W.R. 545 188
Staffordshire Area Health Authority v. South Staffordshire Waterworks Co. [1978] 1 W.L.R. 1387; 122 S.J. 331; [1978] 3 All E.R. 769; (1978) 77 L.G.R. 17 160
Starr v. National Coal Board [1946] K.B. 354 311

l

Starr v. National Coal Board [1977] 1 W.L.R. 653; [1977] 1 All E.R. 243 .... 342, 343, 344, 345, 346
State v. Chapple, 135 Ariz. 281, 660 p.2d 1208 242
Statue of Liberty, The. *See* Sapporo Maru (Owners) v. Statue of Liberty.
Stearine, The (1864) 17 C.B.(N.S.) 56; 11 L.T. 272; 10 Jur.(N.S.) 881 158
Stephenson v. Clift [1988] R.T.R. 171 424
—— v. Stephenson [1985] F.L.R. 1140; (1984) 15 Fam.Law 253 387
—— v. Tyne Commissioners (1869) 17 W.R. 590 137
Stevens v. Simons, *The Times*, November 20, 1987 .... 88, 352
—— v. Stevens [1954] 1 W.L.R. 900; 98 S.J. 404; [1954] 2 All E.R. 381 77
Stojalowski v. Imperial Smelting Corporation (N.S.C.) (1976) 121 S.J. 118 212
Stone (S.) & Sons v. Pugh [1949] 1 K.B. 240 .... 164, 171, 252
Stroud v. Stroud (Practice Note) [1963] 1 W.L.R. 1080; 107 S.J. 273; [1963] 3 All E.R. 539 168
Sturge v. Haldimant (1848) 11 L.T.(O.S.) 28; N.P. 29 .... 127, 143
Subramanian v. Public Prosecutor [1956] 1 W.L.R. 965; 100 S.J. 566 165
Sugden v. Lord St. Leonards (1876) 1 P.D. 154; 45 L.J.P. 1; 34 L.T. 369; 24 W.R. 479 184
Sullivan v. West Yorkshire Passenger Transport Executive [1985] 2 All E.R. 134 .... 36, 50, 281, 282, 356
Suloo v. Redit & Co. Ltd. [1959] N.Z.L.R. 45 142
Sussex Peerage, The, 11 C. & F. 85; 8 Jur. 793 .... 294, 300
Sutcliffe v. Abbott (1902) 20 R.P.C. 50 380
—— v. Thackrah [1974] A.C. 727; [1974] 2 W.L.R. 295; 118 S.J. 148; [1974] 1 All E.R. 859; [1974] 1 Lloyd's Rep. 318, H.L.; reversing [1973] 1 W.L.R. 888 .... 323, 359
Swain v. Edlin-Sinclair Tyre Co. (1903) 20 R.P.C. 435 371
Syers v. Jonas (1848) 2 Exch. 111 159

T., *Re* [1982] 3 F.L.R. 183 396
T. (Minors) (Wardship: Jurisdiction) [1989] 2 W.L.R. 954; 133 S.J. 568; [1989] 1 All E.R. 297; (1989) 87 L.G.R. 735; (1989) 19 Fam.Law 145; (1989) 153 J.P.N. 185; [1989] 2 F.L.R. 212 392
T. (H.H.) v. T. (E.) [1971] 1 W.L.R. 429; 115 S.J. 186; *sub nom.* T. (H.) v. T. (E.) [1971] 1 All E.R. 590 276
Tate & Lyle Food and Distribution Ltd. v. Greater London Council [1983] 2 A.C. 509; [1983] 2 W.L.R. 649; [1983] 1 All E.R. 1159; (1983) 46 P. & C.R. 243; (1983) 81 L.G.R. 4434; [1983] 2 Lloyd's Rep. 117, H.L.; reversing [1982] 1 W.L.R. 970 220
Taylor, *Re* [1972] 2 Q.B. 369 394
—— v. Armand [1975] R.T.R. 225; [1975] Crim.L.R. 227 111
—— v. Barclay (1828) 2 Sim. 213; 7 L.J.(O.S.) Ch. 65 26
—— v. Greening (unreported), May 15, 1956, C.A. 51, 216
—— v. O'Connor [1971] A.C. 115; [1970] 2 W.L.R. 472; 114 S.J. 132; [1970] 1 All E.R. 365; [1970] T.R. 37; 49 A.T.C. 37 .... 134, 281, 282, 286
Technograph Printed Circuits Ltd. v. Mills and Rockley (Electronics) Ltd. [1972] R.P.C. 346 379
Temloc Ltd. v. Errill Properties Ltd. (1989) ConLR 109; (1987) 39 B.L.R. 30; (1988) 4 Const.L.J. 63 360
Tennants Textile Colours Ltd. v. Todd [1989] I.R.L.R. 3; [1988] 7 N.I.J.B. 88 313
Thames and Mersey Marine Insurance Co. v. Gunford Ship Co. [1911] A.C. 529; 80 L.J.P.C. 146; 105 L.T. 312; 16 Com.Cas. 270; 27 T.L.R. 518; 55 S.J. 631 159
Theodor Korner, The (1878) 3 P.D. 162; 47 L.J.P. 85; 38 L.T. 818; 27 W.R. 307 190
Thirkell (Lewis) v. Secretary of State for the Environment (1978) 248 E.G. 685; [1978] J.P.L. 844 318
Thom v. Worthing Skating Rink Co. (1876) L.R. 6 Ch.D. 415 213
Thomas v. Wignall [1987] Q.B. 1098; [1987] 2 W.L.R. 930; 131 S.J. 362; [1987] 1 All E.R. 1185; (1987) 84 L.S.Gaz. 417 286
Thompson (Minors), *Re* [1976] C.L.Y. 1788 66

TABLE OF CASES

Thompson (Minors) v. Charlwood (1969) 113 S.J. 1004 426
—— v. Thompson [1986] 1 F.L.R. 212 398
Thorensen Car Ferries v. Weymouth Portland Borough Council [1977] 2 Lloyd's Rep. 614 160
Thornton v. Royal Exchange Company (1791) Peake 37 168
Tickle v. Tickle [1968] 1 W.L.R. 937; 112 S.J. 397; [1968] 2 All E.R. 154 165
Tingle Jacobs & Co. v. Kennedy [1964] 1 W.L.R. 638n.; 108 S.J. 196; [1964] 1 All E.R. 888n. 423
Tobakin v. Dublin Co. [1905] 2 I.R. 58 195
Tomlinson v. Tomlinson [1980] 1 W.L.R. 322; 124 S.J. 47; [1980] 1 All E.R. 593; (1979) 10 Fam.Law 88 107
Toohey v. Metropolitan Police Commissioner [1965] A.C. 595; [1965] 2 W.L.R. 439; 129 J.P. 181; 109 S.J. 130; [1965] 1 All E.R. 506; 49 Cr.App.R. 148, H.L.; reversing sub nom. R. v. Toohey [1964] 1 W.L.R. 1286 .... 240, 241
Top Shop Estates Ltd. v. Danino (C.); Same v. Tandy Corp. [1985] 1 E.G.L.R. 9; (1985) 273 E.G. 197 .... 255, 259, 324
Torenia, The. See Aktieselskabet de Danske Sukkerfabrikker v. Bajamar Compania Naviera S.A.; Torenia, The.
Townier v. National Provincial and Union Bank of England [1924] 1 K.B. 461; 93 L.J.K.B. 449; 130 L.T. 682; 29 Com.Cas. 129; 40 T.L.R. 214; 68 S.J. 441 196
Town and City Properties Ltd. v. Wiltshier Southam Ltd. (1988) 44 B.L.R. 109 360
Town Centre Securities Ltd. v. Morrison Supermarket (1982) 263 E.G. 435 .... 171, 251
Tracey Peerage Case (1843) 10 Cl. & F. 154; 1 L.T. 310 .... 213, 269
Transport Ministry v. Garry [1973] 1 N.Z.L.R. 120 112
Trendtex Trading Corporation v. Central Bank of Nigeria [1976] 1 W.L.R. 868; 120 S.J. 554; [1976] 3 All E.R. 437; [1976] 2 C.M.L.R. 668 301
Trepca Mines Ltd., Re [1960] 1 W.L.R. 1273; 104 S.J. 979; [1960] 3 All E.R. 304n., C.A.; reversing [1960] 1 W.L.R. 24 74
Trial of Spencer Cowper, Esq. (1699) 13 How.St.Tr. 1106 8
Triplex Safety Glass v. Lancegaye Safety Glass Ltd. [1939] 2 K.B. 395; 108 L.J.K.B. 763; 157 L.T. 576; 54 T.L.R. 90; 55 R.P.C.21; 81 S.J. 982; [1939] 2 All E.R. 693 188
Truman v. Chatham Borough Council; Whitbread Fremlins v. Sittingbourne and Milton Urban District Council (1974) 28 P. & C.R. 326 258
Turner v. Blunden [1986] Fam. 120; [1986] 2 W.L.R. 491; 130 S.J. 184; (1985) 150 J.P. 180; [1986] 2 All E.R. 75; [1986] 1 F.L.R. 69; (1986) 16 Fam.Law 191; (1985) 150 J.P.N. 239 278
—— v. Carlisle City Council (1989) 8 C.L. 259 335
—— v. Secretary of State for Transport (1979) ? P. & C.R. 468 316
Turquand, Ex p., Re Parker (1885) 14 Q.B.D. 636; 54 L.J.Q.B. 242; 53 L.T. 579; 33 W.R. 437 25

U.D.S. Tailoring Ltd. v. B.L. Holdings Ltd. (1981) 261 E.G. 49 253
Ullah v. Hall Line Ltd. [1960] 1 W.L.R. 1320; 104 S.J. 1034; [1960] 3 All E.R. 488; [1960] 2 Lloyd's Rep. 121 222
United Mills Agencies v. Bray (R.E. Harvey) & Co. [1952] 1 T.L.R. 149; 96 S.J. 121; [1952] 1 All E.R. 225n.; [1951] 2 Lloyd's Rep. 631 145
United States v. Amaral (1973) 488 F. 2d 1148 242
—— v. Baller (1975) 519 F. 2d 463 .... 132, 133
—— v. Clifford, 535 F.Supp. 424 264
United States Shipping Board v. Ship St. Albans [1931] A.C. 632 130

Vakauta v. Kelly [1989] A.L.J. 610 212
Valensi v. British Radio Corporation Ltd. [1972] F.S.R. 273, C.A.; [1973] R.P.C. 337; reversing [1971] F.S.R. 66; [1972] R.P.C. 373 .... 374, 375
Valentine's Settlement, Re; Valentine v. Valentine [1965] Ch. 831; [1965] 2 W.L.R. 1015; 109 S.J. 237; [1965] 2 All E.R. 226, C.A.; affirming [1965] Ch. 226 .... 53, 303, 304
Van der Donkt v. Thelluson (1849) 8 C.B. 812; 19 L.J.C.P. 12 .... 299, 302

TABLE OF CASES

Van der Lely (C.) N.V. v. Bamfords Ltd. [1963] R.P.C. 61, H.L.; affirming [1961]
  R.P.C. 296; [1962] C.L.Y. 2283, C.A.; affirming [1960] R.P.C. 169 378
—— v. Watveare Overseas Ltd. [1982] F.S.R. 122 372
Vickers v. Siddell (1890) 7 R.P.C. 293 380
Vose v. Barr [1966] 2 All E.R. 226n. 221

W. (Minors), Re, *The Times*, November 10, 1989 397
——, Re [1990] 1 F.L.R. 203 406
W. (Minors) (Child Abuse: Evidence), Re [1988] F.C.R. 69; [1987] 1 F.L.R.
  297 .... 403, 409
W. and L. (Minors) (Interim Custody), Re (1987) 151 J.P. 222; (1987) 17 Fam.Law
  130; [1987] 2 F.L.R. 67; (1987) 151 J.P.N. 142 385
W. v. Egdell, *The Independent*, November 10, 1989, C.A.; affirming [1989] 2 W.L.R.
  689; 133 S.J. 570; [1989] 1 All E.R. 397 .... 193, 194, 195, 196
—— v. W. [1964] P. 67; [1963] 3 W.L.R. 540; 107 S.J. 533; [1963] 2 All E.R. 841,
  C.A.; affirming 107 S.J. 237; [1963] 2 All E.R. 386 275
—— v. —— [1988] 1 F.L.R. 86 277
—— v. —— (A Minor: Custody Appeal) [1988] 2 F.L.R. 505; (1989) 19 Fam.Law
  63 .... 386, 387
Wahl and Simon-Solitec v. Buhler-Miag (England) Ltd. [1979] F.S.R. 183 372
Wakeford v. Lincoln (Bishop) (1921) 90 L.J.P.C. 174 269
Walker v. Hodgins [1984] R.T.R. 34; [1983] Crim.L.R. 555 424
—— v. Hooper (1978) 21 R.R.C. 155 259
Wallworth v. Balmer [1966] 1 W.L.R. 16; 109 S.J. 936; [1965] 3 All E.R. 721 ...... 19, 20
Walton v. Queen, The [1978] A.C. 788; [1977] 3 W.L.R. 902; 121 S.J. 728; [1978] 1
  All E.R. 542; (1977) 66 Cr.App.R. 25; [1977] Crim.L.R. 747 .... 230, 238
Ward v. Keene [1970] R.T.R. 177 426
—— v. Shell-Mex and B.P. Ltd. [1952] 1 K.B. 280; [1951] 2 T.L.R. 976; 95 S.J. 686;
  [1951] 2 All E.R. 904 324
Waring (F.R.) (U.K.) v. Administraçao Geral do Acucar e do Alcool E.P. [1983] 1
  Lloyd's Rep. 45 27
Warner-Lambert Co. v. Glaxo Laboratories [1975] R.P.C. 354 371
Wass (W. & J.) v. Secretary of State for the Environment and City of Stoke on Trent
  Council [1986] J.P.L. 120 319
Watson v. M'Ewan [1905] A.C. 480 213
—— v. Powles [1968] 1 Q.B. 596; [1967] 3 W.L.R.1 364; 111 S.J. 562; [1967] 3 All
  E.R. 721 .... 281, 284
Watt v. Thomas [1947] A.C. 484; 176 L.T. 498; 63 T.L.R. 314; [1947] 1 All E.R.
  582 212
Waugh v. British Railways Board [1980] A.C. 521; [1979] 3 W.L.R. 150; 123 S.J.
  506; [1979] 2 All E.R. 1169; [1979] I.R.L.R. 364, H.L.; reversing (1978) 122
  S.J. 730 .... 190, 191, 192, 198
Wayland v. Metropolitan Railway Co. [1874] W.N. 96 194
Webb v. Page (1843) 1 Car. & Kir. 23 223
—— v. Webb [1986] 1 F.L.R. 462; (1986) 16 Fam.Law 155 .... 385, 398
Wellington (Duke), Re, Glentaner v. Wellington [1948] Ch. 118; 64 T.L.R. 54; 92
  S.J.11, C.A.; affirming [1947] Ch. 506; [1947] L.J.R.1451; 63 T.L.R. 295; 91
  S.J. 369; [1947] 2 All E.R. 854 305
Welwyn Department Stores Ltd. v. Welwyn Garden City U.D.C. and Pote [1959]
  J.P.L. 438; 52 R. & I.T. 324; 4 R.R.C. 227; 173 E.G. 947 259
Westacott v. Hahn [1917] 1 K.B. 605; 86 L.J.K.B. 956; affirmed [1918] 1 K.B. 495;
  87 L.J.K.B. 555; 118 L.T. 615; 34 T.L.R. 257; 62 S.J. 348 159
Westlake v. Westlake [1910] P. 167; 79 L.J.P. 36; 102 L.T. 396; 54 S.J. 215; 26 T.L.R.
  223 .... 53, 303, 309
Westminster Renslade Ltd. v. Secretary of State for the Environment (1983) 127 S.J.
  444; (1984) 48 P. & C.R. 255; [1983] J.P.L. 454 319
Wetherall v. Harrison [1976] Q.B. 773; [1976] 2 W.L.R. 168; 119 S.J. 848; [1976] 1
  All E.R. 241; [1976] R.T.R. 125; [1976] Crim.L.R. 54 .... 26, 113

liii

TABLE OF CASES

Wexler v. Playle [1960] 1 Q.B. 217; [1960] 2 W.L.R. 187; 124 J.P. 115; 104 S.J. 87; [1960] 1 All E.R. 338; 53 R. & I.T. 38; 58 L.G.R. 120; 5 R.R.C. 359, C.A.; affirming [1959] J.P.L. 127 259
Wheeler v. Le Marchant (1881) 17 Ch.D. 675; 50 L.J.Ch. 795; 44 L.T. 632; 45 J.P. 728 189
White v. Bywater (1887) 19 Q.B.D. 582; 36 W.R. 280; 51 J.P. 821 181
Whitehouse v. Jordan [1981] 1 W.L.R. 246; 125 S.J. 167; [1981] 1 All E.R. 267, H.L.; affirming [1980] 1 All E.R. 650 .... 15, 87, 348
Whitelegg, Re [1899] P. 267; 68 L.J.P. 97; 81 L.T. 234 300
Whiteley, Re [1891] 1 Ch. 558; 60 L.J.Ch. 149; 64 L.T.81; 39 W.R. 248 324
White's Patent (Revocation), Re [1957] R.P.C. 405 373
Wholesale Mail Order Supplies Ltd. v. Secretary of State for the Environment [1976] J.P.L. 163; (1975) 237 E.G. 185 320
Wickers v. Wickers [1952] W.N. 301; [1952] 1 T.L.R. 1473; 96 S.J. 426; [1952] 2 All E.R. 98 393
Williams v. Eady (1893) 10 T.L.R. 41 24
Williamson v. Rider [1963] 1 Q.B. 89; [1962] 3 W.L.R. 119; 106 S.J. 263; [1962] 2 All E.R. 268 64
Willoughby's Case (1597) Cro.Eliz. 566 .... 7, 60
Wilsher v. Essex Area Health Authority [1988] 2 W.L.R. 557; 132 S.J. 418; [1988] 1 All E.R. 871; (1988) 138 New L.J. 78, H.L.; affirming [1987] Q.B. 730; [1987] 2 W.L.R. 425 .... 33, 339
Wilson v. Rastall (1792) 4 Term Rep. 753 195
—— v. Wilson [1903] P. 157; 72 L.J.P. 53; 89 L.T. 77 .... 299, 302
Wilton v. Phillips (1903) 19 T.L.R. 390 182
Winchester City Council v. Secretary of State for the Environment (1979) 77 L.G.R. 715; (1979) 39 P. & C.R. 1; [1979] J.P.L. 620; (1979) 251 E.G. 259, C.A.; affirming (1978) 36 P. & C.R. 455 .... 126, 318
Wingfield, Ex p., Re Florence (1879) 10 Ch.D. 591; 40 L.T. 15; 27 W.R. 346 25
Wooding v. Dowty Rotol (unreported), 1968 C.A. No. 184 351
Woolley v. North London Railway Co. (1869) L.R. 4 C.P. 602; 38 L.J.C.P. 317; 20 L.T. 813; 17 W.R. 650, 797 .... 189, 190
Woolworth (F.W.) v. Moore [1979] J.P.L. 241; (1978) 247 E.G. 999; (1978) 21 R.R.C. 208 .... 250, 259
Worboys v. Acme Investments (1969) 210 E.G. 335; 4 B.L.R. 133; 119 New L.J. 322 .... 355, 365
Working Men's Mutual Society, Re (1882) 21 Ch.D. 831; 51 L.J.Ch. 850; 47 L.T. 645; 30 W.R. 938 223
Worrall v. Reich [1955] 1 Q.B. 296; [1955] 2 W.L.R. 338; 99 S.J. 109; [1955] 1 All E.R. 363 .... 39, 187, 189
Wright v. Bennett (No. 1) [1948] 1 K.B. 601; [1948] L.J.R. 1019; 64 T.L.R. 149; 92 S.J. 167; [1948] 1 All E.R. 411 222
—— v. Doe d. Tatham (1838) 4 Bing.N.C. 489; 5 Cl. & Fin. 670; 2 Jur. 461 ..... 18, 22, 123, 162
—— v. Sydney Municipal Council (1916) 16 S.R.(N.S.W.) 348 172
Wright (John) v. General Gas Appliances Ltd. (1928) 46 R.P.C. 169 379

Yates v. Pym (1816) 6 Taunt. 446 159
Yeomans (Minors), Re (1985) 15 Fam.Law 121 402
Yianni v. Yianni [1966] 1 W.L.R.1 20; 110 S.J. 111; [1966] 1 All E.R. 231n. 66
Yorke v. Yorkshire Insurance Company [1918] 1 K.B. 662; 87 L.J.K.B. 881; 34 T.L.R. 353; 119 L.T. 27 127
Young v. Flint [1987] R.T.R. 300 .... 112, 422

X. (A Minor) (Child Abuse: Evidence), Re [1989] 1 F.L.R. 30 409

Z. (Minors) (Child Abuse: Evidence), Re [1989] 2 F.L.R. 3; (1989) 19 Fam.Law 393; [1989] F.C.R. 440; (1989) 153 J.P.N. 595 .... 403, 405, 406, 410
Zermatt Holdings S.A. v. Nu-Life Upholstery Repairs Ltd. [1985] 2 E.G.L.R. 14; (1985) 275 E.G. 1134 254

Table of Statutes

1806	Witnesses Act (46 Geo. 3, c. 37)	188	1933	Evidence (Foreign, Dominion and Colonial Documents) Act (23 & 24 Geo. 5, c. 4) 294
1837	Wills Act (7 Will. 4 & 1 Vict. c. 26)—			Children and Young Persons Act (23 & 24 Geo. 5, c. 12)—
	s. 21	270		s. 99 20
1853	Evidence (Amendment) Act (16 & 17 Vict. c. 83)—		1938	Evidence Act (1 & 2 Geo. 6, c. 28) 399
	s. 3	187		s. 1 (2) 183, 309
1856	Foreign Tribunals Evidence Act (19 & 20 Vict. c. 113)—		1948	Criminal Justice Act (11 & 12 Geo. 6, c. 58)—
	s. 1	106		s. 41 (1) 84
1861	Foreign Law Ascertainment Act (24 & 25 Vict. c. 11)	294	1949	(5) .... 84 Lands Tribunal Act (12, 13 & 14 Geo. 6, c. 42)—
1865	Criminal Procedure Act (28 & 29 Vict. c. 18)	267		s. 3 .... 68, 256 (5) 258
	s. 8 .... 266, 269		1950	Arbitration Act (14 Geo. 6, c. 27)—
1887	Coroners Act (50 & 51 Vict. c. 71)—			s. 12 (6) (g) 81, 322
	s. 21	321	1954	Landlord and Tenant Act (2 & 3 Eliz. 2, c. 56) 247, 249, 250
	(3) 320, 321			
	s. 23	321		s. 63 (5) 68
	s. 26	322	1956	Sexual Offences Act (4 & 5 Eliz. 2, c. 69)—
1890	Foreign Jurisdiction Act (53 & 54 Vict. c. 37)—			s. 14 (4) 238
	s. 4 .... 24, 26		1957	Homicide Act (5 & 6 Eliz. 2, c. 11) 203
1891	Supreme Court of Judicature Act (54 & 55 Vict. c. 53)—			s. 2 (1) 237
	s. 3	329	1959	Obscene Publications Act (7 & 8 Eliz. 2, c. 66)—
1894	Prevention of Cruelty to Children Act (57 & 58 Vict. c. 41)	20		s. 1 .... 432 (1) .... 431 s. 4 (1) 432
1907	Evidence (Colonial Statutes) Act (7 Edw. 7, c. 16)	294		(2) 431, 434
1911	Perjury Act (1 & 2 Geo. 5, c. 6)—		1961	Land Compensation Act (9 & 10 Eliz. 2, c. 33)—
	s. 1 .... 75, 214			s. 1 256
1921	Tribunals of Inquiry (Evidence) Act (11 & 12 Geo. 5, c. 7)—		1964	s. 2 (3) .... 256 Licensing Act (c. 26)— s. 169 (1) 19
	s. 1	310	1965	Criminal Evidence Act (c. 20)—
1926	Coroners (Amendment) Act (16 & 17 Geo. 5, c. 59)—			s. 1 182
	s. 21	320		Criminal Procedure (Attendance of Witnesses) Act (c. 69)—
	s. 22	321		
	(4) 320, 321			s. 2 83

TABLE OF STATUTES

1967 Welsh Language Act (c. 66)—
  s. 1 74
 Criminal Justice Act (c. 80)—
  s. 9 59
 Leasehold Reform Act (c. 88) 253
1968 Criminal Appeal Act (c. 19)—
  s. 17 (1) (a) 118
  s. 21 (1) 83
  s. 23 (1), (2) 117, 118
  s. 32 77
 Theatres Act (c. 54)—
  s. 3 (1) 431
   (2) 434
 Civil Evidence Act (c. 64) ... 33, 34, 53, 54, 183, 258, 399
  s. 2 (2) 109
   (6) 109
  s. 4 .... 54, 182
   (1) 259
  s. 5 54
  s. 8 (1) 35
   (2) (b) 20
  s. 10 (3) 359
   (4) 359
  s. 15 188
  s. 16 (1) (a) 188
   (3) 187
  s. 18 (1) (b) 322
  Pt. I 54, 57, 121, 150
1969 Family Law Reform Act (c. 46) 272
  s. 20 .... 270, 272
   (1) 271, 272
   (2) 271, 272
   (1A) 272, 273
   (1B) 273
   (2) (b) 273
    (c) 273, 277
   (2A) 272
  s. 21 275
  s. 22 271
  s. 23 (1) 275, 278
  s. 26 276
 Children and Young Persons Act (c. 54)—
  s. 3 (5) 416
   (6) 416
  s. 9 412
   (1) 398
  s. 12A (6) 416
  s. 12B 416
  s. 12C 416
  s. 32A 391
  s. 32B 391
  s. 34 (3) 412
  Sched. 1, para. 4 416

1971 Guardianship of Minors Act (c. 3) 201, 381, 385
  s. 1 402
  s. 5 381
  s. 9 381
 Misuse of Drugs Act (c. 38)—
  s. 37 156
 Tribunals and Inquiries Act (c. 62)—
  s. 10 310
  s. 11 310
 Town and Country Planning Act (c. 78)—
  s. 29 316
  s. 282 (2) 315
1972 Road Traffic Act (c. 20)—
  s. 5 420
   (3) 420
  s. 6 .... 420, 428
   (2) 420
  s. 8 (1) 420
   (7) 425
  s. 10 (2) 420, 421, 427
   (3) (a) 422
   (b) 422
   (4) 425
   (5) 422, 425
   (6) 425
   (8) 422
   (9) 422
 Civil Evidence Act (c. 30) ... 18, 53, 257, 297, 399
  s. 1 (1) 54
   (2) 54, 183
  s. 2 (1) 109
   (3) (b) 120
  s. 3 .... 19, 151
   (1) 121, 150, 151, 233
   (3) 150, 233, 269, 363
  s. 4 (1) 11, 298, 303
   (2) 295, 296, 297
   (b) 296
   (3) 296, 297
   (4) 295
   (5) 296
  s. 5 (2) 322, 359
   (3) 151
 European Communities Act (c. 68)—
  s. 3 (2) 24
  Sched. 1, Pt. I 24
 Local Government Act (c. 7;)—
  s. 250 (2)–(5) 315
1973 Matrimonial Causes Act (c. 18)—
  s. 25 (1) 402
 Guardianship Act (c. 29) . 382, 385
  s. 1 (3) 381

1973	Guardianship Act—*cont.*	
	s. 3 (3)	381
	s. 6 (1)	381
	(2) (*a*)	385
	(3)	386
	(3A)	397
	(6)	381
	Powers of Criminal Courts Act (c. 62)—	
	s. 2	416
	(3)	416
	s. 4A (1)	416
	s. 4B (1)	416
	s. 14 (3)	413
	s. 20	413
	s. 20A	413
	(2)	413
	(4)	413
	s. 46 (1)	415
	(2)	415
1975	Sex Discrimination Act (c. 65)—	
	s. 66 (6)	68
1976	Adoption Act (c. 36)—	
	s. 65 (1) (*a*)	391
1977	Patents Act (c. 37)—	
	s. 104	188
	s. 125 (3)	378
1978	Domestic Proceedings and Magistrates' Courts Act (c. 22)	383
	s. 8	382
	s. 10	382
	s. 12 (3)	382
	(5)	386
	(6)	386, 397
	(7)	383
	(9)	382
1980	Magistrates' Courts Act (c. 43)—	
	s. 30	225
	s. 97	83
	s. 150 (4)	20
1981	Transport Act (c. 56)	420
	Supreme Court Act (c. 54)—	
	s. 32A	352
	s. 33 (1)	80
	(2)	353
	(*b*)	353
	s. 34 (2)	353
	(*b*)	353
	(3)	82
	(*a*)	82
	(6)	82
	s. 35 (1)	80, 353
	s. 54 (8)	73, 329
	s. 68	73
	s. 69 (5)	294
	s. 70	68, 375

1981	Supreme Court Act—*cont.*	
	s. 70—*cont.*	
	(1)	68
	(2)	70
	(3)	68, 374, 375
	(4)	68
	s. 84 (1)	57
1982	Criminal Justice Act (c. 48)—	
	s. 1 (4)	413
	s. 2 (2)	413
	(3)	413
	(6)	413
	Transport Act (c. 49)	420
1983	Mental Health Act (c. 20)	225, 416, 417
	s. 35	417
	(2) (*b*)	417
	(3) (*a*)	417
	(*b*)	417
	(4)	417
	(5)	417
	(8)	417
	s. 36	417
	(3)	417
	(4)	417
	(7)	418
	s. 37	418
	(2)	418
	(3)	418
	(4)	418
	s. 38	418
	(1)	418
	(*b*)	418
	(4)	418
	s. 41	418
	(2)	418
	s. 54 (1)	417
1984	Telecommunications Act (c. 12)—	
	Sched. 2, para. 5	68
	County Courts Act (c. 28)—	
	ss. 26–31	328
	s. 52 (2)	353
	(*a*)	353
	(*b*)	353
	s. 53 (2)	353
	s. 54 (1)	353
	s. 59	328
	s. 63	329
	(1)	69
	(2)	68
	(3)	70
	(4)	68
	(5)	69
	s. 65	73
	s. 68	294
	s. 76	64
	Police and Criminal Evidence Act (c. 60)	124, 261

1984	Police and Criminal Evidence Act—*cont.*		1987	Family Law Reform Act (c. 42)		270
	ss. 19–22	82		s. 1B (*b*)		274
	s. 52	80		s. 17		276
	s. 54 (1)	80		s. 23		270
	s. 55	84		(1)		273
	s. 61	84, 261		(*b*)		273
	s. 62	84		s. 34 (2)		271
	(1) (*a*)	84		Sched. 2, paras. 20–25		270, 272
	s. 66	75	1988	Criminal Justice Act (c. 33)—		
	s. 67 (2)	75		s. 30		183, 184, 185
	s. 76	232		(3)		58, 59
	s. 79	107		(3) (*c*)		58, 59
	s. 81	57	1989	Children Act (c. 41)—		
	s. 86	57		s. 22		273
1985	Prosecution of Offences Act (c. 23)—			s. 89		272
	s. 19 (3) (*b*)	76		s. 96 (3)		183, 397
1986	Family Law Act (c. 55)—			s. 104 (1)		183, 397
	s. 56	272				

Part A: INTRODUCTION

CHAPTER 1

Introduction

A. THE LAW OF EVIDENCE AND EXPERT EVIDENCE

1 A positive body of rules

The evidence given by expert witnesses has traditionally been regarded as an exception to the substantive rule that witnesses in general may not give evidence of opinion but only of fact.[1] The relevant law has been measured largely by the extent to which evidence given by experts departs from that of lay witnesses as to the manner and circumstances in which it may be adduced. There are three particular reasons why such an assumption is inappropriate for present purposes.

First, the exposition of an area of law or legal practice is, for entirely practical reasons of clarity and ease of comprehension, better achieved by a positive, rather than a negative statement of rules. Secondly, it is contended that, aside from this practical aspect, the law relating to expert evidence is, as a matter of logic, more appropriately seen as a set of rules which form a category within the general law of evidence. It may be that these rules have been treated as exceptions to other categories in part because expert witnesses, although they have existed as such for hundreds of years, are nevertheless comparatively recent arrivals on the evidential scene, and have therefore been described largely by reference to pre-existing rules of the law of evidence. Furthermore it will be seen that much expert evidence is, despite being expert evidence properly so-called, not evidence of opinion, so that to describe it generically as an exception to a rule about opinion evidence is to limit its scope in a misleading manner. Thirdly, the modern legal process has come to rely increasingly and very substantially upon expert evidence. There are now, in addition to the limited fields in which such evidence is required as a matter of law,[2] many areas of law and causes of action in which in practical terms the evidence of experts is indispensable.[3] As a consequence of

---

[1] See *e.g.* Lord Mansfield in *Carter* v. *Boehm* (1766) 3 Burr. 1905 and *Folkes* v. *Chadd* (1782) 3 Doug. 157, and J. H. Wigmore, *A. Treatise on the Anglo-American System of Evidence* (3rd ed., 1940), Vol. vii, para. 1918.
[2] *e.g.* proof of foreign law (see Chap. 16).
[3] *e.g.* Official Referee's business, personal injuries, and professional negligence.

this, a body of law has emerged governing the admission and assessment of such evidence in these areas which lends an element of incongruity to persistence with the terminology of exception rather than rule.

Expert evidence is better regarded as evidence which is admissible because it is relevant and of probative value in relation to matters in issue in the case, and therefore as a particular category of such admissible evidence. This approach is more consonant both with the weight of authority and with the actual practice of the courts and tribunals at all levels. It also conforms more closely with the assumptions underlying the extensive procedural rules which now regulate the admission of such evidence in civil proceedings.[4]

2   Relevance and probative value

Expert evidence on a particular matter is admissible if it has both relevance and probative value in relation to it. The question of relevance is decided according to precisely the same criteria as for evidence generally, though the expert evidence may be different in form, in particular where it consists of opinion rather than fact.

Relevance   The legal concept of relevance describes a logical relationship between a piece of information and a proposition which requires proof or disproof. Thus:

> "evidence is relevant if it is logically probative or disprobative of some matter which requires proof."[5]

The question which must be asked is whether the proposed evidence renders "more or less probable,"[6] or tends to prove or disprove, a matter in issue in the case. Many definitions of relevance have been formulated, but even some of the most influential have suffered from defects such as a conflation of the concepts of relevance and standard of proof. Stephen, for instance, describes a fact as relevant if it "proves or renders probable" another fact.[7]

Probative value   Expert evidence is capable of admission where it is not only relevant, but also has a high probative value in relation to issues in the case. This means that it is particularly persuasive in its tendency to prove or disprove particular matters in issue. There is no single criterion by which to judge whether evidence has probative value, and it is obvious that being a relative concept it is a question of degree. The question of

---

[4] In particular R.S.C. Ord. 38.
[5] *D.P.P.* v. *Kilbourne* [1973] A.C. 729 at 756, *per* Lord Simon of Glaisdale.
[6] *Ibid.*, at 756.
[7] Stephen J., *Digest of the Law of Evidence* (12th ed., 1936), article 1.

probative value at the admissibility stage (*i.e.* prior to admitting the evidence) involves a similar process of assessment as the question of weight at the adjudication stage (*i.e.* after all the evidence has been adduced), though at the former stage the hurdle will usually be lower, as the evidence needs only to be capable of being given weight at the adjudication stage. The law of evidence consists largely of rules which have been developed to limit and therefore effectively to define what evidence the law regards as having probative value in situations in which evidence would prima facie be admissible because it was relevant. To take an example, most hearsay is relevant, but extensive rules have developed to admit only that which is likely to have a high probative value. Thus while evidence must be relevant to be admissible, not all relevant evidence is admissible.

Expert and lay witnesses Where expert evidence is admissible it has probative value because:– (i) there are issues in the case which require specialist knowledge or experience for their resolution and (ii) evidence is being adduced from a person who has specialist knowledge or experience appropriate to those issues. By contrast the evidence of lay witnesses would have very little or no probative value on such issues, because they have little or no more specialist knowledge or experience than the tribunal whose task it is to adjudicate upon the facts and can therefore make no contribution to the desired tendency to prove or disprove matters in issue.

Similarly the opinions of lay witnesses are inadmissible, save in certain very limited circumstances,[8] because they have little probative value.[9] Expert opinions, however, have a potentially high probative value. First, the expert witness will probably be experienced in arriving at, expressing and justifying opinions in his specialist field. Secondly, while there is often no method of testing the accuracy of the opinions of lay witnesses except by reference to known facts, which may be scarce on the particular issue, expert opinions can usually be tested in relation both to known facts and to the opinion of an expert witness called by another party in the case. It is the duty of the expert witness:

> "to furnish the judge or jury with the necessary scientific criteria for testing the accuracy of their conclusions, so as to enable the judge or jury to form their own independent judgment by the application of these criteria to the facts proved in evidence."[10]

The identity and qualities of the witness himself therefore assume an importance in relation to the admissibility of expert evidence which make

---

[8] Described, at pp.17–22 below.
[9] See *e.g.* A. Zuckerman, "The So-Called Opinion Rule . . . ," in W. Twining (ed.) *Facts in Law*, (1983), p. 155.
[10] *Davie* v. *Edinburgh Corporation* [1953] S.C. 34, 40.

them, by contrast with the position in relation to other forms of evidence, particularly significant aspects of the question of probative value when specialist issues arise.

B. THE DEVELOPMENT OF EXPERT EVIDENCE

An attempt to trace the historical origins of the modern law of expert evidence, or of the hearing of expert witnesses, is complicated not only by the relative absence of early law reports, but also by the fact that our knowledge of the early courts suggests that it was probably not until about the fifteenth century that the modern notion of the oral witness as the main vehicle for communicating evidence to the court began to appear. Nonetheless it is possible to identify, from some time before this, something akin to expert knowledge being incorporated into the court process,[11] and this can frequently be identified by reference to the nature of the issue before the court.

1 Expert knowledge in the medieval courts

Expert knowledge was certainly assumed to be important to the work of the courts prior to the fifteenth century. It seems likely, however, to have taken the form either of a jury composed of persons with specialist knowledge, or of skilled persons assisting the court, not as witnesses, but more in the manner of assessors.[12] Learned Hand lists a number of cases from the fourteenth century in which it is clear that a jury was empanelled whose members had special knowledge of the trade in respect of which proceedings had been brought,[13] including prosecutions for the use of fishing nets with mesh of a size contrary to trade ordinances,[14] the improper tanning of hides,[15] false tapestry,[16] improper hats and caps,[17] false pewter vessels,[18] false gloves[19] and false wine.[20]

The use of specialist juries, however, was not the only method of

---

[11] See Learned Hand, "Historical and Practical Considerations Regarding Expert Testimony" (1901) 15 *Harvard Law Review* 40, 44.
[12] *Ibid.*, pp. 40–43; W. Holdsworth, *History of English Law* (3rd ed., 1944), Vol. 9, 212–214; J. Thayer, *Cases on Evidence* (revised ed., 1925), p. 672.
[13] Learned Hand, above n. 11, p. 42.
[14] Henry Thomas Riley's *Memorials of London and London Life in the 13th, 14th and 15th centuries* (1868), p. 107 (1313).
[15] *Ibid.*, p. 135 (1320).
[16] *Ibid.*, p. 260 (1350).
[17] *Ibid.*, p. 90 (1311).
[18] *Ibid.*, p. 259 (1350).
[19] *Ibid.*, p. 249 (1350).
[20] *Ibid.*, p. 318 (1364).

obtaining skilled knowledge for the court. In a mayhem case,[21] cited in the later case of *Buckley* v. *Rice Thomas*,[22] surgeons from London were summoned to assist the court as to whether the wound was mayhem or not, as the court was unable to reach a conclusion on the matter.

2 The growth of witness evidence: fact and opinion

The period from the fifteenth century until the seventeenth century was marked by the increasing acceptance of the practice of skilled persons being called to attend upon the court to provide specialist knowledge which the court lacked. Thus in 1493 "masters of grammar" assisted the court in construing a passage of latin in a statute.[23] The case of *Buckley* v. *Rice Thomas*[24] contains some of the earliest reasoned and authoritative judicial dicta on the need for specialist assistance:

> "If matters arise in our law which concern other sciences or faculties, we commonly apply for the aid of that science or faculty which it concerns, which is an honourable and commendable thing in our law."[25]

The jury of skilled persons was still employed in some cases.[26] However there are also clear examples of judicial control over the reception of skilled knowledge by the court, and its use by a lay jury. In *Alsop* v. *Bowtrell*[27] an issue arose as to whether a child born 41 weeks after the death of its mother's husband could be legitimate. Physicians were asked to assist with the matter. The judges appear themselves to have concluded that the physicians' opinions were true and safe to be relied upon, and informed the jury that they could therefore rely on the opinions.[28]

The judges of the seventeenth century, by which time oral evidence by lay witnesses was accepted practice in court, began to formalise the distinction between evidence of fact, or observation, and opinion, or inference. In *Bushell's Case*[29] it was stated that:

> "The Verdict of a Jury and Evidence of a witness are very different things, in the truth and falsehood of them; a witness swears but to what he hath heard or seen, generally or more largely, to what hath

---

[21] (1353) Lib.Ass. 145.
[22] (1554) 1 Plowd. 118.
[23] 1493, Y.B.9.H.VI.16, 8. Cited in *Buckley* v. *Rice Thomas*, above n. 22.
[24] Above n. 22.
[25] *Ibid.*, at 124, *per* Saunders J.
[26] *Willoughby's Case* (1597) Cro. Eliz. 566.
[27] (1619) Cro. Jac. 541.
[28] See Learned Hand, above n. 11, p.56.
[29] (1671) Vaug. 135.

fallen under his senses. But a Juryman swears to what he can infer and conclude . . ."[30]

Wigmore has suggested[31] that the distinction between opinion and factual evidence was not recognised until the eighteenth century, and that it was not until then that the need for personal observation was perceived as essential for the witness of fact.

Bushell's Case suggests that those matters were well established by 1671. There are also, towards the end of the seventeenth century, examples of skilled persons giving evidence under oral examination, in much the form of modern expert evidence. Thus in 1678 physicians gave evidence of the causes of symptoms they had observed at an autopsy,[32] and in 1699 surgeons were asked hypothetical questions about whether a drowned body full of water would sink.[33]

3 The foundations of the modern law of expert evidence

The modern law of expert evidence rests upon an assumption that, in so far as the expert may express opinions or draw inferences, he does so by way of an exception to the rule that witnesses may only give evidence of what they have themselves perceived. This approach was expressed in the dicta of Lord Mansfield in *Carter* v. *Boehm*[34] and the frequently cited decision in *Folkes* v. *Chadd*.[35]

It is in this era that the testimony of skilled witnesses is treated, both in the cases and in textbooks, as a particular class of evidence. An Irish textbook on evidence of 1795, furthermore, employs the modern term "expert":

> "the Proof from the Attestation of Persons on their professional knowledge, we may properly, with the French Lawyers, call Proof by Experts."[36]

Wigmore suggests that the beginning of the nineteenth century saw the first clear judicial recognition of the principle that expert evidence is not admissible where the lay jury is competent to decide the matter itself,[37]

---

[30] (1671) Vaug. 135 at 142, *per* Vaughan C.J.
[31] *A Treatise on the Anglo-American System of Evidence* (3rd ed., 1940), Vol. vii, para. 1917.
[32] *R.* v. *Pembroke* (1678) 6 Howell, State Trials, 1337. See Learned Hand, above n. 11, p. 46.
[33] *Trial of Spencer Cowper, Esq.* (1699) 13 Howell, State Trials, 1106 at 1126–1135. See Learned Hand, above n. 11, p. 46.
[34] (1766) 3 Burr. 1905.
[35] (1782) 3 Doug. 157.
[36] Gilbert's *Law of Evidence*, edition of Capel Lofft, Dublin, 1795, p. 301. See Learned Hand, above n. 11, p. 48.
[37] Wigmore, above n. 31, para. 1917. See *Beckwith* v. *Sydebotham* (1807) 1 Camp. 116; *Durrell* v. *Bederley* (1816) Holt N.P. 283 at 285.

which substantially incorporates the notion that experts should not give evidence upon an ultimate issue, even though this may entail expert knowledge.[38]

C. THE NATURE OF EXPERT EVIDENCE

1 The categories of expert evidence

Lay witnesses may only give one form of evidence, namely evidence of fact, save in those limited circumstances in which they may give evidence of opinion as a convenient way of relating fact to the court or where the opinion is itself an issue in the case. These are discussed in a later part of this chapter.[39] Expert evidence, however, can be divided into a larger number of categories. This is of importance not only for analysing the manner in which it may be adduced, but can also go to the very question whether evidence is expert evidence and therefore admissible only following compliance with R.S.C. Order 38, rule 36.[40]

Five categories of evidence given by experts can be distinguished:

(i) expert evidence of opinion, upon facts adduced before the court;
(ii) expert evidence to explain technical subjects or the meaning of technical words;
(iii) evidence of fact, given by an expert, the observation, comprehension and description of which require expertise;
(iv) evidence of fact, given by an expert, which does not require expertise for its observation, comprehension and description, but which is a necessary preliminary to the giving of evidence in the other four categories;
(v) admissible hearsay of a specialist nature.

The fourth category is not expert evidence properly so-called, but is worthy of inclusion because it often forms an inseparable part of the evidence given by an expert, and is often included within the loose definition of "expert evidence" implied by the ordinary usage of the expression.

---

[38] This rule is now of importance principally in criminal cases; see below, Chap. 7.
[39] See below, pp. 17–22.
[40] See *The Torenia* [1983] 2 Lloyds Rep. 210, 233.

2 Admissibility

Expert evidence is admissible where there are matters in issue before the court which require expertise for their observation, analysis or description. It may be given by any person who has the relevant expertise. In *Buckley* v. *Rice Thomas*[41] it was stated by Saunders J. that:

> "if matters arise in our law which concern other sciences or faculties, we commonly apply for the aid of that science or faculty which it concerns."[42]

Lord Mansfield, in *Folkes* v. *Chadd*,[43] two centuries later, describes the evidence of "men of science"[44] as being admissible before the court. It is not clear whether his use of this term is intended to speak only of disciplines broadly within the natural sciences, and which have some recognised method of analysing and assessing the relevant information. It has been suggested that expert evidence is restricted in approximately this manner.[45] However the practice of the courts, and judicial decisions on particular aspects of the law of expert evidence, indicate that there is no such restriction. These are therefore matters which go to weight not admissibility. To this extent the law is the same now as it was when Saunders J. spoke of a "science or faculty." Whatever meaning Saunders J. attached to the word "science," the additional use of the word "faculty"[46] comprehends a range of specialisms defined by the knowledge, experience and skill of its practitioners, rather than by *a priori* assumptions as to scientific procedure. If Lord Mansfield's use of the word "science" in *Folkes* v. *Chadd* was intended to have a meaning more precise than its latin root "knowledge," it is inadequate as a statement of the present law.[47]

3 What is an expert?

Dictionary definitions of the term "expert"[48] demonstrate that it can be employed both with some particularity and in a more general manner. The adjective has two relevant descriptions: "(i) experienced; (ii) trained

---

[41] (1554) Plowd. 118.
[42] *Ibid.*, at 124.
[43] (1782) 3 Doug. 157.
[44] *Ibid.*, at 159.
[45] See *e.g.* A. Kenny, "The Expert in Court" (1983) 99 L.Q.R. 197.
[46] The *Oxford English Dictionary* gives four relevant definitions of the word 'faculty': (i) an ability or aptitude, whether natural or acquired, for any special kind of action; (ii) a branch or department of knowledge; (iii) that in which any one is skilled; an art, trade, occupation, profession; (iv) the members of a particular profession regarded as one body.
[47] See *e.g. R.* v. *Silverlock* [1894] 2 Q.B. 766 at 769.
[48] *Oxford English Dictionary*.

by experience or practice, skilled, skilful"; as does the noun: "(i) one who is expert or who has gained skill from experience; (ii) one whose special knowledge or skill causes him to be regarded as an authority; a specialist." The term "skilled" when used of persons, is described as meaning "(i) possessed of skill or knowledge; (ii) properly trained or experienced."

There is little doubt that the law follows the first general rather than the second more limited meaning of both the noun and adjectival form of "expert," and of the adjective "skilled," certainly at the stage of admissibility, which is the only one at which it is necessary to decide whether a witness is an expert or not. Once the issue of weight arises, after the evidence has been adduced, the category into which the witness falls is irrelevant to the question whose evidence is to be preferred. Degrees of expertise, or its absence, of course then assume considerable importance.

Possession of expertise In practice there is a broad discretion vested in the court to decide whether or not a person is capable of giving expert evidence. The two most important qualities are the possession of knowledge of the specialism in question, and an ability to use that knowledge by virtue of training and/or experience in that field. It is however the expertise itself, not the route or method by which it was obtained, which is decisive. Thus in *R. v. Silverlock*,[49] a witness expert in the science of handwriting was permitted to give evidence although his profession was that of solicitor:

> "the witness who is called upon to give evidence founded on a comparison of handwritings must be peritus; he must be skilled in doing so; but we cannot say that he must have become peritus in the way of his business or in any definite way. The question is, is he peritus?"[50]

There is no statutory definition as to what constitutes an expert. However, section 4(1) of the Civil Evidence Act 1972, which is concerned solely with the question of proof of foreign law in English courts (which in general must be proved by expert evidence) appears, though its precise intention and purpose are not entirely clear,[51] to suggest that expertise might be derived from "knowledge *or* experience." This is broadly consistent with *R. v. Silverlock*. Although it is not necessary as a matter of law for a skill to have been obtained in a particular manner, or to be the subject of professional practice,[52] it must be specialised to the extent that it exceeds the skills of ordinary people engaged in ordinary pursuits.

---

[49] [1894] 2 Q.B. 766.
[50] *Ibid.*, at 771, *per* Lord Russell C.J.
[51] As to which see below, p. 298.
[52] *R. v. Silverlock*, above n. 49.

Thus, just because a person has been driving for a number of years he may not give evidence as to whether a defendant who had consumed alcohol was thereby rendered unfit to drive.[53]

It is relevant to the question of expertise that an expert witness is usually called for the purpose of drawing inferences from given facts and expressing opinions about matters before the court, unlike lay witnesses. It is the ability of the witness to do this, within a particular specialist field, which therefore justifies the distinction between expert and lay witnesses for evidential purposes. Thus Vaughan-Williams J., in argument in R. v. *Silverlock*, expressed the view that:

> "No one should be allowed to give evidence as an expert unless his profession or course of study gives him more opportunity of judging than other people."[54]

The field of expertise Although the test of expertise in relation to a proposed witness involves an assessment of the qualities of the witness himself, it seems clear that the field of his expressed expertise is not wholly irrelevant to the question of competence to give expert evidence. Thus it can be inferred from the remarks of Vaughan-Williams J. in R. v. *Silverlock*[55] that the field of practice of a witness may not have given him the opportunity to make judgments about the relevant subject-matter. The practice of the courts, however, indicates that this is a question considered more fully at the "weight" than at the "admissibility" stage.[56]

There is though no sound definition of what constitutes an expert discipline, and notwithstanding the references in *Folkes* v. *Chadd* to "matters of science"[57] it is not necessary for the field of expertise to be subject to strictly "scientific" method. Suggestions that the field of expertise must constitute "an organised branch of knowledge"[58] are not supported by the weight of English authority.

Witness of fact A person called primarily as a witness of fact may also be tendered as an expert. Where a police officer was called to the scene of a road accident, had 15 years of experience in the police traffic division, had attended a course in accident investigation and passed an examination in it, and had attended 400 fatal road accidents, he was permitted to give evidence as an expert. This was held to be so:

> "if the subject in which he is giving evidence as an expert is a subject

---

[53] R. v. *Davies (No. 2)* [1962] 1 W.L.R. 1111.
[54] Above n. 49, at 769.
[55] Above n. 49.
[56] See below, pp. 13–14.
[57] Above n. 43, at 159.
[58] *Clark* v. *Ryan* (1960) 103 C.L.R. 486, 501, *per* Menzies J.

in which he has expert knowledge, and if it is restricted and directed to the issues in the case."[59]

The judge added that he must keep "within his reasonable expertise, which is a matter for the judge."[60] The concept of reasonableness is not an easy one to apply in this context, though it has been employed in similar cases, for instance where a police officer was permitted to give evidence as to the nature of the collision, and the likely course of the vehicles after colliding. Inferences were held properly to be drawn from marks on the road and the particular damage to the vehicles if in drawing them the witness kept within his reasonable expertise.[61]

Expertise and weight   As has been suggested above,[62] the general tendency of the courts in practice is not to inquire very rigorously into the question whether evidence is admissible as expert evidence at the admissibility stage.[63] This may be said to be so for three reasons. First, it is obvious from the cases that the test of expertise is not one of great precision, especially because it can depend upon the nature of the matters which require proof, and assumes a wide discretion in the court which considers it. Secondly, it appears to be recognised that the most effective way of assessing expertise is, rather than conducting a difficult exercise based almost entirely upon the limited evidence available as to qualification, experience and skill at the admissibility stage, to hear the witness's substantive evidence and use this as the basis upon which to judge not only the quality of his evidence, but his competence to give it. Thirdly, and following directly from this second point, the degree of expertise revealed by the witness in his evidence is inevitably an important part of the process of attributing weight to the evidence in order to decide the issues. It would indeed be an exercise of some artificiality to attempt to effect complete separation between the question of expertise and that of the persuasiveness of the evidence given by the witness.

This is not to say that a proposed witness who clearly has no specialist knowledge or experience will not be prevented, as he should be, from giving evidence. However, the courts will always be aware that the question of expertise can be further considered at the stage of attribution of weight to the evidence. In a case of unfitness to drive by reason of alcohol consumption, an expert medical witness was called to give his opinion as to the likely quantity of alcohol consumed in the light of the analyst's

---

[59] R. v. *Oakley* [1979] R.T.R. 417, 420, *per* Lord Widgery. The contrary view expressed by the majority in the Australian case of *Nickisson* v. *R.* [1963] W.A.R. 114 was rejected.
[60] R. v. *Oakley*, above n. 59, at 420.
[61] R. v. *Murphy* [1980] Q.B. 434, C.A.
[62] See p. 12.
[63] See below, Chap. 6.

findings in respect of his blood/alcohol content.[64] The witness had not himself conducted any experiments in this area of medicine, and relied on the findings of a British Medical Association special committee which had sat to consider such matters. Lord Parker C.J. took the view that these findings had:

> "been accepted by the medical profession and have become part of the current accepted medical knowledge of the day . . . it may be that while himself not an expert in the matter, his evidence would carry so much the less weight, but so far as admissibility is concerned this court is quite clear that they were properly admitted and referred to."[65]

Where negligence was alleged in the fitting of a security gate,[66] the evidence of the plaintiff's witness, a security consultant, was preferred to that of the witness, a man experienced only in the physical installation of such gates, "called by the defendants as an expert but as such not impressive though no doubt an excellent practical man."[67] The defendant's witness was, however, treated as an expert for the purpose of admissibility.

4 The contradiction within expert evidence

There is a contradiction at the centre of much of the expert evidence which is adduced in court. The expert is not present in order to decide the matter in issue, but to assist the tribunal in so deciding.[68] The evidence is not admissible, certainly in so far as it consists of expert evidence of opinion, unless it treats of matters which are beyond the knowledge and experience of the tribunal. Where there is a conflict of such evidence, this places the tribunal in the position of being required to prefer the evidence of one of two experts who may both have decades of experience and knowledge of the field. In effect there is an assumption that the opinion of the tribunal is to be preferred to that of the expert witness whose evidence is rejected. This may arise, and indeed is more likely to do so, where the matter in issue is one of great controversy within the relevant specialist field. Judge Learned Hand examined this contradiction at the beginning of this century:

> "the whole object of the expert is to tell the jury, not facts . . . but general truths derived from his specialised experience. But how can the jury judge between two statements each founded upon an experi-

---

[64] *R. v. Somers* [1963] 3 All E.R. 808.
[65] *Ibid.*, at 811.
[66] *Dove v. Banham's Patent Locks* [1983] 2 All E.R. 833.
[67] *Ibid.*, at 837. This evidence was clearly rejected on grounds of weight, as opposed to being ruled inadmissible for want of expertise.
[68] See below, Chap. 10.

ence confessedly foreign in kind to their own? It is just because they are incompetent for such a task that the expert is necessary at all . . . When the conflict is direct and open, the absurdity of our present system is apparent. The truth of either combatting proposition lies just in its validity as an inference from a vast mass of experience . . . as to the truth of which trained powers of observation are quite essential, the result themselves of a life of technical training."[69]

There are circumstances in which this problem is unimportant, and indeed some in which an acknowledged division between experts within a specialist field is the very subject of the proceedings. Therefore in many cases of professional negligence the only requirement of the allegedly negligent professional is to persuade the court that there is a body of opinion within the field, which may be a minority view, that would support the methods he employed in the particular case.[70]

In those cases where the contradiction does intrude into the decision-making process, the court can often fall back upon strict observance of the burden and standard of proof, though where the tribunal is not legally qualified the rigour of such observance may on occasion be doubtful. Where, however, the dispute between experts lies at the heart of, or indeed is coextensive with, the main issue in the case, resolution of the conflict by procedural means alone becomes both difficult and inappropriate.

5 Legal method and scientific method

The reception of much expert evidence in court proceedings entails an implicit acceptance of scientific method. In an early authority on the law of expert evidence it was said that:

> "If matters arise in our law which concern other sciences or faculties, we commonly apply for the aid of that science or faculty which it concerns. This is a commendable thing in our law. For thereby it appears that we do not dismiss all other sciences but our own,[71] but we approve of them and encourage them as things worthy of commendation."[72]

A substantial proportion of the law relating to the content of expert evidence arises either from the contradiction described in section 4 above, or

---

[69] Above n. 11, p. 54.
[70] *Bolam* v. *Friern Hospital Management Committee* [1957] 1 W.L.R. 582; *Whitehouse* v. *Jordan* [1981] 1 W.L.R. 246; *Maynard* v. *West Midland Regional Health Authority* [1984] 1 W.L.R. 634.
[71] The judge probably exploys the word 'science' in the sense of 'knowledge.'
[72] *Buckley* v. *Rice Thomas* (1554) 1 Plowd. 118 at 124, *per* Saunders J.

from problems rooted in the polarity of the legal and the scientific method. Aubert has observed that:

> "For the scientist the crux of his method is to make predictions that can, occasionally, be proven false. Such falsification is no disproof of his merit as a scientist. On the contrary, it proves that he is willing to submit himself to the rigours of confrontation with reality, one of his supreme obligations. The supreme obligation of the judge, however, is to avoid wrong decisions while always being willing to decide."[73]

Despite this, the judge must be prepared to be legally decisive in circumstances where there is little scientific consensus on relevant matters requiring technical expertise.[74]

The scientist must, in drawing inferences from observed data,[75] account both for the supporting and contrary indications to his hypothesis, or to the assumptions made prior to the current investigation based on known facts. Different theories of the scientific method emphasise the supporting[76] or contrary[77] indications in varying degrees. Legal theorists, likewise, have taken contrasting views as to the relative importance of the similarities[78] and differences[79] between the legal and the scientific method.[80]

D. THE LIMITS OF EXPERT EVIDENCE

1 Fact and opinion

Expert witnesses may give evidence of various kinds, some of which may also be given by lay witnesses.[81] Experts are however called in the majority of cases primarily in order to express their opinion as to matters in issue in the case. Lay witnesses, save in certain very limited circumstances,[82] may give evidence only of fact and not of opinion. There are many reasons for this, which can be expressed shortly in the form of two objections to such evidence: it tends to usurp the function of the tribunal,

---

[73] V. Aubert, "Understanding Legal Thinking" in C. Campbell and P. Wiles, *Law and Society* (1979) p. 147.
[74] See below, Chap. 10.
[75] Whether in court or in the laboratory.
[76] See *e.g.* T. S. Kuhn, *The Structure of Scientific Revolutions* (2nd ed., 1970).
[77] See *e.g.* K. R. Popper, *The Logic of Scientific Discovery* (1959).
[78] See *e.g.* N. McCormick, *Legal Reasoning and Legal Theory* (1978), p. 103.
[79] See *e.g.* W. Aubert, above n. 73.
[80] See generally, W. Twining, *Theories of Evidence: Bentham and Wigmore* (1985), pp. 156–159; A. Kenny, "The Expert in Court" (1983) 99 L.Q.R. 197.
[81] See above, p. 9.
[82] See below, pp. 17–22.

in that it is the tribunal's task to draw inferences from the facts, and it is inherently unreliable, as it can only be tested by reference to known facts.

While there is inevitably the possibility of these objections also applying to expert witnesses, there are assumptions implicit in the rules of admissibility either that the risks are worth taking, because of the likely benefit of the evidence to the tribunal, or that where expert evidence is concerned such risks can more readily be kept within reasonable limits. Thus a lay tribunal needs the benefit of expertise on matters in issue which require it. Although the tribunal does not itself possess such expertise, the testability of such evidence can be kept within controlled limits by the fact that the evidence of one expert can be measured by reference to contradictory or confirmatory evidence given by an expert in the same field called by the other party, or in limited circumstances by the court.[83]

It is the special character of opinion evidence which has given rise to most of the rules of evidence and procedure which relate particularly to expert witnesses. It is important to distinguish, however, that small class of cases in which witnesses are permitted, in effect, to express an opinion, though they have no expertise of relevance, and to distinguish its purpose from that of expert opinion evidence.

2 Non-expert opinion evidence

There is a respect in which all evidence by individuals of 'facts' which they have perceived by means of their senses is really no more than evidence of opinion. It is an attempt at recollection of matters which they believe they have perceived, and this is no less the case because they feel certain they are right and other witnesses have shared and corroborate that perception.

The general rule for non-expert witnesses is that they may only give evidence as to facts perceived by them through their senses. Evidence which amounts to an opinion about that perceived evidence, or about other facts in issue in that case, is excluded because it is not relevant.[84] The distinction between fact and opinion, however, as has been judicially recognised,[85] is not a particularly clear one.[86] Furthermore, an inference "may be so inescapable that it is of no account whether the witness stops with the observed facts or states the inevitable conclusion to be drawn from them."[87] The question of whether the two are qualitatively different in crucial respects, or whether they simply exist at different points on

---

[83] *e.g.* under R.S.C. Ord. 40; see below, Chap. 3.
[84] See above, p. 5.
[85] See *e.g. Sherrard v. Jacob* [1965] N.I. 151, 156–158.
[86] See *e.g.* P. B. Carter, *Cases and Statutes on Evidence* (1981), p. 501.
[87] *Sherrard v. Jacob*, above n. 85, at 156, *per* Lord MacDermott.

a continuum which runs from factual certainty through near certainty to opinion, is one which suggests itself through much of the case law.

Although there are several exceptions to the rule that non-expert witnesses may not give opinion evidence, these do not extend to the expert's right to give his opinion about facts not perceived by him. Thus it is not the lay witness's opinion itself which is relevant to facts in issue, and therefore admissible, it is the evidence of fact contained within it. The so-called opinion is therefore merely a vehicle by which relevant facts, which otherwise might have been denied it, can be conveyed to the court:

> "The inference may depend . . . on factors which are difficult to rehearse, perhaps even difficult to keep in mind, in their totality . . . the whole mental picture may be of the higher probative value. To state his conclusion in such circumstances may well contribute relevant material for the information of the court which it would lack if the witness were restricted to a recital of what he could remember of the relevant, observed facts."[88]

A distinction can however be drawn between instances in which the expression of an opinion is the only manner in which the facts can be conveyed, and those in which it is simply a convenient means of doing so, or a "compendious mode"[89] of relating the facts. In *Wright* v. *Tatham*[90] evidence was admitted as being "a compendious mode of putting one instead of a multitude of questions to the witness."[91] The question was whether, in the opinion of lay witnesses who had known and had contact with the deceased, he was at the time of such knowledge and contact incapable of making a valid will. It appears to have been understood, however, that the facts allegedly contained within the opinion would be independently tested in cross-examination, as Coleridge J. observed:

> "where the witness to facts is present, it is by no means uncommon to ask directly for his opinion: such a question it would be idle to object to; the objection would only lead to a detailed inquiry into particular facts, which the witness is there ready to go into. Nothing, therefore, would be gained by it. I am not, however, aware that this question has ever, upon argument, been decided to be correct in form."[92]

Civil Evidence Act 1972 The exceptions to the rule against non-expert opinion evidence are generally applicable to criminal as to civil cases. The

---

[88] *Sherrard* v. *Jacob*, above n. 85, at 158, *per* Lord MacDermott.
[89] *Wright* v. *Tatham* (1838) 5 Cl. & Fin. 670 at 721. This is a phrase, of Patteson J., which has frequently been employed since.
[90] *Ibid.*
[91] *Ibid.*, at 721.
[92] *Ibid.*, at 690.

law in respect of civil cases has though now been stated in statutory form by section 3 of the Civil Evidence Act 1972[93]:

> "(2) It is hereby declared that where a person is called as a witness in any civil proceedings, a statement of opinion by him on any relevant matter on which he is not qualified to give expert evidence, if made as a way of conveying relevant facts personally perceived by him, is admissible as evidence of what he perceived.
>
> (3) In this section 'relevant matter' includes an issue in the proceedings in question."

The section purports to do no more than to state the existing common law, and certainly it could not be construed as narrowing the range of non-expert opinion evidence formerly regarded as admissible. It is possible that it might be seen as granting the court a discretion broader than that previously justified by the weight of authority on the question, though there have been no clear judicial indications to this effect. Thus the relevant circumstances continue to divide into the judicially undefined but discernible categories recognised at common law.

Belief or opinion as a fact in issue A lay witness may give evidence of his belief or opinion where such belief or opinion is itself a fact in issue, or is the issue. Thus such evidence will be admitted in a libel action, where the issue (the meaning of the offending words having been agreed) is whether or not the person mentioned in a newspaper story would be identified as the plaintiff in the minds of any persons knowing the circumstances which the newspaper described.[94] Similarly, evidence is admissible to show that words, though not defamatory in their primary meaning, might be understood in their defamatory secondary meaning by persons who know the special facts relating to it.[95]

In criminal proceedings, where it is alleged that the defendant obtained goods by false pretences, evidence of a letter sent to the prosecutor, and of the view taken by the prosecutor on receipt of it, is admissible to show the actual belief of the victim at the time of the fraud, this being an essential element of the offence.[96] In proceedings under section 169(1) of the Licensing Act 1964, pursuant to which it is an offence "knowingly" to sell alcoholic drinks to those under the prescribed age, visual evidence of opinion by the tribunal itself has been permitted.[97] Given that the actual appearance of the person in question inevitably influences another individual's belief as to his age, unless it can be shown that the defendant had

---

[93] Following the recommendations of the Law Reform Committee, 17th Report, Cmnd. 4489 (1970).
[94] *Jozwiak* v. *Sadek* [1954] 1 W.L.R. 275.
[95] *Hough* v. *London Express Newspapers Ltd.* [1940] 2 K.B. 507.
[96] *R.* v. *King* [1897] 1 Q.B. 214.
[97] *Wallworth* v. *Balmer* [1966] 1 W.L.R. 16.

at the material time independent means of discovering the person's appearance, it is clearly relevant.[98]

Fact and opinion inextricably linked: the "compendious mode"[99] If a witness of fact can only give evidence as to that fact by also expressing what amounts to an opinion, the court will not deprive itself of the factual content of the evidence merely on that account. In *Rasool v. West Midlands Passenger Transport Executive*[1] it was sought to adduce as evidence a written statement made shortly after the accident in issue by an eye-witness who at the date of trial could not be found.[2] The statement, in addition to numerous factual details, recorded the opinion of the eye-witness that "the bus driver was in no way to blame for the accident," but was admitted under R.S.C. Order 38, rule 34.[3]

Although there is little suggestion that the categories of evidence admitted under this exception are ever closed, the types of evidence which in practice are frequently sought to be admitted in pursuance of it are fairly limited. The assessment of a person's age, in the absence of conclusive proof such as a birth certificate, is inevitably performed by a combination of factual observation and inferences from it, some of which will be uncontroversial, but others of which will be influenced by opinion. As a matter of procedural practicality, where the age of a child or young person is in issue, and the jurisdiction or powers of the court depend on it, the tribunal must be permitted to make such assessment of an individual's age as is possible in the circumstances, which will include the use of opinion based on observation and any other means available.[4] This is assumed by various statutory provisions.[5] So far as witness evidence of opinion as to age is concerned, in a prosecution for unlawful and wilful neglect of children under the Prevention of Cruelty to Children Act 1894, the evidence of an officer of the National Society for the Prevention of Cruelty to Children was admitted as to the view he had formed about whether some of the children he had observed were under 16.[6] Lord Russell of Killowen C.J., in holding that the production of birth certificates in

---

[98] It seems that such visual evidence is, in the absence of, for instance, a birth certificate, admissible where the sole issue to be determined upon it is an individual's actual age at the material time; see *ibid*.
[99] See above n. 89.
[1] [1974] 3 All E.R. 638.
[2] Civil Evidence Act 1968, s.8(2)(*b*); R.S.C. Ord. 38, rr. 21, 25 and 27.
[3] Finer J. took the view, at 642, however, that "no doubt the court would pay little attention" to the evidence as not being susceptible to cross-examination.
[4] See *Wallworth v. Balmer*, above n. 97. This could be described as an aspect of the "best evidence rule."
[5] *e.g.* Children and Young Persons Act 1933, s.99, Magistrates' Courts Act 1980, s.150(4). It will sometimes be the case that, as for instance with experienced juvenile panels in Magistrates' Courts, the bench is able to employ what is, in effect, its own expert opinion in such matters.
[6] *R. v. Cox* [1898] 1 Q.B. 179.

such cases was not strictly necessary, said that the facts "may be proved by any lawful evidence."[7]

In giving evidence as to a defendant's unfitness to drive through drink, a witness may state his opinion that the defendant was drunk at the material time if he states the facts on which the opinion is based. He may not, however, express an opinion (with or without supporting facts) as to whether or not this condition rendered the defendant unfit to drive.[8] It has on occasion been suggested, though the law at present must be said to be otherwise, that in such cases the witness should only be permitted to state the facts supporting an opinion which he holds, and that the tribunal in question should be left to draw the relevant conclusions from them.[9] This is a view which perhaps has some merit in the case of lay tribunals such as juries which, however emphatically they are instructed to dismiss certain items from their minds, will inevitably find such a sifting process unfamiliar and difficult.

It has also been held that non-experts may give evidence of value, for instance of a broken window in a criminal case, though little judicial reasoning has been applied to the question.[10]

Likenesses and comparisons Evidence which compares one thing with another, even where expressed in the form of an opinion, is admissible in certain circumstances. Thus, photographic evidence has been employed to show the likeness of a child to its alleged father and thereby establish paternity.[11] In other decisions, however, it has been said that such evidence is only to be admitted in exceptional circumstances,[12] though there is little indication as to what these are and to which branches of the law they are confined. Some guidance may perhaps be obtained from *Lucas v. Williams & Sons*,[13] where in copyright infringement proceedings the original picture in question could not be produced, Lord Esher M.R. holding that its production was not strictly necessary:

> " 'Primary' and 'secondary' evidence mean this: primary evidence is evidence which the law requires to be given first; secondary evidence

---

[7] *R. v. Cox* [1898] 1 Q.B. 179 at 180. It could presumably be argued that the NSPCC officer amounted, in the circumstances, to an expert on this issue.
[8] *R. v. Davies (No. 2)* [1962] 1 W.L.R. 1111; *Sherrard v. Jacob* [1965] N.I. 151.
[9] See *e.g.* Kingsmill Moore J., dissenting in *Att.-Gen. v. Kenny* (1959) 94 I.L.T.R. 185. See also A. H. Hudson, "Opinion Evidence of Intoxication" (1961) 77 L.Q.R. 166.
[10] *R. v. Beckett* (1913) 8 Cr.App.R. 204, in which Phillimore J. admitted such evidence, no explanation of which is reported.
[11] *C. v. C. and C.* [1972] 1 W.L.R. 1335. See also *Slingsby v. Att.-Gen.* (1916) 33 T.L.R. 120, H.L.
[12] *Frith v. Frith and Paice* [1896] P. 74. See *R. v. Cook (Christopher)* [1987] Q.B. 417, as to the apparently *sui generis* nature of photofit evidence, despite the obvious objection to it as hearsay.
[13] [1892] 2 Q.B. 113.

is evidence which may be given in the absence of the better evidence."[14]

Evidence of opinion in some circumstances may be admissible under the "compendious mode" principle.[15] It may also be admitted in circumstances where the only ground for so doing, or for so describing the evidence, is that in the nature of things the witness cannot be entirely certain. In *Fryer* v. *Gathercole*,[16] a case concerning the publication of a libellous pamphlet, the witness gave evidence that she had lent her copy to a number of friends and that she believed the one which was returned to her was the same one but that, not having marked it in any way, she could not be sure. Her statement of belief, however, can be said to add nothing to her factual evidence that the pamphlet she lent was, so far as her recollection went, identical to the one which was later returned to her. Furthermore, it is apparently only because the court allowed itself to assume that the expression of uncertainty (a frequent and understandable trait in witnesses) amounts to giving evidence of opinion, because in the nature of the circumstances no one could be absolutely certain, that evidence of belief or opinion proper (*i.e.* that it was in fact the same one) was also admitted. Lord Esher appeared to accept this distinction when he said in *Lucas* v. *Williams*,[17] *obiter*:

> "I am not prepared to say that the infringement could not be proved by calling a witness to say that he knew the original picture, and had seen the picture which was alleged to be a copy of it; and they were both exactly alike."[18]

It is certainly arguable that such evidence would be erroneously described as opinion evidence, but it is no less probative of the relevant issue than that which was admitted in *Fryer* v. *Gathercole*.

3 Judicial notice

The court may take judicial notice of a fact where it is desirable that evidence in relation to it should not be called, and unnecessary that it should be. This principle is primarily and most frequently employed where a particular fact is so notorious in the world at large that to require evidence to prove it would be an inconvenient and unnecessary waste of time and resources.[19] It is also however applied in other limited circumstances, for reasons of public policy. This is so in particular either to

---

[14] [1892] 2 Q.B. 113 at 116.
[15] See *Wright* v. *Tatham* (1838) 5 Cl. & Fin. 670 at 721.
[16] (1849) 4 Exch. 262.
[17] Above n. 13.
[18] *Ibid.*, at 117.
[19] In civil proceedings, matters of which judicial notice may be taken need not be pleaded: *Brandao* v. *Barnett* (1846) 12 Cl. & Fin. 787.

avoid constitutional conflict between the judicial and the executive branches, or to achieve a uniform approach in the courts which would not occur other than by presuming certain facts to exist in certain legal situations. It is in the former area that issues of expert evidence are most likely to intrude.

Facts which are judicially noticeable may lie within the realm of lay or expert evidence. It will be apparent however that, outside the public policy areas mentioned above, something of a paradox arises if it can be said that a particular fact is at once of a class that could require it to be adduced by an expert, by reason of the specialist nature of the subject-matter, and yet so obvious to the world at large that no evidence in respect of it need be called. In order to resolve this paradox, and to establish the circumstances in which expert evidence need not be called, it is necessary to examine the common law doctrine of judicial notice in so far as it treats of matters which would otherwise require to be proven by expert evidence. It will be seen that while matters which lie within the common lay knowledge of the tribunal may be admitted in particular proceedings by the taking of judicial notice, matters of a specialist nature may be so admitted where statute so directs, where there is a reliable source of the information which does not entail calling a witness, or where the doctrine of precedent permits the court to conclude that proof of a matter in previous proceedings has established it beyond doubt.

General Facts may in general be judicially noticed where "no person can raise a question"[20] as to their truth. Evidence which would otherwise be in the nature of expert evidence will be judicially noticed in two principal circumstances. The first is where, although the fact or opinion is not obvious to the court, it is so to all specialists in the field, and there are simple means, possibly recourse to a reference work, of discovering what the evidence would be if it were to be adduced in court. Secondly, such facts or opinions will be judicially noticed where the court is able without such external reference to conclude that, were expert evidence on the point to be adduced, there could not possibly be any dispute about its conclusions. Thus judicial notice may be taken of the fact that two weeks is too short a gestation period for humans.[21] Conversely it may not be taken as to the proposition that 360 days is too long as such a gestation period.[22]

It has been said that the court "takes notice of the ordinary course of nature,"[23] though it may hear expert evidence "as to what the ordinary

---

[20] R. v. *Luffe* (1807) 8 East. 193, 207.
[21] *Ibid.*
[22] *Preston-Jones* v. *Preston-Jones* [1951] A.C. 391.
[23] *McQuaker* v. *Goddard* [1940] 1 K.B. 687 at 700.

course of nature is."[24] Reference to an almanac, however, was not permitted for the purpose of establishing the time of sunset. An astronomer was required to give such evidence.[25]

The categories of facts of which notice may be taken in appropriate circumstances are probably never closed. A number of particular types of evidence which would otherwise be given by expert witnesses are now well established as susceptible to notice. Thus, the practice of professionals in a particular field may be noticed[26] as may certain clear economic facts such as the inflationary loss in the value of money since 1189,[27] though not the nature of a foreign economic system.[28] Notice will be taken of geographical matters,[29] and of time differences.[30] The courts will also notice generally known facts about human nature, for instance that boys may be expected to behave in a mischievous manner if given the opportunity.[31]

Words with a technical meaning Where expert evidence would in usual circumstances be necessary to explain the meaning, or normal usage within the field, of a technical term or phrase, judicial notice may be taken if inquiry can be made precluding the need for evidence to be called. This is so "however technical and obscure"[32] the words, unless there is a material dispute as to their meaning.[33]

Judicial notice as a matter of law In some circumstances judicial notice is taken of particular facts as a matter of law rather than discretion.

Statute Judicial notice of a particular state of affairs may be stipulated by statute.[34] The European Communities Act 1972 provides, by section 3(2), that:

> "Judicial notice shall be taken of the Treaties,[35] of the Official Journal of the Communities and of any decision of, or expression of opinion by, the European Court on any such question as aforesaid;

---

[24] *McQuaker v. Goddard* [1940] 1 K.B. 687 at 700. Notice was there taken of the fact that the camel is not a wild animal in any part of the world, a proposition which it might be supposed required some form of evidence in its support.
[25] *R. v. Crush* [1978] Crim.L.R. 357.
[26] *Re Rosher; Rosher v. Rosher* (1884) 26 Ch.D. 801.
[27] *Bryant v. Foot* (1868) L.R. 3 Q.B. 497 at 506.
[28] *A/S Rendel v. Arcos* [1936] 1 All E.R. 623.
[29] For instance the Ordnance Survey cartographers' practice of representing the centre of a hedge by a line on a map: *Davey v. Harrow Corporation* [1958] 1 Q.B. 60.
[30] *e.g. Curtis v. March* (1858) 3 H. & N. 866, as to the effect of Greenwich Mean Time.
[31] *Williams v. Eady* (1893) 10 T.L.R. 41, 42. See also *Clayton v. Hardwick Colliery Co.* (1915) 32 T.L.R. 159, 160 and *Robinson v. W. H. Smith* (1901) 17 T.L.R. 235.
[32] *Baldwin and Francis v. Patents Appeal Tribunal* [1959] A.C. 663 at 691.
[33] *Ibid.*
[34] See *e.g.* Foreign Jurisdiction Act 1890, s.4. See below pp. 25–26.
[35] The relevant treaties are set out in Part 1 of Sched. 1 to the Act.

and the Official Journal shall be admissible as evidence of any instrument or other act thereby communicated of any of the Communities or of any Community institution."

Custom The circumstances in which judicial notice may be taken are for the most part provided for by authorities which describe the general standard of obviousness or notoriety required of a fact before it may be noticed. Those instances in which a custom may be noticed have however developed in the form of specific authority for specific customs, because of the regularity with which they have been asserted and proved in court.

As such customs almost invariably have a particular legal consequence it is certainly arguable that these decisions are no more than authorities as to the provisions of common law, and that to describe them as judicially noticeable is to ascribe to them, erroneously, a predominantly factual, rather than legal, character,[36] though their application may depend on a factual issue as to the area, for instance of commerce, within which the custom is said to apply. The courts have though seen such custom as appropriately situated within the doctrine of judicial notice so that they must as a matter of law be considered as such.[37]

Custom is judicially noticed where it has been proved so often in court that it is accepted as noticeable.[38] There will be cases, however, where though a custom, for instance as to the terms of employment of domestic servants, is not so notorious as to be judicially noticeable, it can be proved by evidence if to do so does not appear "unreasonable."[39] A custom is unlikely to be noticed where the cases cited in its favour are sparse.[40] Furthermore, where there is doubt over the existence or general application of a custom, it will not be judicially noticed if the precise nature of the custom[41] cannot be stated.[42] Custom will be judicially noticed as to general average,[43] the innkeeper's lien over his guests' chattels in respect of an unpaid bill,[44] the innkeeper's hire of furniture to his guests[45] and the lien of bankers on the securities of their customers.[46]

Territory and sovereignty Where British territorial jurisdiction is in doubt, application is made to the Secretary of State for Foreign Affairs

---

[36] The distinction between law and fact is one which is yet to be jurisprudentially resolved.
[37] *Ex p. Wingfield, Re Florence* (1879) 10 Ch.D. 591, *Edelstein* v. *Schuler & Co.* [1902] 2 K.B. 144 at 155–156, and *Re Chenoweth, Ward* v. *Donelly* [1902] 2 Ch. 488, are possibly not within this category
[38] *Ex p. Turquand, Re Parker* (1885) 14 Q.B.D. 636 at 645.
[39] *Moult* v. *Halliday* [1898] 1 Q.B. 125 at 130. See also *George* v. *Davies* [1911] 2 K.B. 445 at 448.
[40] *Ex p. Powell, Re Matthews* (1875) 1 Ch.D 501 at 507.
[41] Even presumably on matters irrelevant to the point at issue.
[42] *Ex p. Powell, Re Matthews* (1875) 1 Ch.D. 501 at 507.
[43] *Aitchison* v. *Lohre* (1879) 4 App.Cas. 755.
[44] *Mulliner* v. *Florence* (1878) 3 Q.B.D. 484.
[45] *Crocour* v. *Salter* (1881) 18 Ch.D. 30.
[46] *Brandao* v. *Barnett* (1846) 12 Cl. & Fin. 787 at 805.

for guidance as to the government's position on the matter, and judicial notice must be taken of the reply given.[47] Such application is similarly made where the sovereignty or boundaries[48] of a foreign state are uncertain, and again the reply is conclusive.[49] The court may not, however, whether on inquiry or otherwise, take judicial notice of the constitution or economic system of a foreign state. Such matters must be proven by evidence.[50]

E. SPECIALIST OR PERSONAL KNOWLEDGE POSSESSED BY THE TRIBUNAL

Whether or not expert evidence is being adduced, the court or tribunal may have the benefit of specialist or personal knowledge possessed by members of the tribunal which is adjudicating. This may be either fortuitous, in the case of specialist knowledge of members of lay tribunals, or by design, where specialist tribunals are concerned, or where tribunals are expected to employ their knowledge of a locality.

1 Lay tribunals

Benches of magistrates are drawn from the locality of the court in which they sit, and are entitled and expected to draw on their general knowledge of the locality.[51] However, where a justice had specialist medical knowledge of relevance to a matter in issue, it was clearly impossible to proceed "as though he had not got that training, and indeed it would be a very bad thing if he had to."[52] The view has though been expressed that the rule for legally trained tribunals and that for lay tribunals should be different, because the latter "lack the ability to put out of their minds certain features of the case,"[53] though precisely what the difference should be is unclear. Furthermore:

> "the justice with specialised knowledge should not proceed to give

---

[47] Foreign Jurisdiction Act 1890, s.4.
[48] *Duff Development Corporation* v. *Republic of Kelantan Government* [1924] A.C. 797; *Taylor* v. *Barclay* (1828) 2 Sim. 213.
[49] *Foster* v. *Globe Venture Syndicate Ltd.* [1900] 1 Ch. 811. See though *Carl-Zeiss-Stiftung* v. *Rayner and Keeler Ltd.* [1967] 1 A.C. 853 on the difficulties of interpreting the precise effect of the reply.
[50] *A/S Rendel* v. *Arcos* [1936] 1 All E.R. 623.
[51] *Ingram* v. *Percival* [1969] 1 Q.B. 548. See also *Borthwick* v. *Vickers* [1973] R.T.R. 390 at 395, where it was held that such information must be "notorious locally."
[52] *Wetherall* v. *Harrison* [1976] Q.B. 773 at 777, *per* Lord Widgery.
[53] *Ibid.*, at 777. It is worthy of note that benches of magistrates are daily required in non-specialist matters, for instance where the admissibility of a confession is concerned, to put particular features of the case out of their minds.

evidence himself to his fellow justices contradictory to that which they have heard in court."[54]

Judges have taken judicial notice of matters within their own personal knowledge, often gained from their own involvement in previous cases,[55] though they would presumably satisfy themselves that there was no substantial dispute about the matter between the parties before doing so.

2 Specialist tribunals

It is obvious that where tribunals are established to adjudicate or arbitrate in a particular field, and where the members have specialist knowledge or experience of the field, they are expected to employ it in their hearings and deliberations. Thus a trade tribunal may take judicial notice of matters well-known to specialists in the trade.[56] Where the members of the tribunal draw upon a particular piece of specialist knowledge which is in conflict with evidence they have heard, they should draw this to the attention of the parties.[57] While they are:

> "entitled to use their knowledge and experience to fill gaps in the evidence about matters which will be obvious to them but which might be obscure to a layman . . . they ought to draw to the attention of the witnesses the experience which seems to them to suggest that the evidence given is wrong, and ought not to prefer their own knowledge or experience without giving the witnesses an opportunity to deal with it."[58]

The particular function of the tribunal may necessitate its use of specialist knowledge in circumstances where this would be unnecessary in ordinary litigation. Thus rent assessment committees cannot, as a judge can in a civil action, "retire behind the onus of proof and dismiss the plaintiff's claim,"[59] but must fix a fair rent. In the absence of reliable evidence on which to do this, they must "draw on their wisdom, experience and judgment and do the best that they can in the circumstances."[60]

---

[54] *Wetherall v. Harrison* [1976] Q.B. 733 at 778. To permit such a thing would clearly offend against the principles of natural justice.
[55] *McCafferty v. Metropolitan Police District Receiver* [1977] 2 All E.R. 756 at 771; *Glenister v. Glenister* [1945] P. 30 at 36.
[56] *Port Sudan Cotton Co. v. Govindaswamy Chettiar & Sons* [1977] 1 Lloyds Rep. 166; *Bremer v. Toepfer* [1978] 1 Lloyds Rep. 643 at 649; *Waring v. Administraçao Geral do Acucar e oro Alcool E.P.* [1983] 1 Lloyds Rep. 45.
[57] See n. 54, above.
[58] *Dugdale v. Kraft Foods* [1976] 1 W.L.R. 1288 at 1294–1295. See also *Waring v. Administraçao Geral*, above n. 56.
[59] *Metropolitan Properties Co. (F.G.C.) v. Lannon* [1968] 1 All E.R. 354 at 364.
[60] *Ibid.*, at 364.

3 The judge as specialist tribunal

The judge will always be regarded as a specialist on matters of law, but he may also sit as with other tribunals, either by accident or by design, with specialist non-legal knowledge. The county court judge, like the bench of magistrates, is expected to draw upon such local knowledge as he possesses in hearing cases before him,[61] though it is probably impossible to "lay down a formula defining with precision the limits"[62] within which this should be done. Where the judge sat as arbitrator in a workmen's compensation case, he was permitted to take into account his own knowledge of local conditions of wages and employment because his regular hearing of such cases in that locality gave him the knowledge upon which to ground his decision.[63] Such knowledge must, as with judicial notice generally, be "properly applied, and within reasonable limits."[64]

---

[61] *Reynolds v. Llanelly Associated Tin Plate Co.*, [1948] 1 All E.R. 140 at 145.
[62] *Ibid.*, at 145.
[63] *Peart v. Bolckow, Vaughan and Co. Ltd.* [1925] 1 K.B. 399 at 419.
[64] *Keane v. Mount Vernon Colliery Co. Ltd.* [1933] A.C. 309 at 317. It was recognised by Lord Greene in *Reynolds v. Llanelly Associated Tin Plate Co.* [1948] 1 All E.R. 140 at 143 that this "leaves the function of this court [the Court of Appeal] rather vague."

Part B: PRE-TRIAL PRACTICE AND PROCEDURE

CHAPTER 2

Pre-trial Procedure

I CIVIL PROCEEDINGS

A. GENERAL

Examination of the common law principles of evidence suggests that in some respects the evidence of experts is merely a particular application of more general principles, and that in others it is more or less *sui generis*. The rules applicable to pre-trial civil procedure, however, treat expert evidence unequivocally as a class of evidence which is to be regarded entirely differently from others, with its own self-contained code of rules[1] which must in almost all circumstances be complied with before such evidence can be admitted at trial. These are contained largely in R.S.C. Order 38, though other orders do provide individual procedures for particular branches of the law whose exigencies are deemed to require special treatment. Probably the most important of these, and certainly so in terms of volume of litigation, is the procedure for automatic disclosure in relation to personal injuries actions under R.S.C. Order 25, rule 8.[2]

1 County court

The High Court procedure in R.S.C. Order 38, Part IV is expressly applied to the county court by C.C.R. Order 20, rules 27 and 28[3] which provide:

> "27. (1) Except with the leave of the court or where all parties agree, no expert evidence may be adduced at the trial or hearing of an action or matter, unless the party seeking to adduce the evidence has applied to the court to determine whether a direction should be given under rule 37, 38 or 41 (whichever is appropriate) of R.S.C. Order 38, as applied by rule 28 of this

---

[1] *Rover International* v. *Cannon Film Sales* [1987] 1 W.L.R. 1597.
[2] See below, Chap. 19, pp. 336–338.
[3] There is, however, no provision for automatic directions in personal injury cases, and R.S.C. Ord. 25, r. 8 does not apply in the county court.

Order, and has complied with any direction given on the application.

(2) Nothing in paragraph (1) shall apply to expert evidence which is permitted to be given by affidavit or which is to be adduced in an action or matter in which no defence or answer has been filed or in proceedings referred to arbitration under section 64 of the Act.

(3) Nothing in paragraph (1) shall affect the enforcement under any other provision of these rules (except Order 29, rule 1) of a direction given under this Part of this Order.

28. R.S.C. Order 38, rules 37 to 44, shall apply in relation to an application under rule 27 of this Order as they apply in relation to an application under rule 36 (1) of the said Order 38."

2 Rationale

The purpose lying behind the pre-trial rules as to expert evidence is that there should be as much mutual disclosure as is possible between the parties, without trespassing upon the legitimate right of a litigant to gather such evidence as he wishes to, in confidence and with the protection of privilege. In essence this means that almost all expert evidence which is to be relied upon at trial must be disclosed in the absence of good reasons to the contrary. This presumption in favour of disclosure has been reinforced further by the most recent major amendments to the rules.[4] Many justifications can be offered for this policy of openness, and the notes to the relevant rules[5] record a number. They can be reduced however to two general propositions. First, the modern era of litigation has an enhanced emphasis upon reducing delays in the listing and hearing of trials, and in the length of the trials themselves, and a presumption of disclosure is seen to be consistent with these ends. In particular, where there is a common knowledge of the contentions of the parties' expert witnesses, there is always the possibility of narrowing the range of issues and establishing areas of common ground in advance. This possibility may become a likelihood where substantial savings in costs, or anticipated costs, can be ensured at a relatively early stage. Ackner J., in *Ollett* v. *Bristol Aerojet Ltd.*,[6] expressed the view that:

> "the whole purpose of Order 38 is, in relation to expert evidence, to save expense by dispensing with the calling of experts when there is in reality no dispute and, where there is a dispute, by avoiding par-

---

[4] R.S.C. (Amendment) 1987 (S.I. 1987 No. 1423).
[5] R.S.C. Ord. 38, Part IV.
[6] [1979] 1 W.L.R. 1197.

ties being taken by surprise as to the true nature of the dispute and thereby being obliged to seek adjournments."

This was a decision prior to some fairly radical amendments to the rules.[7] However, even prior to those changes it was acknowledged that considerations were entailed in the policy underlying the rules of such pre-trial disclosure.

Secondly, it is implicit in much of the more recent case law that a presumption of disclosure is in the vast majority of cases in the interests of the parties. Offers of settlement are more likely to be made at an earlier stage, and at a realistic level, if the parties can better predict what is likely to happen at trial should the case proceed.

Mutuality It is further recognised that this policy of openness and disclosure is most likely to result in justice between the parties if it is pursued on the basis of strict mutuality. Disclosure must generally apply to the same extent and in the same manner to both parties. Thus, for instance, there is a presumption not only of disclosure of experts' reports, but of their simultaneous disclosure, unless there are persuasive grounds for preferring sequential disclosure.[8] This can be put in the converse way by stating that a presumption of secrecy, or non-disclosure, may give one party an advantage over the other, which often cannot be said to be a wholly legitimate one. It is now beginning to be recognised that the interests of the parties are frequently ill-served by the kind of "forensic blind-man's buff"[9] which has characterised much of the process of obtaining and disclosing expert evidence in the past. The modern rules of pre-trial disclosure reflect this. For medical reports in personal injuries cases, see Chapter 19.

3 Rules constitute a complete code

R.S.C. Order 38 is a complete code of rules relating to the adducing of evidence at trial, and the rules as to expert evidence are a self-contained part of this code. It is not open to parties to litigation to seek to employ provisions concerning evidence in general where the expert evidence rules make specific provision for the point at issue.[10] In *Rover International* v. *Cannon Film Sales*[11] one party sought to adduce an affidavit by an expert witness pursuant to the notice procedure under the Civil Evidence Act 1968 (R.S.C. Order 38, rule 21). Harman J. held that where expert evidence was concerned a party must always seek directions under Order 38, rule 36, and where affidavits were concerned under Order 38, rule 2:

---

[7] See above n. 4.
[8] *Kirkup* v. *British Railways Engineering* [1983] 1 W.L.R. 190. Though see Chap. 19.
[9] *Wilsher* v. *Essex Area Health Authority* [1986] 3 All E.R. 801 at 805, *per* Mustill L.J.
[10] See *e.g.* R.S.C. Ord. 38, r. 41.
[11] [1987] 1 W.L.R. 1597.

PRE-TRIAL PROCEDURE

"Expert evidence is the matter of a separate and specific part of the code relating to evidence contained in R.S.C. Order 38 . . . [which] is a complete code affecting the whole of evidence given at trial . . . the provisions of R.S.C. Order 38 Rule 21 and the Civil Evidence Act 1968 cannot be applied so as to evade completely the provisions of another part of the code of rules in Order 38."[12]

4 Methods of adducing expert evidence under R.S.C. Order 38, rule 36

R.S.C. Order 38, rule 36 provides that: "(1) Except with the leave of the Court or where all parties agree, no expert evidence may be adduced at the trial or hearing of any cause or matter unless the party seeking to adduce the evidence—
    (a) has applied to the Court to determine whether a direction should be given under rule 37, 38 or 41 (whichever is appropriate) and has complied with any direction given on the application, or
    (b) has complied with automatic directions taking effect under Order 25, rule 8(1)(b).
(2) Nothing in paragraph (1) shall apply to evidence which is permitted to be given by affidavit or shall affect the enforcement under any other provision of these Rules (except Order 45, rule 5) of a direction given under this Part of this Order."

There are four principal methods of adducing expert evidence:
    (i) By seeking directions under R.S.C. Order 38, rule 36(1)(a), unless a specific procedure is provided for a particular class of actions.[13]
    (ii) By agreement with all parties[14];
    (iii) Where the court permits a party to adduce evidence by affidavit[15];
    (iv) With the leave of the court.[16]

Of these methods, the first is the one employed in the great majority of cases. Subject to the question of admissibility, it ensures that the expert evidence will be put before the court in one form or another. The second and third methods give no such guarantee, unless agreement is reached at an early stage as to directions, or, exceptionally, an order for affidavit evidence made. Leaving the application until trial is to be avoided unless circumstances dictate otherwise. Even if successful it is likely to result in

---

[12] [1987] 1 W.L.R. 1597 at 1600–1601.
[13] *e.g.* in personal injuries actions (see Chap. 19), automatic directions under R.S.C. Ord. 25, r. 8(1)(b): see R.S.C. Ord. 38, r. 36(1)(b); in patents proceedings (see Chap. 21) the procedure is provided by R.S.C. Ord. 104.
[14] R.S.C. Ord. 38, r. 36(1). See pp. 49–50, below.
[15] R.S.C. Ord. 38, r. 36(2). See pp. 53–54, below, and R.S.C. Ord. 38, r. 2.
[16] R.S.C. Ord. 38, r. 36(1). See p. 36 and Chap. 5., p. 103, below.

an adjournment and an order as to the costs thus thrown away. Agreed orders will usually be incorporated in the court's pre-trial directions in any event.

For these and other reasons, in non personal injuries claims, the seeking of pre-trial directions is almost always the appropriate course to adopt. It should be noted that in personal injuries cases, where the parties do not elect to follow the automatic directions procedure under R.S.C. Order 25, rule 8, the general procedure under R.S.C. Order 38 will apply. For medical reports, see Chapter 19.

B. SEEKING PRE-TRIAL DIRECTIONS

1 General

A party is, in complying with R.S.C. Order 38, rule 36[17], seeking directions as to whether expert's reports should be disclosed (rule 37) or, as will only occur in a small minority of cases, whether the notice procedure relating to documentary evidence[18] should be followed (R.S.C. Order 38, rule 41).

All witnesses giving expert evidence included There is no exhaustive definition of expert evidence for the purposes of R.S.C. Order 38, rule 36. It is clear however that the courts will not adopt a restrictive approach to the matter at the directions stage. It is the nature of the evidence to be adduced which is relevant, not the identity or office of the proposed witness. In *Shell Pensions Trust Ltd.* v. *Pell Frischmann & Partners*,[19] an Official Referee's case, an 'in-house' expert, employed by one of the parties, was held to be subject to the provisions of R.S.C. Order 38, rule 36, the court stating that:

> "The rules in Ord. 38 refer to 'expert evidence' and not to 'evidence given by independent experts.' They apply generally: to independent experts, to so-called 'in-house' experts and to parties themselves."

Disclosure the only issue In making application under R.S.C. Order 38, rule 36(1)(*a*) a party raises only the issue of disclosure. It is not for the master or registrar to decide the issue of admissibility of the expert evidence sought to be adduced. Thus if no order for disclosure is made a party, having once sought directions, is at liberty to call oral expert evidence at trial, subject always to persuading the judge that it is in any event admissible because relevant.

---

[17] Set out at p. 34, above.
[18] Civil Evidence Act 1968, s.8(1), and Ord. 38, rr.20 to 23 and 25 to 33.
[19] [1986] 2 All E.R. 911.

It was for some time suspected that this might not be the case, and a dictum of Lord Denning appeared to suggest that the question of admissibility was, *per se*, a matter for determination at the directions stage, and could not be reopened by the trial judge.[20] Doubts were expressed about the true effect of this decision,[21] and it has now been held, in *Sullivan* v. *West Yorkshire Passenger Transport Executive*,[22] that there is no power to rule on the admissibility of expert evidence at the directions stage.

An order may be made, at the directions stage, as to the number of expert witnesses to be called,[23] but this provision cannot be employed to exclude all expert evidence,[24] and in any event the trial judge may decide to admit more than the number prescribed in the directions by virtue of the general power contained in R.S.C. Order 38, rule 36(1).

2 Procedure

Issues of expert evidence will in the normal course be considered at the directions hearing.[25] A 1974 *Practice Direction*[26] sets out the usual manner in which the question of expert evidence will be considered at the directions hearing, though it has been substantially superseded by the 1987 amendments to the rules themselves which treat the different classes of action uniformly for directions purposes. The master or registrar will in any event record the fact of agreement if the parties have agreed directions, and if not proceed to make the appropriate order.

The wording of rule 36 (1) appears to require all parties to an action or matter to make application, in that it speaks of "the party seeking to adduce the evidence." It is however the clearly established practice of the courts to make orders relating to all parties on specific application by one only. In the usual case, namely where the order will inevitably be for mutual disclosure of expert evidence sought to be relied upon at trial, whether simultaneous or sequential, there could be said to be implied consent on the part of the party making application to the calling (subject to disclosure) of expert evidence by the other parties. The court may furthermore make such directions of its own motion,[27] though it cannot direct a party to call expert evidence at trial. Compliance with directions

---

[20] *Hinds* v. *London Transport Executive* [1979] R.T.R. 103.
[21] See *e.g. Phipson on Evidence* (13th ed., 1982), p. 568.
[22] [1985] 2 All E.R. 134.
[23] R.S.C. Ord. 38, r. 4.
[24] *Sullivan* v. *West Yorkshire Passenger Transport Executive*, above n. 22.
[25] Save where the parties have adopted the automatic directions procedure for personal injuries cases (R.S.C. Ord. 25, r. 8).
[26] [1974] 1 W.L.R. 904.
[27] R.S.C. Ord. 25, r. 3.

so made will be treated as compliance with the requirements of rule 36(1) itself.

Rule 38   Although R.S.C. Order 38, rule 36 does not itself refer to rule 38 the parties, in making application under Order 38, rule 36(1), are raising the possibility[28] of the directions including an order for experts to meet without prejudice before trial pursuant to rule 38.

Time for the rule 36 application   Application under rule 36 may be made at any time. In the majority of cases, however, the hearing of the summons for directions[29] or pre-trial review will be the appropriate time, and even if the parties do not so apply, the court must itself consider at that stage whether directions as to expert evidence should be given.[30] Particular circumstances, however, may suggest that an earlier application is appropriate, and the rules provide for this. Likewise, the application can be made between the hearing of the summons for directions and trial, though this will often be not a new application but a variation or revocation under R.S.C. Order 38, rule 44 as the matter must already have been canvassed at the original directions hearing. Late applications must be made promptly. In third-party proceedings a defendant issuing a late third party summons for directions under R.S.C. Order 16, rule 4 may have the summons dismissed, thus ending the third-party proceedings, if the delay results in the third-party being unable properly to instruct an expert, for example because remedial construction works have been done to premises which prevent investigation of the subject-matter of the claim.[31]

C.   DISCLOSURE OF EXPERTS' REPORTS

R.S.C. Order 38, rule 37(1) provides as follows:

> "Where in any cause or matter an application is made under rule 36(1) in respect of oral expert evidence, then, unless the Court considers that there are special reasons for not doing so, it shall direct that the substance of the evidence be disclosed in the form of a written report or reports to such other parties and within such period as the Court may specify."

---

[28] See R.S.C. Ord. 25, r. 3(*a*), and pp. 51-52, below.
[29] As to the time for which, see R.S.C. Ord. 25, r. 1, which requires the plaintiff to take out the summons within one month of close of pleadings, although this timetable is usually varied by consent.
[30] R.S.C. Ord. 25, r. 3(*a*).
[31] *Courtenay-Evans* v. *Stuart Passey and Associates* [1986] 1 All E.R. 932.

The effect of rule 37 is to create a strong presumption of pre-trial disclosure where parties seek to call expert evidence at trial. The old rule 37 (now revoked in its entirety) related only to personal injuries cases. The new rule 37[32] in fact replaces the old rule 38(1) and (2) (now also revoked),[33] in respect of which most of the relevant authorities were decided.

The 1987 changes in the rules[34] have had two major consequences. First, medical negligence actions are no longer subject to special provisions[35] as to disclosure. Secondly, the very broad measure of discretion as to disclosure[36] of expert evidence generally has been narrowed considerably so that there must now be "special reasons"[37] for not ordering disclosure. There is no specific distinction in the present rules between expert evidence which does and does not go to a factual issue in dispute between the parties. Furthermore, the present rules do not accord any specific relevance to the facts upon which the expert's opinion is based, whether they be hearsay or matters outside the expert's general professional knowledge and experience.

It should be noted that many of the reported decisions on pre-trial procedure in relation to expert evidence concern personal injuries cases. Although such cases are often subject to the separate automatic directions procedure under Order 25, rule 8,[38] it is clear that many of the principles which these decisions expound are of general application and relevance. Furthermore, although the special provisions relating to medical negligence have now disappeared altogether, there is little doubt that

---

[32] See n. 4, below.
[33] *Ibid.* The old rule 38 provided as follows:

> "(1) Where an application is made under rule 36(1) in respect of oral expert evidence to which rule 37 does not apply, the Court may, if satisfied that it is desirable to do so, direct that the substance of any expert evidence which is to be adduced by any party be disclosed in the form of a written report or reports to such other parties and within such period as the Court may specify.
> (2) In deciding whether to give a direction under paragraph (1) the Court shall have regard to all the circumstances and may, to such extent as it thinks fit, treat any of the following circumstances as affording a sufficient reason for not giving such a direction
> (a) that the expert evidence is or will be based to any material extent upon a version of the facts in dispute between the parties; or
> (b) that the expert evidence is or will be based to any material extent upon facts which are neither—
> (i) ascertainable by the expert by the exercise of his own powers of observation, nor
> (ii) within his general professional knowledge and experience."

[34] See n. 32, above.
[35] The old rule 37(3), now revoked.
[36] Disclosure could be ordered when it was thought "desirable to do so."
[37] The words of the old rule 38(2)(*b*)(ii).
[38] Though the parties may elect to adopt the application procedure under R.S.C. Ord. 38, r. 36.

decisions in such cases based on the old rules will continue to be relied upon to the extent that they are consistent with the new, general, rules.

1 Privilege and disclosure

The rules as to disclosure of expert's reports under R.S.C. Order 38 do not, in any manner, dilute the existing law of privilege.[39] Therefore, if an expert's report is prepared for the purpose of existing or contemplated legal proceedings it is privileged and need not be disclosed.[40] If, however, this privilege is enforced, the litigant will in almost all cases forego the possibility of calling that expert's evidence at trial.[41]

This is because in the majority of cases pre-trial disclosure will be ordered in any event pursuant to rule 37, and in the minority of cases where it is not so ordered the justification will very seldom include a claim of privilege, which has not generally been regarded as, *per se*, a sufficient ground for refusing pre-trial disclosure. In any event, if it is proposed to rely on the evidence at trial, all that can be achieved by a refusal to disclose pre-trial is a delay of the inevitable.

There is a limited class of cases, however, in which it has been recognised that a very important professional confidence is in question. Here, although where the justice of the case demanded it the courts have not been slow to order disclosure at trial, the courts have ensured that the professional confidence was breached only to the degree absolutely necessary for the purposes of the legal proceedings.[42] Various devices have been employed in order to achieve this objective, such as preventing all but a party's legal adviser from reading a report,[43] and ordering that certain parts of a document should be concealed.[44] Furthermore, experts have been judicially commended in certain circumstances for refusing to disclose the contents of reports until actually ordered to do so by the court.[45]

There is clearly scope within this very narrow range of circumstances for a contention that there are "special reasons"[46] for not disclosing pre-trial, albeit the trial judge may order full or partial disclosure at trial. An order may be made under R.S.C. Order 38, rule 41 for partial disclosure at the pre-trial stage.[47]

---

[39] As to which, in relation to experts, see Chap. 9.
[40] See *e.g. Worrall v. Reich* [1955] 1 Q.B. 296; *Causton v. Mann Egerton (Johnsons)* [1974] 1 W.L.R. 162.
[41] See R.S.C. Ord. 38, r. 36.
[42] See Chap. 9, pp. 195–202.
[43] *Re M. (Adoption: Parental Consent)* [1973] 1 Q.B. 108.
[44] *Science Research Council v. Nassé* [1980] A.C. 1028.
[45] *R. v. Statutory Visitors to St. Lawrence's Hospital, Caterham, ex p. Pritchard* [1953] 1 W.L.R. 1158.
[46] R.S.C. Ord. 38, r. 37.
[47] See below, p. 44.

2 The principle of disclosure

"The substance of the evidence" Where disclosure is ordered, the party subject to the order must serve upon the other parties "the substance of the evidence . . . in the form of a written report or reports." In most cases it will be convenient for reasons of practicality and cost to disclose the entire report prepared by the expert, which will also probably serve as the foundation of his oral evidence in chief, if not as a substitute for it.

There is frequently merit in serving the entire report pre-trial, in particular because where the reports can be agreed in their central conclusions it may also be possible to avoid the need to call the expert to give oral evidence as to peripheral points of detail.[48] Thus in many instances parties will voluntarily disclose the entirety of their written expert evidence, perceiving it to be in their own interest to do so.

The use of the word "substance" has been described as "ambiguous."[49] It is undoubtedly an open-textured expression, though not perhaps atypically so in the context of Order 38. It gives the master or registrar a measure of discretion which is necessary to the functioning of the disclosure provisions.[50] At the same time it avoids the necessity for parties to attempt to anticipate at the directions stage every particular of the evidence which their expert will give. In a significant number of cases, in any event, the facts upon which opinions are based may change significantly between disclosure and trial, or may not emerge until trial.

The report disclosed must include the expert's opinion, and the facts upon which it is based. It has been stated by Ackner J. in *Ollett* v. *Bristol Aerojet Ltd.*,[51] a decision concerning personal injuries caused by a machine at the plaintiff's work place, that it is wrong to assume that an order requiring the substance of the evidence to be disclosed:

> "is satisfied by the experts merely setting out factual descriptions of the machine and the alleged circumstances in which the accident happened and leaving out any conclusions as to the defects in the machine, the system of work or other relevant opinion evidence. This seems to me to be a total misconception of the ordinary meaning of the word 'substance.' It is also a misconception of the function of an expert. An expert, unlike other witnesses, is allowed, because of his special qualifications and/or experience, to give *opinion* evidence. It is for his opinion evidence that he is called, not for a factual

---

[48] Though not, for example, where in a personal injuries case the position changes materially between disclosure and trial, or the prognosis is very uncertain.
[49] *Phipson on Evidence* (13th ed., 1982), p. 567.
[50] The Rules of the Supreme Court are, with good reason, notably free of the exhaustive definition sections which are a necessary feature of many statutes, but which are often out of place in procedural rules.
[51] *Ollett* v. *Bristol Aerojet Ltd.* (*Practice Note*) [1979] 1 W.L.R. 1197.

description of the machine or the circumstances of the accident, although that is often necessary in order to explain and/or justify his conclusions. When the substance of the expert's report is to be provided, that means precisely what it says, both the substance of the factual description of the machine and/or the circumstances of the accident and his expert opinion in relation to that accident, which is the very justification for calling him."[52]

The report should therefore include the expert's opinion in relation to all matters in issue in the case upon which it is proposed to rely at trial, and the facts (whether related to or perceived by the expert) upon which those opinions are based. In a decision in Official Referee's proceedings, the judge made the following remarks:

"Since the parties have not agreed to exchange statements of fact, the reports need not contain the defendant's intended factual evidence, but doubtless they will have to refer to some facts in order to make the reports intelligible."[53]

Rule 37 lays no general obligation upon the disclosing party to indicate its entire factual case. However, the dictum of Ackner J. in *Ollett* v. *Bristol Aerojet* cited above imposes a higher duty in relation to disclosure of facts than the achievement of "intelligibility" in the report. The approach of Ackner J. is perhaps also more consonant with the purpose of Order 38, and rule 37 in particular. It has been held in *Kenning* v. *Eve Construction Ltd.*[54] that the duty to disclose includes matters detrimental to the case, because the other parties are entitled to cross-examine and the purpose of disclosure is in part to facilitate this. Once called, the expert's duty is primarily to the court. It is wholly wrong for an expert to submit a report to his client with a covering letter containing his "real" or "damaging" opinions.

"Special reasons" Disclosure should be ordered unless there are "special reasons" for not so ordering. There is no further indication, whether express or implicit, in the rules themselves as to what this expression means. It appears clear, however, that the drafting of the present rule 37[55] was intended to have at least four particular consequences. First, there is now a strong presumption that there will be pre-trial disclosure of expert reports. Secondly, it must follow from this that the burden of proof is upon the party which asserts that such disclosure should not take place. Thirdly, the nature of the claim itself, though relevant, is

---

[52] *Ollett* v. *Bristol Aerojet Ltd. (Practice Note)* [1979] 1 W.L.R. 1197.
[53] *Shell Pensions Trust* v. *Pell Frischmann & Partners* [1986] 2 All E.R. 911 at 913.
[54] [1989] 1 W.L.R. 1189. This is discussed further in Chap. 4., pp. 91–92.
[55] Introduced by R.S.C. (Amendment) 1987 (S.I. 1987 No. 1423).

not *per se* a reason for not disclosing.⁵⁶ Fourthly, although non-disclosure will be permitted only in a small minority of cases, there is a clear and more or less unfettered discretion upon the master or registrar to decide upon the facts of the particular case whether "special reasons" are made out for non-disclosure.

The former rule 38(2) directed the court, in considering whether or not disclosure should be ordered, to "have regard to all the circumstances," and then proceeded to grant a discretion to consider two particular circumstances⁵⁷ which could be treated as reasons for refusing pre-trial disclosure. The wording of the old rule 38(2) left some room for doubt as to whether these two circumstances were the only ones which would be sufficient for such a refusal. In *Kirkup v. British Railways Engineering*⁵⁸ it was held by Croom-Johnson J. that the two circumstances were not intended to be exclusive of other possible such reasons, and were merely "guidelines."⁵⁹ The judge observed that, if they had been intended to be exclusive, express words of limitation would be expected.⁶⁰ At no point was Croom-Johnson J.'s interpretation of the rules challenged, though he thought it wise to clarify his reasons for adopting it.⁶¹ It seems reasonable to infer from the drafting of the present rule 37 that a deliberate decision has been made, neither to introduce express words of limitation, nor to reinforce Croom-Johnson J.'s view that the examples given are merely "guidelines," but to dispense with the listing of reasons for non-disclosure altogether, and to leave the matter entirely open for argument depending upon the circumstances of the particular case.

In view of this, it would be misleading to attempt to set parameters within which such "special reasons" might fall. The most that can be done is to record examples of circumstances which have been regarded as having the potential to support the contention that there should be non-disclosure, whether pursuant to previous (and, it should be borne in mind, now revoked) rules, or in the cases. They certainly do not amount, *per se*, to adequate grounds for non-disclosure.

"Special reasons"—some relevant considerations—

   (i) expert evidence based upon a version of the facts in dispute between the parties⁶²;

---

[56] e.g. medical negligence cases under the former rule 37. But see *Naylor v. Preston Area Health Authority* [1987] 1 W.L.R. 958 where Sir John Donaldson M.R. at 968, states that the discretion may be exercised differently in medical cases from those involving other professions. See too R.S.C. Ord. 18, r. 12.
[57] See above n. 33.
[58] [1983] 1 W.L.R. 190.
[59] *Ibid.*, at 194.
[60] *Ibid.*
[61] See [1983] 1 W.L.R. 1165 at 1169, C.A.
[62] The old Ord. 38, r. 38(2)(*a*).

(ii) there is reason for thinking that there is a lack of bona fides or a likelihood of trimming of evidence by a party:
"a refusal of disclosure on these grounds should only occur where there is a solid basis for thinking that it is or may be such a case"[63]
This is most likely to arise in personal injuries cases but it can be envisaged as being relevant in others. It would probably only be a reason for non-disclosure where "the value of such evidence would be lost if (the relevant party) became aware of it before trial"[64];
(iii) expert evidence based upon hypothetical facts which the expert cannot verify from observation or from his own knowledge and experience.[65] This may be a ground for delaying rather than refusing disclosure,[66] or for sequential rather than simultaneous disclosure[67];
(iv) pleadings so general as to make it impossible for the expert to identify the precise issues on which he is to report,[68] or for the party's legal advisers properly to instruct an expert;
(v) the grounds for sequential rather than simultaneous disclosure might be regarded, in a clear case, as reasons for complete non-disclosure.[69] Croom-Johnson J., in *Kirkup* v. *British Railways Engineering*[70] appeared to assume that the considerations relevant to non-disclosure were also relevant to the issue of sequential disclosure. The same could be said to apply in reverse,[71] though perhaps with less force;
(vi) where matters alleged to be privileged in the public interest are contained in the report: see further Chapter 9.

Mutuality It has been generally understood that there is a principle of mutuality underpinning the disclosure of expert evidence.[72] This has the chief consequence that where one party argues successfully that he should not be required to disclose pre-trial, the order will usually be

---

[63] *Naylor* v. *Preston Area Health Authority*, above n. 56, *per* Sir John Donaldson M.R., at 968. See also at 975, *per* Sir F. Lawton.
[64] *Ibid.*, at 975.
[65] See the old Ord. 38, r. 38(2)(*b*), n. 33 above.
[66] See Sir John Donaldson M.R. in *Naylor* v. *Preston Area Health Authority*, above n. 56, at 968.
[67] See below pp. 46–48.
[68] This was regarded by Sir F. Lawton in *Naylor* v. *Preston Area Health Authority*, above n. 56, at 976, as a potential reason for non-disclosure. See too pp. 46–48, below (sequential disclosure).
[69] See below, pp. 46–48.
[70] [1983] 1 W.L.R. 190.
[71] See *e.g.* Sir F. Lawton in *Naylor* v. *Preston Area Health Authority*, above n. 56, at 976, who took the view that very general pleadings might be a ground, not merely for ordering sequential disclosure, but for refusing to order disclosure altogether.
[72] See *e.g. Supreme Court Practice 1991*, Vol. 1, 38/37–39/1.

mutual, *i.e.* neither party will be required to do so. There is no explicit questioning of this principle in the "special reasons" provisions, and it remains to be seen whether the word "special" is regarded as applicable only to the nature of the case or evidence in issue, or whether it could be said in some circumstances to describe the position of one party and not the other.

It probably continues to be the case that mutuality may be abandoned if there are "exceptional circumstances,"[73] and the approach taken by Croom-Johnson J. in *Kirkup* v. *British Railways Engineering*[74] indicates how the competing considerations are likely to be weighed:

> "Mutuality and fairness is one of the reasons for disclosure of expert's reports in personal injury actions, but it is not the only one, nor of such overriding importance that it governs the situation in every case. Other important considerations are the saving of costs and the reasons given by Ackner J. in *Ollett* v. *Bristol Aerojet Ltd.*, *i.e.* the avoidance of surprise and the need to avoid amendments at trial."[75]

3 The extent of the disclosure

Part-Disclosure R.S.C. Order 38, rule 39 provides that:

> "Where the Court considers that any circumstances rendering it undesirable to give a direction under rule 37 relate to part only of the evidence sought to be adduced, the Court may, if it thinks fit, direct disclosure of the remainder."

This provision enables the court to achieve the aim of the rules, namely that there should be disclosure in the majority of cases, by ensuring that disclosure is not completely avoided by a successful contention that rule 37 "special reasons" apply to a limited part of the report. A particular example might be an assertion that a professional confidence, of the limited class which the courts will protect,[76] should be regarded as privileged. The relevant material might very well be contained in a particular paragraph or section of the report, which could be excised for pre-trial purposes, and would remain confidential unless the trial judge ordered that the evidence be adduced at trial.[77]

The court has power at the pre-trial hearing to direct production of the report itself in order to make an order in terms which are as precise as the

---

[73] See *e.g. Supreme Court Practice 1991*, Vol. 1, 38/37–39/1.
[74] [1983] 1 W.L.R. 190.
[75] *Ibid.*, at 194. For medical reports in personal injuries cases, see Chap. 19.
[76] As to which, see Chap. 9, pp. 195–202.
[77] See *e.g. R.* v. *Statutory Visitors to St. Lawrence's Hospital, Caterham, ex p. Pritchard* [1953] 1 W.L.R. 1158.

circumstances allow.⁷⁸ The utility of this power has been recognised in actions, particularly concerning personal injuries, where "lack of bona fides and the likelihood of trimming of evidence" is asserted as a ground for non-disclosure.⁷⁹

Plans and other supplementary documents Where reports are exchanged, they should be accompanied by any plans or other documents which go with the report itself.⁸⁰ The appropriate test is presumably now the "substance" test.⁸¹

Professional literature Experts may in general rely, in forming their opinions for the court, upon research and other findings and literature which are relevant to the issues, even where they do not themselves have direct knowledge of the facts upon which the literature is based.⁸² Order 38 itself makes no specific provision for disclosure (or otherwise) of such materials. The Court of Appeal has however directed in at least one reported case,⁸³ the facts of which do not suggest that the order was appropriate only to the matters in issue in that case, that the references of such relevant literature as the experts could anticipate referring to in court should be disclosed along with their reports. Thus the expert's report:

> "should be accompanied by an identification of any medical or scientific literature, published or unpublished, to which the experts intend to refer."⁸⁴

It is now common practice in medical negligence cases for an order of this kind to be made, providing, for example, for all such literature, reports, articles, extracts from journals and text-books relied on by experts to be listed and exchanged in the same manner as the expert's own report.

It is clearly expected neither that the expert will always be able to anticipate all such material as may be required at trial, nor that he should, merely because such an order is made, attempt to search out material which he does not in fact require for the purpose of forming his opinion on matters in issue. Such an order, therefore:

> "does not mean that if they are taken by surprise and in cross examination wish to rely upon other literature, they should not be able to do so;"⁸⁵

---

⁷⁸ R.S.C. Ord. 24, r. 12.
⁷⁹ *Naylor v. Preston Area Health Authority*, above n. 56, at 968.
⁸⁰ *The Planter* [1955] 1 W.L.R. 898.
⁸¹ See pp. 40–41, above.
⁸² See Chap. 8, pp. 172–181.
⁸³ *Naylor v. Preston Area Health Authority*, above n. 56.
⁸⁴ *Ibid.*, per Sir John Donaldson M.R. at 970.
⁸⁵ *Ibid.*

and neither are experts thereby expected to:

> "conduct a search of medical literature to find any printed material which would support the opinions. What is wanted is disclosure of the printed material upon which the expert has specially relied when making his report."[86]

4 Time for disclosure

In the great majority of cases, the principle of mutuality requires that, where pre-trial disclosure is ordered, it should be simultaneous (however, for medical reports in personal injury cases see Chap. 19). The order will usually provide a time within which this should occur as part of the timetable of pre-trial procedures. However there can be circumstances in which it is desirable for sequential disclosure to take place, though these will be "exceptional."[87] As with non-disclosure, it is not possible to itemise exhaustively the conditions sufficient for sequential disclosure. Almost all the considerations described as relevant in the authorities conform to the notion that:

> "the case for sequential disclosure is based upon the premise that disclosure by the plaintiff's experts will refine and define the issues to which the defendants' experts have to apply their minds."[88]

The following have been regarded as relevant considerations:

(i) A large number of plaintiffs bringing similar actions against one defendant. In *Kirkup* v. *British Railways Engineering*,[89] Croom-Johnson J. expressed the view that, where there were 3,000 claims (in respect of noise-induced hearing loss) at 12 of the defendants' premises:

> "it would be unreasonable to expect the Defendants to have one ready-made standard engineer's report available to be trotted out every time a claim is made against them."[90]

(ii) Complex facts over a long period of time, of which the defendant's expert has no notice until he sees the plaintiff's expert's report. This was the ground on which it appears that the Court of Appeal in *Kirkup* v. *British Railways Engineering*[91] was persuaded to uphold the decision of Croom-Johnson J.:

> "there is a danger in a case of this kind that the defendants will

---

[86] *Naylor* v. *Preston Area Health Authority*, above n. 56, *per* Sir F. Lawton at 976.
[87] *Ibid.*, at 974.
[88] *Ibid.*, at 970.
[89] [1983] 1 W.L.R. 190.
[90] *Ibid.*, at 194.
[91] [1983] 1 W.L.R. 1165.

be called upon to write a thesis upon noise generally in engineering workshops. That will not be of any value to the plaintiffs and it certainly will not be of any value to the trial judge."[92]

(iii) Proofs of witnesses of fact required before expert can give his opinion[93];
(iv) Pleadings too general for the expert witness to identify the precise matters in issue. This has been treated as a reason for sequential disclosure[94] although the defect might be said in some such cases to be in the pleading, not the concept of simultaneous disclosure. It "should be unnecessary if the case has been properly pleaded."[95]
(v) Avoiding amendments to the pleadings[96];
(vi) Saving costs[97];
(vii) Avoidance of surprise necessitating adjournments in the interests of justice[98];
(viii) Facts not verified by the expert himself:

"early disclosure of the substance of an expert's evidence will be of less value in defining the real issues and informing the parties of the true strength or weakness of their respective cases to the extent that it is based upon a hypothetical factual situation which the expert has not himself been able to verify and which is in issue between the parties."[99]

It can be seen that most of these considerations will tend to result in plaintiffs being required to disclose first in the sequence, though this is by no means inevitable. Often however, although it might appear to be advantageous to defendants that this should be so, sequential disclosure may save much time, and thereby reduce the "anguish of uncertainty"[1] surrounding the litigation. In personal injury cases, particularly those defended by insurance companies, it has often in the past been suggested that in the interests of speed and economy, the plaintiff's report should

---

[92] [1983] 1 W.L.R. 1165, per Lawton L.J. at 1170.
[93] *Rahman v. Kirklees Area Health Authority (Practice Note)* [1980] 1 W L R 1244 at 1245, per Cumming-Bruce L.J.
[94] *Kirkup v. British Railway Engineering*, above n. 91.
[95] *Naylor v. Preston Area Health Authority*, above n. 56, at 970. Although it was submitted by the appellants in *Kirkup v. British Railways Engineering*, above n. 91, that the proper remedy was a request for further and better particulars, the Court of Appeal did not refer to the point.
[96] *Kirkup v. British Railways Engineering*, above n. 91, at 194; *Ollett v. Bristol Aerojet* [1979] 1 W.L.R 1197.
[97] *Ibid*. See also *Naylor v. Preston Area Health Authority*, above n. 56, at 968 and 970.
[98] *Ollett v. Bristol Aerojet*, above n. 96.
[99] *Naylor v. Preston Area Health Authority*, above n. 56, at 968.
[1] *Ibid*.

be disclosed first, so that the defendants may consider agreeing it. New rules effective on June 4 1990, principally set out in R.S.C. Order 18, rule 12, provide that sequential disclosure is the norm for medical reports in personal injuries cases. This is discussed fully in Chapter 19.

If there is a principle underlying the practice for all other reports it can, it is submitted, be found in the requirement of rule 37 that where disclosure is ordered, it is the "substance" of the expert evidence which it is proposed to adduce at trial which must be disclosed. It is of benefit to nobody, and least of all perhaps to the party seeking disclosure, if the requirement of simultaneous disclosure simply results in the substance[2] itself not in fact being disclosed, because it is not yet known. Where this can reasonably be avoided by sequential disclosure, therefore, it would be appropriate so to order.[3]

5 Non-mutual disclosure

Are there any circumstances in which the court would order one party only to disclose the substance of its expert evidence while not requiring the other to do so? It has been explained that although the wording of the rules appears specifically to require both parties to make application under rule 36, in practice application by one will be treated as application by all. There is nothing, however, in rule 37 itself, or in Order 38[4] generally, which specifically precludes such an order. Given the strong presumption in favour of disclosure, the occasions on which the court might entertain the submission both that "special reasons" apply and that the principle of mutuality[5] should be abandoned will necessarily be very few. The circumstances in which the issue might arise, such as a claim for privilege in relation to a professional confidence of the limited kind which the courts will protect,[6] could usually be resolved by an order for partial disclosure.[7] The courts have, however, made it clear that the principles of mutuality and fairness, though important to Order 38, are not immutable, and that other considerations, whether of public policy or of practicality in the particular case, may override them.[8]

---

[2] As to which, see pp. 40–42, above.
[3] It has been persuasively suggested that justice would be better served by a presumption of sequential disclosure in most cases: see I. R. Scott, "Experts' reports as particulars of claim" (1984) C.J.Q., 101 at 106–108. See too R.S.C. Ord. 18, r. 12 as amended.
[4] Through *cf.* Chap. 19, pp. 333–336.
[5] See above, pp. 43–44.
[6] As to which see Chap. 9, pp. 195–202, below.
[7] Under R.S.C. Ord. 38, r. 39.
[8] *Kirkup v. British Railways Engineering*, above n. 89, at 194.

6 Revocation, variation and enforcement

Revocation and variation of disclosure orders R.S.C. Order 38, rule 44 provides that:

> "Any direction given under this Part of this Order may on sufficient cause being shown be revoked or varied by a subsequent direction given at or before the trial of the cause or matter."

Wide discretion at every stage of proceedings is maintained by the power in this rule, exercisable by master or registrar at the pre-trial stage, or by the judge at trial. The words "sufficient cause" have not been defined or restricted, though clearly in general the power is to be exercised in a manner consistent with principles developed under R.S.C. Order 38, rules 37 and 38,[9] notably the strong presumption which now exists in favour of disclosure, and in particular of simultaneous disclosure.

Enforcement of disclosure orders R.S.C. Order 38, rule 36(2) provides that:

> "Nothing in paragraph (1) shall ... affect the enforcement under any other provision of these Rules (except Order 45, Rule 5) of a direction given under this part of this Order."

The effect of this provision is to render orders in relation to expert evidence enforceable in the same manner as other procedural provisions, with the exception of committal and sequestration (R.S.C. Order 45, rule 5) which are seen as inappropriately draconian. The remaining forms of sanction, such as stay of the action, dismissal of the action, and striking out of the defence, provide the court with powers adequate to ensure compliance. The court also has the sanction of a wholly or partially adverse order as to costs where directions for disclosure are complied with out of time.[10]

D. AGREEMENT NOT TO SEEK DIRECTIONS AS TO DISCLOSURE

R.S.C. Order 38, rule 36 requires application to be made to the court for appropriate directions as a condition of calling expert evidence at trial, but also provides that parties may agree to adduce such evidence at trial without seeking directions. This will usually result from an agreement by both parties voluntarily to disclose to each other the reports of their

---

[9] See above, pp. 37–44.
[10] *Cable v. Dallaturca* (1977) 121 S.J. 795.

experts, in the expectation, frequently, that the evidence itself can be agreed. The parties may also, however, agree that there be no application for directions and no pre-trial disclosure, but that the parties should be at liberty to call such evidence at trial. They may agree too the precise number and type of such witnesses who may be called at trial, though the trial judge, as the judge of admissibility, may exclude such evidence if it is not relevant.

E. OTHER DIRECTIONS

1 Number of experts

R.S.C. Order 38, rule 4 provides that:

> "The Court may, at or before the trial of any action, order that the number of medical or other expert witnesses who may be called at the trial shall be limited as specified by the order."

This provision for limiting the number of expert witnesses who may be called at trial clearly contemplates that the order may be made either at the directions stage by the master or registrar, or at trial by the trial judge. Where it is the trial judge who so orders, he may make such order as he wishes subject to the question of admissibility and therefore relevance, and this is discussed in Chapter 5. The court may not however give directions limiting the areas of subject-matter upon which the expert may speak, a fact which has been judicially regretted.[11]

It follows from the fact that the question of admissibility is for the trial judge alone that the master or registrar cannot prevent a party from adducing expert evidence. He may clearly however, under R.S.C. Order 38, rule 4, restrict the number of expert witnesses. It has been held, though, in *Sullivan* v. *West Yorkshire Passenger Transport Executive*,[12] that he may not limit the number to none, thereby effectively prejudging the issue of admissibility. He may of course choose not to order disclosure of reports, but this does not preclude a party from adducing expert evidence at trial. Orders as to numbers of experts on the issue of liability are inappropriate if liability is admitted in the pleadings.[13]

Rule 4 leaves open the possibility, on its face, that the master or registrar might limit the number of experts to, for example, one, where there is in one action a number of issues requiring different forms of expertise, perhaps an engineer and a consultant orthopaedic surgeon in a road acci-

---

[11] *Murray Pipework Ltd.* v. *UIE Scotland Ltd.* (1990) Const. L.J. 56 at 58.
[12] [1985] 2 All E.R. 134.
[13] *Brown* v. *Merton, Sutton and Wandsworth Area Health Authority* [1982] 1 All E.R. 650.

dent case where issues of liability and quantum are in issue. Rule 4 makes no particular allowance for this possibility. The interpretation in practice is to limit the number of witnesses to one in respect of any particular form of expertise which is demonstrated to be relevant.

Taxation of costs An order made under R.S.C. Order 38, rule 4 does not fetter the jurisdiction of the taxing master to determine whether the numbers of witnesses called was reasonable.[14] Conversely, the fact that no such order as to number was made is not "to be regarded as indicating that the calling of an expert witness is necessarily to be regarded as unreasonable."[15]

Although 'in-house' experts, though not independent, are "experts" for the purposes of Order 38,[16] it has been held that they do not qualify as experts for the purpose of taxation of costs.[17]

2 Meeting of experts without prejudice

R.S.C. Order 38, rule 38(3) provides that:

> "In any cause or matter the Court may, if it thinks fit, direct that there be a meeting 'without prejudice' of such experts within such periods before or after the disclosure of their reports as the Court may specify, for the purpose of identifying those parts of their evidence which are in issue. Where such a meeting takes place the experts may prepare a joint statement indicating those parts of their evidence on which they are, and those on which they are not, in agreement."

This provision, introduced comparatively recently,[18] does not yet have the benefit of an established practice. It is an example of the developing policy of openness in pre-trial procedure.[19] Although described in the notes to the rule as a "significant step,"[20] the rule has been drafted in a somewhat tentative manner, which leaves its practical consequences open to development by the courts. This is discussed further in Chapter 4.

No directions need be sought as to this particular provision, as R.S.C. Order 38, rule 36 does not make reference to rule 38. The master or

---

[14] *Atwell* v. *Minister of Public Building and Works* [1969] 1 W.L.R. 1074.
[15] *Ibid.*, at 1076.
[16] *Shell Pensions Trust* v. *Pell Frischmann & Partners* [1986] 2 All E.R. 911.
[17] *Taylor* v. *Greening* (unreported), June 15, 1956, C.A. Though see further Chap. 11.
[18] R.S.C. (Amendment No. 2) 1986 (S.I. 1986 No. 1187).
[19] See above, pp. 32–33.
[20] *Supreme Court Practice 1991*, Vol. I, 38/37–39/6.

registrar must however consider the matter pursuant to the general requirement in R.S.C. Order 25, rule 3.[21] There is a complete discretion in respect of the exercise of the power, and there are no grounds upon which such an order must be made, or matters which must be taken into account before so ordering. It should also be noted that the order can be made in any case where there is expert evidence, not only where directions are sought pursuant to rule 36.

Joint statement The experts may prepare a joint statement at or following a "without prejudice" meeting. The master or registrar is not specifically empowered to direct that such a statement be prepared, even conditional upon agreement being reached as to some part of the expert evidence. It was held in *Graigola Merthyr* v. *Swansea Corporation*,[22] a case involving lengthy and complex expert evidence, that:

> "the expert advisers of the parties, whether legal or scientific, are under a special duty to the Court in the preparation of such a case to limit in every possible way the contentious matters of fact to be dealt with at the hearing."

Clearly, thus, even though a statement cannot be ordered by the master or registrar, once the experts attend such a meeting they are duty-bound to identify areas of agreement. It follows that, in order to be of utility for the purpose of limiting issues at trial, such agreement should be recorded in writing. The notes to rule 38[23] observe that such a statement has the effect of removing the "without prejudice" protection of any matter stated to be agreed. The conduct and status of without prejudice meetings and joint statements is discussed in detail in Chapter 4.

F. OTHER METHODS OF ADDUCING EXPERT EVIDENCE

The seeking of directions as to disclosure of the substance of proposed oral evidence under R.S.C. Order 38, rule 36(1) is the usual method of adducing expert evidence at trial. As has already been observed, however, there are other means of doing so,[24] which will only be appropriate in particular and limited circumstances.

---

[21] And see *Practice Direction* [1974] 1 W.L.R. 904.
[22] [1928] 1 Ch. 31 at 38, *per* Tomlin J.
[23] See further the cases discussed in Chap. 4, at pp. 92–99.
[24] See above p. 34.

1 Oral evidence

Automatic directions in personal injuries cases In many of the more straightforward claims for damages for personal injuries the procedure under R.S.C. Order 25, rule 8 will be appropriate.[25]

Leave of the court Whether or not directions have been sought under R.S.C. Order 38, rule 36(1), the court has a complete discretion over the admission of expert evidence.[26] This discretion will however be sparingly exercised where no persuasive reasons are offered for failure to seek directions, particularly where the application is left until trial.[27]

2 Written evidence

Expert evidence, like lay witness evidence, is regarded by the courts, unless agreed, as best given orally, as the oral hearing provides the best opportunity for other parties to test its quality and for the tribunal to judge its weight. Thus R.S.C. Order 38, rule 1, which applies to all witnesses, provides that:

> "Subject to the provisions of these rules and of the Civil Evidence Act 1968 and the Civil Evidence Act 1972, and any other enactment relating to evidence, any fact required to be proved at the trial of any action begun by writ by the evidence of witnesses shall be proved by the examination of the witnesses orally and in open court."

In limited circumstances, however, expert evidence may be admitted in written form.

Affidavit evidence R.S.C. Order 38, rule 36(2) excludes from the requirements of R.S.C. Order 38, Part IV any evidence which is permitted to be given by affidavit. This is mainly concerned with orders under R.S.C. Order 38, rule 2, but also extends to certain limited jurisdictions and interlocutory procedures in which affidavit evidence is the conventional method of adducing evidence. Expert affidavit evidence has occasionally been admitted, usually for reasons of expediency, where its content appears to be relatively uncontroversial or the witness is abroad.[28] Affidavit evidence of opinion, however, was not admitted where it was based upon hearsay supplied to the expert (in this case a statutory inspector in winding-up proceedings), which could not be

---

[25] See below Ch. 19, pp. 336–338.
[26] R.S.C. Ord. 38, r. 36(1).
[27] This is discussed in more detail in Chap. 5, p. 103.
[28] See *e.g. Re Arton* [1896] 1 Q.B. 509; *Westlake v. Westlake* [1910] P. 167; *Re Valentine's Settlement* [1965] Ch. 831.

verified by the court, unless it constituted a "record" under section 4 of the Civil Evidence Act 1968.[29]

Expert evidence contained in a statement   R.S.C. Order 38, rule 41 provides:

> "Where an application is made under rule 36 in respect of expert evidence contained in a statement and the applicant alleges that the maker of the statement cannot or should not be called as a witness, the Court may direct that the provisions of rules 20 to 23 and 25 to 33 shall apply with such modifications as the Court thinks fit."

This incorporates into the Order 38 procedure the provisions of section 1 of the Civil Evidence Act 1972:

> "(1) Subject to the provisions of this section, Part 1 (hearsay evidence) of the Civil Evidence Act 1968, except section 5 (statements produced by computers) shall apply in relation to statements of opinion as it applies in relation to statements of fact, subject to the necessary modifications and in particular the modification that any reference to a fact stated in a statement shall be construed as a reference to a matter dealt with therein.
> (2) Section 4 (admissibility of certain records) of the Civil Evidence Act 1968, as applied by subsection (1) above, shall not render admissible in any civil proceedings a statement of opinion contained in a record unless that statement would be admissible in those proceedings if made in the course of giving oral evidence by the person who originally supplied the information from which the record was compiled; but where a statement of opinion contained in a record deals with a matter on which the person who originally supplied the information from which the record was compiled is (or would if living be) qualified to give oral expert evidence, the said section 4, as applied by subsection (1) above, shall have effect in relation to that statement as if so much of subsection (1) of that section as requires personal knowledge on the part of that person were omitted."

Thus the hearsay provisions of the Civil Evidence Act 1968 apply to expert opinion (and factual) evidence, save that computer evidence is excluded, and records under section 4 are only subject to these provisions in so far as the original supplier of the information would himself be qualified to give expert evidence if called before the court. The court can modify the provisions as to the manner in which such evidence is adduced, and the discretion is not limited by the words of R.S.C. Order 38, rule 41. It is presumably intended, however, that the modifications

---

[29] *Savings & Investment Bank* v. *Gasco Investments (Netherlands) B.V.* [1984] 1 W.L.R. 271.

should be limited to ensuring that the other parties are given as many of the advantages of R.S.C. Order 38, Part IV as is possible in the circumstances.

It is clear that the use of the hearsay provisions of the Civil Evidence Act 1968 will be justified in a relatively small number of cases involving expert evidence. For unlike a witness of fact, whose evidence will probably be lost to the court entirely if not so admitted, in most instances a different expert can be instructed to replace one who cannot or should not be called. Situations justifying its use would include those where the expert's opinion was based upon personal inspection of the subject matter of the action, which is no longer in existence or unable to be further inspected, or where the expert practises within a very limited specialism, other experts in which are difficult to obtain. In any event a party will usually be better advised to seek a different expert witness, as the court will inevitably tend to be more impressed by a credible live witness called by the other party than by a statement which is not subject to cross-examination and unable to respond to the factual evidence which emerges at trial.

It has been observed[30] that although statute would prima facie render it possible for a party to say that although its expert could give oral evidence at trial, it was simply proposed that he should not, the party preferring to adduce written evidence only, this result is effectively precluded by the fact that directions must be sought under R.S.C. Order 38, rule 36 before adducing any expert evidence,[31] and the remainder of R.S.C. Order 38, Part IV does not permit the court to make such a direction.

3 Court expert

R.S.C. Order 40 permits the court, upon application by the parties, to appoint a court expert, and describes the appropriate procedure.[32]

G. NO PROPERTY IN EXPERT EVIDENCE

1 Adducing the expert's report of another party

R.S.C. Order 38, rule 42 provides that:

> "A party to any cause or matter may put in evidence any expert report disclosed to him by any other party in accordance with this part of this Order."

This provision, though wide, does not includes reports voluntarily dis-

---

[30] *Phipson on Evidence*, (14th ed., 1990) pp. 819–820.
[31] See *Rover International v. Cannon Film Sales* [1987] 1 W.L.R. 1597.
[32] See below, Chap. 3, pp. 60-65.

closed by another party. It is confined to reports disclosed pursuant to R.S.C. Order 38, Part IV,[33] although this presumably includes reports disclosed following agreement of the parties under rule 36(1). This latter situation must be distinguished from totally voluntary disclosure. The party so doing must then decide whether to rely solely upon the other party's report, or whether additional expert evidence is necessary. Dicta as to what constitutes an "agreed" report[34] will assist with the question whether the latter course is a practicable one.

2. No property in an expert witness

Subject to the question of privileged communications,[35] the law takes the view that the obtaining of the fullest possible evidence for the benefit of the court outweighs any question of loyalty or other claim which a party may have upon a witness. In *Harmony Shipping Co. S.A. v. Saudi Europe Line*[36] a handwriting expert was, in rather unusual circumstances, consulted by both parties to an action. It was held by Lord Denning M.R. that "an expert witness falls into the same position as a witness of fact,"[37] for the reason that:

> "the court is entitled, in order to ascertain the truth, to have the actual facts which he has observed adduced before it and to have his independent opinion on those facts."[38]

The general rule, which applies to all evidence which might be given by an expert, subject to legally recognised privilege, is therefore that:

> "there is no property in an expert witness as to the facts he has observed and his own independent opinion on them."[39]

It is not possible to circumvent this general principle by agreement or otherwise and a contract purporting to restrain an expert witness from giving evidence for another party would not be enforced by the courts, as it would be contrary to public policy.[40]

II CRIMINAL PROCEEDINGS

A party to criminal proceedings in the Crown Court[41] who wishes to adduce expert evidence at trial must comply with the Crown Court

---

[33] See *Mallick v. Allied Schools Agency Limited, The Times*, March 4, 1980, C.A.
[34] See below, Chap. 4, pp. 88–89, and Chap. 19, pp. 348–353.
[35] As to which see Chap. 9 below.
[36] [1979] 1 W.L.R. 1380.
[37] *Ibid.*, at 1385.
[38] *Ibid.*, at 1385.
[39] *Ibid.*, at 1386. See further pp. 104–106 below.
[40] *Ibid.*, at 1386.
[41] No special rules exist for magistrates' court proceedings.

(Advance Notice of Expert Evidence) Rules 1987,[42] which provide as follows:

> "1. These Rules may be cited as the Crown Court (Advance Notice of Expert Evidence) Rules 1987 and shall come into force on 15th July 1987.
>
> 2. These Rules shall not have effect in relation to any proceedings in which a person has been committed for trial or ordered to be retired before 15th July 1987.
>
> 3.—(1) Following the committal for trial of any person, or the making of an order for his retrial, if any party to the proceedings proposes to adduce expert evidence (whether of fact or opinion) in the proceedings (otherwise than in relation to sentence) he shall as soon as practicable, unless in relation to the evidence in question he has already done so—
>
>> (a) Furnish the other party or parties with a statement in writing of any finding or opinion which he proposes to adduce by way of such evidence; and
>>
>> (b) Where a request in writing is made to him in that behalf by any other party, provide that party also with a copy of (or if it appears to the party proposing to adduce the evidence to be more practicable, a reasonable opportunity to examine) the record of any observation, test, calculation or other procedure on which such finding or opinion is based and any document or other thing or substance in respect of which any such procedure has been carried out.
>
> (2) A party may by notice in writing waive his right to be furnished with any of the matters mentioned in paragraph (1) above and, in particular, may agree that the statement mentioned in sub-paragraph (a) therefore may be furnished to him orally and not in writing.
>
> (3) In paragraph (1) above, 'document' has the same meaning as in Part I of the Civil Evidence Act 1968.
>
> 4.—(1) If a party has reasonable grounds for believing that the disclosure of any evidence in compliance with the requirements imposed by rule 3 above might lead to the intimidation, or attempted intimidation, of any person on whose evidence he intends to rely in the proceedings, or otherwise to the course of justice being interfered with, he shall not be obliged to comply with those requirements in relation to that evidence.
>
> (2) Where, in accordance with paragraph (1) above, a party considers that he is not obliged to comply with the requirements

---

[42] (S.I. 1987 No. 716). Made pursuant to the Police and Criminal Evidence Act 1984, s.81, and the Supreme Court Act 1981, ss.84(1) and 86.

imposed by rule 3 above with regard to any evidence in relation to any other party, he shall give notice in writing to that party to the effect that the evidence is being withheld and the grounds therefor.

5. A party who seeks to adduce expert evidence in any proceedings and who fails to comply with rule 3 above shall not adduce that evidence in those proceedings without the leave of the court."

Thus unless the parties agree to the contrary,[43] written disclosure of the proposed expert evidence must be made as soon as practicable after committal.[44] In default of compliance, the leave of the court will be required for its adduction at trial.[45] If it is asserted that good reason exists for non-disclosure,[46] written reasons for this must be given to the other party.[47] It has been observed that these obligations are effectively only relevant to the defence where, as is the almost invariable case, the prosecution is already under a duty to disclose the evidence of all its proposed witnesses in advance.[48] Furthermore it can have the indirect effect of requiring the defence, in many such instances, to disclose a part of its factual case in advance.[49]

A party may seek to adduce expert evidence in the form of a report only. This requires the leave of the court, which must take into account the matters set out in section 30 of the Criminal Justice Act 1988, which provides as follows:

"(1) An expert report shall be admissible as evidence in criminal proceedings, whether or not the person making it attends to give oral evidence in those proceedings.

(2) If it is proposed that the person making the report shall not give oral evidence, the report shall only be admissible with the leave of the court.

(3) For the purpose of determining whether to give leave the court shall have regard—

(a) to the contents of the report;

(b) to the reasons why it is proposed that the person making the report shall not given oral evidence;

(c) to any risk, having regard in particular to whether it is likely to be possible to controvert statements in the report if the person making it does not attend to given oral evidence in the proceedings, that its admission or exclusion will result in unfairness to the accused or, if there is more than one, to any of them; and

---

[43] S.I. 1987 No. 716, r. 3(2).
[44] Ibid., r. 3(1).
[45] Ibid., r. 5.
[46] Ibid., r. 4(1).
[47] Ibid., r. 4(2).
[48] See R. May, *Criminal Evidence* (1986), p. 137.
[49] Ibid.

(d) to any other circumstances that appear to the court to be relevant.

(4) An expert report, when admitted, shall be evidence of any fact or opinion of which the person making it could have given oral evidence.

(5) In this section "expert report" means a written report by a person dealing wholly or mainly with matters on which he is (or would if living be) qualified to give expert evidence."

The evidence of any witness, including an expert, may also be adduced under section 9 of the Criminal Justice Act 1967 in written form if it is signed with a declaration that its contents are true and no other party serves notice within seven days requiring the maker to attend court to give oral evidence. The disclosure rules set out above are however not displaced by this provision. It is not clear with what degree of strictness the courts will apply the provisions of section 30 of the Criminal Justice Act 1988. However there must in most cases where expert evidence is challenged be a "risk", under section 30(3)(c), of "unfairness to the accused", if cross-examination is thereby denied to him. Furthermore where an expert is dead, beyond the seas or otherwise unable to give evidence, it is highly unlikely that no other expert can be found to express an opinion on known facts.[50]

---

[50] See *R. v. McGuire* (1985) 81 Cr.App.R. 323. This decision is discussed further in Chap. 8, pp. 184–185.

CHAPTER 3

Court Appointed Experts

The most frequent method of obtaining specialist expertise and knowledge for the court is for the parties, usually after seeking directions as to disclosure,[1] to call such expert witnesses as they choose, subject to the court's control over their competence[2] and number,[3] and the relevance of the evidence they propose to give. However there may be circumstances in which the court itself wishes to have the benefit of expert assistance from persons other than witnesses called by the parties, either upon application of the parties, or of its own motion, or it may follow from the nature of the proceedings that such assistance will usually be required. Various provisions, both statutory and at common law, provide for the circumstances under which this may occur.

The history of the use of experts by the courts shows that the balance has shifted substantially away from court-appointed experts, who may now only be employed in limited circumstances. Indeed, until about the seventeenth century almost all expert assistance to the court was by way not of witnesses called by the parties,[4] but either of special juries or experts called in by the court of its own motion.[5]

A. THE COURT EXPERT

In the overwhelming majority of cases any expert witness called to give evidence will do so as the witness of one of the parties, usually also having been engaged by that party to prepare a report and then to appear as a witness. There is however provision, under R.S.C. Order 40, for the court, though not of its own motion, to obtain the services of an expert witness, whether in the absence of other expert evidence where there is

---

[1] See above, Chap. 2.
[2] See above pp. 10–12.
[3] R.S.C. Ord. 38, r. 4.
[4] See Chap. 1, pp. 6–9.
[5] See *e.g. Willoughby's Case* (1597) Cro. Eliz. 566; *Alsop v. Bowtrell* (1619) Cro. Jac. 541.

nevertheless a need for it, or where the parties' experts express such diametrically opposed opinions, or interpretations of given facts, that the court is unable to choose between them. It is apparent that such a deadlock will not necessarily be resolved by the appointment of a further expert. He may merely reinforce the existing polarity, but not in a manner which persuades the judge that one pole is to be preferred to the other. Equally he may take a form of *via media* between the opinions expressed which is legally inconclusive. The latter problem might on some occasions be circumvented by that formal adherence to the rules as to burden and standard of proof which is the evidentially correct resort of the courts in such circumstances.

1 Power to appoint a court expert

R.S.C. Order 40, rule 1 provides that:
>"(1) In any cause or matter which is to be tried without a jury and in which any question for an expert witness arises the Court may at any time, on the application of any party, appoint an independent expert or, if more than one such question arises, two or more such experts, to inquire and report upon any question of fact or opinion not involving questions of law or of construction.
>
>An expert appointed under this paragraph is referred to in this Order as a "court expert."
>
>(2) Any court expert in a cause or matter shall, if possible, be a person agreed between the parties and, failing agreement, shall be nominated by the court.
>
>(3) The question to be submitted to the court expert and the instructions (if any) given to him shall, failing agreement between the parties, be settled by the court.
>
>(4) In this rule "expert," in relation to any question arising in a cause or matter, means any person who has such knowledge or experience of or connection with that question that his opinion on it would be admissible in evidence."

The power of the court to appoint a court expert may only be exercised on the application of a party to the proceedings and not therefore of its own motion. This severely limits its ambit and excludes circumstances in which the judge is unsupported by the parties, dissatisfied with existing expert evidence, or concerned at its absence in a case which appears to demand it. It is unlikely therefore to be employed where there is the prospect of substantial conflict between experts on the question in respect of which such an appointment might otherwise be made. The utility of Order 40 will often therefore be confined to obtaining information which is not the subject of major controversy in the case, but where issues of time and costs are of relative importance.[6]

The appointment may be made "at any time."[7] It is conceivable thus that a party which had not hitherto considered expert evidence to be necessary, either on a particular issue, or at all, might at a late stage seek to persuade the court to exercise its power in the interests of justice. The wording of rule 1(2) suggests that this is not the type of situation anticipated as being within the scope of the order, but it is equally clear that it is not specifically excluded. Where there has been full disclosure of reports, however, it is unlikely that such an application would meet with an enthusiastic reception.

Expert The definition of "expert" contained in rule 1(4) does not significantly add to or narrow the somewhat unspecific authorities on the meaning of the word outside the bounds of Order 40. It does however serve to emphasise that it is the present state of "knowledge or experience" of the individual which is decisive *per se*, and not the particular route or means by which such knowledge or experience was obtained.[8]

2 Procedure

The decision having been taken, upon application,[9] to appoint a court expert, and the question or questions on which he is to report having been settled, the court writes to the expert whose name, if he consents to the appointment, then appears in the order, and he prepares his report. If the fee is not agreed by the parties, it will be fixed by the court, and each party will pay half subject to the future course of the action. The remaining procedure provided for under R.S.C. Order 40 is as follows:

> "2.—(1) The court expert must send his report to the court, together with such number of copies thereof as the court may direct, and the proper officer must send copies of the report to the parties or their solicitors.
> (2) The court may direct the court expert to make a further or supplemental report.
> (3) Any part of a court expert's report which is not accepted by all the parties to the cause or matter in which it is made shall be

---

[6] In some such circumstances the court may take judicial notice of a particular fact. See above Chap. 1, pp. 22–26.
[7] R.S.C. Ord. 40, r. 1(1).
[8] The *Supreme Court Practice 1991* notes to R.S.C. Ord. 40 (at 40/1–6/1) observe that the former rule (R.S.C. Ord. 37A, r. 11) includes as "experts": scientific persons, medical men, engineers, accountants, actuaries, architects, surveyors and other *specially skilled persons* (emphasis added).
[9] By summons. See 33 *Atkin's Court Forms* (2nd ed.) (1981 issue) 340, Form 36. And see Form 37 for a form of order.

treated as information furnished to the court and be given such weight as the court thinks fit.

3. If the court expert is of opinion that an experiment or test of any kind (other than one of a trifling character) is necessary to enable him to make a satisfactory report he shall inform the parties or their solicitors and shall, if possible, make an arrangement with them as to the expenses involved, the persons to attend and other relevant matters; and if the parties are unable to agree on any of those matters it shall be settled by the court.

4. Any party may, within 14 days after receiving a copy of the court expert's report, apply to the court for leave to cross-examine the expert on his report, and on that application the court shall make an order for the cross-examination of the expert by all the parties either:

(a) at the trial, or

(b) before an examiner at such time and place as may be specified in the order.

5.—(1) The remuneration of the court expert shall be fixed by the court and shall include a fee for his report and a proper sum for each day during which he is required to be present either in court or before an examiner.

(2) Without prejudice to any order providing for payment of the court expert's remuneration as part of the costs of the cause or matter, the parties shall be jointly and severally liable to pay the amount fixed by the court for his remuneration, but where the appointment of a court expert is opposed the court may as a condition of making the appointment, require the party applying for the appointment to give such security for the remuneration of the expert as the court thinks fit.

6. Where a court expert is appointed in a cause or matter, any party may, on giving to the other parties a reasonable time before the trial notice of his intention to do so, call one expert witness to give evidence on the question reported on by the court expert but no party may call more than one such witness without the leave of the court, and the court shall not grant leave unless it considers the circumstances of the case to be exceptional."

As has been indicated, R.S.C. Order 40 is most likely to be employed in respect of matters as to which there is little controversy, certainly as far as the content of the evidence itself is concerned, though of course the parties may well assert that it has different consequences in law. The order does however acknowledge the possibility that the report may not fit into this pattern, either wholly or in part. Thus rule 2(3) ensures that any "information"[10] not so accepted is nevertheless available to the court. Furthermore, rule 6 enables a party wishing to call evidence in rebuttal to do so on giving reasonable notice, though leave is required where more than one expert is sought to be called on each side, and exceptional circumstances must be shown. It would follow from the fact that this may be done in relation to "the question reported on by the court expert" that where under rule 1 more than one court expert has been called because more than one "question" arises, the commensurate number of experts may be called in rebuttal without the leave of the court.

3   County court

There is no equivalent procedure in the County Court Rules to that contained in R.S.C. Order 40. Despite this, where lacunae arise in relation to county court practice, the county courts must be governed by the High Court practice where the latter covers the point in issue. By section 76 of the County Courts Act 1984:

> "In any case not expressly provided for by or in pursuance of this Act, the general principles of practice in the High Court may be adopted and applied to proceedings in a county court."

Does the term "general principles," though, include specific orders, such as R.S.C. Order 40, where no equivalent exists in the County Court Rules? In *McCreagh* v. *Frearson*[11] it was held that individual rules of the High Court are not necessarily included thereby, but only guiding principles. This suggests that no equivalent power exists in the county court though the common law position is the same.

There can, however, be no objection to the parties to a county court action consenting to a direction that the report of a single expert be obtained. In county court actions, where the costs issue is frequently of comparable importance to that of damages (or any other relief sought), this may render practicable the adducing of necessary expert evidence which otherwise would have been absent.

4   Use of Order 40

Despite its ostensible advantages, R.S.C. Order 40 is little used.[12] Lord Denning has speculated upon the reasons why:

---

[10] The report is described not as evidence but as "information" though it may be given "weight" by the court as may evidence proper.

[11] (1921) 91 L.J.K.B. 365. See also *Williamson* v. *Rider* [1963] 1 Q.B. 89.

[12] It has been suggested judicially that the provision might be more frequently employed: see *Partington and Son* v. *Tameside Metropolitan Borough Council* (1985) 32 B.L.R. 150 at 164.

"I suppose that litigants realise that the court would attach great weight to the report of a court expert, and are reluctant thus to leave the decision of the case so much in his hands. If his report is against one side, that side will wish to call its own expert to contradict him, and then the other side will wish to call one too. So it would only mean that the parties would call their own experts as well. In the circumstances the parties usually prefer to have the judge decide on the evidence of experts on either side, without resort to a court expert."[13]

Litigants and their advisers will understandably often take the view that the very fact that a court expert is appointed gives the appointee an appearance of impartiality which is difficult to dislodge, even if unwarranted, albeit the parties may apply to cross-examine.[14] The prospect of his taking an adverse view is therefore a greater risk than the almost inevitable fact that the opposing party will, as the court knows, only call its own expert if his evidence is largely favourable to its case. Hence court experts are not often appointed. The provisions of Order 40 are regarded by the masters as almost wholly anachronistic, and if any such orders have been made in recent years, they are negligible in number.

The widespread use of experts not retained by the parties themselves is in any event, perhaps, not desirable in a legal system which retains an adversarial, or accusatorial, rather than inquisitorial system of justice. For this system depends for its success upon each party putting its case in the strongest legitimate manner possible, and this applies to expert evidence as much as to any other, however much the theory of the complete impartiality of experts persists. The appointment of a court expert, on any controversial issue, always creates the risk that a party's strongest points are never put to the tribunal at all, unless the parties elect to call their own witnesses, a step which tends to defeat any purpose which the court expert may have.

B. POWER OF THE COURT TO CALL EXPERT WITNESSES

The procedure for appointing a court expert under R.S.C. Order 40 may only be invoked upon application of one of the parties.[15] There are procedures pursuant to which the court may obtain expert assistance for the court,[16] but these do not involve the calling of an expert as a witness

---

[13] *Re Saxton (deceased)* [1962] 1 W.L.R. 968 at 972.
[14] R.S.C. Ord. 40, r. 4.
[15] *Ibid.*, r. 1(1).
[16] See parts C, D, and E of this chapter.

proper, save under limited and specific powers.[17] It is clear that in a not insignificant number of cases the judge has been dissatisfied, either with the absence of expert evidence on an issue, or more usually with its conflicting content. Such an objection can only be resolved by a technical adherence to the rules as to burden and standard of proof.

1 The general rule and its exceptions

There is a general rule that the judge may not, of his own motion, summon witnesses of fact not called by the parties. In *Re Enoch and Zaretsky Bock*[18] it was held that the judge might not call a lay witness not called by the parties other than with the consent of both parties. This general rule is subject to the exception that in criminal cases involving the liberty of the subject the court's overwhelming duty to do justice gives it the power to call witnesses itself,[19] though this should not be done after the defence case is closed, unless the need for it arises *ex improviso*: in circumstances which no human ingenuity could foresee.[20] Although this exception applies principally to criminal cases, it has been said to apply to aspects of civil actions, such as committal proceedings, which have a quasi-criminal character.[21]

There is also a line of cases involving children which indicates that the court will take such steps in circumstances where the interests of the child demand it,[22] though this will usually be achieved by the mechanism of requesting the Official Solicitor to act for this purpose on the child's behalf.[23] This follows partly from the need to avoid a multiplicity of expert examinations of the child where the parties cannot agree how or by whom this should be performed.[24] The judge may also have the power to call a witness (and presumably if necessary an expert) when tracing a kidnapped child.[25]

Despite the law as expressed in the old authorities, the approach in practice may be somewhat different, and many judges would consider that the inherent jurisdiction of the court permitted them to call any witness where this was in the interests of justice, subject to the right of the parties to cross-examine.

---

[17] See part E of this chapter.
[18] [1910] 1 K.B. 327.
[19] *R. v. Harris* [1927] 2 K.B. 587; *R. v. Holden* (1838) 8 Car. & P. 606 (surgeon who examined murder victim not called by prosecution, called by judge.)
[20] *Ibid*. See below, Chap. 5, pp. 114–118.
[21] *Yianni v. Yianni* [1966] 1 W.L.R. 120.
[22] This being the paramount consideration both in statute and at common law in most such cases.
[23] See *e.g. Re R. (P.M.) (An infant)* [1968] 1 All E.R. 691n. And see below, Chap. 22, pp. 393–395.
[24] *Re S. (Infants)* [1967] 1 All E.R. 202 at 209, *per* Cross J.
[25] *Re Thompson (Minors)* [1976] C.L.Y. 1788.

2 Expert witnesses

The authorities which provide the general rule with regard to witnesses of fact contain no indications that the position might be any different in relation to expert witnesses. Indeed most refer expressly to "witnesses". Such an expression, without more, clearly includes experts. There are no recent authorities which suggest that the courts have more extensive powers in respect of expert than of lay witnesses. Furthermore the court expert procedure,[26] which might be thought to have been designed to meet those situations in which the judge himself wished to call expert witnesses, specifically requires a party to make application. R.S.C. Order 40 could have been drafted so as to permit the judge to call expert witnesses of his own motion in limited and defined circumstances, but was not.

There are some old decisions which suggest that such a power could exist. It is unlikely however that these support the existence today of a general power to call expert witnesses without the consent of the parties. In many instances it is not clear whether or not the parties in fact opposed the judge's proposed course,[27] or indeed that the judge was not invoking a different power, for instance to refer the matter, or a specific issue, to a referee.[28] Other such cases can be explained or ignored on the grounds that they date from the period when it was the general and accepted practice of the courts to call their own experts[29], that the decision concerned arbitration proceedings[30], or that the practice of the judge in calling a sculptor friend to give evidence[31] was disapproved generally on appeal.[32] It appears therefore that the court now has no such general power,[33] and that the R.S.C. Order 40 procedure governs the court's powers in this respect.[34] As has been discussed, however, it is likely that many judges would in practice rely upon the inherent jurisdiction of the court to support their view that justice could only be done by

---

[26] Under R.S.C. Ord. 40.
[27] *Kennard* v. *Ashman* (1894) 10 T.L.R. 213; *Hindson* v. *Ashby* [1896] 2 Ch. 1 at 21 (judge ordered experts called by parties to take photographs).
[28] *Colls* v *Home and Colonial Stores* [1904] A.C. 179 at 192 (the judge stressed that his remarks were obiter); *Mellin* v. *Monaco* (1877) 3 C.P.D. 142 at 149; *Badische Anilin Und Soda Fabrik* v. *Levinstein* (1883) 24 Ch.D. 156; *Att.-Gen.* v. *Birmingham Tame and Rea District Drainage Board* [1912] A.C. 788.
[29] *Pickering* v. *Barkley* (1648) Sty. 182.
[30] *Eastern Counties Railway Company* v. *Eastern Union Railway* (1863) 3 De G. J. and S. 610.
[31] *Slingsby* v. *Att.-Gen.* (1916) 32 T.L.R. 364, C.A.
[32] *Slingsby* v. *Att.-Gen.* (1916) 33 T.L.R. 120.
[33] *The Harbinger* (1852) 8 L.T. 612 suggests that it might, but is so briefly reported as to lack any indication of the *ratio decidendi*.
[34] See J. Basten, "The Court Expert in Civil Trials—a Comparative Appraisal" (1977) 40 M.L.R. 174.

themselves calling an expert witness, despite the absence of authoritative support for such a course.

C. ASSESSORS

Although the circumstances in which the court may of its own motion call expert witnesses are very limited, it nevertheless has in civil actions a complete discretion to appoint assessors to sit with it,[35] in order to assist upon those aspects of the case which require specialist knowledge for their comprehension and adjudication. In addition to this general power, there are provisions of a similar kind within specific High Court jurisdictions, such as the Patents Court,[36] the Admiralty Court,[37] and the Lands Tribunal.[38] These are dealt with below in the discussions of expert evidence in those fields.[39] There is also special provision for the appointment of assessors (to include a taxing officer and a practising solicitor) in disputes as to the taxation of costs.[40]

1 The power to appoint assessors

High Court The general power is contained in section 70(1) of the Supreme Court Act 1981:

> "In any cause or matter before the High Court the court may, if it thinks it expedient to do so, call in the aid of one or more assessors specially qualified, and hear and dispose of the cause or matter wholly or partially with their assistance."

The word "expedient" in effect gives the court a complete discretion in the exercise of this power. The manner of their appointment and use is governed by R.S.C. Order 33, rule 6:

> "A trial of a cause or matter with the assistance of assessors under section 70 of the Act shall take place in such manner and on such terms as the court may direct."

This provision appears to grant to the court a similarly unfettered dis-

---

[35] Supreme Court Act 1981, s.70(1).
[36] "Advisers" are appointed under the Supreme Court Act 1981, s.70(3) and (4).
[37] R.S.C. Ord. 75, r. 25(2).
[38] Lands Tribunal Act 1949, s.3; Lands Tribunal Rules 1975 (S.I. 1975 No. 299), r. 35.
[39] See below, Chap. 21, pp. 374–375 (patents), Chap. 18, pp. 328–329 (admiralty) and Chap. 13, pp. 256–259 (Lands Tribunal). Assessors may also be appointed under the Sex Discrimination Act 1975, s.66(6) (C.C.R. Ord. 49, r. 17(3)), the Telecommunications Act 1984, Sched. 2, para. 5 (CCR Ord. 50, r. 18A), the Landlord and Tenant Act 1954, s.63(5) (C.C.R. Ord. 43, r. 13), and R.S.C. Ord. 33, r. 2(d), (Official Referee's business).
[40] R.S.C. Ord. 62, r. 35(5); C.C.R. Ord. 38, r. 24(7); C.C.R. Ord. 13, r. 11; County Court Act 1984, s.63(2) and (4).

cretion. Numerous judicial decisions however significantly circumscribe the exercise of the power.[41]

County court The equivalent power in the county court is provided by section 63 of the County Courts Act 1984:

> "(1) In any proceedings the judge may, if he thinks fit on the application of any party, summon to his assistance, in such manner as may be prescribed, one or more persons of skill and experience in the matter to which the proceedings relate who may be willing to sit with the judge and act as assessors . . . .
>
> (5) Where any person is proposed to be summoned as an assessor, objection to him, either personally or in respect of his qualification, may be taken by any party in the prescribed manner."

The procedural provisions are contained in C.C.R. Order 13, rule 11:

> "(1) A party to any proceedings who desires an assessor to be summoned to assist the judge at the hearing shall, not less than 14 days before the day fixed for the hearing, file an application in that behalf.
>
> (2) The proper officer shall submit to the judge any application made under paragraph (1) and, if the judge grants the application, the proper officer shall give to the parties notice stating the name of the person proposed to be summoned as assessor.
>
> (3) A party who objects to the person proposed to be summoned as assessor shall, within 4 days after the service on him of the notice under paragraph (2), give to the proper officer notice of his objection stating the grounds thereof and on receipt of the notice the proper officer shall fix a day for the hearing of the objection and give notice thereof to the parties including, except in the notice to the party objecting, a statement of the grounds of the objection.
>
> (4) Where no notice of objection is given within the time limited or where an objection has been heard and an assessor has been selected, the applicant shall deposit in the court office such sum as the registrar thinks reasonable in respect of the assessor's fee for the day of hearing and thereupon the proper officer shall summon the assessor.
>
> (5) If an application for an assessor is refused, the proper officer shall give notice of the refusal to the parties.
>
> (6) An order summoning an assessor may be varied or revoked by the judge on application or of his own motion.

[41] See below, pp. 70–72.

(7) An assessor shall be entitled to such fee for attending court as would be allowed on taxation in respect of an expert witness. (8) Where the hearing of proceedings in which an assessor has been summoned is adjourned, the party on whose application the assessor was summoned shall forthwith deposit in the court office such sum as the registrar thinks reasonable in respect of the assessor's fee for the day of the adjourned hearing."

Remuneration and costs Section 70(2) of the Supreme Court Act 1981 provides that:

"The remuneration, if any, to be paid to an assessor for his services under subsection 1 in connection with any proceedings shall be determined by the court, and shall form part of the costs of the proceedings."

County court remuneration and costs are governed by section 63(3) of the County Courts Act 1984.

2   The nature and function of assessors

Assessors act as "expert guides of the court."[42] They may be appointed whenever the judge must adjudicate upon a case, or limited issues within a case, involving specialist matters. If necessary, rather than risk the lengthening of the hearing or an ill-informed decision on account of the judge's lack of familiarity with such matters, the case should be adjourned to permit one or more assessors to sit.[43]

Assessors may well be appointed in similar circumstances to those in which expert evidence is adduced,[44] and the assessors themselves may provide similar expertise to the court. However they are not expert witnesses. Assessors are not sworn, and cannot be cross-examined.[45] Although they are not witnesses, neither do assessors form part of the court.[46] Lord Denning has explained the purpose of their appointment thus:

"the court is equipping itself for its task by taking judicial notice of all such things as it ought to know in order to do its work properly."[47]

So, in a nautical case, an assessor was used to explain the significance of

---

[42] *Owners of S.S. Melanie* v. *Owners of S.S. San Onofre* [1919] W.N. 151, H.L.
[43] *Esso Petroleum* v. *Southport Corporation* [1956] A.C. 218.
[44] Though far less frequently in most fields of practice.
[45] *The Queen Mary* (1947) 80 Lloyd's Rep. 609 at 612. And see *Earwicker* v. *London Graving Dock Company Limited* [1916] 1 K.B. 970, C.A.
[46] *The Koning Willem II* [1908] P. 125 at 137.
[47] *Baldwin and Francis* v. *Patents Appeal Tribunal* [1959] A.C. 663 at 691.

particular lines on a sea-chart,[48] again as a form of substitute for what the court might otherwise judicially notice. Assessors may however assist with the more contentious aspects of the proceedings,[49] so long as the facts require specialist knowledge which the court would otherwise lack. They may not however participate in the proceedings other than by giving the judge such advice as he may require,[50] and are precluded from examining witnesses or advocating one party's case:

> "He is an assessor to assist the learned judge upon points as to which his expert knowledge may render assistance; he is not there to conduct an examination or a cross-examination ... his duty is simply and solely that of assisting the learned judge by his expert knowledge to arrive at a proper conclusion ... he is not a witness ... he cannot be cross-examined, and he certainly ought not to take up the position of cross-examining witnesses at length; and he ought not to take up the case as if he were leading counsel for one side or the other."[51]

There is however no reason why the judge should not make his own questioning of witnesses more effective by taking the assessor's advice upon its content. The assessor:

> "may, in proper cases, suggest to the judge questions which the judge himself might put to an expert witness with a view to testing the witness's view or to making plain his meaning."[52]

Furthermore, although the evidence must be assessed by the judge, the assessor may assist:

> "as to the proper technical inferences to be drawn from proved facts, or as to the extent of the difference between apparently contradictory conclusions in the expert field."[53]

Informing parties of advice There is no obligation upon the court to inform the parties of advice received from assessors. However there is equally no objection to so doing, and the practice has been judicially approved especially where the advice is likely to affect the judge's conclusions.[54]

---

[48] *Mercer* v. *Denne* [1905] 2 Ch. 538 at 544.
[49] Frequently, in nautical cases, questions involving the standard of seamanship to be expected in particular circumstances.
[50] *Earwicker* v. *London Graving Dock Company Limited* [1916] 1 K.B. 970, C.A.
[51] *Ibid.*, at 975.
[52] *Richardson* v. *Redpath Brown* [1944] A.C. 62 at 70.
[53] *Ibid.*
[54] *Ibid.*, at 71.

3 Expert evidence where assessors sit

Although expert evidence has been heard in some cases in which assessors have sat,[55] the general rule is that such evidence may not be heard in respect of matters in issue upon which the assessors are competent to assist the court,[56] whether upon affidavit[57] or orally. In a case concerning a collision at sea, in which nautical rights of way required explanation to the court, Trinity Masters sat as assessors.[58] No other evidence of nautical opinion was permitted because:

> "it would be most inconvenient, and injurious to the ends of justice, if in cases where the court always has the benefit of, and derives the greatest assistance from, the opinions on nautical points of the Trinity Masters, the proceedings were allowed to be incumbered by any evidence by way of opinion on such points."[59]

4 Assessors advise but do not decide

However much attention the judge pays to the advice of the assessor, the decision upon each issue, and the case itself, is for the judge alone, as the assessor does not sit as part of the court, merely as adviser to it.[60] It is "the duty of the judge to form his own judgment whatever that judgment may be."[61] The judge must not "surrender" his view to the assessors: this would both be wrong in principle and create the danger that assessors might themselves disagree.[62] In a workman's compensation case, the judge had succumbed to the temptation of "substituting the mind of the medical assessor for his own"[63] to the extent that the assessor had effectively decided the medical issue. Furthermore the credibility of the witnesses is not a question for assessors, who sit to advise on questions within their special competence.[64] The judge should be:

> "unaffected in questions of credibility of evidence by the opinion of those whose nautical skill upon all questions of seamanship he has the great advantage at the trial."[65]

---

[55] See A. Dickey, "The Province and Function of Assessors in English Courts" (1970) 33 M.L.R. 494, p. 503.
[56] *The Assyrian* (1890) 63 L.T. 91; *The Kirby Hall* (1883) 8 P.D. 71 at 76; *The Ann and Mary* (1843) 2 Wm. Rob. 189.
[57] *The No* (1853) 1 Sp. Ecc. & Ad. 184.
[58] *The Ann and Mary* above, n. 56.
[59] *Ibid.*, at 197.
[60] *The Australia* [1927] A.C. 145; *The City of Berlin* [1908] P. 110 at 118. See *The Marinegra* [1959] 2 Lloyd's Rep. 65 for a useful review of the authorities.
[61] *The Gannet* [1900] A.C. 234 at 236.
[62] *Ibid.*
[63] *Ancrum* v. *Cooperative Wholesale Society* (1945) 172 L.T. 248.
[64] *The Koning Willem II* [1908] P. 125.
[65] *Ibid.*, at 137.

5 Court of Appeal

The Court of Appeal may hear an appeal with assessors in a suitable case.[66] Where the Court of Appeal is reviewing the decision of a court of first instance which sat with assessors it may take into account not only the judge's decision, but also any advice he received from assessors, as the judge's view may only be explicable by reference to advice thus taken.[67]

D. REFEREES

The court may, both in the High Court and the county court, refer particular matters, often involving complicated matters of technical fact, to a referee.[68] The referee may be a person with a special expertise in the particular field. He will adjudicate upon the case in the manner and to the extent that the court has directed in making the reference. Official Referees' business is considered elsewhere.[69] Because they act in a judicial or quasi-judicial capacity, referees may not be called as witnesses in the relevant proceedings.[70]

E. HEARINGS IN CHANCERY CHAMBERS

R.S.C. Order 32, rule 16 provides, in Chancery cases, that:

> "If the Court thinks it expedient in order to enable it better to determine any matter arising in proceedings in chambers, it may obtain the assistance of any person specially qualified to advise on that matter and may act upon his opinion."

No practice is prescribed as to the precise manner in which this may be done,[71] but it cannot have the effect of removing from the court the responsibility for the decision itself:

> "Reports of this nature although entitled to great weight as affording independent testimony, cannot be considered as awards, or in any other light than as furnishing materials for the information and guidance of the Court."[72]

---

[66] Supreme Court Act 1981, s.54(8); R.S.C. Ord. 59, r. 10.
[67] *Hattersley* v. *Hodgson* (1905) 21 T.L.R. 178.
[68] Supreme Court Act 1981, s.68; R.S.C. Ord. 36; County Courts Act 1984, s.65; C.C.R. Ord. 19, rr. 7–10.
[69] See below, Chap. 20.
[70] *Broder* v. *Saillard* (1876) 24 W.R. 456.
[71] R.S.C. Ord. 62, r. 25 enables the taxing master to fix the appropriate fees.
[72] *Ford* v. *Tynte* (1864) DeG. J. & S. 127 at 131.

F. EXPERTS REGULARLY APPOINTED BY THE COURTS FOR SPECIFIC PURPOSES

Courts dealing with particular types of case on a regular basis are statutorily empowered to appoint experts to assist the court, either as representatives of a party (such as the professional guardian ad litem in the case of a child in proceedings involving children)[73] or in respect of a particular aspect of the case (such as the social enquiry report prepared by a probation officer for sentencing purposes in criminal cases).[74] Two particular classes of person, interpreters and shorthand writers, are regularly employed by the courts, or sometimes by the parties themselves, to assist in the operation of the court. They can properly be described as expert witnesses in that they provide expert advice to the court, which can be evidentially challenged and is in evidential form, and which the court itself does not have the specialist knowledge or ability to provide.

1 Interpreters

The language of the courts in England and Wales is English.[75] Parties who do not understand or cannot communicate the language fully enough to participate in the proceedings to the necessary degree may use an interpreter,[76] and translators may be employed where foreign documents are concerned.[77] Although it is the right of any such person to use an interpreter, they may not be employed for purposes other than that of interpreting what is said, except at the discretion of the court. Where a foreigner is unrepresented, therefore, the court has a discretion whether to permit him to open his case through an interpreter,[78] in those courts where only the litigant in person or counsel may speak otherwise than as a witness. The manner of the interpretation is also in the discretion of the court. Thus the court may decide whether the evidence should be translated as it is given, or in some other way.[79] It has also been said that it is undesirable for the interpreter to speak from the well of the court, though the court may in its discretion permit this.[80] It is wrong for the interpreter to have an association with persons involved in the case which might raise the possibility of bias. So, where a person faced an allegation of obtaining a pecuniary advantage by deception at a Chinese restaurant, a

---

[73] See below, Chap. 22, pp. 391–396.
[74] See below, Chap. 23, pp. 412–416.
[75] Welsh may be spoken in the Welsh courts: Welsh Language Act 1967, s.1.
[76] This includes the deaf and dumb: *R. v. Whitehead* (1866) 10 Cox 234.
[77] As to the use of interpreters by examiners, see *Marquis of Bute v. James* (1886) 33 Ch.D. 157.
[78] *Re Trepca Mines Ltd.* [1960] 1 W.L.R. 24.
[79] *In the Estate of Fuld* [1965] 1 W.L.R. 1336.
[80] *Ibid.*

Chinese waiter at the restaurant, the servant of the alleged victim, was inappropriate as an interpreter.[81] It should be observed that in many instances the court in practice permits persons not wholly independent of one or other party to act as interpreter but the usual, and it is suggested, correct practice, is that this should be avoided where substantial conflicts of evidence must be resolved by the court. The interpreter is subject to the law of perjury to the same extent as ordinary witnesses.[82] Interpreters who act not only in the courtroom itself, but also in conferences and other discussions outside it will often be privy to information which, passing as it does between lawyer and client, is privileged. The interpreter in these circumstances is bound by the same privilege as the lawyer, because he is merely the "instrument" of communication with the lawyer.[83]

Interpreters will often be required to act, in criminal cases, from the earliest stages of the prosecution process. There are relevant provisions in the Codes of Practice under the Police and Criminal Evidence Act 1984.[84] The codes provide that the same interpreter should not be employed both at the police station and in court,[85] and if the practice is not observed the court may take this into account in deciding any issues to which such failure may be relevant.[86] It has been held that a police officer cannot give evidence of what the defendant said where the answers were given through an interpreter. The interpreter must be called to prove the words used.[87] It is good practice for interpreters to make full notes of such interviews in case there be a dispute as to what was said.[88]

It is essential, in criminal court proceedings, that the defendant understands what is being said against him, and that his own case is properly put. Where it was clear that a defendant did not fully understand questions put through an interpreter at his trial the conviction was quashed.[89] Where a person who does not fully understand English is represented by counsel at trial, the evidence must be translated if the defendant does not in fact understand.[90] There is a discretion to forego translation of the evidence if the defendant indicates, either himself or through his counsel, that he does understand and does not wish to have evidence translated, if

---

[81] *R.* v. *Mitchell* [1970] Crim.L.R. 153, C.A. There is no good reason why the same should not apply in civil proceedings.
[82] Perjury Act 1911, s.1.
[83] *Du Barré* v. *Livette* (1791) Peake 77 at 111.
[84] See section 66 of the Act, Code C (Detention Treatment and Questioning of Persons by Police Officers) and Code D (Identification of Persons by Police officers).
[85] Code C, paragraph 14A.
[86] Police and Criminal Evidence Act 1984, s.67(2).
[87] *R.* v. *Attard* (1958) 43 Cr.App.R. 90.
[88] See *Archbold*, (43rd ed.) para. 4–12.
[89] *R.* v. *Imrie* (1917) 12 Cr.App.R. 282.
[90] *R.* v. *Lee Kun* (1916) 11 Cr.App.R. 293. As to matrimonial proceedings see *Kashich* v. *Kashich* [1951] W.N. 557.

the judge is satisfied that he substantially understands the case to be made against him.[91] Where the accused is not represented, the judge has a discretion to allow non-translation of part of the evidence if he indicates that he understands it and does not wish to have it translated.[92] There is no oath prescribed, but the following form is often used:

> "I swear by Almighty God that I will well and truly interpret and explanation make to the court and the witness of such matters and things as shall be required of me to the best of my skill and understanding."

Provisions exist as to witness allowances in county court[93] and criminal proceedings,[94] and as to costs in criminal proceedings.[95] Special provisions exist for Welsh proceedings.[96]

2 Shorthand writers

The main purpose of shorthand notes of court proceedings is to provide an accurate transcript of what was said for the purpose of any appeal which results from the decision in the case.[97] In the majority of such cases the shorthand writer is appointed by the court. They may also, however, be of importance where, during the hearing of the evidence, some doubt arises as to what was said earlier, for instance if a witness being cross-examined disputes a previous answer.[98] In such circumstances the shorthand writer may be asked to read out to the court the note taken of the relevant passage.

Where a decision is relevant as a precedent in a subsequent case, and it is not recorded in a law report, a shorthand note may be referred to, even though because of the passage of time the original note-taker cannot transcribe.[99] The shorthand writer is *sui generis* in some respects, occupying as he does a position neither of being part of the court nor a witness. This has implications for the law of privilege, and it has been said that "an official shorthand writer [may refer] to his notes at trial, even though copies of these may be privileged from production to a non-party who has subpoenaed him."[1] The court may order the impounding of the

---

[91] *Ibid.*
[92] *Ibid.* The same rules apply for deaf and dumb persons.
[93] C.C.R. Ord. 38, r. 16.
[94] Costs in Criminal Cases (General) Regulations 1986 (S.I. 1986 No. 1335).
[95] Prosecution of Offences Act 1985, s.19(3)(*b*).
[96] Welsh Courts (Oaths and Interpreters) Rules 1943 (S.R. and O. 1943 No. 683), as amended; Welsh Courts (Interpretation) Rules 1972 (S.I. 1972 No. 97).
[97] As to interviews, see *R.* v. *Veltheim* (1908) 148 C.C.C. Sess. Pap. 583.
[98] See *R.* v. *O'Connell* (1844) Arm. & Tr. 165.
[99] *Renshaw* v. *Dixon* [1911] W.N. 40.
[1] *James* v. *James, ex rel.*, May 21, 1919: see *Phipson on Evidence* (14th ed., 1990), para. 12–42.

shorthand-writer's notes in court where there is a danger that, for instance, a secret process may be disclosed.[2]

Practice in the High Court is governed by R.S.C. Order 68 for cases in the Queen's Bench and Chancery Divisions and in the Admiralty Court. The Matrimonial Causes Rules 1977[3] make specific provision for Family Division cases. Order 68 provides for an official shorthand writer to take a note of all oral evidence and of judgment,[4] unless the judge otherwise directs.[5] Any party may then, subject to paying the prescribed charges, obtain a transcript of the note.[6] The costs of a shorthand-note of previous proceedings may be allowed insofar as it is relevant in the present proceedings.[7] The rules also provide for the cost of transcription to be avoided where the judge's own note is adequate for the purposes of an appeal.[8] The use of this rule whenever possible has been judicially encouraged.[9] Order 68 applies only to proceedings in open court, but parties to proceedings in chambers may also agree to a note being taken.[10] Examiners may also obtain the services of a shorthand writer.[11]

In criminal cases, a shorthand note is taken in courts from which an appeal lies to the Court of Appeal.[12] The Criminal Appeal Rules 1968 provide for the circumstances in which a tape recording may be substituted for a shorthand note,[13] and for the judge to make appropriate arrangements when neither is possible.[14] The parts of the trial which need to be recorded are defined.[15] The rules also regulate the provision of transcripts and payment for them,[16] and for the certification by the shorthand writer or transcriber of the correctness and completeness of the record.[17] A party may need leave to obtain a transcript of more than the evidence directly relevant to the points of appeal.[18]

There is a duty upon counsel and officers of the court to inform the judge if there is reason to believe that a shorthand-note will not be taken

---

[2] *Badische* v. *Levinstein* (1883) 24 Ch.D. 156.
[3] S.I. 1977 No. 344, r. 53.
[4] And the judge's summing up in jury matters.
[5] R.S.C. Ord. 68, r. 1(1).
[6] *Ibid.*
[7] *Bright's Trustee* v. *Sellar* [1904] 1 Ch. 369. And see *Supreme Court Practice 1991*, Vol. 1, 62/12/12.
[8] R.S.C. Ord. 68, r. 2.
[9] *Stevens* v. *Stevens* [1954] 1 W.L.R. 900.
[10] *Re Hilloary and Taylor* (1887) 36 Ch.D. 262 at 267. See also *Supreme Court Practice 1991*, Vol. 1, 32/15/3.
[11] *Supreme Court Practice 1991*, Vol. 1, 39/11/2.
[12] Criminal Appeal Act 1968, s.32.
[13] S.I. 1968 No. 1262, r. 18(1).
[14] *Ibid.*, r. 18(3).
[15] *Ibid.*, r. 18(2).
[16] *Ibid.*, r. 19.
[17] *Ibid.*, r. 20.
[18] *R.* v. *Lurie* [1951] W.N. 493.

by a competent person,[19] so that the judge may make an appropriate direction,[20] and a similar duty if it becomes clear that a transcript is an inadequate record of the proceedings.[21] However an inadequate note is not a ground of appeal *per se*.[22] The judge should not amend the transcript before submission to the Court of Appeal.[23] It is important that the shorthand-note only includes such material as was put before the court, although other documents may be shown to the shorthand-writer to assist with factual accuracy when evidence of antecedents and previous convictions is given:

> "a copy of the proof of evidence shall be given to the shorthand writer when the officer is called to prove the contents. He may use it to check his note, but must transcribe only so much as is given in evidence."[24]

---

[19] *R. v. Payne and Spillane* [1971] 1 W.L.R. 1779.
[20] Under Rule 18 of the Criminal Appeal Rules 1968.
[21] *R. v. Payne and Spillane*, above n. 19.
[22] *R. v. Le-Caer* (1972) 56 Cr.App.R. 727. And see *R. v. Elliott* (1909) 2 Cr.App.R. 171.
[23] *R. v. Kluczynski* [1973] 1 W.L.R. 1230, C.A.
[24] *Practice Direction (Crime: Antecedents)* [1966] 1 W.L.R. 1184, para. 3.

CHAPTER 4

Preparation and Presentation of Expert Evidence

A. PRESERVATION, INSPECTION, TESTS ETC. IN RELATION TO THE SUBJECT-MATTER OF PROCEEDINGS

The adducing of expert evidence frequently depends upon the opportunity for an expert witness to examine material which, or a person who, is the subject of proceedings. It may also be necessary, or at least advantageous, for tests or experiments to be carried out upon the subject-matter or a sample from it. The subject-matter may be in the possession or under the control of another party. It may be the other party himself, or his medical or bodily condition may be a relevant issue. Documents may be required, either for what they record,[1] or in order to establish their genuineness or some other fact about how they came to be made. In general if tests are carried out in a laboratory or by other scientific means an expert may give evidence of work carried out by persons under his control and supervision,[2] or by another analyst or scientist of equal status who is duplicating the test for greater accuracy or safety.[3] There is no reason why he should not be questioned in cross-examination as to the degree to which the witness can properly be satisfied of the results obtained by his colleagues. Parties may adduce the results of scientific experiments performed by experts on material identical or similar to the actual subject-matter of the case in both criminal[4] and civil proceedings.[5]

1 Civil proceedings

The courts have numerous powers as to the subject-matter of proceedings before trial, though these are subject to specific provisions in relation to cases of personal injuries or death, and patents cases.[6] The chief

---

[1] For medical reports in personal injury actions see Chap. 19, p. 353.
[2] *R. v. Kershberg* [1976] R.T.R. 526.
[3] *R. v. Tate* [1977] R.T.R. 17.
[4] *R. v. Heseltine* (1873) 12 Cox C.C. 404.
[5] *Bigsby v. Dickinson* (1876) 4 Ch.D. 24.
[6] See R.S.C. Ord. 104, rr. 11 and 12.

statutory powers are contained in the Supreme Court Act 1981, which is mirrored as to the relevant provisions in the County Courts Act 1984.[7] As to the inspection etc. of property before the commencement of the action, section 33(1) provides:

> "On the application of any person in accordance with rules of court, the High Court shall, in such circumstances as may be specified in the rules, have power to make an order providing for any one or more of the following matters, that is to say—
> (a) the inspection, photographing, preservation, custody and detention of property which appears to the court to be property which may become the subject-matter of subsequent proceedings in the High Court, or as to which any question may arise in any such proceedings; and
> (b) the taking of samples of any such property as is mentioned in paragraph (a), and the carrying out of any experiment on or with any such property."[8]

The procedure for obtaining such orders is contained in R.S.C. Order 29, rule 7A, which requires an originating summons supported by affidavit specifying the property proposed to be subject to the order. Its relevance should be demonstrated by reference to a draft pleading if this is practicable.[9] Such an order may not be made if it would result in the disclosure of information relating to a secret process, discovery or invention not in issue in the proposed proceedings,[10] or if it would be likely to be otherwise injurious to the public interest.[11]

Control over relevant property after commencement of the action is governed by the court rules. R.S.C. Order 29, rule 2(1) provides that:

> "On the application of any party to a cause or matter the Court may make an order for the detention, custody, or preservation of any property which is the subject-matter of the cause or matter, or as to which any question may arise therein, or for the inspection of any such property in the possession of a party to the cause or matter."[12]

The court has a broad discretion to order samples or observation of, or experiments upon, property which may be in issue, provided for by R.S.C. Order 29, rule 3(1):

> "Where it considers it necessary or expedient for the purpose of obtaining full information or evidence in any cause or matter, the

---

[7] The procedural rules are identical: see C.C.R. Ord. 13, r. 7(1)(g).
[8] See also County Courts Act 1984 (C.C.A. 1984), s.52.
[9] R.S.C. Ord. 29, r. 7A(3).
[10] R.S.C. Ord. 29, r. 7A(6).
[11] Supreme Court Act 1981, s.35(1); C.C.A. 1984, s.54(1).
[12] Applied to the County Courts by C.C.R. Ord. 13, r. 7(1)(b).

Court may, on the application of a party to the cause or matter, and on such terms, if any, as it thinks just, by order authorise or require any sample to be taken of any property which is the subject-matter of the cause or matter or as to which any question may arise therein, any observation to be made on such property or any experiment to be tried on or with such property."[13]

Arbitrators have co-extensive powers.[14] The power to order inspection, in all cases, includes a power to order the removal of an obstruction preventing full or any inspection. Where a wall inhibited inspection of the workings of a mine which was the subject of the proceedings, demolition of the wall was permitted.[15]

Medical inspections will not be ordered unless they are clearly warranted by the facts of the case.[16] In Chancery proceedings, for example where an unborn child may become entitled to trust monies, the writ *de ventre inspiciendo* may issue for examination of a mother who claims to be pregnant.[17] The courts will not force persons to undergo a medical or other bodily inspection against their will, it being an assault if they do not consent, though in some cases the court will draw an adverse inference from such a refusal.[18] The legal issues are of course paramount, and the relevant law may not justify any such inference.[19]

A document will be treated as "property" if it is its physical characteristics (such as authenticity), rather than the information it contains, which are in issue.[20] Orders under rules 2 and 3 can be facilitated, in an appropriate case, by authorising a party to "enter upon any land or building in the possession of any party to the cause or matter."[21] In addition to these powers under the rules the court has inherent jurisdiction to make an order permitting a party to enter upon the defendant's premises or property and seize items or documents, known as an Anton Piller order.[22] There is a substantial body of recent authority charting the development of this order. Because of the usual circumstances, namely that it is made *ex parte* in relation to matters which have not been fully

---

[13] Applied to the county courts by C.C.R. Ord. 13, r. 7(1)(e). An experiment is "something that [the expert witness] has seen which has been produced for the purpose of [the] action": *British Celanese Ltd. v. Courtaulds Ltd.* (1933) 50 R.P.C. 63 at 84.
[14] Arbitration Act 1950, s.12(6)(g).
[15] *Bennett v. Griffiths* (1861) 3 E. & E. 467.
[16] *Agnew v. Jobson* (1877) 13 Cox C.C. 625, *cf. Mitchell v. Stephens* (1894) 63 L.J. 389. As to personal injuries cases, see Chap. 19.
[17] *Re Blakemore* (1845) 14 L.J. Ch. 336.
[18] *S. v. B.* [1905] 21 T.L.R. 219.
[19] See *e.g. Re Betts* (1887) 19 Q.B.D. 39 (not misconduct in bankruptcy proceedings).
[20] *Re Saxton* [1962] 1 W.L.R. 859. If the latter is the case the appropriate application is one for discovery: *Huddleston v. Control Risks Information Services Ltd.* [1987] 1 W.L.R. 701.
[21] R.S.C. Ord. 29, rr. 2(2) and 3(2).
[22] *Anton Piller A.G. v. Manufacturing Processes Ltd.* [1976] Ch. 55.

canvassed before the court, it will only be granted in circumstances of the clearest apparent necessity.

Personal injuries and death In existing proceedings for personal injuries or death the court has slightly different powers in relation to relevant property. The general power in R.S.C. Order 29 rules 2 and 3 permits the court to order the detention, custody or preservation of any relevant property, whether or not it is in the ownership or possession of another party, but for its inspection only if it is in another party's possession. In cases of personal injuries or death inspection may also be ordered of property not in the ownership or possession of a party.[23] Similar provisions exist in all cases as to the taking of samples and the performance of experiments, save that where orders are made in cases of personal injuries and death no specific provision exists as to observation.[24] The general power in R.S.C. Order 29, rule 3 does not however exclude cases of personal injuries and death.

2 Criminal proceedings

Property relevant to criminal procedures The powers of the police in relation to seizure of property are contained in the Police and Criminal Evidence Act 1984.[25] In addition there are common law duties which arise out of the general powers of the police. It has for some time been the position that the police have a duty to preserve for the court things which constitute evidence relating to a crime.[26] Furthermore where a witness produces an item it is the duty of the court, or any police officer in whose charge the court places it, to preserve it for the purposes of justice thereafter.[27] It has been suggested that this may be too broad a statement of the position, though without a specific indication as to what the law in fact therefore is.[28]

The Court of Appeal gave guidance as to the protection of such items, and their availability for defence purposes such as expert investigation, in R. v. *Lambeth Metropolitan Stipendiary Magistrate, ex p. McComb.*[29] It was there held that once an item becomes an exhibit (here in committal proceedings) the court has a duty to preserve it for the purposes of justice and a fair trial, and to take care to preserve it from loss and damage. The court must permit the defence reasonable access for the purposes of

---

[23] Supreme Court Act 1981, s.34(3)(*a*); R.S.C. Ord. 29, r. 7A(2).
[24] Supreme Court Act 1981, s.34(3)(6).
[25] See ss.19–22.
[26] R. v. *Lushington, ex p. Otto* [1984] 1 Q.B. 420.
[27] *Ibid.*, at 423–424.
[28] R. v. *Uxbridge J.J., ex p. Sofaer* (1987) 85 Cr.App.R. 367 at 378.
[29] [1983] 2 W.L.R. 259.

inspection and examination, and for production. The court may entrust exhibits to the police or the Director of Public Prosecutions, imposing such restrictions as are proper in the circumstances. If the court does not impose any restrictions, the custodial body must deal with the exhibit in the best interests of justice. The defence can apply to the court for an order that exhibits be made available for inspection or testing before trial.[30] This presumably includes the taking of samples. There is a general protection as to these matters in that if the defence has been refused access to exhibits the court may refuse to permit the prosecution to adduce them in evidence, "in the exercise of its inherent power to make all such orders as are necessary to secure a fair trial."[31] It is submitted that this power extends not only to preventing the exhibit itself from being produced in court, but also to not permitting witnesses (whether expert or otherwise) to answer questions based upon their observation of the item or a part of it.

The defence may also seek the production of any object by issuing a summons requiring a person to attend and produce the item at court.[32] The Registrar of Criminal Appeals has a duty to make documents or things available for inspection by the appellant or respondent in appeal proceedings.[33] In Crown Court proceedings, the rules now provide for proper opportunities for expert examination of relevant property in any case where the other party seeks to adduce expert evidence in relation to it.[34]

Automatic recordings Where a typist produces a transcript of a tape-recording, evidence of its accuracy may be given by the typist, who is treated as an expert for that limited purpose.[35] It has been held in New Zealand that where a tape-recording of a conversation was difficult to understand if it was played back in normal circumstances, a police-officer may write a transcript if he has listened repeatedly to it and understands what is said.[36] He becomes a "temporary expert in the sense that by repeated listening to the tapes he has qualified himself *ad hoc*."[37] While there is no doubting the desirability of adducing evidence in this way it may be questioned whether, as both these decisions assume, the witness thereby becomes a "temporary expert." The witness, with no

---

[30] [1983] 2 W.L.R. 259 at 271.
[31] *Ibid.*, at 272.
[32] Criminal Procedure (Attendance of Witnesses) Act 1965, s.2; Magistrates' Courts Act 1980, s.97.
[33] Criminal Appeal Act 1968, s.21(1); Criminal Appeal Rules, 1968, rr. 7 and 8.
[34] Crown Court (Advance Notice of Expert Evidence) Rules 1987, set out in full in Chap. 2, pp. 27–28.
[35] *Hopes and Lavery* v. *H.M. Advocate* (1960) J.C. 104 C.J.
[36] *R.* v. *Menzies* [1982] 1 N.Z.L.R. 40.
[37] *Ibid.*, at 49.

special expertise, is merely doing for convenience what the jury could do for itself if it had the time, and then giving factual evidence of it.

Plans A police constable or person with prescribed qualifications may prepare a plan as evidence in criminal proceedings, as to the "relative position of the things shown on the plan."[38] Distances must however be strictly proved. A copy of the signed certificate accompanying the plan must be served seven days before the hearing.[39] The certifier can be required to attend court by notice served three days before trial, or within such other period as the court allows. Architects and the members of four other professional institutions may certify.[40]

Medical and other personal examinations The accused in criminal proceedings cannot in general be required to undergo a medical examination, and a doctor who carries out such an examination assaults the accused.[41] The Police and Criminal Evidence Act 1984 contains extensive provisions as to the circumstances in which the person of the accused may be examined. Intimate searches may be performed for Class A drugs or items capable of causing physical injury to himself or others.[42] This must be done by a medical practitioner or nurse, although if this is not practicable the search may be performed by a police officer of the same sex. Intimate samples of the body for evidential or investigatory purposes may be taken, though only by a medical practitioner where items or substances other than urine or saliva are sought.[43] Inferences may be drawn from refusal to give consent, which is required for such a sample to be taken.[44] Fingerprints may only be taken in general by consent, but this is subject to wide exceptions.[45]

B. EXPERTS' REPORTS

There are no general legal rules as to the form of experts' written reports. The parties will usually in civil proceedings be required before adducing expert evidence at trial to disclose the "substance" of the expert's evidence to the other parties in the form of one or more written reports.[46] There are also disclosure provisions for Crown Court criminal proceed-

---

[38] Criminal Justice Act 1948, s.41(1).
[39] *Ibid.*, s.41(5)(*a*).
[40] Evidence by Certificate Rules 1961 (S.I. 1961 No. 248), r. 1.
[41] *Agnew* v. *Jobson* (1877) 13 Cox C.C. 625.
[42] Police and Criminal Evidence Act 1984, s.55.
[43] *Ibid.*, s.62.
[44] *Ibid.*, s.62(1)(*a*).
[45] *Ibid.*, s.61. As to fingerprints generally see below, Chap. 14, pp. 261–262.
[46] R.S.C. Ord. 38, r. 37.

ings. These are more fully discussed in Chapter 2. In practice parties almost invariably serve a full report as prepared by the expert.[47] The only legitimate area of non-disclosure relates to opinions which have not yet been formed by the expert. This may be for two principal reasons.

First, the usual order in civil proceedings, other than those involving personal injuries, is for mutual disclosure of reports, so that when the expert prepares his own report he has no opportunity to consider the opinions of experts for the other parties. The reports may subsequently be agreed. If they are not, there is still scope for each expert, short of full agreement, or agreement upon individual material points, to modify his opinions having seen the other side's report. Where this is the case the expert would often be well advised to prepare a supplementary report for voluntary service on the other parties. If an expert witness has genuinely altered his views it is usually less damaging to his client to do so openly in advance than in oral evidence at trial. If it must be done orally at trial it is important that the modifications are fully notified to counsel so that the matter can be dealt with in examination in chief, rather than under apparently effective cross-examination. Of course the timing of a voluntary supplementary report is a matter of careful judgment. Negotiations with a view to settlement may be in train and may appear to justify late disclosure. Any costs advantages of agreed evidence may however be lost if concessions are made too late.

The second situation in which the expert's opinions are legitimately not fully disclosed is where the evidence at trial is a necessary prerequisite to the expression of a final opinion. This likelihood can be reduced by an order for exchange of lay witnesses' proofs of evidence.[48] However in a number of cases evidence of fact at trial can materially contribute to the expert's views. Thus in personal injuries cases with a psychological or psychiatric aspect a medical witness may benefit from the opportunity to observe the plaintiff in the witness box, and similarly in criminal proceedings with such features. In many criminal cases expert witnesses for the prosecution, and indeed for the defence, may not have had notice of the accused's case on the facts. Furthermore, witnesses of fact whose evidence has been disclosed in civil or criminal proceedings may depart from their proofs or statements under cross-examination.

1 Drafting the report

Requirements as to the content of reports in specific legal fields and jurisdictions are discussed in the chapters below relating to them. Some considerations are however more generally applicable. The expert should draft the report in a manner appropriate to its forensic purpose. His duty

---

[47] As to the inclusion of plans, references to learned articles etc., see Chap. 2, p. 45.
[48] R.S.C. Ord. 38, r. 2A.

is not to represent the interests of his client, but to express his views honestly and as fully as is necessary for the purposes of the case. A combative tone is inappropriate and only serves to undermine the likelihood of its conclusions being accepted. Criticism of the personality or conduct of other expert witnesses is not justified unless clearly relevant and undeniably supported by the facts. The expert should attempt therefore not to allow his opinions to be coloured by sympathy for his client or his client's case. The protection of the party against adverse expert opinions is his liberty to engage, if he can afford it, any number of experts to prepare reports, and dispense with those which are inconvenient to his case.

There is a wholly distinct sense, however, in which the expert can and should assist his client's case. His report can be presented in a form in which its conclusions, which represent the expert's true opinion, are most likely to be readily accepted by the tribunal which is to hear the case, or which may cause the other parties' experts and legal advisers to reconsider their current stance. Its form may also assist his client's advocate in putting the merits of his case to the court. These considerations are particularly important where the expert is engaged to prepare a report upon complex and technical matters of fact.

First, the report should recognise the shape and emphasis of the client's case. A good place to start is with the pleadings, if these are already in existence. These should have been settled principally so as to ensure that every matter alleged is pleaded, but will also usually set out the case in as persuasive a manner as possible, perhaps, where chronology is not of the essence, starting with the stronger points and separating them from the rest. There is no objection to an expert following that example in his report, and indeed it facilitates the presentation of the case at trial. An expert should however avoid using legal expressions creatively. Adjectives such as "defective" and "inadequate" should be used with great care, and expressions with a substantial legal content going to the heart of the case, such as "negligent" or "in breach of contract" should be wholly avoided in reports, and only employed, if the questions eliciting them are permitted, in oral evidence in court. In the more complex cases it is usually best not to settle any pleadings until the expert has reported, unless expert material can comfortably be confined to a schedule.

Secondly, the expert should strive to be as systematic as possible. Where large quantities of technical facts or figures require recording, they are best placed in schedules, with appropriate cross-references to the main conclusions in the body of the report. These are of enormous assistance to the legal advisers, both in presenting the case at trial, and also pre-trial in agreeing matters of fact or opinion, and in preparing factual evidence for hearing. The body of the report should be categorised, classified and sub-divided, preferably in numbered points or paragraphs, to as great a degree as is possible within the confines of the subject-matter.

Thirdly, where there is communication with experts for the other parties, whether pursuant to directions of the court or otherwise, experts and solicitors should attempt in complicated cases to agree, if not the substance of the evidence, at least the form in which it is to be presented. There is little more wasteful of time and costs than the necessity for lawyers or the expert to spend long hours cross-referencing schedules which were prepared in a different form. This is often unavoidable, particularly where mutual disclosure of reports is the first indication the experts have of how the other experts have categorised and scheduled their evidence. Particular forms of proceedings, such as construction claims, may deal with such difficulties by way of devices such as Scott schedules. Any scope for agreement as to such matters of form at an early stage should be explored.

Fourthly, the expert must consider the likely readership of the report. Will the case be heard by a specialist tribunal, *e.g.* an arbitrator with relevant expertise, an official referee or patents judge who hears similar cases, or a judge whose relevant expertise is confined to the law? Or will it be heard by a lay bench or jury? It must also be comprehensible to the lawyers, who may or may not be familiar with the specialist terms and concepts employed. If in doubt the expert should aim for the lowest common denominator of expertise among the readership, and this is likely in civil cases to be the intelligent non-specialist who is nevertheless experienced in the comprehension, digestion and explanation of technical material. Excessive use of jargon should be avoided where possible.[49]

Report drafted by counsel   The practice has long been adopted by some solicitors of instructing counsel to settle experts' reports in cases where they are of great importance and, though perhaps well prepared as a technical report, not well suited to the needs of litigation. There is little doubt that the practice has also been used in order to improve upon the report by excision and amendment, or the use of descriptive words which have some direct relation with the legal matters which require proof. The courts have expressed some disapproval of the practice,[50] and there is certainly a strand of judicial opinion which views it as wholly inappropriate.[51] The practice has nonetheless continued, and perhaps unfairly so if some practitioners have regarded the judicial disapproval as in effect binding while others have not. Barristers are now however professionally

---

[49] See *Jones* v. *Griffith* [1969] 1 W.L.R. 795 at 802.
[50] See *Whitehouse* v. *Jordan* [1981] 1 W.L.R. 246 at 256–257, *per* Lord Wilberforce.
[51] See *e.g. Kelly* v. *London Transport Executive*, [1982] 2 All E.R. 842 at 851, *per* Lord Denning M.R.

entitled to settle experts' reports,[52] which at least has the merit of introducing a degree of uniformity where counsel are instructed. Members of the Bar must use their discretion as to the extent to which they preserve the distinction between improving the expression of an opinion and changing its meaning. Certainly where there is a danger of the latter a conference with the expert should be arranged so that the expert can confirm personally that what is being said on his behalf accords precisely with his views. The expert should in any event review the report settled by counsel and insist upon its amendment as necessary.

2 Agreeing reports

Much of the authority relating to the agreeing of experts' reports concerns the agreement of medical reports in personal injuries cases. This is discussed fully in Chapter 19. Some considerations are relevant only to medical reports, but others are of more general application, or at least partially so. The chief consideration for the solicitor is to ensure that reports are not agreed by the parties where their substance does not in fact agree. The practice is now becoming more widespread, particularly with the formal introduction of "without prejudice" meetings,[53] of experts drawing up an agreed statement as to those respects in which their views coincide and conflict. In many cases, particularly with small amounts of money in issue, the pressure of costs considerations may lead to solicitors 'agreeing' reports which do not concur in all material respects.

The reports if agreed should not only concur on all matters in issue but must also be capable of use by the court without expert assistance.[54] Where this is not the case the parties must ensure that experts attend to explain the implications of their views in the light of the legal issues. If a party wishes to give or adduce evidence of fact contrary to the expert's conclusions, or at variance with the factual assumptions the expert made when writing a report which was then agreed, consideration will need to be given to calling the expert at trial.[55] Likewise the facts may themselves change. The condition of a plaintiff in personal injuries proceedings may alter radically before trial. It may be possible to agree amended reports immediately before trial, but where there is doubt as to this the experts should appear at the hearing. Although he must try the case on the evidence, the judge is not bound by expert evidence even where it is contained in agreed reports[56] though the circumstances are likely to be few

---

[52] Bar Code of Conduct, para. 606, and Annexe H, para. 5.8.
[53] R.S.C. Ord. 38, r. 37. These are discussed below.
[54] *Proctor* v. *Peebles* [1941] 2 All E.R. 80.
[55] See *Gilson* v. *Howe* (unreported), 1970, C.A. No. 46.
[56] *Eachus* v. *Leonard* (1968) 106 S.J. 918; *Stevens* v. *Simons, The Times*, November 20, 1987.

in which such a judicial course is taken, and the judge must have some evidential or other legal basis for his decision. A party may if it chooses adduce the report of another party in evidence.[57]

Changes in the facts, or in the way a party puts its case, may justify the calling of experts even though reports have been agreed. It has however been said that the courts should not allow evidence to be adduced to show that an expert has changed his mind since the reports were agreed.[58] Different considerations may apply in criminal proceedings, and the view has been taken that medical reports as to the accused's state of mind, certainly where it is relevant to his guilt, should not be agreed.[59]

C. DUTIES OF THE EXPERT WITNESS

Experts, like all witnesses, have a duty to state what is, or what they believe to be, the truth about matters upon which their opinion or their recollection is being sought. There are particular pressures upon experts, who are frequently in more than one sense professional witnesses, to give evidence which is either intentionally false or, though correct, misleading by omission. The methods by which the courts deal with overt bias and perjury are discussed in Chapter 10.[60]

There is however, apart from the question of bias, conscious or unconscious, the question of whether the expert has any duty in respect of the manner in which he gathers, prepares and presents his evidence. This question is not easily answered by reference to authority, and in any event the consequences for the expert of its breach are elusive, save that his evidence may be less sympathetically received by the court, and that in an extreme case the party by whom he is called may be penalised in costs. It has been suggested that in certain classes of case a special duty arises out of the relationship with a client, but this appears to be confined to the conduct of a potential defendant or other professional involved in pre-action events. One judge has said:

> "I personally think that in professional negligence cases, and in particular in medical negligence cases, there is a duty of candour resting upon the professional man."[61]

There is judicial support for the proposition that there is a duty upon expert witnesses to limit the issues before the court to those essential for

---

[57] R.S.C. Ord. 38, r. 42. See further Chap. 2, at pp. 55–56.
[58] *Pursell v. Railway Executive* [1951] 1 All E.R. 536.
[59] *Hill v. Baxter* [1958] 1 Q.B. 277.
[60] At pp. 213–215.
[61] *Naylor v. Preston Area Health Authority* [1987] 1 W.L.R. 958 at 967, *per* Lord Donaldson M.R.

the resolution of the dispute. Tomlin J. has said that experts are under a "special duty to the Court"[62] as to this when preparing evidence for trial. In another case he expressed the view that:

> "in the preparation of these cases, it is the duty of those who are concerned for either side as experts, whether legal or scientific, to minimise in every way they can the issues of fact that have to be determined by the court."[63]

The judge criticised the practice, for which he blamed both lawyers and experts, of avoiding pre-trial contact between experts which might indicate, before substantial trial costs were incurred, that there was in fact little scientific dispute between the parties. Given that there is now specific provision in civil proceedings[64] for without prejudice meetings of experts, a duty to meet cannot be said to exist independently of any specific order the court may in its discretion make.

1 Evidence contrary to the case

Unlike the lawyers, the expert witness has a principal and overriding duty, not to the party by whom he is retained, but to the court. Sir Roger Ormrod has suggested, extra-judicially, despite this difference, that the expert witness should have a duty, analogous to that of barristers, to disclose to the court opinions of which the court is not aware which are clearly contrary to his own.[65] This is usually of course achieved by the very fact that other parties call their own experts, whose reports will not be agreed if there is material conflict. Sir Roger Ormrod has further expressed the view that:

> "the one essential of all expert evidence is a frank statement of the limits of accuracy within which he is speaking, and a readiness to indicate, whether asked or not, what his evidence does *not* prove or suggest as likely."[66]

It would undoubtedly assist the court in its evaluation of evidence if the expert was under a clear duty in respect of these matters. A failure to provide the full picture, however, with misleading results, may well be made possible, or facilitated, by counsel's failure, when examining in chief, to insist or permit that all the serious limitations of the evidence are made known. Where full reports are prepared and disclosed pre-trial, as is usual, this danger can be reduced, but only, again, if the expert, instructed by the party's legal adviser, explains in the report itself what

---

[62] *Graigola Merthyr* v. *Swansea Corporation* [1928] 1 Ch. 31.
[63] *Att.-Gen.* v. *Ringwood Rural District Council* (1928) 92 J.P. 65 at 67.
[64] R.S.C. Ord. 38, r. 38.
[65] "Scientific Evidence in Court," (1968) Crim.L.R. 240.
[66] (1972) 12 Med. Sci. Law., 9.

are the limits to the evidence in terms of accuracy and of probative value in relation to those issues upon which an opinion is expressed. At present, however, it cannot be said that any such specific duty exists.

Disclosure The question of what an expert is duty-bound to tell the court has been opened up somewhat by the decision in *Kenning* v. *Eve Construction Ltd*.[67] In that case, an expert sent his report to his client's solicitors, enclosing a letter pointing out some of the problems with the client's case. The solicitors, by mistake, enclosed the letter when disclosing the report to the plaintiff's solicitors. Privilege was asserted, but Michael Wright Q.C. held that the duty to disclose the "substance" of the expert's evidence in a personal injuries case, under R.S.C. Order 25, rule 8(1)(*b*) included any opinion the expert might hold contrary to the interests of his client. The letter did have privileged status, but this was deemed to be waived unless the defendant elected not to call that expert. The purpose of disclosure was to facilitate cross-examination, and material relevant for that purpose should be disclosed. Michael Wright Q.C. acknowledged that it was a widespread practice for such letters to accompany reports, although the previous practice of providing two separate reports, one favourable and one full, was shown clearly to be contrary to the rules by the decision in *Ollett* v. *Bristol Aerojet Ltd*.[68]

He indicated furthermore that his intrepretation of the duty left the solicitor with a simple choice. He must:

> "make up his mind whether he wishes to rely upon that expert, having balanced the good parts of the report against the bad parts. If he decides that on balance the expert is worth calling, then he must call him on the basis of all the evidence that he can give, not merely the evidence that he can give under examination-in-chief, taking the good with the bad together. If, on the other hand, the view that the solicitor forms is that it is too dangerous to call that expert, and he does not wish to disclose that part of his report, then the proper course is that that expert cannot be called at all."[69]

It seems likely that the effect of this decision, however correct in principle and desirable in fact, will be to ensure that such adverse evidence or information is relayed orally rather than in a document,[70] although this would not be sufficient to exclude it from the duty of disclosure.

The decision in *Kenning* v. *Eve Construction Ltd*. is confined to the questions of disclosure and privilege. It does however contain within it the seeds of a more general duty upon experts to bring to the court's

---

[67] [1989] 1 W.L.R. 1189.
[68] [1979] 1 W.L.R. 1197.
[69] *Kenning* v. *Eve Construction Ltd.*, above n. 67, at 1195.
[70] As was argued by counsel for the defendant.

attention matters which are contrary to his client's case and which may assist other parties. This is the inescapable consequence of its premises. It remains to be seen whether the higher courts see fit to state this general duty in clear and comprehensive terms.

D. CONTACT WITH COUNSEL

Counsel instructed in a case in which expert witnesses are to be called by his client has certain duties in relation to the circumstances in which he may speak to the expert. These are set out in the Code of Conduct of the Bar at paragraph 607:

> "607.1 Save in exceptional circumstances and subject to paragraphs 607.2 and 609 a barrister in independent practice and if he is to appear as an advocate an employed barrister must not discuss a case in which he may expect to examine any witness:
> (a) with or in the presence of potential witnesses other than the lay client character witnesses or expert witnesses;
> (b) with the lay client character witnesses or expert witnesses in the absence of his professional client or his representative.
> 607.2 In a civil case a practising barrister may in the presence of his professional client or his representative discuss the case with a potential witness if he considers that the interests of his lay client so require and after he has been supplied with a proper proof of evidence of that potential witness prepared by the witness himself or by his professional client or by a third party."

E. WITHOUT PREJUDICE MEETINGS OF EXPERTS

Where the parties propose to call experts the court may, by R.S.C. Order 38, rule 38, provide that the experts meet without prejudice, either before or after exchange of reports. The practice of so doing was commenced in the Official Referees' Courts,[71] in the early 1980s, by consent of the parties, although no doubt ad hoc arrangements between the parties had been made previously from time to time. The court's power to require such a meeting, in all civil cases where directions are given as to expert evidence, should diminish that reluctance in litigants to discuss the merits of the case which is rooted in a concern not to appear too consensual or weak. R.S.C. Order 38, rule 38 provides that:

---

[71] See *Richard Roberts Holdings Ltd.* v. *Douglas Smith Stimson* (1989) 47 B.L.R. 113 at 123.

"In any cause or matter the Court may, if it thinks fit, direct that there be a meeting "without prejudice" of such experts within such periods before or after disclosure of their reports as the Court may specify, for the purpose of identifying those parts of their evidence which are in issue. Where such a meeting takes place the experts may prepare a joint statement indicating those parts of their evidence on which they are, and those on which they are not, in agreement."

The court can therefore order such a meeting to take place, but it is for the experts to decide, with or without reference to their clients and the legal advisers, whether or not to prepare a joint statement. There is no duty upon the parties to seek directions as to such a meeting but the master or registrar must consider it of his own motion,[72] and this will usually be done at the directions hearing at which the issue of disclosure is considered.

1 Before or after exchange

The meeting may be ordered to take place either before or after the exchange of reports. The nature of the case, and of the facts to be proved by expert evidence, will determine which is preferable. If the experts are required to meet after exchange there is a danger that, having put their views in writing, they may be unwilling to alter them. This tendency might arise out of a concern not to disappoint a client who thought he could rely on his expert to hold to the opinions which he originally expressed, or the fear of a loss of professional standing if he appears forced to admit error or the superiority of another expert's view.

On the other hand in more complicated cases, such as construction claims with large numbers of alleged defects to consider, a meeting may be pointless if the experts do not have final or draft reports available both to consider before the meeting and to provide a focus for the beneficial conduct of the meeting itself. Certainly if the meeting can usefully take place before formal disclosure of reports it will often be possible to avoid the need for the preparation of supplementary or amended reports, which can interrupt a pre-trial timetable and may necessitate late amendments to the pleadings.

2 Meeting during trial

Rule 38 probably does not contemplate the possibility of a without prejudice meeting occurring on the first day of or otherwise during the trial, providing as it does for meetings "within such periods before or after disclosure" as the court may specify. It is clear from the decision of Newey J.

---

[72] R.S.C. Ord. 25, r. 3.

in *Richard Roberts Holdings Ltd. v. Douglas Smith Stimson*[73] that difficulties may arise as to the status and nature of meetings between experts which do, whether or not the court is notified, take place at the time of trial. One particular problem which can arise is the extent to which the experts may in such meetings agree matters conclusively on behalf of the parties. In relation to pre-trial meetings, this question is addressed below.[74] In *Richard Roberts Holdings* Newey J. concluded that in assessing the status of a meeting at trial the court may have regard to the existence and nature of any pre-trial meetings, though these will not be conclusive.[75]

The court will also however be aware of the additional difficulty faced by a party at trial.[76] For, by contrast with the position following a pre-trial meeting of experts, if a party is not minded to agree matters which the expert conceded without prejudice at the meeting, he will not have the luxury of dispensing with the services of the unsympathetic witness and engaging another, because the trial is current. Indeed the judge may already have heard some evidence from him.

It is submitted that while the court should not ignore the existence of pre-trial meetings in such circumstances, or the wording of any order providing for them, it should principally examine the trial meeting on its own merits. Rule 38 does not easily bear the interpretation that it might include trial meetings, particularly because of its provision for periods before or after exchange within which meetings may take place, and meetings at trial between experts will take place not in the ordinary course of things, but for a specific purpose, usually at the behest of the parties. It is that purpose, and any express words which state or reflect it, which should govern the status of such a meeting, in addition to any particular instructions or authority which the expert may be invested with, which should be made clear by the parties before the meeting begins.[77]

3 Pre-trial without prejudice meeting

Save for the use of the term "without prejudice," there is no indication in rule 38 as to what may be the status of the pre-trial meeting, and the consequences of anything said thereat in the absence of specific provision by the parties beforehand. Clearly, once the experts have decided to prepare a written statement, questions arise as to the true status of that document, and these are considered below.

The mere fact that an order has been made that a meeting should take

---

[73] Above n. 71.
[74] See pp. 95–97.
[75] *Ibid.*, at 126.
[76] *Ibid.*, at 126.
[77] *Ibid.*, at 126.

place does not supply the experts with authority of any kind to bind their principals. In *Carnell Computer Technology Ltd., v. Unipart Group Ltd.*[78] Fox-Andrews J. expressed the view that:

> "The only authority the experts had to reach agreement ... was vested in them by my directions. I find that an expert has no implied or ostensible authority to agree facts orally or in any form other than in a joint report where an order exists."[79]

It is submitted that this *obiter dictum* properly describes the position, in so far as it states that mere participation in a joint meeting does not give experts implied or ostensible authority as to anything, though the contrary proposition that the judge's directions, or any joint statement, does or may imply authority is open to question, and this is discussed below.

If the parties agree that their experts may bind them other than in a joint written statement, no doubt the experts can so bind them, and likewise a decision can be made that the meeting is open, so that any admissions or inconsistencies can be put to an expert in cross-examination at trial. Newey J., in *Richard Roberts Holdings*,[80] took the view that in relation to meetings during trial the parties' intentions would have to be inferred if not expressly indicated.[81] The same would not be true of pre-trial meetings pursuant to directions: if there is no express agreement the meeting is, as provided for by rule 38, wholly without prejudice save for any question which may arise in respect of a joint written statement.

4 Joint written statement

Rule 38 provides that where the court makes a direction that the experts meet without prejudice, they "may" prepare a joint written statement:

> "indicating those parts of their evidence on which they are, and those on which they are not, in agreement."

The court cannot therefore direct that the experts do so, and it amounts to no more than an opportunity which may be taken. If it is taken, however, certain consequences may follow, though the matter cannot be said to have been judicially settled. The position where the parties have made an agreement about the status of such a statement before the meeting is clear, though it is unlikely that legal advisers would take the risk of such a course without a final liberty to amend the statement once they and their clients had seen it. What, though, is the position where no such agreement is made?

---

[78] (1988) 45 B.L.R. 100.
[79] *Ibid.*, at 108.
[80] Above n. 71.
[81] *Ibid.*, at 126.

One view holds that while the experts may speak orally entirely without prejudice, once they commit their opinions jointly to paper, the matters thus recorded not only become 'open,' they also bind the parties. In *Carnell Computer Technology*[82] Fox-Andrews J. expressed his approach in this way:

> "the importance of a written report is ... fundamental. It obviates the possibility of conflict between experts as to what was or was not agreed. The preparation of such a report brings home to each expert the fact that he is agreeing conclusively certain facts or opinions on behalf of his client."[83]

The judge repeated this general approach in a subsequent decision.[84] Newey J., in *Richard Roberts Holdings*,[85] took a contrary view: merely by recording matters in a joint written statement the experts neither bind the parties nor 'open' its contents for exploration at trial.[86] The latter approach appears more likely to gather support in future, although all the reported judicial pronouncements upon this issue have, strictly, been *obiter dicta*. A number of considerations, both legal and practical, suggest that this will be the case:–

(i) The words of rule 38 do not confer on the court the power to bind the parties in the absence of their express consent. The rule might well be *ultra vires* if it purported to do so, because it would:

> "not be dealing with procedure, but with the substantive rights of persons under the law of agency."[87]

This provides reason to doubt the view expressed in *Carnell Computer Technology* that "the only authority the experts had to reach agreement ... was vested in them by my directions,"[88] if this statement was intended to suggest that court directions do indeed provide such authority.

(ii) Rule 38 permits a direction only as to "without prejudice" meetings.[89]

(iii) The court cannot in any event order that a joint written statement be prepared other than by consent, so that any authority could only arise by clear consent of the parties.

(iv) To hold otherwise is to misconceive the function of expert witnesses:

---

[82] Above n. 78.
[83] *Ibid.*, at 109.
[84] *Murray Pipework Ltd.* v. *UIE Scotland Ltd.* (1990) Const. L.J 56 at 58.
[85] Above n. 71.
[86] *Ibid.*, at 125.
[87] *Ibid.*, at 125.
[88] Above n. 78, at 108.
[89] *Richard Roberts Holdings*, above n. 71, at 125.

> "it would be quite alien to the role of expert witnesses that they should have an automatic power to bind parties at the conclusion of 'without prejudice' meetings. An 'expert' does not represent a party in the way that a solicitor represents his client; he is principally a witness and his duties are to explain to the court (and no doubt to those who instruct him) technical matters and to give objective 'opinion' evidence."[90]

(v) if such meetings, or joint written statements, could without more bind the parties, they and their legal advisers would inevitably either oppose meetings altogether, or give their experts instructions not to prepare a joint written statement and to avoid agreement of any kind.[91] This is clearly contrary to the spirit of rule 38, which as Fox-Andrews J. has observed, "is to produce as wide an area of consensus between the experts"[92] as is possible.

(vi) experts may arrive at agreements using expressions with legal consequences which they do not fully appreciate and would not intend: the parties' legal advisers must therefore have the opportunity to review both the content and the exact form of such agreements before they have binding effect.

Subsequent agreement to be bound There is nothing preventing the parties, having read the joint written statement, from agreeing to be bound by it or from drawing up an agreed statement, having received their expert's account of what occurred at the meeting. Such an agreed statement can be drawn up by or with the assistance of the parties' legal advisers, preferably incorporating specific reference to those pleaded issues which are no longer in issue, or only so in a limited respect, such as quantum.

5 The expert's evidence in court

The expert may agree matters in a without prejudice meeting, either orally or in writing. By doing so, as has been seen, he neither binds the party retaining him, in the absence of express authority, nor 'opens' the matters agreed for disclosure in court. He cannot therefore be cross-examined upon inconsistencies between his evidence at trial and what he may have agreed or said in the pre-trial meeting, unless a joint written statement is agreed by the parties to go before the court. So long as he has not genuinely changed his mind in the interim, however, it would be

---

[90] *Richard Robert Holdings*, above n. 71, at 125.
[91] Though see J. Bray, *et al.*, "The Law and Practice of Without Prejudice Meetings" (1990) Const. L.J. 23, p. 29, which expresses a more optimistic view.
[92] *Murray Pipework Ltd.* v. *UIE Scotland Ltd*, above n. 84, at 59.

wrong for him to give evidence contrary to the position he adopted at the meeting. In *Richard Roberts Holdings* the judge observed that although such dubious professional practice could not avail the other parties at trial:

> "other sanctions might be invoked against him. If he is a member of a profession, complaint might be made to its governing body; further or alternatively if he is a member of an association of consultants or of experts he might be reported to it."[93]

He would in theory, too, be open to perjury proceedings, though these are in the case of opinion evidence subject to particular difficulties which are discussed in Chapter 10.[94]

Party's position A party whose expert makes admissions or agreements contrary to material aspects of his case at a without prejudice meeting must either amend his pleaded case, concede that part of the pleaded case, or cease to retain the expert.[95] The last course presents difficulties which increase substantially the closer to trial the meeting takes place. In any event some costs will be at risk.

6 Conduct of the without prejudice meeting

There is no provision in the rules for the manner in which the without prejudice meeting is to take place, though where the parties consent, as is now common, to an order including a provision that the experts prepare a joint written statement if this is possible, they should apply their minds to the desirability and possibility of so doing, at least for subsequent confirmation by the parties. The usual, though not invariable, order is for reports to be exchanged only after the without prejudice meeting takes place. This does however mean that the experts will attend the meeting 'blind': without knowing what the opposing expert will say, though they may frequently already have spoken informally before meeting.

In the more factually straightforward cases, this presents little difficulty. In a more complex case, such as a construction dispute with many allegations of defects or variations, the meeting may not be profitably conducted without clear points of reference. If a schedule has already been prepared or pleaded this may provide a useful starting point, although frequently such schedules cannot be finalised until the experts have met and reported, at least where reports are directed to follow not precede the meeting. Certainly in complex cases one expert, probably the plaintiff's in most cases, should ensure that the relevant material is set out in sys-

---

[93] Above n. 71, at 125–126.
[94] At pp. 214–215.
[95] *Richard Roberts Holdings*, above n. 71, at 126.

tematic form, whether or not as a 'draft report', in order that each point can be identified, discussed, and perhaps marked as "in issue" or "agreed" in whole or in part. The defendant's expert can then raise any matters not canvassed by the plaintiff's expert. In most cases little will be lost by sending the other party's expert a copy of the document or draft report in advance of the meeting. In major cases more than one meeting may well prove necessary. In those involving buildings or land a meeting on site may be a useful focus for part of the discussion.

Part C: EVIDENCE AT TRIAL

CHAPTER 5

The Expert Witness At Trial

A. PRE-TRIAL DISCLOSURE AND LEAVE TO ADDUCE EXPERT EVIDENCE

In civil proceedings and Crown Court criminal proceedings there are provisions as to pre-trial disclosure of expert's reports.[1] In the case of civil actions, the requirement is usually the seeking of directions as to such disclosure,[2] which will now most frequently result in an order for mutual disclosure. In criminal cases in the Crown Court, the report must actually be disclosed,[3] save in exceptional circumstances.[4] If a party has not complied with these rules, the leave of the court is required if expert evidence is to be adduced at trial,[5] unless the parties agree otherwise[6] or there has been either an order for affidavit evidence[7] or compliance with automatic directions in personal injuries cases.[8]

The court will exercise its discretion as to leave where there has been a failure to comply with the rules, in relation to all the circumstances of the case. If adjournments are absolutely necessary, adverse costs orders may be made.[9] Whether or not a party requires such leave because of a failure to comply with the rules, the court must still be satisfied as to admissibility. If the proposed evidence is irrelevant, because expert evidence is unnecessary to any matter in issue, or the witness is not competent because not expert, it may be ruled inadmissible despite compliance with the rules. In practice such assessments are, save in the clearest cases, made after the evidence has been heard, by the appropriate attribution of weight when the court makes its decision.

---

[1] See Chap. 2.
[2] R.S.C. Ord. 38, r. 36; C.C.R. Ord. 20, r. 27.
[3] Crown Court (Advance Notice of Expert Evidence) Rules 1987 (S.I. 1987 No. 716), r. 3.
[4] Ibid., r. 4.
[5] Ibid., r. 4; R.S.C. Ord. 38, r. 36; C.C.R. Ord. 20, r. 27.
[6] R.S.C. Ord. 38, r. 36; C.C.R. Ord. 20, r. 27, Crown Court (Advance Notice of Expert Evidence) Rules 1987, above n. 3, r. 3(2).
[7] R.S.C. Ord. 38, r. 36(2); C.C.R. Ord. 29, r. 27.
[8] R.S.C. Ord. 38, r. 36(1)(b); R.S.C. Ord. 25, r. 8.
[9] Cable v. Dallaturca (1977) 121 S.J. 795.

B. COMPETENCE AND COMPELLABILITY

1 Competence

In general the law as to competence of witnesses of fact[10] applies to experts too, whether they give evidence of fact, opinion or both. In addition to this, however, the expert witness must be competent in the appropriate expert discipline. This essentially consists of two qualifications, familiarity with the specialist field relevant to the matters in issue upon which the evidence is to be given, and the requisite level of expertise, whether it be gained through learning or experience.[11]

2 Compellability

As with the question of competence, the expert witness is in general, and certainly in so far as he gives evidence of fact, subject to the law applicable to lay witnesses.[12] In practice the question is not frequently of importance in relation to experts, because unlike witnesses of fact, who may uniquely have observed material facts, a party will usually have a number of possible experts to choose from, and a reluctant expert is likely to be damaging rather than helpful to a party's case. This does not necessarily apply in a field in which there is a very limited number of experts, or where a particular expert has inspected subject-matter which is no longer available, and requires expertise for its comprehension and analysis.

In *Seyfang* v. *Searle (G.D.) & Co.*[13] Cooke J. considered the circumstances in which an expert would be compelled to give evidence. To the extent that he is a witness to a fact in issue in the case, he is usually compellable,[14] and in this respect is little different from any other witness. The same does not however apply to evidence of opinion, unless he has some particular and important factual link with the case:

> "the English courts will not as a general rule require an expert to give expert evidence against his wishes in a case where he has had no connection with the facts or the history of the matter in issue."[15]

It is clear that any question of confidentiality which arises may be relevant, as is any inconvenience to the proposed witness:

> "that principle will apply with particular force where the expert can-

---

[10] See *Phipson on Evidence* (14th ed., 1990) paras. 9–02 *et seq.*
[11] For a detailed discussion of these points see Chap. 1, pp. 10–14, and Chap. 6, pp. 121–131.
[12] See *Phipson on Evidence* (14th ed., 1990) paras. 9–14 *et seq.*
[13] [1973] 1 Q.B. 148.
[14] *Ibid.*, at 151.
[15] *Ibid.*, at 152.

not give the evidence required of him without a breach of confidence, and where the preparation of the evidence required of him would require considerable time and study. This . . . principle, if it be correct, establishes a distinction between expert evidence and evidence as to matters of fact."[16]

The courts will set aside a *subpoena* in such circumstances:

"the court has a discretion not to compel an expert to give evidence against his wishes when he has no connection with the facts or the history of the matter in issue: see *Seyfang* v. *Searle and Co.*"[17]

Where, though, important factual evidence may be lost to the court if the expert does not give evidence, the court may compel him to give evidence[18]:

"In the case of expert witnesses legal professional privilege attaches to confidential communications between the solicitor and the expert, but it does not attach to the chattels or documents upon which the expert based his opinion, nor to the independent opinion of the expert himself: see *Harmony Shipping* . . . the court is entitled, in order to ascertain the truth, to have the actual facts which the expert has observed adduced before it in considering his opinion."[19]

This principle applies to civil as it does to criminal proceedings.[20] The circumstances in which such a situation is likely to arise may well justify the court in exercising its discretion to admit expert evidence at trial notwithstanding a failure to apply for directions to disclose, or to disclose, before trial.

No property in an expert witness In *Harmony Shipping Co. S.A.* v. *Saudi Europe Line Ltd.*[21] a handwriting expert was consulted by the plaintiff and then by the defendant, in relation to the same document. He had in the interim forgotten that he had already advised the plaintiff. His opinion was favourable to the defendant's case. When the defendant subpoenaed the expert to attend court as a witness, the plaintiff asserted that he could not first advise one party and then give evidence at another's behest. Lord Denning upheld the defendant's right to do so, stating that "an expert witness falls into the same position as a witness of fact."[22] Thus, although some of the evidence which the expert could give might

---

[16] [1973] 1 Q.B. 148 at 152.
[17] *Lively* v. *City of Munich* [1976] 1 W.L.R. 1004 at 1010, *per* Kerr J.
[18] *R.* v. *King* [1983] 1 W.L.R. 411.
[19] *Ibid.*, at 414, *per* Dunn L.J.
[20] *Ibid.* See also *Corbett* v. *Corbett* (*Orse. Ashley*) [1971] P. 83 (nullity proceedings).
[21] [1979] 1 W.L.R. 1380.
[22] *Ibid.*, at 1385.

be protected by the plaintiff's privilege, he could give the two kinds of evidence necessary to the defendants:

> "the court is entitled, in order to ascertain the truth, to have the actual facts which he has observed adduced before it and to have his independent opinion on these facts."[23]

Even though, therefore, the opinion expressed to both parties, and to the court, was to the same effect, (that the document in question was probably a forgery), the opinion, which he continues to hold, is "independent" of the privilege and therefore available to the court:

> "there is no property in an expert witness as to the facts he has observed and his own independent opinion on them."[24]

Furthermore, the plaintiff could not seek to pre-empt this outcome by express agreement with the expert:

> "a contract by which a witness bound himself not to give evidence ... would be contrary to public policy and would not be enforced by the court."[25]

Foreign proceedings In *Seyfang* v. *Searle*,[26] the court was concerned with an application that a doctor in England be examined and produce documents for the purpose of an action in the United States.[27] It was held that, given that the doctor had no direct personal connection with the facts in issue, the court should not permit this procedure to be used in effect as a method of compelling a non-party to disclose documents, the request for which was:

> "so widely worded as to amount in effect to an order for discovery ... equally authoritative evidence might ... be obtained ... from witnesses in the United States."[28]

C. THE CALLING OF EXPERT WITNESSES

A party may in general call its witnesses in whatever order it likes.[29] It is the usual practice for expert witnesses to be called after witnesses of fact,

---

[23] [1979] 1 W.L.R. 1380 at 1385.
[24] *Ibid.*, at 1386. A Canadian decision, *McDonald* v. *Bestway* (1972) 27 D.L.R. (3d) 253, is less forthright about the logic of the division between the advice actually given and the "independent" opinion.
[25] *Harmony Shipping*, above n. 21, at 1386.
[26] Above n. 13.
[27] Under the Foreign Tribunals Evidence Act 1856, s.1.
[28] *Seyfang* v. *Searle*, above n. 13, at 152.
[29] *Briscoe* v. *Briscoe* [1968] P. 501; *Barnes* v. *B.P.C. (Business Forms) Ltd.* [1975] 1 W.L.R. 1565 at 1568.

because they may be required to express opinions upon facts given in evidence beforehand. However it has been suggested that the High Court, under its inherent power to regulate its own business, may direct the order in which witnesses are called, though at present this is limited to the Commercial Court.[30] It is particularly important that, where the expert evidence is to consist of one professional person's view of the professional competence of another, the expert witness should hear the latter under examination in chief and cross-examination before expressing his opinion. In criminal cases parties are at liberty to call witnesses in the order they wish, but the defendant should be called before his other witnesses "unless the court in its discretion otherwise directs,"[31] because "he ought to give his evidence before he has heard the evidence and cross-examination of any witness he is going to call."[32] The circumstances in which parties may call an expert witness after the close of their case are discussed below.[33]

Experts, unlike lay witnesses, may in all cases sit in court to hear the evidence of other witnesses before they have themselves given evidence.[34] The view has been expressed that this is a matter for the court's discretion.[35] While undoubtedly the court may regulate its own proceedings, and may exclude any person from the court, this discretion should perhaps only be exercised in the most exceptional circumstances in the case of experts. A judge has written of an unreported case in which medical experts gave evidence as to fits suffered by an individual and were then discharged after giving their evidence. While giving his evidence, subsequently, the individual in fact suffered a fit, and the benefit of expert observation of it was lost. The symptoms had to be described by lay persons present in court at the time.[36] This was an unusual case, but the evidence of experts is often undoubtedly markedly more useful to the court if, for instance, a doctor observes a plaintiff, who he may have interviewed only briefly in his surgery, giving lengthy evidence of his symptoms and suffering in a personal injuries case. In other cases the expert may have had no contact at all with witnesses of fact before the trial.

The prosecution in a criminal case need not call any particular witness, albeit relevant, whether lay or expert, though it has been suggested that any witness essential to the unfolding of the narrative should usually be

---

[30] *Bayerrische Ruckversicherung Aktien-Gesellschaft* v. *Clarkson Puckle Overseas Limited, The Times,* January 29, 1989, per Saville J. And see *Supreme Court Practice, 1991,* Vol. I, 72/A19 and 72/A24. See further Chap. 18, p. 330.
[31] Police and Criminal Evidence Act 1984, s.79.
[32] *R.* v. *Morrison* (1911) 6 Cr.App.R. 159 at 165.
[33] See below Part F, pp. 114–116.
[34] *Tomlinson* v. *Tomlinson* [1980] 1 W.L.R. 322 at 327.
[35] *R.* v. *Bexley Justices, ex p. King* [1980] R.T.R. 49. See also, *Moore* v. *Lambeth County Court Registrar* [1969] 1 W.L.R. 141. The court may permit a medical witness to attend to a juror who has fallen ill: *R.* v. *Newton* (1849) 13 Q.B.D. 716 at 735.
[36] Sir G. Thesiger, (1975) 15 Med. Sci. Law, pp. 3–8.

called.[37] It has a duty to ensure that all witnesses who gave evidence at committal, and appear on the back of the indictment, are present at trial, though it need not call them if it takes the view that the interests of justice would not thus be best served.[38] The prosecution must also disclose to the defence the existence of any material witness it does not propose to call, though it need not disclose any written statement made by that person.[39] It is normal and good practice, however, voluntarily to disclose any such statement.[40] The judge may decide to call witnesses not called by the prosecution if this would be in the interests of justice. Where three surgeons had examined a murder victim, and the prosecution only called two of them as witnesses, the third, whose name did not appear on the back of the indictment, was called by the judge "for the furtherance of justice."[41] The court has a discretion whether to grant an adjournment for prosecution expert witnesses whose statements have been served on the defence to attend at the defence's request.[42]

In criminal cases it is important that, if an expert is to be called, the members of the jury are not misled as to his opinions. Thus where the defence of diminished responsibility is raised by a defendant without medical witnesses, the prosecution should not simply tender its own for cross-examination, but invite the defence to examine them in chief, so that their evidence is not distorted.[42a]

D. EXAMINATION IN CHIEF

1 Establishing the expert's qualifications

It is conventional for the expert witness, having taken the oath, to give evidence of his experience and qualifications, often at some length, both in order to establish that he has the requisite type and standard of expertise for admissibility purposes, and in order that, when the court comes to attribute weight to the evidence of the experts called by all parties, his expertise is established. This is particularly important because much expert evidence consists not of direct factual observation, which can be tested in obvious ways by cross-examination, but of opinion. Although the reasons for expressing an opinion can of course be given, it is frequently the case that the expert relies substantially upon the less tangible combination of knowledge and experience which he has gathered during

---

[37] *Seneviratne* v. *R.* [1936] 3 All E.R. 36.
[38] *R.* v. *Oliva* [1965] 1 W.L.R. 1028.
[39] *R.* v. *Bryant and Dickson* (1946) 31 Cr.App.R. 146.
[40] Code of Conduct of the Bar, Annexe H, para. 1.4(d).
[41] *R.* v. *Holden* (1838) 8 Car. & P. 606 at 609.
[42] *R.* v. *Gallagher* (1983) Crim.L.R. 335.
[42a] *R.* v. *Bardoe* [1969] Crim.L.R. 185.

his career in order to give weight to his views. The formal qualifications and other achievements which mark the possession of that knowledge and experience are therefore essential constituents of the expert's evidence. It is usual for the advocate calling the expert witness to lead this preliminary part of the evidence, merely asking the witness to confirm that the curriculum vitae recited to the court is correct.

2 Adducing the expert's report

In most cases the expert will have written a report before the trial, and usually this will have been disclosed to the other parties, either by direction or by agreement.[43] The provision in the Civil Evidence Act 1968, section 2(2)(b), preventing witnesses in civil cases from adducing most written statements before giving their oral evidence in chief does not apply to expert's reports which have been disclosed, by virtue of the Civil Evidence Act 1972, section 2(1), pursuant to which R.S.C. Order 38, rule 43[44] provides:

> "Where a party to any cause or matter calls as a witness the maker of a report which has been disclosed in accordance with a direction given under rule 37 or 38, the report may be put in evidence at the commencement of its maker's examination in chief or at such other time as the Court may direct."

No specific provision has been made for situations where the report has not been disclosed, either by agreement or pursuant to a court order. The practice is to permit the advocate to adduce the report at any time (usually after leading the qualifications evidence), as with the disclosed reports which are caught by R.S.C. Order 38, rule 43.[45] In fact the reports will frequently have been read before the maker is called, either because the plaintiff's advocate has read them in his opening speech, or the judge may indicate that he has had the opportunity of reading them, whether before the trial or during an adjournment. However the evidence is adduced the expert must in his examination in chief state the facts upon which his opinion is based.[46]

The expert may be tendered for cross-examination upon his report alone, without additional oral examination, or after only limited questioning:

> "as a general rule the report of an expert witness can be read as his

---

[43] See Chap. 2 above.
[44] Applied in the county court by C.C.R. Ord. 20, r. 27.
[45] Though the principle *expressio unius, exclusio alterius* might be thought to lead to a different result.
[46] R. v. *Turner* [1975] Q.B. 834 at 840.

evidence in chief, subject only to supplementary questions necessary for explanation or amplification of the report."[47]

Where there has been an order for pre-trial disclosure, this will have included a direction that the "substance"[48] of the expert's evidence be disclosed. Leave is required to call any evidence not thus disclosed,[49] and this will not be given without good reason:

> "when the Court has ordered that the evidence of an expert witness should be shown to the opposing party (almost always a mutual exchange of reports) that order encompasses all the evidence which the witness intends to give in his evidence in chief. Supplementary expert evidence is not admissible without the leave of the Court. For my part I would hesitate long before giving such leave, because the supplementary evidence may take the other party by surprise and be evidence which the opposing counsel has had no opportunity to consider."[50]

It may be that a less rigorous approach is appropriate in criminal cases, where the liberty of the subject is in question.[51] Undoubtedly however there is a somewhat indistinct line between explanation and amplification, on the one hand, and evidence upon new material, which may on occasion be inconspicuously adduced under the guise of the former.[52]

The other party's expert's report   R.S.C. Order 38, rule 42 permits a party to adduce in evidence the disclosed report of another party:

> "a party to any cause or matter may put in evidence any expert report disclosed to him by any other party in accordance with [R.S.C. Order 38, Part IV]."

This may be done whether or not the party adduces expert evidence from its own witness.

3   Refreshing memory

Experts may refresh their memory from near contemporaneous records as may lay witnesses, where matters of fact are concerned. The record

---

[47] *The Capitaine Le Goff* [1981] 1 Lloyd's Rep. 322 at 325, *per* Sheen J. In criminal proceedings on issues such as diminished responsibility, it may be advisable for the expert to express his opinions in chief orally: see *R. v. Bardoe* [1969] Crim.L.R. 185.
[48] R.S.C. Ord. 38, r. 37.
[49] *Ibid.*, r. 36.
[50] *The Capitaine Le Goff*, above n. 47, at 325.
[51] The Crown Court (Advance Notice of Expert Evidence) Rules 1987 (S.I. 1987 No. 716) requires disclosure of "any finding or opinion which he proposes to adduce" (rule 3(a)).
[52] Just as re-examination can on occasion be employed as a device to re-open the examination in chief.

need not be exclusively that of the witness. A doctor was therefore permitted to refresh his memory from a pro-forma completed by a police officer, as it was a joint record of what they had both observed.[53] Experts may frequently, because they are required in their work to prepare reports, make notes which are then typed or printed. In *Horne* v. *Mackenzie*[54] a surveyor's manuscript report to his employees was printed. Although the printed version was not a precise transcript of the manuscript, he was permitted to refresh his memory from it at trial, because it contained the substance of what he had observed. An expert may also remind himself of the contents of a textbook, where it has contributed to his opinion.[55]

4 Hostile witness

The conventional view of expert witnesses is that, although they are called by a party, they do not share that party's interest, and therefore give independent and fair evidence to the court. Undoubtedly however there are occasions when experts depart from this ideal, whether because of a conscious or unconscious desire to assist one party, or because their personal or professional pride renders them unwilling to be dislodged from particular positions they have adopted within the discipline, whether inside or outside court. There will be very isolated occasions when this manifests itself in a desire to damage the case of the party calling him during examination in chief, in which case he may be cross-examined by that party's counsel as a hostile witness:[56]

> "a hostile witness is a witness who, from the manner in which he gives his evidence, shows that he is not desirous of telling the truth to the court."[57]

Application to treat a witness as hostile may be made as soon as he displays unmistakeable signs of hostility,[58] though the court should decide which parts of the evidence are worthy of belief.[59]

The opinions of experts are perhaps less susceptible of clear identification as being falsely given than is the case with lay evidence of fact, but where this amounts to hostility an expert may be cross-examined upon his opinion.[60] In *R.* v. *Cook*[61] an expert was permitted to be cross-

---

[53] *Taylor* v. *Armand* [1975] R.T.R. 225.
[54] (1839) 6 Cl. & F. 682.
[55] As to reference to such hearsay sources, see Chap. 8 below. And see *Phipson on Evidence* (14th ed., 1990), para. 12–41.
[56] *Oakes* v. *Uzzell* [1932] P. 19.
[57] *Coles* v. *Coles* (1866) L.R. 1 P. & D. 70.
[58] *R.* v. *Pestano* (1981) Crim.L.R. 397.
[59] *Ibid.*
[60] *R.* v. *Cook* (1907) 147 C.C.C. Sess. Pap. 466.
[61] *Ibid.*

examined by the party calling him after advancing a theory so extraordinary that he could not possibly have believed in it. A witness can probably be cross-examined about his general bias towards the party calling him.[62]

E. CROSS-EXAMINATION

1 Disputed evidence must be challenged

Just as a party must in cross-examination challenge evidence of fact given in chief by a lay witness which is not accepted, so the opinions of an expert must be challenged if they are to be disputed. Where an expert for the defence in a criminal case gave difficult technical evidence, the court said the case must proceed despite prosecution counsel's request for an adjournment on the ground that he did not understand and therefore could not challenge it.[63] It was held on appeal that if crucial evidence is to be disputed in final speeches, it must be clearly stated to the witness, while he is in the witness-box, that the evidence is not accepted, albeit no detailed questioning takes place. In *R. v. Hart*,[64] a case concerning lay witnesses, it was stated that the:

> "witness should be challenged in the witness box or, at any rate. . . . it should be made plain, while the witness is in the box, that his evidence is not accepted."[65]

2 The tribunal's role

The judge, bench or jury may have specialist knowledge relevant to the expert evidence being given, which may in part conflict with it. There is no objection to the bench using its own specialist knowledge in questioning the witness:

> "it is a matter of the most elementary learning that judges every day, both in England and Ireland, ask questions suggested by their special knowledge, whether local or scientific."[66]

It is important however that any such specialist knowledge, if it is likely

---

[62] *R. v. Chapman* (1838) 8 C. & P. 558 at 559. And see Cross, *Evidence* (6th ed. 1985), pp. 287–288.
[63] *Transport Ministry v. Garry* [1973] 1 N.Z.L.R. 120 (S.C.).
[64] (1932) 23 Cr.App.R. 202.
[65] *Ibid.*, at 207. It has been suggested that there is a right to cross-examine as to evidence of an expert which was unnecessary to the prosecution in a criminal case: *Young v. Flint* [1987] R.T.R. 300. The appropriate course would perhaps be for the court to indicate that it would disregard the evidence so that cross-examination was unnecessary.
[66] *R. v. Antrim* [1895] 2 I.R. 603.

to contribute to the decision, be explained to the parties and expert witnesses.[67] It has been held that a bench was entitled to consider a relevant report, which was not before the court, where the analyst witness, as to extraneous matter in caper-tea, admitted that he had read the report too.[68] The court may examine an expert as to his views upon a particular passage in a scientific pamphlet and invite his comments, even though he has not adopted it as part of his evidence. However it should not use such works in other circumstances solely "for the purpose of displacing or criticising the witness's testimony."[69]

The court must ensure that it understands the technical evidence given by an expert witness. It may in cross-examination question his answers, or seek clarification of them. However a judge must not intervene so often that, in effect, he takes cross-examination out of the hands of counsel,[70] and it:

> "loses much of its effectiveness in counsel's hands if the witness is given time to think out the answer to awkward questions."[71]

3 Credit

Expert witnesses may, like lay witnesses, be cross-examined as to credit. It is important that this is confined to relevant material:

> "since the purpose of cross-examination as to credit is to show that the witness ought not to be believed on oath, the matters about which he is questioned must relate to his likely standing after cross-examination with the tribunal which is trying him or listening to his evidence."[72]

Experts may be challenged as to credit in relation to their opinions as they may in respect of facts. Thus, where the issue is the value of agricultural land:

> "in some cases it *may* be necessary to examine a Court valuer, not as to the details of his valuation or the principles upon which he acted, but to rebut untrue evidence of statements made by him which, if true would be evidence that erroneous principles had been acted upon by him in his valuations generally or on that of the particular farm under consideration."[73]

So experts may be asked to justify or deny particular opinions expressed

---

[67] Ibid. And see *Wetherall v. Harrison* [1976] 1 Q.B. 773, 777.
[68] *Shortt v. Robinson* (1899) 63 J.P. 295.
[69] *Davie v. Edinburgh Corporation*, 1953 S.C. 34, 41.
[70] *Jones v. National Coal Board* [1957] 2 Q.B. 55.
[71] Ibid., at 65, *per* Denning L.J.
[72] *R. v. Sweet-Escott* (1971) 55 Cr.App.R. 316, 320, *per* Lawton J.
[73] *Gosford v. Alexander* [1902] 1 I.R. 139, 143.

on other occasions so long as they may cast doubt upon the opinions expressed in the present case, and this includes evidence given in other, similar cases.[74] The issue of whether a professional man acted in good faith in forming a particular opinion is one for the jury (or other trier of fact).[75] Evidence therefore from other professionals should not go directly to the issue of good faith, though presumably their views may be sought as to the quality of the relevant opinion because it is relevant to the main issue.

A witness may be asked about his attitude to the parties, if it is suggested that he is biased.[76] Where such bias is alleged, unlike most other forms of allegation,[77] evidence in rebuttal may be brought, and the witness's answer need not be accepted.[78] An expert may be questioned, and evidence in rebuttal adduced, that he is or was not in a fit physical or mental state to express a proper opinion, for instance because he is a drunkard.[79] If, however, the cross–examination is becoming vexatious, it may be stopped,[80] particularly if it is remote from the relevant issues.[81] A police surgeon will not be assumed to be acting unfairly in the interests of the police, and as their agent, unless the same is proved by evidence.[82] The party calling a witness must not allow the court to think that he has a status that he does not have, or conceal the fact that he has been professionally disciplined, for instance where a police officer has been reduced in rank from Chief Inspector.[83] The same must apply where experts have undergone a reduction in professional status.

F. EVIDENCE AFTER CLOSE OF CASE

1 Civil

In civil cases, the circumstances in which it will be justified for a party to call expert evidence after the close of its case will be few. This is both because of the fact that directions as to disclosure will or should have been sought if not agreed,[84] thus making it clear to both parties exactly what the issues requiring expert evidence are, and because detailed plead-

---

[74] *British Hartford Fairmont Syndicate Ltd.* v. *Jackson* (1932) 49 R.P.C. 495 at 532.
[75] *R.* v. *Smith* [1974] 1 All E.R. 376.
[76] *Att.-Gen.* v. *Hitchcock* (1847) 1 Exch. 91.
[77] As to which see *Phipson on Evidence* (14th ed., 1990), paras. 12–34 to 12–37.
[78] *Att.-Gen.* v. *Hitchcock*, above n. 76. For a detailed discussion of cross-examination as to credit, see *Phipson on Evidence* (14th ed., 1990), paras. 12–20 *et seq.*
[79] *Alcock* v. *Royal Exchange Assurance* (1849) 13 Q.B. 292.
[80] *R.* v. *Treacey* [1944] 2 All E.R. 228.
[81] *Ibid.*
[82] *R.* v. *Nowell* [1948] 1 W.L.R. 830.
[83] *Meek* v. *Fleming* [1961] 2 Q.B. 366.
[84] R.S.C. Ord. 38, r. 36.

ings should have put both parties on notice as to the factual and legal issues to be raised. Furthermore in a substantial number of cases the expert witnesses will have met without prejudice before trial and narrowed or clarified the issues.[85] There is however a general discretion in the judge to admit further evidence, where the interests of justice require it, if there is good reason for the failure to adduce at the proper time.[86]

2 Criminal

The prosecution may only call evidence after the close of its case when the need for it arises *ex improviso*: where no human ingenuity could foresee the need for it.[87] It has been said that "this rule of practice is only a general rule ... there may be occasions for departing from it,"[88] but it is unclear what these circumstances might be.[89] The *ex improviso* doctrine will not avail a prosecution case which has simply failed to anticipate the defendant's defence.[90] Thus where the defendant merely set up an alibi defence, asserting that he was not at the scene of the alleged crime, it was held that this was a possibility which the prosecution could and should have foreseen.[91] It might however be reasonable for the prosecution not to call evidence where it only seemed of marginal relevance before the defence case was heard.[92] The matter is always one for the discretion of the court, so that even if the matter does clearly arise *ex improviso* leave may nevertheless be refused.[93]

Expert evidence is subject to the same rules, though where it is in the nature of formal evidence, such as an analyst's certificate, the discretion may be exercised more liberally so long as there is no danger of injustice to the defendant.[94] The courts will not employ their discretion to compensate for a failure by the prosecution to call expert evidence which was at all times available to it, for instance where a handwriting expert had reported on documents in a forgery case[95]:

> "all that was being done was to seek to remedy an obvious deficiency in the evidence in support of the case for the prosecu-

---

[85] R.S.C. Ord. 38, r. 38.
[86] *Doe* v. *Bower* (1851) 16 Q.B. 805.
[87] *R.* v. *Harris* [1927] 2 K.B. 587, 594.
[88] *R.* v. *Cleghorn* [1967] 2 Q.B. 584, 590.
[89] See *R.* v. *Scott* (1984) 148 J.P. 731.
[90] *R.* v. *Liddle* (1930) 21 Cr.App.R. 3.
[91] *Ibid.* See also *Middleton* v. *Rowlett* [1954] 1 W.L.R. 831. The 'alibi warning' will now usually cover this particular possibility.
[92] *R.* v. *Levy and Tait* (1966) 50 Cr.App.R. 198 at 202.
[93] *R.* v. *Harrington (John)* (1984) 6 Cr.App.R.(S.) 182.
[94] *R.* v. *Tate* [1977] R.T.R. 17; but *cf. Pigott* v. *Sims* [1973] R.T.R. 15.
[95] *R.* v. *Day* [1940] 1 All E.R. 402.

tion . . . although the material upon which that evidence was to be given had been in the hands of the prosecution from the beginning."[96]

G. EVIDENCE AFTER TRIAL

1 Civil

In civil proceedings a party may only call additional evidence after trial in the limited circumstances set out in R.S.C. Order 59, rule 10(2):

> "The Court of Appeal shall have power to receive further evidence on questions of fact, either by oral examination in court, by affidavit, or by deposition taken before an examiner, but, in the case of an appeal from a judgment after trial or hearing of any cause or matter on the merits, no such further evidence (other than evidence as to matters which have occurred after the date of the trial or hearing) shall be admitted except on special grounds."

Where relevant matters have occurred after the date of the trial or hearing, they must to be admissible substantially affect a basic assumption made at the trial.[97] Expert evidence is often required in cases involving children, whose physical and emotional development after trial will be of interest to the Court of Appeal (or to the original court if there is specific provision for the matter to return there).

Where such relevant changes are not advanced, a party must show "special grounds," which have been said to require three conditions to be satisfied:

> "first, it must be shown that the evidence could not have been obtained with reasonable diligence for use at the trial; secondly, the evidence must be such that, if given, it would probably have an important influence on the result of the case, though it need not be decisive; thirdly, the evidence must be such as is presumably to be believed, or, in other words, it must be apparently credible though it need not be incontrovertible."[98]

---

[96] *Ibid.*, at 404.
[97] *Murphy v. Stone–Wallwork (Charlton) Ltd.* [1969] 1 W.L.R. 1023; *Mulholland v. Mitchell* [1971] A.C. 666.
[98] *Ladd v. Marshall* [1954] 1 W.L.R. 1489 at 1491. See also *Roe v. Robert McGregor and Sons Limited* [1968] 1 W.L.R. 925. A solicitor does not fail to use due diligence where evidence comes to light after trial because of an expert's late discovery of it: *Gibbs v. Bartlett, The Times*, April 20, 1989.

2 Criminal

The Court of Appeal can hear evidence not adduced at trial by section 23 of the Criminal Appeal Act 1968. This provides two main powers:

(i) under section 23(2), the court 'shall' hear credible and admissible evidence tendered to them, if there is a 'reasonable explanation' for the failure to adduce it at trial;

(ii) under section 23(1), the court 'may' compel a witness to attend and be examined, and receive any tendered witness evidence, if 'they think it necessary or expedient in the interests of justice.

The first power, unlike the second, is clearly not discretionary, and must be exercised if the prerequisites exist.[99]

Although the terms of section 23 make no distinction between expert and other evidence, it seems that the courts will be particularly restrictive, in relation to expert evidence, in interpreting the words "reasonable explanation."[1] Thus although section 23(2) is mandatory in form, the first hurdle, of providing a reasonable explanation for failing to adduce at trial, will be particularly high in the case of expert evidence. In *R. v. Lomas*[2] defence solicitors in a murder case had attempted to obtain the services of an experienced leading pathologist, but had found all save one, who was unfavourable to the defence case, prevented by other commitments from appearing at trial. They were therefore obliged to retain a relatively inexperienced pathologist, who at trial agreed with the prosecution expert. After the defendant was convicted an experienced leading pathologist expressed an opinion favourable to the defence case. The Court of Appeal held that:

> "although the section in its terms appears wide enough to embrace fresh evidence of scientific or medical opinion, it seems to this court that only in most exceptional cases would it be possible to say that there was any reasonable explanation for not adducing such evidence at trial."[3]

However, the court took the view in this case that:

> "the appellant's advisers took reasonable steps to secure the necessary medical evidence before trial and had from their proposed witness a report, which in certain important respects assisted their case, and it was reasonable, particularly with the long vacation about to begin, not to ask for an adjournment to obtain the advice of a more experienced pathologist. They could not foresee that when the time

---
[99] See *R. v. Melville* [1976] 1 W.L.R. 181.
[1] *R. v. Lomas* [1969] 1 W.L.R. 306.
[2] *Ibid.*
[3] *Ibid.*, at 310.

came their expert would find himself unable to disagree in any respect with [the prosecution pathologist]."[4]

It should usually be clear to the parties that expert evidence is necessary in the particular case. In this it is different from lay witness evidence, which may well only emerge after trial. There will however be unusual circumstances such as those in R. v. *Lomas* in which a reasonable explanation for not adducing it exists. In another murder case, a doctor happened to be observing the trial, and heard evidence of experts with which he disagreed. A possible mode of death (by immersion in water) was suggested after the trial which had not occurred to the witnesses. The doctor's opinion was admitted.[5] Evidence was not however heard under the section, in the case of R v. *Melville*,[6] where pre-trial psychological reports had suggested that the defendant was capable of standing trial. After conviction, he was further examined, and some relevant abnormalities of mind were found casting doubt on the opinions first expressed. It was held that the evidence could not be admitted under section 23(2) because the fresh evidence was not "really overwhelming."[7] It is clear then that it will not avail a defendant simply to find an expert after trial who disagrees with the evidence adduced for him at trial, although section 23(1) can be employed to admit expert evidence in an appropriate case.[8]

The general discretion under section 23(1) will be employed largely by reference to the cogency and strength of the new evidence, as suggested by R. v. *Melville*.[9] The Court of Appeal must also consider the question, having exercised the discretion in the defendant's favour, whether to order a new trial. In R. v. *Morgan*[10] a forensic scientist employed by the Home Office stated categorically at trial that a footprint had been made by a particular shoe. It emerged after trial that a number of his laboratory colleagues had disagreed, and took the view that although this was possible, it was not certain. It was impracticable to hold a new trial as some of the forensic evidence had by that time been destroyed. The conviction was therefore quashed.

---

[4] R. v. *Lomas* [1969] 1 W.L.R. 306, at 310.
[5] R. v. *Harding* (1936) 25 Cr.App.R. 190.
[6] [1976] 1 W.L.R. 181.
[7] *Ibid.*, at 186.
[8] R. v. *Frankum* (1983) 5 Cr.App.R.(S.) 259.
[9] R. v. *Melville*, above n. 6; see too R. v. *Lattimore and others* (1975) 62 Cr.App.R. 53.
[10] [1978] 1 W.L.R. 735. This case was in fact referred to the Court of Appeal under s. 17(1)(*a*) of the Criminal Appeal Act 1968, not s. 23.

CHAPTER 6

The Nature and Admissibility of Expert Evidence

A. NATURE AND ADMISSIBILITY

1 The nature of expert evidence

In Chapter 1 it was suggested that the evidence given by expert witnesses can usefully and logically be divided into five categories.[1] There is no authority which expressly supports this overall categorisation, and indeed it has been suggested elsewhere that the only expert evidence properly so-called is expert opinion evidence.[2] This, it is submitted, is too restrictive. In practical terms the need for precise definition is limited, and its most likely relevance is in connection with the seeking of directions as to disclosure, in the absence of which a party may be prevented from adducing expert evidence before the court. The decision in *The Torenia*[3] lends some limited support to the view that expert evidence is properly seen in broad terms.

In *The Torenia* a party sought to adduce the evidence of a witness at trial. No directions had been sought as to disclosure pursuant to R.S.C. Order 38, rule 36. There is no doubt that the proposed witness, the captain of a merchant ship, was competent to give expert evidence. It was argued however that the evidence he would give was confined to fact which, not being expert evidence, required no directions as to disclosure. The proposed evidence was as to observations he had made over a number of years of "damage to deep tanks or deep tank structures and bulkheads in cargo service," and of his "experience of not using deep tanks while sailing in ballast conditions."[4] Hobhouse J. held that this was properly described as expert evidence, and considered that there were in this case three evidential categories to be identified:

> "In a case of this kind one can analyse the matter in this way: First, evidence is adduced which can be described as direct factual evidence, which bears directly on the facts of the case. Second, there is opinion evidence which is given with regard to those facts as they have been proved; and then, thirdly, there is evidence which might

---

[1] See Chap. 1, p. 9. The fourth category is not strictly expert in nature.
[2] See *e.g. Reckitt and Coleman v. Barden* [1987] F.S.R. 407 at 408.
[3] [1983] 2 Lloyd's Rep. 210.
[4] *Ibid.*, at 232.

be described as factual, which is used to support or contradict the opinion evidence. This is evidence which is commonly given by experts, because in giving their expert evidence they rely upon their expertise and their experience, and they do refer to that experience in their evidence. So an expert may say what he has observed in other cases and what they have taught him for the evaluation of the facts of the particular case. So also experts give evidence about experiments which they have carried out in the past or which they have carried out for the purposes of their evidence in the particular case in question."[5]

Hobhouse J. gave four principal reasons for adopting this view.[6] First, the Civil Evidence Act 1972, appears to assume that expert evidence can include evidence of fact.[7] Secondly, a distinction is unrealistic when, as often happens, the expert may employ both fact and opinion in order to describe observations he has made. Thirdly, there is a distinction between facts in issue in the case, and collateral facts of a kind relied on by an expert in support of his opinions. Fourthly, it is desirable in general that such expert factual evidence be subject to directions given by the court. In Chapter 1 it was suggested that two further categories of evidence, which can be distinguished from those identified by Hobhouse J., need to be considered. These are expert evidence explaining technical matters or words to the court, and admissible expert hearsay evidence. There is nothing in the judge's *ratio decidendi* however which would tend to exclude the existence of these categories, and he did state that his categories related particularly to cases "of this kind,"[8] in which only the limited categories which he discussed arose for consideration.

It is suggested however, that it is not strictly necessary for opinion evidence of any kind to be given for evidence to be described as expert evidence, despite the contrary view.[9] In reality though, whatever the form of the evidence, its purpose was in effect the furnishing of an opinion to the court. An opinion can be described as "the inference of a fact from other ascertained facts."[10] It was argued in *The Torenia* that the captain, in giving evidence of the various examples of tanks and damage thereto which he had seen, was doing no more than giving evidence of facts, and that he was not drawing an inference of fact from them. Although the judge did not analyse the matter in this way, it is clear that the purpose of providing the court with this range of facts was to furnish it with a gener-

---

[5] [1983] 2 Lloyd's Rep. 210 at 233.
[6] *Ibid.*, at 233–234.
[7] See s.2(3)(*b*). Though the preamble, on which the judge also relied, is less clear as to this, as in speaking of "opinion" it may include admissible lay opinion.
[8] *The Torenia* [1983] 2 Lloyd's Rep. 210 at 233.
[9] *e.g. Reckitt and Coleman* v. *Barden*, above n. 2.
[10] P. Gillies, "Opinion Evidence" 1986 Aust.L.J. 597 at 598.

alisation about damage to tanks in different conditions. Expert witnesses and triers of fact may draw inferences from facts, lay witnesses may not. The trier of fact is being invited to draw an inference of an expert nature (*i.e.* a generalisation about damaged tanks). Any evidence, though factual in form, which provides the court with a generalisation as to expert subject matter, can be properly treated as expert opinion evidence, because its clear purpose is the generalisation, not the bare facts themselves. The question which must be asked, then, is whether the inference to be drawn from the facts is of its nature an 'expert' inference or not. If, for instance, the matter can be resolved by a simple mathematical calculation,[11] unlike the evidence in *The Torenia* and most such cases, it is certainly arguable that it is not.

2 Admissibility

The only statutory provision as to the general admissibility of expert evidence is section 3(1) of the Civil Evidence Act 1972:

> "Subject to any rules of court made in pursuance of Part 1 of the Civil Evidence Act 1968 or this Act, where a person is called as a witness in any civil proceedings, his opinion on any relevant matter on which he is qualified to give expert evidence shall be admissible in evidence."

From this it can be seen that the only two requirements are the relevance of the evidence and the competence of the expert witness to give it. This begs more questions than it answers.

It was observed in Chapter 1 that evidence is generally treated as admissible if it is relevant and of high probative value in relation to an issue.[12] It is obvious that expert (or any other evidence) which directly concerns an issue in the case is relevant to it. It only becomes admissible however, (subject to any exclusionary rules), if it is of high probative value. A lay witness can demonstrate this by perceiving relevant events or facts directly, subject to his ability to observe and remember accurately. The expert, who often has no close personal connection with the facts of the case, may only be able to demonstrate this by the knowledge and skill which he as an individual brings to the case. These qualities are usually of little probative value if they are shared by the triers of fact. Thus the expert's evidence is admissible only if he imports into the proceedings an expertise which is both relevant to matters in issue, and of a kind which

---

[11] See *Reckitt and Coleman* v. *Barden*, above n. 2. Though see below, Chap. 15, pp. 283–284 and 289–290 for reasons why such evidence may in any event be expert evidence.
[12] See Chap. 1, pp. 4–5.

THE NATURE AND ADMISSIBILITY OF EXPERT EVIDENCE

the triers of fact cannot supply unassisted. In *Buckley* v. *Rice Thomas*[13] it was stated that:

> "if matters arise in our law which concern other sciences or faculties, we commonly apply for the aid of that science or faculty which it concerns."[14]

Just as the triers of fact are unable to form a view as to specialist matters unassisted, so the evidence of lay witnesses is inadmissible, because it is of very little probative value in relation to specialist issues, as was observed in *Folkes* v. *Chadd*[15]: "in matters of science no other witnesses can be called."[16] The modern law is merely a development of these principles. In *R.* v. *Turner*[17] Lawton L.J. held that expert evidence was only admissible as to matters outside "ordinary human experience."[18] From the facts of *Turner* it can be seen that ordinary human experience is regarded as being fairly wide, to include for example an understanding of how a "deep emotional relationship" and "profound grief" could lead to an "explosive release of blind rage." It is assumed, in *Turner* and other cases on the admissibility of psychiatric evidence in criminal cases, that although jurors may not have specific personal experience of the kind of behaviour with which the court is concerned they can, where the defendant is not suffering from a mental abnormality, extrapolate from their knowledge of how normal humans generally behave, to comprehend the events in the particular case, extraordinary though they may be. The jury is:

> "a body of men and women who are able to judge ordinary day-to-day questions by their own standards, that is, the standards in the eyes of the law of theoretically ordinary reasonable men and women."[19]

The principle in *Turner* has, by a narrow majority, been disapproved as an all-embracing rule by the Australian decision in *Murphy* v. *R.*[20] The majority there expressed the view that the distinction between normal and abnormal human conditions is by no means clear, and that jurors may need assistance from experts in relation to the behaviour of persons who, though 'normal', have a mental disability which is highly relevant to the case. In *Murphy* the relevant defendant signed a confession, but

---

[13] (1554) Plow. 118.
[14] *Ibid.*, at 124.
[15] (1782) 3 Doug. K.B. 157.
[16] *Ibid.*
[17] [1975] 1 Q.B. 834.
[18] *Ibid.*, at 841.
[19] *R.* v. *Chard* (1971) 56 Cr.App.R. 268 at 270–271.
[20] (1989) 63 Aust.L.J. 422.

alleged at trial that, because of his very limited intellectual capacity, he could not have understood what he was alleged to have admitted. Evidence was sought to be adduced at trial from a psychologist to show that at normal reading speed, he would have understood only about 25 per cent. of its contents.

On appeal the expert evidence was held to have been wrongly excluded by the trial judge. The abnormal/normal distinction, Mason C.J. said:

> "tends to obscure the fact that in a particular case evidence may be offered to which the distinction has no relevance."[21]

The evidence was admissible because it was relevant to two issues. First, his general level of linguistic ability and comprehension, and the fact that he was an exceptionally slow reader, comprehending only a small fraction of meaning at normal reading speed.[22] Secondly, it was irrelevant that his problems were the result of environmental factors rather than an innate mental defect,[23] if the jury would be assisted by expert explanation of their significance. It is submitted that the approach of the court in *Murphy* is of considerable assistance in the analysis of the need, particularly of jurors, but not only so, for instruction in relation to psychological and other evidence as to unfamiliar aspects of the behaviour of "normal" people,[24] though *Turner* must be said to continue to represent the English law.

It is the content of the evidence which is proposed to be given which ultimately determines its admissibility in relation to an issue which may justify its use. In *Wright* v. *Tatham*[25] it was held that the fact that the case involved the competency of a testator did not *per se* support the admission of expert evidence, but that:

> "where you can bring the decision of that question, as you sometimes may, to depend upon deductions from scientific premises, you may hear those deductions, expressed as opinions by scientific men."[26]

The issue itself may though determine admissibility. In *Ramadge* v. *Ryan*,[27] a libel case, the conduct of a physician was in issue. Expert evidence might have been admissible as to breaches of specific rules of conduct of the medical profession, but was not appropriate here because the question was whether a physician had honourably and faithfully dis-

---

[21] (1989) 63 Aust. L.J. 422 at 431.
[22] *Ibid.*, at 437.
[23] *Ibid.*, at 438.
[24] See also Chap. 12.
[25] (1838) 5 C. & F. 670.
[26] *Ibid.*, at 690.
[27] (1832) 9 Bing. 333.

charged his duty to the medical profession, which was a point "on which the jury were as capable of forming a judgment as the witness himself."[28]

The justification for adducing the evidence must spring from the expertise of the witness, not the witness himself. One of the usual features of a science or other specialism is that certain common assumptions are shared by its practitioners as to the way in which it is carried out. Where evidence, though rooted in the expertise of the witness, is in fact determined entirely by considerations extraneous to the expert's specialism, it is unlikely to be admitted. So in *Ramadge* v. *Ryan* the answer to the question "might depend altogether on the temper and peculiar opinions of the individual witness."[29] Where a pathologist gave evidence that an attack on a murder victim was "frenzied," adding that this was a personal not a medical opinion, the judge was held to have erred in directing the jury that this was expert opinion.[30]

The fact that a professional man has acted in a professional capacity in relation to persons or facts in issue in the case does not make his evidence, *per se*, expert evidence. So the lawyer who acted as such for Charles Manson and his followers in the United States could give evidence as to their beliefs, but this was not in the nature of expert evidence.[31] Furthermore an expert's opinions in relation to the legal issues and merits of the case are of low probative value in themselves. Where an expert's report was "merely giving arguments in favour of the plaintiff on the issues of negligence and causation and so forth," it was not expert evidence and was inadmissible.[32]

Evidence wrongfully obtained Whatever the relevance and probative value of the evidence looked at objectively, it may be inadmissible if the manner of its being obtained is contrary to statute,[33] or was in circumstances where consent to perform a medical procedure should have been obtained and was not, and this is deemed oppressive to a defendant.[34] Such a failure may or may not affect the quality of the evidence itself.

B. FIELDS OF EXPERTISE

The question "what is an expert?" was examined in Chapter 1. Frequently there is little difficulty with the related question whether the field

---

[28] (1832) 9 Bing. 333 at 336.
[29] *Ibid.*, at 336.
[30] *R.* v. *Cook* (1982) Crim.L.R. 670.
[31] *Process Church of the Final Judgment* v. *Hert Davis*, *The Times*, January 29, 1975, C.A.
[32] *Hinds* v. *L.T.E.* [1979] R.T.R. 103 at 105.
[33] *e.g.* 1984 Police and Criminal Evidence Act.
[34] *R.* v. *Payne* (1963) 47 Cr.App.R. 122.

of expertise in which he is competent is appropriate to the case in support of which his evidence is being adduced. Difficulties can arise however as to its relevance in relation to specific issues within the case, and where, although a witness has an expertise, he either lacks the theoretical understanding of his subject which would enable him properly to draw inferences from facts, or the practical experience required to translate his knowledge and training into practical consequences. Furthermore the courts must evolve principles to govern the admission of evidence of scientific or other fields not yet entirely accepted by other expert practitioners, or by the courts.

1   Admissible fields of expertise

Attempts have been made to define the components of a 'scientific' or other discipline admissible as evidence in court.[35] As was suggested in Chapter 1, and as will be seen hereafter, the examples of cases in which expert evidence has been admitted range so widely that it is impossible to reduce them to particular forms of specialist practice. It is arguably possible to do this in a meaningful manner where strictly scientific disciplines are concerned, but there is little doubt as to the general and particular admissibility of these in any event. The contentious cases are those which do not subscribe to particular and established forms of specialist procedure, but which nevertheless often are and should be admissible.

As will be seen, however, it is possible to view the authorities as demonstrating that the more marginal and less methodical or established fields of expertise are usually only admitted in relation to a very specific and limited point in issue in the case. Frequently too such evidence will, although as has been seen the distinction is not a clear one, be closer to factual evidence than the opinion evidence usually given by experts in court. In other than those marginal cases it can be said that an admissible expert discipline should be such that, when a practitioner gives evidence which is inferential in nature, the reasoning process is one which would be substantially shared by other practitioners in the field, and is therefore rooted in the knowledge and method of the expert discipline, not in some whim of the witness which relates more to his personality and disposition than to the expertise which he professes. This is logically so because, if it were not the case, the central justification for expert evidence, namely the ability of the expert, by reason of the expertise itself, to analyse particular facts, would be absent.[36] It is not necessary however for the discipline to have been reduced to documented or organised knowledge. Most expert disciplines do in fact conform to this pattern, but it is inadequate by way of definition both upon analysis of

[35] See *e.g.* A. Kenny, "The Expert in Court," (1983) 99 L.Q.R. 197.
[36] See *Ramadge* v. *Ryan*, above n. 27.

the authorities, and because the primary requirement of the expertise is that it resides in the expert himself, in consequence of which he is competent to give evidence as a witness.

Ultimately however, it is the needs of the case which define the admissibility of the evidence, and therefore of a field of expertise. Even matters as apparently subjective as taste in art can be subject to expert opinion if, as in the case of charitable gifts for educational purposes, the court is unable, by factual evidence or by taking judicial notice, to decide the matter before it unassisted.[37] A market researcher may not be entitled to give expert evidence as to a purely mathematical calculation,[38] though the position may be different if he is explaining to the court the margin of error in particular sampling techniques.[39]

Issue determines admissibility As has been seen, nowhere either by statute or in the cases is a clear general principle established as to what constitutes an appropriate field of expertise for admission in court proceedings. Equally, however, it can be seen from the cases that a wide range of such fields, from the most established scientific discipline, to the most practical and unscholarly form of employment, have been admitted by the courts. What these cases suggest, with varying degrees of clarity, is what is logical, namely that it is the issue which determines the admissibility of the particular field. If the issue requires a sophisticated level of inferential reasoning in the expression of an opinion on a central question in the proceedings, a witness will not be heard, or if he is heard little weight will be attached to his evidence, if his field is one which does not itself require, in its regular study or practice, a similar level and type of inferential reasoning. Where, however, the issue is more in the nature of fact, albeit fact of a specialist kind, a witness whose specialist field does not entail inferential reasoning of a sophisticated kind may be permitted to give evidence. This is particularly so where an "expert" gives evidence of common knowledge or practice within a particular field, without the necessity for explaining this by a process of reasoning involving the justification for, in addition to the expression of, an opinion.[40] The two chief principles governing the exercise of discretion in such circumstances are, first, that the proposed evidence should have a high probative value in relation to the particular issue, which it will not have if a reasoning process is required which is foreign to the proposed witness and to his field of expertise, and secondly that there is no substantial danger of

---

[37] *Re Pinion* [1965] Ch. 85, 107. In other fields such as planning, however, matters of aesthetic taste should not usually be decided upon expert evidence: see *Winchester County Council* v. *Secretary of State for the Environment* (1979) P. & C.R. 113.
[38] *Reckitt and Coleman* v. *Barden*, above n. 2.
[39] *GE Trade Mark* [1969] R.P.C. 418 at 446, *per* Graham J.
[40] See *e.g. Smith* v. *Cook* (1876) 1 Q.B.D. 79.

prejudice. This danger arises principally with juries, and to a lesser extent with magistrates, who may find difficulty in dismissing from their minds opinions expressed by witnesses ill-equipped to engage in such reasoning processes.

2 Appropriate expertise

It is a matter in the discretion of the court to decide, not only whether a witness is an expert, but also whether his expertise is appropriate to the needs of the case. While it is obvious that an accountant cannot give evidence on medical matters, other divisions may be less clear. In some fields the court may be constrained by the availability of experts. In all circumstances the needs of the court in relation to the particular issue prevail, and the only clear guiding principle is that the witness must bring to the case a relevant expertise which the court requires and lacks. It is the issue or issues on which the expert is to give evidence which is relevant, not the general subject-matter of the case. So in an insurance case, a doctor was permitted to give evidence as to the materiality of particular information, because:

> "the importance or otherwise of that which should be disclosed to a life insurance company may well be appreciated only by doctors or surgeons."[41]

Generalists It will sometimes be the case that a witness expert in a broad field is asked to give evidence on a particular subject, within the general discipline, with which he has either no familiarity or no practical working acquaintance:

> "it is competent to the witness to give us his judgment, if he can speak to the practice of a long series of years. He may prove what is the proper way of dealing with ships; and it is not necessary that he should have been personally engaged in the trade to form an opinion as a matter of judgment. A medical man may give an opinion on a professional point, though the case may never have occurred within his own experience. It is a scientific opinion, and he may give it just as a man in a particular trade may give evidence of the usage of the trade, though he may never have been there."[42]

It is apparent from this dictum that the ability of a generalist to give evidence of specialist matters outside his specific experience is not confined only to scientific fields, where a common method prevails, but applies in all fields of expert evidence. Despite this, the court may feel that the

---

[41] *Yorke* v. *Yorkshire Insurance Company* [1918] 1 K.B. 662.
[42] *Sturge* v. *Haldimant* (1848) 11 L.T.O.S. 28, N.P. 29, *per* Pollock C.B.

expert's lack of particular knowledge is in the circumstances of the case such a shortcoming that the evidence would be more prejudicial than beneficial, particularly where a jury is sitting, inclined as it may be, regardless of warnings by the judge, to attach great weight to the utterances of a witness described as an expert.

The important factor in such cases is that the expert must, by his knowledge, training and experience in general, have an ability to comprehend, explain and draw inferences within a specialism that is not his own, but which has probative value because it is markedly superior to the fact-finding tribunal's ability to do so. So a medical man with no experience of alcohol and blood analysis may give evidence of alcohol destruction rates based entirely on British Medical Association tables.[43] Here, his medical training gives him an advantage over most lay people both because his experience of BMA publications generally will enable him to attest to their accuracy, and because his medical knowledge enables him to explain their consequences in relation to a particular individual's metabolism.

It is important to establish that the specialist field concerned is squarely within the general expertise of the witness, otherwise such justifications diminish almost to vanishing point. In a Canadian case a doctor was called to give evidence as to the distance a shot was fired from the body which a bullet had entered.[44] He had no experience of such matters, but had studied books on the subject, which gave guidance as to judging distance from the size of the wound and the jagged nature of its edge. A dissenting minority took the view that although the question was in part medical, it was also a ballistic one which rested on the bore of the gun and related points.[45] These ballistic questions a medical man had no competence to assess. The evidence was admitted, despite this objection, on the ground that the witness by his training had a considerable advantage over the jury,[46] although the court was undoubtedly influenced by the fact that no contrary evidence (ballistic or otherwise) was called. The dissentients however, it is suggested, correctly identified the appropriate principle, that a generalist should confine himself to specialisms which are unarguably within his general field.

Theory and practice There is nothing in principle preventing an expert with only theoretical knowledge of a field from expressing an opinion which entails the translation of theory into practical consequences for the matter before the court, though his inexperience will go to the question of weight. The court may however say that the expert must either have

---

[43] *R. v. Somers* (1963) 48 Cr.App.R. 11.
[44] *Preeper v. R.* (1888) 15 S.C.R. 401.
[45] *Ibid.*, at 410.
[46] *Ibid.*, at 417 and 420.

practical experience of the particular matter before the court, or alternatively that he must be able to call upon some practical experience in an analogous field which, given his theoretical overview of the general discipline, enables him to make inferences in practical terms.

In *Clark* v. *Ryan*,[47] a leading Australian decision, the expert issue before the court was the behaviour of articulated lorries on roads when driven with varying degrees of care, as compared with ordinary motor cars. Dixon C.J. held that a witness experienced in the actual use of such lorries might give specific evidence of how, in his experience, they behave when driven in a particular way. Alternatively it would in principle have been admissible to hear evidence from a scientist as to the physics involved, though the judge doubted how beneficial this would have been to a jury. It was not however an appropriate case for a person in neither of these categories to give practical evidence as to a lorry's likely behaviour in particular circumstances.[48]

In cases with a medical element the courts have been particularly resolute in excluding the evidence of persons who are not doctors by training. In *Nightingale* v. *Biffen*,[49] which concerned arsenic poisoning in the course of employment, a research student in toxicology was not permitted to give evidence as to whether particular individuals were suffering from such poisoning. This was despite the fact that his work had given him a familiarity with such symptoms, particularly in the industrial context. Similarly a social psychologist was not permitted to give evidence as to whether an individual suffered from a disease, defect or abnormality of mind because not being a medical man, he had "no experience of personal diagnosis."[50]

There is no necessity in principle for the evidence which is to be given to constitute subject-matter which is part of the normal practice of the witness's calling. So an engraver was called, in a prosecution as to the forging of a will, to state that he had been able to find pencil marks which had subsequently been erased.[51] A medical attendant at lunatic asylums, whose function was to visit the institutions and report on them as to standards of hygiene, was permitted to give evidence as to the sanity at the time of his visit of a particular inmate,[52] another apparent example of the willingness of the courts to permit those with a medical training to give evidence on almost any question within the medical field. The dictum of Lord Mansfield in *Folkes* v. *Chadd*,[53] that:

---

[47] (1960) 103 C.L.R. 486.
[48] *Ibid.*, at 490–491. See also below n. 65.
[49] (1925) 18 B.W.C.C. 358, C.A.
[50] *R.* v. *Mackenney* (1981) 76 Cr.App.R. 271 at 275.
[51] *R.* v. *Williams* (1838) 8 C. & P. 434.
[52] *Martin* v. *Johnston* (1858) 1 F. & F. 122.
[53] Above n. 15.

"the opinion of scientific men upon proven facts may be given by men of science within their own science"

was cited to exclude the evidence of land surveyor as to to the relative positions of ships involved in a collision at sea.[54]

Limited practical issue The courts will admit the evidence of persons with little obvious scientific or analogous expertise, where the issues necessitate assistance upon a limited practical point, requiring little or no inferential reasoning, so long as their evidence is confined to that point. So a prostitute can give evidence as to the meaning within her trade of a particular abbreviation.[55] In negligence proceedings relating to animals:

"a large body of witnesses, comprising people acquainted with marsh land, said that in their opinion it was imprudent to turn young horses among horned cattle."[56]

In some circumstances a person of no discernible training and expertise will be regarded as an expert, because his particular circumstances place him in a better position than the court. Thus the evidence of a person who saw a particular post mark regularly was preferred to that of a trained postmistress who, though expert in post marks generally, worked in a different office and was unfamiliar with the particular post mark in question.[57] Such near non-experts will probably, however, be confined to evidence which is more factual than inferential in form and content. The value of the evidence in *Smith* v. *Cook*[58] may well have resided in the large number of witnesses giving essentially factual evidence as to their own practice rather than in inferential reasoning performed by any one of them, though it cannot be said that this and similar cases can be explained solely on that ground.

Secondary occupation The court will always analyse the actual expertise offered by the witness in relation to the issues in the case. Although in some instances, particularly in the medical field, the courts have shown themselves to be influenced primarily by the professional title the witness carries, this is in general not relevant, save in the process of assessing the content of the expertise. In *R.* v. *Silverlock*[59] a solicitor who also had an interest in handwriting analysis was admitted as an expert in the latter, because it was the expertise itself which the court was concerned with, not his title or main occupation. Witnesses can call upon expertise

---

[54] *United States Shipping Board* v. *Ship St. Albans* [1931] A.C. 632 P.C.
[55] *Shaw* v. *D.P.P.* [1962] A.C. 220 at 227.
[56] *Smith* v. *Cook* (1876) 1 Q.B.D. 79.
[57] *Abbey* v. *Lill* (1829) 5 Bing. 299 at 304.
[58] Above n. 56.
[59] [1894] 2 Q.B. 766.

derived either from "professions or pursuits."[60] Police officers are usually not regarded as experts. There are good policy reasons for this, in that they so frequently give evidence as to fact in criminal cases that a general guiding principle is appropriate. They may however demonstrate an expertise as to a particular area of police practice by training and repeated experience, though it will not be sufficient for this experience to have been gained only in the course of the case.[61] Such a "quasi-expert" would tend to bias in the knowledge he put before the court,[62] quite apart from the low level of expertise such circumstances would imply. Police officers with training and experience in particular specialisms such as the investigation of traffic accidents[63] have been treated as experts, and in a Canadian case a police officer was permitted to give evidence as to the functioning of a piece of equipment used for calculating the speed of a car, though he could not properly be described as an expert witness.[64] He had considerable experience of the instrument, and had conducted tests and experiments with it, but had no detailed understanding of the scientific principles of its operation. Although he was expressly declared not to be an expert, he was nonetheless permitted to give evidence of an inferential nature.

Fact and opinion It has been suggested that a strict division can be made between experts with a 'scientific' or similar background, who are permitted to perform inferential reasoning in court, and others, who are not.[65] The cases discussed in this chapter suggest that although the courts tend towards such a position, it cannot be so stated as an all-embracing rule. Particular aspects of this question are examined further in the next chapter.

3 Novel sciences: the "twilight zone"

A particular field of expertise may be of doubtful admissibility either because it is relatively young, for instance a forensic science which has grown out of recent basic scientific progress, or because the courts have traditionally been wary of accepting its usefulness in the trial process. Conversely, a field may be so well established, either as a reliable scientific or other discipline, or as a useful forensic tool, that no question arises as to its admissibility so long as it is relevant to issues in the case. The English law has proceeded on this question not according to any established principles—the authorities are bereft of clear suggestions as

---

[60] *Beckwith* v. *Sydebotham* (1807) 1 Comp. 116.
[61] *R.* v. *Crouch* (1850) 4 Cox 163.
[62] *Ibid.*, at 164.
[63] *R.* v. *Oakley* [1979] R.T.R. 417.
[64] *Dickie* v. *Saari* (1973) 43 D.L.R. (3d.) 207.
[65] See *Clark* v. *Ryan*, above n. 47.

to what these might be—but by gradually accepting particular fields into the legal fold over a period of time, to the effective, though not in theory absolute, exclusion of those which have not benefitted from this process.

By way of contrast, courts in other jurisdictions have attempted to state some general principles, particularly in relation to the reception of novel scientific practices. The United States courts are regularly asked to consider relatively untried scientific procedures which are asserted as capable of making a contribution within the forensic sphere. The established United States authority is *Frye* v. *United States*,[66] which contains a statement as to the manner in which such new sciences should be approached:

> "Just when a scientific principle crosses the line between the experimental and demonstrable stages is difficult to define. Somewhere in this twilight zone, the evidential force of the principle must be recognised, and while the courts will go a long way in admitting expert testimony deduced from a well-recognised scientific principle or discovery the thing from which the deduction is made must be sufficiently established to have gained general acceptance in the field in which it belongs."[67]

In the more recent decision in *United States* v. *Baller*,[68] in which the court had to consider the development of many newly discovered or adopted scientific processes since the decision in *Frye*, more detailed principles were set down. These are of additional interest in that they were expressly approved and adopted in the Australian case of *R.* v. *Gilmore*,[69] a decision concerning the admissibility of spectrographic voice analysis. The court's approach in *U.S.* v. *Baller* can be expressed in terms of five specific guidelines[70]:

(i) "there must be a demonstrable, objective procedure for reaching the opinion";
(ii) there must exist "qualified persons who can either duplicate the result or criticize the means by which it was reached, drawing their own conclusions from the underlying facts";
(iii) "deciding whether these conditions have been met is usually within the discretion of the trial judge";
(iv) "absolute certainty of result or unanimity of scientific opinion is not required for admissibility";
(v) "unless an exaggerated popular opinion of the accuracy of a particular technique makes its use prejudicial or likely to mislead the

---

[66] (1923) 293 F. 1013.
[67] *Ibid.*, at 1014.
[68] (1975) 519 Fed. 2d. 463.
[69] [1977] 2 N.S.W.L.R. 935 at 939.
[70] From dicta at 466–467.

jury, it is better to admit relevant scientific evidence in the same manner as other expert testimony and allow its weight to be attacked by cross-examination and refutation."

It cannot be said that these guidelines represent the English law. However they contain little, if anything, which is actually inconsistent with the manner in which the English courts have received such evidence. The final guideline, which represents something approaching a presumption of admissibility, only has its effect if the other guidelines are adhered to. In particular the dangers are very much reduced if there are other practitioners within the field who can be called upon both to advise the advocate on fruitful lines of cross-examination, and to give evidence either in rebuttal of the validity of the entire discipline, or to explain those aspects of it which can safely be treated as reliable. A number of relevant considerations are suggested by the general approach of the English courts:

(i) The matter is, at root, one of probative value. Expert evidence is only admissible if the evidence of the particular expert is significantly probative of issues which the triers of fact would, left with the established facts and their own knowledge, be unable to determine because they are outside "ordinary human experience."[71] Subject to the question of a presumption of the kind suggested by the fifth of the *Baller* guidelines, the party seeking to call such evidence must show that it is capable of having probative value. Having done so, he must show that this is not outweighed (particularly where juries are concerned) by its prejudicial effect, or by doubts as to its validity or accuracy which outweigh the probative value which is contended for it. These may be doubts as to the fundamentals of the field itself, or as to its application to the facts of the particular case.

(ii) The courts acknowledge a process over time by which particular scientific techniques become accepted, initially within the scientific community, and then by the courts.[72] The two do not run hand in hand, both because the courts are not primarily a forum for the accreditation of the experimental sciences, and because the legal process, entailing as it does a process of evidential proof, makes additional demands upon a scientific discipline.

(iii) A discipline need not be simply accepted or rejected for evidential purposes. It may have a limited use in the court process, either because of its nature, or because of its limitations as compared with conventional evidential methods. So for example actuarial

---

[71] *R. v. Turner* [1975] 2 Q.B. 834; see also [1956] Crim.L.R. 655.
[72] *Ibid.*, at 843; *D.P.P. v. A. & B.C. Chewing Gum Ltd.* [1968] 1 Q.B. 159 at 164.

THE NATURE AND ADMISSIBILITY OF EXPERT EVIDENCE

techniques may be admitted as a check upon the judge's own calculations in cases of damages for future loss, but are not in general to be employed as the chief basis of calculation.[73]

(iv) A scientific technique may be treated as admissible, but only subject to specific warnings to lay triers of fact as to the need for clearly understood and forensically unambiguous results.[74]

(v) The courts may admit expert evidence in a field which is of doubtful susceptibility to expertise, if its findings can be put before the court in such a way that the court can itself analyse each element in the reasoning or calculation process. Thus evidence of surveys by market researchers is received in patent, copyright and passing-off cases, subject to full disclosure of every aspect of the survey both to other parties and to the court, by which means the court can monitor the scientific, logical and evidential validity of each element.[75]

(vi) The courts will not generally compromise established evidential principles, which are themselves a safeguard of the reliability of the expert evidence to which they apply. Although the hearsay rule has been modified somewhat in respect of certain types of expert evidence, the rule does operate to prevent, in practice, the reception of much evidence derived from the technique of hypnosis,[76] for example, quite apart from any question as to its inherent unreliability.

---

[73] *Taylor* v. *O'Connor* [1971] A.C. 115; *Mitchell* v. *Mulholland* [1972] 1 Q.B. 65; *Auty* v. *National Coal Board* [1985] 1 W.L.R. 784. See below, Chap. 15, pp. 279–286.
[74] *Gumbley* v. *Cunningham*, [1988] Q.B. 170; *Smith* v. *Geraghty* [1986] R.T.R. 222 at 232. See below, Chap. 24, pp. 426–430.
[75] *Imperial Group plc.* v. *Philip Morris Ltd.* [1984] R.P.C. 293; *Scott Ltd.* v. *Nice-Pak Products Ltd.* [1988] F.S.R. 125. See below, Chap. 15, pp. 289–293.
[76] See below, Chap. 12, pp. 242–243.

CHAPTER 7

The Form and Content of Expert Evidence

Just as there are considerations specific to expert witnesses governing the general admissibility of their evidence in the particular case, which were discussed in Chapter 6, so the courts exercise special control over the manner in which such witnesses give their evidence, both as to the questions they may be asked, and as to the ways in which they may answer them. Experts may of course give the evidence that lay witnesses may, and in so far as they do so, the usual rules of evidence apply. The character of expert evidence lies in particular in the expressing of opinions, or the drawing of inferences from known (or, as will be seen, assumed)[1] facts.

The courts have adopted a fairly liberal approach to the manner in which experts may give their evidence. This is most evident in proceedings where the judge is the trier of fact (*i.e.* most civil cases) but the daily practice of the criminal courts also discloses a tendency to the view that so long as the expert is able materially to assist the court with specialist knowledge, experience or methods of analysing fact, this opportunity should not be denied to it by formalistic rules about the method by which such evidence is delivered.[2] It follows from this approach that, so long as some fundamental evidential principle is not thereby undermined, the classes of such methods are never closed,[3] and that new scientific developments, or the exigencies of a particular case, may lead the court to consider that evidence should be adduced in novel ways, subject always to the overriding discretion of the judge to exclude evidence which bears the hallmarks of unfairness or prejudice. The point at which such dangers are most likely to arise is where the expert's judgment begins to trespass upon the ability of the court to arrive at its own view of the issues. Experts, however eminent or persuasive, are only witnesses with a specific role:

> "their duty is to furnish the Judge or jury with the necessary scientific criteria for testing the accuracy of their conclusions, so as to

---
[1] See below section C, "Hypothetical Questions," pp. 147-150.
[2] See in particular section D, "Questions on an Ultimate Issue," pp. 150–155.
[3] *M'Fadden* v. *Murdock* (1867) Ir.R. 1 C.L. 211 at 218.

enable the Judge or jury to form their own independent judgment by the application of these criteria to the facts proved in evidence."[4]

A. OPINION AND FACT

1 Facts in issue

Precision Some types of fact are susceptible to the expression of very precise expert opinions, while many are not. The degree of precision appropriate to the matter in issue will depend upon its nature. Issues such as the rental value of premises can often only be ascertained by an "intelligent guess,"[5] though it has been suggested that while an "element of surmise" is often necessary, this is not the same as a guess.[6] Specific statutory provisions may require certainty or near-certainty, and the criminal standard of proof often has the effect of demanding the same. In general, however, the question is whether the evidence has that degree of probative value which renders the opinion likely to be of substantial assistance to a trier of fact without expertise. So long as it fulfils this requirement, the uncertainties or qualifications surrounding it do not affect its admissibility.

Laying the factual foundation for an opinion The opinion of an expert, however correct, is of no use to the court unless it is clearly formed by inference from facts which have been or are to be proved in evidence. The expert must always, in expressing an opinion, indicate which facts he relies upon:

> "counsel calling an expert should in examination in chief ask his witness to state the facts upon which his opinion is based. It is wrong to leave the other side to elicit the facts by cross-examination."[7]

The courts have in certain instances said that the expert should, even where inferences from facts are agreed, give oral evidence, so that for instance a jury hearing evidence as to a defence of diminished responsibility in a murder case[8] may be quite clear as to the process of reasoning from facts to expert inferences.

The factual foundation of an expert opinion may be laid simply by referring to facts which a party will prove independently in evidence. The expert may himself do so, however, by a process which amounts in effect

---

[4] *Davie v. Edinburgh Magistrates* (1953) S.C. 34 at 40.
[5] *Ireland v. Taylor* [1949] 1 K.B. 300 at 309.
[6] *Lewis v. Port of London Authority* (1914) 111 L.T. 776 at 778.
[7] *R. v. Turner* [1975] 1 Q.B. 834 at 840. See also *Samuels v. Flavel* [1970] S.A.S.R. 256 at 260.
[8] *R. v. Ahmed Din* (1962) 46 Cr.App.R. 269.

to corroboration, though this should be distinguished from situations in which corroboration is required in law.[9] He may refer to experiments he conducted repeating as closely as possible the facts as alleged by one of the parties, and compare the result to that alleged by the parties to have occurred in the case.[10] He may, to add weight to his opinion, show that a professional practice which he states to be common is one which he has himself acted in accordance with on specific occasions.[11] If the expert witness was himself involved in a personal capacity in the facts giving rise to the proceedings, he may show that he acted at all times consistently with the opinion he is now expressing.[12] Where the expert himself observed the facts upon which he based his opinion, there is no particular requirement as to how he came to observe them. Although, therefore, a doctor visited a lunatic asylum to report on the standard of hygiene, he was subsequently able to give opinion evidence as to the sanity of a patient.[13] It has been suggested that there is a distinction between a practical man giving evidence of his experience (for example of how trailers behave on the roads), and that of a witness using theoretical knowledge, the former giving evidence only of fact, the latter of opinion.[14] This strict distinction appears not to be an entirely helpful one. No two accidents are the same, and the description of normal behaviour characteristics, however untheoretical in form, always involves elements of generalisation and inference.

In general an expert need not have observed facts himself in order to express an opinion upon them, though the probative value and weight of the evidence may be affected by this where it would be usual for him to have done so. A pathologist may express a view as to cause of death, despite not having personally examined the body, if the wounds are described to him.[15] A ship surveyor was permitted to express a view as to the seaworthiness of a ship from descriptions of its state proved by others.[16] In specific areas of law the courts may however develop a practice as to such matters. An example is the evidence of psychiatrists as to the sanity of a criminal at the time of the offence, or of a testator when making a will. These are examined in Chapter 12 below.

While the expert may support his opinion by referring to specific facts, however, the reverse does not apply. A fact not observed by the expert witness is not proved because he expresses an opinion upon it, save that

---

[9] See *Phipson on Evidence* (14th ed., 1990), paras. 14–02 to 14–06.
[10] *R. v. Heseltine* (1873) 12 Cox 404.
[11] *Birrel v. Dryer* (1884) 9 App.Cas. 345.
[12] *Stephenson v. Tyne Commissioners* (1869) 17 W.R. 590. The court described such conduct as corroboration of his opinion.
[13] *Martin v. Johnston* (1858) 1 F. & F. 122.
[14] *Clark v. Ryan* (1960) 103 C.L.R. 486.
[15] *R. v. Mason* (1912) 7 Cr.App.R. 67.
[16] *Beckwith v. Sydebotham* (1807) 1 Camp. 116.

the expert may in some circumstances properly be asked which of two or more factual consequences he thinks more likely to have flowed from a given factual situation.[17] Facts must, subject to certain exceptions peculiar to expert evidence,[18] always be independently proved.[19]

2 Formation and use of the opinion

Generalisation The opinion which the expert is asked to express is frequently of the kind: "X is what tends to happen in similar circumstances, therefore Y is what I would expect to happen (or to have happened) in the particular circumstances of this case." The first stage in this reasoning process is the formation of a generalisation,[20] which may arise in a number of ways, such as drawing upon experience, reasoning from theoretical principles accepted within an expert discipline, reference to statistics or other data accepted within such a discipline, or most often a combination of these.

To the extent that a witness purports to base his view entirely upon experience, the experience can be described as no more than evidence of fact (*i.e.* a number of facts which he has witnessed over a period). If he does not proceed to express an opinion in terms, the court is then in effect left with a generalisation. It has been judicially suggested, as has already been seen, that this is not expert evidence of opinion.[21] The English courts have seen this as a false dichotomy: where the obvious purpose of the evidence is the furnishing of a generalisation, it is misleading and artificial to describe it as evidence of fact *simpliciter*.[22] Furthermore this kind of generalisation from experience is not confined to particular sciences or professions. It is admissible:

> "wherever peculiar skill and judgement, applied to a particular subject, are required to explain results, or trace them to their cause."[23]

Thus a shopkeeper may generalise as to the cause and amount of wastage of goods sold in small quantities.[24]

Factual comparisons Rather than, or in addition to, relying upon his general experience, the expert may seek to base his opinion upon a comparison between the facts of the present case and those of another similar set of facts of which he is aware. It is important to distinguish the two,

---

[17] See below section C, "Hypothetical Questions," pp. 147–150.
[18] See Chap. 8.
[19] R. v. *Turner* above n. 7.
[20] See R. Eggleston, *Evidence Proof and Probability* (2nd ed., 1983), 141 *et seq.*
[21] *Clark* v. *Ryan*, above n. 14.
[22] *The Torenia* [1983] 2 Lloyd's Rep. 210 at 233.
[23] *M'Fadden* v. *Murdock*, above n. 3, at 218.
[24] *Ibid.*

for there is always a danger of specific factual comparisons, as to which original evidence of the facts compared may be necessary, being admitted under the guise of the expert's general experience. In a case concerning the rental valuation of a farm the valuer relied upon his knowledge of the rents of other farms in the area,[25] and the view was expressed that:

> "if by former experience he has acquired a knowledge, not merely of the rent paid for one particular farm, but . . . of the rents generally paid therein, it is part of his knowledge . . . and . . . may be taken into consideration by him . . . however, only when it is part of his own antecedent knowledge—when . . . it has become part of his mental equipment. It cannot be the result of inquiries made for the purpose."[26]

An expert may always make specific comparisons where the example is one of which he can himself give original evidence. Thus in *Folkes v. Chadd*[27] the expert was permitted to refer to harbours nearby the one in question which he himself knew of. It was said further that such specific comparisons were only admissible if the harbour described was indeed directly comparable (*i.e.* without embankments). In *Metropolitan Asylum District v. Hill*[28] this aspect of the decision in *Folkes v. Chadd* was criticised. The absence of similarity in purported comparisons was not a question of admissibility, but of weight. In *Metropolitan Asylum District v. Hill* the question was whether a hospital was responsible for causing a high level of disease in its neighbourhood. It was sought to give evidence of comparison with another district, similar in all respects save that it contained no hospital and the level of disease was lower. In the event the court held that the evidence was not substantial or well documented enough to be relied upon.[29] However it was held that in principle, such evidence is admissible, even where it is a dissimilarity (as to the existence of a hospital and the level of disease) that is relied upon, not a similarity.

The kind of evidence which is admissible will, it is submitted, depend not on some artificial distinction between similarity and dissimilarity, but on what evidence is justified by the facts of the particular case. The types of inference to be drawn from the comparisons in *Folkes v. Chadd* and *Metropolitan Asylum District v. Hill* were very different, and the words of Lord Mansfield in the former case certainly permit the interpretation that he was only explaining what was appropriate in the particular case. Further it was certainly arguable that a type of comparison which was of

---

[25] *Gosford v. Alexander* [1902] 1 I.R. 139.
[26] *Ibid.*, at 143. See also *English Exporters v. Eldonwall* [1973] Ch. 415, discussed at length in Chap. 8, pp. 169–172.
[27] (1782) 3 Doug. K.B. 157.
[28] (1882) 47 L.T. 29.
[29] *Ibid.*, at 33.

no assistance to the court was inadmissible (as opposed merely to lacking weight) because it had no probative value in relation to the facts, and was therefore irrelevant. Where there is doubt, however, the courts will usually resolve it by admitting the evidence, then if appropriate ascribing little weight to it.

In a particular case, evidence of comparison may be admissible on one issue, but not on another. In considering whether a book is obscene, a jury may hear evidence from an expert comparing it with accepted literary works in order to establish the "public good" defence,[30] but may not hear such expert comparison evidence in relation to the question of obscenity itself, for this is a matter wholly for the jury to assess on the basis of their own view of the work in question.[31] Where a defendant faced a charge of maliciously damaging a building by an explosion of dynamite, thereby endangering life, an expert was not permitted to give evidence of damage to buildings other than that named in the indictment for the purpose of proving the danger to life.[32] The evidence was nevertheless admitted to demonstrate the general nature of the explosion.

Applying expertise to the facts An expert can only justify his being called by bringing to the facts of the case the advantage of his learning or experience. "Mere opinion"[33] is of no use to the court unless it arises out of the expertise. His evidence will be inadmissible if it simply consists of arguments in favour of one party which counsel "can give as well or better."[34] A defendant's conviction was quashed where he raised the provocation defence, and the prosecution's pathologist described the attack as "frenzied," as he was not speaking as an expert in so doing.[34a] If the expert evidence can only be such as would be derived from experience of particular factual situations with which the witness, though an expert, is not familiar, he should not give that kind of evidence,[35] though unless such an objection is clear the court will usually resolve the matter by the attribution of weight rather than by refusing to admit it at all. It is open to the party calling an expert, however, to decide how to present his evidence, and how directly to apply his evidence to the facts. So in M'Fadden v. Murdock[36]:

> "it was competent to the Plaintiff either to apply, by the witness's own statements, his skill and experience to the particular facts

---

[30] R. v. Penguin Books [1961] Crim. L.R. 176.
[31] R. v. Reiter [1954] 2 Q.B. 16. See also Chap. 25, p. 434.
[32] R. v. McGrath and McKevitt (1881) 14 Cox 598.
[33] Carter v. Boehm (1766) 3 Burr. 1905 at 1918.
[34] Hinds v. London Transport Executive [1979] R.T.R. 103 at 105.
[34a] R. v. Cook (1982) Crim.L.R. 670.
[35] Clark v. Ryan (1960) 103 C.L.R. 486 at 491.
[36] (1867) Ir.R.I.C.L. 211 at 218. Above n. 3.

proved at the trial, or to prove, in general terms, the result of his skill and experience as applied to the class of subjects to which the matter in controversy belonged, and to leave it to the jury to apply that general evidence to the facts which they should determine to have been proved before them."[37]

B. OPINION AND STANDARDS

1 Standards of professional conduct

Opinion an issue In negligence cases, and contractual claims entailing allegations as to some breach of professional standards, experts may give evidence upon the standard of conduct to be expected from a prudent and competent, or sometimes a specially skilled, person practising in the same field. In some such cases, the opinion itself is in effect the issue, in that the defendant professional may have a complete defence if he can show that a representative of a "responsible body" of skilled practitioners within the field approves of the practice he adopted.[38] This may be so where there is a genuine division within the specialist field about how particular procedures should be performed, and a practitioner will not be held negligent "merely because there is a body of opinion which would take a contrary view."[39] In such a case the evidence of the expert has the purpose of demonstrating what those who practise in accordance with the view to which he subscribes believe is the appropriate procedure. It has been suggested that this precludes evidence of what the witness himself would have done in the particular circumstances. In *Midland Bank v. Hett, Stubbs and Kemp*,[40] a case concerning solicitors' negligence, Oliver J. said of such evidence:

> "if there is some practice in a particular profession, some accepted standard of conduct which is laid down by a professional institute or sanctioned by common usage, evidence of that can and ought to be received. But evidence which really amounts to no more than an expression of opinion by a particular practitioner of what he thinks that he would have done had he been placed, hypothetically and without the benefit of hindsight, in the position of the defendants, is of little assistance to the court; whilst evidence of what, as a matter of law, the solicitor's duty was in the particular circumstances of the

---

[37] *M'Fadden v. Murdock* (1867) Ir.R.I.C.L. 211 at 220.
[38] *Bolam v. Friern Hospital Management Committee* [1957] 1 W.L.R. 582.
[39] *Ibid.* at 587.
[40] [1979] Ch. 384.

case is, I should have thought, inadmissible, for that is the very question which it is the court's function to decide."[41]

Oliver J. here supplies three gradations of such evidence, the first admissible, the second of doubtful utility (though not apparently inadmissible), and the third inadmissible. In a subsequent passage he said of the evidence of practising solicitors:

"I doubt the value, or even the admissibility, of this sort of evidence, which seems to be becoming customary in cases of this type."[42]

The judge appears here to be distinguishing cases of solicitors' negligence from others, and it may be that this is in part because judges, as professional lawyers, feel themselves able to assess such questions,[43] though this might not be so obviously so for a very narrow legal specialism. There have been suggestions in cases concerning professions other than lawyers that evidence of what the witness would himself have done in the defendant's place should be avoided.[44] The real position is that in saying what course of action would be taken in particular circumstances by members of his school of thought an expert witness is in effect giving evidence as to his own practice. If he is to apply this to the facts of the particular case, and it is often of benefit to the court to have such assistance, he is doing little other than saying what he would have done in the circumstances. Of course some experts may, for reasons for instance of professional courtesy, stop short of actually saying "he did it that way: I would have done it this way." It is however an exercise of some artificiality to make the distinction as a matter of admissibility, and it may be that the appropriate way to manage the difficulties of hindsight is simply to deal with them openly in evidence, and to invite the expert to consider what effect the advantage of hindsight may have upon the opinion he expresses.

Opinion not an issue Some cases concerning professional standards justify the reception of expert opinion, but in circumstances in which the opinion in itself is not sufficient to conclude the issue of breach of duty, being, if accepted, merely evidence which contributes to the court's decision. The division between this class of cases and those discussed previously is not always a clear or an easy one. However where the issue is not whether there is a responsible body of opinion which subscribes to a

---

[41] [1979] Ch. 384 at 402.
[42] *Ibid.*
[43] See *e.g.* Jackson and Powell, *Professional Negligence* (2nd ed., 1987), pp. 210–211. See also, however, *Fletcher* v. *Winter* (1862) 3 F. & F. 138, in which a lawyer gave evidence as to whether a step taken in an action by another lawyer was wholly useless.
[44] See *e.g. Suloo* v. *Redit & Co. Ltd.* [1959] N.Z.L.R. 45 at 67, in which despite expressing such a view the court proceeded to consider the witness's evidence as to his own practice.

particular view or practice, but what is generally accepted as the prudent approach or practice in particular circumstances, the court is concerned less with the opinions of expert witnesses *per se* than with the general conclusions to be drawn from their evidence. An unresolved conflict of expert evidence may, in the former case, decide the matter, in the sense that the court may be persuaded that there are several responsible bodies of opinion, it being sufficient that the allegedly negligent defendant subscribed to the practice of one of them. In the latter case if such a conflict arises the court must resolve it.

In this second category of cases it is clear that evidence of what the witness would have done in particular circumstances is of even less assistance to the court,[45] and arguably inadmissible because irrelevant:

> "when a plaintiff seeks to establish the general practice in a particular profession it will be of little avail to him to call a member of that profession merely to give evidence of the witness's own practice."[46]

Witnesses must nevertheless be wary of trespassing on ultimate issues,[47] particularly the concept of negligence, which is a question of mixed fact and law for the court. The witness may however give evidence which in substance, though not form, answers the final question whether an act was negligent:

> "the plaintiff's counsel might state to the witness what had been done, and might ask him if an officer of competent skill would have done so."[48]

The counterpart of the fact that, in expressing opinions as to a generally accepted view within the profession, witnesses should not refer to what they would themselves have done in specified circumstances, is that they need not necessarily have personal experience of the matters of which they speak,[49] although its absence may go to weight. They may indeed refer to articles or other professional literature to support their view.[50] Even though they do not have direct experience of the matters in question they can speak with some authority either because they can assess such secondary evidence as being consistent with their scientific or professional knowledge, or because they can speak of it as emanating from a trustworthy source. Equally, though again this will go to weight, different though analogous experience may be sufficient to ground an opinion

---

[45] *Berthon v. Loughman* (1817) Stark 258.
[46] *McLaren Maycroft v. Fletcher* [1973] 2 N.Z.L.R. 100 at 108 citing *Chapman v. Walton* (1833) 10 Bing. 57.
[47] See below, pp. 150–155.
[48] *Malton v. Nesbit* (1824) 1 C. & P. 70 at 72.
[49] *Sturge v. Haldimant* (1848) 11 L.T.O.S. 28 at 29.
[50] *H. v. Schering Chemicals Limited* [1983] 1 W.L.R. 143 at 145. See Chap. 8, pp. 172–181.

about a general practice. So the practice in the colonial fruit trade may be admitted as evidence of the practice in the London fruit trade.[51]

In specific areas of law, outside the field of negligence, the courts may develop a particular practice as to how expert witnesses are to give evidence of the practice of their colleagues. The extent to which they may refer to their own practice, or what they would have done in given circumstances, will depend upon the nature of the issue. Thus the question of non-disclosure in insurance cases, in which the issue is the materiality of the information to the prudent underwriter, despite some conflicting authority is usually to be resolved by reference only to the general practice of underwriters of prudence.[52] The distinction may be one of form rather than substance where a broker is asked whether a prudent broker would have procured the alterations to the policy which had been agreed in that case.[53] The distinction is more meaningful where the question relates to a class of information on the basis of which insurance brokers or underwriters habitually make decisions. The more individual and unusual the circumstances, the less probative will be evidence as to a general practice, because the witness is in effect compelled to imagine what he would have done in the same situation. Cases such as that in which the evidence of one group of experts was preferred to that of another, because they had themselves in the past underwritten ships in a manner consistent with the view they were now expressing, are probably to be explained on the ground that the concern of the court was principally with the credit or bona fides of the witnesses rather than with extrapolating some general practice from particular actions.[54]

Criminal proceedings may justify the reception of evidence of opinion more specifically related to the particular conduct of a professional, such as a doctor.[54a]

Setting standards of care The standard of care in professional negligence proceedings is to be set by the courts, but upon evidence as to practice and regulation within the particular profession. It may be misleading and of little use to the court to adduce evidence of eminent practitioners in the field where the issue is the standard of the ordinary competent practitioner.[55] It is always open to the courts to conclude that a professional practice which is general, or institutionally recommended, is not the legal standard, and indeed the usual prudent practice may go further

---

[51] *Fleet* v. *Murton* (1871) L.R. 7 Q.B. 126.
[52] *Horne* v. *Poland* [1922] 2 K.B. 364 at 365; *Scottish Shire Line Ltd.* v. *London and Provincial Marine and General Insurance Co. Limited* [1912] 3 K.B. 51 at 70.
[53] *Chapman* v. *Walton*, above n. 46.
[54] *Birrell* v. *Dryer* (1884) 9 App.Cas. 345.
[54a] *R.* v. *Whitehead* (1848) 3 C. & K. 202.
[55] *Chin Keow* v. *Government of Malaysia* [1967] 1 W.L.R. 813 at 817, P.C.

than the law requires.[56] Likewise the evidence may appear conclusively to show that the defendant met accepted professional standards, but the court:

> "is not necessarily bound by such evidence for the court must retain its own freedom to conclude that the general practice of a particular profession falls below the standard required by the law."[57]

The courts will always be influenced by accepted codes of practice, whether governmental in origin or promulgated through a particular professional institution. The effect of governmental codes is usually, in practical evidential terms, to shift the burden of proof where there is a relevant departure therefrom, so that the defendant, in a construction design case:

> "must show that the design is capable of rational analysis and is adequate and safe."[58]

To say that the evidential burden may shift in this way is really no more than to acknowledge the great weight of such a code in negligence proceedings. The court always, however, sets the standard in law, and codes may be of limited use if they are not directly in point, or are out of date in relation to a more recent method of design which is the subject-matter of the proceedings.[59]

2 Opinion concerning group reactions

Experts may as has been seen express an opinion, depending upon the issues before the court, as to whether a particular practice is a competent one supported by some other colleagues, and as to the general practice, belief or state of knowledge within the profession as a whole. There is also however a limited category of cases in which an expert may express an opinion about how other colleagues would behave in particular circumstances. In cases concerning trade marks, passing-off and copywright,[60] an expert may be permitted to give evidence:

> "about the likely reactions of others in relation to matters which are within his or her sphere of work,"[61]

---

[56] *United Mills Agencies v. Harvey, Bray and Co.* [1951] 2 Lloyd's Rep. 631 at 643.
[57] *McLaren Maycroft v. Fletcher*, above n. 46, at 108. See also *Greaves v. Baynham Meikle and Partners* [1975] 1 W.L.R. 1095 at 1102; *Sidaway v. Board of Governors of the Bethlem Royal Hospital* [1984] Q.B. 493 at 513–514; *Re The Herald of Free Enterprise, The Independent*, December 18, 1987. This question is discussed in J. Holyoak, "Raising the Standards of Care" (1990) 10 Legal Studies 201.
[58] *Bevan Investments Ltd. v. Blackhall and Struthers* [1973] 2 N.Z.L.R. 45. See also *Greaves v. Baynham Meikle*, above n. 57.
[59] *Independent Broadcasting Authority v. E.M.I. and B.I.C.C.* (1980) 14 B.L.R. 1, H.L.
[60] As to surveys in relation thereto see Chap. 8, pp. 165–167 and Chap. 15, pp. 289–293.
[61] *Soda Stream Ltd. v. Thorn Cascade Co. Ltd.* [1982] R.P.C. 459 at 468.

He may do so because his knowledge and experience of the field permits him to judge that:

> "according to his experience of how the business in which he is and has been conducted, traders or customers will adopt certain characteristics or practices,"[62]

though the weight of such evidence will need to be carefully considered.[63] It is only admissible in relation to specific legal issues of the kind described, concerning the marketing or sale of products or other things to large groups of people. It is not admissible as to the likely reaction of others (whether expert or not) in relation to the specific facts of, for instance, an insurance case.[64] Such evidence will only be admissible on issues where:

> "the question is not what the private opinion of the individual may be, as to the probable course of his conduct in a particular case, but what in his judgment the general opinion would be amongst those conversant with such matters."[65]

3 Non-professional standards

Expert witnesses may not give evidence as to standards which the judge or lay trier of fact is able to assess. Thus the guilt of criminals, the state of mind of normal persons,[66] the concept of reasonableness and other such issues are not the province of the expert. This is discussed further in Part D below. Some issues may appear to be illuminated by expert evidence in ways which they would not be without it, but if the standard is a lay standard the evidence will usually be inadmissible unless it is on a specific point ancillary to the main issue.[67] The question whether pollution from coking ovens constitutes a nuisance is not to be resolved by asking the opinion of experts who can detect such pollution by the use of sophisticated scientific instruments, because the injury must be "visible to ordinary persons."[68]

However, the nature of the issue before the court may demand the use of expert evidence upon such apparently subjective questions as artistic merit. A court deciding whether a gift of the contents of the donor's own artistic studio was educational and therefore charitable would benefit from expert opinion, because although tastes differed, there was "an

---

[62] *George Ballantine and Son Ltd.* v. *Ballantyne Stewart and Co. Ltd.* [1959] R.P.C. 273 at 280.
[63] *Ibid.*
[64] *Campbell* v. *Rickards* (1883) 5 B. & Ad. 840 at 846.
[65] *Berthon* v. *Loughman* (1817) 2 Stark 258 at 259.
[66] See below Chap. 12.
[67] See *e.g. D.P.P.* v. *A. & B.C. Chewing Gum* [1968] 1 Q.B. 159, discussed below, p. 152.
[68] *Salvin* v. *North Brancepeth Coal Company* (1874) 31 L.T. 154.

accepted canon of taste" of which the court did not take judicial knowledge.[69] In libel proceedings an expert was permitted to give evidence as to what view the Jockey Club would be likely to take of the conduct of one of its members in withdrawing a horse from a race to facilitate an alleged gambling fraud.[69a]

C. HYPOTHETICAL QUESTIONS

Lay witnesses of fact, save in very limited circumstances,[70] may only speak of what they have perceived through their senses. Expert witnesses may of course draw inferences and express opinions, and this will almost always be in part, and often wholly, in respect of facts not perceived by the expert. Such facts will, however they are to be proved, frequently not be agreed, so that asssumptions cannot be made as to how the court will find upon the disputed facts. Many of the questions which are put to experts as to matters of opinion are therefore of necessity hypothetical in form. Whenever an opinion is expressed by an expert, its factual basis must be adduced in examination in chief,[71] whether the factual basis be a fact which is part of that party's case, or one (presumably part of the other party's case) which is hypothetically assumed. The expert witness must not be placed in the position of apparently being invited to comment on the truth or bona fides of a particular witness's evidence,[71a] though he may of course observe that one hypothesis as to the facts is more probable than another, if his expertise is prerequisite to such an opinion. The distinction between the two is sometimes not a simple one, but difficulties can be avoided by clear questioning from the advocate.

Some jurisdictions have specific statutory provisions as to the form in which hypothetical questions must be put.[72] Although no such provisions exist in English law, the court should prevent lines of questioning which appear to give the expert too much freedom to trawl evidence of fact for material in support of his opinion. In *Ferrers' Case*,[73] in which the expert issue was whether the defendant was a lunatic at the time he committed a homicide, the court had heard lengthy evidence from witnesses of fact citing examples of peculiar behaviour at about the time of the offence. Counsel was prevented from asking the medical witnesses the general question whether any and if so which of these circumstances

---

[69] *Re Pinion* [1965] Ch. 85 at 107.
[69a] *Greville v. Chapman* (1844) 5 Q.B. 731.
[70] As to which see Chap. 1, pp. 17–22.
[71] *R. v. Turner* [1975] 1 Q.B. 834 at 840.
[71a] See *Re S. and B. (Minors), The Independent*, June 1, 1990.
[72] *e.g.* United States Federal Rules of Evidence, rr. 703 and 705.
[73] (1790) 19 How.St.Tr. 885.

indicated lunacy.[74] He was however permitted to ask whether lunacy was indicated by specific types of behaviour, such as "quarrelling with friends without cause,"[75] or "drinking coffee hot out of the spout of the pot."[76] The expert was allowed to answer this final inquiry by reference to the particular offender, not merely to lunatics generally, by saying "I should think it one [a symptom of lunacy] in the present case; it is not a general one."[77] Hypothetical questions should therefore be confined to individual items of evidence, and not involve an overview of a range of evidence.

It has been seen that while most facts can be perceived by expert witnesses just as they can by lay witnesses others may require expertise for their observation.[78] Hypothetical questions may, if appropriate, be put to an expert witness in respect of either category of fact.[79] The question of how precise must be the correspondence between the evidence of fact adduced and the hypothetical questions put has not been examined at length in the English cases, though it has received some attention in other jurisdictions, where it has been concluded that some divergence is not necessarily fatal and does not render the evidence thus adduced inadmissible. It has been said to be a question of whether the hypothetical material creates a "fair climate" for the opinions expressed, there being no requirement that the questions put are "precisely consonant" with the evidence of fact.[80] This approach is made necessary by taking a realistic view of the evidence of fact often adduced in court. Thus in an American case:

> "there was some evidence to support every hypothetical question to which objection was made. Such evidence was not always complete, was sometimes hazy as to time, distance and other vital words, but in general, furnished a fair climate for the consideration of the views of the expert witnesses."[81]

This does not entail that advocates are thereby necessarily entitled to diverge from existing evidence of fact in putting their hypothetical questions. It has been said in an Australian decision that:

> "discrepancies may be fatal, in some cases even slight discrepancies may be fatal; in other cases even broad departures are not likely to affect the force of the expert opinion."[82]

---

[74] (1790) 19 How. St. Tr. 885.
[75] *Ibid.*
[76] *Ibid.*
[77] *Ibid.*
[78] Chap. 1, p. 9. See too *Salvin* v. *North Brancepeth Coal Co.*, above n. 68.
[79] See *Beckwith* v. *Sydebotham*, above n. 16; *R.* v. *Mason*, above n. 15.
[80] *Paric* v. *John Holland Constructions Pty. Ltd.* [1984] 2 N.S.W.L.R. 505 at 509–510.
[81] *Culver* v. *Sekulich* (1959) 80 Wyoming 437 at 458.
[82] *Paric* v. *John Holland Constructions Pty. Ltd.* above n. 80, at 510.

Whether this represents the law in this country is unclear. The approach appears to be an acceptable and helpful one if three points are made. First, no party should, without more, diverge in its hypothetical questions to an expert from the evidence of fact. Such a course should always be justified by elements in the evidence of fact (such as uncertainty or impression) which necessitate such a departure. Secondly, whether such a course is proper will also always depend upon whether the expert opinion which relies upon it is undermined by any such discrepancy, which is a question to be decided on the facts of the particular case. Thirdly, expert opinion is only admissible if it is relevant to matters in issue. If it is founded upon facts which have not been or will not be even approximately proved it should not be given.

Hypothetical questions may be put in particular forms for particular purposes. A form frequently used in relation to forensic evidence, though by no means confined thereto, is to ask whether certain forensic findings are consistent with particular hypothetical facts.[83] This is most useful where the expert evidence, while not indicating only one possible set of facts, does nonetheless indicate a limited number of such sets, of which that set put hypothetically is one. This is often, though imprecise, forensically significant. While, as has been seen, an expert witness may not express an opinion as to whether a witness of fact is telling the truth, he may by means of hypothetical assumptions give evidence which may be used to impugn the credibility of a witness of fact. So where a defendant said that he had originally forgotten events at the time of the alleged offence, but that later, on driving past the scene, he recollected events in his favour, a psychiatrist was permitted to state that such a process did not conform to any known pattern of hysterical amnesia.[84] He was not permitted to offer the opinion, however, that the evidence was a fabrication even though this was the inevitable inference from his evidence. In most cases concerning professional practice, an expert may not hypothesise as to how he personally would have acted in particular circumstances, but only as to what professionals generally, or a significant group of competent professionals, would probably have done.[85] The hypothetical question is frequently the only way of adducing expert evidence as to a person's state of mind at the time of performing a particular act, such as committing an alleged offence,[86] or making a will.[87] Even where a doctor has been absent from court, thereby having had no chance to observe an alleged offender whose state of mind is in issue, nor

---

[83] *R. v. Smith* (1915) 31 T.L.R. 617 at 618.
[84] *R. v. Eades* [1972] Crim. L.R. 99.
[85] *Hatch v. Lewis* (1861) 2 F. & F. 467 at 475; *Berthon v. Loughman*, above n. 45. See also above, pp. 141–144.
[86] See Chap. 12, pp. 229–235.
[87] See Chap. 12, pp. 245–246.

THE FORM AND CONTENT OF EXPERT EVIDENCE

to listen to the evidence of witnesses of fact who observed the offender at the material time, he may have such matters put to him hypothetically,[88] and any deficiencies in the resulting opinion go to weight not admissibility.[89]

D. QUESTIONS ON AN ULTIMATE ISSUE

It has historically been the rule at common law, in both civil and criminal proceedings, that no witness may give evidence on an ultimate issue in the case. The rule has, however, always suffered from the difficulty of defining an ultimate issue,[90] and this has been reflected in the tendency of the courts, often for very good practical reasons, either to ignore it altogether, or to permit witnesses to give answers in careful words which appear to avoid being caught by the exclusion, though their true effect is to offend against the rule.[91] Expert evidence of opinion is particularly susceptible to such difficulties, because it involves that mental process of inference from facts which constitutes the usual function of the courts. There is now express statutory provision for the giving of expert evidence upon an ultimate issue, in sections 3(1) and (3) of the Civil Evidence Act 1972. This section is confined however to civil proceedings, and despite suggestions that the criminal courts should become subject to similar provisions,[92] this has not yet occurred. Even in respect of civil cases, however, as will be seen, the ramifications of the old common law rule cannot be entirely ignored.

1 Civil proceedings: statute

Section 3 of the Civil Evidence Act 1972 provides that:

> "(1) Subject to any rules of court made in pursuance of Part I of the Civil Evidence Act 1968 or this Act, where a person is called as a witness in any civil proceedings, his opinion on any relevant matter on which he is qualified to give expert evidence shall be admissible in evidence.
>
> (3) In this section "relevant matter" includes an issue in the proceedings in question."

---

[88] *R. v. Fisher* [1961] O.W.N. 94.
[89] *Ibid.*, at 97.
[90] *Cross on Evidence* suggests abandoning any such definition altogether (pp. 445–6).
[91] There have been occasional judicial attempts to stem the tide: see *Graphic Arts Co. v. Hunters Ltd.* (1910) 27 R.P.C. 677 at 687.
[92] See Criminal Law Revision Committee, 11th report, Cmnd. 4491 (1972), para. 64.

The Act does however additionally provide by section 5(3) that:

> "Nothing in this Act shall prejudice—
> (a) any power of a court, in any civil proceedings, to exclude evidence (whether by preventing questions from being put or otherwise) at its discretion."

Both the term "relevant matter" in section 3(1) and the general discretion preserved by section 5(3) ensure that the effect of the Act is not to permit a party to call expert evidence on an ultimate issue without more. It must be justified by being relevant. This was a clear concern of the Law Reform Committee in its seventeenth Report,[93] which recommended that expert evidence should not be held inadmissible "upon the ground only"[94] that it is adduced in relation to an issue in the proceedings.

The opinion of an expert will often be inadmissible not because it is upon an ultimate issue, but because it is in any event irrelevant, having little or no probative value. It will have a low probative value in particular if it concerns an issue, as many ultimate issues do, which the trier of fact is as capable of deciding as an expert. Thus although the ultimate issue rule itself is abolished, one of its traditional justifications in principle remains, namely that evidence is inadmissible if it tends to usurp the function of the tribunal. This it will not do, however, if the issue in question contains an element which requires expertise for its comprehension or reasoning,[95] in which event section 3 permits expert evidence to be given. Thus section 3 does not, it is suggested, open wide a door previously closed or left only slightly ajar by the common law. It simply permits otherwise admissible expert evidence as to specialist matters not to be denied to the court merely because it trespasses upon an ultimate issue in the case.

2 Criminal proceedings

The Criminal Law Revision Committee[96] has expressed the view that the practice of the criminal courts should be identical to that introduced in the civil courts by section 3 of the Civil Evidence Act 1972.[97] It recommended thus both because it felt that principle was now far behind practice in that the ultimate issue rule for expert witnesses was often simply ignored, and because it thought it to be evident that "this is a subject on

---

[93] Cmnd. 4889 (1970).
[94] *Ibid.*, at para 63.
[95] *Buckley v. Rice Thomas* (1554) 1 Plowd. 118.
[96] 11th Report, Cmnd. 4991 (1972).
[97] Others have adopted a similar position. See *e.g.* J. D. Jackson, "The Ultimate Issue Rule: One Rule Too Many" [1984] Crim. L.R. 75.

which it is desirable that the law in the two kinds of proceedings should be in accord."[98] It has further taken the view that "it would now probably be held that the prohibition no longer exists."[99] The decision in *D.P.P. v. A.& B.C. Chewing Gum*[1] was cited in support of this proposition. The recommended statutory changes have not however been introduced although the practice of many criminal courts could almost be said to assume that they have. The dangers of allowing an expert witness to usurp the court's function are correctly perceived as more immediate in criminal cases, in spite of the control of the judge over what is put before, and considered by, the jury.

The reality of the practice in the criminal courts was described by Lord Parker C.J. in *D.P.P. v. A. & B.C. Chewing Gum*[2] as follows:

> "with the advance of science more and more inroads have been made into the old common law principles. Those who practise in the criminal courts see every day cases of experts being called on the question of diminished responsibility, and although technically the final question 'Do you think he was suffering from diminished responsibility?' is strictly inadmissible, it is allowed time and time again without any objection. No doubt when dealing with the effect of certain things on the mind science may still be less exact than evidence as to what effect some particular thing will have upon the body, but that, as it seems to me, is purely a question of weight."[3]

Lord Parker C.J. did not however express this view merely as an ex post facto recognition of a practice which could not be reversed. He admitted expert evidence as to the effect of the allegedly obscene material in the case upon different age groups of children on the broad ground that:

> "any jury and any justices need any help they can get, information which they may not have."[4]

It is important too to note that in the judge's opinion the common law may indeed be shaped by progress made in the scientific world, and that general rules which purport to deny such specific developments are often either ignored by the lower courts, or circumvented on other grounds.

The position at common law was for a long period expressed in *R. v. Wright*,[5] in which it was held that a medical witness, giving evidence as to the sanity of the defendant when committing an offence, might not

---

[98] Above n. 96, para. 266. This latter justification was not further explained.
[99] *Ibid.*, para. 268.
[1] [1968] 1 Q.B. 159.
[2] *Ibid.*
[3] *Ibid.*, at 164.
[4] *Ibid.*, at 165.
[5] (1821) Russ. & Ry. 456.

express an opinion as to whether the particular facts before the court constituted an act of insanity. He could however state what types of behaviour demonstrated insanity in persons generally, from which the jury could draw inferences in the particular case.[6]

There is little doubt however that such a distinction is not now rigorously observed, and given that expert evidence of this kind is to be put before a jury, it may be suspected that the often casuistic distinction between the general and the particular is either ignored by juries, or seen as a distinction of form rather than substance. It has been suggested too that some defences in criminal proceedings can in effect only be raised by adducing expert evidence, and that:

> "it would put an insuperable difficulty in the way of the defence whenever they were trying to establish insanity"[7]

if such evidence were to be excluded by an ultimate issue or other analogous rule.

3 Application of the rule

Human nature Expert evidence is inadmissible on questions which primarily consist of an assessment of human nature, in general and without abnormality.[8] Thus in passing-off and trademark cases, where the issue for the court to determine is frequently the effect of a particular form of visual or other representation upon prospective purchasers, evidence has not generally been admissible as to whether such a person would be likely to be deceived, for it is not probative of the issue to call a witness:

> "to give what is in truth expert evidence as to human nature, because what they are asked in this form of question is, not what would happen to them individually, but what they think the rest of the world would suppose or believe."[9]

These are matters which are "incapable of scientific proof",[10] as to which no expertise is likely to be of real assistance to the court, quite apart from any ultimate issue which they may involve. It has been said that there is no such thing as an expert in human nature.[11] This may be unduly restrictive, as psychological evidence is now admitted in limited circum

---

[6] (1821) Russ. & Ry. 456 at 457–458.
[7] *R. v. Holmes* [1953] 1 W.L.R. 686 at 688, *per* Lord Goddard. See also pp. 233–235.
[8] See below, Chap. 12.
[9] *Bourne v. Swan & Edgar Ltd.* [1903] 1 Ch. 211 at 224. See also *Payton v. Snelling* [1901] A.C. 308.
[10] *R. v. Byrne* (1960) 44 Cr.App.R. 246 at 258.
[11] *Royal Warrant Holders Association v. Edward Deane and Beal Ltd.* [1912] 1 Ch. 10.

stances, but indicates the general disposition of the courts, even now, towards this kind of evidence.

Lay standards Standards which are the very question for the court to decide are not to be subject to expert evidence, unless there is a clear specialist aspect to it which is indivisible from the assessment of the standard itself. So where the issue was whether a collision at sea could have been avoided with the exercise of proper care, a nautical witness was permitted to answer because it was "a question having reference to a matter of science and opinion."[12] In *D.P.P.* v. *A & B. C. Chewing Gum*,[13] however, a distinction was drawn between questions as to the effect which allegedly obscene literature would have on particular age groups of young children, and the question whether such literature would "tend to deprave and corrupt" such children. The latter, final question was one "entirely for the justices."[14] Similarly, an analyst was wrongly permitted to give evidence as to whether a bottle label was "calculated to mislead" about its contents, because the question is whether the general public would be misled, as to which he has no particular expertise.[15] It has been said however that, while the court must form its own standard of quality in judging whether a "cordial" drink is properly so described, it may receive the expert evidence of an analyst about its actual contents.[16]

Questions of reasonableness are always for the court. There may however be limited circumstances in which expert evidence as to specific practices may assist with the decision. So where the court is considering whether a clause in a contract of employment is in restraint of trade, it may receive expert evidence as to the precautions employers in the field customarily take to protect themselves from injury by a departing employee.[17]

Credibility of witnesses An expert may not in general give evidence as to whether a witness is, in his or her opinion, telling the truth. This is clearly for the court. A psychiatric social worker has however been said to be permitted to state whether a witness's account of events was credible, as part of her opinion as to that person's general psychiatric state, though not to go the small step further and to express an opinion as to whether the witness is telling the truth as to particular fact.[18]

---

[12] *Fenwick* v. *Bell* (1844) 1 C. & K. 312.
[13] [1968] 1 Q.B. 159.
[14] *Ibid.*, at 164
[15] *Concentrated Foods* v. *Champ* [1944] 1 K.B. 342 at 350.
[16] *Broughton* v. *Whittaker* [1944] 1 K.B. 269; but see *Collins* v. *Barking Corporation* [1943] K.B. 419.
[17] *Haynes* v. *Doman* [1899] 2 Ch. 13 at 24.
[18] *Re S. & B. (Minors), The Independent*, June 1, 1990.

E. THE MEANING OF WORDS

The great majority of words or phrases from which the courts are required to elicit a meaning are either those with a specific legal meaning, or general words in common usage. In the case of the former a legal tribunal, or lay tribunal advised by judge or justices' clerk, must clearly identify the meaning, and where the latter are concerned it is the task of the court as the trier of fact to arrive at its own conclusion, unassisted by evidence, save that dictionaries may be employed if they assist.[19] In other circumstances, however, it may appear to be of benefit to call an expert witness as to meaning, or as is more likely to ask an expert, already giving evidence as to other matters in the case, to express a view on meaning in the light of his experience and skill. Save in limited and specific circumstances, though, an expert's views are inadmissible and should not be canvassed. In *Lovell and Christmas* v. *Wall*,[20] Cozens-Hardy M.R. identified these circumstances thus:

> "If a document is in a foreign language, you may have an interpreter. If it contains technical terms, an expert may explain them. If, according to the custom of a trade or the usage of the market, a word has acquired a secondary meaning, evidence may be given to prove it."[21]

This is a succint summary of the position, but somewhat too simplistic as a complete statement of the law, which must be described by reference to the different contexts in which contentious words and phrases may be found.

1 Statute

Statutes are of course in general to be construed upon legal principles without the assistance of evidence, expert or otherwise. Where statutory words have a clear ordinary meaning, but can also be given a different technical meaning, the court will not admit expert evidence.[22] However certain statutes do contain technical words from a particular non-legal area of expertise. It is only if the court is satisfied that such expertise is essential for its construction, or its construction by reference to the technical subject-matter of the case, that evidence will be admitted.[23] So

---

[19] This is by way of judicial notice, however: see Chap. 8, p. 181.
[20] (1911) 104 L.T. 85.
[21] *Ibid.*
[22] *Camden* v. *I.R.C.* [1914] 1 K.B. 641 at 648.
[23] *London and North-East Railway* v. *Berriman* [1946] A.C. 278 at 294.

expert evidence was admitted as to whether cannabis leaves were part of the "flowering and fruiting tops"[24] of the plant.[25] The principle is very limited, and has been regarded as too narrow to permit engineers to assist in the interpretation of certain statutory words in relation to a statutory railway plan.[26]

2 Legal documents

Legal documents which come before the court for construction, usually contracts or deeds, are subject to the same general rule as statutes, namely that their meaning in law is a matter for lawyers, and not therefore to be subject to expert evidence. There are however three circumstances in which expert evidence may, or arguably may, be adduced on matters of construction. First, where it is alleged that there is a custom in a particular trade that words have a particular contractual meaning, evidence of those conversant with trade usage may be adduced, for instance to prove that the phrase "1,000 rabbits" was intended to mean 1,200.[27] Experts from the colonial broking trade were permitted to give evidence that the word "vermicelli" contractually denoted "sound vermicelli" in the trade.[28] However counsel's questioning of such witnesses should proceed step by step, first laying the foundation for the question as to meaning by establishing that there is a customary usage in the trade, because the effect of the evidence is to alter the meaning of a written document.[29]

Secondly, where words are clearly of a technical nature which the court would not understand without assistance, expert evidence may be adduced. Items bequeathed in his will by a statuary bore obscure and specialist names, and expert assistance as to their meanings was permitted.[30] The insurance expression "perils of the seas" can however be interpreted unassisted, and an expert's opinion as to liquid loss from casks on a ship must be confined to the actual cause of the loss, and should not extend to whether such loss was covered by the words of the insurance policy.[31] Some expressions, though consisting of words used in ordinary parlance, may only be comprehensible in context by reference to particular geographical or other circumstances. Expert evidence was therefore admitted in relation to the words "in turn to deliver" in a charterparty, because in context they bore no obvious meaning without knowledge of

---

[24] Misuse of Drugs Act 1971, s.37.
[25] *Harding* v. *Hayes* [1974] Crim. L.R. 713.
[26] *Dowling* v. *Pontypool Co.* (1874) L.R. 18 Eq. 714.
[27] *Lovell and Christmas Ltd.* v. *Wall*, above n. 20, at 88.
[28] *Curtis* v. *Peek* (1864) 13 W.R. 230.
[29] *Ibid.*
[30] *Goblet* v. *Beechey* (1829) 3 Sim. 24.
[31] *Crofts* v. *Marshall* (1836) 7 C. & P. 597, N.P.

the regulations and practice of the particular port concerned, in this case Algiers.[32]

There is a third category of circumstances in which the precise extent of the principle is difficult to state. This is where words carry an ordinary meaning which the court can elucidate unassisted, but one party asserts that although no trade custom (in the legal sense) is advanced, the words were intended to bear a special meaning.[33] It has been said that contracts are unlike statutes in sometimes requiring evidence of a "technical meaning."[34]

In *Myers* v. *Sarl*,[35] which concerned the construction of a contract, the court admitted expert evidence to prove a special meaning, and took the view that where such a meaning was established, this was prima facie what the parties intended, unless the document as a whole suggested otherwise.[36] The courts will however not be slow to decide from the character of a word that it could not have been intended in any special sense, and that it presents no difficulties of construction demanding evidence. The expression "showground" in a trust document was regarded as clearly being a word of "normal parlance" and "not a term of art requiring expert assistance."[37] The evidence of an insurance expert was not admitted to show the "practical difficulties" which arose from insurance liability imposed by the clear words of a term in the RIBA form of building contract.[38] It was asserted that these difficulties tended to show that the words could not have been intended to impose liability thus. The court expressed the view *obiter* that such evidence could only, and then only arguably, be admissible if there was a "latent ambiguity" in the use of a word "in its context."[39]

Patent specifications   There is a considerable body of law on the questions whether and to what extent expert evidence may be adduced as to the meaning of technical and other terms in the specification. This is fully discussed in Chapter 21.

Foreign legal documents   Expert witnesses may be called to assist the court where foreign legal documents are in issue. They may translate, explain the meaning of terms of art, assist with any special principles of law and advise the court as to the rules of construction which would be

---

[32] *Robertson* v. *Jackson* (1845) 2 C.B. 412.
[33] See *Crosfield* v. *Techno-Chemical Laboratories* (1913) 29 T.L.R. 378 at 379.
[34] *Camden* v. *I.R.C.* [1914] 1 K.B. 641.
[35] (1860) 3 E. & E. 306.
[36] *Ibid.*, at 320.
[37] *Brisbane City Council* v. *Queensland* [1978] 3 W.L.R. 299 at 306, P.C.
[38] *Gold* v. *Patman and Fotheringham* [1958] 1 W.L.R. 697.
[39] *Ibid.*, at 704.

employed in the courts of the relevant country.[40] They may not however assist with the actual construction of the document.[41] The distinction may be a somewhat casuistic one, as they may assist with the meaning of technical legal terms, for example in a French will,[42] and this may extend to evidence given:

> "in order to express to an English mind the meaning which is conveyed to a Portuguese mind by the words used,"[43]

where such words are of a technical kind, whether legal or scientific. Clearly this could on occasion in effect dispose of the matter in issue upon the document. What the expert may clearly not do is to construe the document in its entirety, or any entire provision within it, unless this is composed entirely of technical matters:

> "it is for the court to construe the document, having fortified itself with the permissible evidence."[44]

So although the court may be assisted as to French "rules of construction" and "technical terms," such assistance must not extend to opinion "as to its meaning after those aids have been taken into account."[45]

3 Non-legal statements

Where documents come before the court which are not subject to legal principles of construction, expert evidence is in general admissible as to special meanings understood by those in a particular field or trade. So evidence was permitted to show that a letter stating that a ship would sail from St. Domingo in October would be understood in the relevant commercial field to mean not before October 25.[46] In criminal proceedings, where a question of intention turns upon a special meaning understood by the writer and recipient of a threatening letter, evidence as to the special meaning may be adduced.[47] The same could no doubt apply to oral statements.

F. CONTRACT

The circumstances in which expert evidence may assist in the construction of a contract are limited. A contract is a legal document, or state-

---

[40] *Duchess Di Sora* v. *Phillips* (1863) 10 H.L.C. 624.
[41] *Ibid.* See also *The Stearine* (1864) 17 C.B. (N.S.) 56.
[42] *Re Cliff's Trusts* [1892] 2 Ch. 229 at 232.
[43] *Chatenay* v. *Brazilian Submarine Telegraph Co.* [1891] 1 Q.B. 79 at 85.
[44] *Rouyer Guillet et Compagnie* v. *Rouyer Guillet and Company* [1949] 1 All E.R. 244 n.
[45] *Ibid.*
[46] *Chaurand* v. *Angerstein* (1791) Peake 61.
[47] See *R.* v. *Hendy* (1850) 4 Cox C.C. 243 (not concerned with expert evidence).

ment, which it is for the judge to interpret. Indeed the circumstances in which extraneous evidence of any kind is admissible are few, as the agreement must in general stand on its own as evidence of the intention of the parties. The principal respects in which expert evidence in relation to meaning may be adduced are where a customary meaning within a particular market or trade is alleged, and where the court wishes to place itself in the "factual matrix" of the parties. These are discussed below. In addition the court may in respect of particular forms of contract require expert evidence as to the meaning of a given general expression on the facts of the particular case, though it will usually attempt to hear the evidence in such a way as to prevent the witness from expressing a view of a specific legal meaning. Questions frequently arise where insurance contracts are concerned, about what should be disclosed by the insured at the time of insurance. There is no settled rule as to when expert evidence must or may be called as to the materiality of a particular fact, and of course the court may conclude that a fact is obviously material without assistance. This is so *a fortiori* where an arbitrator, who probably has relevant expertise, is concerned.[48] While however expert evidence may be called as to materiality, the general practice of underwriters cannot affect a specific statutory duty.[49]

1 Custom

Evidence of those who practise in a particular trade or market may be adduced to prove a special meaning for words used in a contract. This may not be done however where the customary meaning advanced conflicts with other express words of the agreement.[50] The custom must be certain and notorious, and not in the circumstances unreasonable.[51] Custom may also be used to add words or terms to a contract where it is shown on evidence that this is general within the trade or market.[52] There are large numbers of reported cases dealing with the particular circumstances in which customary meanings may be advanced, and these substantive questions of contract law are discussed in the more comprehensive works on the law of contract. The extent to which judicial notice of a custom may be taken without evidence is discussed in Chapter 1.[53]

---

[48] *Locker and Woolf Ltd.* v. *Western Australian Insurance Co. Ltd.* (1935) 153 L.T. 334.
[49] *Thames and Mersey Marine Insurance Co.* v. *Gunford Ship Co.* [1911] A.C. 529 at 538–539.
[50] *Yates* v. *Pym* (1816) 6 Taunt 446; *Westcott* v. *Hahn* [1918] 1 K.B. 495. The witness may not have to practice in the particular market: see *Adams* v. *Peters* (1849) 2 Car. & Kir. 723.
[51] *Devonald* v. *Rosser* [1906] 2 K.B. 728.
[52] *Syers* v. *Jonas* (1848) 2 Exch. 111; *Produce Brokers Co. Ltd.* v. *Olympic Oil & Cane Co. Ltd.* [1916] 1 A.C. 314.
[53] At pp. 25–26.

2 Factual matrix

There is no doubt of the admissibility of expert evidence where a particular custom consistent with the agreement is alleged. The court may, however, in less easily defined circumstances, admit evidence from those with experience of the particular factual matrix[54] within which the parties were operating at the time they made the contract. This must however be distinguished from evidence of the parties' negotiations or intentions, which:

> "ought not to be received, and evidence should be restricted to evidence of the factual background known to the parties at or before the date of the contract, including evidence of the 'genesis' and objectively the 'aim' of the transaction."[55]

There is no clear guidance as to when the courts should admit such evidence, though it appears clear that it will usually be in commercial circumstances,[56] and that it is not limited to the analysis of particular terms, but may be employed in relation to whether there was an intention to create legal relations,[57] in other words as to whether a contract existed at all at a particular time. Lord Denning has defined the doctrine in somewhat loose terms,[58] but it is submitted that it is Lord Wilberforce's approach which is most authoritative, as developed in *Prenn* v. *Simmonds*[59] and *Reardon Smith Line* v. *Yngvar Hanson Tangen*.[60] He explained the need for such evidence, in the latter case, as follows:

> "When one speaks of the intention of the parties to the contract, one is speaking objectively—the parties cannot themselves give direct evidence of what their intention was—and what must be ascertained is what is to be taken as the intention which reasonable people would have had if placed in the situation of the parties."[61]

Lord Wilberforce then continued to explain the proper approach of the court to the use of such evidence:

> "what the court must do must be to place itself in thought in the same factual matrix as that in which the parties were . . . in the

---

[54] *Reardon Smith Line Ltd.* v. *Yngvar Hansen Tangen* [1976] 1 W.L.R. 989.
[55] *Prenn* v. *Simmonds* [1971] 1 W.L.R. 1381 at 1385, *per* Lord Wilberforce.
[56] *Thoresen* v. *Weymouth Portland Borough Council* [1977] 2 Lloyd's Rep. 614. As to the insurance market, see *Insurance Company of Pennsylvania* v. *Grand Union Ins. Co.*, [1990] 2 Lloyd's Rep. 208 at 222–223.
[57] *Thoresen* v. *Weymouth Portland B.C.*, above n. 56.
[58] *Staffordshire Area Health Authority* v. *Staffordshire Waterworks Co.* [1978] 1 W.L.R. 1395.
[59] Above n. 55.
[60] Above n. 54.
[61] *Ibid.*, at 996.

search for the relevant background; there may be facts which form part of the circumstances in which the parties contract in which one, or both, may take no particular interest, their minds being addressed to or concentrated on other facts so that if asked they would assert that they did not have these facts in the forefront of their mind, but that will not prevent those facts from forming part of an objective setting in which the contract is to be construed."[62]

The witness becomes therefore a kind of contextual officious bystander, informing the court of commercial facts which the parties would have declared obvious if their minds had been addressed to them at the time. When considering the factual matrix, however, it is inappropriate to divide the contract into different limbs, as the aim is to identify the single "obvious commercial purpose" of the entire agreement.[63] Furthermore, although the reception of such evidence must be properly limited, the courts will not artificially distinguish "reasoning from result," and evidence should be heard as to the entire factual context.[64]

---

[62] *Reardon Smith Line Ltd.* v. *Yngvar Hansen Tangen* [1976] 1 W.L.R. 989 at 997.
[63] *Hyundai Co. Ltd.* v. *Pournaras* [1978] 2 Lloyd's Rep. 502 at 506, *per* Roskill L.J.
[64] *Insurance Company of Pennsylvania* v. *Grand Union Insurance Co.*, above n. 56.

CHAPTER 8

Hearsay

In order for expert evidence to be adduced to its full beneficial extent, and to avoid a whole series of fictions about how experts formulate their opinions, it is necessary for a very particular approach to the hearsay rules to be adopted in so far as they bisect with the law of expert evidence. The use of hearsay by experts occurs both at an explicit level, at which particular hearsay sources are specifically referred to or produced in evidence, and at an implicit level, at which it is assumed that many of the expert's views will be informed by knowledge gained externally to the case, and in particular from the books, articles, papers and statistics through which the learning of a specialist discipline is disseminated among its members. There are statutory provisions in relation to experts for circumstances in which a party wishes to adduce an expert's written statement, but asserts that the expert himself cannot or should not be called as a witness. These are discussed in Chapter 2. The evidence must always be relayed to the court through the agency of an expert, whether in written form under the rules, or orally. A lay witness should not be asked questions which he can only answer by consulting an expert and repeating his opinion.[1]

It has long been recognised that the fact that an opinion is expressed by an expert lends no additional weight to any facts upon which it is based if he has no direct knowledge of those facts:

> "the cautious rules by which the rejection of evidence is determined, affect as well the most weighty opinions, as the most worthless gossip, unless vouched by the indispensable sanction of an oath; a certain few and well-known cases only excepted."[1a]

Expert witnesses can of course give direct evidence of fact. They may also give such evidence of admissible hearsay as may lay witnesses. In so far, however, as they give evidence of what would if they were not expert witnesses be inadmissible hearsay, they do not prove it as a fact although it may, as a constituent part of their opinion, have probative value. This is

---

[1] *Rofe* v. *Kevorkian* [1936] 2 All E.R. 1334
[1a] *Wright* v. *Doe. d. Tatham* (1838) 4 Bing. N.C. 489 at 509.

clear from the decisions in *H. v. Schering Chemicals Ltd.*[2] and *English Exporters (London) Ltd. v. Eldonwall Ltd.*[3]

A. HEARSAY EVIDENCE OF FACT

1 Facts in issue

In a number of circumstances an expert witness may need to give evidence of fact, not perceived by him, which is itself in issue in the proceedings, or which has been obtained specifically for the proceedings. It is necessary, however, for the evidence of fact to be the prerequisite for the expression of an expert opinion, or the expert analysis upon which an opinion can be based. The witness may not, simply because he is an expert, give evidence as to hearsay matters which would be inadmissible coming from a lay witness, unless it has this nexus with expert opinion evidence. The hearsay evidence itself may or may not be in the nature of expert evidence. However the fact that a person with expertise gave the expert witness the information makes it no more admissible to prove the fact itself.[4] Facts must always be proved by original evidence:

> "where an expert relies on the existence or non-existence of some fact which is basic to the question on which he is asked to express his opinion, that fact must be proved by admissible evidence."[5]

In *R. v. Abadom*[6] it was held that persons who had given an expert witness information as to such basic facts must themselves be called as witnesses, whether or not they were experts.[7] It is necessary for such facts to be established at the outset:

> "counsel calling an expert should in examination in chief ask his witness to state the facts upon which his opinion is based. It is wrong to leave the other side to elicit the facts by cross-examination."[8]

Scientific teamwork It is recognised that much laboratory work, for example providing chemical analysis of blood and urine samples taken in connection with drink-driving offences, is in reality performed with the participation of a number of scientists, who may have different roles on a permanent basis, or may perform the same functions as each other from

---

[2] [1983] 1 W.L.R. 143.
[3] [1973] Ch. 415.
[4] *R. v. Turner* [1975] Q.B. 834. An accountant witness cannot give evidence as to the contents of account books he has studied, merely because they were prepared by an accountant: they must be produced and proved (*Johnson v. Kershaw* (1847) 1 De G.E. Sm. 260).
[5] *R. v. Abadom* [1983] 1 W.L.R. 126 at 131.
[6] *Ibid.*
[7] *Ibid.*
[8] *R. v. Turner*, above n. 4, at 840.

time to time. Although it is always open to the court to be evidentially dissatisfied as to such arrangements in the particular case, the court will hear expert evidence from an analyst who did not himself perform all the constituent parts of the analysis, but supervised assistants who did.[9] It is probably necessary however that the analyst who attends court is himself able to understand and carry out those parts of the analysis which he did not in fact perform. Experts may not, as has been observed, simply tell the court what someone else told them, merely because they are both in fact experts.[10]

Doctors and patients Much of a doctor's diagnosis and prognosis is based not only upon what he observes, but also upon what he is told by a patient, or by an individual he is examining for the purposes of preparing a medical report. If, however, those facts are contested, they are not established as facts merely by the doctor's evidence of what he was told. In R. v. Turner[11] Lawton L.J. expressed the view that:

> "it is not for this court to instruct psychiatrists how to draft their reports, but those who call psychiatrists as witnesses should remember that the facts upon which they base their opinions must be proved by admissible evidence. This elementary principle is frequently overlooked."[12]

As to the establishment of the basic facts, therefore, the doctor has no advantage over the lay witness:

> "hearsay evidence does not become admissible to prove facts because the person who proposes to give it is a physician."[13]

The court will usually hear such hearsay evidence, if it is the basis of the expert's opinion. However, if the facts are disputed, and not proved by admissible original evidence, the court will give little weight to them,[14] and therefore probably to the opinion itself.[15] In R. v. Bradshaw [15a] Lord Lane L.C.J. expressed the following view:

> "if the doctor's opinion is based entirely on hearsay and is not sup-

---

[9] *Stone & Sons* v. *Pugh* [1949] 1 K.B. 240; *R.* v. *Kershberg* (1976) R.T.R. 526. See also *English Exporters (U.K.) Ltd.* v. *Eldonwall Ltd.* [1973] 2 W.L.R. 435 at 439. As to use by an expert of comparison with results obtained by a colleague on the subject-matter of the proceedings, see *R.* v. *Tate* [1977] R.T.R. 17.
[10] *R.* v. *Abadom* [1983] 1 W.L.R. 126 at 131.
[11] [1975] Q.B. 834.
[12] *Ibid.*, at 840. See too the Canadian case of *R.* v. *Abbey* (1982) 138 D.L.R. 202, in which a psychiatrist's evidence of what the defendant said was ruled inadmissible because the defendant elected not to give evidence at all.
[13] *Ramsay* v. *Watson* (1961) 108 C.L.R. 643 at 649.
[14] *Ibid.*, at 649.
[15] *R.* v. *Turner*, above n. 4, at 840.
[15a] (1985) 82 Cr.App.R. 79 at 83.

ported by direct evidence the judge will be justified in telling the jury that the defendant's case (if that is so) is based upon a flimsy or non-existent foundation and that they should reach their conclusion bearing that in mind."

Furthermore, Lord Lane indicated that it was entirely acceptable for the judge to tell the jury that the defendant could have given such evidence if he had chosen to. The opinion would though nonetheless be admissible.[15b] A doctor may always however give evidence of what, for instance, a psychiatric patient said, if it is part of the behaviour the psychiatrist is observing, and evidence of the state of mind of the patient. This is so on ordinary evidential principles because the expert is not purporting to prove that what the patient said was true.[16]

The courts will hear such evidence from psychiatrists even though the diagnosis is different from the condition for which a defendant thought he was being examined. A defendant who ran the defence of automatism to a murder charge was seen by psychiatrists who, partially on the basis of what he said to them, concluded that there was no evidence of automatism, but that there were signs of diminished responsibility. This was not unfair, because the defendant knew that he was being examined for some abnormality of mind, and both conditions were such.[17] It has been held that doctors may adduce evidence of contemporaneous statements as to their state of health as part of the *res gestae*.[18] This must, however, be contemporaneous, and not consist of an account of how, some time previously, the condition was contracted.[19] There may be circumstances in which the contrary applies, and the patient may give evidence of what the doctor said, though these will be limited.[20] Furthermore the patient will always be permitted to confirm or deny what the doctor alleges the patient said.[21]

Evidence of an expert as to what a defendant or witness said while under the influence of hypnosis or a truth drug is not generally admissible, and this is discussed further in Chapter 12. One of the objections to such evidence is that it may offend against the rule prohibiting self-serving statements.[21a]

Surveys conducted for the proceedings It is recognised that in certain types of case, particularly concerning patents, copywright, passing-off

---

[15b] *Ibid.*
[16] *Subramanian* v. *Public Prosecutor* [1956] 1 W.L.R. 965. See also *R.* v. *Bradshaw* [1985] Crim.L.R. 733, and the discussion of psychiatrists' evidence in Chap. 12, pp. 232–233.
[17] *R.* v. *(Stanley) Smith* (1979) 69 Cr.App.R. 378.
[18] *Aveson* v. *Kinnaird* (1806) 6 East. 188.
[19] *Amys* v. *Barton* [1912] 1 K.B. 40.
[20] *Tickle* v. *Tickle* [1968] 2 All E.R. 154 at 158.
[21] *R.* v. *(Stanley) Smith*, above n. 17.
[21a] See *Fennell* v. *Jerome Property Maintenance Ltd.*, *The Times*, November 26, 1986.

and others with an economic element, the opinion of a cross-section, or particular but large group, of the public is a fact in issue in the proceedings. The immense practical and financial difficulties of insisting upon all such persons giving original evidence as witnesses have resulted in an acceptance that hearsay survey evidence may be given to the court, so long as a competent expert can confirm and explain how the results were obtained.[22]

It has been held that evidence of this kind is not in fact hearsay. In *Customglass Boats Ltd. v. Salthouse Brothers Ltd.*.[23] a New Zealand passing-off action, Mahon J. took the view that such evidence is admissible:

> "as proving an external fact, namely, that a designated opinion is held by the public or a class of the public, this not being a matter of hearsay at all."[24]

This dictum has since been supported by Falconer J. in *Lego System Actieselskab v. Lego M. Lemelstrich Ltd.*,[25] where he stated that such evidence:

> "is not hearsay at all, but is evidence proving an external fact, namely that a particular opinion was held by the public or a class of the public."[26]

It is submitted however that this is not the case. The evidence proves that a particular opinion was expressed by the sample, not that it held such an opinion. This distinction was observed by King J. in an Australian decision, *Mobil Oil Corporation v. Registrar of Trade Marks*[27]:

> "all that such evidence ... can prove is that certain opinions were expressed by the individual persons interviewed."[28]

Despite this it is clear that survey evidence is and should be admissible in appropriate cases. So long as there are adequate safeguards as to the manner in which such evidence is collected and presented, there is little danger of the problems inherent in most hearsay evidence. This is particularly so where competent experts can advise the court as to the statistical limitations of the response to the survey. Such safeguards are considered below.[29] There can be little doubt that such evidence is hearsay, however. As the purpose of the exercise is to prove that the individ-

---

[22] *General Electric Co. v. General Electric Co. Ltd.* [1972] 1 W.L.R. 729.
[23] [1976] R.P.C. 589.
[24] *Ibid.*, at 595.
[25] [1983] F.S.R. 155.
[26] *Ibid.*, at 179.
[27] (1983) 51 A.L.R. 735.
[28] *Ibid.*, at 738.
[29] Chap. 15, pp. 289–293.

uals in the survey do in fact hold the opinions they express (from which it is inferred that a proportion of the general public or a particular group of persons does) it falls precisely within the hearsay objection. It should be acknowledged that such evidence in cases requiring it is to be treated as *sui generis* and admissible as an exception to the hearsay rule, subject to the appropriate safeguards.

Research as to a society of individuals There are expert disciplines in which a researcher may need to speak to people, and perhaps in large numbers, in order to gather the raw material upon which an overall view is to be based. In *Milirrpum* v. *Nabalco Pty.*[30] evidence of an anthropologist was admitted, despite the fact that he had spoken to large numbers of aboriginals who were not called as witnesses, as to their laws and social organisation. It was held that the expert was not entitled to give evidence in the form "Munggurrawuy told me that his was Gumatz land."[31] However the expert could give evidence in the form:

> "I have studied the social organisation of these aboriginals. This study includes observing their behaviour; talking to them, reading the published work of other experts; applying principles of analysis and verification which are accepted as valid in the general field of anthropology. I express the opinion as an expert that proposition X is true of their social organisation."[32]

The basis upon which this was accepted was that the gathering of evidence in this manner is intrinsic to anthropology as a discipline,[33] and the judge drew an analogy between a chemist's concern with the behaviour of elements and the anthropologist's concern with human behaviour.

It may be said that market research surveys fall logically into an analogous category.[34] However a distinction can be drawn between the anthropologist, whose purpose is to analyse the society of individuals rather than the individuals themselves, and the market researcher, whose chief purpose is to assess how individuals react to a particular product, albeit these individual reactions may subsequently be represented in statistical (*i.e.* general) form. It is the individuals who buy.

Prior report on facts in issue by another expert It will frequently be necessary for expert witnesses to rely upon a report or other material prepared by an expert, who will probably not be a witness, and this they

---

[30] (1971) 17 F.L.R. 141.
[31] *Ibid.*, at 161.
[32] *Ibid.*
[33] *Ibid.*
[34] See above, pp. 165–167.

may do in order to demonstrate the information upon which they base their opinion. This will not however have the effect of proving the facts relied upon by the first expert. A doctor, asked whether adultery could be inferred from the fact that a wife had syphilis not contracted from her husband:

> "expressed an opinion, based no doubt upon records of examination of the patient by other doctors, upon the case sheets, and so forth, that it was primary infection, and was a case in all probability of infection by sexual intercourse."[35]

However this did not assist in the matter of proof of the facts themselves:

> "evidence of the character of the disease from which she was suffering should be given by those who had personally examined her when she first came to the hospital."[36]

It has been held that a shipbuilder can be called to express an opinion concerning the seaworthiness of a ship, though he was not present at the survey,[37] although it must be assumed that he was not thereby being permitted to establish the condition of the ship as a matter of fact. This was achieved by a survey report, which was admitted for other, unstated, reasons. If an expert seeks to refer in court to a report not prepared by him, he cannot thereby avoid its being put in evidence, and used by other parties.[38] It has also been held, on the principle (arising out of the best evidence rule) that records of events before living memory may be adduced, that Brunel's engineering records of a particular site (a matter in issue in the case) could be referred to by expert engineer witnesses.[39] Such reports may be excluded for other reasons, for instance where counsel's opinion upon a trust deed was inadmissible for the purposes of construction because to adduce it would offend against the parol evidence rule.[40]

Prior reports will frequently be referred to in court, though not by way of establishing the primary facts to which they refer, particularly in personal injuries and other cases involving medical witnesses. Guidance has been given as to how this should be done:

> "it would be useful when a medical report was being prepared for the purpose of agreement with the other side if a doctor who drew on information obtained from some other doctor were to annex an

---

[35] *Ramsdale v. Ramsdale* (1945) 173 L.T. 393 at 394.
[36] *Ibid.*
[37] *Thornton v. Royal Exchange Company* (1791) Peake 37.
[38] *Stroud v. Stroud* [1963] 1 W.L.R. 1080.
[39] *East London Rail Company v. Conservators of the River Thames* (1904) 90 L.T. 347.
[40] *Rabin v. Gerson Berger* [1986] 1 W.L.R. 526.

extract from another doctor's report or state in some greater detail what the view expressed by that doctor was."[41]

Expert acting pursuant to statutory powers Although there have been suggestions that the reports of statutorily appointed company inspectors may be admissible as to the facts upon which they report,[42] the relevant cases are probably not authority for that general proposition.[43] Reports of this kind express an opinion upon facts, and as such are not admissible to prove those facts.[44] It has however been said that the report of a statutorily appointed professional tribunal may be treated as conclusive, otherwise a court looking at the same facts might come to a different view, on the same facts, in relation to a question of professional misconduct.[45]

Weight An expert may refer to the opinions of other experts in order to add weight to his own opinion, and this may include opinions expressed in previous cases, for example before a statutory tribunal, to show that his "was not an isolated opinion, but was shared by other members of the profession."[45a]

2 Fact extrinsic to the proceedings: comparison

Expert witnesses will almost always, whether consciously or not, in expressing an opinion call upon their knowledge of similar circumstances to the facts of the particular case. This may simply be a convenient way of analysing information, or it may be the way in which professionals in the field perform their tasks as a matter of usual practice. Thus valuers of land and buildings consider neighbouring properties, and similar properties in other areas, in arriving at an appropriate rental value for the land in question. If therefore they are asked their opinion on the rental value of land in civil proceedings, such comparisons are an important part of the process.

The expert's knowledge of other values may have come about in a number of ways, some of which may if they are sought to be adduced in evidence offend against the hearsay rules. In *English Exporters (London) Ltd., v. Eldonwall Ltd.*[46] Megarry J. considered these sources of knowledge, and gave a fully reasoned judgment as to the extent to which they

---

[41] *Peters v. Harding* (1963) 107 S.J. 852.
[42] *Re Armvent Ltd.* [1975] 1 W.L.R. 1679; *Re St. Piran* [1981] 1 W.L.R. 1300.
[43] *Savings and Investment Bank v. Gasco* [1984] 1 W.L.R. 271.
[44] *Ibid.*
[45] *Hill v. Clifford* [1907] 2 Ch. 236.
[45a] *R. v. Deputy Industrial Injuries Commissioner, ex p. Moore* [1965] 1 Q.B. 456 at 483.
[46] [1973] Ch. 415.

are admissible. Although the case itself concerned valuation evidence, its principles are no less applicable to expert evidence in general. Megarry J. divided this evidence into four categories, stating that the witness:

> "(a) may express the opinions that he has formed as to values even though substantial contributions to the formation of those opinions have been made by matters of which he has no first-hand knowledge;
>
> (b) may give evidence as to the details of any transactions within his personal knowledge, in order to establish them as matters of fact; and
>
> (c) may express his opinion as to the significance of any transactions which are or will be proved by admissible evidence (whether or not given by him) in relation to the valuation with which he is concerned; but
>
> (d) may not give hearsay evidence stating the details of any transactions not within his personal knowledge in order to establish them as matters of fact."[47]

Of these it can be seen that categories (b) and (d) concern direct evidence of fact. The expert may give evidence of fact within his own knowledge as may any witness:

> "If he has first-hand knowledge of a transaction, he can speak of that. He may himself have measured the premises and conducted the negotiations which led to a letting of them at £x, which comes to £y per square foot; and he himself may have read the lease and seen that it contains no provisions, other than some particular clause, which would have any material effect on the valuation; and then he may express his opinion on the value. So far as the expert gives factual evidence, he is doing what any other witness of fact may do, namely, speaking of that which he has perceived for himself."[48]

However, although he proposes to give expert evidence, he is caught by the ordinary rule against hearsay where his knowledge of the particular valuation is derived from a source which he cannot confirm from his own knowledge:

> "it seems to me quite another matter when it is asserted that a valuer may give factual evidence of transactions of which he has no direct knowledge, whether per se or whether in the guise of giving reasons for his opinion as to value. It is one thing to say 'From my general experience of recent transactions comparable with this one, I think

---

[47] [1973] Ch. 415 at 423.
[48] *Ibid.*, at 421.

the proper rent should be £x': it is another thing to say 'Because I have been told by someone else that the premises next door have an area of £x square feet and were recently let on such-and-such terms for £y a year, I say the rent of these premises should be £z a year.'"[49]

These principles are clearly an extrapolation from the rules relating to lay witnesses, which are no different at root, but only in their particular implications, where experts are concerned. However Megarry J. made it clear that in practice a less than rigorous adherence to these rules may be permitted for reasons of practicality:

"No doubt in many valuation cases the requirement of first-hand evidence is not pressed to an extreme: if the witness has not himself measured the premises, but it has been done by his assistant under his supervision, the expert's figures are often accepted without requiring the assistant to be called to give evidence.[50] Again, it may be that it would be possible for a valuer to fill a gap in his first-hand knowledge of a transaction by some method such as stating in his evidence that he has made diligent enquiries of some person who took part in the transaction in question, but despite receiving full answers to his enquiries, he discovered nothing which suggested to him that the transaction had any unusual features which would affect the value as a comparable."[51]

However this appears to be little more than a recognition of the right of another party to consent to what would otherwise be admissible evidence being admitted in these forms. If the evidence adduced by these less formally sound methods was of importance in the case and in issue, there would be no obligation on an opposing party to accept evidence in this form and the matters in issue would need to be proved in the proper manner, however laborious this might be.[52] For even though, as is often the case, the expert witness may have obtained his hearsay knowledge from other professionals whom he knows well and trusts implicitly, such evidence is open to the two major objections to all inadmissible hearsay evidence: the court cannot satisfy itself that the information contains no errors of importance, and the other parties are deprived of the opportunity to cross-examine the original provider of the information, both upon those positive parts of the evidence which may be in error or misleading, and as to those matters which have not been referred to at all

---

[49] [1973] Ch. 415 at 421. If hearsay evidence is wrongly adduced as to comparables (or indeed as to other matters), it must be objected to at the time, otherwise it may be admitted: *Town Centre Securities Ltd. v. Morrison Supermarket* (1982) 263 E.G. 435 at 436–437.
[50] Cf. *Stone & Sons v. Pugh* and *R. v. Kershberg*, above n. 9.
[51] Above n. 49.
[52] See also *R. v. Abadom* [1983] 1 W.L.R. 126 at 131.

and which may lead the court to view the evidence given in chief in a different light.[53]

In order to ensure that the court is not misled as to this, Megarry J. in *English Exporters* v. *Eldonwall* took the view that a list of comparables should not be submitted to the court unless each comparable on it is to be proved by admissible evidence:

> "for counsel to put in a list of comparables ought to amount to a warranty by him of his intention to tender admissible evidence of all that is shown on the list."[54]

This evidence may of course come from the expert witness himself, or from other witnesses of fact, who may or may not themselves be experts. The same must apply wherever a party's expert case is put on the basis of information extrinsic, though purportedly relevant, to the facts in issue.[55] However in many cases the parties can avoid the need for such lengthy evidence to be called by full mutual pre-trial disclosure and consequent agreements based upon discussions between the parties' experts.[56]

Extrinsic facts as part of the expert's "mental equipment"[57] There can be no objection, and it would be idle to suggest otherwise, to the expert, whether valuer or not, taking into account facts of which he is aware which give an indication, by means of comparison, as to the view he should take of the facts in issue in the proceedings. It has been suggested that the expert is confined to transactions of which he has personal experience, and must not make specific inquiries for the purpose.[58] However the better view is that the expert is not required to attempt the artificial and often practically impossible task of sifting out those influences upon his opinion of which he does not himself have direct knowledge.[59]

B. EXTRINSIC MATERIALS AND THE EXPERT'S OPINION

The opinion which an expert expresses upon a matter will consist of many different contributory elements. These will include his training,

---

[53] See *English Exporters* v. *Eldonwall*, above n. 46, at 422.
[54] *Ibid.*, at 423.
[55] See also *Wright* v. *Sydney Municipal Council* (1916) 16 S.R.N.S.W. 348.
[56] Possibly under R.S.C. Ord. 38, r. 38. And see *English Exporters* v. *Eldonwall*, above n. 46, at 423.
[57] *Gosford* v. *Alexander* [1902] 1 I.R. 139, 143.
[58] *Ibid.*, at 143.
[59] *English Exporters* v. *Eldonwall*, above n. 46, at 420.

experience, knowledge and analytical skills. He will during his career, in most instances, have read large quantities of professional literature in learned journals, reports and other such sources. These elements are largely indivisible from his opinion, which is no less valuable or receivable because of this. He may also wish to refer to a specific such extrinsic source in detail for the purpose of supporting his evidence, though it makes no reference to facts in issue in the case. While the court could not prevent the expert from taking its contents into account in giving his opinion evidence, it might object to specific reference to it on the ground that it was inadmissible as hearsay. The courts have therefore developed principles upon which such sources may or may not be received or referred to in evidence.

1   Extrinsic materials as general influence upon expert's opinion

The courts, as they realistically must, have taken a robust view of the expert's ability to rely on documentary sources relating to matters which do not constitute, but do nevertheless bear upon and assist with the analysis of, facts in issue in the proceedings. Wigmore has described the advantages of their contribution, and the reasons why the hearsay objection, that such sources cannot be tested before the court, is outweighed by the advantage of obtaining an opinion informed by them:

> "No one professional man can know from personal observation more than a minute fraction of the data which he must every day treat as working truths. Hence a reliance on the reported data of fellow scientists, learned by perusing their reports in books and journals. The law must and does accept this kind of knowledge from scientific men. On the one hand, a mere layman, who comes to court and alleges a fact which he has learned only by reading a medical or a mathematical book, cannot be heard. But, on the other hand, to reject a professional physician or mathematician because the fact or some facts to which he testifies are known to him only upon the authority of others would be to ignore the accepted methods of professional work and to insist on finical and impossible standards. Yet it is not easy to express in usable form that element of professional competency which distinguishes the latter case from the former. In general, the considerations which define the latter are (a) a professional experience, giving the witness a knowledge of the trustworthy authorities and the proper source of information, (b) an extent of personal observation in the general subject, enabling him to estimate the general plausibility, or probability of soundness, of the views expressed, and (c) the impossibility of obtaining infor-

mation on the particular technical detail except through technical data in part or entirely."⁶⁰

The danger of errors, irrelevancies and misleading information being employed unchecked is inevitable. However Megarry J. in *English Exporters* v. *Eldonwall*⁶¹ was of the view that the expert's ability to identify such things, combined with a process whereby the good would cancel out the bad, left the court, through an inarticulate sifting function performed by the expert witness, with information which, if it could not always be relied upon, could at least on balance be said to benefit the court. There was therefore no objection to a valuer employing such sources:

> "textbooks, journals, reports of auctions and other dealings, and information obtained from his professional brethren and others, some related to particular transactions and some more general and indefinite, will all have contributed their share. Doubtless much, or most, of this will be accurate, though some will not; and even what is accurate so far as it goes may be incomplete, in that nothing may have been said of some special element which affects values. Nevertheless, the opinion that the expert expresses is none the worse because it is in part derived from the matters of which he could give no direct evidence. Even if some of the extraneous information which he acquires in this way is inaccurate or incomplete, the errors and omissions will often tend to cancel each other out; and the valuer, after all, is an expert in this field, so that the less reliable the knowledge that he has about the details of some reported transaction, the more his experience will tell him that he should be ready to make some discount from the weight that he gives it in contributing to his overall sense of values. Some aberrant transactions may stand so far out of line that he will give them little or no weight. No question of giving hearsay evidence arises in such case; the witness states his opinion from his general experience."⁶²

Textbooks Books which cover a particular expert discipline, or a field within it, are not admissible *per se* unless the court is taking judicial notice of a fact recorded in it. A fact in issue can never therefore be evidentially proved merely by reference to a textbook:

> "if a landlord complained of a farmer for not properly cultivating his land, he could not refer to books in order to show in what way

---

⁶⁰ J. Wigmore, *A Treatise on the Anglo-American System of Evidence*, (3rd ed., 1940), Vol. 2, para. 665(b); cited in *Borowski* v. *Quayle* [1966] V.R. 382 at 386–387.
⁶¹ Above n. 46.
⁶² *Ibid.*, at 420.

the land ought to be cultivated, for that must be proved before the jury."[63]

In so far as textbooks may be employed this must occur through the agency of an expert witness,[64] and counsel may not simply read passages of a medical textbook to the court.[65] An expert witness may, in giving his opinion, which must be his own, indicate that it is founded in part upon textbooks which he has read:

> "I do not think that the books themselves can be read; but I do not see any objection to your asking Sir Henry Halford his judgment, and the grounds of it, which may be, in some degree, founded on books, as part of his general knowledge."[66]

There is little difficulty where the expert is merely reminding himself of material with which he was in the past conversant, or reading in detail on a professional topic with which he is only familiar in general terms. However it is less desirable for a witness to become an 'instant expert' on a subject which only has a remote connection with the area of his professional practice and expertise. In a Canadian case,[67] a medical expert, trained and practising in the medical field, was called to give evidence on the distance from which a shot had been fired at a body. He made it clear that he had no personal experience of such a question, but had studied books on the subject. From one such book he had learned that this distance could be assessed by reference to the size of the wound and the jagged nature of its edge. It was held that he could give such evidence because it did concern "a question of medical science or skill,"[68] and was not a purely ballistic issue, and the majority disregarded the fact[69] that such medical evidence might be said to be dependant upon ballistic questions such as the bore of the gun used. The question, said the majority, is whether the medical expert, with the benefit of having read textbooks on the subject, is at an advantage over the jury in assessing the evidence, and held that he was.[70] The decision can in part be explained by the court's concern that no other expert evidence was before it.

A part of the reason why such difficulties arise is that the courts tend not to look very rigorously at the level and type of the expert's skill and

---

[63] *Darby* v. *Ouseley* (1856) 1 H. & N. 1.
[64] *R.* v. *Taylor* (1874) 13 Cox 77.
[65] *R.* v. *Crouch* (1844) 1 Cox 94. Counsel may of course refer to legal textbooks, although it has been observed that care should be taken not to place too much reliance upon cited references without looking at the original sources: *Johnson* v. *Agnew* [1980] A.C. 367 at 395–396.
[66] *Collier* v. *Simpson* (1831) 5 C. & P. 73.
[67] *Preeper* v. *R.* (1888) 15 S.C.R. 401.
[68] Ibid., at 408.
[69] Observed by the two dissenting judges.
[70] *Preeper* v. *R.* (1888) 15 S.C.R. 401 at 417.

experience when deciding admissibility, on the basis that it can be fully assessed in the attribution of weight to the evidence of the various witnesses. Where, as in *Preeper* v. *R.*[71] the case is before a jury, it may be questioned whether the jurors can realistically be relied upon to analyse such issues in a discriminating manner once the evidence has been given.

2 Extrinsic materials specifically cited

It has been seen that there is and can be no objection to an expert drawing upon his reading of materials within his discipline, and that it would be pointless to attempt some kind of artificial distinction between his own general views and those of others who may have influenced him. The same would not necessarily apply however where an expert witness makes specific reference to an article, report or statistical table, prepared by others for purposes other than the proceedings in question, and seeks to cite it as specific authority or support for an opinion he expresses. Apart from any other possible objection, the fact that it contains prima facie inadmissible hearsay raises considerable difficulties, which cannot be surmounted by the assertion that it is merely a general contributor to his knowledge and experience, upon which he then draws when expressing his professional opinion.

On the other hand such materials, though not prepared for the proceedings themselves, can have a very high potential probative value in the case. This is clearly not a sufficient reason for admissibility, because much inadmissable lay hearsay evidence shares the same quality, but is excluded because the court is unable to probe the memory and bona fides of the person who would give original evidence. The position with experts, however, can be contrasted in two respects. First, the expert cannot be prevented in any event from relying on particular extrinsic materials, perhaps without disclosing them, in giving his opinion. Given this is so, this part of his opinion is at least open to scrutiny by the court, and by advocates and experts acting for the other parties, if it is clearly accepted as citeable without objection. The second ground for distinguishing such materials arises from the very reason why expert evidence is admissible at all, namely that the expert, because of his knowledge, training and experience, is said to be at a significant advantage over a lay tribunal when analysing and drawing inferences from technical information within his field. This gives him the ability to act as a filter through which extrinsic materials can be used by the court, in that he is able to assess their quality (which may be demonstrated by his direct evidence that they are widely accepted as authoritative within the special-

---

[71] Above n. 67.

ist field) and their particular relevance to the proceedings before the court.

In *R. v. Abadom*,[72] the court examined both the circumstances in which, and the conditions under which, such materials might be employed. The decision is concerned with criminal proceedings, but the central principles are equally applicable to civil actions. The appellant was charged with a robbery, which had included the smashing of a window pane. He denied that he had been present. A principal scientific officer at the Home Office forensic laboratories stated that small pieces of glass found in a pair of shoes belonging to the appellant shared the same refractive index as glass from the broken window. The Home Office Central Research Establishment prepared, on a routine basis, statistics relating to glass analysed scientifically. The expert, using these statistics, was able to say that only four per cent. of all glass had the same refractive index as that discovered in the shoes and the broken pane. This was clearly persuasive evidence that the appellant had been at the scene of the crime.[73] The evidence having been admitted at trial, he was convicted.

The Court of Appeal, for which Kerr L.J. gave the judgment of the court, found that this evidence had been correctly admitted, and upheld the conviction. The expert was experienced in the field of glass analysis, and was therefore able to understand and explain the precise manner in which the refractive index had been calculated, and in which the statistics had been prepared.[74] As someone familiar with the statistics, he would be able to confirm that they had been collected and published in a scientifically sound manner. Furthermore as to the actual fact in issue, namely the probability of the two fragments of glass being the same, four per cent., the expert had himself calculated it, albeit employing the figures in the Home Office statistics, which would indisputably be hearsay if adduced evidentially. A number of points emerge from the *ratio decidendi* of Kerr L.J.'s judgment:

(i) One of the purposes of the expert witness is to bring specialist knowledge within the field, which otherwise would be denied to it, before the court:

> "the process of taking account of information stemming from the work of others in the same field is an essential ingredient of the nature of expert evidence."[75]

(ii) The opinion expressed by experts in court will be improved by a knowledge of the published work in the specialism:

---

[72] [1983] 1 W.L.R. 126.
[73] Though in the absence of other corroborative evidence it is certainly not conclusive. There would still be a large quantity of this glass in existence.
[74] *Cf. Customglass Boats Ltd. v. Salthouse Brothers Ltd.*, above n. 23.
[75] *Ibid.*, at 131.

> "It is part of their duty to consider any material which may be available in their field, and not to draw conclusions merely on the basis of their own experience, which is inevitably likely to be more limited than the general body of information which may be available to them."[76]

(iii) Evidence as to probabilities is useful to the court in certain circumstances. This will often require the use of statistical sources, which frequently by their very nature involve a hearsay element in their collation:

> "Relative probabilities or improbabilities must frequently be an important factor in the evaluation of any expert opinion and, when any reliable statistical material is available which bears upon this question, it must be part of the function and duty of the expert to take this into account.
> However, it is also inherent in the nature of any statistical information that it will result from the work of others in the same field, whether or not the expert in question will himself have contributed to the bank of information available on the particular topic on which he is called upon to express his opinion. Indeed, to exclude reliance upon such information on the ground that it is inadmissible under the hearsay rule, might inevitably lead to the distortion or unreliability of the opinion which the expert presents for evaluation by a judge or jury. Thus, in the present case, the probative value or otherwise of the identity of the refractive index as between the fragments and the control sample could not be assessed without some further information about the frequency of its occurrence. If all glass of the type in question had the same refractive index, this evidence would have virtually no probative value whatever. The extent to which this refractive index is common or uncommon must therefore be something which an expert must be entitled to take into account, and indeed must take into account, before he can properly express an opinion about the likelihood or unlikelihood of the fragments of glass having come from the window in question. The cogency or otherwise of the expert's conclusion on this point, in the light of, *inter alia*, the available statistical material against which this conclusion falls to be tested, must then be a matter for the jury."[77]

(iv) If an expert does in fact rely upon specific extrinsic materials in

---

[76] *Customglass Boats Ltd.* v. *Salthouse Brothers Ltd.*, above n. 23 at 131.
[77] *Ibid.*, at 129–130.

arriving at his opinion, it is both unfair and misleading for these not to be placed squarely before the court. There is a greater danger that the expert may distort the contents of the material.[78] Furthermore the material may not have been published, in which case if specific reference is not made to it in evidence, the court will be unaware of it unless another expert witness refers to it:

> "Once the primary facts on which their opinion is based have been proved by admissible evidence, they are entitled to draw on the work of others as part of the process of arriving at their conclusion. However, where they have done so, they should refer to this material in their evidence so that the cogency and probative value of their conclusion can be tested and evaluated by reference to it. . . . But it does not seem to us, in relation to the reliability of opinion evidence given by experts, that they must necessarily limit themselves to drawing on material which has been published in some form. Part of their experience and expertise may well lie in their knowledge of unpublished material and in their evaluation of it. The only rule in this regard, as it seems to us, is that they should refer to such material in their evidence for the reasons stated above."[79]

(v) Different considerations from those appropriate in cases of purely lay witness evidence may apply where expert evidence of opinion, including some reference to hearsay materials, is given.[80] Thus *Myers* v. *Director of Public Prosecutions*[81] can be distinguished, said Kerr L.J. In *Myers* v. *D.P.P.* records as to indelible numbers stamped on car engines were sought to be adduced to show that certain stolen cars were those which had been connected with the accused. The evidence was held not to be admissible. Kerr L.J. distinguished *Myers* v. *D.P.P.* on the grounds *inter alia* that no expert had given evidence as to these records, and that any connection they displayed between the cars stolen and those connected with the accused was a question of fact, not as in *Abadom* a question of opinion.

The evidence, however, which resulted from the calculations of the expert in *Abadom* was of a mathematical probability. Although no doubt evidence of opinion was employed in assessing the validity and cogency of the statistics used, this is as much a question of fact, and a fact in issue, as the relationship between car engine numbers with which the court in

---

[78] *Customglass Boats Ltd.* v. *Salthouse Brothers Ltd.*, above n. 23.
[79] *Ibid.*, at 131.
[80] *Ibid.*, at 130.
[81] [1965] A.C. 1001.

Myers v. *D.P.P.* was concerned.[82] It is clear that the expert could, if the statistical evidence was not specifically to be referred to, be asked in general terms to give an approximate estimate of the likelihood of glass of the same refractive index being found in two different places and it is obviously preferable, given this, that he should both disclose the statistics of which he is aware and come to a precise conclusion ("four per cent.") if one is possible, rather than an informed guess ("a small but not insignificant likelihood" or some such phrase).

(vi) It is nevertheless essential that the basic facts upon which the calculations are based, whether requiring expertise for their perception or not, should be proved by admissible original evidence:

"where an expert relies on the existence or non-existence of some fact which is basic to the question on which he is asked to express his opinion, that fact must be proved by admissible evidence."[83]

Published statistical tables   It was established in *Abadom* that an expert may cite and rely upon records of data assembled by persons who are not witnesses before the court even though these have not been published. The courts have over a long period accepted that experts may refer to statistical and other tables and references commonly used and accepted within a particular profession, such as tables listing established destruction rates for alcohol[84] and setting out the average duration of life on actuarial principles.[85] The witness may do this even though he has not trained in the particular profession whose members compiled and calculated the figures, though if they are disputed this will go to weight.[86] So a doctor may refer to alcohol destruction rate tables, though he is not trained as a chemical analyst,[87] and an accountant may refer to actuarial tables though, despite some knowledge of insurance, he is not an actuary.[88] It has been suggested in a Canadian case that this is so even though the expert does not himself understand the scientific basis upon which the figures were compiled so long as he can confirm that insurance companies use the mortuary tables in question on a regular basis,[89] and

---

[82] See too J. James, "A Clear Cut Case" (1984) 47 M.L.R. 103.
[83] *Ibid.*, at 131. See also *English Exporters (London) Ltd.* v. *Eldonwall* [1973] Ch. 415 at 421; *R.* v. *Turner* [1975] Q.B. 834 at 840; R. Pattenden, "Expert Opinion Evidence Based on Hearsay" [1982] Crim.L.R. 85, published before the decision in *Abadom*.
[84] *R.* v. *Somers* (1964) 48 Cr.App.R. 11.
[85] *Rowley* v. *London and North Western Railway Company* (1873) L.R. 8 Ex. 222.
[86] *R.* v. *Somers*, above n. 84.
[87] *Ibid.*
[88] *Rowley* v. *London and North-Western Railway Company*, above n. 85.
[89] *Canadian Pacific Railway* v. *Jackson* (1915) 52 S.C.R. 281.

though the English cases do not expressly state as much, their facts appear to be consistent with such a proposition.

Adoption of extrinsic materials   An expert may in appropriate circumstances simply adopt a passage in a book, pamphlet or table, though unless he specifically does so the court cannot employ passages from a pamphlet "for the purpose of displacing or criticising the witness's testimony."[90] Uncited passages may however be put to the expert in cross-examination for his comment.[91]

C. HEARSAY MATERIALS ADMISSIBLE WITHOUT EXPERT EVIDENCE

1   British Pharmacopoeia

This standard medical reference work is admissible to prove the proper contents of drugs and other medical compounds.[92] It is not conclusive, however, and may be rebutted by persuasive evidence contrary to its text.[93]

2   Dictionaries

Dictionaries may be employed by the court to assist with the meaning of words, but this is by way of judicial notice, not expert evidence:

> "dictionaries are not to be taken as authoritative exponents of the meaning of words used in Acts of Parliament, but it is a well-known rule of courts of Law that words should be taken to be used in their ordinary sense, and we are therefore sent for instruction to these books."[94]

Their use may go beyond simple meaning, though still only within the bounds of judicial notice:

> "dictionaries may properly be referred to in order to ascertain not only the meaning of a word. . . . but also the use to which the thing (if it be a thing) denoted by the word is commonly put."[95]

---

[90] *Davie* v. *Edinburgh Magistrates* [1953] S.C. 34 at 41.
[91] *Ibid.*
[92] *Dickins* v. *Randerson* [1901] 1 K.B. 437; *White* v. *Bywater* (1887) 19 Q.B.D. 582.
[93] *Boots* v. *Cowling* (1903) 88 L.T. 539. See too *Hudson* v. *Bridge* (1903) 88 L.T. 550.
[94] *R.* v. *Peters* (1886) 16 Q.B.D. 636.
[95] *Coca-Cola Company of Canada Ltd.* v. *Pepsi-Cola Company of Canada Ltd.* (1942) 59 R.P.C. 127, 133; *Re Demuth Ltd.'s Application* (1948) 65 R.P.C. 342.

3 Others

A death certificate is admissible as to the fact and date of death[96] though not as to its cause.[97] Maps are not evidence of any fact existing at the time they were shown, unless they were drawn pursuant to a statutory power, or constitute a statement of reputation.[98] Rights of way cannot therefore usually be proved thus. Photofit pictures are *sui generis* and the hearsay rules do not apply to them.[99]

D. ADMISSIBILITY BY STATUTE

1 General

Experts' reports which would normally be hearsay unless proved by the maker may be admitted under specific statutory provisions. Thus medical records held by private hospitals might, though the point has not been decided, be admissible in criminal proceedings as "business records."[1] A National Health Service hospital is not however a "business" for these purposes.[2] An autopsy report was held not to be an official record, and not therefore to be admissible *per se*, under a Bahamanian statute.[3] Research documents and articles are not "records" within the meaning of section 4 of the Civil Evidence Act 1968. It was the intention of the act only to include records:

> "Which historians would regard as original or primary sources, that is, documents which either give effect to a transaction itself or which contain a contemporaneous register of information supplied by those with direct knowledge of the facts."[4]

The report of an inspector appointed pursuant to statute to investigate a company's affairs is not a "record" within section 4, because it is not an original or primary source, but expresses opinions upon facts proved by others.[5] Where a document containing expert opinion is a "record" within section 4, the person who originally supplied the information for

---

[96] *Wilton* v. *Phillips* (1903) 19 T.L.R. 390.
[97] *Bird* v. *Keep* [1918] 2 K.B. 692.
[98] *Att.-Gen.* v. *Horner (No. 2)* [1913] 2 Ch. 140; *Pipe* v. *Fulcher* (1958) 1 E. & E. 111; *Hammond* v. *Bradstreet* (1854) 10 Ex. 390.
[99] *R.* v. *Cook* (1987) 84 Cr.App.R. 369.
[1] Criminal Evidence Act 1965, s.1.
[2] *R.* v. *Crayden* [1978] 1 W.L.R. 604, 607.
[3] *Newbold* v. *R.* [1983] 3 W.L.R. 375 P.C.
[4] *H.* v. *Schering Chemicals Ltd.* [1983] 1 W.L.R. 143 at 146.
[5] *Savings and Investment Bank* v. *Gasco.* [1984] 1 W.L.R. 271.

the record must himself have been competent to give oral expert evidence under section 1(2) of the Civil Evidence Act 1972.[6]

Section 1 of the Evidence Act 1938 provides for the admissibility in criminal proceedings of documents compiled in the course of a trade or business "where direct oral evidence of a fact would be admissible" and a statement in the document tends "to establish that fact." The Court of Appeal has taken the view that this could extend to an expert statement of opinion.[7] It is submitted, however, that the dissenting judgment of Edmund-Davies L.J. is to be preferred. He considered that the opinion alone of an expert could not be admissible *per se* because:

> "The maker of the statement must have had personal knowledge of the matters dealt with by the statement."[8]

It requires too creative a construction of the statutory section to extend this to expert opinions. Some limited judicial support for this approach has since been forthcoming, though it was stated to be "inconclusive."[9]

2   Civil proceedings involving children

Particular difficulties arise in proceedings in which the welfare of a child is in issue, and there are specific rules governing the admissibility of hearsay evidence in such cases.[10] These are discussed in Chapter 22.[11]

3   Criminal Proceedings

Section 30 of the Criminal Justice Act 1988 provides for hearsay evidence of experts to be adduced in certain circumstances. This is discussed in Chapter 2.[12]

E.   ADDUCING HEARSAY EVIDENCE OF AN EXPERT AT COMMON LAW

In relation to civil proceedings, the circumstances in which hearsay evidence of an expert may be adduced are governed by statute and rules of court, and these are discussed in Chapter 2. In criminal proceedings in

---

[6] As to the general applicability of the Civil Evidence Act 1968 to expert evidence, see Chap. 2.
[7] *Dass* v. *Masih* [1968] 1 W.L.R. 756, *per* Lord Denning and "provisionally" Salmon L.J.
[8] *Ibid.*, at 767.
[9] *R.* v. *Wood Green Crown Court, ex p. P.* [1982] 4 F.L.R. 206 at 216, *per* McCullough J.
[10] Children (Admissibility of Hearsay Evidence) Order 1990 (1990 S.I. No. 143), introduced pursuant to the Children Act 1989, s.96(3) and s.104(1).
[11] At pp. 396–399.
[12] At pp. 58–59.

the Crown Court there is now a statutory discretion to admit hearsay evidence of an expert's report, subject to the requirements of section 30 of the Criminal Justice Act 1988, and this is also discussed in Chapter 2. There remain two circumstances however where the common law exceptions to the rule against hearsay in criminal proceedings may be relevant, namely proceedings in a magistrates' court, which are not covered by section 30, and matters in the Crown Court where it is not an expert's "report", within the terms of section 30, which is sought to be adduced.

It is clear however that opinion evidence is to be treated on a wholly different footing from that of fact. In *R. v. McGuire*[13] a scientific officer attended in the course of his employment to investigate a fire in an arson case, and prepared a report which contained both observations of fact, and opinions about the cause of the fire based on those facts. He died before the trial commenced. The Court of Appeal held that the trial judge was correct to rule the statement of fact admissible, but not those of opinion. The prosecution had sought to adduce the evidence pursuant to the common law exception which applies where the maker of the statement was acting under a duty at the time, which the fire officer clearly was.

The Court of Appeal gave four principal reasons for ruling that the evidence of opinion could not be adduced under that exception.[14] First, the justification for admitting factual evidence in such circumstances, namely that otherwise the evidence would be denied to the court, does not apply to an expert's opinion, because another expert can almost always be found to express one, upon the admissible evidence of fact. It might also be observed that if another expert cannot be found to express the same opinion, this is in itself good reason to exclude the evidence in any event. The Court of Appeal noted that the House of Lords in *Myers v. D.P.P.*[15] had cited with approval the words of Sir George Jessel in *Sugden v. Lord St. Leonards*[16] to the effect that the maker of the statement must have had a "peculiar means of knowledge"[17] of the relevant matters to justify admission. An opinion does not sit comfortably within this requirement.

Secondly, the Court of Appeal saw as an important basis of the general exception the mechanical nature of note-taking when under a duty, which is in itself some guarantee of accuracy. There is "nothing mechanical or routine about an opinion."[18] Correct though this undoubtedly is, it may be questioned just how mechanical or routine is an expert's scientific

---

[13] (1985) 81 Cr.App.R. 323.
[14] *Ibid.*, at 330.
[15] [1965] A.C. 1001.
[16] (1876) 1 P.D. 154.
[17] *Ibid.*, at 241.
[18] *R. v. McGuire*, above n. 13, at 330.

investigation of "facts," which are thus admissible, but which may require considerable expertise for their observation and identification.

The Court of Appeal's third reason was that an opinion is not subject to the kind of check by an employer which is at the heart of the assumption that a "duty" carries with it some guarantee of truth. Finally it was noted from the authorities that contemporaneity was treated as an indication of reliability. Paradoxically, an opinion might be said to be reliable exactly because it was the result of some reflection, and hence inevitably some delay between observation and statement.

In fact in *R. v. McGuire* the statement was contained in the form of a report, so that the provisions of section 30 of the Criminal Justice Act 1988 would now govern its admissibility. It is not inconceivable however that an expert might make factual notes, not in the form of a report, whether prepared for the court or otherwise, and also make notes of his inferences from, or opinions upon, those facts. The latter would clearly not be admissible in such circumstances.

CHAPTER 9

Privilege and Confidentiality

The expert witness is subject to the general law of privilege to the same extent and in the same manner as any other witness, though some aspects of it have a special significance for the expert. Questions of privilege are unlikely to arise in relation to opinions given by experts in court, although it is not inconceivable that they might. They occur primarily in relation to facts, or documents produced by the expert, upon which his opinion may be based. In addition, particular difficulties spring from the conflict between the general, though not absolute, principle that all relevant evidence should be available to the court, and the ethical or contractual duty of the expert external to the particular proceedings. These may be said to arise out of his employment or from codes of behaviour imposed both from without by the professional bodies or organisations to which most experts belong and from within by the expert's own perception of his ethical duty. It will be seen that the law makes few confessions to such codes, whatever their origin. It is not the purpose of this chapter to give a full account of the law of privilege, but to identify those aspects of it which particularly affect the adducing of expert evidence.

A. THE LAW OF PRIVILEGE

In general, whoever asserts that privilege arises, the only person or body who can enforce it is the litigant,[1] or the client in the case of 'legal adviser' privilege, to which special rules apply. Once evidence becomes, or is adjudged to be, privileged, it remains so for all subsequent purposes in the litigation.[2] Where evidence which is prima facie privileged becomes known by another party to litigation, that party is permitted to give secondary evidence of it, as the court is not concerned with how this came about. The most likely such circumstance is where a document falls into the hands of the opposite party by accident (or possibly by subterfuge), and for this reason, experts, who frequently prepare and produce

[1] *Schneider* v. *Leigh* [1955] 2 Q.B. 195.
[2] *Calcraft* v. *Guest* [1898] 1 Q.B. 759. Though this general principle should arguably be qualified by the discussion at pp. 195–202 below.

documents for the purposes of litigation, are susceptible to such misfortune.[3]

Privilege can be waived and thereby cease to take effect in respect of particular evidence, either by conduct of the parties, or in effect by operation of law, such as the rules as to disclosure of expert's reports.[4] It has been suggested that a waiver can be created by "implied understanding" between the parties, for instance where one party discloses a medical report to the other without expressly stating that the disclosure is conditional upon mutual disclosure.[5] This approach is put on the basis that to hold otherwise would not constitute "fair dealing," because a party should not be permitted to "play with a 'poker' face with the cards hidden from view."[6] The present position, however, is probably that in the absence of express waiver, or waiver by operation of law, no such implied waiver arises. Waiver in respect of one privileged document does not without express waiver extend to other documents treating of the same subject-matter in a particular case.[7] If, however, a document records a conversation and is subject to waiver, other documents recording the content of that conversation lose their privilege.[8] Agreement to exchange reports does not amount to an implied waiver in relation to reports which it is not intended to rely upon at trial.[9]

Despite the general principle that privilege is that of the litigant, two particular forms of privilege attach, atypically, to the witness. As such, there is no reason to suppose that they are not applicable to experts to the same extent as they are to any other witness. First, in criminal proceedings only,[10] a witness is not compellable to disclose any communication with his or her spouse during the marriage.[11] Secondly, any witness may avail himself of the privilege against self-incrimination. Thus

> "no one is bound to answer any question if the answer thereto would, in the opinion of the judge, have a tendency to expose the deponent to any criminal charge, penalty or forfeiture which the judge regards as reasonably likely to be preferred or sued for."[12]

---

[3] An injunction may be obtainable as a matter of discretion to restrain the use of an expert's report: *Webster* v. *James Chapman and Co.* [1989] 3 All E.R. 939 at 944–947.
[4] R.S.C., Ord. 38, Pt. IV. As to the relationship between privilege and the duty of full disclosure, see *Kenning* v. *Eve Construction Ltd.* [1989] 1 W.L.R. 1189
[5] By Lord Denning in *Causton* v. *Mann Egerton* [1974] 1 W.L.R. 162 at 167.
[6] *Ibid.*, at 167.
[7] *Ibid.*, per Stamp L.J. and Roskill L.J. See also *Worrall* v. *Reich* [1955] 1 Q.B. 296 and *Re Saxton* [1962] 1 W.L.R. 968. In the latter case Lord Denning was in the majority, despite his subsequently expressed views. The position may be different where a document is specifically adduced at trial: *General Accident* v. *Tanter* [1984] 1 W.L.R. 100.
[8] *General Accident* v. *Tanter* [1983] 1 W.L.R. 100.
[9] *McGuinness* v. *Fairbairn Lawson* (1966) S.J. 870.
[10] See the Civil Evidence Act 1968, s.16(3).
[11] Evidence (Amendment) Act 1853, s.3. See *Bent* v. *Allot* (1580) Cary 94.
[12] *Blunt* v. *Park Lane Hotel Ltd.* [1942] 2 K.B. 253 at 257, per Lord Goddard.

Witness privilege applies to the production of documents as it does to oral evidence. Where a notary was at risk of losing his professional status he was able to invoke the privilege not to produce a document to the court.[13] The privilege is available to a corporation at risk of criminal proceedings in its capacity as legal person.[14] No privilege can be invoked against potential civil penalties or proceedings.[15]

A witness, including presumably an expert witness, may claim a lien over a document against a party requiring its production in court,[16] where for instance the witness has not been paid fees for services rendered. The witness cannot withhold production where the lien is in respect of a third party.[17]

1 Communications between party and legal adviser

Communications, whether oral or written, between a legal adviser and his client are privileged where their purpose is the obtaining of legal advice, and where they are made in respect of litigation which has been commenced or which is in the client's contemplation. This is so whether the client communicates with a solicitor,[18] barrister,[19] or a legal adviser employed by a company or other organisation.[20] The entire communication is privileged. The courts have resisted attempts to suggest that the parts of a communication which do not strictly treat of privileged matters can be separated from the whole and thereby become subject to disclosure.[21] A patent agent is, for limited purposes, also capable of conferring privilege upon his lay client.[22]

2 Privileged communications with third parties

Where the evidence of an expert is sought to be adduced at trial, it must usually be disclosed by way of report before trial. The rules of court governing such disclosure are discussed in Chapter 2. It has been held in *Kenning* v. *Eve Construction Ltd*[23] that where disclosure is ordered, this includes any part of the expert's opinion relevant to cross-examination, and this duty is not evaded by asking the expert to submit his assessment

---

[13] *Nelme* v. *Newton* (1819) 2 W. & J. 186. See also *Spokes* v. *Grosvenor Hotel* [1897] 2 Q.B. 124.
[14] *Triplex Safety Glass* v. *Lancegaye Safety Glass Ltd.* [1939] 2 K.B. 395.
[15] Witnesses Act 1806; Civil Evidence Act 1968, s.16(1)(a).
[16] *Re Hawkes* [1898] 2 Ch. 1.
[17] *Ibid.* See also *Re Aveling Barford, The Independent,* August 31, 1988, (solicitor's lien).
[18] *Berd* v. *Lovelace* (1577) Cary 62.
[19] *Dennis* v. *Codrington* (1580) Cary 100.
[20] *Crompton Amusement Machines Ltd.* v. *Customs & Excise Commissioners* [1972] 2 Q.B. 102.
[21] *Re Sarah C. Getty Trust* [1985] Q.B. 956.
[22] Patents Act 1977, s.104; Civil Evidence Act 1968, s.15.
[23] [1989] 1 W.L.R. 1189.

of the weakness of his client's case inconfidence in a separate document. His entire opinion loses its privilege. This is discussed further in Chapter 4.[24]

Privilege attaches however to all communications by a litigant, or his lawyer, with a third party, where it is for the purpose of actual or prospective litigation. Reports of experts are no exception: see *Worrall* v. *Reich*.[25] In a significant proportion of such cases, the third party will be an actual or potential expert witness. The general principle in relation to documents, which applies nevertheless to all forms of communication, was described in *Wheeler* v. *Le Marchant*[26]:

> "documents are protected where they have come into existence after litigation commenced or in contemplation, and when they have been made with a view to such litigation, either with a view to obtaining advice as to such litigation, or of obtaining evidence to be used in such litigation, or of obtaining evidence which might lead to the obtaining of such evidence."

It can be seen from this passage that although the communication must have this connection with actual or prospective litigation, the ambit of such communications is fairly broad. Unlike the all embracing lawyer/client privilege discussed above, third party communications need not have been initiated directly, or even indirectly, by a lawyer,[27] although it is obvious that they will often have been so:

> "it is not necessary that they should have come into existence at the instance of the lawyer. It is sufficient if they have come into existence at the instance of the party himself."[28]

It is essential, however, that litigation be in existence or in actual contemplation. Where, following an accident, officers of a company prepared a report on the accident, it was not privileged, even though "litigation generally, and almost inevitably, follows an accident of this sort."[29] Where however a surveyor prepared a report to assist without prejudice negotiations with the express purpose of avoiding litigation, it was held not to be a discoverable document.[30] There are numerous examples of the operation of the rule where expert witnesses, or more frequently potential expert witnesses, are parties to such a communication. Thus,

---

[24] At pp. 91–92.
[25] [1955] 1 Q.B. 296.
[26] (1881) 17 Ch.D. 675 at 681.
[27] See *Bustros* v. *White* (1876) 1 Q.B.D. 423.
[28] *Buttes Gas and Oil Co.* v. *Hammer* [1981] Q.B. 223 at 243, *per* Lord Denning.
[29] *Woolley* v. *North London Railway Co.* (1869) L.R. 4 C.P. 602.
[30] *Rabin* v. *Mendoza* [1954] 1 W.L.R. 271.

communications of scientists,[31] doctors,[32] marine surveyors,[33] and salvage experts[34] have been held to be privileged where litigation was in existence or contemplation.

Previous litigation   The question whether privilege can be asserted in respect of a document prepared in connection with other legal proceedings was examined in *The Aegis Blaze*.[35] In 1980, cargo was damaged aboard a ship, and the owners of the ship instructed surveyors to report. The instruction was in contemplation of litigation so that the report was clearly privileged in relation to that litigation. In 1981 a different cargo was damaged aboard the same ship. The cargo owners sought disclosure of the report on the 1980 incident. It was held by the Court of Appeal that no privilege could be asserted in the second litigation unless the party (or his successor) claiming it was a party to both sets of litigation. If however the party was common to both, and there was sufficient connection between the two cases for the document to be relevant to the second, privilege could be asserted, and could only be lost by waiver. There need not, however, be a substantial connection between the subject matter of the two cases, although the issue of disclosure could not arise unless there was some common material of relevance to both.

Interpreters   Interpreters are in a somewhat anomalous position in that, in theory, they act merely as the mouthpiece of the client for the assistance of the court, and of others, for the benefit of the client. The interpreter is bound to treat relevant communications as privileged in the same manner as the legal adviser is required to.[36]

The "dominant purpose" rule   Communications may have as only one of their purposes the pursuance of actual or prospective litigation. There have been numerous judicial attempts to formulate a test suitable for deciding whether privilege should attach to a multi-purpose communication. In *Waugh v. British Railways Board*,[37] a decision of the House of Lords which is the leading authority on this question, it was stated by Lord Simon that previous authority was so divergent as to leave the House of Lords with a number of options, making it appropriate to consider the matter "on grounds of principle and convenience, unem-

---

[31] *Woolley v. North London Railway Co.*, above n. 29.
[32] *Friend v. London, Chatham & Dover Railway Co.* (1877) 2 Ex. D. 437.
[33] *The Theodor Korner* (1878) 3 P.D. 162.
[34] *Adam Steamship Co. Ltd. v. London Assurance Co.* [1914] 3 K.B. 1256.
[35] [1986] 1 Lloyd's Rep. 203.
[36] *Du Barré v. Livette* (1791) 1 Peake 78.
[37] [1980] A.C. 521.

barrassed by previous authority, which . . . constitutes diverse springboards."[38]

In *Waugh* v. *British Railways Board*, a report had been prepared for the Board following a railway accident, for the dual purpose of obtaining legal advice and of improving safety. It was held that the report was not privileged, because to be so it would need to have had as its "dominant purpose" the obtaining of legal advice with a view to litigation. In laying down this test the House of Lords was adopting the words of Barwick C.J. in the Australian case of *Grant* v. *Downs*.[39]

Lord Russell of Killowen was attracted by the simplicity of the "sole purpose" test for practical purposes, but recognised that:

> "the standard of sole purpose would be in most, if not all, cases impossible to attain . . . to impose it would tilt the balance of policy in this field too sharply against the possible defendant."[40]

Both he and Lord Simon were further persuaded by the fact that the "dominant purpose" test has been successfully applied and interpreted in other fields of law, such as bankruptcy and conspiracy.[41]

Lord Edmund-Davies also entertained the possibility of a less restrictive test, but excluded this on policy grounds:

> "the public interest is, on balance, best served by rigidly confining within narrow limits the cases where material relevant to litigation may be lawfully withheld . . . in as much as the only basis of the claim to privilege in such cases as the present one is that the material in question was brought into existence for use in legal proceedings, it is surely right to insist that, before the claim is conceded or upheld, such a purpose must be shown to have played a paramount part."[42]

It can be seen from this passage that although the court did not regard itself as constrained by previous authority, it was concerned nevertheless to root its decision firmly in the principles upon which the law of privilege rests, and in the limited justification for depriving the tribunal of relevant evidence which those principles assume. This was reinforced by the insistence that the dominant purpose is not to be assessed by reference to the manner in which a communication is described.[43] Thus the fact that a document is described on its face as being for the purpose of litigation is not to be regarded as conclusive, though no doubt it is not wholly irrelevant. *Waugh* v. *British Railways Board* therefore provides a formidable barrier to litigants who seek to use the law of privilege as a substantially

---

[38] *Waugh* v. *British Railways Board*, above n. 37, at 534.
[39] (1976) 135 C.L.R. 674.
[40] *Waugh* v. *British Railways Board*, above n. 37, at 545.
[41] *Ibid.*, at 537 and 545.
[42] *Ibid.*, at 543.
[43] *Ibid.*, at 539, *per* Lord Edmund-Davies.

procedural device for withholding relevant evidence. It appears that the dominant purpose rule will be strictly applied. Where, in a case since *Waugh*,[44] assessors prepared a report on premises subject to a loss for an insurance company, it was held not be privileged, because its dominant purpose was to decide "whether or not they should rely upon the clause of the policy in order to repudiate liability,"[45] a decision which it might be thought has considerable proximity to the contemplation of litigation.

Privilege where there are several prospective defendants It has been recognised that even where the result is to deny a plaintiff the opportunity to discover which of a number of prospective defendants was negligent, their privilege will be protected once litigation is contemplated. In *Lee* v. *South West Thames Regional Health Authority*[46] an infant plaintiff suffered burns. He was taken first to one hospital, in the North East Thames Regional Health Authority, then transferred to another (in the Hillingdon Area Health Authority) by ambulance, then returned by ambulance to the first hospital. He suffered brain damage, probably through oxygen deprivation, which may have occurred during an ambulance journey. The ambulance was under the control of the defendant regional health authority. As a result of the plaintiff's application for pre-trial discovery,[47] the defendant authority disclosed the existence of a memorandum prepared by its employees in contemplation of litigation, but to enable the Hillingdon authority to take legal advice as to its liability to the plaintiff.

The defendant's privilege was upheld, as Hillingdon would otherwise lose its own privilege, and effectively thereby be prevented from freely gathering evidence without risk of disclosure to the plaintiff. The judge at first instance[48] took the view that the defendants were merely acting as agents, in obtaining the memorandum, of the Hillingdon authority, albeit the defendants were reporting on actions of their own employees which might have been tortious.

Although the decision in *Schneider* v. *Leigh*,[49] appeared to present an obstacle to upholding the decision of Skinner J. at first instance in *Lee*, it was distinguished by the Court of Appeal in that the two causes of action in that case, which were themselves quite different, did not arise out of the same facts. In *Schneider* v. *Leigh* an expert witness in relation to a tort claim had allegedly libelled the plaintiff in the tort claim, and disclosure was sought for the purposes of the libel action. This is an unusual

---

[44] *Melik & Co.* v. *Norwich Union Fire Insurance Society and Kemp* [1980] 1 Lloyd's Rep. 523.
[45] *Ibid.* at 525, *per* Woolf J., citing *Waugh* v. *British Railways Board*, above n. 37.
[46] [1985] 1 W.L.R. 845.
[47] Under R.S.C. Ord. 24, r. 7A.
[48] *Lee* v. *South West Thames Regional Health Authority* [1985] 1 W.L.R. 845 at 848.
[49] [1955] 2 Q.B. 195.

set of circumstances, and one which, quite properly, the Court of Appeal in *Lee* did not allow to dictate the principles upon which the appeal should be decided. Despite this, Lord Donaldson M.R. although satisfied that the outcome in *Lee* was good law, reached it with "undisguised reluctance,"[50] in that it effectively prevented the plaintiff from finding out which of a number of potential defendants was the appropriate one to sue. In an *obiter* speculation as to how such plaintiffs might achieve such disclosure, he floated the interesting, though as yet untested suggestion that the decision of the House of Lords in *Sidaway* v. *Board of Governors of the Bethlem Royal Hospital and the Maudsley Hospital*[51] could be of assistance. The principle formulated in *Sidaway*, that a patient may compel his doctor to answer questions as to proposed treatment, he proposed, might be extended to compel disclosure *ex post facto*, where the treatment did not proceed satisfactorily, of what in fact occurred.

3 Expert evidence not attracting privilege

There is, as was discussed in Chapter 5, no property in an expert witness.[52] Thus, whatever privilege may arise between a party and an expert witness, the court cannot be deprived of the expert's opinion,[53] or the facts on which it is based. It is however conceivable that the expert who discloses may be in breach of an implied term of his contract with the party for whom he acts if he deliberately or negligently allows his opinion to be known by another party. If another party wishes to call the expert as to these matters, the party who originally instructed the expert cannot prevent him. In *W.* v. *Egdell*[54] it was held at first instance that this even extends to a document brought into existence for the purpose of the legal proceedings because, once it has been put before the expert for his opinion, it becomes "part of the facts on which the opinion is based."[55] There is:

> "a clear and important distinction to be drawn between, on the one hand, instructions given to an expert witness and, on the other hand, the expert's opinion given pursuant to those instructions."[56]

This may however be somewhat misleading. For while, as was established in *Harmony Shipping Co. S.A.* v. *Saudi Europe Line*[57] an expert's

---

[50] *Lee* v. *South West Thames Regional Health Authority*, above n. 48.
[51] [1985] A.C. 871.
[52] *Harmony Shipping Co. S.A.* v. *Saudi Europe Line* [1979] 1 W.L.R. 1380. See Chap. 5.
[53] *R.* v. *King* [1983] 1 W.L.R. 411.
[54] [1989] 2 W.L.R. 689. This decision was upheld by the Court of Appeal: [1990] 1 All E.R. 835. See below, pp. 195–196.
[55] *Ibid.*, at 717.
[56] *Ibid.*
[57] [1979] 1 W.L.R. 1380. See also *R.* v. *King*, above n. 53, at 414.

actual opinion cannot be withheld from the court merely because it was once expressed to one of the parties in contemplation of litigation, an expert's report or other communication with a party which contains opinion is privileged as a whole, unless the court orders that it be disclosed as a condition of adducing it at trial, or supports such disclosure in the public interest.[58]

Furthermore, the purpose of privilege is specifically to prevent another party to proceedings from obtaining discovery or knowledge of particular material. Thus, where a third party has a claim on, for instance, a report on a mental patient, the fact that it was prepared for the legal proceedings does not prevent its disclosure to the Home Office, where the public interest demands this.[59]

4 Party-party communications

Communications between opposite parties, or their agents, are not in general privileged. In a number of cases this has had implications for the conduct of potential expert witnesses, for instance in accident cases in which an allegedly negligent company's medical officer has had conversations with the plaintiff. Where, in a fatal accident case,[60] the defendants sent a doctor to assess the plaintiff's medical condition before he died, and an agent to discuss compromise of the matter, it was held by Cockburn C.J. that:

> "when confidential communications have taken place between you and your agent, who has been sent to report and inquire about the subject matter of the litigation, you are not in general to be compelled to tell your adversary what the result of the inquiries may be. But when you send your agents to see and negotiate with the other party, whatever passes at such interviews ought to be made known, and the other party, or those representing him, have a right to inspect the communications respecting them."[61]

The facts of this case demonstrate the distinction in law between party-party communications, and those between a party and his agent, where litigation is in existence or contemplation.[62] In a similar Irish case, where defendants sent an agent to see the injured plaintiff, and obtained a signed statement from him as to the way in which the accident occurred,

---

SF[58] The Court of Appeal upheld the decision at first instance in *W. v. Egdell*, but on different grounds: see [1990] 1 All E.R. 835.
[59] See also *Hunter v. Mann* [1974] Q.B. 767; *W. v. Egdell*, above n. 54.
[60] *Baker v. London & South Western Railway Co.* (1867) L.R. 3 Q.B. 91.
[61] *Ibid.*, at 93. See also *Wayland v. Metropolitan Railway Co.* [1874] W.N. 96.
[62] Though *quaere* the situation where the agent merely relates to his principal the content of a conversation with the opposite party; *cf. General Accident Fire and Life Assurance Co. v. Tanter* [1983] 1 W.L.R. 100.

there was no privilege attaching to the document.[63] The court was also able to find, quite separately from this, that as the plaintiff had signed the statement it was his document, so that he was entitled to possession of it. See though, the discussion in Chapter 2 of the position in relation to without prejudice meetings of experts pursuant to R.S.C. Order 38, rule 37.

B. PROFESSIONAL CONFIDENCES OF EXPERT WITNESSES

1 The principal rule

Practitioners of many professions, and among them a substantial number of expert witnesses, work within the confines of an ethical system which includes a rigorous approach to the question of confidentiality. The requirements of professional bodies, though they do not usually have the force of law, act as a sanction almost as powerful as the law in that the personal consequences of a departure from them can be equally severe. Sustained attempts have been made to move the law into a position where it protects at least the most important of these confidences through privilege. In general, however, the courts have resisted such suggestions, and it is notable that even where the law of privilege does protect professional confidences, it does so primarily for policy reasons of a broad "public interest," rather than through a desire to protect the relationship between the individual professional and his particular client.[64] This has been judicially regretted, as early as the eighteenth century:

> "there are cases, to which it is much to be lamented that the law of privilege is not extended; those in which medical persons are obliged to disclose the information which they acquire by attending in their professional characters."

It has been suggested that there are some professional enterprises, such as psychiatry, of which confidentiality is such a central feature that they would often be rendered ineffective if they were not guaranteed protection.[65] However, although such confidentiality is recognised as being of importance, it can be breached if the public interest favours disclosure, quite apart from the needs of litigation. Thus in *W. v. Egdell*, in which a psychiatrist was instructed by solicitors acting for a mental patient to examine him for the purpose of a mental health tribunal hearing, it was

---

[63] *Tobakin v. Dublin Co.* [1905] 2 I.R. 58.
[64] See *e.g. D. v. N.S.P.C.C.* [1977] 2 W.L.R. 201. Doctors may not have a duty to assist the police in their inquiries about a patient though they should not mislead: *Rice v. Connolly* [1966] 2 Q.B. 414.
[65] *Wilson v. Rastall* (1792) 4 Term Rep. 753 at 760, *per* Buller C.J.

held by the Court of Appeal that the confidence could be breached if the public interest was served by that report being made available to the hospital authority responsible for the patient, and indeed to the appropriate government department.[66] The Court of Appeal confirmed that the courts must in such cases engage in an exercise of balancing the public interest in disclosure against the interest in confidentiality, which is not only the interest of an individual but also a public interest worthy of protection. There can however be no general rule as to which public interest prevails: it will always be a question of fact for the court. In W v. *Egdell* the interest of the public in protection from dangerous mental patients was held to be paramount. The same has been held to apply where a psychiatrist showed his report, prepared for the defence for sentencing purposes, to the prosecution.[67] Albeit, the defence could have elected not to produce it, he was not in breach of his duty of confidence, because the public interest in knowing that the defendant's mental condition made him a danger to his family outweighed any such duty.

The courts have frequently found questions of public interest, for example in the proper administration of justice, to override an acknowledged need to preserve professional confidences in particular circumstances,[68] and have threatened to imprison individuals who refused to answer relevant questions in court.[69]

2 The exceptions

Statutory or other necessity Particular aspects of the law may be subject to variations of the usual disclosure rules, either because statute so provides, or because a particular jurisdiction of the court entails it. In adoption cases the guardian *ad litem*'s report is confidential.[70] It has been said judicially that this "exception to standard procedural practice is to protect the interests of the child."[71] Similarly the wardship jurisdiction, because of its particular administrative character, for the purpose of protecting the welfare of the child, as distinct from a simple dispute between parties, vests in its judges a discretion to act in accordance with this purpose by requiring confidentiality to be protected where necessary.[72] Lord Devlin observed that it is:

---

[66] [1990] 1 All E.R. 835, C.A.
[67] R.v. *Crozier*, The Independent, May 11, 1990.
[68] The following examples of such cases were cited by Bingham L.J. in *W.* v. *Egdell*, above n. 66, at 848–849: *Att.–Gen.* v. *Mulholland* [1963] 2 Q.B. 477 at 489–490; *Chantrey-Martin and Co.* v. *Martin* [1953] 2 Q.B. 286; *Hunter* v. *Mann* [1974] Q.B. 767; *Tournier* v. *National Provincial and Union Bank of England* [1924] 1 K.B. 461 at 473 and 486. See too *R* v. *Smith* [1971] 1 W.L.R. 1445 (psychiatrists).
[69] *Nuttall* v. *Nuttall and Twyman* (1964) S.J. 605.
[70] Adoption Rules 1984 (S.I. 1984 No. 265), r. 6(11).
[71] *Re M.* [1973] 1 Q.B. 108 at 121.
[72] *Official Solicitor* v. *K.* [1965] A.C. 201.

"erroneous to suppose that because the inquiry is judicial, all the ordinary principles of a judicial inquiry must be observed."[73]

The court's discretion The law of privilege is principally a creature of the common law. As such it is perhaps unsurprising that the inherent power of courts to control their own proceedings should lend to the law of privilege a fairly broad area of discretion where procedural and evidential matters are concerned. This discretion is exercised in two ways.

(i) *Damage-limitation* Where it has been decided, whether after argument upon the point or by consent, that a particular communication does not attract privilege in respect of the proceedings, the evidence must be adduced and put before the court. Where the communication is, despite this, acknowledged to be of a genuinely sensitive nature, it may be protected in a number of ways so that it remains as confidential as is possible in the circumstances. Thus officials who have prepared reports on mental defectives have been judicially supported in their refusal to disclose their contents until actually ordered to do so by the court.[74] In adoption proceedings, a mother about whom serious criticisms were made in the guardian *ad litem*'s report was prevented from reading the report, but her legal adviser was permitted to see it.[75] This was described as a "commonsense and excellent" practice.[76] The court may itself look at documents in issue before deciding whether disclosure should occur.[77] It may order that documents or parts of them should be physically covered.[78] A hearing or part of it may be held *in camera*, though it is recognised that good reason must be shown for such a step:

> "to justify an order for hearing *in camera* it must be shown that the paramount object of securing that justice is done would really be rendered doubtful of attainment if the order were not made."[79]

The court may further take action to ensure that damaging disclosure cannot occur after the court's use for the evidence has ended. The court shorthand writer's notes have been ordered to be impounded in court where they would have disclosed the nature of the secret scientific process in issue between the parties.[80] A general protection for such communications is afforded by the fact that discovery is, unless the contrary is

---

[73] *Official Solicitor v. K.*, above n. 72 at 239.
[74] R. v. *Statutory Visitors to St. Lawrence's Hospital, Caterham, ex p. Pritchard* [1953] 1 W.L.R. 1158.
[75] *Re M.* [1973] Q.B. 108.
[76] *Re K. (Infants)* [1963] Ch. 381 at 397.
[77] *Burmah Oil v. Bank of England* [1980] A.C. 1090; *Science Research Council v. Nassé* [1980] A.C. 1028.
[78] *Science Research Council v. Nassé*, above n. 77.
[79] *Scott v. Scott* [1913] A.C. 417, 439, *per* Lord Haldane.
[80] *Badische v. Levinstein* (1883) 24 Ch.D. 156.

ordered, only granted for the purposes of the action itself.[81] This is of most use where particular documents are sought to be protected:

> "those who disclose documents on discovery are entitled to the protection of the court against any use of the documents otherwise than in the action in which they are disclosed."[82]

Submissions that this rule is ineffectual where the proceedings were in open court and the document was read out by witnesses or counsel have been rejected.[83]

(ii) *The balancing discretion* Where privilege is asserted in furtherance of a public interest recognized by the courts as a matter of law, there is a necessary duty upon the court to weigh that public interest against the need of the court to hear all relevant evidence. This is discussed in detail below.[84] There is additionally however, even where such issues do not arise, a discretion in the court to weigh the need for confidentiality against the importance of the particular evidence to the court, and to conclude that evidence which is not prima facie privileged should not be disclosed or adduced, because of its relative unimportance to the facts in the case, though it is of some arguable relevance. It is important to distinguish these two categories, because the exercise of the discretion is sometimes expressed judicially in terms of a weighing of the 'public interest.' Thus the former limited class of cases can be described as treating of the public interest as a matter of law, in order to distinguish it from the latter, discretionary consideration of the public interest, with which this discussion is partially concerned.[85]

The discretion, though it is always available to the court, is only to be exercised in a manner consistent with the general principles upon which the law of privilege operates, and the courts must:

> "start from the basis that the public interest is, on balance, best served by rigidly confining within narrow limits the cases where material relevant to litigation may be lawfully withheld."[86]

Furthermore, as with judicial discretion generally, "if it comes to the forensic crunch . . . it must be law, not discretion, which is in command."[87]

The discretion will not be employed in order to exclude evidence which, though confidential, is clearly of relevance and importance to

---

[81] *Riddick v. Thames Board Mills* [1977] 1 Q.B. 881, C.A.
[82] *Distillers Co. (Biochemicals) Ltd. v. Times Newspapers Ltd.* [1975] Q.B. 613 at 621, *per* Talbot J.
[83] *Harman v. Secretary of State for the Home Office* [1983] A.C. 280.
[84] See pp. 199–202.
[85] This distinction is based upon dicta in *D. v. N.S.P.C.C.* [1977] 2 W.L.R. 201.
[86] *Waugh v. British Railways Board* [1980] A.C. 521 at 534.
[87] *D. v. N.S.P.C.C.*, above n. 85, at 227, *per* Lord Simon.

matters in issue. It is where such evidence, though relevant is of only marginal importance to the case that it will be exercised. Thus:

> "if a doctor, giving evidence in court, is asked a question which he finds embarrassing because it involves him talking about things which he would normally regard as confidential, he can seek the protection of the judge and ask the judge if it is necessary to answer. The judge, by virtue of the overriding discretion to control his court which all English judges have, can, if he thinks fit, tell the doctor that he need not answer the question. Whether or not the judge would take that line, of course, depends largely on the importance of the potential answer to the issues being tried."[88]

It would be a proper exercise of the discretion for the judge to conclude that evidence was "very unlikely to affect the decision of the case",[89] though it was relevant. Ultimately, given that each party is prima facie entitled to disclosure of all relevant evidence, the court must consider whether disclosure is necessary for disposing of the proceedings fairly as between the parties.[90] It might be thought that this does little more than to reaffirm the principle that the court is only concerned with evidence which has real probative value. It has however been held that the discretion may operate to exclude evidence which is clearly relevant, and therefore of at least theoretical probative value, but which is not necessary for fairly disposing of the present case.[91]

3 Public interest as a matter of law

There is a limited class of cases in which the public interest, used not in its colloquial sense but as a term of art, is said to outweigh the interest of the courts, and the parties to litigation, in disclosure of all relevant evidence. The principles elicited by this class of cases are of considerable importance to expert witnesses, in a number of areas of professional practice, particularly where the certain ability to keep confidences is central to aspects of such practice. Modern authority[92] has confirmed the view that certain categories of such confidences are protected as a matter of law, not discretion.[93] As such it is.

> "a point which the court is bound to take of its own motion if it thinks that it arises."[94]

---

[88] *Hunter v. Mann* [1974] 1 Q.B. 767 at 775, *per* Lord Widgery.
[89] *Campbell v. Tameside Metropolitan Borough Council* [1982] Q.B. 1065.
[90] *Science Research Council v. Nassé* [1980] A.C. 1028.
[91] *Burmah Oil v. Bank of England* [1980] A.C. 1090.
[92] *D. v. N.S.P.C.C.*, above n. 85.
[93] *Ibid.*, at 229.
[94] *Buttes Gas and Oil Co. v. Hammer* [1981] Q.B. 223 at 252, *per* Donaldson L.J.

Although this protection is conveniently considered as an aspect of the law of privilege, it is not clear that it amounts to privilege properly so called. Lord Reid has said:

> "I do not think that the right to withhold the documents depends or flows from any privilege. It arises from the public interest. . . ."[95]

This is more than a merely theoretical distinction, because privilege itself, whoever in fact seeks its protection, can only reside in a party to actual or prospective litigation, not a witness who may seek to protect a confidence.[96] Any person may assert the public interest immunity if they are being required to give evidence or produce documents.

The confidences which have been established as being subject to such protection have been confined within narrow limits by the courts. Police informants are in general protected, as are those who supply information to the Gaming Board[97] although the immunity may be lifted where the relevant evidence is crucial to establishing the innocence of a criminal.[98] State secrets such as those which might be useful to an enemy are also subject to immunity.[99] It is clear that the national economic interest is in general terms a public interest susceptible of such protection, though the extent to which, and circumstances in which this is so are by no means settled.[1]

The immunity from disclosure which perhaps has the most extensive implications for expert witnesses is that relating to communications made in pursuance of the welfare of children.[2] This is a public interest which the courts are bound to recognise as a matter of law, though it is also governed by an indeterminate, though undeniable, area of discretion. The leading authority is the House of Lords decision in *D. v. National Society for the Prevention of Cruelty to Children*[3] which, though confined on its facts to information relating to the welfare of children, analysed in some depth the legal basis upon which the public interest immunity rests. It is thus possible to draw from it some of the more general principles which are likely to influence the willingness of the courts to extend the immunity to other communications in the future.

In *D. v. N.S.P.C.C.* an anonymous informant had told an N.S.P.C.C. inspector about a mother's maltreatment of her 14 month old child.[4] The

---

[95] *R. v. Home Secretary, ex p. Lewes Justices* [1973] A.C. 388 at 402.
[96] See *Schneider v. Leigh*, above n. 1.
[97] *R. v. Home Secretary, ex p. Lewes Justices* [1973] A.C. 388.
[98] *Conway v. Rimmer* [1968] A.C. 910.
[99] *Duncan v. Cammell Laird* [1942] A.C. 624. See also *Buttes Gas and Oil Co. v. Hammer* [1981] Q.B. 223, (communications with a foreign state on territorial matters not to be disclosed).
[1] See *Burmah Oil v. Bank of England* [1980] A.C. 1090.
[2] *D. v. N.S.P.C.C.*, above n. 85.
[3] *Ibid.*
[4] The information, it later transpired, was erroneous.

inspector conducted an investigation, as a result of which the mother brought an action in negligence for nervous shock allegedly caused by the manner of the inspector's investigation. It was asserted that it was central to the mother's prospects of establishing such a case that the informant's identity should be disclosed. It was however held to be in the public interest that it should not be, and that an immunity attached to those who informed bodies statutorily charged with the welfare of neglected and maltreated children such as local authorities, the police and the N.S.P.C.C. Three principles emerge from the decision in *D. v. N.S.P.C.C.*

First, the categories of public interest are, though limited, never closed:

> "the maxim *expressio unius, exlusio alterius* is not a canon of construction that is applicable to judgments."[5]

Lord Simond cited with approval a previous decision, which identified the role of the courts in relation to matters of public policy as being:

> "to expound, and not to expand, such policy. That does not mean that they are precluded from applying an existing principle of public policy to a new set of circumstances, where such circumstances are clearly within the scope of the policy."[6]

Secondly, despite this capacity of the courts to apply the principle to new subject-matter, it must be clearly established that there is a public interest in that which is sought to be protected by the immunity. The only method thus far accepted as incontrovertibly establishing this is the express words or clear implication of a statute, such the Gaming Act 1968, by which:

> "Parliament decided that it is in the public interest that there should be certain measures of control, of supervision and of restriction of gaming activities."[7]

In *D. v. N.S.P.C.C.*, the N.S.P.C.C., with statutory powers to investigate the neglect and maltreatment of children, had been given clear sanction to further the public interest in the welfare of children[8] which is itself enshrined in numerous statutes[9]:

> "the public interest to be protected is the effective functioning of an organisation authorised under an Act of Parliament to bring legal proceedings for the welfare of children."[10]

Lord Simon thought it irrelevant to this point that a body (such as the

---

[5] *D. v. N.S.P.C.C.*, above n. 85, at 209, *per* Lord Diplock.
[6] *Kender v. St. John Mildmay* [1938] A.C. 1 at 38.
[7] *R. v. Home Secretary, ex p. Lewes Justices*, above n. 97, at 403, *per* Lord Morris.
[8] *D. v. N.S.P.C.C.*, above n. 85, at 228.
[9] *e.g.* Guardianship of Minors Act 1971.
[10] *D. v. N.S.P.C.C.*, above n. 85, at 210, *per* Lord Diplock.

N.S.P.C.C.) has only powers and not (like local authorities) also duties in relation to children.[11]

Thirdly, although these immunities exist as a matter of law, they are also subject to a substantial area of discretion as to their application in the particular case. Disclosure will be ordered if potential damage to an established public interest is not clearly identified:

> "if, on balance, the matter is left in doubt, disclosure should be ordered."[12]

This could be said to do no more than place the burden of showing that disclosure should not take place upon the person asserting a public interest in non-disclosure. It is clear though that even where a clear general public interest exists, for example, in the confidentiality of local authority records in relation to children, the courts will order disclosure in the particular case.[13]

It is worthy of note, however, that Lord Edmund-Davies was favourably disposed in his speech to a broad approach to the problem, by contrast with the narrower view of his colleagues. Such an approach would give the court, in any case where a confidential relationship arose, a discretion to decide whether the public interest would be better served by non-disclosure. This, by contrast with the discretion already discussed, which does not spring from a public interest asserted as a matter of law, would not be confined to cases where the contested evidence was, though strictly relevant, of only marginal importance to resolution of matters in issue in the case. This broad approach, however, has not found authoritative support, despite the considerable sympathy with which it would clearly meet in some non-legal professional circles. It would amount to a significant development of the law, going as it does to the root of established principles of the law of privilege. The process of deciding, however, what is an area of public interest worthy of the protection of the courts (*i.e.* the prior question), is one which can take on an appearance remarkably similar to the broad discretionary approach advocated by Lord Edmund-Davies:

> "if I have to weigh in the balance the risk of gaming clubs getting into the wrong hands against the risk of a respectable citizen occasionally being denied the privilege of running a gaming club, I have no doubt that in the public interest the latter rather than the former risk ought to be accepted."[14]

---

[11] *D. v. N.S.P.C.C.*, above n. 85, at 228.
[12] *Ibid.*, at 233, *per* Lord Edmund-Davies. See also *Official Solicitor v. K.* [1965] A.C. 201.
[13] *Re D* [1970] 1 W.L.R. 599; *Re M* [1990] 2 F.L.R. 36. See further Chap. 22, pp. 399–401.
[14] *R. v. Home Secretary, ex p. Lewes Justices*, above n. 97, at 413, *per* Lord Salmon.

CHAPTER 10

The Evidential Value of Expert Evidence

A. BURDEN AND STANDARD OF PROOF

1 Burden of proof

Expert evidence, although frequently an important element of a party's case, is usually not prerequisite to the establishment of a cause of action or a prosecution, or the raising of a defence. In criminal cases, the high standard of proof may have the effect of requiring expert evidence to be called for the prosecution in order to cover what would otherwise be doubt resulting in acquittal. In prosecutions in relation to drink/driving offences, the evidence of an analyst will be necessary to establish the level of alcohol in the body.[1] Certain sentences may only be imposed on particular classes of offender after the obtaining of reports from a probation officer[2] or doctor.[3] Despite the fact that expert evidence is seldom a formal legal requirement, it is recognised that it may in practical terms be essential for a party to adduce it. So, while the Homicide Act 1957 does not in terms require medical evidence in support of a defence of diminished responsibility, it is nevertheless "a practical necessity if that defence is to begin to run at all."[4] Similar considerations apply to the defence of insanity.[5] Such psychiatric evidence is discussed in Chapter 12.

Expert evidence may be necessary where particular exhibits are to be adduced in evidence, if their comprehension or description requires expertise. Thus analysts are necessary to identify particular drugs, though not if there is an admission as to their identity.[6] A bench of magistrates should not measure tyres with a tyre gauge without expert evidence as to the proper manner of its use.[7] Where a particular form of punishment, known as piqueting, was in issue, and it was unfamiliar to the court, it should have been illustrated to the court by a witness familiar with its practice.[8] The plaintiff's injured finger in a road accident case

---

[1] See below, Chap. 24, pp. 421–423.
[2] See below, Chap. 23, pp. 412–416.
[3] See below, Chap. 23, pp. 416–419.
[4] R. v. Dix (1982) 74 Cr.App.R. 306 at 311. See also R.. v. Byrne (1960) 44 Cr.App.R. 246; Att-Gen. for South Australia v. Brown [1960] A.C. 432.
[5] R. v. Holmes (1953) 37 Cr.App.R. 61.
[6] Bird v. Adams [1972] Crim.L.R. 174; R.. v. Chatwood [1980] 1 W.L.R. 874.
[7] R. v. Tiverton Justices, ex p. Smith [1981] R.T.R. 280.
[8] R. v. Picton (1804) 30 How.St.Tr. 226 at 480.

could not be shown to the jury in the absence of a medical witness to explain the nature of the injury.[9]

2 Standard of proof

There is no direct method of correlating the standard of proof in criminal and civil cases to the varying degrees of certainty which scientists and other experts ascribe to their findings. The criminal standard is susceptible of no precise mathematical description,[10] such as a 99 per cent. probability, and although the civil standard can be meaningfully described as 51 per cent. probability this is often difficult to translate into terms equivalent to those of scientific results or estimates. In most cases, of course, the expert evidence, whether it be in the form of a generally expressed opinion or of a numerically represented set of scientific results, must be taken together with the factual evidence in the case, to which it is meaningless to ascribe precise numerical probabilities. In *R. v. Bracewell*,[11] Ormrod L.J. drew the distinction between scientific proof and legal proof.[12] The fact that a proposition is not absolutely certain in scientific terms need not entail that there is a doubt in respect of the criminal standard of proof:

> "the available data may be inadequate to *prove* scientifically that the alternative hypothesis is false, so the scientific witness will answer 'No, I cannot exclude it,' though the effect of his evidence as a whole can be expressed in terms such as 'But for all practical purposes (including the jury's) it is so unlikely that it can safely be ignored.' "[13]

In the great majority of such cases subject to the criminal standard of proof it will be the combination of the scientific with other factual evidence which permits a finding beyond reasonable doubt. Where there is only scientific evidence, represented in probabilistic terms, the court should not "transmute a mathematical probability into a forensic certainty."[14] Furthermore it should not be regarded as inevitable that there is a doubt, upon the criminal standard of proof, merely because two experts disagree. The jury may prefer the evidence of one to that of

---

[9] *Curtler v. London Tramway Company Ltd.*, *The Times*, February 13, 1891. The report does not however make clear whether or not this was because, liability being in issue, it was sought to demonstrate the cause of the accident by inference from the nature of the injury.
[10] See R. Coleman and H. Walls, "The Evaluation of Scientific Evidence" [1974] Crim.L.R. 276; H. Walls, "What is Reasonable Doubt?" (1971) Crim.L.R. 458.
[11] (1979) 68 Cr.App.R. 44.
[12] *Ibid.*, at 49.
[13] *Ibid.*
[14] *Re J.S. (A Minor)* [1981] Fam. 22 at 28.

another, and to suggest otherwise would be "heresy."[15] It is submitted, however, that the jury should be warned that such a course would only be appropriate where the evidence of one expert has been substantially discredited on matters in issue.

It has been suggested in a number of cases, to which the civil standard of proof would ordinarily apply, that because of the gravity of the matter, or the implications of the evidence for the reputation, whether professional or personal, of an individual, a more stringent standard of proof may apply.[16] Such cases frequently involve the assessment of important expert evidence, particularly though not only where the conduct of professionals is concerned. The true effect of these cases, however, is probably not to change the standard of proof itself, but merely to demonstrate that the courts will not act except upon weighty and persuasive evidence where the consequences of their decisions have more than purely legal implications.

B. WEIGHT

1 Admissibility and weight

It has been seen from previous chapters that even where a serious question arises as to whether expert evidence, or the evidence of a particular proposed expert witness, should be admitted, the evidence is often heard by the court in any event. This is so for a number of reasons. First, it is often difficult to decide whether extensive proposed evidence is admissible without hearing the bulk of it, though as almost universally, reports are now prepared and disclosed, this problem looms less large. Secondly, however, even with the existence of a report, which could be drafted by a legal adviser,[17] it is difficult to judge the competence of a witness to give expert evidence without hearing the substance of his oral evidence. The lack of formal qualifications, such as degrees, is not conclusive as to competence in many cases. Thirdly, the doubtful admissibility of expert evidence can usually be effectively resolved by according to it little or no weight at the adjudication stage. There are substantial dangers, however, where issues are considered by justices, juries and other fact-finding tribunals without legal training. Juries are likely to be profoundly influenced by an ostensibly impressive expert witness, what-

---

[15] R. v. *Sodo* [1975] R.T.R. 357.
[16] See *e.g. Re J.S. (A Minor)*, above n. 14; *Re G. (A Minor)*, *The Times*, July 20, 1987; *Hornal* v. *Neuberger* [1957] 1 Q.B. 247; *Bater* v. *Bater* [1951] P. 35; *Re Dellow's Will Trusts* [1964] 1 W.L.R. 451. See also A. Khan and A. Wolfgang, "Standard of Proof in Medical Negligence" (1984) 52 Medico-Legal Journal 117.
[17] See Chap. 4, pp. 87–88.

ever efforts the judge may make in his summing-up to counteract this tendency.

The appeal courts will always pause before criticising a trial judge who has himself seen an expert giving evidence in court, and has permitted his evidence to be considered by the jury. However, it has been said that it was wrong to permit the evidence of a handwriting expert to go before a jury where it consisted of an opinion that a disputed signature was that of the defendant, without any reasons being given,[18] and a new trial was ordered where, on a matter upon which there was scientific controversy, a jury had made findings in the absence of "satisfactory" evidence in support of them.[19]

2 Conflicting expert evidence

Save that the court is usually in the former case dealing with opinions as well as facts, there is no difference in substance between the assessment of expert and other evidence. The credit of the witness, as revealed by the content of his evidence, his demeanour in court and his manner of answering questions are all relevant, though with experts the court is seldom concerned with the telling of specific deliberate untruths, but more often with either a predisposition towards the case of the party calling him, or towards a professional position which he has adopted and is reluctant to be shifted from, despite evidence to the contrary. The substance of the evidence, likewise, must be weighed and accorded value. Although the impressiveness of an expert's qualifications and experience are always relevant, they must not be employed as a substitute for the need to analyse the content of conflicting evidence by reference to the facts in the case.

There are no rules of law concerning the precedence to be accorded as between the practitioner and the theorist: their relative merits must always be judged according to the needs of the particular case. Furthermore, subject to the question of admissibility, there is no *a priori* qualitative difference between different fields of expertise for evidential purposes,[20] though of course particular disciplines may be more appropriate for the analysis of specific issues than others. Similarly, the evidence of one expert is not necessarily superior to that of another because he has a greater familiarity with the subject matter of the case. A court, hearing evidence as to the mental condition of a respondent wife in divorce proceedings, preferred the evidence of a medical witness, who had only examined her once, to that of doctors who had charge of her over a period of years, particularly (but apparently not only) because the rel-

[18] R. v. *Hipson* [1969] Crim.L.R. 85.
[19] *Metropolitan Asylum District* v. *Hill* (1882) 47 L.T. 29 at 33.
[20] See *e.g. Milirrpum* v. *Nabalco Pty Ltd.* (1971) 17 F.L.R. 141.

evant period was outside that during which any of the expert witnesses had examined her.[21]

The court may resolve the matter not by the substance of the opinion, but by taking account of the circumstances in which the expert came to express it. In proceedings concerning expert mining issues, the opinion of one group of experts was preferred because they had expressed it before it was known that legal proceedings would ensue[22]:

> "they were called in to advise the defendants before any contest arose ... for the more advantageous conduct of the mine, but not to assist them in the litigation."[23]

An expert of less eminence may however, by the opportunity of personal observation, be in a better position to express a view than a number of eminent specialists who could express only theoretical opinions after the event.[24]

If the court admits expert evidence of opinion it must be taken to have done so because it is unable, without such evidence, to decide upon matters of a specialist nature. While the court may, therefore, decide between the views of conflicting experts, either by simply preferring one opinion to another, or by reference to the influence of facts found in the case upon these opinions,[25] it may not adopt a specialist position or theory which has not been posited before the court by any expert[26]:

> "if the medical evidence is equivocal, the court may elect which of the theories advanced it accepts. If only two medical theories are advanced, the court may elect between the two or reject them both; it cannot adopt a third theory of its own, no matter how plausible such might be to the court."[27]

3 Opinion and fact

Evidence of opinion and fact has important differences. Neither has evidential precedence over the other in general terms, although in individual cases it may be obvious that the issues will be decided predominantly or exclusively by evidence of one kind or the other. Facts may outweigh opinions, either because an opinion is based on facts which are dis-

---

[21] *Sofaer* v *Sofaer* [1960] 1 W.L.R. 1173. Conversely, the court may prefer the evidence of persons with both specialist knowledge and familiarity with the subject-matter, such as that of witnesses as to value, who knew a ship before it went down: *The Iron Master* (1859) Sw. 441.
[22] *Abinger* v. *Ashton* (1873) L.R. 17 Eq. 358.
[23] *Ibid.*, at 375.
[24] *Brock* v. *Kellock* (1861) 43 Griff. 38 at 68.
[25] See below, pp. 208–209.
[26] *McLean* v. *Weir* (1977) 3 C.C.L.T. 87.
[27] *Ibid.*, at 101.

proved, or because facts which are proved show the opinion itself to be erroneous. Conversely, the evidence of an expert witness may demonstrate conclusively that a particular version of the facts offered by a witness must be substantially wrong. In the final analysis of course the facts are always predominant because they, not the opinions, are what a party must prove or disprove, and opinion ultimately has the sole purpose of making it possible to establish that a state of factual affairs has existed, exists or is likely to exist, providing the court with the specialist framework within which to make such assessments. The duty of the expert witness:

> "is to furnish the Judge or jury with the necessary scientific criteria for testing the accuracy of their conclusions, so as to enable the Judge or jury to form their own independent judgment by the application of these criteria to the facts proved in evidence."[28]

Expert evidence alone There is no reason in principle why an action should not be tried on expert evidence alone, though this will always be against a matrix of agreed facts as to the surrounding circumstances. Liability for an accident may be decided entirely on expert evidence, the court deciding which expert gives the most convincing account of what occurred.[29] Where negligence is prima facie established by the maxim *res ipsa loquitur*, it can be rebutted solely by expert evidence,[30] though this cannot be achieved by employing expert evidence to suggest a number of hypotheses, only some of which do not entail negligence,[31] particularly where an employer must show that he in fact took reasonable steps to prevent an industrial accident.[32] In a criminal case, the judge should consider a submission of no case to answer upon the usual principles although the only evidence is scientific.[32a]

Expert evidence and evidence of fact The duty of the court is to consider the expert evidence in the light of the facts, not in isolation from them,[33] and where a case involves substantial elements both of opinion and factual evidence the court may accord as much weight to each as it sees fit. The judge should permit a jury to hear all relevant expert evidence, where the decision is in part one of fact, such as the capacity of a child to give evidence.[34] Although for the purposes of admissibility and procedure a distinction is drawn between the two kinds of evidence, all

---

[28] *Davie v. Edinburgh Magistrate* (1953) S.C. 34 at 40.
[29] *Dawson v. Murex* [1942] 1 All E.R. 483.
[30] *Pearson v. North Western Gas Board* [1968] 1 All E.R. 669.
[31] *Moore v. Fox and Sons* [1956] 1 Q.B. 596.
[32] *Ibid.*
[32a] *R v. Penman* (1985) 82 Cr.App.R. 44.
[33] See *Davie v. Edinburgh Magistrate*, above n. 28.
[34] *R. v. Reynolds* [1950] 1 K.B. 606.

evidence is really evidence of opinion, and the court must simply decide whether to rely on that which originates in lay perception or expert knowledge and skill.[35] Where the court believes certain factual witnesses, it may simply adopt the view of the expert whose approach is consistent with those witnesses.[36] Where the results of two analyses of a motorist's urine were so far apart that the defence expert believed they must have related to different samples, raising the question whether the wrong container had been sent to him, the jury was entitled to assess all the evidence, both as to the mechanics of how the containers were sent, and as to the substance of the expert opinion evidence.[37] Where the prosecution was unable to call psychiatric evidence as to a defence of diminished responsibility, because the defendant when interviewed by the psychiatrist denied any involvement in the offence, the jury was entitled nevertheless to reject thereby uncontradicted defence psychiatric evidence if there was factual evidence as to the accused's state of mind with which to compare it.[38] There must however be factual evidence adequate to support the jury's finding.[39]

Preferring non-expert evidence   The law makes no general distinction as to the value of expert and non-expert witness evidence,[40] though in the individual case it may be obvious that one sheds more light on matters in issue than the other. Although facts predominate in the sense that the purpose of expert evidence is in effect only to point to the likelihood of a particular state of affairs or set of facts, the court is entirely at liberty as to which class of evidence it prefers. So where the court was required to assess the effect of blasting operations on some houses which had suffered damage, it was said that, although the judge:

> "was free to place his main reliance on the evidence of those who described what they 'saw, felt and heard,' there is no binding authority which required him to give mechanical preference to that class of evidence as against scientific evidence in determining the weight of evidence."[41]

Attempts have occasionally been made to state a hierarchy of evidence on particular issues. Thus where the value of a lost ship fell to be decided, in the absence of clear evidence of its market value, it was held that the most

---

[35] See *R.* v. *Wells* [1976] Crim.L.R. 518.
[36] *Clark* v. *Clark* [1939] P. 228.
[37] *R.* v. *Dawson* [1976] R.T.R. 535. However, see also *Gordon* v. *Thorpe* [1986] Crim.L.R. 61, *Newton* v. *Woods* (1987) 151 J.P. 436 and the discussion in Chap. 24, pp. 423–424.
[38] *R.* v. *Kiszko* [1979] Crim.L.R. 465.
[39] *Aitken* v. *McMeckan* [1895] A.C. 310.
[40] *Shawinigan* v. *Naud* [1929] 4 D.L.R. 57.
[41] *Porter* v. *Bell* [1955] 1 D.L.R. 62 at 68.

probative evidence was the expert opinion of those who knew the ship when afloat, followed by the expert opinion of those conversant with shipping generally, with factual evidence of its original cost and insurance value being of inferior weight.[41a] Whatever the merits of such an analysis in the particular case, this cannot be said to be an appropriate general approach, and such preconceived orders of importance find little support in the authorities.[41b]

It is only where the nature of the issues logically demands that expert evidence predominates that a jury can be said wrongly to have decided as to the evidence of witnesses of fact. Even if two experts are of the highest expertise, their evidence may, once weighed by the jury, be discarded, particularly where the experts are concerned with an area of scientific uncertainty, such as the state of a man's mind when committing an offence.[42] Conversely, where there can be virtual scientific certainty, and the expert evidence all points to one conclusion, the jury should not adopt a scientific theory of its own.[43]

The facts and issues in a case may demonstrate that witnesses of fact have a clear advantage over any expert,[44] and this will justify rejection on grounds of weight of the expert evidence. Where a witness as to central facts is also an expert, his evidence will often be difficult to dislodge, even if a number of specialists of eminence take a different view.[45] If factual evidence is unchallenged as fact, it cannot be upset by opinion evidence, and although a party which did not cross-examine a witness, who stated that he saw an individual writing particular words, was permitted to call expert evidence in rebuttal, it had no weight because:

> "that evidence being unimpeached ... [it] could be no counterbalance to the direct evidence of the attesting witness."[46]

The court should always be guided by the issues in the particular case as to how to apportion weight between factual and opinion evidence, and then consider the actual weight of each item of evidence. Courts may differ as to the first part of this process. Thus the courts have taken different views as to the necessity,[47] or otherwise,[48] of relying on expert evidence as to the state of mind of an alleged criminal. The court may feel constrained by authority as to its approach in particular categories of case,[49]

[41a] *The Iron Master*, above n. 21.
[41b] See though *The Harmonides* [1903] P. 1 at 5–6, and *The Clyde* (1856) Sw. 23.
[42] *R. v. Rivett* (1950) 34 Cr.App.R. 87.
[43] See *Anderson v. R.* [1972] A.C. 100; *McLean v. Weir*, above n. 26.
[44] See *Bowden v. Bowden* (1917) 62 S.J. 105.
[45] *Brock v. Kellock*, above n. 24.
[46] *Newton v. Ricketts* (1861) 9 H.L.C. 262 at 266.
[47] *R. v. Byrne* (1960) 44 Cr.App.R. 246 at 258.
[48] *R. v. Rivett*, above n. 42.
[49] *McLoughlin v. O'Brien* [1983] A.C. 410.

but in general the courts will look at the particular needs of the case before them. So where the welfare of children is concerned the courts will be heavily reliant upon psychiatric evidence in the case of an abnormal child, but will be less reluctant to make its own judgment in the light of all the evidence, non-expert included, where the child is happy and normal.[50]

Directions to the jury It is of particular importance that juries are fully and properly directed as to how to weigh expert evidence, and on its relationship to evidence of fact. They must not be invited to disregard the opinion of an expert witness and form their own opinion on specialist matters.[51] Conversely, juries must be directed clearly that they should only accept expert evidence because they are persuaded by it,[52] not because of the absence of evidence to the contrary.[53] A jury was wrongly directed that it should accept medical evidence unless the doctor "by his own conduct shows that his evidence ought not to be accepted" because this:[54]

> "then puts him into a position in which, in the absence of reasons for rejecting his evidence, his evidence ought to be accepted."[55]

The criminal standard of proof necessitates close attention to a jury direction where the acceptance of a prosecution expert's evidence renders a guilty verdict logically (if not practically) inevitable. In such circumstances the only two courses which would avail the defendant of the protection of the standard of proof would be a direction either that the jury must feel sure as to the prosecution expert's evidence, or that it should assume that the defence expert is correct and therefore to base its verdict exclusively on the non-expert evidence.[56]

4 Weight on appeal

Just as the appeal courts are reluctant to interfere with decisions which depend in part upon observation of the manner in which lay witnesses give their evidence, so they will not criticise without good reason an assessment of the relative weight to be accorded to expert and other evi-

---

[50] *J. v. C.* [1970] A.C. 668 at 726.
[51] *Anderson v. R.*, above n. 43. See also *McLean v. Weir*, above n. 26. The prosecution has a duty, which the court should enforce if counsel does not, to decide whether an expert witness not present at trial should be called, lest the jury reaches a decision on specialist matters without specialist assistance: *R. v. Hipson* [1969] Crim.L.R. 85.
[52] *R. v. Matheson* (1958) Cr.App.R. 145 at 152.
[53] *R. v. Lanfear* [1968] 1 All E.R. 683.
[54] *Ibid.*, at 684, *per* Diplock L.J.
[55] *Ibid.*
[56] *R. v. Platt* [1981] Crim.L.R. 332.

dence, or to the conflicting evidence of experts. Undoubtedly demeanour looms less substantial as a method of assessment of experts. However, suggestions that it may be simply irrelevant where experts are concerned[57] are probably wrong. It was observed by Brandon L.J. in *Joyce* v. *Yeomans*[58] that the trial judge does have significant advantages over the appellate court:

> "In my judgment, even when dealing with expert witnesses, a trial judge has an advantage over an appellate court in assessing the value, the reliability and the impressiveness of the evidence given by experts called on either side. There are various aspects of such evidence in respect of which the trial judge can get the 'feeling' of a case in a way in which an appellate court, reading the transcript, cannot. Sometimes expert witnesses display signs of partisanship in a witness box or lack of objectivity. This may or may not be obvious from the transcript, yet it may be quite plain to the trial judge. Sometimes an expert witness may refuse to make what a more wise witness would make, namely, proper concessions to the viewpoint of the other side. Here again this may or may not be apparent from the transcript, although plain to the trial judge. I mention only two aspects of the matter, but there are others."[59]

However, an appeal court should not come to a different conclusion, in respect of any evidence, unless satisfied that the trial judge's advantage in this respect could not alone account for the divergence of view.[60] It has been suggested that there is a crucial distinction in this respect between the "perception" and "evaluation" of facts.[61] Although the two processes are clearly to be approached somewhat differently by appeal courts, both the decision in *Joyce* v. *Yeomans*[62] and a recognition of the partisan pressures upon some expert witnesses suggest that the appeal courts should always look at the individual case rather than be guided by some supposed general principle or tendency. In an appropriate case the appeal courts will say that both the expert and the other evidence in the case were insufficient to found the decision or finding at first instance.[63] A trial judge may also be successfully appealed where he bases his assessment of experts upon his knowledge of them from other cases, to the exclusion of the merits of their evidence in the present proceedings.[63a]

---

[57] *Stojalowski* v. *Imperial Smelting Corporation* (N.S.C.) (1976) 121 S.J. 118.
[58] [1981] 1 W.L.R. 549.
[59] *Ibid.*, at 556.
[60] *Watt* v. *Thomas* [1947] A.C. 484 at 487.
[61] *Benmax* v. *Austin Motor Co.* [1955] A.C. 370.
[62] Above n. 58.
[63] *Aitken* v. *McMeckan*, above n. 39.
[63a] *Vakauta* v. *Kelly* [1989] A.L.J. 610 H.C.

C. BIAS

It has long been recognised by the courts that bias is not the preserve of lay witnesses, and that experts may display it in their evidence. Indeed in many respects the incentives for experts to favour one party contrary to their actual belief are substantial. First, expert witnesses are paid for their evidence. Secondly, they may be retained on a regular basis by a particular client or group of clients in different cases. Thirdly the expert may hope to gain favour with a client generally, perhaps because he hopes that non-legal professional engagements may be forthcoming or continue. Lord Campbell noted that the temptation to bias was strong even for "respectable witnesses,"[64] and took the view that scientific witnesses should not in general be accorded much weight.[65] Lord Jessel M.R. recalled a case while he was in practice at the bar in which a party had commissioned 68 expert's reports until a favourable one was obtained.[66] His practice on the bench was to treat experts with some scepticism.

The criminal courts will quash convictions which are based upon forensic evidence tainted by bias. In *Preece* v. *H.M. Advocate*[67] a Home Office forensic scientist, not asked by counsel about the blood group of the victim, declined to tell the court, knowing that his conclusions about the case were unwarranted and misleading without information as to the blood group. The conviction was quashed as the evidence "fell short of the standards of accuracy and objectivity of an expert witness."[68] As a result of this and other cases proposals have been made from time to time for pre-trial exchange of expert's reports in criminal cases, and for meetings between experts to discuss their findings.[69] Some such provisions have now been introduced.[70]

A part of the difficulty in relation to biased or false expert evidence is the absence of remedies for the victim or of other personal consequences for the expert witness. There is in general no action for damages against a witness who gives false evidence in criminal proceedings.[71] The immunity of police officers from civil action for perjury in court proceedings has been said to extend to the preparation, pre-trial, of a report for the Director of Public Prosecutions.[72] Presumably forensic scientists act-

[64] *Tracey Peerage Case* (1843) 10 Cl. & F. 154 at 177.
[65] *Ibid.*, at 191. See also *Davidson* v. *Davidson* (1860) 22 S.C. 749 at 751–752.
[66] *Thom* v. *Worthing Skating Rink Co.* (1876) L.R. 6 Ch.D. 415.
[67] [1981] Crim.L.R. 783.
[68] *Ibid.*
[69] See *e.g.* Sir R. Ormrod, "Scientific Evidence in Court" [1968] Crim.L.R. 240; A.R. Brownlie, "Expert Evidence in the Light of Preece v. H.M. Advocate" (1982) 22 Med. Sci.Law 237.
[70] Crown Court (Advance Notice of Expert Evidence) Rules 1987: see Chap. 2, pp. 57–58.
[71] *Hargreaves* v. *Bretherton* [1959] 1 Q.B. 45.
[72] *Marrinan* v. *Vibert* [1963] 1 Q.B. 528. See too *Watson* v. *M'Ewan* [1905] A.C. 480.

ing for the Home Office or the police are subject to the same protection. Experts will also be immune to civil action arising out of negligence if the act was part of the criminal investigation process.[73] This immunity covers:

> "the collection and analysis of material relevant to the offence or possible offence under investigation ... not ... merely ... the preparation of the witness's formal statement or proof of evidence."[74]

Actions against experts in civil cases alleging negligence or fraud will usually fail because of difficulties in the proof of causation. Litigation is subject in any event to such uncertainties that the courts will be very slow to say that the outcome would have been different if particular evidence had or had not been given.

5 Perjury

The question whether experts are subject to perjury proceedings for giving false evidence is open to some doubt. Any witness may be prosecuted for perjury if he:

> "wilfully makes a statement material in that proceeding, which he knows to be false or does not believe to be true."[75]

Experts are not excluded *per se* from this liability, so that they may clearly be prosecuted for wrong statements of fact which come within the terms of the section as interpreted by the case law. This must logically extend to statements of fact which require expertise in the observation or perception of the facts.

Some of the older authorities suggest that where opinion is concerned, experts may not be open to such prosecution. Of opinion evidence generally, it has been said that:

> "although the evidence is given on oath, in point of fact the person knows he cannot be indicted for perjury, because it is only evidence as to a matter of opinion."[76]

It has also been said that a witness could not be prosecuted for perjury where the truth or falsehood of the statement depended on the construction of a deed.[77] It is submitted however that these authorities are misleading. In *Folkes* v. *Chadd*[78] it was said that:

---

[73] *Evans* v. *London Hospital Medical College* [1981] 1 W.L.R. 184.
[74] *Ibid.*, at 192.
[75] Perjury Act 1911, s.1.
[76] *Abinger* v. *Ashton* (1873) L.R. 17 Eq. 358 at 373. See also *Adams* v. *Canon* (1621) 1 Dyer 53b.
[77] *R.* v. *Crespigny* (1795) 1 Esp. 280.
[78] (1792) 3 Doug. 157.

"hand-writing is proved every day by opinion; and for false evidence on such questions a man may be indicted for perjury."[79]

This remark was *obiter*, but although it may well refer to the evidence of lay witnesses familiar with the handwriting of a particular person, there is no logical distinction between this and expert opinion. More recent authority suggests that opinion may indeed be the subject of perjury proceedings, if an opinion is not genuinely held.[80] Some of the older authorities support the principle that a witness may be subject to perjury proceedings if he states that he "believes" something to be the case when in fact he believes otherwise.[81] This is a state of mind strongly analogous to (and difficult to distinguish from) opinion, whether expert or otherwise. The view has also been expressed that:

> "the state of a man's mind is as much a fact as the state of his digestion. It is true that it is very difficult to prove what the state of a man's mind at a particular time is, but if it can be ascertained it is as much a fact as anything else."[82]

What is undoubtedly the case is that such proceedings will be extremely infrequent, because of the enormous difficulties of proof to the criminal standard.[83]

---

[79] *Ibid.*, at 159. See also *R. v. Pedley* (1784) 1 Leach 325.
[80] *R. v. Schlesinger* (1847) 10 Q.B. 670.
[81] *Ockley v. Whitlesbye* (1622) Palm. 294; *R. v. Mawbey* (1796) 6 Term. Rep. 619 at 637.
[82] *Edgington v. Fitzmaurice* (1885) 29 Ch.D. 459 at 483.
[83] See *R. v. Schlesinger*, above n. 80.

CHAPTER 11

Costs and Fees

A. CIVIL PROCEEDINGS

The general principles upon which costs are recoverable in relation to the expense of engaging experts before and at trial are no different from those relating to ordinary witnesses and other evidential costs, principally set out in R.S.C. Order 62 and C.C.R. Order 38.[1] The court or the taxing master may disallow costs where they were not necessarily or properly incurred,[2] and specific orders in appropriate cases may be made requiring the solicitor to repay monies to his client or to indemnify other parties.[3] The expert himself has no locus standi to make representations at a taxation hearing, though the taxing master has a discretion to hear him in a case involving substantial fees.[4] The solicitor has a duty to use his best endeavours on the expert's behalf at such hearings.[5]

1 The necessity for expert evidence

In general costs follow the event, and the successful party should recover all reasonably incurred costs. The issue may arise however as to whether expert evidence was necessary in order to achieve the result, and whether the person called was in fact an expert. These matters must be decided on general principles as to admissibility and expertise, and the test is the purposive one applied in *The Torenia*,[6] so that if the purpose of expert factual observations is the drawing of inferences, it will be regarded as expert evidence proper. Although 'in-house' experts are experts for the purposes of pre-trial disclosure,[7] it has been held that they may not qualify on taxation as experts.[8] It is submitted however that there can be no fixed rule as to this, and that the taxing master should exercise his discretion bearing in mind whether the witness had in any event to give factual evidence on a party's behalf, the extra expert preparation involved,

---

[1] R.S.C. Ord. 62 applies where C.C.R. Ord. 38 is silent.
[2] R.S.C. Ord. 62, rr. 11 and 28.
[3] Ibid.
[4] *Cementation v. Keaveney*, The Times, July 21, 1988.
[5] Ibid.
[6] [1988] 2 Lloyd's Rep. 210.
[7] *Shell Pensions Trust v. Pell Frischmann* [1986] 2 All E.R. 911.
[8] *Taylor v. Greening* (unreported), May 15, 1956, C.A.

the nature of the expert evidence he gave, and whether other expert witnesses were called.[9]

No generalisations should be made as to the classes of expert who do and do not warrant remuneration as such. The issues in the case must be analysed to decide whether the particular witness's evidence was necessary, and whether he had expertise relevant to it. Thus a claims consultant may be regarded as an expert in construction cases, if not generally, at least in relation to specific issues such as delay, if there are a number of possible causes of the delay and the court requires assistance as to which were operative.[10] The court will if necessary separate those expert costs which are fully allowable, and those which are only partially so or not at all. In *Mitchell* v. *Mulholland*[11] Edmund-Davies L.J. expressed the view that each witness must be individually considered, to decide whether the costs were either necessary or proper for the attainment of justice or enforcing the rights of a party, or otherwise reasonably incurred.[12] Thus in a personal injuries case involving calculations of future pecuniary loss, the court concluded that no costs were recoverable in relation to an economist, whose evidence had been unnecessary, and that one third of the costs of an actuary[13] and a chartered accountant were recoverable because their evidence was only of limited value, and much of it had been based on that of the economist.[14] Costs have been disallowed where the only function of an expert witness was to give evidence as to ordinary English words,[15] which is irrelevant and inadmissible. An interpreter may be regarded as an expert for such purposes where a foreign party is involved,[16] although there are specific provisions as to interpreters.[17]

A solicitor giving evidence of fact in relation to the case is regarded as a "professional"[18] not an "expert" witness.[19] Where a person, not an expert, has been properly engaged to perform some evidence-gathering exercise before trial, costs may be recovered in relation to his expenses even though such costs would normally be recovered as part of an expert's "qualifying" fee.[20] Thus although an expert who was conducting a chemical analysis of discharge into a river would normally collect

---

[9] See the discussion in section 2 below.
[10] *J. Longley and Co. Ltd* v. *South-West Regional Health Authority* (1983) 24 B.L.R. 56 at 62–63.
[11] (1973) 117 S. J. 307.
[12] See *Société Anonyme Pêcheries Ostendaises* v. *Merchants' Marine Insurance Co.* [1928] 1 K.B. 750.
[13] As to the admissibility of such evidence, see Chap. 15.
[14] *Mitchell* v. *Mulholland*, above n. 11.
[15] *Halvanon Insurance* v. *Jewett Duchesne* [1987] 4 C.L. 245.
[16] *Earl Shrewsbury* v. *Trappas* (1862) 31 L.J. Ch. 680.
[17] See Chap. 3, p. 76.
[18] For which a different scale applies.
[19] *Chamberlain* v. *Stoneham* (1889) 24 Q.B.D. 113.
[20] *Att.-Gen.* v. *Birmingham Drainage Board* (1908) S. J. 855.

his own samples, or arrange for a colleague to do so, and receive an expert's qualifying fee for work preparatory to the expression of an opinion, there was nothing to prevent a party engaging instead a non-expert to perform the task of collecting samples, and obtaining costs in relation thereto.[21] The expert would then receive a fee only for his work thereafter.

Number of experts There is no determinate number of experts appropriate to a particular class of case, although conventions may have developed in relation to some, and there is a general discretion as to whether the number called was justified in the circumstances. The master may before trial give directions as to number,[22] as may the judge at trial, but it is only when their evidence has been heard and judgment given that their necessity can properly be assessed. The taxing master is not bound by pre–trial directions or rulings at trial,[23] and the absence of an order as to the number of expert witnesses ought not:

> "to be regarded as indicating that the calling of an expert witness is necessarily to be regarded as unreasonable."[24]

Some early cases suggested that there may be a general rule that only two experts should be allowed for costs purposes unless there were "exceptional" circumstances,[25] but they are preceded by authority which, it is suggested, reflect the modern position, which is that if an expert witness was heard and examined without objection, this is a good though not conclusive indication that his evidence was relevant and properly adduced, however many other experts were called.[26]

2   Costs and damages

The work performed by an expert witness before trial may take many forms, and the question may arise whether his fees and any attendant expenses should be recovered as part of a substantive damages claim, or as costs of the action. He may perform advisory or other work at a time when litigation was not even contemplated, some of which can be used for the purposes of proceedings. He may, once proceedings have started, be asked to prepare a report for litigation purposes, which also has some practical use beyond the litigation. The taxing master has a wide discretion as to what is properly covered by costs, and he may exercise it to

---

[21] *Ibid.*
[22] Under R.S.C. Ord. 38, r.4. See Chap. 2, pp. 50–51.
[23] *Atwell* v. *Minister of Public Building and Works* [1969] 1 W.L.R. 1074.
[24] *Ibid.*, at 1076.
[25] *Graigola Merthyr Co.* v. *Swansea Corporation* [1927] W.N. 30; *Frankenburg* v. *Famous Lasky Film Service* [1931] 1 Ch.428.
[26] *Maxim* v. *Godson* [1916] 1 Ch. 21.

treat as "incidental"[27] to the action matters between the accrual of the cause of action and the issue of proceedings.[28] This principle should be no less applicable to expert evidence in general, and has been supported in the case of medical examinations.[29]

An expert's fees are recoverable as damages on the ordinary causation rules appropriate to the cause of action (usually the tortious or the contractual test). Thus the fees of an engineer in a construction case, where the parties agreed to adopt the remedial works he recommended, were recoverable as damages as being "incurred as a natural consequence of the defendant's breach."[30] The courts generally adopt a practical approach to the matter, avoiding too theoretical a view of the division between damages and costs. It is possible to analyse all the costs of litigation logically as flowing from the cause of action:

> "all the costs of litigation which arise out of a breach of contract are, in a sense, the result of that breach, but not all such costs are recoverable as damages."[31]

The courts appear thus to exclude as a head of damages items which are clearly recoverable as costs. Cairns L.J. in *Bolton* v. *Mahadeva*[32] adopted this practical, rather than strict analytical approach in dismissing a damages claim in relation to an expert's report:

> "so far as the Defendant's claim in respect of fees for the report which he obtained from his expert is concerned, it seems to me quite clear that that report was obtained in view of a dispute which had arisen and with a view to being used in evidence if proceedings did become necessary, and in the hope that it would assist in the settlement of the dispute without proceedings being started. In those circumstances, I think that the judge was right in reaching the conclusion that the report was something the fees for which if recoverable at all, would be recoverable only under an order for costs."[33]

Only in limited circumstances can damages be recovered in relation to matters after the commencement of proceedings, and these do not include the situation in which the taxing master disallows particular items as costs.[34]

---

[27] R.S.C. Ord. 62, r.2(4).
[28] See *Ross* v. *Caunters* [1980] Ch. 297; *Société Anonyme Pêcheries Ostendaises* v. *Merchants' Marine Ins. Co.*, above n.12.
[29] *Jones* v. *Davies* [1914] 3 K.B. 549, C.A.
[30] *Peak Construction (Liverpool) Ltd.* v. *McKinney Foundations* (1970) 69 L.G.R. 1 at 10.
[31] *Hutchinson* v. *Harris* (1978) 10 B.L.R. 19 at 39.
[32] [1972] 1 W.L.R. 1009.
[33] *Ibid.*
[34] *Cockburn* v. *Edwards* (1881) 18 Ch.D. 449.

The fact however that an item could, if so claimed, properly be recovered as damages, does not preclude its being recovered as costs if it is a proper item and can be justified as to quantum.[35] In *Manakee* v. *Brattle*[36] a surveyor was engaged to prepare plans and specifications for the purpose of inviting tenders for works to remedy a defective cesspool. Proceedings were then issued in relation to the defects. The court took the view that the surveyor's pre-action work was properly allowed as costs. A quantity surveyor was also engaged after the writ was issued, to deal with the substantial divergence between the parties as to the proper costs of the work. It can be inferred from the language of the judgment, although so much is not clearly stated, that these fees would not have been recoverable as costs if they had been incurred prior to the issue of the writ, presumably because the question of the resolution of the divergence in costs can only be relevant once the question of damages arises.

It is submitted that an approach consistent with most of the cases, which do not taken together present a clear principle, is to allow by way of damages any expert work prior to the issue of proceedings which is wholly referable to remedying the damage, albeit it may also have some subsequent forensic use. If the items of work performed by the expert are clearly divisible in a logical manner, then one part should be recoverable as damages and the other as costs. Any report or other expert work performed after the issue of proceedings, or clearly in contemplation thereof, which is principally for the purpose of the litigation, should be recoverable in costs even though it may have an incidental practical use beyond the litigation.[37] This approach is consistent with the views of Cairns L.J. in *Bolton* v. *Mahadeva*[38] and with the description of reports as having a "main purpose" in *Hutchinson* v. *Harris*.[39] The taxing master however always has a discretion to look at the proceedings in the round and conclude that an item is "incidental" to the proceedings though it could have been recovered as damages but was not.[40]

A party may, in addition to or instead of engaging an independent expert to perform duties relevant to the litigation, direct its own staff to do the work. Managerial time spent rectifying the consequences of a tort in respect of which proceedings are brought can be an item of special damage and claimed as such.[41] Items which would clearly be recoverable as costs if an independent expert was engaged may also be so recoverable if a company engages its own staff to perform this work.[42] Thus where a

---

[35] *Manakee* v. *Brattle* [1970] 1 W.L.R. 1607.
[36] *Ibid.*
[37] This is the practice in relation to medical reports in personal injuries cases.
[38] Above n.32.
[39] Above n.31, at 39.
[40] *Manakee* v. *Brattle*, above n.35.
[41] *Tate and Lyle Food and Distribution Ltd.* v. *G.L.C.* [1982] 1 W.L.R. 149.
[42] *Re Nossen's Letter Patent* [1969] 1 W.L.R. 638.

company in patent proceedings itself performed experiments for litigation purposes, the fees and salaries of those performing them were allowed.[43] Some of these would no doubt have been "in-house" experts in any event.[44] The company was also entitled to recover as costs expenditure on materials used in the experiments, but not sums representing overheads for the cost of running the buildings in which, and the machines on which, the experiments were run, as they were not occasioned by the litigation itself and would have been incurred in any event.[45]

3 Pre-trial considerations

In most litigation it will be clear at an early stage that expert evidence will be necessary, as will its likely parameters. Thus in most personal injuries cases one specialist in the relevant medical discipline is essential, with possible additional experts where there are secondary consequences of a physiological or psychological nature. Where counsel is instructed his advice may be taken as to this, but of course the solicitor must exercise his own independent judgment too.[46] Usually the need can be agreed between the parties, even if the evidence cannot. The courts are perhaps more hesitant than they could be in penalising parties and their solicitors where dilatory or unreasonable behaviour occurs in relation to expert evidence. The possibility, however, is always there.

Thus, where an offer of settlement is forthcoming in a personal injury case but would have been so sooner if the plaintiff's solicitors had disclosed a medical report when it was first requested, thus saving costs, the plaintiff's costs in the interim may be disallowed.[47] The question is:

> "whether there really could have been any good ground for saying that the plaintiff might be harmed and/or was risking anything by disclosing this report at that stage."[48]

There are of course often disputes about when medical reports should be disclosed, particularly if it is suspected that an insurance company seeks the report not to make an early offer but simply to gain as much information about the plaintiff as possible, both generally, and for the purposes of obtaining and assessing their own medical evidence. If there is no such reason, and there is no likelihood of prejudice by disclosure, costs may be risked. Furthermore where a personal injuries case does proceed to hearing, a party may though successful be penalised, for

---

[43] Re Nossen's Letter Patent [1969] 1 W.L.R. 638.
[44] As to which, see *Shell Pensions Trust* v. *Pell Frischmann*, above n.7.
[45] *Ibid.*
[46] *Davy-Chieseman* v. *Davy-Chieseman* [1984] Fam. 48.
[47] *Vose* v. *Barr* [1966] 2 All E.R. 226.
[48] *Ibid.*, at 228.

example as to half his costs,[49] for late disclosure of experts' reports. Solicitors may be ordered to pay costs personally if a case is stood out in consequence of their non-compliance with directions as to expert evidence and discovery.[50]

In Legal Aid cases, authority may need to be obtained specifically before instructing an expert. Where this is done, and a limited authority is given, a solicitor may properly incur greater costs if the general provisions of the regulations permit and justify it.[51] The court, when considering the merits of decisions by parties to adduce expert evidence, or whether to appoint a Court Expert (which is seldom done), must not be influenced by the costs implications of the fact that one party only is legally aided.[52]

4 Considerations at trial

Costs in general follow the event. It is a wholly proper exercise of discretion, however, to disallow, or make an adverse order in relation to, the costs of adducing evidence upon limbs of the claim which failed. Thus, if witnesses are called exclusively as to issues upon which a party does not succeed, costs may be disallowed in relation to them.[53] This must be so *a fortiori* in relation to expert evidence, which is costly and as to which specific pre-trial directions are usually either made or agreed.

A successful party will always be at risk as to witnesses who, in the event, are not called at trial though they attend, and costs relating to the expenses of an expert whose only function at trial was to advise the party and its legal advisers as to technical matters will almost certainly be disallowed.[54] A witness who is kept at court for days and then not called is there "unnecessarily" and therefore probably not subject to a costs allowance.[55] However it may be possible to justify the presence of an expert during the evidence of the other witnesses if his own evidence may depend upon its content. If an expert is to attend court purely to advise, a specific order should be sought for an allowance for his fees.[56] Where experts attend appeal hearings they will almost certainly be regarded for costs purposes as superfluous to the litigation, unless leave to adduce additional evidence has been obtained.[57] The mere fact that an expert

---

[49] *Cable* v. *Dallaturca* (1977) 121 S.J. 795. The provisions of R.S.C. Ord. 18, r. 12 (1A) now alter the position as to the sequence of disclosure.
[50] *Countrywide Properties* v. *Moore, The Times,* January 30, 1987.
[51] *Ullah* v. *Hall Line Ltd.* [1960] 1 W.L.R. 1320.
[52] *Re Saxton (Deceased)* [1962] 1 W.L.R. 968.
[53] *Brown* v. *Houston* [1901] 2 K.B. 855.
[54] *Consolidated Pneumatic Tool Co.* v. *Ingersoll Sergeant Drill Co.* (1908) 25 R.P.C. 574. See also *Longley* v. *S.W.R.H.A.,* above n.10, at 63.
[55] *Wright* v. *Bennett* [1948] 1 All E.R. 410.
[56] *Consolidated Pneumatic Tool Co.* v. *Ingersoll,* above n. 54.
[57] *Ibid.*

was not called to give evidence does not of course mean that his evidence was bound to be unnecessary, and an allowance may be made.[58] There is no general principle that cancellation fees are allowable, for example where an expert arranges his schedule to permit a court attendance which proves unnecessary at a late stage, though the court's discretion has been exercised to allow this on particular facts.[59]

Unlike witnesses of fact, who have a public duty to attend court, expert witnesses are entitled to insist on their monetary compensation before giving evidence,[60] although usually this is dealt with by way of solicitor's undertaking. An expert witness who has not been properly compensated, or had binding arrangements made for compensation, need not give any oral evidence, even if he has been sworn, and will not in refusing to do so be in contempt of court,[61] because the courts will protect his right to a fee in advance. This is in part because it is seen as necessary to preclude the possibility of payment dependant upon the kind of evidence he actually gives.[62]

5 The expert's fees

The allowances awarded by the courts observe a distinction between "expert" and "professional" witnesses, the latter being professionals called to give factual evidence, although the observation of the fact may require expertise. Experts are entitled to a "qualifying" fee, for preparation, including perusal of any documents, site visits and views,[63] any inspections, experiments or sampling performed, and necessary communication and conferences with the client and his legal advisers. They are entitled in addition to an allowance for time spent at court[64] and any expenses for travel incidental to preparation and court attendances, and for time spent preparing reports. The allowance is time-based, though related to the witness's level of expertise and levels of reward in the field in which he practices. He is not entitled to an allowance calculated on other than a time basis, whatever the method by which he normally charges. Thus surveyors who charge fees in their usual work as a percentage of the value of the property concerned are not entitled to an allowance assessed on this basis.[65] An agreement to be paid from the proceeds

---

[58] An issue may arise as to the point at which this became clear.
[59] *Reynolds* v. *Meston*, (unreported), February 24, 1986, Q.B.D.
[60] *Webb* v. *Page* (1843) 1 Car. & Kir. 23.
[61] *Re Working Men's Mutual Society* (1882) 21 Ch.D. 831.
[62] *Clark* v. *Gill* (1854) 1 K.& J. 19.
[63] See *Great Western Railway Co.* v. *Carrpalla* [1909] 2 Ch. 471.
[64] Though see above p. 222, n. 55.
[65] *Drew* v. *Josolyne* (1888) 4 T.L.R. 717; *Debenham* v. *King's College Cambridge* (1884) Cab. & El. 438. See also *Faraday* v. *Tamworth Union* (1916) 86 L.J. Ch. 436.

of the litigation if it is successful may be champertous, though not in a tribunal which is not a court of law.[66]

Costs may be claimed in relation to time spent by the expert reading the case papers and preparation for giving evidence, though this will be moderate in amount.[67] There is no general principle that such an allowance must be made, and no doubt it will depend upon the size and complexity of the case. Certainly where there is, as is common, a long time lapse between the expert's preparation of his report or other qualifying work and the date of trial it would seem unjust to deprive an expert of compensation for time he would undoubtedly, and properly, spend in reviewing the case. By contrast in a small case the expert can often remind himself of the necessary facts at court while waiting to be called, particularly given that the purely factual witnesses will normally precede his own oral evidence.

6 Assessors and Court Experts

Opposite presumptions appear to apply in relation to cases in which assessors or a Court Expert are appointed. Thus expert witness costs should not be disallowed where the court sits with assessors,[68] unless the judge specifically so orders.[69] However where a Court Expert is appointed the costs of expert witnesses are not allowable unless the trial judge certifies the reasonableness of calling the witness.[70]

7 Arbitrations and tribunals

Particular arbitration agreements or rules may make provision for costs of expert witnesses, but generally arbitrators have a discretion to order costs as they see fit, and will not and should not depart substantially from the principles observed in the courts. They may disallow the costs of a successful party which employs an excessive number of experts or indeed lawyers.[71] This possibility may be more rigorously pursued in arbitrations than in court proceedings, given the assumption that the arbitrator has some expert knowledge. However arbitrators in other than the simplest cases should usually use their expertise better to comprehend the expert evidence, not to dispense with it altogether.[72] Thus expert evidence should generally be allowable in costs.[73]

---

[66] *Pickering* v. *Sogex Services (U.K.) Ltd.* (1982) 20 B.L.R. 66.
[67] *Smith* v. *Buller* (1875) L.R. 19 Eq. 473.
[68] As to costs of nautical assessors see *Practice Direction* [1987] 2 Lloyd's Rep. 563.
[69] *Rigolli* v. *London Borough of Lambeth*, (unreported), December 5, 1977.
[70] R.S.C. Ord. 62, Appendix 2, r.3(2).
[71] *Rosen* v. *Dowley* [1943] 2 All E.R. 172.
[72] See *Longley* v. *S.W.R.H.A.*, above n.10, at 63.
[73] *Ibid.*

B. CRIMINAL PROCEEDINGS

Where the court makes an order for costs to be paid from central funds, or from one party to another, costs relating to expert evidence are taxed upon general principles of relevance and reasonableness, which do not depart substantially from the principles in civil proceedings. One point of difference, however, is that while it is usually clear whether or not a particular witness's evidence was necessary for a successful prosecution, because the requisite elements of the offence must each be proven, the same causative connection cannot often be made where the accused is acquitted, as this may have been for any of a number of reasons. If a defendant receives a favourable costs order any evidence admitted at trial by the judge must be regarded as necessary to the defendant's case if he is acquitted. There are guidelines for taxation officers as to expert evidence,[74] and they have a broad discretion. Agency fees incurred in obtaining the appropriate expert will not usually be recoverable.[75]

Specific orders as to costs are however the exception rather than the rule in criminal proceedings, and expert witnesses are more likely to be compensated by way of allowances pursuant to the appropriate regulations. These divide expert witnesses into two categories, "professional" witnesses, which are lawyers, accountants, doctors, dentists or vetinary surgeons called to give evidence of fact (which may of course require expertise for its observation) and "expert" witnesses proper. Different sets of regulations, and scales of allowance, apply to witnesses called by the Crown Prosecution Service[76] and witnesses called by the defence, the judge or a private prosecutor.[77] They are in general entitled to an allowance for attending trial, travel and overnight subsistence. A separate allowance is made to experts for preparation of a report, but other preparation for trial is included in the attendance allowance in an ordinary case, though the circumstances may justify a separate allowance. These regulations also apply to interpreters and doctors giving oral evidence under section 30 of the Magistrates' Courts Act 1980,[78] and to doctors preparing reports under the Mental Health Act 1983.[79] There are provisions, for both professional and expert witnesses, as to substitute or locum staff where the witness must engage these to continue his professional practice in his absence. All allowances are calculated on a strictly compensatory basis and thus are not subject to income tax.

---

[74] Taxation Officers' Notes for Guidance, paragraphs 128–135.
[75] R. v. Powar (1984) Taxation Compendium, S22.
[76] Crown Prosecution Service (Witnesses' Allowances) Regulations 1988; Serious Fraud Office (Witnesses' Allowances) Regulations 1988. (S.I. 1988 No. 1863).
[77] Costs in Criminal Cases (General) Regulations 1986 (S.I. 1986 No. 1335).
[78] Ibid., reg.20(2).
[79] Ibid., reg. 25.

There are also provisions relating to legally aided defendants.[80] Authority may be sought from the Area Committee for particular expenditure in relation to expert evidence, so that no question may subsequently be raised as to whether it was properly incurred.[81]

---

[80] Legal Aid in Criminal and Care Proceedings (Costs) Regulations 1989 (S.I. 1989 No. 343).
[81] *Ibid.*, regs. 7(4) and 9(7).

Part D: METHODS OF PROOF

CHAPTER 12

Psychiatric and Psychological Evidence

Psychiatric evidence is now widely received in the courts, and some cases substantially depend upon it. Psychological evidence is much less commonly used in the criminal courts, though it does have a limited role in civil cases, particularly in proceedings concerning the mental and educational development of children. Psychiatric evidence may be used in criminal cases on issues from the start to finish of the proceedings, including the place of detention of a mentally abnormal person before trial, fitness to plead, mental responsibility for the offence, and sentence. The statutory control of psychiatric evidence in the sentencing process is discussed in Chapter 23. Difficult issues may also arise from the practitioner's duty of confidence towards a patient, and these are discussed further in Chapter 9.

A. CRIMINAL PROCEEDINGS: EXPERT EVIDENCE AS TO THE STATE OF MIND OF THE ACCUSED

1 The abnormality rule

Where the issue is the state of mind of the accused at the time of an alleged offence, the general rule[1] is that expert evidence as to his mental state may not be called unless it be contended that it was "abnormal."[2] This is because members of the jury, whose task it is to assess the witnesses, are said to be able to judge unassisted matters which are within "ordinary human experience."[3] Mental illness is not within this experience.[4] Lawton L.J., in *R. v. Turner*,[5] took the view that the doctrine laid down in *Folkes v. Chadd*,[6] namely that expert evidence is only admissible as to scientific matters likely to be outside the experience and knowledge of a jury, was equally applicable to psychiatric evidence in criminal cases.

---
[1] But see below pp. 238–240 as to the position of co-defendants.
[2] *R. v. Chard* (1971) 56 Cr.App.R. 268, C.A.
[3] *R. v. Turner* [1975] 1 Q.B. 834 at 841.
[4] *Ibid.*
[5] *Ibid.*
[6] (1782) 3 Doug. 157.

Provocation, the defence in *Turner*, was squarely within the ordinary jury man's experience and knowledge.[7] It follows from this that where the defendant is held in custody before trial, and examined in prison by a psychiatrist, the report should not be disclosed to the prosecution or defence if it raises no question of insanity or abnormality.[8]

Abnormality There is no clear definition of what the courts regard as the kind of mental abnormality justifying the adducing of expert evidence. The logical approach to the matter is that taken in *R. v. Smith*,[9] in which the defence was one of automatism, and in particular of sleep-walking. The court decided the matter not by reference to some supposedly objective mental standard, but by asking the question whether such behaviour was "within the realm of the ordinary juryman's experience."[10] On this basis the jury was entitled to the benefit of evidence by way of medical explanation of the defence. Lane L.J. took the view that if he, had he been the trier of fact, would have required expert assistance, as he would have done, the jury should not be denied it.

In *Turner* the defence was one of provocation. The provocation was said to have arisen out of "profound grief" rather than any "formal psychiatric illness."[11] Although this was said to have led to an "explosive release of blind rage,"[12] it did not warrant expert evidence:

> "jurors do not need psychiatrists to tell them how ordinary folk who are not suffering from any mental illness are likely to react to the stresses and strains of life."[13]

Lawton L.J. evidently took the view that individuals with those kinds of psychological features which simply render them more vulnerable to commit crimes when faced with particular circumstances are not abnormal in any sense that jurors are unable to comprehend. Thus a man who was "quick-tempered" or possessed of a "florid imagination"[14] was well able to be properly assessed by a jury unassisted.

There are, however, no fixed parameters of the rule, and the court's discretion must be exercised on the facts of each case. Thus a psychiatrist was permitted to give evidence, in relation to a defence of diminished responsibility in a murder case, that the defendant had an extremely immature personality.[15] It will always be relevant to identify the precise

---

[7] Furthermore, it bears the test of "reasonableness," which is for the jury alone: *R. v. Camplin* [1978] A.C. 705.
[8] *R. v. Howard* (1957) 42 Cr.App.R. 23.
[9] (1979) 69 Cr.App.R. 378.
[10] *Ibid.*, at 385.
[11] Above n. 3, at 839–840.
[12] *Ibid.*, at 841.
[13] *Ibid.*
[14] *Ibid.*
[15] *Walton v. R.* [1978] A.C. 788, P.C.

issue upon which the evidence is being adduced. Thus where, on a charge of attempting to procure an act of gross indecency, the prosecution adduced a letter, written by the defendant, in evidence and asked the jury to draw inferences from it, the defence was permitted to call a psychiatrist to rebut the presumption that a man intends the natural consequences of his acts, by showing that the defendant suffered from a psychoneurosis which, at times of great stress, resulted in his submitting to an irresistable desire to get himself into trouble.[16] The Canadian case of *R. v. Lupien*[17] demonstrates a fairly broad view of admissibility. There was no expert evidence as to the defendant's state of mind at the time of the offence. Despite this psychiatric evidence was called to show that he had a violent defence mechanism in relation to homosexual acts, with which the case was concerned, and would not knowingly participate in them. The expert evidence was held admissible because it demonstrated an absence of capacity to form the requisite intent. Clearly this is a psychological condition which a jury would not be expected to understand without expert assistance, though the position where such evidence goes to the issue of the intent displayed at the time of the offence is less certain.

As has been seen the courts, with good reason, have avoided setting particular limits to the admission of expert evidence in these cases by reference to some given medical standard of normality. However this has proved more difficult where the suggestion that the defendant's condition is abnormal amounts only to the assertion that his intelligence quotient is very low. Thus it has been said that an I.Q. which, though low, is within the range of normality as understood by psychologists, does not justify the adducing of expert evidence.[18] Suggestions that the more liberal Australian approach[19] be adopted have been rejected.[20] Other judges, however, have been less certain as to the possibility or validity of identifying the limits of this "range,"[21] though the fact that the disputed evidence is a confession made by a juvenile may justify a less restrictive approach.[22]

It is worthy of observation that the adoption of a strict approach to the question of I.Q. (*i.e.* identifying those with a figure over a given level as 'normal') may have the opposite effect to that intended by the courts in cases such as *Turner*. For the chief and justified concern of the courts is that the fact-finding process should not be surrendered to professionals such as psychiatrists, but should remain the province of the courts. By subscribing to a rule of admissibility which depends entirely on a figure

---

[16] *R. v. Riley* [1967] Crim.L.R. 656.
[17] [1970] S.C.R. 263.
[18] *R. v. Masih* (1986) Crim.L.R. 395.
[19] *Schultz v. R.* [1981] W.A.R. 171.
[20] *R. v. Masih*, above n. 18.
[21] *R. v. Silcott, per* Hodgson J.: see M. Beaumont, "Psychiatric Evidence: Over-Rationalising the Abnormal" (1988) Crim.L.R. 290.
[22] *Ibid.*

(the bottom end of the "normality" range) which is not only fairly arbitrary, but also assessed entirely by psychiatrists themselves, the court is in effect depriving itself of the ability to assess the individual case. If, however, the evidence is adduced with no such assumptions, the court is free to reject or accept it in an entirely untrammelled manner on the basis of the weight of the evidence, both of fact and of opinion, alone.

The Australian decision in *Murphy* v. *R.*[22a] has more recently analysed an important aspect of this issue, but with a somewhat different approach. The defendant in question had signed a confession. The trial judge prevented him from adducing the evidence of a consultant psychologist to show that he was of such limited intellectual capacity that he could not have comprehended more than a small percentage of the confession he purported to be making. On appeal it was held by a narrow majority that the judge was wrong to exclude such evidence. The 'normal/abnormal' distinction was not useful in such a case, because such a distinction may have little or no meaning in relation to questions such as literacy and vocabulary usage. Psychiatrists and psychologists may be able to give evidence of matters in relation to 'normal' people which are nevertheless outside lay knowledge and experience. This was particularly so in that the expert was here able to say that, at normal reading speed, the defendant would have understood only 25 per cent. of what he was reading. It was furthermore irrelevant to the question of admissibility that his problems may have arisen from environmental factors rather than from some innate mental defect.

Confessions are subject to specific statutory control.[23] In jury trials, the issue of the voluntariness of a confession is one for the judge alone, and confessions have been excluded where, upon medical evidence, it was shown that the symptoms of hypoglaecaemia in a diabetic included an increased susceptibility to suggestion,[24] that a drug, Pethidin, could affect a confession's voluntariness,[25] and that a defendant became emotionally disturbed and hysterical when overwhelmed by difficulties.[26] Even though a judge does not exclude a confession the defence may yet seek to cast doubt upon its contents, and the usual principles of admissibility would apply.

2 Admissible psychiatric evidence

Where it is accepted by the court that the issues in the case justify the reception of psychiatric evidence, there remains a question as to the con-

---

[22a] (1989) 63 Aust.L.J. 422.
[23] Police and Criminal Evidence Act 1984, s.76.
[24] R. v. *Powell* [1980] Crim.L.R. 39.
[25] R. v. *Davis* [1979] Crim.L.R. 167.
[26] R. v. *Kilner* (1976) Crim.L.R. 740.

trol of the precise answers the witness may give. This is rightly regarded as particularly important in the case of juries, whose members have little experience in the separation of items of evidence, and may find it hard to exclude from consideration things which a professional witness has said, however forcefully the judge requests them to do so in his summing-up.

Psychiatrists perform a large proportion of their examination by conversation with the individual concerned. In so far as what the individual says during examination is adduced only to show his state of mind, the psychiatrist may state in court what was said. However the hearsay rule is no less applicable than elsewhere in relation to statements concerning facts in issue in the case, which must be proved by separate, admissible, evidence.[27] If the defendant elects not to give evidence, but a medical witness has stated facts, upon which he bases his opinion but of which he has no direct knowledge, which are crucial to the defence case, the judge is justified in telling the jury that the defence case rests on a "flimsy or non-existent foundation," and may comment that the defendant could have given evidence on the relevant points if he had wished to.[28] The evidence of a medical man who has not examined the defendant, but only seen him give evidence in court, is probably admissible,[29] though it would be of doubtful value.

Ultimate issue[30] Frequently the evidence given by a psychiatrist may if accepted have the effect of giving the defendant a complete defence or of deciding the main issue before the court, for example whether the verdict should be guilty of murder or manslaughter. However while this is not an objection to expert evidence in civil actions,[31] the legislature has thus far not seen fit to remove the exclusion in relation to criminal trials. Despite this, it is the case that psychiatrists daily give evidence in court which, in substance if not in form, decides the issue if it is accepted. The courts are faced with the difficulty of, on the one hand, avoiding "trial by psychiatrists"[32] and, on the other, ensuring that the defendant, given that an issue is raised requiring psychiatric evidence, may put his case in full. Where, as is often the case, the *actus reus* of the offence is admitted, but not the *mens rea*, it is particularly difficult fairly to prevent the psychiatrist from expressing an opinion upon the very matter which the jury must determine. The old practice is as stated in R. v. *Wright*[33]:

---

[27] R. v. *Turner*, above n. 3, at 840. See also R. v. *Abbey* (1982) 138 D.L.R. 202 and the discussion in Chap. 8, pp.164–165.
[28] R. v. *Bradshaw* (1985) 82 Cr.App.R. 79 at 83.
[29] R. v. *Searle* (1831) 1 Moo. and Rob. 75; R. v. *Wright* (1821) Rus. and Ry. 456.
[30] For a full discussion of this question see Chap. 7, pp. 150–154.
[31] Civil Evidence Act 1972, s.3(1) and (3).
[32] R. v. *Turner*, above n. 3, at 842.
[33] (1821) Russ. and Ry. 456.

> "a witness of medical skill might be asked whether, in his judgment, such and such appearances were symptoms of insanity ... and that by such questions the effect of his testimony in favour of the prisoner might be got at in an unexceptionable manner. Several of the judges doubted whether the witness could be asked his opinion on the very point which the jury were to decide, *viz.* whether, from the other testimony given in the case, the act as to which the prisoner was charged was, in his opinion, an act of insanity."[34]

Not long after the decision in *Wright*[35] a doctor was permitted to say whether the defendant knew the difference between right and wrong,[36] but it was also, in a case where the doctor had not examined the defendant,[37] but had only sat through the evidence in court, held improper to ask whether the defendant was in fact of unsound mind when he committed the offence:

> "the proper mode is to ask what are the symptoms of insanity, or to take particular facts, and, assuming them to be true, to say whether they indicate insanity on the part of the prisoner."[38]

The permitted question here avoids the ultimate issue in form though not in substance.

More recent cases, however, while not laying down a clear rule, indicate that the distinction observed in *Wright* is now regarded as too strict. In *R. v. Holmes*,[39] an insanity case, it was regarded as acceptable for the witness to be asked in cross-examination whether the defendant knew the nature of his act and that it was wrong[40]:

> "it would put an insuperable difficulty ... in the way of the defence whenever they were trying to establish insanity,"[41]

held Lord Goddard, if such evidence were not to be admitted. The answer to this question, it can be seen, effectively decides the case if the evidence is accepted, though it stops short of the question which was objected to in *R. v. McNaghten*,[42] namely whether the defendant was in fact insane at the time of the offence, which is a question partly of observed fact.

In another nineteenth century case, where the defendant was suscept-

---

[34] *Ibid.*, at 457–458.
[35] *Ibid.* at 457–458
[36] *R. v. Higginson* (1843) 1 C. & K. 129 at 130.
[37] Though this factor does not seem to have determined the inadmissibility of the question.
[38] *R. v. Frances* (1849) 4 Cox 57 at 58.
[39] (1953) 37 Cr.App.R. 61.
[40] *Ibid.*
[41] *Ibid.*, at 64.
[42] (1843) 1 C. & K. 130 n.

ible to occasional fits of insanity, the question arose whether the offence was committed during such a fit.[43] A medical witness was permitted to give evidence as to the "state of her mind" in general, though not as to her "responsibility" for the particular offence.[44] It is not entirely clear whether the evidence was excluded only on the ground that the expert would otherwise be giving evidence of fact which he had not perceived, quite apart from the question whether he should as an expert be entitled to make the link between the mental condition and responsibility for the offence.[45]

The modern practice is to permit experts to speculate, upon hypothetical facts, as to whether or not the defendant's alleged behaviour at the time of the offence in itself indicates the mental abnormality which the defence is asserting. It is perhaps too casuistic a process to attempt to distinguish between this and the practice, objected to in the nineteenth century cases, of saying that because certain behaviour occurred, therefore the defendant cannot have had the mental responsibility which the prosecution must prove. Whichever is the appropriate description of what is permitted, there is little doubt that the permitted evidence of the psychiatrist, if accepted, often effectively decides the issue if the hypothesis is also proved.[46] Thus in R. v. Holmes,[47] a psychiatrist was allowed to answer the questions, on the issue of insanity, whether the defendant knew the nature of his act, and whether his conduct indicated that he knew it was against the law. To hold otherwise:

> "would put an insuperable difficulty. . . . in the way of the defence whenever they were trying to establish insanity."[48]

A similarly liberal approach is also now taken in relation to the defence of diminished responsibility to a murder charge. This defence is divided into three elements, all of which the defence must prove on the balance of probabilities: (a) that there was an abnormality of mind, (b)(i) which arose from arrested or retarded development of mind or any inherent causes or was induced by disease or injury, and (b)(ii) which was such as substantially impaired the defendant's mental responsibility for his acts in doing or being a party to the killing.[49] Psychiatric evidence may be called in relation to all three of these questions.[50]

---

[43] R. v. Richards (1858) 1 F. & F. 87.
[44] Ibid., at 88.
[45] See also R. v. McNaghten (1843) 1 C. & K. 130 n. Though see the judge's remarks at 136.
[46] Though see R. v. Byrne (1960) 44 Cr.App.R. 246, discussed below, pp. 237–238.
[47] (1953) 37 Cr.App.R. 61.
[48] Ibid., at 64.
[49] See R. v. Byrne, above n. 46.
[50] R. v. Dix (1982) 74 Cr.App.R. 306 at 311; R. v. Vernege (1982) Crim.L.R. 598.

3 Necessity for expert evidence

There is no rule of law that any particular form of evidence is required in relation to defences arising out of the allegedly abnormal mental state of the defendant. Despite this in reality expert evidence is essential given the onus of proof which lies upon the defence.[51] Where the issue of diminished responsibility arises in relation to a murder charge, expert evidence has been said to be a "practical necessity if that defence is to begin to run at all."[52] Where the defence of automatism is raised, the defendant's evidence, unsupported by medical evidence, will "rarely" be sufficient.[53] This arises partly out of its unfamiliarity to triers of fact, and partly from the fact that it is so often dishonestly raised in circumstances where the evidence of *actus reus* is clear-cut. Devlin J. has said:

> "I do not doubt that there are genuine cases of automatism and the like, but I do not see how the layman can safely attempt without the help of some medical or scientific evidence to distinguish the genuine from the fraudulent."[54]

Similarly, a defence of insanity in the form of an "uncontrollable impulse" has been said to demand medical evidence.[55]

Defendant's choice Difficult issues may arise where a defendant is probably suffering from a relevant abnormality, which could be illuminated by expert evidence, but does not wish such evidence to be adduced on his behalf. The Court of Appeal in *R. v. Kooken*[56] has doubted whether the judge may call evidence of diminished responsibility in such circumstances. The Court of Appeal answered the question whether such a course was necessary or expedient in the interests of justice by saying that it could not be, albeit the defendant is not mentally sound. It is submitted that this question might in many cases be answered differently, given that the defendant's mental condition may deprive him or her of the ability to assess its necessity or expediency for him or herself, and given the judge's general discretion in criminal cases to call witnesses himself where the interests of justice demand it.[56a]

4 Assessment of the evidence

Whatever the issues, and however technical the evidence justifying the calling of an expert, the jury is free to accept or reject expert evidence.

---

[51] *R. v. Layton* (1849) 4 Cox 149.
[52] *R. v. Dix* (1982) 74 Cr.App.R. 306 at 311.
[53] *Bratty* v. *Att.-Gen. for Northern Ireland* [1963] A.C. 386 at 413.
[54] *Hill* v. *Baxter* [1958] 1 Q.B. 277 at 285.
[55] *Att.-Gen. for South Australia* v. *Brown* (1960) 44 Cr.App.R. 100 at 112–113.
[56] (1982) 74 Cr.App.R. 30 at 35.
[56a] See *R. v. Holden* (1838) 8 Car.& P. 606 at 609

However where the expert evidence is unchallenged, the jury should only base a verdict which contradicts the expert opinion upon cogent evidence of fact.[57] If there is no evidence to contradict it, the jury can only accept the expert evidence.[58] Where there is medical evidence of opinion that the defendant was labouring under diminished responsibility, but the defendant's evidence does not support the hypothesis upon which the opinion is based, the jury can reject that opinion though it is uncontradicted.[59] Where the expert witnesses do not agree,[60] or the evidence requiring specialist explanation cannot by its nature be conclusive, the jury may decide the issue itself. Thus a judge has expressed the view on the evidence before the court that:

> "this is not a case where a scientific witness can say with certainty, as in the case of a bodily disease. . . . that a disease exists."[61]

Where the defence of diminished responsibility is run, the court must consider the wording of section 2(1) of the Homicide Act 1957 which, as explained above,[62] has been described in R. v. Byrne[63] as consisting of three elements ((a), (b)(i) and (b)(ii)). Having found ((a) and b(i)) that the defendant had a relevant abnormality of mind, it must then consider whether this "substantially impaired his mental responsibility" in killing or being party to a killing ((b)(ii)). In Matheson[64] it was stated that the jury could differ from an expert on this issue, but only upon separate evidence supporting that course.[65] In Byrne,[66] Lord Parker L.C.J. took the view that this question was one:

> "of degree, and essentially one for the jury. Medical evidence is, of course, relevant, but the question involves a decision not merely whether there was some impairment of the mental responsibility of the accused for his acts, but whether such impairment can properly be called 'substantial,' a matter upon which juries may quite legitimately differ from doctors."[67]

The position appears therefore to be that where there is clear medical evidence that there was substantial impairment, this should, unless there are cogent facts to contradict it, be accepted to the extent that there is

---

[57] R. v. Matheson (1958) 42 Cr.App.R. 145 at 152.
[58] R. v. Bailey (1961) Crim.L.R. 828.
[59] R. v. Kiszko (1979) 68 Cr.App.R. 62.
[60] R. v. Jennion [1962] 1 W.L.R. 317 at 321.
[61] R. v. Rivett (1950) 34 Cr.App.R. 87.
[62] At p. 235.
[63] Above n. 46.
[64] Above n. 56.
[65] Ibid., at 152.
[66] Above n. 46.
[67] Ibid., at 258.

impairment which could be described as "substantial." If the medical expert describes it as substantial, but the jury having heard his evidence does not agree with this description, they may reject his evidence as to the description. The same would apply if the expert took the view that the impairment of responsibility, though present, was not "substantial." Impairment clearly need not be "total" to be "substantial."[68]

The jury's discretion to reject the expert's view of impairment is particularly suitably exercised where the issue is one which is "incapable of scientific proof."[69] The same approach has been taken in relation to the phrase "severe impairment of intelligence and social functioning" under section 14(4) of the Sexual Offences Act 1956, concerned with the inability of a woman with such impairment to consent to sexual acts. However persuasive the expert evidence, the jury may reject the expert's view as to its conformity with the statutory words. This was illustrated graphically in *R. v. Hall*[70]:

> "We are unable to accept that a medical expert's opinion that a woman of, say, 30, with the intelligence of a girl of five is not severely impaired is of any real weight, if indeed admissible at all. If, having heard such evidence, the jury observe the victim happily playing with toys suitable for a child of five, unable to cope with toys for slightly older girls, and only able to converse like a child of five, the doctor's opinion cannot be regarded as being preferable to the observation of the jury."[71]

It is desirable if not essential that where the defence of diminished responsibility is being raised, the jury should hear the medical evidence themselves,[72] and in a case on automatism it was said that "agreed medical reports so often used in civil actions have no place in criminal courts."[73] The judge should probably not, however, himself call evidence as to diminished responsibility, it has been held,[74] though given that the judge has a discretion to call evidence in criminal cases in the interests of justice[75] this cannot be said to be an inflexible rule.

5 Evidence of disposition: co-defendants

The general rule, as has been discussed, is that psychiatric or other expert evidence of a defendant's state of mind is not admissible unless it is for

---

[68] *R. v. Lloyd* (1960) 50 Cr.App.R. 61.
[69] *R. v. Byrne*, above n. 46, at 258.
[70] (1988) 86 Cr.App.R. 159.
[71] *Ibid.*, at 162. See also *Walton v. R.*, above n. 15, at 794.
[72] *R. v. Ahmed Din* (1962) 46 Cr.App.R. 269.
[73] *Hill v. Baxter*, above n. 54, at 281.
[74] *R. v. Kooken* (1982) 74 Cr.App.R. 30.
[75] *R. v. Harris* (1927) 20 Cr.App.R. 86.

the purpose of proving or disproving mental abnormality. A limited apparent exception to this rule has emerged, largely as a result of the decision in *Lowery* v. *R.*[76] Two co-defendants were charged with murder, which was accepted as having been committed by one or both of them, but each blamed the other. One co-defendant was permitted to call a psychologist, in order to demonstrate that the other was the more aggressive and dominating personality. The psychologist employed techniques known as the *Rorschach* test and the *Thematic Apperception* test. The evidence was held to be admissible, because relevant, to show that one of them "had a personality marked by aggressiveness," whereas the other "had a personality which suggested that he would be led and dominated by someone who was dominant and aggressive."[77] The court did not analyse in detail the basis upon which this evidence should be admitted, though it appears that the particular facts of the case were thought to warrant it. Certainly the evidence appears to have been probative of the issue of who was more likely to have committed the offence, and clearly the tests performed by the psychologist provided the jury with specialist knowledge and skill which it otherwise would have lacked. It is difficult however to see it as consistent with *Turner*,[78] in that the fact that some people have a more dominating and aggressive personality than others is precisely the kind of "normal" feature of humanity which juries are said to be able to comprehend from their own experience, and of course the jury would be able to see the defendants themselves giving evidence so long as they did not exercise their right not to do so.

Furthermore there seems to be little reason why, if questions of aggressiveness and dominance are to be the subject of expert evidence, this should not be extended to single defendants. No doubt there are many circumstances in which a single defendant might wish to call evidence to show that he was not the kind of person who would commit a crime, of violence for example, which suggests particular character traits in its perpetrator. The fact that co-defendants are involved is not perhaps a sufficiently cogent reason *per se* for excluding such expert evidence in other cases. Certainly the mere fact that co-defendants accuse each other of an offence has not been seen as sufficient, even if it be necessary, for the calling of expert evidence as to this sort of disposition. Where co-defendants were charged with arson, it was regarded as inadmissible to show a propensity to arson in one defendant,[79] though this course was justified in part upon the ground that the chief defence of the other was that he was elsewhere at the time the crime was established as having been commit-

---

[76] [1973] 3 W.L.R. 235.
[77] *Ibid.*, at 247.
[78] Above n. 3.
[79] *R.* v. *Neale* (1977) 65 Cr.App.R. 304 at 307.

ted.[80] The judge in a murder trial involving co-defendants refused to admit expert evidence in rebuttal of an accusation that one co-defendant had a history of mental illness, and in particular fits or brainstorms.[81]

B. CRIMINAL PROCEEDINGS: WITNESS RELIABILITY

1 Psychiatric evidence as to witness's mental abnormality

In certain circumstances expert evidence may be called to show that a witness, whether it be the defendant or another, is lying, either about the facts of the offence itself, or about his ability to recollect them. In *R. v. Eades*[82] the defendant in a road traffic prosecution claimed completely to have forgotten the circumstances when questioned by police, but to have experienced a sudden recollection of events, to his advantage, when later driving past the scene. The prosecution was held properly to have called psychiatric evidence to show that hysterical amnesia, the only possible cause of such memory lapses, would not permit the sudden recovery of memory in this manner. It was treated as an admissible extension of the rule in *Toohey v. Metropolitan Police Commissioner*[83] (concerned with witnesses other than the defendant), because the prosecution was merely availing itself of the practice, approved in *Toohey*, of calling "a witness to impugn the reliability of an opponent's witness on medical grounds."[84]

In *Toohey*, the prosecution's main witness was a 16 year old boy, who had allegedly been assaulted by the defendant. Evidence was held admissible, from a medical expert, to show that the witness was more prone to hysteria than normal people, and that the defendant's account, that the witness had been drunk and had become hysterical, might well have been correct. It was held that medical evidence was also admissible to show that the capacity of a witness to give reliable evidence was affected by an illness or abnormality of mind:

> "when a witness through physical (in which I include mental) disease or abnormality is not capable of giving a true or reliable account to the jury, it must surely be allowable for medical science to reveal this vital hidden fact to them."[85]

---

[80] *Ibid.*, at 307.
[81] *R. v. Rimmer and Beech* [1983] Crim.L.R. 250. The report of this case does not illuminate the grounds for such a ruling.
[82] [1972] Crim.L.R. 99.
[83] [1965] A.C. 595.
[84] *R. v. Eades*, above n. 82.
[85] *Toohey v. Metropolitan Police Commissioner*, above n. 83 at 608.

In a case of alleged child sexual abuse a psychiatric social worker was permitted to give evidence that a witness she had counselled was giving a credible account of her history, and as to her capacity to fantasise.[86] She could not however state that in her opinion she was or was not telling the truth on any given issue in the case. The court recognised that there was a fine line only between the two.

In *R. v. MacKenney*[87] it was held however that a man with psychology training, but "no experience of direct personal diagnosis,"[88] was not competent to give evidence about witness reliability. The court regarded the *Toohey* principle as permitting expert evidence only as to a "disease or defect or abnormality of mind that affects the reliability of his evidence."[89] Evidence from a psychologist was not admissible on this issue because psychiatry was the "branch of medical science dealing with diseases and disorders of the mind."[90] Clearly a "disease" should be identified by an expert with medical training. The same might not necessarily apply where a "defect" or "abnormality" was concerned. The court in *MacKenney* was however taking a restrictive view of those terms and relating them to a specific medical condition.

Unlike *Toohey*, however, the court in *MacKenney* did not think it necessary, should psychiatric evidence be available, for the witness to be alleged to be "totally incapable of giving accurate evidence."[91] The mental condition need only "substantially affect the witness's capacity to give reliable evidence."[92] This is probably the better view of the question, as it can seldom be said of a witness that he is absolutely incapable of giving a true or reliable account of events. Such a requirement would in effect exclude this class of evidence in the vast majority of cases, even where there were real and legitimate doubts about a witness's mental state.

These rules are analogous to, if not a part of, the principle that a witness who is physically incapable of giving proper evidence should not do so, and that expert opinion on this question is admissible. Thus a deaf and dumb witness might give evidence through an expert interpreter, though this will not be permitted if, despite the expert's opinion, it is clear to the court that the witness cannot understand the proceedings.[93] Similarly, doctors may be required to express an opinion as to whether a witness is too ill to give evidence,[94] in the interests both of his own health and of assessing the reliability of his evidence.

---

[86] *Re S. and B. (Minors), The Independent*, June 1, 1990.
[87] (1981) 76 Cr.App.R. 271.
[88] *Ibid.*, at 275.
[89] *Ibid.*, at 274.
[90] *Ibid.*, at 275.
[91] *Ibid.*, at 276.
[92] *Ibid.*, at 276.
[93] *R. v. Whitehead* (1866) 10 Cox C.C. 234.
[94] *R. v. Chapman* (1838) 8 C. & P. 558.

2 Normal witnesses: psychology

Numerous studies, involving psychologists, have been performed into the reliability of witnesses without any mental or physical illness or abnormality.[95] In particular, significant results have been obtained in relation to the reliability of eye witness evidence of identification. Expert evidence as to this is clearly inadmissible on present authority, and the courts are limited to the safeguard of warning the jury as to the dangers of accepting identification evidence when it is uncorroborated by independent facts.[96] In the United States the courts have begun to receive such evidence in those limited circumstances, in the discretion of the trial judge, where it can be shown to assist the jury.[97] Other jurisdictions have however resisted such developments, in conformity with the English law.[98]

3. Ancillary scientific techniques

A number of scientific techniques have been developed, both within and outside the psychiatric discipline, as methods either of distinguishing between honest and dishonest recollection, or of enhancing honest but defective memory. As will be seen, such techniques all share the difficulty, in addition to doubts about their probative value, of frequently requiring the court to ignore the rule against previous consistent statements.[99] This difficulty might in some cases not prove insuperable if the evidence was adduced in the form of expert opinion that the defendant or witness was in general terms speaking frankly about a subject.[1] A further substantial objection is that such techniques tend to usurp the function of the tribunal, which must include the assessment of the veracity of a witness.

Hypnosis The technique of hypnosis, usually performed for forensic purposes by a psychiatrist with this special skill, can be employed both for the dishonest, and the honest but forgetful, witness. It is most likely to be employed for the latter. The police have for a number of years used hypnotists in order to assist in the process of pre-trial investigation, but

---

[95] See *e.g.* D. Farrington, K. Hawkins and S. Lloyd-Bostock, *Psychology, Law and Legal Processes* (1979), pp. 167–206; S. Lloyd-Bostock and B. Clifford, eds., *Evaluating Witness Evidence* (1983); S. Lloyd-Bostock, ed., *Psychology in Legal Contexts* (1981).
[96] R. v. *Turnbull* [1977] Q.B. 224.
[97] See *U.S.* v. *Amaral* 488 F.2d 1148 (9th Cir. 1973); *State* v. *Chapple* 135 Ariz. 281, 660 p. 2d 1208.
[98] See *e.g. R.* v. *Smith* [1987] V.R. 907.
[99] See *e.g. Fennell* v. *Jerome Property Maintenance Ltd.*, *The Times*, November 26, 1986.
[1] See *Re S. and B. (Minors)*, *The Independent*, June 1, 1990

the technique has probably not been employed in court proceedings.[2] Such attempts as have been made to adduce such evidence have been rejected by the courts.[3] It has been said that this situation should continue, at least while there is so much scientific disagreement both about the technique itself, and the proposition that a witness is more likely to be truthful under hypnosis.[4] It has been received in limited circumstances in other jurisdictions, for instance where the defendant experienced amnesia in relation to events in issue.[5] The defendant was hypnotised in court. This was not treated as evidence, but the answers of the defendant and the hypnotists to subsequent questions was. The technique was found to be a proper scientific procedure of which the defendant was entitled to the benefit. There have been proposals for the reception of hypnosis in this country, though in circumstances where the subject was hypnotised out of court.[6] It would often however raise the difficulty that the evidence could only be adduced in the inadmissible form of a previous consistent statement, and legislation would probably be required to alter this state of affairs.[7]

Truth drugs The use of so-called "truth drugs," such as sodium pentathol, is fairly widespread in some fields, such as the military. In the legal sphere it is unlikely that they would be employed other than as an adjunct to psychiatric practice. Thus they would constitute a technique by which a psychiatrist could enhance his other forensic and analytical skills, administered strictly under his control, with the results used evidentially through the agency of the psychiatrist himself giving evidence. The English courts have not generally received such evidence, although there are isolated, and somewhat haphazardly reported, examples of its admission. There are no dicta of authority from the higher courts capable of establishing a principle in relation to the admission of such evidence. Although there is little doubt that such drugs have specific uses in non-legal contexts, their advantages in the forensic context are uncertain, in part because few psychiatrists would assert more than a rather greater tendency to tell the truth than otherwise when under their influence. This throws some doubt on the probative value of evidence obtained with their use.[8]

The reported instances of its admission in this country suggest that the

---

[2] See A. Serly, "A Trance to Remember" *The Law Magazine*, June 12, 1987, 33. See too *Fennell* v. *Jerome Property Maintenance Ltd.*, above n. 99.
[3] *R.* v. *Wagstaff* [1983] Crim.L.R. 152.
[4] *Ibid.*, at 157.
[5] *R.* v. *Pitt* (1968) D.L.R. (2d) 513.
[6] L. Howard and A. Ashworth, "Some Problems of Evidence Obtained by Hypnosis" (1980) Crim.L.R. 469.
[7] See *R.* v. *Mackay* [1967] N.Z.L.R. 139.
[8] *Ibid.*

courts will only receive evidence to which the use of truth drugs has contributed in relation to the issue of the accused's state of mind at the time of the alleged offence.[9] Thus evidence of what was said after the administration of oxygen and carbon-dioxide was admitted where the accused was thus assisted in re-living a repressed incident.[10] The psychiatrist concluded however that the accused was insane at the time of the offence, which would in itself render the psychiatrist's evidence admissible.

Other jurisdictions, such as New Zealand and the United States, have been cautious in the admission of such evidence upon issues other than the state of mind of the accused at the time of the offence.[11] Furthermore, as with hypnotically induced evidence, there are difficulties with the general evidential principles as to previous consistent statements.[12] Where the administering of such drugs is permitted, there should be professional observers acting for the other parties present.[13] There is little reliable authority for the admissibility of truth drug assisted evidence[14] in relation to the question whether a witness is telling the court the truth, and on general principles it would seem to be inadmissible, as the jury is the assessor of bona fides in a witness who is not mentally abnormal.[15] It has been said to be inadmissible as a matter of principle,[16] despite the fact that it has apparently been heard on isolated occasions without the authoritative support of the higher courts. Such evidence was admitted in a case, heard by a recorder, of theft from the body of a dead person.[17] However it was asserted, though the jury did not accept it, that the accused had suffered from "dissociation," whereby the shock of seeing a dead body prevented him from recalling the events. This is a mental condition, analogous to automatism, in relation to which a jury would benefit from expert assistance.

Polygraph The use of the polygraph, or lie-detector machine, is the subject of no reported English decision. However it is unlikely that such evidence would be admissible on general principles, as it performs little more than the jury's function, and probably does not illuminate particular aspects of an individual's mental state, whether at the time of the offence or otherwise. Furthermore in practice such machines are frequently operated by persons, who although no doubt expert in their use,

---

[9] See (1954) 98 S.J. 794 (Nottingham case).
[10] *R. v. Barker*: see H. Walton, "The 'Truth Drug' " [1954] Crim.L.R. 423.
[11] See *R. v. Mackay* above n. 7 (N.Z.), and D. Mathieson, "The Truth-Drug: Trial by Psychiatrist" (1967) Crim.L.R. 645.
[12] *R. v. Mackay*, above n. 7, at 151.
[13] *Ibid*.
[14] Though see [1954] Crim.L.R. 482, as to the Northern Ireland case of *R. v. Gordon* (1953).
[15] *R. v. Meehan* (1970) J.C. 11.
[16] *Fennell v. Jerome Property Maintenance Ltd.*, above n. 99.
[17] *R. v. Spencer, The Times*, January 21, 1960.

have no psychiatric or other medical expertise,[18] thus arguably placing their evidence outside the ambit of existing authorities on the admission of evidence of state of mind, such as *Turner*.[19] In Canada there is limited authority for their use,[20] but also contradictory and probably better authority in *Phillion v. R.*[21] to the effect that polygraph evidence is not admissible. Although that decision was based in part upon the obviously unsatisfactory fact that the defendant, having submitted pre-trial to favourable polygraph tests, elected not to give evidence of any kind at trial, it appears nevertheless to be a clear rejection of the general use of such machines, because of the evidential rule as to previous consistent statements, the absence of medical training in most operators and the absence of a scientific consensus as to reliability.[22]

C. CIVIL PROCEEDINGS: SANITY

The evidence of psychiatrists and psychologists may be admissible in, for example, personal injuries cases concerning injuries with a mental aspect, and no special rules relate to the admissibility of such evidence. Where the issue before the court is the sanity or otherwise of an individual at a particular time, particularly where a will or contract is concerned, an expert may give evidence as to sanity, but only, it appears, where he has personally examined the individual.[23] If he is expressing his opinion on the basis of observations put to him as having been made, he must only "give general scientific evidence on the cause and symptoms of insanity" and "confine himself to general scientific principles."[24] In order for a direct opinion to be expressed as to the insanity of the individual, although the expert must have examined him, this need not have been done for the purpose of considering his sanity, and a medical expert whose visit to an asylum was solely for the purpose of a hygiene inspection was permitted to give evidence of the sanity of an inmate.[25] However strong the medical evidence, though, for example as to capacity to contract, the jury or court must always·

---

[18] See *Phillion v. R.* (1977) 74 D.L.R. (ed) 136 at 140.
[19] [1975] 1 Q.B. 834.
[20] *R. v. Wong* [1977] 1 W.W.R. 1.
[21] Above n. 18.
[22] *Ibid.*, at 140. Though see p. 141 *et seq.* as to the United States approach. See also E. Harnon, "Evidence Obtained by Polygraph: An Israeli Perspective" (1982) Crim.L.R. 340.
[23] *Bainbrigge v. Bainbrigge* (1850) 4 Cox 454.
[24] *Ibid.*
[25] *Martin v. Johnston* (1858) 1 F. & F. 122.

"form their own judgment upon it, not disregarding, but not relying upon, the opinions of the medical men."[26]

---

[26] *Lovatt* v. *Tribe* (1862) 3 F. & F. 9 at 11. See also *Richmond* v. *Richmond* (1914) 111 L.T. 273 at 274.

CHAPTER 13

Valuation of Land and Buildings

When issues concerning the valuation of land and buildings come before the courts, or another legal forum, they almost always include questions of expert evidence. The most common issues are those relating to annual or other periodic values attached to land, such as rent or rates, rather than the freehold value. The expertise involved is almost invariably that of a surveyor, who may well be a specialist within the particular sector concerned, such as office buildings, agricultural lettings etc. The forms of dispute which have given rise to most of the legal authority are those relating to the rent for business premises, whether under the Landlord and Tenant Act 1954 or pursuant to a rent review clause in the lease. There is also a body of law relating to rating and other cases in the Lands Tribunal, as to which special procedural provisions apply. A substantial proportion of valuation disputes are resolved by arbitration, either pursuant to an arbitration clause or by consent.

There has also developed a practice of jointly instructing an independent expert acceptable to the parties to reach a valuation by which the parties will then agree to be bound.[1] This kind of arrangement has no legal status as a tribunal subject *per se* to review by the courts. It is a contractual agreement between the parties and the independent expert, and any recourse to the courts is limited to the legal rights which arise out of that agreement.[2] The agreement may procure a "speaking" valuation, in which the expert gives reasons for his decision and the calculations by which he arrives at his final figure, or a "non-speaking" valuation in which nothing but the valuation itself is communicated to the parties. A non-speaking valuation probably cannot be impugned so long as the valuation is performed by the right man of the right property and in good faith.[3] Even where more is required pursuant to the agreement, the courts will not purport to lay down detailed directions as to what the valuer should take into account in performing the valuation.[4] The courts will however be quicker to find negligence in a valuer supplying a mortgage

---

[1] A detailed examination of this subject is beyond the scope of this book.
[2] *Burgess v. Purchase & Sons (Farms)* [1983] Ch. 216.
[3] *Ibid.*, at 11.
[4] *Forte and Co. v. General Accident Ltd.* [1986] 2 E.G.L.R. 115. See also *Compton Group Ltd. v. Estates Gazette Ltd.* (1977) 36 P. & C.R. 148.

valuation for one party if he has failed to apply any of the clear principles of the discipline.[5]

A. ADMISSIBILITY

1 Relevant considerations

It is a matter of valuation expertise and practice as to how to value a particular piece of land and the buildings upon it. The higher courts will not without good reason interfere with the decision of a court at first instance, arbitrator or tribunal which has assessed the valuation evidence and come to a conclusion upon it. There is a very substantial body of case law as to the relationship between actual valuation practice, which is a matter for the witness, and the requirements of the particular statute or contract pursuant to which the valuation is made.[6] Where the question is what the particular land would be worth on the open market, the principal method is the use of comparables.[7] However these are only as useful as their similarities with the subject property, and it may be necessary to carry out a valuation exercise based upon the value of the property itself in commercial terms.

Thus a caravan site, which may be unique in the area, could be rated on the basis of likely profits.[8] In rent cases under the Landlord and Tenant Act 1954 the tenant's business accounts are generally not relevant, and therefore not discoverable documents,[9] though the position might well be different where there were no comparables and the premises were peculiarly adapted for a specific purpose.[10] Furthermore there are certain types of business, such as racecourses, petrol stations and theatres, whose rent as a matter of valuation does generally depend on actual takings, so that evidence of these would be highly relevant, but this could never apply to shop premises with no peculiar features.[11] Trading figures must be shown to be directly relevant to a particular issue.[12]

In rent review cases it may be necessary to consider matters occurring after the review date, but the specific relevance of such evidence must be demonstrated. To admit such evidence in general would be:

---

[5] *Corisand Developments* v. *Druce* (1978) 248 E.G. 315.
[6] See *e.g.* Bernstein and Reynolds, *Handbook of Rent Review* and Woodfall, *Landlord and Tenant*.
[7] Discussed below.
[8] *Garton* v. *Hunter* [1969] 2 Q.B. 37.
[9] *Barton* v. *Longacre Securities Ltd.* [1982] 1 W.L.R. 398.
[10] *Ibid.*
[11] *Ibid.*
[12] *Harewood Hotels* v. *Harris* [1958] 1 W.L.R. 108.

"to introduce into the valuation a species of foreknowledge which would not be available to any willing buyer or willing seller."[13]

It has been said however that if the rent of a comparable property was reviewed the day after the review date for the subject property it must be relevant, as must such evidence in the subsequent period, the only question being as to weight the longer the period is.[14] The position would be different where the subsequent evidence is used to judge how likely it was at the date of the original valuation that some future event would occur.[15] This logical approach would exclude evidence as to whether, for example, a change of use was in fact subsequently permitted, when the issue at the review date was the likelihood of such permission without the benefits of foreknowledge.

Depending upon the issue, it may be possible to demonstrate rateable value as being relevant to a rent valuation, particularly where there is an absence of other, usually more persuasive indicators.[16] The tenant's rights and his prospects of success in exercising them are always relevant, whether, for example, these be renewal rights under the Landlord and Tenant Act 1954[17] or contractual obligations of the landlord to grant consent to a reasonable change of use.[18] It is important both in assessing the facilities of the subject premises, and in analysing the similarities of comparables, to have the fullest possible information as to the nature and extent of the premises. Where therefore a landlord's surveyor had valued premises in evidence without having seen all the rooms because of the tenant's inadvertance, it was a reasonable exercise of discretion to order a new trial, as the evidence could not with reasonable diligence have been available at the first hearing.[19]

2 Comparables

The chief method of valuation for a new or reviewed rent is the comparable, and where good evidence of comparable properties is available other evidence may be regarded as inadmissible, or at least of negligible weight. Usually, where experts are instructed on both sides, each valuer will prepare a list of comparables, and depending upon the size and nature of the particular market, these may or may not overlap. Much of the value of such evidence is in the remarks made by a valuer about those comparables adduced in support of the other party's contended value. It

---

[13] *Gaze v. Holden* (1983) 266 E.G. 998. See also *Divan Estates Ltd. v. Rossette Sunshine Savouries Ltd.* (1982) 261 E.G. 364.
[14] *Segama N.V. v. Penny Le Roy Ltd.* (1984) 269 E.G. 322.
[15] *Ibid.*, at 326.
[16] See *e.g. Jeffereys v. Hutton* (1956) 168 E.G. 203; *Robinson v. Shaw* (1956) 167 E.G. 192.
[17] *Pivot Properties v. Secretary of State for the Environment* (1980) 41 P. & C.R. 248.
[18] *Aldwych Club v. Copthall* (1962) 185 E.G. 289.
[19] *Skrzypkowski v. Silvan Investments* [1963] 1 W.L.R. 525.

VALUATION OF LAND AND BUILDINGS

is thus essential for details of comparables to be exchanged, and this is usually done by consent by way of schedule, quite apart from the court or arbitrator's powers to require this.[20] The parties may agree the facts contained in the schedules notwithstanding a possible hearsay objection.[21] Comparables are also used in rating proceedings, though the view was once expressed that such evidence is "practically valueless" because of the variations in circumstances between properties in the same area.[22]

In rent cases under the Landlord and Tenant Act 1954 the use of comparables is essential save in circumstances in which the subject premises are unique. Care must be taken however to adduce only that evidence of comparison which is directly relevant. Where evidence of comparison was adduced from other traders in the same arcade as the subject property, they were permitted to give evidence that their rents were too high and that the level of trade resulting from their position in the arcade was not as good as they had expected it to be when they agreed the lease.[23] The Court of Appeal held that the only admissible evidence from such people was to the effect that their particular position was not a good one for trade purposes. Any other evidence was of "very limited value" and therefore not merely of little weight, but inadmissible.[24]

It is essential when considering comparables to be aware of every aspect of their circumstances. A property which is superficially similar in position and nature may be useless as a comparable if the rent is subject to peculiarly onerous or favourable terms in the lease as to user and repairs.[25] The lease of a particularly good comparable may not have been finally agreed, but if a firm offer has been made, and can be proved, the comparison is of considerable weight.[26] It is suggested that strict proof should often be insisted upon in such a case as information as to the state of such negotiations, even where given and received in good faith, can be very unreliable.

The valuation technique of 'zoning' is widely used for comparisons of value per square foot of properties of different sizes, particularly retail premises of different depths from the shop-front. It has been said however to be of limited value in relation to small shops of similar size, as to which direct comparisons can be made without the technique of zoning,[27] which does introduce a somewhat artificial formulaic element into

---

[20] See *Handbook of Rent Review*, Form F6, for a specimen schedule.
[21] As to which, see below pp. 251–252.
[22] *Pointer v. Norwich Assessment Committee* [1922] 2 K.B. 471; *Cartwright v. Sculcoates Union* [1900] A.C. 150.
[23] *Rogers v. Rosedimond Investments Ltd.* (1978) 247 E.G. 467.
[24] *Ibid.*
[25] See *Re 52, 54 and 56 Osnaburgh Street* [1957] C.L.Y. 1947; *Aldwych Club v. Copthall*, above n. 18.
[26] See *Re 52, 54 and 56 Osnaburgh Street*, above n. 25.
[27] *F. W. Woolworth v. Moore* (1978) 21 R.R.C. 208.

the calculation. Despite this, zoning is a very useful forensic technique, in addition to its professional acceptance among valuers, in that it provides an established and uniform method of analysing comparables adduced by different experts.

Hearsay An expert valuation witness may obtain information about comparables from a wide variety of sources, which fall into three principal categories. First, he will use where possible properties in relation to which he has had a personal professional involvement. In such a case he may give direct evidence of the particulars of the property and the agreement reached in relation to it, refreshing his memory from or producing documents where necessary. Secondly, he will hear of properties through professional channels, particularly a colleague in his own or a familiar firm. In these circumstances he may not give evidence in relation to the comparable property. The other party may not require proof of such particulars however if the expert has satisfied himself that the information he has been given is correct by checking with a fellow professional he knows and trusts. Thirdly, there may be properties of which he hears and as to which he cannot be certain that the particulars about which he has information are correct, although he believes them to be so. Here his client will almost certainly be put to proof of every aspect of the property and the terms of the lease if one currently exists. It can substantially undermine a valuer's opinion if his most persuasive comparables are evidentially inadmissible.

Objections to such evidence must be taken at the hearing, and a failure to do so will usually constitute a waiver of any subsequent remedy in relation to it.[28] The provisions as to proof of hearsay in the Civil Evidence Act 1968 are procedural, not substantive, so that once an arbitrator hears such evidence without objection, he may properly rely upon it.[29] The position is different however where there is a risk that an arbitrator may have taken hearsay evidence into account without giving both parties the opportunity to make representations about it.[30]

The fullest examination of the impact of the hearsay rules upon the adducing of hearsay evidence of comparables is the judgment of Megarry J. in *English Exporters (London) Ltd.* v. *Eldonwall Ltd.*[31] This is discussed at length in Chapter 8[32] and the reader is referred to that discussion for an analysis of the evidential principles which apply. The two specific forms of evidence which Megarry J. stated that a valuer may give

---

[28] *Town Centre Securities Ltd.* v. *Wm. Morrison Supermarkets Ltd.* (1982) 263 E.G. 435. See also *Rogers* v. *Rosedimond Investments Ltd.*, above n. 23, at 469.
[29] *Town Centre Securities*, above n. 28, at 436.
[30] *Shield Properties and Investments Ltd.* v. *Anglo-Overseas Transport Co. Ltd.* (1924) 273 E.G. 69.
[31] [1973] Ch. 415.
[32] At pp. 169–172.

are factual evidence of transactions in which he has himself been involved, and opinion evidence as to those transactions which have been or will be proved by other admissible evidence. In addition he may bring to his opinion his general experience of values in cases of a similar kind, some of which he may have been personally involved with, and others of which he may have absorbed through conversations with clients and other valuers or though professional literature. This is very largely what, when combined with training and judgment, constitutes his expertise, namely his professional experience.

Megarry J. emphasised that a valuer could give direct evidence of a comparable only by personal involvement.[33] Thus, if he had read the lease, he could describe its contents. If he had measured the property, he could give evidence of dimensions. The judge supposed that if the valuer had not himself measured the comparable property, but had left it to an assistant, his evidence would be accepted without the necessity of calling the assistant.[34] In fact this procedure is probably acceptable on general principles of expert evidence.[35] Megarry J. also referred to the likelihood that a valuer who had filled a gap in his direct knowledge by diligent enquiries would not be pressed to prove this directly,[36] though the judge was presumably not suggesting that a party may not put the valuer to strict proof on a material matter in dispute. Of course there is nothing to prevent the expert from employing forbidden information (*i.e.* what he has been told about the letting of a particular property) as part of his general experience, by simply not mentioning it. However eminent and respected he is, though, the court is unlikely to be satisfied of his evidence as to value without his analysis in oral evidence of specific comparables. Megarry J., aware of the dangers of a less than strict approach to hearsay, particularly perhaps in arbitrations, took the view that:

> "for counsel to put in a list of comparables ought to amount to a warranty by him of his intention to tender admissible evidence of all that is shown on the list."[37]

B. WEIGHT

1 Method of valuation

Unless the relevant statute or contract provides for it, there is no simple method of valuation which the witness must adopt.[38] The most that can

---

[33] *English Exporters (London) Ltd. v. Eldonwall Ltd.* [1973] Ch.415 at 421.
[34] *Ibid.*
[35] See *Stone v. Pugh* [1949] 1 K.B. 526; *R. v. Kersberg* (1976) R.T.R. 526.
[36] *English Exporters (London) Ltd. v. Eldonwall Ltd.*, above n. 33, at 421.
[37] *Ibid.*, at 423.
[38] *Guppy's Properties Ltd. v. Knott* (1977) 245 E.G. 1023.

be said is that the governing legislation may require certain matters to be assumed or taken into account, but this does not dictate the professional approach to be taken. Likewise the tribunal is free to adopt the course which it prefers. Although valuation is performed by mathematical means, it is not rigorously scientific or rational in the sense that so long as the correct steps are taken, the right answer will result: "valuation is not a science, it is an art."[39] There is therefore no need for the tribunal to give precise reasons for arriving at a given figure:

> "in the very nature of things the reasons, in the scientific sense, are not possible in such an instance."[40]

It is perfectly acceptable for all the evidence, of both fact and opinion, to be considered as a matter of impression, rather than making a finding that the result is dictated by a specific method of calculation:

> "the appropriate way to arrive at the correct figure is to bear in mind all the factors that are adduced before me, bear in mind all the figures that are put before me, to bear in mind the very helpful expert assistance of [the expert witnesses] but to weigh all those factors together as a matter of judgment, not as a matter of calculation."[41]

The same approach has been suggested as appropriate for Rent Assessment Committees:

> "at the end of the day they are entitled to put everything in the pot and stir it all together, and what comes out as the cooked dish is the fair rent as they find it."[42]

However the evidence given by the experts, and the decision made by the tribunal, must be an assessment of the value of the actual property in the actual market. Where therefore in a case under the Leasehold Reform Act 1967 expert valuers, rather than expressing an opinion upon the evidence before the Lands Tribunal, considered themselves bound to calculate on the basis of a method known as the 'adverse differential' which had been approved in previous Lands Tribunal decisions, an appeal to the Court of Appeal was successful.[43] A Lands Tribunal decision of Sir Eric Sachs emphasises the need for experts to maintain an open mind:

> "experts in a specialised field of valuation must beware of becoming so attached to a convenient formula which can appropriately be applied in a number of instances that it imprisons their reasoning in

---

[39] *Ibid.*, at 1023–1024.
[40] *Ibid.*
[41] *U.D.S. Tailoring Ltd.* v. *B. L. Holidays Ltd.* (1981) 261 E.G. 49 at 50.
[42] *Midanbury Properties Ltd.* v. *H. T. Clark and Sons,* (1981) 259 E.G. 565 at 566.
[43] *Official Custodian for Charities* v. *Goldridge* (1973) 26 P. & C.R. 191 at 213–214.

cases where that formula is not at all appropriate. Moreover, a formula which has merits in terms of stable currency and stable rates of interest may cease to have merit when stability no longer exists."[44]

The tribunal, whether it consists of lawyers or valuers, or both, will usually be required to reach its decision in precise terms, by naming a single figure, or a number of single figures, for varying situations. The fact that this is so, however, should not encourage witnesses in attempts at precision where this is not possible, or may be misleading. It should be recognised that in performing its task, which as discussed above is one of general impression in many cases, the tribunal may be assisted, and persuaded, more effectively by evidence which adopts this realistic and pragmatic approach, rather than by treating the valuation exercise as an "exact science, as a mathematical calculation, which it is not."[45] It may, moreover, constitute sound valuation practice in particular circumstances to express the market value of premises as being within a range of figures, rather than as a precise figure. If the court so finds, it should accept this evidence, and determine its legal consequences.[46]

2 The tribunal's own expertise

Many of the persons hearing land valuation matters are themselves valuation experts, and are selected in order that they may bring their expertise to bear upon the proper resolution of the dispute. There is however a distinction between decision by independent expert, which is not a quasi-judicial but a purely contractual arrangement, and that by an arbitrator, whose obligations flow from statute and from the rules of natural justice which are enforceable in the courts. Other statutory tribunals such as the Lands Tribunal and Rent Assessement Committees have their own rules pursuant to statute, and again have enforceable obligations as to natural justice. The obligations of an arbitrator are to an extent dictated by the nature of the procedure adopted. Even where the arbitration is by written evidence only, however, the same general principles apply: the arbitrator must consider the evidence, of fact and opinion, submitted to him by the parties, and must arrive at his decision upon that evidence.[47] Where an arbitrator relied in such an arbitration upon two matters which were never referred to by the surveyors acting for the parties, and never put to them by the arbitrator in a meeting he had with them, Bingham J. took the view that he was using his expertise in an illegitimate manner.[48] The arbitrator relied in making his award upon the level of expenditure

[44] *Gallagher Estates* v. *Walker* (1973) 28 P. & C.R. 113.
[45] *Midanbury Properties Ltd.* v. *H. T. Clark and Sons*, above n. 42, at 566.
[46] *Carreras Ltd.* v. *D. E. & J. Levy* (1970) 215 E.G. 707.
[47] *Zermalt Holdings* v. *Nu-Life Upholstery Repairs Ltd.* [1985] 2 E.G.L.R. 14.
[48] *Ibid.*

required to bring the premises up to an acceptable structural and decorative standard, and upon his view that the smaller 'comparables' placed before him could not be regarded as properly comparable. These were both specific matters of fact and opinion relating to the individual case. Bingham J. held that the arbitrator was entitled to rely upon his expertise as to "general matters," but that where he did so in relation to "specific matters" concerning the subject premises, as these were, natural justice required that his views be:

> "exposed for the comments and submissions of the parties . . . If he is to any extent relying on his own personal experience in a specific way then that again is something that he should mention so that it can be explored."[49]

No disclosure is necessary in relation to the arbitrator's general expert knowledge, but it has been said that if he forms a view contrary to the evidence which would take the parties by surprise, he should notify them.[50] An arbitrator should have notified claimants, where the respondents did not appear at the arbitration, that he took the view that their claim was grossly inflated.[51] He is not entitled to use his expert knowledge to provide evidence which a party chose not to adduce itself.[52] An arbitrator was wrong to do his own pedestrian count outside retail premises without informing the parties that he would,[53] as was a Lands Tribunal member who went to the subject property and listened for levels of noise and vibrations as an uncalled "witness"[54]: they should use their expertise to evaluate the evidence, not to supply it.[55] The arbitrator or other tribunal member may have very specific knowledge, which may be relied upon entirely, so long as it is notified to the parties. Where a surveyor member of the Lands Tribunal for Scotland had inspected the subject land before buildings upon it were demolished, the Tribunal was entitled to accept the evidence of the expert witness with whose opinion his observations were most consistent, to the effect that the buildings had been in very poor condition.[56] The tribunal's local knowledge may be used, and should be, even to the exclusion of the expert evidence, if this is warranted,[57] although if such a radical course is proposed the witnesses should always have the opportunity to deal with such an opinion.

---

[49] Ibid., at 15.
[50] Fox v. Wellfair (1982) 263 E.G. 589 and 657.
[51] Ibid.
[52] Ibid.
[53] Top Shop Estates Ltd. v. C. Danino [1985] 1 E.G.L.R. 9.
[54] Hickmott v. Dorset County Council (1977) 35 P. & C.R. 195.
[55] Top Shop Estates Ltd. v. C. Danino, above n. 53.
[56] Braid Investments Ltd. v. East Lothian District Council (1981) 259 E.G. 1088 and 260 E.G. 75.
[57] See e.g. Barratt v. Harrison (1956) 167 E.G. 761.

VALUATION OF LAND AND BUILDINGS

In arbitrations, particularly of a minor kind, it is sometimes the case that a surveyor or other professional who is intimately involved in a particular transaction or building works is contractually designated as arbitrator in the event of a dispute. He is only excluded from so acting if he is a necessary witness in the arbitration,[58] and the fact that he has made adverse remarks about the merits of one party is not an exclusory factor.[59]

Rent Assessment Committees are not expected to give detailed judgments and may reject expert evidence without giving reasons, or select a figure for rent advanced by no expert before them, again without giving reasons.[60]

C. LANDS TRIBUNAL

1 Pre-hearing procedure

The evidential rules of the Lands Tribunal are governed principally by the Lands Tribunal Rules 1975.[61] The provisions as to expert witnesses in cases under section 1 of the Land Compensation Act 1961, contained in section 2(3) of that Act, are repeated in almost identical terms in rule 42(2) of the rules. Rule 42 provides as follows:

> "(1) This rule applies to any proceedings except appeals from decisions of local valuation courts under Part II and applications for certificates under Part VI.
> (2) Not more than one expert witness on either side shall be heard unless otherwise ordered:
> Provided that, where the proceedings include a claim for compensation in respect of minerals or disturbance of business, as well as in respect of land, one additional expert witness on either side of the value of the minerals or, as the case may be, on the damage suffered by reason of the disturbance may be heard.
> (3) An application for leave to call more than one, or more than one additional, expert witness may be made to the registrar in accordance with the provisions of rule 45 or to the Tribunal at the hearing.
> (4) Where more than one party intends to call an expert witness, every such party shall, within 28 days after being so requested by the

---

[58] *Freeman* v. *Chester R.D.C.* [1911] 1 K.B. 783; *Bristol Corporation* v. *Aird* [1913] A.C. 241.
[59] *Hogg* v. *Belfast Corporation* [1919] 2 Ir. Rep. 305.
[60] *Metropolitan Property Holdings* v. *Laufer* (1974) 29 P. & C.R. 172. See also *Guppy's Ltd.* v. *Sandoe* (1975) 235 E.G. 689 at 693 and *Midanbury Properties Ltd.* v. *H. T. Clark and Sons*, above n. 42.
[61] S.I. 1975 No.299, as amended. The rules are made pursuant to the Lands Tribunal Act 1949, s.3.

registrar, send to the registrar a copy of each of the following documents relating to the evidence to be given by the expert witness, together with sufficient copies for service upon the other parties—
  (i) every plan and valuation of the land or hereditament which is the subject of the proceedings (including particulars and computations in support of the valuation) which it is proposed to put in evidence;
  (ii) either a statement of any prices, costs or other particulars and any plans relating to a property or properties other than that land or hereditament which are proposed to be given in evidence in support of the valuation, or a statement that no such prices, costs, particulars or plans will be relied upon.

(5) The registrar shall, within 7 days after receiving all the documents required to be supplied by the parties under paragraph (4) above, send to each party copies of the documents supplied by the other party.

(6) If an application for leave to call more than one, or more than one additional, expert witness is made at the hearing and is granted by the Tribunal, or if at the hearing any party seeks to rely upon any plans, valuations or particulars which appear to the Tribunal not to have been sent to the registrar in accordance with this rule, the Tribunal may adjourn the hearing on such terms as to costs or otherwise as it thinks fit."

This rule contains the necessary provisions as to disclosure of expert evidence, with the result that it is unnecessary for the disclosure provisions of the High Court rules to apply. Thus:

"Nothing in the Civil Evidence Act 1972, or in rules of court made under it, shall prevent expert evidence from being adduced before the Tribunal by any party notwithstanding that no application has been made to the tribunal for a direction as to the disclosure of that evidence to any other party to the proceedings."[62]

The particulars submitted pursuant to rule 42(4) should contain the substance of the expert evidence to be adduced, not merely a summary of it, in relation to each comparable.[63] However it is not necessary or even desirable for the proposed expert's entire proof of evidence to be submitted, merely the particulars required by the rule. Thus the inferences which the expert witness will draw from the comparables, and any opinions he holds as to comparisons between them, need not be thus disclosed. This is not of any real disadvantage to the parties, because the expert's opinion at the hearing should take fully into account the com-

---

[62] Lands Tribunal Rules 1975, r. 39(3).
[63] See *Marchi-Stevenson Ltd.* v. *Edwards* (1958) 3 R.R.C. 289.

VALUATION OF LAND AND BUILDINGS

parables adduced by the other party. The parties are not excluded from adducing at the hearing evidence as to the rental or other relevant value of comparables where agreement was not reached and the value fixed until after the date for disclosure of particulars to the Tribunal.[64] However the late evidence is much more likely to be treated favourably if such notice as is possible has been given to the other party and to the Tribunal.[65] Where proceedings are under rule 33A (*i.e.* without a hearing), rule 33A(8) provides that written representations may be adduced from experts in the same manner as evidence under rule 42.

Section 3(5) of the Lands Tribunal Act 1949 makes provision for costs. A substantial proportion of non-legal costs in many matters before the Lands Tribunal will be constituted by the fees of surveyors and other relevant professionals. These may be made up both of fees relating to matters prior to the hearing and preparation for it, and those directly flowing from the reference to the Lands Tribunal. In a compensation case the pre-reference costs were held to be recoverable as part of the substantive compensation where they were sustained as a direct result of a dispossession.[66]

2 Admissibility and weight of evidence

Expert witnesses before the Lands Tribunal may be examined and cross examined in the usual manner, and any relevant evidence may be adduced subject to compliance with rule 42 as discussed above. Such compliance, however, does not admit the relevant particulars in evidence, it merely creates the conditions for their admissibility. Any document must be produced by a witness if not agreed between the parties, and no questions to a witness may be based upon it until it is properly before the Tribunal.[67] He can always, of course, be questioned as to matters within his own direct knowledge.[68]

Surveyors frequently have without prejudice conversations prior to the hearing, either informally or by specific arrangement of the parties with a view to compromise or a narrowing of issues. It has been emphasised that care should be taken not to make a practice of disclosing facts in such discussions on the understanding that they will not be employed at the hearing, unless it is clear that they will not be relevant.[69] The Civil Evidence Act 1968 applies to the adducing of hearsay and documentary evidence

---

[64] *Estate of J. M. Routh* v. *Central Land Board* (1957) 8 P. & C.R. 290, C.A.
[65] *Ibid.*
[66] *London County Council* v. *Tobin* (1959) 10 P. & C.R. 79. See too *Truman* v. *Chatham Borough Council* (1974) 28 P. & C.R. 326; *Mahood* v. *Department of the Environment for Northern Ireland* (1985) 277 E.G. 652.
[67] *Chinnery* v. *Basildon Development Corporation* [1970] R.V.R. 530.
[68] *Ibid.*
[69] *Provincial Theatres Ltd.* v. *Holyoak* (1969) 15 R.R.C. 198.

generally, though a fairly liberal approach may be adopted to the notice provisions where there is little or no prejudice.[70]

Any evidence as to valuation is admissible so long as it is relevant, although evidence of rent returns obtained after lodging of an objection to an appellant's proposal for a rent reduction has been excluded.[71] Comparables are generally admissible, though their weight may be diminished by distance from the subject property.[72] There is no requirement in principle, however, that a comparable be in the same district as the subject property, or as that for which the valuation officer acts.[73] Zoning should be employed only where it is demonstrably necessary, and not where a direct comparison of premises is possible without the intervention of a mathematical technique of that kind.[74] Comparables may, though admissible, be rejected as carrying no weight if the circumstances justify using a different indicator of value, such as the money market. However the land market should usually be central to the expert evidence, with the money market "only as a factor."[75]

The Tribunal itself has expertise, and frequently directly related to matters in issue in the case. It has a broad discretion to apply this expertise generally to matters before it. It must however, as must arbitrators, use the expertise to evaluate the evidence, not to supply it.[76] Members must take care not to visit sites and assess the evidence on that basis without notifying the parties, and even if they do so with notice should be mindful that their own observations should not be substituted for the evidence save in the clearest case.[77] Evidence emerging after the hearing, even though relevant, will usually not be admitted where the issues it raises were not canvassed at the original hearing.[78]

---

[70] See *e.g. Gredby v. Newham* (1973) 26 P. & C.R. 400 at 414–415: land-use records admitted pursuant to the Civil Evidence Act 1968, s.4(1).
[71] *Lach v. Williamson* (1957) 2 R.R.C. 347; *Scott v. Thompson* [1958] 3 R.R.C. 261.
[72] *Walker v. Hooper* (1978) 21 R.R.C. 155.
[73] *Morgan v. Bishop's Stores* (1963) 10 R.R.C. 128; *Sleet v. Holman* (1966) 12 R.R.C. 329; *Kidd v. Sellick* (1977) 20 R.R.C. 250.
[74] *F. W. Woolworth. v. Moore*, above n. 27.
[75] *Gallagher Estates v. Walker*, above n. 44.
[76] *Top Shop Estates Ltd. v. C. Danino*, above n. 53. See also *Hickmott v. Dorset County Council*, above n. 54. There is provision, by Rule 35 of the Lands Tribunal Rules 1975 (S.I. 1975 No. 299) for the appointment of assessors.
[77] *Bagnall v. Baker* (1972) 17 R.R.C. 387.
[78] *Welwyn Department Stores Limited v. Welwyn Garden City U.D.C.* (1958) 4 R.R.C. 227; *Wexler v. Playle* (1959) 5 R.R.C. 359.

CHAPTER 14

Forensic Sciences and Techniques

A. CRIMINAL INVESTIGATION AND PROOF

Forensic science has generally been regarded as the employment of particular scientific techniques in the investigation and prosecution of criminal offences. Although it is not by definition unconcerned with civil proceedings, in practice it is used overwhelmingly in the criminal field, though there are non-criminal proceedings which have some use for it, of which questions of parentage in matrimonial and other proceedings are probably the most important. These are considered later in this chapter. There is a substantial literature, both in books and learned journals, on the technical aspects of forensic science, which are beyond the scope of this work.

There are in fact relatively few legal rules, whether statutory or otherwise, determining the admissibility and use of forensic science in the courts. Many of the rules in fact employed are imposed as a matter of policy by the Home Office[1] in its role as employer and manager of the state's forensic science professionals. This means that, provided that the prescribed scientific procedures have in fact been complied with, much forensic scientific evidence is of a high probative value merely by virtue of its being placed before the court. Despite this, there has hitherto been a lack of proportion between the resources and adversarial advantages available to prosecution and defence in criminal cases. This arises in part from the fact that it is scientists acting for the police who almost invariably conduct the initial investigations,[2] both at the scene of the crime, and subsequently in the laboratory. The courts have traditionally exercised very little control over this aspect of a prosecution, and defence scientists have often been unable independently to test these initial findings in a satisfactory manner. They have frequently been reliant upon theoretical challenges[3] to the evidence which are not only intrinsically imperfect, but which may also appear unconvincing to a jury because of the clear disadvantage under which the defence expert labours. Some of

---

[1] Or by particular groups of professionals, such as the Fingerprint Society.
[2] Of which the collection of samples is a crucial part.
[3] Often, because of partial or non-disclosure, at short notice.

these difficulties have been addressed in part by the legislature,[4] but many deficiencies remain.[5]

Because of the inevitable fact that experts called by the parties may not have been involved in the investigation or analysis of crime until a late stage, the admissibility of forensic evidence is unaffected by the expert's lack of contact with the physical evidence with which the court is concerned,[6] though this may go to the question of weight. Juries are susceptible to two particular dangers: an inability to comprehend complex scientific evidence, and a tendency, often derived from the first difficulty, to accept what is said by an apparently impressive and authoritative expert witness, regardless of the merit of the content of his evidence. For this reason there is a heavy onus of responsibility upon the judge to explain in simple, though not simplistic, terms the competing scientific theories or findings on offer in a particular case. He should in doing so endeavour to avoid advancing a theory of his own which has not been fully canvassed before the scientific witnesses.[7] It is now becoming clear that lay witness identification evidence is unreliable in a high degree,[8] and for this reason among others the apparent certainties of the scientific method must be handled with great care, particularly where the criminal standard of proof is concerned.

1 Fingerprints

The comparison of fingerprints has long been the most commonly used method of forensic scientific identification. It is the practice of fingerprint professionals to draw conclusions for forensic use by the prosecution (though not necessarily for investigatory purposes) only if there are 16 common ridge characteristics in the two samples.[9] The Police and Criminal Evidence Act 1984 now provides a procedure for the taking of control samples of an individual's fingerprints.[10] Despite the recent development of DNA typing, sometimes confusingly known as genetic or DNA fingerprinting, the use of fingerprints proper is likely to remain pre-eminent as a method of identification clearly satisfying the criminal standard of proof where the body fluids or other material necessary for DNA tests are unavailable. Fingerprints can also be used for investigation purposes where no suspect has been identified, by virtue of the extensive fingerprint records kept by the police.

---

[4] See Chap. 2.
[5] See *e.g.* Sargent and Hill, *Criminal Trials: The Search For Truth*, Fabian Research Series, No. 348.
[6] R. v. *Mason* (1912) 76 J.P. 184.
[7] R. v. *Smith* (1915) 11 Cr.App.R. 229 at 239.
[8] See *e.g.* the research cited at Chap. 12, p. 242, n. 95.
[9] As to this and other matters of scientific policy and practice, see D. Campbell, "Fingerprints: A Review" (1985) Crim.L.R. 195.
[10] Police and Criminal Evidence Act 1984, s.61; *cf. Callis* v. *Gunn* [1964] 1 Q.B. 495.

A criminal court may convict on fingerprint evidence alone,[11] no corroboration being required. The courts will be scrupulous however to ensure that the fingerprint, in the absence of other evidence, proves the offence itself, not merely some connection with the subject-matter of the offence. On a charge of receiving a stolen car, a defendant's conviction was quashed where his fingerprint was found on the back of the driving mirror of the car in question.[12] He could merely have been a passenger in the car, and this would not *per se* amount to the possession which proves the offence. As with all expert evidence, the decision as to its determination of the issues is a matter for the court. As a matter of law there is no reason why the court should not perform its own comparison of fingerprints,[13] however in practice the prosecution would not now seek to adduce such evidence without expert evidence to a proper standard. In other jurisdictions indeed it has been said that expert evidence is essential,[14] and it is likely that the Court of Appeal would support this view in criminal cases. It has been suggested that it may be wrong for an expert to state that a fingerprint is unique in the world,[15] but no rule has been laid down. Where a jury is involved the judge should be particularly wary of permitting the witness to make assertions going to the standard of proof which are not clearly supported by scientific evidence before the court, though this could include secondary sources of a statistical or other nature.[16]

2 Tracking dogs

The use of dogs specially trained to track particular individuals by scent has a long history. In the overwhelming majority of cases in which such dogs are used their function is confined to the investigation of the crime and the apprehension of a suspect, who is then prosecuted on the basis of independent forensic or other evidence. There are however occasional sets of facts which dictate that the handler of the dog may need to be called to prove an essential element in the case. Evidence of this kind has been admitted in the English courts, though the exact conditions of admissibility are not reported.[17] Such evidence has also been admitted in the Scottish courts, with judicial notice having been taken of the fact that different people have different scents,[18] and in Northern Ireland.[19] It has

---

[11] R. v. *Castleton* (1910) 3 Cr. App.R. 74.
[12] R. v. *Court* (1960) 44 Cr.App.R. 242.
[13] See R. v. *Bacon* (1915) 11 Cr.App.R. 90, in which the court was assisted by a police officer, who was presumably (in the then state of the art) regarded as an expert.
[14] See R. v. *O'Callaghan* [1976] V. R. 676.
[15] *Ibid.*
[16] See R. v. *Abadom* [1983] 1 W.L.R. 126.
[17] See R. v. *Webb* [1954] Crim.L.R. 49.
[18] *Patterson* v. *Nixon* (1960) S.L.T. 220 at 224.
[19] R. v. *Montgomery* [1966] N.I. 120.

also generally been admitted in other jurisdictions, with exceptions,[20] and the appropriate principles have been explored in Commonwealth jurisdictions.

The dog handler must be an expert, and should clearly be able to show that the dog is properly trained, in addition to proving his own ability to handle the dog.[21] It has been said that he must show:

> "that the dog was by virtue of its breeding and training able to track a human being by his particular scent."[22]

Such evidence does not offend against the hearsay rule,[23] as the handler is merely giving evidence of the dog's conduct. The suggestion has been made that such a dog is properly viewed as a "tracking instrument" activated by the "appropriate word of command."[24] It has been correctly observed that this is a misleadingly simplistic view of the behaviour of an animal, however highly trained.[25] It is particularly dangerous because many people have what has been described as a "superstitious faith"[26] in a dog's abilities, which might lead a jury to accept uncritically what was apparently shown by the dog's behaviour. In R. v. Montgomery[27] one of the judges spoke of the "common knowledge"[28] which ordinary people possess about what dogs can do, without any apparent concern at the possibility that this may extend to wholly subjective assessments of canine capability. The court considered that no special jury warning was necessary beyond the usual advice as to the weight of evidence.[29]

Evidence as to tracking dogs can clearly be of use to the court. Its admission should perhaps however be conditional upon two matters: first, that the handler is an expert who has satisfied the court as to the dog's training and ability with "scrupulous thoroughness,"[30] and secondly, where the evidence is to be considered by a jury, that the judge gives a clear and specific warning as to the dangers of relying upon evidence which depends upon an animal for its existence.

3 Other admissible forensic scientific evidence

There is a number of other types of scientific evidence which are routinely admitted in criminal proceedings. These may be existing branches of

---

[20] See *e.g. R. v. Tupedo* [1960] A.D. 58 (South Africa).
[21] *R. v. Haas* (1962) 35 D.L.R. 172.
[22] *Ibid.*, at 176.
[23] *R. v. Lindsay* [1970] N.Z.L.R. 1002 at 1005.
[24] *R. v. Montgomery*, above n. 19, at 126.
[25] See F. Newark, "What the Dog Said" (1966) 82 L.Q.R. 311; G. McCormack, "The Admissibility of Tracker Dog Evidence" (1985) Crim.L.R. 202.
[26] *R. v. McCartney* [1976] 1 N.Z.L.R. 472.
[27] Above n. 24.
[28] *Ibid.*, at 126.
[29] *Ibid.*, at 125.
[30] *R. v. Lindsay*, above n. 23, at 1005.

science adapted for use in the forensic sphere, or areas of analysis created and used almost exclusively for such purposes. Examples are the analysis of fibres and hairs, blood/alcohol levels, drugs and glass, the grouping of blood stains and the investigation of arson.[31] Evidence as to footmarks has been received over a very long period, and even in the nineteenth century strict requirements were imposed as to the manner in which the comparison was performed before the evidence was admitted.[32] Such matters might today go to weight rather than admissibility.

4 New forensic sciences

The categories of admissible scientific techniques are never closed in principle. However there is a somewhat ill-defined process whereby new sciences, or perhaps more often sciences newly recruited for use in the forensic forum, become accepted as generally admissible in court,[33] subject of course to the expertise of the proposed witness being established. This is explored at greater length in Chapter 6.[34] Examples of sciences which have been advanced as evidentially sound but which the courts, whether in this or in other jurisdictions, have yet unequivocally to accept as admissible are: hypnosis,[35] truth drugs[36] and the polygraph[37] (or lie-detector) and voice-printing.[38] Forensic odontology has been received, but has been said not yet to be reliable enough alone to support a positive identification.[39] This list is by no means exhaustive.

Linguistic analysis A growing body of research into the propensity of individuals to use particular words in a specific manner or with a predictable frequency, either in spoken or written form, has suggested that this may in future be a fruitful area of forensic interest. "Forensic linguistic analysis" has been rejected for evidential use in the United States.[40] "Stylometry" has been said in Australia to be receivable in principle, and properly described as a science, though rejected in the particular case because of the difficulty of comparing unlike samples.[41] Commentators have suggested that the widespread forensic use of such techniques may

---

[31] For an account of the scientific progress made in these fields see P.H. Whitehead, "Ten years of Forensic Science, 1974–1983" (1984) Crim.L.R. 663.
[32] R. v. Shaw (1830) 1 Lew. 116; R. v. Heaton (1832) 1 Lew. 116.
[33] R. v. Turner [1974] Q.B. 834 at 843.
[34] At pp. 131–134.
[35] See Chap. 12, p. 242.
[36] See Chap. 12, p. 243.
[37] See Chap. 12, p. 244.
[38] Not yet accepted in the U.S.: see People v. King [1969] A.T.L.A. Newsletter 16 (California).
[39] Lewis v. R. (1987) 88 F.L.R. 104 (Australia).
[40] U.S. v. Clifford 543 F. Supp. 424 at 430. (W.D. pa. 1982).
[41] R. v. Tilley [1985] V.R. 505.

be inhibited less by their intrinsic defects or lack of scientific method than by the difficulty of obtaining appropriate samples, within the original evidence of a particular case, for their accurate use. Large amounts of text may be required for firm conclusions to be drawn.[42] The document in issue and the control document should normally have been made under similar circumstances.[43] It appears to be accepted that such methods have not yet established themselves as reliable enough to be universally admissible for evidential purposes.[44]

5 Visual images of suspects

A sketch or photofit of a suspect prepared by a police officer or other person for the purpose of identification may be adduced in evidence.[45] Although it may be said in effect to offend against the rules as to self serving statements, the Court of Appeal in *R. v. Cook*[46] has said that this is not a proper objection because the adducing of such a picture in evidence does not depend upon "a recital by the witness when giving evidence of what that person said to the police officer composing it."[47] Furthermore such visual images are analogous to photographs,[48] "another form of the camera at work, albeit imperfectly,"[49] and hence *sui generis*.[50] The rule against hearsay applies only to written statements.[51]

The issue of whether what is in fact involved is a question of expertise requiring expert evidence appears not to have been considered by the courts, although the court in *R. v. Cook* expressed the view that where a sketch is concerned:

> "the police officer is merely doing what the witness could do if possessing the requisite skill."[52]

Similarly, it may be said, a photofit entails expertise, both in its design and in its use. The courts have rejected the suggestion that, albeit such evidence is admitted, it should be subject to the "Turnbull" warning, amounting though it does to eyewitness identification evidence.[52a]

---

[42] See R. Totty et al, "Forensic Linguistics" (1987) 27(1) Journal of the Forensic Science Society 13.
[43] B. Niblett and J. Boreham, "Cluster Analysis in Court" (1976) Crim.L.R. 175. The authors refer to an unreported case at the Old Bailey in which the evidence of a "stylistic analysis" expert was called.
[44] See R. Totty et al, above n. 42, and A. Kenny, "The Expert In Court" (1983) L.Q.R. 197.
[45] R. v. Cook [1987] 2 W.L.R. 775.
[46] Ibid.
[47] Ibid., at 780–781.
[48] As to which see R. v. Tolson (1864) 4 F. & F. 103 at 104.
[49] R . v. Cook, above n. 45, at 781.
[50] Ibid. at 781.
[51] Ibid.
[52] Ibid.
[52a] R. v. Constantinou [1989] Crim.L.R. 571.

B. HANDWRITING

Evidence relating to handwriting, adduced for the purpose of establishing the identity of the writer, or excluding particular persons from having written it, may be given both by lay witnesses who are familiar with the writing of the person in question[53] and by experts, though the form in which they give the evidence will be different. The expertise of the expert need not have been attained in any particular prescribed manner, a principle explained in a leading case on expertise not only in the handwriting field, but also generally, *R. v. Silverlock*[54]:

> "the witness who is called upon to give evidence founded on a comparison of handwritings must be peritus; he must be skilled in doing so; but we cannot say that he must have become peritus in the way of his business or in any definite way. The question is, is he peritus? Is he skilled? Has he an adequate knowledge?"[54a]

1 Criminal proceedings

The comparison of different examples of handwriting in criminal cases is governed by section 8 of the Criminal Procedure Act 1865:

> "comparison of a disputed writing with any writing proved to the satisfaction of the judge to be genuine shall be permitted to be made by witnesses; and such writings, and the evidence of witnesses respecting the same, may be submitted to the court and jury as evidence of the genuineness or otherwise of the writing in dispute."

"Writing proved . . . to be genuine" It is apparent from the wording of the section that before any comparison may occur, the "control" sample must be proved to be genuine, a matter for the judge. Despite authority to the contrary[55] it is now clear from the decision in *R. v. Ewing*[56] that the judge must be satisfied as to the genuineness of the allegedly genuine document to the criminal, not the civil, standard of proof.[57] Thus the prosecution must prove its case on both documents, separately, beyond reasonable doubt.

"Witnesses" The word "witnesses" in section 8 is capable of including both lay and expert witnesses, and indeed there is no objection to the

---

[53] *R. v. Derrick* (1910) 5 Cr.App.R. 162.
[54] [1894] 2 Q.B. 766.
[54a] *Ibid.*, at 771.
[55] *R. v. Angeli* [1979] 1 W.L.R. 26.
[56] [1983] Q.B. 1039.
[57] Following *Blyth v. Blyth* [1966] A.C. 643.

adducing of evidence from either. In the period since the Criminal Procedure Act of 1865 there has been a recurrent question as to whether disputed handwriting should go before a jury without expert assistance (*i.e.* in addition to the evidence of a lay witness familiar with the defendant's writing, or simply looking at the two documents). In *R. v. Harvey*[58] it was stated by Blackburn J. that:

> "the evidence is very weak, and I do not think the jury ought to act upon it without the assistance of an expert."[59]

It is not clear from this whether the judge intended to convey that expert assistance should only be insisted upon where the evidence was weak, or in all cases. A later decision assumed the former:

> "this Court does not decide that expert evidence in such cases is necessary, and the observations of Blackburn J. in *Harvey* do not so decide, but it is clear from the nature of things that to leave a question of handwriting to a jury without assistance is a somewhat dangerous course."[60]

The judge added that if the court itself found "striking similarities" between two documents the position might be different.[61]

The modern courts have however been more cautious, and it now seems that where disputed handwriting is in issue, expert evidence should be supplied to assist.[62] In *R. v. Tilley* it was somewhat confusingly stated that in providing thus, the court was following the earlier case of *R. v. Rickard*,[63] which it appeared not to be doing in every particular. In *R v. O'Sullivan* it was accepted however that very often the disputed documents are an essential part of the prosecution case, and must therefore go before the jury in any event. Where this occurs the judge should warn it of the dangers of doing any comparison unassisted.[64] Ultimately though the jury cannot be prevented from drawing such inferences.[65]

The decisions in *R. v. Tilley* and *R. v. O'Sullivan* express the law on these questions. However handwriting comparisons have been permitted by the courts in other limited circumstances. Thus where defence counsel invited the jury to draw comparisons knowing of the decision in *R. v. Til-*

---

[58] (1869) 11 Cox 546.
[59] *Ibid.*, at 548.
[60] *R. v. Rickard* (1919) 13 Cr.App.R. 140 at 143.
[61] *Ibid.*
[62] *R. v. Tilley* (1961) 45 Cr.App.R. 360; *R. v. O'Sullivan* (1969) 53 Cr.App.R. 272.
[63] Above n. 60.
[64] *R. v. O'Sullivan*, above n. 62.
[65] *Ibid.*, at 282. The relevant part of the decision in *R. v. Stannard* [1965] 2 Q.B. 1, which might suggest a different approach, is of doubtful correctness: see *R. v. O'Sullivan*, above n. 62, at 282.

ley,⁶⁶ the judge took the view that the court could form an opinion as to whether the defendant, a man of limited education, could sustain over a period a practice of writing in many different styles.⁶⁷ It is suggested that in the ordinary comparison case, even if the court thinks it can discern a "striking similarity"⁶⁸ between examples of handwriting, expert evidence should be adduced.

Handwriting expert There is, as has been stated, no prerequisite to handwriting expertise other than the appropriate level of skill.⁶⁹ Police officers, however, are not *per se* handwriting experts,⁷⁰ even where they have given evidence (prima facie wrongly) in other trials as experts.⁷¹ Furthermore a police officer, or any other person whose experience is confined to the analysis of writing in the case in question, is not an expert⁷²:

> "knowledge so obtained, that is to say, for such a specific purpose, and under such a bias, is not such as to make a man admissible as a *quasi-expert* witness."⁷³

Jury warning Where documents are necessarily in evidence in criminal proceedings, and the handwriting upon them is in dispute, expert assistance should be obtained, as has been seen, before any inferences are drawn as to the identity of the writer. If however an expert is not available, the jury should be warned by the judge as to the dangers of drawing such inferences unassisted.⁷⁴ In the final analysis though the jury which has such documents before it cannot actually be prevented from doing so:

> "as a matter of practical reality all that can be done is to ask them not to make the comparisons themselves and to have vividly in mind the fact that they are not qualified to make comparisons."⁷⁵

It is wrong for the judge to invite the jury to consider particular features of the handwriting, even where it is inevitable that they will consider this issue.⁷⁶

---

[66] *R. v. Smith* (1968) 52 Cr. App.R. 648.
[67] *R. v. Smith* (1909) 3 Cr.App.R. 87. See too *R. v. Hope* (1955) 39 Cr.App.R. 33.
[68] *R. v. Rickard*, above n. 60, at 143.
[69] *R. v. Silverlock*, above n. 54.
[70] *R. v. Harvey*, above n. 58.
[71] *R. v. Wilbain and Ryan* (1863) 9 Cox 448.
[72] *R. v. Crouch* (1850) 4 Cox 163.
[73] *Ibid.*, at 164.
[74] *R. v. O'Sullivan* above n. 62, at 282.
[75] *Ibid.*
[76] *R. v. Smith* (1968) 52 Cr.App.R. 648 at 652.

Ex improviso The issue of disputed handwriting cannot be said to arise *ex improviso*, thus justifying the calling of expert evidence by the prosecution after it has closed its case, where the prosecution had samples of the defendant's admitted handwriting in its possession throughout the trial.[77]

2 Civil proceedings

Expert evidence as to handwriting is admissible in civil cases on the same principles as in criminal proceedings, though the particular provisions of section 8 of the Criminal Procedure Act 1865, and the decisions upon it, do not of course apply. Thus expert evidence is never essential in principle,[78] as in criminal proceedings lay witnesses who have over a long period been familiar with the handwriting in issue, and its writer, may be called. Some early decisions suggest that this type of evidence will be more persuasive as a matter of weight than that of an expert, though these are also explicable on the grounds that the expert advanced was biased[79] or had only a brief opportunity to analyse the writing in question.[80] Because he is not giving evidence of fact, the expert may not give evidence to the effect that two documents were written by the same person,[81] or that a particular person wrote a particular document.[82]

It has also been held that the expert is limited to pointing out similarities and drawing conclusions therefrom,[83] but it must be presumed that he may now express an opinion upon an ultimate issue to the effect that in his view two documents were written by the same person.[84] If the writing on one document is of known authorship, this effectively permits all such evidence forbidden in the early cases. If such comparisons are to be made, both samples must be in court.[85]

Issues which may be canvassed A handwriting expert may give evidence as to the time at which a document was probably written.[86] Evidence to the effect that a particular document is in a disguised hand is probably receivable,[87] though this has been doubted,[88] and it has been

---

[77] *R. v. Day* (1940) 27 Cr.App.R. 168. See Chap. 5, pp. 114–116.
[78] *Re Clarence* (1909) 54 S.J. 117.
[79] *The Tracy Peerage* (1843) 10 Cl. & Fin. 154 at 190–191.
[80] *The Fitzwalter Peerage* (1842–4) 10 Cl. & Fin. 193 at 201.
[81] *R. v. Cator* (1802) Esp. 117.
[82] *Wakeford v. Bishop of Lincoln* (1921) 90 L.J.P.C. 174.
[83] *Ibid.*
[84] Civil Evidence Act 1972, s.3(3).
[85] *Arbon v. Fussell* (1862) 3 F. & F. 152.
[86] *Re Hindmarch* (1867) L.R. 1 P. & D. 307; *The Tracy Peerage*, above n. 79.
[87] *R. v. Cator* (1802) 4 Esp. 117.
[88] *Gurney v. Langlands* (1822) 5 B. & Ald. 330.

suggested that it would be of little weight.[89] There seems to be no logical reason however why the evidence of a convincing expert witness should not be accepted on such a point, given that much comparison evidence consists of identifying attempts to disguise handwriting.

Wills Act 1837, section 21 Words in wills may only be construed by the courts if they are, in the terms of section 21, "apparent." Such words are "apparent" even though they can only be read by an expert using specialist techniques.[90] Such techniques must not however consist of a material interference with the will itself, such as the use of chemical agents to remove ink from its surface.[91] Furthermore an expert may not give evidence of what he can read by the use of infra-red light where this technique involves the taking of a photograph of the will, because the words are not then "apparent" on the face of the original document, but only on a copy of it.[92]

C. SCIENTIFIC TESTS OF PARENTAGE IN CIVIL PROCEEDINGS

Whenever the question of parentage is in issue in civil proceedings, the court has power to order relevant persons to undergo blood tests. The Family Law Reform Act 1987 (F.L.R.A. 1987) also makes provision for bodily samples of other kinds to be tested,[93] though the relevant sections had not been introduced at the time of writing.

1 Ordering scientific tests

The power to order blood tests is provided by section 20 of the Family Law Reform Act 1969 (F.L.R.A. 1969) which provides as follows:

> "(1) In any civil proceedings in which the paternity of any person falls to be determined by the court hearing the proceedings, the court may, on an application by any party to the proceedings, give a direction for the use of blood tests to ascertain whether such tests show that a party to the proceedings is or is not thereby excluded from being the father of that person and for the taking, within a period to be specified in the direction, of blood samples from that person, the mother of that person and any party alleged to be the father of that person or from any, or any two, of those persons. A court may at

---

[89] *Gurney* v. *Langlands* (1822) 5 B. & Ald. 330.
[90] *Ffinch* v. *Combe* [1894] P. 191.
[91] *Re Horsford* (1874) L.R. 3 P. & D. 211 at 215.
[92] *Re Itter* [1950] P. 130.
[93] F.L.R.A 1987 s.23 and Sched. 2, paras. 20–25.

any time revoke or vary a direction previously given by it under this section.

(2) The person responsible for carrying out blood tests taken for the purpose of giving effect to a direction under this section shall make to the court by which the direction was given a report in which he shall state
  (a) the results of the tests;
  (b) whether the party to whom the report relates is or is not excluded by the results from being the father of the person whose paternity is to be determined; and
  (c) if that party is not so excluded, the value, if any, of the results in determining whether that party is that person's father;
and the report shall be received by the court as evidence in the proceedings of the matters stated therein.

(3) A report under subsection (2) of this section shall be in the form prescribed by regulations made under section 22 of the Act.

(4) Where a report has been made to a court under subsection (2) of this section, any party may, with the leave of the court, or shall, if the court so directs, obtain from the person who makes the report a written statement explaining or amplifying any statement made in the report, and that statement shall be deemed for the purposes of this section (except subsection (3) thereof) to form part of the report made to the court.

(5) Where a direction is given under this section in any proceedings, a party to the proceedings, unless the court otherwise directs, shall not be entitled to call as a witness the person responsible for carrying out the tests taken for the purpose of giving effect to the direction, or any person by whom any thing necessary for the purpose of enabling those tests to be carried out was done, unless within fourteen days after receiving a copy of the report he serves notice on the other parties to the proceedings, or on such of them as the court may direct, of his intention to call that person; and where any such person is called as a witness the party who called him shall be entitled to cross-examine him.

(6) Where a direction is given under this section the party on whose application the direction is given shall pay the cost of taking and testing blood samples for the purpose of giving effect to the direction (including any expenses reasonably incurred by any person in taking any steps required of him for the purpose), and of making a report to the court under this section, but the amount paid shall be treated as costs incurred by him in the proceedings."

When the 1987 provisions are introduced,[94] they will have the effect of amending subsections (1) and (2) as follows:

[94] Pursuant to F.L.R.A. 1987, s.34(2).

"(1) In any civil proceedings in which the parentage of any person falls to be determined, the court may, either of its own motion or on an application by any party to the proceedings, give a direction—
  (a) for the use of scientific tests to ascertain whether such tests show that a party to the proceedings is or is not the father or mother of that person; and
  (b) for the taking, within a period specified in the direction, of bodily samples from all or any of the following, namely, that person, any party who is alleged to be the father or mother of that person and any other party to the proceedings;
and the court may at any time revoke or vary a direction previously given by it under this subsection.
(2) The person responsible for carrying out scientific tests in pursuance of a direction under subsection (1) above shall make to the court a report in which he shall state—
  (a) the results of the tests;
  (b) whether any party to whom the report relates is or is not excluded by the results from being the father or mother of the person whose parentage is to be determined; and
  (c) in relation to any party who is not so excluded, the value, if any, of the results in determining whether that party is the father or mother of that person;
and the report shall be received by the court as evidence in the proceedings of the matters stated in it.
(2A) Where the proceedings in which the parentage of any person falls to be determined are proceedings on an application under section 56 of the Family Law Act 1986, any reference in subsection (1) or (2) of this section to any party to the proceedings shall include a reference to any person named in the application."

The consequential provisions,[95] which will be introduced at the same time as the 1987 amendments set out above, have the chief effect of substituting any references to "blood samples" in the F.L.R.A. 1969 with "bodily samples," and to "blood tests" with "scientific tests," to reflect the language of the section as amended.

However since the enactment of the 1987 Act a further amendment, this time brought fully into effect, has been made to section 20 by the Children Act 1989,[96] and this adds the following subsections:

"(1A) Where—
  (a) an application is made for a direction under this section; and

---

[95] F.L.R.A. 1987, Sched. 2, paras. 20–25.
[96] Children Act 1989, s.89.

(b) the person whose paternity is in issue is under the age of eighteen when the application is made,

the application shall specify who is to carry out the tests.

(1B) In the case of a direction made on an application to which subsection (1A) applies the court shall—

(a) specify, as the person who is to carry out the tests, the person specified in the application; or

(b) where the court considers that it would be inappropriate to specify that person (whether because to specify him would be incompatible with any provision made by or under regulations made under section 22 of this Act or for any other reason), decline to give the direction applied for."

A substantial part of the reason for these actual, and prospective, amendments is the discovery and development of the technique of DNA testing,[97] which among other applications makes it possible to be more precise about blood connections than is the case with the traditional blood tests, although these too have undergone considerable improvement in quality and in the precision of their findings.

In particular, DNA testing, if performed accurately, permits a prediction that a particular person is related to another to a very high degree of probability, which for forensic purposes may be regarded as certainty. Once the 1987 amendments are given effect, although under section 20(2)(b) the analyst will have to indicate his conclusions in exclusory rather than inclusory terms, he will also by section 20(2)(c) be required to indicate the extent to which the analysis permits the positive identification of a particular person as parent of the child in question. The court will be able to act of its own motion,[98] and to order all persons who are parties to the proceedings to undergo scientific tests.[99]

The changes already introduced by the Children Act 1989, however, do have the effect of permitting DNA testing, because a number of DNA analysts have now been approved for blood testing purposes,[1] as have their higher fees.[2] In paternity cases, unlike many criminal cases, the ability to test blood satisfies the need in the vast majority of cases, because there is no reason why a party without a genuine religious or medical objection should not give a blood sample. In criminal proceed-

---

[97] See *e.g.* P. Werrett and J. Lygo, "DNA Profiling" 1987 L.S.Gaz. 3637; R. Yaxley, "Genetic Fingerprinting" (1988) 18 Fam.Law 403; R. White and J. Greenwood, "DNA Fingerprinting and the Law" (1988) 51 M.L.R. 145.
[98] The prospective s.23(1).
[99] The prospective s.23(1)(b).
[1] Home Office Circular 41/1989.
[2] Blood Tests (Evidence of Paternity) (Amendment) Regulations 1990 (S.I. 1990 No. 359); Blood Tests (Evidence of Paternity) (Amendment) (No 2) Regulations 1990 (S.I. 1990 No 1025).

ings, of course, the prosecution may only have a small bodily sample available from the scene of the crime, usually not blood.

The applicant must specify who is proposed as analyst, and the court must either support or dismiss the entire application.[3] Specific procedural rules govern procedure in the various courts, namely R.S.C. Order 112,[4] C.C.R. Order 47, rule 5 and the Magistrates' Courts (Blood Tests) Rules 1971.[5] The performance of the blood test, in relation to all courts, is regulated by the Blood Tests (Paternity) Regulations 1971.[6]

2   The court's discretion

It is always a question of fact in the circumstances of the particular case as to whether the court should order tests of parentage, either upon application or of its own motion.[7] Where it is considering the need for the appointment of the Official Solicitor or another guardian *ad litem*, such questions can often be postponed until after the test results have been obtained, as they may effectively dispose of the case.[8] The House of Lords took the view in *S. v. S.; W. v. Official Solicitor*[9] that, certainly where issues of legitimacy were concerned, it was generally in the child's best interests for the full truth to be known and established by the court, and that the court should have the best evidence available to it. Lord Reid went so far as to say that:

> "to prevent a blood test is to suppress the evidence that it would yield."[10]

The court should, in Lord Reid's view, order a blood test in the case of a young child unless satisfied that it was against his interests, though the position may be different where an older child is reluctant to submit to it. However the general principle is that knowledge is better than ignorance in cases of doubt:

> "the court must protect the child, but it is not really protecting the child to ban a blood test on some vague and shadowy conjecture that it may turn out to be to its disadvantage: it may equally well turn out to be for its advantage or at least do it no harm."[11]

---

[3] F.L.R.A. 1987, s.1B(*b*).
[4] And see *Practice Note* [1972] 1 W.L.R. 353.
[5] S.I. 1971 No. 1991.
[6] S.I. 1971 No. 1861, as amended.
[7] A registrar has jurisdiction as to blood tests, but should usually refer a dispute to the judge: *R. v. R.* [1973] 1 W.L.R. 1115.
[8] *Practice Note* [1975] 1 W.L.R. 81.
[9] [1972] A.C. 24.
[10] *Ibid.*, at 45.
[11] *Ibid.*, at 45, *per* Lord Reid.

It may be relevant for the court to ask the question whether the degree of certainty which the proposed test can provide in the particular case justifies its being ordered. Where it may be inconclusive, it can be undesirable if it invites the child to question his confidence in his mother.[12] However to resolve such an issue on the basis of a formalistic application of the burden and standard of proof is almost always unsatisfactory:

> "there is nothing more shocking than that injustice should be done on the basis of a legal presumption when justice can be done on the basis of fact."[13]

The power to order tests only arises where parentage is a live issue in the proceedings. The desire of an adult to know the truth cannot displace the child's interest if this demands that the child's present belief is not disturbed.[14] The court will be wary too of an oblique motive, such as that of a husband who simply wishes to establish for his own reasons that his wife has committed adultery.[15] Likewise it will rarely be justified where only an issue such as access remains to be decided.[16]

Testing a child There can be no general rule removing the court's discretion on the basis of the child's own views. Clearly a very young child can safely be ignored,[17] save that the court may wish to ask itself what his view might have been were he old enough to hold one. The general approach appears to be that the court will take the expressed views of an older child into account, but will not be fettered by them. Thus a 14 or 15 year old's preference should be considered, but is "never decisive."[18]

The court should however not require the child to be tested until after the relevant adults have submitted to a test, because if they refuse the child may have suffered unnecessarily.[19] Where the Official Solicitor or other guardian *ad litem* does not consent to a child being tested, the court will of course pay such an opinion considerable attention, but is not bound by it.[20]

The reluctant party The court cannot force any adult party to undergo a blood test,[21] but may draw adverse inferences from a failure to do so.[22]

---

[12] M. v. M. and G. [1969] 1 W.L.R. 843. See also *Hodgkiss v. Hodgkiss* [1984] F.L.R. 563 and P. v. P. (1969) 113 S.J. 343.
[13] *Holmes v. Holmes* [1966] 1 W.L.R. 187 at 188. See also *Re L.* [1968] P. 119.
[14] *Hodgkiss v. Hodgkiss*, above n. 12.
[15] M. v. M. and G., above n. 12.
[16] *Re J.S. (A Minor)* [1981] Fam. 22 at 29.
[17] See S. v. S., above n. 9, *per* Lord Reid at 45.
[18] B. v. B. [1968] P. 466 at 473; see too L. v. L. (1968) 112 Sol. Jo. 840.
[19] *Re J.S.*, above n. 16, at 29; P. v. P., above n. 12; *Re L.*, above n. 13.
[20] *Re L.*, above n. 13.
[21] See F.L.R.A. 1969, s.21; W. v. W. [1964] P. 67.
[22] F.L.R.A. 1969, s.23(1).

The court has a general jurisdiction to order a stay of proceedings wherever it is just and reasonable,[23] but appropriate though this may be in, for example, personal injuries proceedings, in family cases it may be wholly wrong to refuse to decide the matter on this basis. There may be limited circumstances, however, in which a similar effect can be achieved by some other interlocutory order. Thus Sheldon J. granted an injunction preventing a mother from leaving the country until she provided a sample for testing.[24]

3 Standard of proof

The results of scientific tests of parentage are usually expressed in probabilistic terms, and it thus becomes necessary to consider how such findings affect the standard of proof. Of course in many cases there will be other evidence of fact before the court, such as evidence of a mother that she had sexual intercourse with the putative father at about the material time, to which can be added the test results. Presumptions of law as to legitimacy can be rebutted by such evidence.[25]

How a court assesses evidence expressed in probabilistic terms is entirely for its discretion so long as all the evidence is considered. However the higher courts appear not simply to translate a percentage chance shown by a scientific test into an equivalent finding on the balance of probabilities. This was the approach of the court in legitimacy proceedings, in which it was for the husband to establish illegitimacy, but the non-scientific evidence did not permit the court to conclude on the balance of probabilities that the husband was the father, nor that, as the husband asserted, the wife had committed adultery.[26] Blood test evidence showed that one in every nine or 10 men, among Western Europeans, could have been the father, including the husband. The court took the view that this evidence did "go some way towards making it probable"[27] that the husband was the father, and therefore "on a narrow balance"[28] found that the husband had failed to discharge the onus upon him.

It has also been held that although the purpose of section 26 of the F.L.R.A. 1969 was to dispense with the need for findings beyond reasonable doubt,[29] the standard of proof should not necessarily be that of a commercial or negligence action, but should be commensurate with the seriousness of the issue.[30] This approach, which might be thought to lack

---

[23] *Edmeades* v. *Thames Board Mills* [1969] 2 Q.B. 67. See too *S.* v. *S.* above n. 9, at 46–47.
[24] *Re J.* [1988] 1 F.L.R. 65.
[25] F.L.R.A. 1969, s.26. See though F.L.R.A. 1987, s.17.
[26] *T.* v. *T.* [1971] 1 W.L.R. 429.
[27] *Ibid.*, at 433.
[28] *Ibid.*
[29] Thus overruling decisions such as *F.* v. *F.* [1968] P. 506.
[30] *Serio* v. *Serio* (1983) 4 F.L.R. 756, C.A.

the certainty and predictability which would be an advantage in such proceedings, led the court to conclude that a test result showing an 88.5 per cent. probability in favour of paternity by the putative father was not useful as a significant pointer to paternity. The court also expressed the view that the mathematical probability disclosed by the test result should be relied upon at the expense of the analyst's comment upon it,[31] and that this should then be combined with other evidence of fact, in itself inconclusive, to ground a finding of paternity to the requisite standard. Such an approach, that the standard of proof is affected by the gravity of the issue, paternity being a "grave" issue, has since been supported by Latey J.,[32] though the facts underlying the decision do not assist with an understanding of the practical results of this principle. Latey J. was concerned with circumstances in which two men had sexual intercourse with one woman over the period of possible conception. The paternity index for one showed a 97·4 per cent. probability of paternity, while the other was infertile. This set of facts would presumably lead to one result whatever the standard of proof, indicating as it did a "virtual certainty"[33] of paternity.

Ormrod L.J. adopted a similar position upon the question of the application of the civil standard of proof to statistical findings in concluding that indeed the court should be guided by the nature of the issue before the court and that:

> "in deciding the balance of probability, the court must take into account the gravity of the decision and determine 'the degree of probability which is proportionate to the subject-matter.' "[34]

He confirmed too that it was wrong to apply a statistical probability to the standard of proof in a simple mathematical sense:

> "the concept of 'probability' in the legal sense is certainly different from the mathematical concept; indeed it is rare to find a situation in which these two usages co-exist although, when they do, the mathematical probability has to be taken into the assessment of probability in the legal sense and given its appropriate weight."[35]

The fact that the courts have clearly approved a 'floating' standard of proof in parentage matters in any event confounds such attempts as might be made to presume equivalence between the legal and the mathematical concepts of probability. Scientific tests will always be signifi-

---

[31] Though see now F.L.R.A. 1969, s.20(2)(c) as prospectively amended, above p. 272.
[32] W. v. W. [1988] 1 F.L.R. 86 at 88.
[33] Ibid.
[34] Re J. S. (A Minor), above n. 16, at 29.
[35] Ibid.

cant, however, whether as primary evidence or as corroboration,[36] where they have probative value in a statistically high degree.[37]

Adverse inferences Where tests are ordered, while as has been described the courts cannot force adults to comply, inferences may be drawn from a failure to do so.[38] The same applies where an adult prevents a child from being tested.[39] Such a refusal can also constitute evidential corroboration where a statute requires it,[40] though there must be no reasonable excuse for the refusal.[41]

---

[36] *Turner* v. *Blunden* [1986] 2 W.L.R. 491.
[37] *Ibid.*
[38] F.L.R.A. 1969, s.23(1).
[39] *Re L.* [1968] P. 119 at 159.
[40] *McV.* v. *B.* [1988] 2 F.L.R. 67.
[41] *B.* v. *B.* and *E.* [1969] 1 W.L.R. 1800 at 1803.

CHAPTER 15

Mathematical, Statistical and Financial Calculations

A. ACTUARIAL EVIDENCE

The courts are frequently required to make assessments of the life expectancy of an individual. This is usually for the purpose of calculating damages for future loss, and almost always in the context of a claim arising out of personal injuries or a fatal accident. The particular difficulty the court faces has two aspects. First, it must arrive at a number of years representing the period the individual is expected to live. It is obvious that in most cases a particular number of years cannot be proven, on the balance of probabilities, to be the individual's likely span, because the chance that he will live for, say, 23, 24, 26 or 27 years in fact far outweighs the chance that he will live for exactly 25. Nevertheless a figure must be chosen which is fair and just in the circumstances, in so far as the evidence permits. Secondly, the court is almost invariably attempting to provide the individual with an annual sum, calculated by reference to pecuniary needs he did not have before the accident in question (in a personal injuries case),[1] and to an assessment of what his income would have been had he not suffered personal injuries or death. This annual figure, however, must be converted into a single lump sum to form the court's damages award, unless the parties can agree a 'structured settlement'.

1 Actuarial calculations

Actuaries practise their science on the basis of probabilities, most often but not exclusively in the context of insurance. Their raw material is the facts of the particular life in question, and the actuarial tables habitually used within the profession for making calculations. The science in the context of damages awards consists of selecting the appropriate tables, and making mathematical calculations by applying them to the facts of the individual's life and the sums of money required on an annual basis. As has been seen, however, the figure selected as the appropriate number of years of the life cannot be said to be probable in the sense that the individual in the case is more likely than not to live for that number of years precisely. It is the product of a generalisation, based upon the calculated

---

[1] Though not in the case of a fatal accident.

future of all members of the class which has been selected as best representing the individual in the case. In this generalised manner, therefore, it takes account of the chance that the individual will live for fewer years than expected. This includes the chance, particularly important where loss of future earnings calculations are concerned, that he will die before his proposed retirement date. The calculation can never be entirely 'just' or 'fair' for the particular individual, because it is based in part upon the future of the class he is deemed to belong to, but in so far as the particular individual's future is unknown (which is usually to a considerable extent) it represents a 'justice' or 'fairness' which is informed by the experience of the actuarial profession (which prepares the tables over time), the expertise of the actuary who performs the particular calculation, and the fact that the individual is being placed in no worse (and no better) a position than other members of the class he is in.[2] Actuarial calculations can incorporate varying assumptions as to future economic inflation and interest rates.

2 Admissibility of actuarial evidence

Actuarial evidence has long been received in the courts. In *Rowley v. London and North Western Railway Company*[3] an accountant who, though not an actuary, had experience of insurance, was permitted to give such evidence, based upon the Carlisle actuarial tables. Blackburn J. held that it was admissible because:

> "with the view of ascertaining the probable duration of a particular life at a given age, it is material to know what is the average duration of the life of a person of that age."[4]

This average, however, was only a starting point, and was subject to variation dependent upon evidence as to the health of the life in question.[5] The courts have however dispensed with such evidence where it was not strictly relevant, as where the question of number of years was outweighed by the need to assess the quality of the life, as opposed to its mere quantity.[6] This could equally well be done on a "common-sense" basis.[7]

Since these decisions the courts have, almost universally, while never expressly stating that actuarial evidence is *per se* inadmissible, held that it is not in general to be relied upon, and is to be used only for limited pur-

---

[2] For a fuller explanation of these principles in a legal context, see J. H. Prevett, "Actuarial Assessment of Damages: The Thalidomide Case" (1972) 35 M.L.R. 140 and 257.
[3] (1873) L.R. 8 Ex. 221. See also *M'Donald v. M'Donald* (1880) 5 App.Cas. 519.
[4] *Ibid.*, at 226.
[5] *Ibid.*, at 226.
[6] *Benham v. Gambling* [1941] A.C. 157 at 163.
[7] *Rose v. Ford* [1937] A.C. 826.

poses. The majority in *Fletcher* v. *Autocar*,[8] and the court in *Mitchell* v. *Mulholland*[9] declined to found their main calculations as to future loss upon actuarial principles. This appears mainly to be on the ground of imprecision, the courts being:

> "quite unconvinced that . . . the actuarial approach . . . affords the court such a precise tool as it would desire to have in its hand . . . "[10]

This general approach was more recently confirmed in *Auty* v. *National Coal Board*[11] by the Court of Appeal. Although the court's attitude stems in part from the fact that it held that interest should not be taken into account in the damages calculations (thus making the actuarial evidence, which did take account of interest, unhelpful), it nevertheless left no doubt as to its general disposition towards such evidence, Purchas L.J. describing the case as:

> "a skirmish late in a campaign which has been waged for two decades or more to inject into the art of assessment of compensation for future loss the techniques of the actuary. This is not to say that actuarial evidence is inadmissible. Unhappily, where compensation for future loss is involved, its value is almost invariably diminished if not extinguished by uncertainties."[12]

It has been suggested, and not entirely without reason, that the unwillingness of the courts to welcome actuarial evidence more vigorously rests at least in part upon a failure wholly to comprehend it,[13] despite the assertion of one judge that "judges are well qualified to avoid the snares of such evidence."[14] In particular, the courts have complained that actuarial calculations do not take account of the chance that the individual plaintiff may live for a different number of years than the figure obtained from actuarial calculations, with the particularly important consequence that the chance that he may not reach the proposed age of retirement is ignored.[15]

Despite this judicial resistance, it is clear that actuarial evidence is not wholly inadmissible on future loss issues:

> "there is no reported case which says that a judge cannot and should

---

[8] [1968] 2 Q.B. 322.
[9] [1972] 1 Q.B. 65. See too *Taylor* v. *O'Connor* [1971] A.C. 115 at 140.
[10] *Watson* v. *Powles* [1968] 1 Q.B. 596 at 605–606, *per* Winn L.J., cited in *Mitchell* v. *Mulholland* above n. 9, at 76.
[11] [1985] 1 W.L.R. 784. See also *Hodgson* v. *Trapp* [1988] 3 W.L.R. 1281 at 1298.
[12] *Ibid.*, at 808.
[13] See *e.g.* Kemp and Kemp, *The Quantum of Damages*, Vol. 1, paras. 8–006 *et seq.*
[14] *Sullivan* v. *West Yorkshire Passenger Transport Executive* [1985] 2 All E.R. 135 at 136, *per* Stephenson L.J.
[15] See *e.g. Mitchell* v. *Mulholland*, above n. 9, at 85–86, and *Auty* v. *National Coal Board*, above n. 11, at 798, *per* Waller L.J.

not look at actuarial evidence, although there are strong indications that its value in a court of law is very limited."[16]

However the courts have made it equally clear that it will usually fulfil a merely ancillary role:

"actuarial aids are sometimes helpful, but they are not the be-all and end-all of this difficult matter."[17]

The actuarial method has been said to provide "useful arithmetical data which a judge should have in mind."[18] The courts have repeatedly limited actuarial calculations to use by the judge "as a check on his own calculations, but no more,"[19] as a "cross-check"' rather than the "'primary basis'" of calculation,[20] and as:

"ancillary aids for the purpose of checking the appropriateness of the amount of damages which has been arrived at by employing the normal method with or without adjustments."[21]

Salmon L.J., dissenting from the majority in *Fletcher* v. *Autocar*,[22] has taken a somewhat unfashionable judicial view, however. Actuarial calculations in his view are "a matter about which it is impossible to generalise"[23] and although it is in some cases "of no real help and only adds unnecessarily to the expense and time involved in the trial,"[24] "there are some cases, and . . . this is one of them, in which the actuarial evidence is of great value."[25] Salmon L.J. went on to use the actuarial evidence as the "primary" basis of his calculations as to loss of future earnings consequent upon personal injuries. There is little sign that this approach has gained many judicial adherents since.[26]

Limitations of actuarial evidence Although it may be that the courts have been too resistant to the assistance which actuarial calculations can afford to the courts in certain types of case, nevertheless its limitations have to be recognised. Actuaries can see into the future of a particular individual no more than judges, and the calculations, though sound at the time, may in fact prove dramatically wrong in retrospect. Further-

---

[16] *Sullivan* v. *West Yorkshire Passenger Transport Executive*, above n. 14, at 136, *per* Stephenson L.J.
[17] *S.* v. *Distillers* [1970] 1 W.L.R. 114 at 123. approved in *Mitchell* v. *Mulholland*, above n. 9, at 85.
[18] *Fletcher* v. *Autocar*, above n. 8, at 346, *per* Diplock L.J.
[19] *Mitchell* v. *Mulholland*, above n. 9, at 85.
[20] *Sullivan* v. *West Yorkshire Passenger Transport Executive*, above n. 14, at 137.
[21] *Taylor* v. *O'Connor* [1971] A.C. 115 at 140, *per* Lord Pearson.
[22] Above n. 8.
[23] *Ibid.*, at 355.
[24] *Ibid.*, at 355.
[25] *Ibid.*, at 355.
[26] See *Auty* v. *National Coal Board*, above n. 11.

more, monetary calculations which make allowance for interest[27] and inflation are inappropriate where, on legal principle, these elements are to be excluded. In particular, however, actuarial calculations as to the length of the life in question are only advantageous where the court has little more relevant information about the individual than is available about the other people in the class to which he has been allocated. Thus, in an extreme example, in the case of "a man known to be on his death bed with consumption,"[28] the court which has this information before it is clearly in as good a position as anyone to make the relevant calculation unassisted, and this will be so, to a lesser extent, where the court has any significant information as to the health of the individual which the actuary has not taken into account, or which is far more significant than generalised probabilities. In most cases, however, the actuary can incorporate such assumptions into his method, and indeed can confine himself if necessary, but still with benefit to the court, to assessing the appropriate lump sum to yield a particular annuity where the length of the life is ascertained by entirely non-actuarial means.

It is also important to recognise, as has been seen, that actuarial calculations, proceeding as they do upon the basis that the individual life is merely one of a substantial class of persons, are only fair to the plaintiff (and indeed to the defendant) in a generalised probabilistic way, placing the life, after allowances for facts known about it, in a position no better and no worse than others in the same class. Although this results in a degree of accuracy of prediction which in many cases cannot be improved upon, it is unsatisfactory to the legal mind in the sense that much of the material which contributes to the calculation consists of information about lives unconnected with the plaintiff, which are not the subject of evidence, and which indeed are in effect hearsay.[29] Thus in a real sense the case has not been proven upon evidence of fact, or upon direct inferences, whether expert or otherwise, from that fact.[30]

3 Will actuarial evidence be more extensively received in the future?

The limited extent to which the courts will receive actuarial evidence in future loss cases may be founded in part upon a failure, or a reluctance, fully to understand its principles. However there are suggestions in the cases that this attitude springs from a feeling that ultimately actuaries are

---

[27] See *Mitchell* v. *Mulholland*, above n. 9, and *Auty* v. *National Coal Board*, above n. 11.
[28] An example referred to in *M'Donald* v. *M'Donald* (1880) 5 App.Cas. 519 at 533, and see also p. 532.
[29] Though see Chap. 8, pp. 176–181, as to the admissibility of statistical tables produced by an expert witness.
[30] As is suggested below, however, the same can be said to apply to the courts' traditional method of calculating future loss.

merely performing mathematical calculations, and these the court can equally perform itself.[31] There are also repeated examples in the cases of an argument which proceeds from the undoubted fact that actuarial calculations are imperfect and speculative, to the more doubtful proposition that the courts' traditional method is therefore to be preferred to actuarial tables, which are "a very imprecise and therefore non-scientific mode of assessing damages."[32] These assumptions can be questioned on a number of grounds:

(*i*) As Salmon L.J. observed in *Fletcher* v. *Autocar*[33]:

"the normal method is nothing else than a rough and ready way of producing the actuarial result."[34]

The actuarial calculations are likely to be more accurate however because they are performed by persons who are experts in the field, using tables which contain the sum of actuarial data and experience over a long period. This was recognised as long ago as the decision in *Rowley* v. *London and North Western Railway Company*.[35] In fact the courts make frequent reference to tables of similar cases.[36] These, though useful, are compiled on the basis of reported cases alone from a necessarily small sample. There is frequently no directly comparable case to the one in question.

(*ii*) The fact that in a number of decisions[37] the courts have indicated that actuarial calculations may be used as a check on the court's own figures suggests both that they do have some validity and that the courts are often unsure of the results of the traditional method.

(*iii*) The fact that the calculation is, ultimately, a purely mathematical or statistical one should be no bar to adducing the evidence of an actuary. The courts frequently hear the evidence of accountants which, though lengthy and detailed, is mathematically much simpler than many actuarial calculations. Furthermore, it cannot be assumed that all lawyers have been educated to an advanced level in statistical and probabilistic method.

(*iv*) The application of generalised data to the circumstances of a particular individual is a specialist task, and one which the actuary is expert in performing.[38] Because of his training and experience he has an advan-

---

[31] See *e.g. Fletcher* v. *Autocar*, above n. 8, at 347, *per* Diplock L.J.
[32] *Watson* v. *Powles* [1968] 1 Q.B. 596 at 606, *per* Winn L.J., cited with approval in *Mitchell* v. *Mulholland*, above n. 9, at 76.
[33] Above n. 8.
[34] *Ibid.*, at 357.
[35] Above n. 3, at 226.
[36] Such as those in Kemp and Kemp, *The Quantum of Damages*.
[37] Cited above.
[38] See Prevett, above n. 2, at 148, on 'bridging this gap.'

tage compared to the lawyer extrapolating from tables of precedents[39] in relation to the particular case.

(v) The courts without actuarial evidence are denied the use of actuarial tables. These require expertise in their selection, in their use, and in their application to specific circumstances. They are the product of the daily performance of such calculations by professionals over a long period, and are the distillation of quantities of data far beyond anything contained within the confines of legal precedent. They do of course contain hearsay material, but where produced and explained by an actuary should be admissible under the rule in *R. v. Abadom*.[40]

(vi) Those bodies, composed at least in part of lawyers, which have considered the question of the admissibility and use of actuarial evidence have concluded in favour of its more extensive employment.[41]

(vii) The objection that actuarial calculations are "uncertain" and "conjectural" is odd. By no means all of the expert evidence daily adduced in the courts has the benefit of certainty or near-certainty. Medical evidence as to prognosis, adduced often enough in the same personal injuries cases as raise loss of earnings issues, can be highly speculative, and the medical witnesses usually concede this. It is protected from prejudicial consequences by the ability of other parties to cross-examine and to call their own witnesses in rebuttal.

Despite all of these factors, actuarial evidence is only as good as the way it is presented to the court. It is, for instance, almost impossible for an actuary while in the witness box to perform alterations to his detailed calculations on the basis of alternative hypotheses which may be put to him.[42] The party which does not anticipate this difficulty runs the risk that the court will simply ignore its evidence because it cannot be adapted to facts found during the trial and which the actuary was unable to include in his calculations. The actuary must persuade the court that not only is the method relevant, but the calculations themselves are "sound and precise,"[43] It is submitted that, although Salmon L.J. was in the minority in *Fletcher v. Autocar*,[44] he was not wrong in principle in expressing the view that actuarial calculations are "a matter about which it is impossible to generalise."[45] Thus, although the weight of authority is against its use in future loss claims, it is always open to a party to present convincing evidence, and justify its reception in the particular case. In

---

[39] Such as those in Kemp and Kemp, *The Quantum of Damages*.
[40] (1983) 76 Cr.App.R. 48, C.A.
[41] See e.g. Prevett, above n. 2 and Kemp and Kemp, *The Quantum of Damages*, above n. 13.
[42] See Prevett, above n. 2, at 259.
[43] *Mitchell v. Mulholland* above n. 9, at 79, and *Auty v. N.C.B.*, above n. 11, at 797.
[44] Above n. 8.
[45] *Ibid.*, at 355. The parties are of course at liberty to agree figures for future loss on the basis of actuarial evidence, as in the increasingly used 'structured settlement': see Kemp and Kemp, *The Quantum of Damages*, Vol. 1, para. 6A–008.

doing so, that party inevitably risks an adverse costs order.[46] However given the considerable weight of authority to the effect that actuarial evidence is frequently useful to the court as a check against its own calculations[47] it may often be possible to justify it on this ground alone.

B. ACCOUNTANCY

The expert evidence of accountants is employed across a broad spectrum of legal issues, and questions of complex financial calculation may be raised in relation to many different forms of legal proceedings.[48] Four general categories of evidence can be identified as constituting fields in which accountancy techniques may play a significant part. First, accountants may be called to give evidence as to the professional standards of other accountants, usually in negligence or breach of contract claims, and this is discussed below. Secondly, they may give evidence as to the financial activities of firms and companies, for instance in relation to insolvency, share dealings or, in the criminal sphere, commercial fraud, particularly by reference to the accounts and account books of the organisation in question. Thirdly, they may be tax specialists giving evidence as to the financial consequences of the relevant law, in relation to companies or individuals, though judges may on some issues take the view that expert evidence is unnecessary.[49] Fourthly, they may give evidence on the quantum of damages in any case which calls for complicated calculations with which the court needs assistance, or cases in which some degree of speculation is required, such as future loss claims in personal injury cases. Where such evidence tends towards the actuarial, however, care must be taken as to admissibility, as can be seen from the first part of this chapter.

In some of these fields the accountant's expertise may overlap with that of others, particularly in the company sphere, and care should be taken to ensure that the accountant keeps within his own area of specialism. Equally, different kinds of expert may be able to give admissible evidence on the same points, so that where the issue was the appropriate

---

[46] Whether at trial or on taxation.
[47] See above pp. 281–282.
[48] See, as to the various accountancy techniques which may be called upon in the legal sphere, D. Chilvers and C. Lemar, *Litigation Support and Financial Assessment of Damages*, (1988).
[49] In personal injuries cases raising questions of future loss, judges have often preferred the broad brush of the multiplier to the supposed precision of experts: see *Thomas* v. *Wignall* [1987] 1 All E.R. 1185; *Taylor* v. *O'Connor* [1971] A.C. 115 at 134. Increasing use is now being made of accountants in the formulation of 'structured settlements' as to future loss in personal injuries cases, which have been judicially approved: see Kemp and Kemp, *The Quantum of Damages*, Vol. 1, para. 6A–008.

manner of calculating the amount of company profits for distribution, and in particular how items of expenditure and loss are subtracted, evidence was admitted from both an accountant and a practising businessman.[50] The accountant is subject of course to the usual rules of evidence. When, as is frequently the case, his evidence depends very largely upon examination of account books an accountant may only give evidence as to their contents if the books themselves have been properly adduced in evidence.[51]

The courts may also use the general practice of accountants as a method of assessing, particularly in tax-related proceedings, what is a proper commercial approach to statutory provisions. The courts are not bound by any evidence they hear as to this, but:

> "where, however, there is evidence which is accepted by the court as establishing a sound commercial accountancy practice conflicting with no statute, that normally is the end of the matter."[52]

The question, therefore, whether a payment is of a capital or a revenue nature "must be answered in accordance with sound accountancy principles,"[53] although the judge must ultimately decide what these are.[54]

Professional negligence Accountants may give evidence as to the proper standards to be expected of practising accountants in a particular sphere, whether in negligence or in contractual claims. As with other forms of professional negligence, the courts are slow to make a finding that an accountant has not reached the requisite standard of care, and will usually expect persuasive evidence from a professional of standing before doing so. Where he must choose between experts at the adjudication stage he will be influenced by the experience and expertise of the witnesses. He will also attribute weight to the evidence of an accountant whose own practice is particularly relevant to matters in issue. Thus the evidence was preferred, in a case concerning the drawing up of accounts, of an accountant who was the head of his firm's technical services unit, which was responsible for setting and monitoring standards of accounting and auditing within the firm.[55]

In all proceedings as to professional negligence it is for the court to set the standard of care, not the witnesses, however good their qualifications for expressing opinions. Thus auditors may assist the court as to

---

[50] *Bond* v. *Barrow* [1902] 1 Ch. 353.
[51] *Johnson* v. *Kershaw* (1847) 1 De G. & Sm. 260.
[52] *Odeon Associated Theatres* v. *Jones* [1972] 2 W.L.R. 331 at 337.
[53] *Ibid.*, at 336.
[54] *Ibid.* See also *Heather* v. *P-E Consulting Group* [1973] Ch. 189.
[55] *Lloyd Cheynham & Co. Ltd.* v. *Littlejohn & Co.* [1987] B.C.L.C. 303 at 306.

"matters of practice," but not as to what an auditor is "bound as a matter of law to do."[56] As with other professional disciplines, the court will always be guided by the expert evidence, and will not therefore purport to set down immutable principles or conclusive lists of requirements for particular fields of professional practice. Thus, as to auditing practice, the court was able to describe "at least five" principles which would always be of importance,[57] but these were not exhaustive.

Codes of practice within the profession, such as the Statements of Accounting Practice, will always be of considerable weight. Though not conclusive, they may well in effect raise a presumption of negligence if they are materially departed from, which can only be rebutted by the clearest evidence:

> "while they are not conclusive, so that a departure from their terms necessarily involves a breach of their duty of care, and they are not, as the explanatory forward makes clear, rigid rules, they are very strong evidence as to what is the proper standard which should be adopted and unless there is some justification, a departure from this will be regarded as constituting a breach of duty."[58]

There are obviously good reasons for taking the view that a standard generally and formally endorsed within the profession, and thus codified, is the appropriate one. In addition, in the commercial sphere third parties are entitled to assume that accounts have been prepared in accordance with some established and known standard.[59]

Audit A question which is particularly susceptible of being raised in claims relating to negligent auditing is the degree to which the auditor may accept at face value the documents and other information which he is given in the course of the auditing exercise where there might be reason to doubt that they properly reflect the matters which the audit will record. The expert evidence must direct itself to the appropriate standards. The duty of an auditor, it has been said, is "verification not detection,"[60] so that his task is essentially confirmatory rather than investigatory. Nonetheless he must come to his task "with an inquiring mind."[61] It is not negligent to fail in performing an audit to be "suspicious" if the auditor is "reasonably careful,"[62] and:

---

[56] *Nelson Guarantee Corporation Ltd.* v. *Hodgson* [1958] N.Z.L.R. 609. See also *Pacific Acceptance Corporation Ltd.* v. *Forsyth* (1970) W.N. (N.S.W.) 29 at 75.
[57] *Nelson* v. *Hodgson*, above n. 56, at 612.
[58] *Lloyd Cheynham* v. *Littlejohn*, above n. 55, at 313, *per* Woolf J.
[59] *Ibid.* See too Chap. 7, pp. 144–145.
[60] *Re City Equitable Fire Insurance Co. Ltd.* [1925] 1 Ch. 407.
[61] *Fomento Ltd.* v. *Selsdon Fountain Pen Co. Ltd.* [1958] 1 W.L.R. 45.
[62] *Re Kingston Cotton Mill Co. (No. 2)* [1896] 2 Ch. 279 at 284.

"where there is nothing to excite suspicion very little inquiry will be reasonably sufficient."[63]

The expert evidence as to negligence must reflect these standards. In general, if the auditor is satisfied that he can confirm what he is told, he has investigated enough. If, however, there is ground for suspicion raised by something he observes in performing that task, he may well be in breach of duty, in negligence and otherwise, if he then fails to pursue the matter or seek independent confirmation which would satisfy the reasonably prudent auditor.

C. MARKET RESEARCH SURVEYS

Surveys are conducted as to the opinions or reactions of the public or a particular section of the public in relation to particular products, both as an incident to the commercial marketing of the product, and for the specific purpose of legal proceedings, most often in patent, copyright and passing-off actions. Such evidence is clearly admissible in general and is regularly received in the courts. The fact that a survey was not performed for the proceedings themselves does not *per se* exclude it from reception in the proceedings.[64] There has been some controversy about whether or not the results of such surveys, when adduced other than by calling all the (usually numerous) participants in the survey to give evidence, is hearsay, whether admissible or otherwise. The weight of authority appears to be in favour of the view that it is not hearsay,[65] though this has been questioned.[66] These issues are discussed in Chapter 8.[67] There is no doubt, however, that whatever their evidential status, such surveys are admissible,[68] and the question which then arises is as to the safeguards which should be insisted upon before such evidence is permitted to be adduced in court, or having been adduced, attributed some weight.

Surveys of this kind are usually conducted by market researchers working for a specialist market research company. It was held in *Reckitt and Coleman v. Barden*[69] that a market researcher called to give evidence was not an expert, and that the provisions in the rules as to pre-trial

---

[63] *Re London and General Bank (No. 2)* [1895] 2 Ch. 673.
[64] *Reckitt and Coleman v. Barden* [1987] F.S.R. 407 at 408.
[65] *Customglass Boats Ltd. v. Salthouse Brothers Ltd.* [1976] R.P.C. 589; *Lego System Aktieselskab v. Lego M. Lemelstrich Ltd.* [1983] F.S.R. 155.
[66] *Mobil Oil Corporation v. Registrar of Trade Marks* (1983) 51 A.L.R. 735.
[67] At pp. 165–167.
[68] *G.E. Trade Mark* [1970] R.P.C. 297, H.L.; *Lego System Aktieselskab v. Lego M. Lemelstrich Ltd.* above n. 65.
[69] Above n. 64.

directions and disclosure need not therefore be complied with. The judge expressed the view that the witness:

> "is not going to give any evidence whatsoever which is a matter of opinion in the slightest. He is, as it were, the reporting head of a computer into which the raw data produced for the purposes of the survey had been fed . . . he does not require any particular expertise to say that this is the result of the enquiries. He will not . . . say a single sentence which will start with the words 'in my opinion,' and it seems to me that that is really the essence of 'expert evidence."[70]

It is a doubtful proposition that evidence can only be expert evidence if it consists of matters of opinion.[71] In any event, in many cases involving surveys the assistance of a market researcher who supervised the survey will be needed in order to investigate the manner in which the survey was conducted, in which conclusions were drawn from the responses recorded, and as to the consequences of sampling and other errors which are almost unavoidable in the conduct of large surveys. It is established that:

> "the court can receive the evidence of statistical experts . . . in so far as they comment generally on the replies to questionnaires and the methods of conducting the surveys."[72]

Furthermore a description by a professional market researcher of the manner in which the survey was conducted (for instance as to the steps that were taken to reduce sampling error) is, though arguably evidence of fact not opinion, nevertheless in the nature of expert evidence unless it is of the most mundane kind. Evidence may also be given by persons in a particular trade as to the likely opinions or practices of others in the trade,[73] and in interlocutory proceedings such evidence may be adduced upon affidavit, although the deponents thereto must be called at trial.[74]

Conduct and disclosure of the survey   Whether or not survey evidence is regarded as hearsay, it clearly carries some of the risks inherent in hearsay evidence. In particular the court is unable to confirm for itself that the maker of the alleged statement said what is alleged and either meant what the words suggest in themselves or intended them to carry the meaning attributed to them by the party adducing the evidence. Whitford J., in *Imperial Group plc* v. *Philip Morris Ltd.*[75] made detailed stipula-

---

[70] *Ibid.*, at 408.
[71] See Chap. 1, p. 9 and Chap. 6, pp. 119–121.
[72] *General Electric Trade Mark* [1969] R.P.C. 418 at 446, *per* Graham J.
[73] *George Ballantine and Son Ltd.* v. *Ballantyne Stewart and Co. Ltd.* [1959] R.P.C. 273 at 280.
[74] *Sodastream Ltd.* v. *Thorn Cascade Co. Ltd.* [1982] R.P.C. 459.
[75] [1984] R.P.C. 293.

tions, which have subsequently been confirmed,[76] as to the safeguards upon which the courts should insist, both in the collection and evaluation of the data, and in its disclosure, when receiving survey evidence. In some particulars these requirements have been repeated and expanded in other cases, notably *Customglass Boats Ltd. v. Salthouse Brothers Ltd.*[77] and *Scott Ltd. v. Nice-Pak Products Ltd.*[78] Nine specific requirements can be identified:

(i) *Sample selection*

"The way in which the interviewees are selected must be established as being done by a method such that a relevant cross section of the public is interviewed."[79]

"There must be evidence that the answers were drawn from a true cross-section of that class of the public or trade whose impression or opinion is relevant to the matter in issue."[80]

(ii) *Sample size*   The sample must be:

"of a size which is sufficient to produce some relevant result viewed on a statistical basis."[81]

(iii) *Fairness and good-faith*   The survey must be conducted fairly within the limits necessarily imposed by a survey.[82] Questions must not be based on a false premise or a deceit, or have the effect of trapping interviewees into giving particular answers.[83]

(iv) *Neutral questions*   Interviews should certainly not contain leading questions, and should endeavour to be entirely neutral in the response they suggest:

"it is very difficult in connection with an exercise such as this to think of questions which, even if they are free from the objection of being leading, are not in fact going to direct the person answering the question into a field of speculation upon which that person would never have embarked had the question not been put."[84]

---

[76] *Scott Ltd. v. Nice-Pak Products Ltd.* [1988] F.S.R. 125.
[77] Above n. 65.
[78] Above n. 76.
[79] *Imperial Group plc. v. Phillip Morris Ltd.* above n. 75, at 302.
[80] *Customglass Boats Ltd. v. Salthouse Brothers Ltd.* above n. 65, at 595.
[81] *Imperial Group plc. v. Phillip Morris Ltd.*, above n. 75, at 302.
[82] *Ibid.*
[83] *Scott v. Nice-Pak*, above n. 76, at 130–131.
[84] *Imperial Group plc. v. Phillip Morris Ltd.*, above n. 75, at 303. See also *Scott v. Nice-Pak*, above n. 76, at 130–131.

MATHEMATICAL, STATISTICAL AND FINANCIAL CALCULATIONS

> "There must be a formulation of questions cast in such a way as to preclude a weighted or conditional response."[85]

(v) *"Don't know" option* The interviewer should, in addition to other possible answers to questions, have a "don't know" or "doubtful" option, so that those who are undecided are not wrongly categorised as having answered in a specific manner.[86]

(vi) *Recording the answer in full* Many surveys require the interviewer merely to place the answers given to questions into particular predetermined categories. However:

> "the exact answers given and not some sort of abbreviation or digest of the exact answer should be recorded;"[87]
> "there must be clear proof that the answers were faithfully and accurately recorded."[88]

(vii) *Coding* Answers are often coded, whether by computer or manually, both for the assessment of results overall, and sometimes for the purpose, during the interview, of deciding which question to ask next. Parties must show that this has been done properly and accurately.[89]

(viii) *Instructions to interviewers* The court must be made aware of:

> "exactly what instructions were given to persons carrying out the interviews."[90]

(ix) *Pre-trial disclosure* Before trial, a party must make:

> "the fullest possible disclosure of exactly how many surveys they have carried out, exactly how those surveys were conducted and the totality of the number of persons involved ... [and] the totality of all answers given to all surveys."[91]

This may have the effect in many cases of rendering marginal the doubtful proposition that a market research professional may not be an expert for pre-trial disclosure (or other) purposes.[92]

---

[85] *Customglass Boats Ltd.* v. *Salthouse Brothers Ltd.*, above n. 65, at 595.
[86] *Scott* v. *Nice-Pak*, above n. 76, at 133.
[87] *Imperial Group plc.* v. *Phillip Morris Ltd.*, above n. 75, at 303.
[88] *Customglass Boats Ltd.* v. *Salthouse Brothers Ltd.*, above n. 65, at 595.
[89] *Imperial Group plc.* v. *Phillip Morris Ltd.*, above n. 75, at 303; *Scott* v. *Nice-Pak*, at 132–133.
[90] *Imperial Group plc.* v. *Phillip Morris Ltd.*, above n. 75, at 303.
[91] *Ibid.*
[92] See *Reckitt and Coleman* v. *Barden*, above n. 64.

Market research survey evidence is clearly admissible *per se*, so that failure to observe these procedures will go to the question of weight rather than admissibility,[93] though it has been suggested that a serious failure to comply, particularly if it raises the question of good faith, can render such evidence inadmissible.[94] Notwithstanding this, it is clearly a risk-laden venture to proceed to trial with survey evidence, costly as it is to compile and assimilate, which departs in any substantial sense from the requirements which have been listed.[95]

---

[93] See *Customglass Boats Ltd.* v. *Salthouse Brothers Ltd.*, above n. 65, at 595.
[94] *Scott* v. *Nice-Pak*, above n. 76, at 135.
[95] See *Scott* v. *Nice-Pak*, above n. 76, at 130–135.

CHAPTER 16

Proof of Foreign Law

A. GENERAL

Where any issue of foreign law[1] arises before an English court, in which it is required to adjudicate upon the effect of the foreign law, there is a general rule that it must be proved upon evidence as a fact.[2] With a number of exceptions, the rule requires that the fact be proved by expert evidence.[3] There are many areas of practice in which expert evidence is usually, in practical terms, essential, and some specific statutory provisions which require it. However the proof of foreign law is perhaps the only broad field in which the adducing of expert evidence is usually required as a matter of legal principle.

B. THE EXCEPTIONS

1 Miscellaneous statutes

Certain statutes provide for the court to find foreign laws to have a particular effect in particular circumstances, or prescribe the procedure by which the foreign law is to be ascertained.[4] In such cases, expert evidence before the English court will not in general be necessary.

2 Previous decisions of the English courts

The doctrine of judicial notice cannot be applied to foreign law,[5] although the courts have occasionally taken a contrary view where a state of legal affairs was "notorious,"[6] for example that roulette is not

---

[1] Scots law is foreign law.
[2] *Concha* v. *Murrietta* (1889) 40 Ch.D. 543. Though where a jury is sitting, the judge assesses matters of foreign law: Supreme Court Act 1981, s.69(5); County Courts Act 1984, s.68.
[3] *The Sussex Peerage* (1844) 11 C. & F. 85.
[4] See *e.g.* British Law Ascertainment Act 1861; Evidence (Colonial Statutes) Act 1907; Evidence (Foreign, Dominion and Colonial Documents) Act 1933.
[5] See *e.g. Rendel* v. *Arcos* [1937] 3 All E.R. 577.
[6] *Saxby* v. *Fulton* [1909] 2 K.B. 208 at 211.

unlawful in Monte Carlo.[7] The rule at common law was that previous decisions of English courts on points of foreign law were not precedents for subsequent cases, and that the foreign law had to be strictly proved afresh in each case, however similar the circumstances. Section 4(2) of the Civil Evidence Act 1972 has made considerable incursions into this principle, by providing for circumstances in which, in civil though not in criminal cases,[8] decisions of certain courts can be adduced in evidence in subsequent proceedings:

> "Where any question as to the law of any country or territory outside the United Kingdom, or of any part of the United Kingdom other than England and Wales, with respect to any matter has been determined (whether before or after the passing of this Act) in any such proceedings as are mentioned in subsection (4) below, then in any civil proceedings (not being proceedings before a court which can take judicial notice of the law of that country, territory or part with respect to that matter)—
> (a) any finding made or decision given on that question in the first-mentioned proceedings shall, if reported
> or recorded in citable form, be admissible in evidence for the purpose of proving the law of that country, territory or part with respect to that matter; and
> (b) if that finding or decision, as so reported or recorded, is adduced for that purpose, the law of that country, territory or part with respect to that matter shall be taken to be in accordance with that finding or decision unless the contrary is proved:
> Provided that paragraph (b) above shall not apply in the case of a finding or decision which conflicts with another finding or decision on the same question adduced by virtue of this subsection in the same proceedings."

The courts the decisions of which may be so adduced in evidence are set out in section 4(4):

> "The proceedings referred to in subsection (2) above are the following, whether civil or criminal namely:
> (a) proceedings at first instance in any of the following courts, namely the High Court, the Crown Court, a court of quarter sessions, the Court of Chancery of the county palatine of Lancaster and the Court of Chancery of the county palatine of Durham;

---

[7] Ibid.
[8] Although previous decisions of some criminal courts can be adduced in civil proceedings: Civil Evidence Act 1972, s.4(4).

(b) appeals arising out of any such proceedings as are mentioned in paragraph (a) above;

(c) proceedings before the Judicial Committee of the Privy Council on appeal (whether to Her Majesty in Council or to the Judicial Committee as such) from any decision of any court outside the United Kingdom."

Section 4(2) thus provides for the admission in evidence of such a previous decision, if it is reported or recorded in citable form.[9] This is not irrebuttable proof of the foreign law, but raises a presumption which must be rebutted, presumably by expert evidence, by the party which asserts that the law is different.[10] If two or more previous decisions are adduced in evidence pursuant to section 4(2), and they conflict, the foreign law must be proved by expert evidence in the usual way.[11] Section 4(2) provides that where any "question" arises in relation to the law on a particular "matter," the machinery of section 4 may be employed. These open-textured expressions afford the judge considerable discretion in the matter of whether a previous decision is on all fours with the case before him, particularly as no two sets of facts, however analogous, can be identical.

There must be citable record of the previous decision upon which reliance is placed, pursuant to section 4(5):

"For the purposes of this section a finding or decision on any such question as is mentioned in subsection (2) above shall be taken to be reported or recorded in citable form if, but only if it is reported or recorded in writing in a report, transcript or other document which, if that question had been a question as to the law of England and Wales, could be cited as an authority in legal proceedings in England and Wales."

Procedure under section 4(2) is set out at section 4(3):

"Except with the leave of the court, a party to any civil proceedings shall not be permitted to adduce any such finding or decision as is mentioned in subsection (2) above by virtue of that subsection unless he has in accordance with rules of court given to every other party to the proceedings notice that he intends to do so."

The relevant rules of court under section 4(3) in the High Court are provided by R.S.C. Order 38, rule 7:

"(1) A party to any cause or matter who intends to adduce in evi-

---

[9] As to which see s.4(5).
[10] Ibid., s.4(2)(b).
[11] As to which see below, pp. 298-309.

dence a finding or decision on a question of foreign law by virtue of section 4(2) of the Civil Evidence Act 1972 shall—
- (a) in the case of an action to which Order 25, rule 1 applies, within 14 days after the pleadings in the action are deemed to be closed, and
- (b) in the case of any other cause or matter, within 21 days after the date on which an appointment for the first hearing of the cause or matter is obtained,

or in either case, within such other period as the Court may specify, serve notice of his intention on every other party to the proceedings.

(2) The notice shall specify the question on which the finding or decision was given or made and specify the document in which it is reported or recorded in citable form.

(3) In any cause or matter in which evidence may be given by affidavit, an affidavit specifying the matters contained in paragraph (2) shall constitute notice under paragraph (1) if served within the period mentioned in that paragraph."

The County Court Rules under section 4(3) are contained in C.C.R. Order 20, rule 25:

"(1) Subject to the provisions of this rule, a party who intends to adduce in evidence a finding or decision on a question of foreign law by virtue of section 4(2) of the Civil Evidence Act 1972 shall, not less than 14 days before the day fixed for the trial or hearing or within such other period as the court may specify, serve notice of his intention on every other party to the proceedings.

(2) The notice shall specify the question on which the finding or decision was given or made and specify the document in which it is reported or recorded in citable form.

(3) In any action or matter in which evidence may be given by affidavit, an affidavit specifying the matters contained in paragraph (2) shall constitute notice under paragraph (1) if served within the period mentioned in that paragraph.

(4) Unless in any particular case the court otherwise directs, paragraph (1) shall not apply to an action or matter in which no defence or answer has been filed."

It is clear that a number of cases decided before section 4 of the Civil Evidence Act 1972 came into force are now of little or no value where they directly contradict section 4(2).[12]

---

[12] *e.g. Bater* v. *Bater* [1907] P. 333; *McCormick* v. *Garnett* (1854) 5 De G. M. & G. 278.

C. PROVING FOREIGN LAW BY EXPERT EVIDENCE

1 Competence of expert witnesses

Unnecessary to be a qualified legal practitioner in the relevant country The Civil Evidence Act 1972, section 4(1), provides:

> "It is hereby declared that in civil proceedings a person who is suitably qualified to do so on account of his knowledge or experience is competent to give expert evidence as to the law of any country or territory outside the United Kingdom, or of any part of the United Kingdom other than England and Wales, irrespective of whether he has acted or is entitled to act as a legal practitioner there."

In so far as section 4(1) provides that an expert witness need not be a legal practitioner in the relevant country, it does no more, indeed considerably less, than to restate the existing common law.[13] It is unclear whether the intention of the section is merely to achieve this limited objective, or whether the words "suitably qualified on account of his knowledge or experience" are also intended to replace the substantial body of case law which exists on the question of competence to prove foreign law. It seems likely that, even if this broader interpretation is appropriate, the existing common law guidelines will not be lightly abandoned, and may well be the best indication of the manner in which the question of competence will be approached.

Mere academic study not sufficient Where a witness derives his knowledge of foreign law purely from a course of academic study, he is not competent as an expert. Thus study at a foreign university is not sufficient[14] even if the course covered matters before the court.

Practitioners in a country other than that in respect of which evidence of foreign law is sought to be adduced are in the same position, as where an English barrister practising in Canadian appeals to the Privy Council was not competent on a question of Canadian law, because:

> "his knowledge of any parts of that law besides those which actually come before him in the course of litigation can only have been acquired, as any other person may acquire it, by study, and the knowledge so acquired will not make his evidence admissible."[15]

It can be inferred from this passage that if the witness could have shown personal experience of the particular point in issue, he would have been

---

[13] *Brailey v. Rhodesia Consolidated Ltd.* [1910] 2 Ch.D. 95.
[14] *Bristow v. Sequeville* (1850) 19 L.J.Ex. 289; *Re the Goods of Bonelli* (1875) 1 P.D. 69.
[15] *Cartwright v. Cartwright and Anderson* (1878) 26 W.R. 684 at 685.

regarded as competent.[16] If this inference is made, the decision sits more happily with cases in which the witness had never practised, whether in law or in any field entailing knowledge of law, in the relevant foreign country, but was nevertheless regarded as competent. In *Brailey* v. *Rhodesia Consolidated Ltd.*[17] the evidence of an expert in Roman-Dutch law at the Incorporated Council of Legal Education in London was admitted although he had never practised in Rhodesia. He had made a special study of its application to the British colonies for teaching purposes, though. This was presumably regarded as categorically different from study for the mere purpose of obtaining an academic qualification.[18]

Evidence has also been admitted from a lawyer who had only studied but never practised in Italy, and whose job as counsel to the Italian Consulate in London was to advise Italians in England about their legal rights and about documents required for execution in Italy.[19] The matter in issue concerned the Italian law of contract and tort, as to his knowledge of which the case report gives no indication. It may be however that because his clients were Italian his position was regarded as being analogous to that of practising lawyers in Italy. For when a lawyer does practise in the relevant foreign country, the courts do not appear to inquire closely into the relevance of the content of his practice to matters in issue. Presumably in most cases a trained lawyer practising in the relevant jurisdiction is capable of acquainting himself with matters in which he does not specialise to a level sufficient for the purposes of the English court.

Not only lawyers are competent Although he must be conversant with the law of which he speaks,[20] it is not necessary for a witness to be a trained, qualified or practising lawyer to give evidence of foreign law.[21] Where a person's business or profession has given him knowledge or experience of the law, in a foreign country, his evidence may be admissible. In *Van Der Donkt* v. *Thelluson*[22] a Belgian hotel keeper in London had previously been a merchant in stocks and bills of exchange in Belgium, thus acquiring practical knowledge of the Belgian law of bills and notes, upon which he was entitled to give evidence, as he was:

> "a person having special and peculiar means of knowledge of the Law of Belgium with regard to bills of exchange and promissory notes ... in as much as he had been carrying on a business which

---

[16] This appears to be the distinction between the witness in *Cartwright* (above n. 15), and that in *Wilson* v. *Wilson* [1903] P. 157 (see below p. 302).
[17] [1910] 2 Ch.D. 95.
[18] *Cf. Bristow* v. *Sequeville*, above n. 14.
[19] *Rose-Troup* v. *Sleeping Car Co., The Times,* January 31, 1911.
[20] *R.* v. *Naguib* [1917] 1 K.B. 359.
[21] *Van Der Donkt* v. *Thelluson* (1849) 8 C.B. 812.
[22] *Ibid.*

made it his interest to take cognisance of the foreign law, he does fall within the description of an expert."[23]

It is clear however that, certainly where non-lawyers are concerned, the witness must be shown to have knowledge of the particular aspect of foreign law which is before the court:

> "all persons, I think, who practise a business or profession which requires them to possess a certain knowledge of the matter in hand, are experts, so far as expertness is required."[24]

Thus, a Nigerian banker was competent on the legality of certain bank notes in Nigeria,[25] a Chilean notary could give evidence as to the law relating to executors in Chile,[26] and an English merchant who traded in Chile, and had observed the formalities of marriage being performed, could give evidence on the limited matter of completion of a parish marriage register.[27] Scottish marriage law, however, was not properly proved by the evidence of a tobacconist, albeit his business was in Scotland.[28]

Nature of office may demonstrate competence The general rule, as already stated,[29] is that non-lawyers must demonstrate actual knowledge of the relevant area of foreign law. Where, however, the witness holds an office which of its nature entails knowledge of the aspect foreign law in issue, the court will conclude that the witness is in fact competent on the question, without necessarily inquiring whether he is in fact competent. In *The Sussex Peerage*[30] it was stated that:

> "the witness is in a situation of importance; he is engaged in the performance of important and responsible public duties and connected with them, and in order to discharge them properly, he is bound to make himself acquainted with the law of marriage. That being so, his evidence is of the nature of that of a Judge. It is impossible to say that he is incompetent."[31]

The office need not be of a particular kind. Where a point of Persian law required proof, a Persian embassy official was permitted to give evidence. The court heard that there were no lawyers in Persia, but that all members of the diplomatic service were required to be thoroughly versed in

---

[23] *Van Der Donkt v. Thelluson* (1849) 8 C.B. 812 at 825, *per* Maule J.
[24] *Ibid.*
[25] *Ajami v. Comptroller of Customs* [1954] 1 W.L.R. 1405, P.C.
[26] *Re Whitelegg* [1899] P. 267.
[27] *Abbot v. Abbott and Godoy* 4 S.W. & T.R. 254.
[28] *R. v. Brampton*, (1808) 10 East. 282 at 287.
[29] Above, pp. 298–300.
[30] (1844) 11 C. & F. 85.
[31] *Ibid.*, at 134.

the law.[32] Similarly a legal adviser to the Maltese government was regarded as inevitably competent on a question of Maltese law.[33]

The court will inquire into whether the nature of the office gives the witness knowledge of the specifically legal aspects of the subject under discussion. Thus it has been said that the evidence of an ambassador from the relevant country:

> "may be the best evidence of the practical workings of the machinery of government in the country which he represents. But I see no reason why his evidence of the law of his country should have some special persuasive power."[34]

It is equally apparent from this passage that high office, such as ambassadorial status, does not *per se* invest the evidence of the witness with an authority it might authorise lack. Where matters of weight are concerned, the court will draw its conclusions upon the merits of the evidence itself.[35]

Issue determines competence The court should consider, when adjudicating upon the admissibility of the evidence of a proposed witness, whether his knowledge is likely to be of assistance to the court on exactly the point at issue, not merely in the general area of inquiry. In *Ajami* v. *Comptroller of Customs*[36] it was said that:

> "not only the general nature, but also the precise character of the question upon which expert evidence is required, have to be taken into account when deciding whether the qualifications of a person entitle him to be regarded as a competent expert."[36a]

In *Ajami* a bank manager, with long experience of which bank notes were legal tender in Nigeria, was permitted to give evidence on the limited point whether certain particular notes were legal tender in Nigeria at the material time.

Practical considerations relevant Although the admissibility of expert evidence is a question of fact to be decided upon legal principle, the courts do take account of purely practical considerations, such as witness availability. Thus, the court hearing that there were no lawyers in Persia, the evidence of a diplomat was accepted, it having been established that

---

[32] *In the Goods of Dost Aly Khan* (1880) 6 P.D. 6.
[33] *Gossage* v. *Gossage and Heaton* 78 S.J. 551. See too *Associated Shipping Services Ltd.* v. *Department of Private Affairs of the Ruler of Abu Dhabi, The Independent*, August 14, 1990.
[34] *Trendtex Trading Corporation* v. *Central Bank* [1976] 3 All E.R. 437 at 441, per Donaldson J.
[35] See below, pp. 302–303.
[36] [1954] 1 W.L.R. 1405, P.C.
[36a] *Ibid.*, at 1408.

all Persian diplomats must have knowledge of the law.[37] Where the only legal expert available charged a prohibitive fee, the court accepted affidavit evidence from an ex-Governor of Hong Kong who deposed to having knowledge upon the legal question in issue.[38] In a case in which, although there were some Maltese lawyers who would have the relevant knowledge, there were practical difficulties in getting them to court, the evidence of an English lawyer with the relevant knowledge was accepted.[39]

The courts have been prepared to accept a less than rigorous adherence to established competence rules where the nature of the matter in issue demands it, and the alternative would be to proceed without evidence at all, through no fault of the parties. This is broadly analogous to the "best evidence rule" in the general law of evidence:

> "normally an expert should have recent practical experience as well as academic qualifications ... but I am satisfied that the particular question with which I am concerned could not have arisen in a Russian court, that nobody could be better qualified to give evidence on this branch of Russian law than Dr. Dobrin, and that I at any rate have no qualifications at all to do so."[40]

Counsel not to act as witness It is perhaps a situation that is particularly susceptible of occurrence in the field of proof of particular foreign laws that counsel appointed to represent a party to proceedings may also be competent to act as an expert witness in the matter. It is however improper for this to occur and separate arrangements must be made.[41]

Weight It is apparent from the discussion of witness competence that, although certain reasonably clear principles emerge from the cases, the admissibility of expert evidence on questions of foreign law is subject to a considerable breadth of discretion, and that practical considerations may sometimes weigh almost as heavily as questions of legal principle.[42] As with expert evidence generally however, the courts will often in practice, when in doubt as to whether a particular witness is relevantly expert, admit the evidence, and if the level of expertise appears not to be high reflect this by placing little reliance upon it as a matter of weight.[43] It has indeed been suggested, further to this, that the relevance of practice (as

---

[37] *In the Goods of Dost Aly Khan*, above n. 32.
[38] *Cooper-King* v. *Cooper-King* [1900] P. 65.
[39] *Wilson* v. *Wilson* [1903] P. 157.
[40] *Re Banque des Marchands de Moscou* [1958] Ch. 182 at 202.
[41] *R.* v. *Secretary of State for India* [1941] 2 K.B. 169.
[42] See *e.g Re Banque des Marchands de Moscou*, above n. 40.
[43] See *e.g Van Der Donkt* v. *Thelluson*, above n. 21, at 826.

opposed to academic study) to expertise is only to be considered at this latter stage,[44] though this view does not find wide support in the cases.

2 Form of expert evidence of foreign law

Oral evidence usually required The usual rule, as with expert evidence generally, is that where a question of foreign law is in issue between the parties, oral evidence of the witness at trial is required.

Affidavit evidence Rules of court as to affidavit evidence by experts in civil cases[45] apply equally to witnesses on questions of foreign law. Other procedural provisions may prescribe the adducing of affidavit evidence within particular areas of practice. A *Practice Direction*[46] has been issued in relation to proof of foreign law in non-contentious probate matters. After citing section 4(1) of the Civil Evidence Act 1972 it provides as follows:

> "This provision, which comes into force on 1st January 1973, overrides the requirement of rule 18 of the Non-Contentious Probate Rules 1954 that only in special circumstances may the registrar accept an affidavit of law made by a person who has not practised as a barrister or advocate (or, in the case of certain countries, as a solicitor) in the country whose law is in question. An amendment of the rule will be sought in due course, but the provisions of section 4(1) will in any event apply in non-contentious probate matters as from 1st January 1973. Affidavits of law made by a person qualified under section 4(1) to give evidence must set out particulars of the knowledge and experience claimed by the deponent to make him competent to give expert evidence of the law of the country in question. As in the case of a barrister or advocate, an affidavit made by the person claiming to be entitled to the grant or his attorney, or the spouse of either, will not be accepted."

Affidavit evidence of foreign law is admitted only in exceptional circumstances, and the courts have frequently, though admitting it, made it clear that it is not in most circumstances a proper method of proof.[47] It is more likely to be admitted, though even then "reluctantly," where the evidence is uncontradicted by the other party.[48] Where a foreign lawyer, who was

---

[44] *Lazard v. Midland Bank* [1933] A.C. 289 at 298.
[45] R.S.C. Ord. 38, r. 36(2); C.C.R. Ord. 20, r. 27(2).
[46] *Practice Direction* [1972] 3 All E.R. 912. See Non-Contentious Probate Rules 1954 (S.I. 1954 No. 796) r. 18.
[47] See too, however, *Re Arton* [1896] 1 Q.B. 509 at 511 n.; *Westlake v. Westlake* [1910] P. 167, in which affidavit evidence was admitted, though with no indication in the judgments as to the basis on which this was done.
[48] *Re Valentine's Settlement* [1965] Ch. 831.

probably competent, swore an affidavit the main substance of which was the report of a United States judgment exhibited to it, the court admitted it saying "[we] strongly deprecate this mode of providing evidence of foreign law."[49] In the event the judgment so adduced was irrelevant to the matter in issue and the party adducing the evidence failed, so that the question of the weight to be attributed to it did not arise.

Certificates The courts have occasionally accepted a certificate of the ambassador from the country in respect of which the law must be proved, though there is little discussion in the reports upon which any principle could be stated.[50] It is clearly however an exception to the usual rule that oral evidence is necessary, and would need to be justified on the facts of the case. No doubt the fact that the case was not contested, or in particular that the point of foreign law was not in issue between the parties, would be of some importance.[51]

Interrogatories Interrogatories on questions of foreign law may be admissible where it is shown that the subject of the interrogatories is competent to give expert evidence on the matters in issue.[52]

Foreign law texts Copies may be admitted of foreign statutes, which the court may have to construe itself, with the assistance of expert witnesses.[53] Where an application to adduce a foreign law book conflicts with the rule that in general oral expert evidence must be called, it will not usually be granted.[54] However, the French vice-consul was permitted to produce a textbook of French codes with commentary thereon, the court having accepted the evidence of the witness that it would be admissible in the French courts for proof of the matter in issue.[55] The courts "strongly deprecate" the adducing of a foreign law report merely by exhibiting it to an affidavit.[56]

3 Evidence experts may give as to questions of foreign law

Effect not content The purpose of receiving expert evidence on points of foreign law is not merely to place the content of the law before the court, but to obtain the expert's opinion as to its effect. In *Baron de Bode's Case*[57] it was observed by Lord Denman C.J. that:

---

[49] *Callwood v. Callwood* [1960] A.C. 659.
[50] *Krajina v. Tass Agency* [1949] 2 All E.R. 274; *Re the Goods of Klingemann* 32 L.J.P. 16; *In the Goods of Oldenburg* (1884) 9 P.D. 234.
[51] See *Re Valentine's Settlement* [1965] Ch. 831.
[52] *Perlak v. Deen* [1924] 1 K.B. 111.
[53] See below pp. 306–309.
[54] *The Perth Peerage* (1848) 2 H.L.C 865 at 874.
[55] *Lacon v. Higgins* (1822) Stark 178;
[56] *Callwood v. Callwood* [1960] A.C. 659.
[57] (1845) 8 Q.B. 208 at 250–251.

"properly speaking, the nature of such evidence is not to set forth the contents of the written law, but its effect and the state of law resulting from it. The mere contents, indeed, might often mislead persons not familiar with the particular system of law."

Where a foreign statute or other legislative provision requires interpretation, expert evidence will often be necessary as to the manner in which the relevant legal system would approach the task. Thus evidence has been adduced as to the "Russian meaning" of Russian legislation,[58] and a New York lawyer has described the construction employed by the New York courts of words which, though they have an ordinary meaning in the English language, are also terms of art with a different meaning in New York.[59] The same applies where contracts are concerned, and a Chilean lawyer's opinion has been given of the Chilean construction of contractual terms.[60]

No foreign precedent Where a matter of foreign law must be resolved in the English courts, the expert witness is usually required to inform the court of what the law is, if it is contained in clear legislative form, and of the interpretation of the legislation adopted where the courts of the foreign country have considered the particular aspect of it which is in issue in the English case. Similarly where a foreign country has a system analogous to the common law, to the extent that the courts themselves make, or develop, principles of law, the witness will give evidence of the approach of the foreign courts. If the evidence is accepted, the judge states the foreign law accordingly.

Where, however, there is no clear guidance in foreign sources of law, the court cannot simply ignore the question. Thus where there is no foreign precedent on the particular point or the authorities, such as they are, conflict, the court must, with the assistance of expert evidence, decide the matter itself.[61] Where there was no decision of the Spanish Supreme Court on a point of Spanish law, the court accepted expert opinion evidence as to what decision the Supreme Court would probably arrive at were the matter to be heard before it.[62]

Doubtful foreign precedent The following approach was taken by the court where there was reason to doubt the correctness of an American decision on a matter in issue:

"The witnesses for the plaintiffs have given evidence that this decision of Mr. Justice Noyes is incorrect in American law and

---

[58] *Princess Paley Olga* v. *Weisz* [1929] 1 K.B. 718.
[59] *Dreyfus* v. *I.R.C.* [1954] 1 Ch. 672.
[60] *St. Pierre* v. *South American Stores* [1937] 3 All E.R. 349.
[61] *Lloyd* v. *Guibert* [1865] L.R. 1 Q.B. 115.
[62] *Re Duke of Wellington* [1947] Ch. 506.

inconsistent with other authorities. The defendants' witnesses have given evidence to the contrary, and both have cited authorities in support of their respective contentions. It seems to me that we must consider whether in our opinion this decision was correct and must consider it as a question of fact upon the evidence. If this were not so, evidence as to foreign law would be useless wherever there was a decision of any foreign Judge on the point, and our Courts could only follow that decision as a binding authority. This is not the position of our Courts in such a matter."[63]

Judicial reliance on expert evidence of foreign law It is clear that, where a point of foreign law requires to be settled for the purposes of a court action in this country, in general expert evidence must be adduced to prove it. Furthermore the purpose of that evidence is not for the witness merely to produce the relevant foreign sources of law, but to express his opinion as to the way in which the sources would be treated in a foreign court, and of the true effect of the foreign law on the facts with which the English court is concerned.[64] Where there is competent and convincing expert testimony, which is either uncontradicted, or contradicted only by testimony which is not both competent and convincing, the judge will accept it, and apply it to the facts of the case before him. Where however the judge is not placed in this position, the manner in which he should proceed is not so clear, and two schools of thought appear to have emerged in the cases. These can usefully be described as the "constructionist" and the "factual" approaches.

According to the constructionist view, the task in which the English court is engaged when assessing points of foreign law is essentially that of construing foreign written laws in a similar manner to that in which it construes English legislation and contracts, and in which it assesses the relevant precedents. Thus, where there is no satisfactory expert evidence, or an unresolvable conflict between expert witnesses, the judge must proceed to construe the foreign law himself.

It has been held that even where expert evidence has been adduced, the court can look at the written passages in question and come to its own view.[65] Perhaps the most thorough going expression of this view is contained in the judgment of Scrutton L.J. in *Buerger* v. *New York*,[66] in which he states that even if expert evidence as to the meaning of an aspect of Russian law is uncontradicted, the English court may still reject this evidence and prefer its own interpretation[67]:

---

[63] *Guaranty Trust of New York* v. *Hannay* (1918) 87 L.J.K.B. 1223 at 1231.
[64] *Baron de Bode's Case* (1845) 8 Q.B. 208 at 250–251.
[65] *De Beeche* v. *South American Stores* [1935] A.C. 148.
[66] (1927) 96 L.J.K.B. 930.
[67] *Ibid.*, at 936.

> "I can see no reason why a court is bound to accept the evidence of an expert witness as to fact, when he supports it by a document the plain words of which render his opinion impossible."[68]

Where, in a case on a point of French law, the opinions of the expert witnesses were "directly opposed to each other,"[69] the judge elected to look at French cases and textbook passages adduced by the witnesses, and to decide the matter on the basis of his own reading of the decision in a French case. In *Concha* v. *Murrietta*[70] it was held that, where expert witnesses referred in their evidence to passages in the legal code of the country concerned, it would be:

> "most unreasonable to hold that we are not at liberty to look at those passages and consider what is their proper meaning."[71]

There is also however a suggestion that this may only occur where the expert evidence is both unsatisfactory and conflicting.[72]

The factual view, by contrast, proceeds according to the assumption which underlies the general evidential principles upon which foreign law is adduced. This is that, even though what are being considered are in themselves questions of (foreign) law, the English court must treat them for evidential purposes as questions of fact. It is also rooted in the perception that the English judge, learned though he may be in the domestic law, has no particular standing to express opinions about the law of foreign countries, even where he has the sources of the foreign law available to him. This view was frankly expressed by Roxburgh J. when he said that, whatever the competence of the expert in court to give evidence on Russian law, it was clear "that I at any rate have no qualifications at all to do so."[73]

A fairly uncompromising version of this approach is that of McNair J., who refused to incline to the constructionist view despite his clear distaste for the expert evidence which he was asked to accept:

> "there being no evidence to the contrary I feel constrained to accept this as the true view, however unreasonable it may be, though I confess I have reached this conclusion with considerable reluctance and hesitation, especially as I formed the view that Mr. Page (under the pressure of cross-examination) perhaps unconsciously was at times inclined to depart from the position of a dispassionate expounder of the law and assumed the role of an advocate."[74]

---

[68] (1927) 96 L.J.K.B. 930 at 937.
[69] *Bremer* v. *Freeman* (1857) 1 Deane Ecc. Rep. 192.
[70] (1889) 40 Ch.D. 543.
[71] *Ibid.*, at 550.
[72] *Ibid.*, at 550. See *Bremer* v. *Freeman*, above n. 69.
[73] *Re Banque des Marchands de Moscou* [1958] Ch. 182 at 202.
[74] *Rossano* v. *Manufacturer's Life Insurance Co.* [1963] 2 Q.B. 352 at 381.

It has also been stated, in an equally strict adoption of this approach, that the judge should decline to read the foreign law sources at all, even as an aid to assessing the merits of the expert evidence:

> "if he reads them, they may appear to him to accord with the testimony or to differ from it. If, in his view, they accord with it, nothing is gained. If, in his view, they differ from it, he, being ignorant of the foreign law, cannot weigh his opinion against the clear and uncontradicted opinion of the witness."[75]

There are also dicta which, though clearly sympathetic to the factual approach, indicate a slightly less rigid adherence to its purest form, accepting that the judge may read and analyse the foreign law texts, but only for limited purposes:

> "the text of the foreign law if put in evidence by the experts may be considered, if at all, only as part of the evidence and as a help to decide between conflicting testimony."[76]

It has also been emphasised that the appropriate way of resolving the dilemma thus thrown up is resort to the burden and standard of proof:

> "the court must accept that evidence, unless obviously false or discredited in some way, in which event, too, the plaintiff would fail because he has not on his part proved the applicable law in fact, if it be not what has been proved by these witnesses ... The rule is that the foreign law applicable to a case must be taken from the statement of the expert witness as to what the law is, and not from text books or codes referred to by him."[77]

The judge in this Irish case did, however, concede that there might be limited circumstances in which departure from this strict rule might be permissible, though the court should "use great caution" in doing so.[78]

It is submitted that although a certain flexibility of approach, of a kind suggested in O'Callaghan v. O'Sullivan,[79] is not entirely out of place given the unique nature of evidence of foreign law, it is properly regarded evidentially as fact not law for the purposes of proof, an assumption that underpins almost all the authorities. Thus the factual approach is clearly, as a matter of principle, to be preferred if the general principle is not to be undermined. There is little doubt, however, that once the foreign law texts themselves are before the court, judges will on occasion be persuaded that they are not entirely incompetent to arrive at a view themselves, especially where the expertise of the witnesses appears

---

[75] Nelson v. Bridport (1846) 8 Beav. 527 at 541.
[76] Lazard v. Midland Bank [1933] A.C. 289 at 298.
[77] O'Callaghan v. O'Sullivan [1925] 1 I.R. 90 at 119.
[78] Ibid.
[79] See above, n. 77.

questionable as a matter of evidential weight, if not at the admissibility stage.

No expert evidence There are isolated instances in which the courts have dispensed with the requirement of expert evidence altogether, despite the need for a finding on a matter of foreign law. Where there was no issue between the parties as to the validity of a Guernsey marriage, and the marriage certificate was before the court, it was assumed that the marriage was valid.[80] Scarman J. took the view that an adjournment to obtain the evidence would involve undue delay and expense, so that section 1(2) of the Evidence Act 1938 entitled the court not to require the attendance of a witness.[81] It seems likely that if the question had been in issue between the parties a different view would have been taken.

Where, similarly, the parties agreed to dispense with expert evidence, the judge was asked, and agreed, to interpret foreign law on English principles of construction.[82] These are assumed to apply if it is not proved that foreign principles differ.

The court will not inquire into acts done in a sovereign capacity.[83] However expert evidence is necessary in relation to the validity, in a dispute involving private rights, of an act done by a citizen purporting to act on behalf of a sovereign or sovereign state.[84]

---

[80] *Henaff* v. *Henaff* [1966] 1 W.L.R. 598.
[81] *Ibid.*, at 600. The contrary decision in *Westlake* v. *Westlake* [1910] P. 167 was distinguished on the ground that it was decided prior to the introduction of the Evidence Act 1938.
[82] *Jabbour* v. *Custodian of Israeli Absentee Property* [1954] 1 W.L.R. 139 at 147–148.
[83] *Duke of Brunswick* v. *King of Hanover* (1848) 1 H.L.C. 1. See too *Bultes Gas and Oil Co.* v. *Hammer* [1982] A.C. 888.
[84] *Dubai Bank Ltd.* v. *Galadari, The Independent,* June 20, 1990.

CHAPTER 17

Tribunals Not Governed by the Strict Rules of Evidence

A. STATUTORY TRIBUNALS AND INQUIRIES

The rules of procedure and admissibility of expert evidence for statutory tribunals are by no means uniform. Whether or not they are governed by court rules of evidence depends upon the provisions, usually regulations promulgated by statutory instrument, which govern the individual tribunal.[1] The instrument appointing a tribunal may provide that the High Court rules apply.[2] Some, such as the Lands Tribunal[3] and Planning Inquiries,[4] have specific and unique rules relating to expert evidence, while others have none. Industrial tribunals[5] have no specific provision for expert evidence to be adduced by the parties, and are not governed by the strict rules of evidence, though there is a general duty to admit evidence which is relevant, which includes expert evidence if the issue warrants it. There are many tribunals which share these characteristics, and which have no duty to admit expert evidence as a matter of course, but must consider it on the merits if it is sought to be adduced: a policy to exclude it would lead to intervention by the courts.[6] A number of tribunals, such as the Pensions Appeal Tribunal, have special procedural and evidential rules relating to particular classes of expertise, such as medical evidence, and have a fairly broad discretion as to how to use the evidence so long as their governing rules, and the principles of natural justice, are observed.[7]

There are two particular features of tribunals and inquiries which inform the approach of the courts to the review of their functions. First, most operate on the premise that at least one of the parties is likely not to be legally represented, so that informality is at the heart of their operation, in so far as this does not conflict with the needs of justice.[8] Secondly, the members of the tribunal or inquiry are very often appointed either pursuant to a statutory requirement or to a general

---

[1] Tribunals and Inquiries Act 1971, s.10 and 11.
[2] Tribunals (Evidence) Act 1921, s.1.
[3] See Chap. 13, pp. 256–259.
[4] See below, pp. 313–320.
[5] See below, pp. 311–313.
[6] See *R. v. Income Tax Commissioners* (1911) 27 T.L.R. 353.
[7] See *Jackson v. Minister of Pensions* [1946] 2 All E.R. 500.
[8] See *Aberdeen Steak Houses Group plc v. Ibrahim* [1988] I.C.R. 550.

policy, because they have some specialist knowledge or expertise in relation to the matters which they will hear. Where they do possess this, they are expected to use it. The main proviso is that where this leads them to doubt evidence which they have heard, in a specific respect which goes to a matter in issue, they must notify the party or the witness that this is so, before allowing this knowledge to affect the result of the hearing.[9]

There are old authorities which appear to adopt a stricter view, to the effect that in no circumstances may members of the panel do more than use their specialist knowledge and expertise for the purpose of comprehending expert evidence adduced before them,[10] and these may be explained in part by the specific provision for medical evidence made by their governing rules. In so far as this is not a full explanation, and it appears not to be, the position is probably no longer the same. In those tribunals and inquiries which have a local significance which is relevant to the matters heard before it, members with local knowledge are encouraged to use it, though natural justice would again demand notice to a party whose evidence was thus rejected.[11]

B. INDUSTRIAL TRIBUNAL

Procedure in industrial tribunals is governed by the Industrial Tribunals (Rules of Procedure) Regulations 1985,[12] and these make no specific provision for the manner in which most expert evidence may be adduced. Schedule 1 prescribes rules for most proceedings in the tribunal, and clause 8(2) provides a general right to call witnesses. There is also provision for assessors with specialist knowledge to sit with the tribunal,[13] although the panel is usually composed of two persons in addition to the chairman with particular industrial or employment experience. There is also a power, in equal value claims only, for the tribunal itself to instruct an independent expert,[14] and this is discussed below.

The general right to call witnesses is subject to the power of the tribunal to conduct the proceedings "as it considers most suitable to the clarification of the issues before it."[15] This reflects the fact that the strict law of evidence does not apply. Most tribunals, chaired by a lawyer,

---

[9] *Dugdale v. Kraft Foods Ltd.* [1977] I.C.R. 48 at 54; *Hammington v. Berber Sportcraft Ltd.* [1980] I.C.R. 248.
[10] *Moxon v. Minister of Pensions* [1945] K.B. 490; *Starr v. National Coal Board* [1946] K.B. 354.
[11] *Crofton Investment Trust Ltd. v. Greater London Rent Assessment Committee* [1967] 2 Q.B. 955.
[12] S.I. 1985 No. 16.
[13] Clause 5(3).
[14] Sched. 2, clause 7A.
[15] Sched. 1, clause 8(2).

adhere closely to the rules of evidence and to the normal court procedure for calling and testing the evidence, while attempting to preserve that air of informality which is intended to permit unrepresented parties to pursue their cases at no disadvantage. It has been said however that to allow this informality to be reflected in too relaxed an approach to the principles of evidence is counter-productive.[16] The courts have indicated that these principles are a sound guide to good practice, and should not simply be ignored.[17] There is furthermore a general duty, which will be enforced by the Employment Appeal Tribunal, to admit admissible evidence, and the industrial tribunal must receive evidence which is probative of an issue in the case.[18] Thus if there is an issue requiring expertise, the tribunal cannot properly refuse to hear an expert witness called by one of the parties.

Quite apart from the power, seldom exercised, to appoint assessors, the panel may, and is expected to, use its experience of industrial and employment matters in order to assess the evidence,[19] whether it be expert opinion or factual evidence. Where however there is a particular matter of fact or opinion, requiring specialist or expert knowledge, which a member of the panel having expert or specialist knowledge concludes against a party's admitted evidence, the party calling the evidence must be informed.[20] Thus the party and any relevant witness should be aware both that the panel member has this knowledge, and of the conclusion he uses it to draw, if this is contrary to the evidence adduced.[21] This is because the knowledge in effect, becomes evidence itself, and natural justice must be observed. A tribunal was therefore wrong to rely on such knowledge where it:

> "was not merely used for weighing up, or assessing, or interpreting the evidence but it was substituted for the evidence, or as part of the evidence, and that had never been put to the employee or his representative so that it could be dealt with."[22]

The industrial tribunal has the same power as the county court to order discovery.[23] Thus any relevant matters which may fall within the province of expert evidence not subject to privilege must be disclosed if the tribunal so orders. If a medical report has been prepared other than for the

---

[16] *Aberdeen Steak Houses Group plc* v. *Ibrahim*, above n. 8.
[17] *Ibid.* See also *Snowball* v. *Gardner Merchant* [1987] I.C.R. 719 at 722.
[18] *Aberdeen Steak House* v. *Ibrahim*, above n. 8; *Rosedale Mouldings Ltd.* v. *Sibley* [1980] I.C.R. 387.
[19] *Dugdale* v. *Kraft Foods Ltd.* [1977] I.C.R. 48 at 54.
[20] *Ibid.*
[21] *Ibid.*
[22] *Hammington* v. *Berber Sportcraft Ltd.* [1980] I.C.R. 248.
[23] Industrial Tribunals (Rules of Procedure) Regulations 1985, r. 4.

purpose of the litigation itself, and it is relevant to the issues, it must be disclosed. There is no right to disclose only its conclusions.[24]

1 Equal value claims

In these proceedings alone the tribunal may engage an independent expert, pursuant to the rules, to investigate and report upon the equal value issue.[25] The tribunal must however, before doing so, decide whether or not there are reasonable grounds for determining that the work is of equal value.[26] This procedure has been observed to be unfortunate in the delays it necessarily occasions in the resolution of the case.[27] The tribunal probably has no power to require applicants to submit to interview by the independent expert. If there were such a power, the tribunal would not be criticised for exercising its discretion against so ordering, and refusing to draw adverse conclusions from the applicant's failure to consent to such an interview.[28] The tribunal, in commissioning a report, makes no undertaking as to its findings. It may reject the independent expert's conclusions entirely,[29] though this should usually be done on the basis of cogent evidence upon which an alternative conclusion can stand. The courts have taken a pragmatic approach to the admissibility of statistics relating to the employment market, but they are probably generally admissible if the issue justifies their use.[30]

C. PLANNING INQUIRIES

Procedure at planning inquiries is governed by rules introduced in 1988. These in part formalise practices which were often previously pursued by consent, and also make new provision as to the manner of the hearing of evidence at the inquiry itself. The Town and Country Planning (Inquiries Procedure) Rules 1988[31] replace the 1974 rules of the same name,[32] and the Town and Country Planning Appeals (Determination by Inspectors) (Inquiries Procedure) Rules 1988[33] replace the Town and County Planning Appeals (Determination by Appointed Persons) (Inquiries Procedure) Rules 1974.[34] The Department of the Environment has issued a

---

[24] *Ford Motor Co. Ltd.* v. *Nawaz*, The Times, February 10, 1987.
[25] Sched. 2, clause 7 A.
[26] *Sheffield Metropolitan District Council* v. *Siberry* [1989] I.C.R. 208. See also *Reed Packaging* v. *Boozer* [1988] I.C.R. 391 at 399.
[27] *Sheffield Metropolitan District Council* v. *Siberry*, above n. 26.
[28] *Lloyd's Bank plc* v. *Fox* [1989] I.C.R. 80.
[29] *Tennants Textile Colours Ltd.* v. *Todd* [1989] I.R.L.R. 3.
[30] *Rice* v. *Civil Service Commission* [1977] I.R.L.R. 291, E.A.T.; *cf. Fletcher* v. *Clay Cross (Quarry Services) Ltd.* [1978] I.R.L.R. 361, C.A.
[31] S.I. 1988 No. 944.
[32] S.I. 1974 No. 419.
[33] S.I. 1988 No. 945.
[34] S.I. 1974 No. 420.

circular[35] which describes the background and purpose of the present rules, with a number of annexes covering specific aspects and providing guidance as to good, though not binding, practice in relation to matters on which the rules are silent or only partially prescriptive. The rules are described in the circular as the "Secretary of State Rules" (S.S.R.) and the "Inspectors Rules" (I.R.) respectively, and the same appellation is adopted here. The provisions of one set of rules are substantially but not wholly repeated in the other.

1 Pre-inquiry procedure

The rules provide for a pre-inquiry meeting, which is broadly the equivalent of a directions hearing or a pre-trial review. This does not automatically take place, but only if the Secretary of State,[36] where appropriate, or the inspector,[37] thinks it desirable. It is not intended to occur as a matter of course, but where the inquiry is likely to be lengthy, to involve complex and technical expert evidence, or to receive submissions from a large number of different parties.[38] It may be employed to explore the possibility for expert witnesses to agree matters of fact such as the description and planning history of the site, and generally to narrow areas in dispute.[39] Where major planning inquiries are concerned, the inspector may wish, having seen the outline statements,[40] to consider whether he should invite individuals with relevant expert knowledge to participate in relation to issues which it appears will not be fully or properly covered by other participants.[41] It may also be possible to agree facts and methodologies relating to the environmental effects of the proposals.[42]

The practice of giving evidence by the reading of a proof or written statement has long been an informally adopted method of adducing evidence, though subject to two main difficulties: first, that of notice, and secondly, that of reconciling the conflict between the desire to save time at the hearing itself and the need for the substance of a witness's evidence to be openly available, for challenge if necessary, to all parties. The rules now anticipate these problems by the employment of two documents, a "written statement" and a "written summary." Any proposed witness intending to give evidence by reading a written statement must now send it to the inspector,[43] three weeks before the inquiry, or if there is a time-

---

[35] Circular 10/88.
[36] S.S.R., r. 5(1).
[37] S.S.R., r. 7(1); I.R., r. 7(2).
[38] Circular 10/88, Annex 5, para. 1.
[39] *Ibid.*, para. 4.
[40] S.S.R., r. 5.
[41] Circular 10/88, Annex 1, para. 18.
[42] *Ibid.*, para. 19.
[43] S.S.R., r. 13(1); I.R., r. 14(1).

table laid down under rule 8, three weeks before the evidence is to be given.[44] Copies must be sent to the parties at the same time.[45] The Inspectors may also require a "written summary" of the statement.[46] The statement must have annexed to it any documents, or the relevant parts of them, to which it refers.[47] At the inquiry itself, the witness gives evidence in chief by simply reading the summary, although the inspector may direct otherwise.[48]

The inspector is usually a person able to understand technical evidence, particularly with the assistance of expert witnesses and counsel who, as laymen in the specialist field, have had to comprehend it for the purposes of the inquiry. The Secretary of State may however appoint an assessor to advise the inspector, though his advice must not travel outside his remit and into the general merits of the inquiry.[49]

2 Procedure at the inquiry

The inspector has a complete discretion, subject to the dictates of natural justice, to determine the procedure at the inquiry, save in so far as the rules make express provision.[50] So long as the skeleton of rules is complied with, and the fundamentals of natural justice are observed, the inspector need not follow slavishly the practice of civil litigation in the courts:

> "to 'over-judicialise' the inquiry by insisting on observance of the procedures of a court of justice which professional lawyers alone are competent to operate effectively in the interests of their clients would not be fair."[51]

This philosophy is obviously of particular relevance to issues which concern a large number of individuals and groups, many of whom may not be legally represented.

The inspector has a general power to summons witnesses to give evidence or produce documents as to matters in issue at the inquiry.[52] He may also allow any person to appear on behalf of a group or a number of individuals having a similar interest in the inquiry.[53] Any "person

---

[44] S.S.R., r. 13(2); I.R., r. 14(2).
[45] S.S.R., r. 13(3); I.R., r. 14(3).
[46] S.S.R., r. 13(1); I.R., r. 14(1).
[47] S.S.R., r. 13(5); I.R., r. 14(5).
[48] S.S.R., r. 13(4); I.R., r. 14(4).
[49] S.S.R., r. 9; I.R., r. 9.
[50] S.S.R., r. 14(1); I.R., r. 15(1).
[51] *Bushell* v. *Secretary of State for the Environment* [1980] 3 W.L.R. 22 at 29.
[52] Town and Country Planning Act 1971, s.282(2), applying the Local Government Act 1972, s.250(2)–(5).
[53] S.S.R., r. 11(4); I.R., r. 11(4).

entitled to appear" may call evidence, but only the applicant,[54] local planning authority and party present pursuant to section 29 of the Town and Country Planning Act 1971 may cross-examine as of right,[55] the calling and challenging of evidence by others being at the inspector's discretion.[56] The inspector may refuse to permit the adducing of any evidence which is irrelevant or repetitious, although a person not permitted to give oral evidence can submit written evidence before the close of the inquiry.[57]

Where it is proposed to call witnesses to give evidence by way of written statement, the pre-inquiry "written summary" procedure, as already described, must be followed. The witness gives his evidence by reading aloud the summary only,[58] though the inspector may direct otherwise.[59] If this procedure is adopted, the witness may tender his full written statement in evidence and be cross-examined upon it as if it were evidence he had given orally in chief. This can save a great deal of time in the case of expert witnesses who may be presenting a large quantity of technical data, all of which may be necessary to prove the logic of an argument, but only some of which needs to be challenged. If all parties are legally represented and have been so for a period before the inquiry, this can be achieved by the agreement of facts and inferences, but the same is clearly not applicable where unrepresented persons and groups appear at the inquiry, some without long notice.

Annex 6 of the Department of the Environment Circular[60] stresses the need for advocates to ensure that written evidence put before the inquiry is mutually consistent and not repetitious,[61] although of course inconsistent evidence adduced by a party is sometimes unavoidable and often illuminating. It is observed in Annex 6 that parties can take substantial steps with expert evidence to ensure that much of the technical and background matter appears in annexes to the main statement.[62] The inspector may find it helpful to hear the evidence of all expert witnesses issue by issue, rather than in the conventional manner, where discrete technical points arise, though this need should have been identified at a pre-inquiry meeting or otherwise in advance of the inquiry.[63] There are specific provisions too as to the manner in which a representative of the Secretary of

---

[54] Or appellant.
[55] See *Nicholson* v. *Secretary of State for the Environment* (1977) 76 L.G.R. 693; *Turner* v. *Secretary of State for Transport* (1979) P. & C.R. 468.
[56] S.S.R., r. 14(3); I.R., r. 15(3).
[57] S.S.R., r. 14(4); I.R., r. 15(4).
[58] S.S.R., r. 13(4); I.R., r. 14(4).
[59] *Ibid.*
[60] Circular 10/88.
[61] *Ibid.*, para. 11.
[62] *Ibid.*, para. 12.
[63] *Ibid.*, para. 9.

State may attend and give evidence.[64] Any written representations must be submitted at the inquiry if not submitted beforehand, and the inspector has a discretion as to whether or not to take these into account.[65]

It is a matter for the inspector as to whether witnesses may refuse to answer questions in cross-examination.[66] The inspector may however adopt any method of examination or other procedure which is fair, and particularly at inquiries dealing with substantial local policy issues at which many individuals and groups may seek a voice it is:

> "quite fallacious to suppose that ... the only fair way of ascertaining matters of fact and expert opinion is by the oral testimony of witnesses who are subjected to cross-examination on behalf of parties who disagree with what they have said."[67]

Where expert evidence is given, there will usually be substantial cross-examination of the witness by those parties entitled to cross-examine in any event. Others however may wish to challenge his evidence. Lord Diplock expressed the view in *Bushell* v. *Secretary of State for the Environment*[68] that where this is so:

> "the relevant circumstances in considering whether fairness requires that cross-examination should be allowed include the nature of the topic upon which the opinion is expressed, the qualifications of the maker of the statement to deal with that topic, the forensic competence of the proposed cross-examiner, and, most important, the inspector's own views as to whether the likelihood that cross-examination will enable him to make a report which will be more useful to the minister in reaching his decision than it otherwise would be is sufficient to justify any expense and inconvenience to other parties to the inquiry which would be caused by any resulting prolongation of it."[69]

3 Admissibility

The procedural rules discussed above can be employed by the inspector to govern the admissibility of evidence if he wishes to do so. He should however be guided by the general principles as to admissibility which are applied in planning matters, and his decision may be subject to review in

---

[64] S.S.R., r. 12(1)–(4); I.R., r. 12(1)–(4). He need not answer questions as to the merits of government policy.
[65] S.S.R., r. 14(10); I.R., r. 15(10).
[66] See *Accountancy Tuition Centre* v. *Secretary of State for the Environment* (1977) J.P.L. 792, and comment thereon.
[67] *Bushell* v. *Secretary of State for the Environment*, above n. 51, at 29.
[68] Above n. 51.
[69] *Ibid.*, at 30.

the courts if he fails to recognise these. Hearsay is generally admissible, though as where it is admissible in the courts, it should seldom be used uncorroborated on an important matter in issue, and this is no less true of technical questions subject to expert evidence.[70] Statistics and other figures may be persuasive unproved if an expert witness can explain them convincingly or give personal credence to their source, but where there is no explanation as to their origin they are of little probative value.[71]

An inspector is entitled to refuse to admit expert evidence as to the purely aesthetic merits of a planning proposal, because these are not matters of scientific or technical substance.[72] Inspectors do however in their discretion often admit such evidence, particularly where the aesthetic merits of a major planning proposal are the subject of public controversy. Cross-examination on such questions may be of limited use.[73] Political questions are not in principle relevant to planning inquiries, although in reality it is very difficult to state definitive lines of demarcation. What is undoubtedly true is that, as Lord Diplock stated in *Bushell*, policy issues which are exclusively so are not best resolved at an inquiry, which is not merely an instrument of local democracy. Similarly, something which is exclusively a political or policy issue is probably not susceptible of expert evidence as understood by the courts, although no doubt most experts would have an opinion to express if asked.

What the inspector must at all times attempt to observe is natural justice, particularly in relation to those, such as appellants, with a direct interest in the decision. What this entails though is fairness as between the parties, not an adherence to the evidential rules of the civil courts. Thus where a planning authority placed a letter, in the nature of hearsay, before an inquiry, and the inspector preferred its content to the sworn evidence of witnesses for the owners, there was no objection to his doing so, because the letter was openly before the inquiry, and the owners were free to comment upon it or call rebuttal evidence.[74] Any logically probative evidence is admissible and may be given weight.[75] It is not necessarily unfair to prevent a party from cross-examining upon evidence.[76] A party should always be given the opportunity to make representations as to planning matters which the inspector will rely upon but which were not ventilated at the inquiry.[77] An inspector did not give a "fair crack of the whip" to owners, subject to a compulsory purchase order, where he

---

[70] See *Knight's Motors* v. *Secretary of State for the Environment* [1984] J.P.L. 584.
[71] *French Kier Developments* v. *Secretary of State for the Environment* [1977] 1 All E.R. 296.
[72] *Winchester City Council* v. *Secretary of State for the Environment* (1979) 39 P & C.R. 1.
[73] Circular 10/88, Annex 6, para. 14.
[74] *T.A. Miller Ltd.* v. *M.H.L.G.* [1968] 1 W.L.R. 992.
[75] *Ibid.*, at 995.
[76] *Ibid.*, at 995.
[77] *Lewis Thirkwell* v. *Secretary of State for the Environment* [1978] J.P.L. 844.

observed a sheared through tell-tale at the site, and drew conclusions from it about the foundations of the buildings which had not been canvassed at the hearing.[78] This kind of specific technical finding, which might be a matter of controversy between expert witnesses, can only fairly be considered upon evidence.

4 Weight

The inspector may make a site visit[79] and draw general conclusions as to matters which have been or will be canvassed at the hearing. He may also rely upon his own knowledge of comparable matters, such as recent experience of the noise emitted from dog kennels.[80] Where he makes a site visit with the possibility that it may affect his decision he should always announce at the hearing that he will do or has done so.[81] There can be little objection to this so long as the time and circumstances at which the site visit is made are not atypical in relation to issues at the inquiry.[82] The parties should have the opportunity to make representations as to this.

The inspector is often an expert in relation to the issues, sometimes in a very specific but more often in a general sense, and he may having heard and read the evidence use that expertise to come to a conclusion on technical matters totally contrary to the expert evidence,[83] *a fortiori* where the technical matters are mixed with questions of non-specialist judgment and common-sense, such as the effect of noise on people.[84] It is well known that the effect of noise on different people is variable, and the measurement of noise levels by scientific instruments is simply the imperfect best that science can do in a very subjective field.[85] This is so even though the evidence is unchallenged.[86] To suggest otherwise, and that he must accept uncontradicted expert evidence, is a "complete and total fallacy"[87]:

> "the inspector (who is a man of experience, and, above all, specialised qualifications, who is sent to assess a problem of this kind) is

---

[78] *Fairmount Investments v. Secretary of State for the Environment* [1976] 2 All E.R. 865 at 874.
[79] S.S.R., r. 16; I.R., r. 17.
[80] *Ainley v. Secretary of State for the Environment* (1987) J.P.L. 33.
[81] *London Borough of Southwark v. Secretary of State for the Environment* [1987] J.P.L. 36.
[82] *Wass v. Secretary of State for the Environment* [1986] J.P.L 120.
[83] *Westminster Renslade Ltd. v. Secretary of State for the Environment* [1983] J.P.L. 454.
[84] *Ibid.*, at 456.
[85] *Mason v. Secretary of State for the Environment* [1984] J.P.L. 332 at 333.
[86] *Ibid.*
[87] *Kentucky Fried Chicken (G.B.) Ltd. v. Secretary of State for the Environment* (1977) 245 E.G. 839, *per* Lord Widgery.

supposed to use his own knowledge and, if I may say so, common-sense as well."[88]

This is so however great the expertise and distinction of the particular witnesses.[89] It is a complete misconception to take the view that matters of professional opinion in planning inquiries require the sort of factual support in evidence required in a criminal case.[90]

D. CORONER'S COURT

Proceedings before coroners are inquisitorial in nature, and the rules of evidence and procedure follow from that fact. There may be persons interested in the outcome of the proceedings, particularly those connected with an individual who died in questionable circumstances who wish to make assertions or challenge evidence given, but this can only be done within the limitations of an inquisition.

1 Admissible expert evidence

There are four principal methods of adducing expert evidence before a coroner at an inquest, and save in relation to the third, where a jury itself requires evidence,[91] only the coroner himself has the right to call witnesses to give the evidence.

Post-mortem examinations by a pathologist Examinations of the deceased post-mortem, requested by the coroner, must be conducted by a legally qualified medical practitioner,[92] in practice a pathologist. By section 21(2) of the Coroners' Act 1887 the coroner may direct a post-mortem examination, and may by section 21(1) summon him to give evidence at an inquest as to how the deceased came to his death. It must not be conducted by a doctor against whom improper or negligent treatment of the deceased is alleged.[93] The coroner may alternatively decide to request a post-mortem examination without an inquest, by section 21 of the Coroners' (Amendment) Act 1926, where there is reasonable cause to suspect sudden death from an unknown cause, but the coroner believes an inquest will be unnecessary. The result of the examination is then submitted to the coroner in writing. The coroner cannot dispense with an

---

[88] *Kentucky Fried Chicken (G.B.) Ltd.* v. *Secretary of State for the Environment*, see above n. 87.
[89] *Ibid.*
[90] *Wholesale Mail Order Supplies Ltd.* v. *Secretary of State for the Environment* [1976] J.P.L. 163 at 164, *per* Lord Widgery.
[91] Coroners' Act 1887, s.21(3).
[92] See Coroners' Rules 1984 (S.I 1984 No. 552), r. 6(1).
[93] Coroners' Act 1887, s.21(2). See also Coroners' (Amendment) Act 1926, s.22(4).

inquest, section 21(2) provides, if he has reasonable cause to suspect that the deceased died a violent or unnatural death, or in prison, or in any other place so provided for by statutes other than the 1887 Act.

There is provision for the situation where the coroner has already decided to hold an inquest, and then seeks a post-mortem examination, under section 22 of the 1926 Act. The pathologist can further be asked to make a special examination, by way of analysis, test or otherwise. The pathologist may then express an opinion upon these matters at the inquest.[94]

Deceased's doctor If the deceased was attended by a medical practitioner of any kind, either at his death, or during his last illness, the coroner may summon the doctor as a witness to give evidence as to the manner in which the deceased came to his death.[95] If the deceased was not so attended, the coroner may adduce the relevant evidence from a pathologist.[96]

Jury requires evidence There is a little used power of juries at an inquest, where a majority is satisfied that, on the evidence adduced before them thus far, the cause of death has not been satisfactorily explained.[97] The jury may in writing require the coroner to summon a pathologist, named by them, to perform a further post-mortem examination. This is the only method of adducing evidence other than at the behest of the coroner himself.

Other experts The coroner is at liberty to call any evidence which will assist in determining the matters before him, and this may include the opinion of experts other than those already described. It may be a medical specialist other than a pathologist, an analyst required to perform a test for the pathologist, or an expert as to some aspect of the non-medical circumstances in which the deceased died, for example an engineer where the deceased was killed by coming into contact with machinery.

2 Procedure and practice

The coroner can enforce his power to call witnesses by summons,[98] and impose fines if witnesses disobey. There are procedural rules by which the coroner is bound,[99] with specific provisions relating to the adducing of

---

[94] Coroners' (Amendment) Act 1926, s.22(4).
[95] Coroners' Act 1887, s.21(1).
[96] *Ibid.*
[97] Coroners' Act 1887, s.21(3).
[98] *Ibid.*, s.21 and s.23.
[99] Coroners' Rules 1984 (S.I. 1984 No. 552).

documentary evidence,[1] but so long as he complies with the rules he may decide how and to what extent evidence is to be adduced.[2] The coroner may thus admit hearsay, for example.[3] However his conduct is subject to review by the higher courts, and if he has adopted evidential procedures which clearly exclude probative evidence, or place undue weight upon indirect or other doubtful evidence, the inquest may be quashed. In *R. v. Coroner for Inner London North District, ex parte Linnane*[4] the Divisional Court held that the coroner had exercised his discretion in a manner which was wrong in law. The coroner had refused to call a doctor tendered by the son of the deceased, on the grounds that it was inappropriate for a coroner to call a medical witness proffered by an interested person, and that because he himself had relevant knowledge of infectious diseases, such evidence was unnecessary. These grounds were held to be bad, because there was no reason in principle why a member of the deceased's family should not submit a medical witness for the coroner's consideration. Furthermore the coroner's own knowledge was irrelevant given that the jury was the tribunal of fact and the coroner could not also act as expert witness.

Where medical witnesses are summoned by the coroner he is responsible for their fees.[5] Neither the finding at the inquest nor the evidence recorded is admissible as evidence of fact or opinion in subsequent proceedings,[6] save that a witness in other proceedings may be cross-examined as to what was said or done.[7]

E. ARBITRATIONS

Arbitrations in general are governed by the rules of evidence which apply in the courts.[8] Furthermore the same applies to specific provisions and procedures relating to expert evidence.[9] Two chief factors, however, have the consequence that the adducing of expert evidence in arbitrations frequently does not follow the pattern in the courts. First, the arbitration may be subject to express or implied provisions arising out of a relevant

---

[1] Coroners' Rules 1984 (S.I. 1984 No. 552) r. 37.
[2] *R. v. Divine, ex p. Walton* [1930] 2 K.B. 29 at 36.
[3] *R. v. Greater Manchester Coroner, ex p. Tal* [1985] Q.B. 67 at 84–85.
[4] *The Independent*, July 31, 1990.
[5] Coroners' Act 1887, s.26.
[6] *Bird* v. *Keep* [1918] 1 K.B. 692 at 699.
[7] *Barnett* v. *Cohen* [1921] 2 K.B. 461.
[8] Civil Evidence Act 1968, s.18(1)(*b*).
[9] Civil Evidence Act 1972, s.5(2). They also have powers to order such things as the preservation and inspection of property in issue: Arbitration Act 1950, s.12(6)(*g*).

arbitration agreement.[10] Secondly, arbitrators are very frequently persons who are themselves experts in the field in which the dispute arises. Subject to any express or implied term, arbitrators are bound to observe the rules of evidence no less than judges.[11] In some arbitrations, however, such as straightforward disputes as to the quality of goods, it may be sufficient for the arbitrator simply to view the goods himself, and decide the matter without evidence.[12]

Arbitrators are frequently appointed exactly because they have expertise in the subject-matter of the arbitration, and this may or may not preclude the need for expert evidence from witnesses.[13] If he is competent to do so, and particularly where he was appointed under rules presuming a relevant specialist competence, he may in a quality arbitration decide, without expert evidence, not only questions of quality, but also the issue of damages flowing from a breach of contract.[14] However the matter is to be decided not upon a general discretion in the arbitrator, but on the basis that any further evidence is in the circumstances unnecessary. Where it can be shown that expert evidence was necessary in order to permit the matter to be canvassed properly, the award may be set aside if the arbitrator fails to admit such evidence.[15] He may hear expert evidence upon an ultimate issue in the arbitration.[16] Where expert witnesses are called, the arbitrator may of course reject their evidence and rely upon his own general skill and experience.[17] However he should not in such circumstances adopt a theory of his own, or employ his own knowledge of specific relevant facts, and act on them, without putting this to the parties so that their experts have the opportunity of commenting on it.[18]

Even if the arbitrator is himself a competent specialist, this does not *per se* warrant the conclusion that expert evidence is unnecessary, particularly in a complex dispute, and a party should not be penalised in costs for calling an expert merely because the arbitrator is a competent

---

[10] In particular, it may provide for arbitration according to the rules of the body which drafted and published the contract, such as the Joint Contracts Tribunal in building cases. Some of these rules and procedures are discussed in the chapters relating to specific areas of legal practice.
[11] *Re Enoch and Zaretsky, Bock and Co.* [1910] 1 K.B. 327.
[12] *Arenson v. Arenson* [1977] A.C. 405 at 431. See also *Sutcliffe v. Thackrah* [1974] A.C. 727 as to independent experts, whose duties are limited to those arising out of their contract of engagement.
[13] *Mediterranean and Eastern Export Co. Ltd. v. Fortress Fabrics Ltd.* [1948] 2 All E.R. 186; *Eads v. Williams* (1854) L.J. Ch. 531.
[14] *Mediterranean and Eastern Export Co. v. Fortress Fabrics*, above n. 13, at 188.
[15] *Johnston v. Cheape* (1817) 5 Dow. 247.
[16] *Anderson v. Wallace* (1835) 3 Cl. & F. 26. As to the nature of an ultimate issue in relation to expert evidence, see Chap. 7, pp. 150–154.
[17] *Fox v. Wellfair* [1981] 2 Lloyd's Rep. 514.
[18] *Ibid.*

TRIBUNALS NOT GOVERNED BY THE STRICT RULES OF EVIDENCE

specialist.[19] The purpose of appointing specialists as arbitrators is not chiefly so that they can decide the case unassisted, it is also, in a complex case, exactly so that they can understand and weigh the merits of such expert evidence as is adduced by the parties.[20] They should use their expertise principally to understand and evaluate the evidence, not to supply it.[21]

In general the arbitrator, as with a judge in court proceedings, may not call his own witnesses unless the parties consent.[22] However the arbitration agreement may expressly or impliedly provide otherwise, and the particular form of arbitration may lead the reviewing court to accept that the arbitrator may consult third parties, with or without subsequent notice to the parties. Thus it has been held that arbitrators could call in a competent expert to assist with the valuation of the stock of a partnership and the partnership itself, and adopt his opinions if they wished.[23] Arbitrators who could not agree as to a rental and commencement date for the lease of a mill were not criticised by the courts for placing the matter in the hands of an umpire, also a person with special knowledge, who did not hear any submissions from the parties.[24] The court concluded that the parties had not sought a formal arbitration with evidence on each side, but the specialist opinion of the arbitrators, to settle the dispute quickly and inexpensively.[25] Where such a mutual intention of the parties cannot be presumed, an arbitrator who appoints an independent surveyor to report to him as to value should give the parties the opportunity to call evidence and treat the opinion he has solicited as evidence before the arbitration.[26]

Arbitrators may be called as witnesses to give evidence in court as to matters which occurred in and at the time of an arbitration which are within their own knowledge. They may not, however, be asked to state the reasons why they arrived at their award,[27] whether or not these include matters of specialist knowledge or expert evidence.

---

[19] *James Longley* v. *S.W. Thames Regional Health Authority* (1983) 25 B.L.R. 56 at 63.
[20] *Ibid.*
[21] *Top Shop Estates Ltd.* v. *C. Danino* [1985] 1 E.G.L.R. 9 at 11.
[22] *Re Enoch*, above n. 11.
[23] *Anderson* v. *Wallace* (1835) 3 Cl. & F. 26 at 41. See too *Emery* v. *Wase* (1801) 5 Ves. 846.
[24] *Bottomley* v. *Ambler* (1877) 38 L.T. (N.S.) 545.
[25] *Ibid.*, at 546.
[26] *Gray* v. *Wilson* (1865) 35 L.J.C.P. 123; *Re Eastern Counties Railway Co.* (1863) 2 New Rep. 441.
[27] *Duke of Buccleuch* v. *Metropolitan Board of Works* (1872) L.R. 5 H.L. 418 at 433; *Ward* v. *Shell-Mex and B.P. Ltd.* [1951] 2 All E.R. 904; *Re Whiteley* [1891] 1 Ch. 558.

CHAPTER 18

Specific commercial jurisdictions

A THE RESTRICTIVE PRACTICES COURT

Evidence as to matters of competition law has a special character because the issues relate only in part to specific events. The courts may well be concerned with straightforward matters of fact, such as whether an agreement was in fact reached between groups of companies, though even this may have to be established largely by inference from subsequent behaviour and activity in the market. They will also usually be concerned however with more generalised questions about the effect of such decisions upon the market as a whole, whatever the relevant market may be, in so far as they have commercial and consumer consequences. These are issues of a broad economic nature, and not easily susceptible of proof by direct evidence of the usual kind. The Restrictive Practices Court, though chaired by a judge, consists for its substantive proceedings also of lay members, who though not lawyers may well themselves have expertise of particular relevance to the issues in the case.

1 Adducing expert evidence

Procedure is governed by the Restrictive Prices Court (Amendment) Rules 1976,[1] the principal evidential provisions of which also apply in resale prices proceedings.[2] A general power to summon witnesses is provided by rule 40. By rule 36 the Court can direct the admission of:

> "scientific, technical or statistical information . . . by the production of specified scientific, technical, economic or trade publications or works of reference containing such information."

Thus there is no bar, subject to relevance, to hearsay evidence[3] being adduced as to general, or if relevant fairly specific economic questions. However, where particular matters of fact are in issue, the Court may well not admit indirect evidence or may attribute little weight to it. Thus an expert economist was not permitted to give evidence as to the practi-

---

[1] S.I. 1976 No. 1897, as amended by S.I. 1982 No. 871.
[2] Restrictive Practices Court (Resale Prices) Rules 1976 (S.I. 1976 No. 1899), r. 13.
[3] As to the preparation and presentation of documentary evidence, see *Practice Direction* (*Restrictive Practices: Evidence*) (1984) I.C.R. 703. See also R.S.C. Ord. 41.

cal workings of the book trade, though he was able to express opinions about the economic principles applicable to the factual situation described by booksellers and others involved in the trade itself.[4]

A particular difficulty where hearsay is concerned is the adducing of evidence of market behaviour and conditions in foreign countries, for the purpose of comparing the national market. In general the Court will hesitate to hear evidence of the position in a foreign country where lengthy investigation would be necessary to establish the merits of the comparison.[5] There is though no principle to this effect and the Court will consider the proposed evidence on its merits. In the *Chocolate and Sugar Confectionary Reference*[6] the Court was concerned with tables of consumer prices of chocolate and confectionary in seven foreign countries, with comparisons to English prices. The rules permitted the reception of the evidence, it was held, and it would not be excluded solely on that ground.[7] The Court chose not to admit the evidence, however, because:

> "there are so many factors which would be relevant in order to make that evidence of weight in regard to any issue that we have to decide, and ... those factors would not be covered by evidence that is to be laid before us."[8]

The evidence was therefore not "of sufficient relevance or weight to justify its being admitted."[9] The Court would, however, admit:

> "any parts of it which it may emerge are direct evidence, that is to say, evidence that would be admissible under the strict rules of evidence."[10]

The Court emphasised that it was not seeking to lay down any rule or principle as to this.[11] It appears therefore to have used the rule as to hearsay not as an objection in principle, because it is specifically admissible in such proceedings, but as a convenient and proper threshold for deciding which evidence was or was not of a high enough probative value to justify admission in the particular case. The Court has relied upon evidence as to foreign markets where satisfied as to its probative value.[12] It is desirable that a party proposing to rely on such evidence pleads this

---

[4] *Re Net Book Agreement* (1962) L.R. 3 R.P. 246.
[5] See *Re Cement Makers' Federation Agreement* (1961) L.R. 2 R.P. 241 at 266; *Re Motor Vehicle Distribution Scheme Agreement* (1961) L.R. 2 R.P. 173.
[6] (1967) L.R. 6 R.P. 325.
[7] *Ibid.* at 337.
[8] *Ibid.*
[9] *Ibid.*
[10] *Ibid.*
[11] *Ibid.*
[12] See *Re Net Book Agreement*, above n. 4. at 314.

intention, with reference to the particular countries as to which it will be adduced.[13]

There will be much evidence which is or should be unchallenged in most cases, and parties should not insist on proof where it achieves little. A partially adverse costs order was made where a party was put to proof of a general medical contention that it is important that shoes fit the wearer's feet.[14] Furthermore much evidence is incapable of precise quantitative assessment, and the Court will not demand this in relation to such issues as the benefits of an agreement, the quality of goods, or the improvement in production techniques resulting from an exchange of information between organisations.[15] A party merely has a duty to put any available and relevant material before the Court in as helpful a form as possible.[16]

2 Trade witnesses

Where large numbers of trade witnesses are giving evidence of a repetitive nature, often in order to prove a market pattern, the Court will encourage measures to short-circuit the need for full cross-examination of all witnesses. Thus a party challenging their evidence need not challenge each trade witness in a particular class of such witnesses on each point.[17] The Court will not in such circumstances speculate on what the other trade witnesses might have said if asked.[18]

Parties should avoid any behaviour which may tend to discourage persons in the trade from giving information or evidence. Thus where surveys are performed, questions should not be included which may tend to have that effect.[19] Likewise, the Court will take a strong view of articles or other publications which may deter people from giving evidence.[20] Information which is price-sensitive or otherwise of a confidential nature will be protected by the Court where necessary, and it may in its discretion permit witnesses giving oral evidence to write down sensitive information on paper.[21] Such witness reticence is of course wholly unjustified where agreements of a restrictive nature are being investigated, and the Court will be swift to infer from the circumstances, and from the evidence of witnesses deprived by the absence of material documents of the

---

[13] *Chocolate and Sugar Confectionery Reference*, above n. 6. at 338.
[14] *Re Footwear Reference* (1968) L.R. 6 R.P. 398.
[15] *Re Net Book Agreement*, above n. 4, at 309.
[16] *Ibid.*
[17] *Practice Note* (1958) L.R. 1 R.P. 114.
[18] *Ibid.*
[19] *Practice Note* (1961) L.R. 2 R.P. 168. As to surveys, see Chap. 15, pp. 289–292.
[20] *Re Doncaster and Retford Co-operative Societies' Agreement* (1960) L.R. 2 R.P. 129.
[21] *Re Phenol Producers' Agreement* (1960) LR. 2 R.P. 49.

SPECIFIC COMMERCIAL JURISDICTIONS

opportunity to refresh their memories, that a restrictive agreement has been made.[22]

B. ADMIRALTY PROCEEDINGS

The procedure relating to the Admiralty jurisdiction of the High Court is contained in R.S.C. Order 75. Some county courts also have an Admiralty jurisdiction, as to which there are specific provisions.[23] The jurisdiction is one of the few in which assessors are regularly employed.[24] Where they are not, and the case is tried upon conventional expert evidence, there is an established presumption that expert's reports or statements are subject to pre-trial disclosure, for agreement if possible,[25] on pain of a possible special order as to costs if this is not done.[26] The report should be accompanied by any other reports, plans, models, calculations or other material necessary for its comprehension.[27]

The Court may order pre-trial inspection of the ship, or any other property, by the parties, witnesses or assessors. This is a specific provision under the Admiralty procedure,[28] but is without prejudice to the general powers of the court in respect of inspection and allied matters.[29] Orders as to inspection have been made in relation to issues concerning the condition of the ship,[30] port procedures[31] and lighting.[32]

Evidential questions relating to expert witnesses are decided upon general principles. However the logs of lightships and lighthouses can be admitted by affidavit from an officer of Trinity House.[33] There are also provisions as to adducing the ship's log,[34] the contents of which may be very much in issue where questions of seamanship are concerned.

Nautical assessors As has been observed assessors are, atypically in relation to civil proceedings generally, an established feature of Admiralty trials. The assessors are usually Elder Brethren of Trinity House. The question whether they should be appointed should be decided at the

---

[22] *Re Motor Vehicle Distribution Scheme Agreement* (1961) L.R. 2 R.P. 173.
[23] As to Admiralty proceedings in County Courts, see the County Courts Act 1984, ss.26–31 and s.59, and C.C.R. Ord. 40.
[24] See below.
[25] *Practice Direction (Admiralty) Evidence of Expert Witnesses* [1968] 1 W.L.R. 312.
[26] *Ibid.*
[27] *Ibid.* See also *The Planter* [1955] 1 W.L.R. 898.
[28] R.S.C. Ord. 75, r. 28.
[29] R.S.C. Ord. 29, rr. 2 and 3. See further Chap. 4 pp. 79–82, above.
[30] *The Marathon* (1879) 4 Asp. 75.
[31] *The Sound Fisher* [1937] 58 Lloyd's Rep. 135.
[32] *Duke of Buccleuch* (1889) 15 P.D. 86.
[33] *The Maria Das Dores* (1863) Brown and Lush. 27.
[34] *Practice Note (Evidence: Ship's Log)* [1953] 1 W.L.R. 262.

directions stage.[35] They may also be appointed in county court proceedings,[36] and in appeals to the Court of Appeal[37] and the House of Lords.[38] Usually if the court below sat with assessors the Court of Appeal will do so too,[39] though the higher court may consider any views which were expressed by the assessors who sat below.[40]

The usual practice of the court if assessors are appointed is to dispense with expert evidence on the matters in respect of which the assessors have expertise relevant to the facts of the case, and this is a general rule in the case of nautical assessors.[41] A departure from this rule may however be justified by special circumstances, such as recent changes in the system of work on particular vessels of which assessors may not yet be aware. [42] Furthermore questions as to the value of a lost ship, which have to do with commercial as well as nautical considerations, will also require expert evidence in many cases. In the absence of clear evidence of current market value, however, the best evidence may be that of persons in the trade who knew the vessel before it went down.[43]

C. THE COMMERCIAL COURT

The procedure and practice of the Commercial Court are governed by the Guide to Commercial Court Practice.[44] As with Official Referees' business, pre-trial matters are dealt with by the judges of the court, so that questions as to the admissibility and form of expert evidence can be conveniently dealt with at an early stage if necessary.

The practice relating to the pre-trial disclosure of expert evidence is contained in paragraph 15 of the Guide. The general provisions of R.S.C. Order 38, Part IV continue to apply. Experts' reports should normally be exchanged a reasonable time after factual witness statements are exchanged,[45] so that their opinions can be based upon the full factual evidence to be adduced. Because of the desirability of reducing or eliminating expert issues, no leave will be given, on the summons for directions, to adduce expert evidence unless it appears inevitably to be necessary.[46]

---

[35] R.S.C. Ord. 75, r. 25(3).
[36] See County Courts Act 1984, s.63.
[37] Supreme Court Act 1981, s.54(8); R.S.C. Ord. 59, r. 10.
[38] Supreme Court of Judicature Act 1891, s.3.
[39] *Practice Direction* [1965] 1 W.L.R. 853. A party seeking a variation of this practice should say so in his notice of appeal.
[40] *The City of Berlin.* [1908] P. 110.
[41] *The Gazelle* (1842) 1 W. Rob. 471.
[42] *The St. Chad* [1965] 1 Lloyd's Rep. 107.
[43] *The Iron Master* (1859) S.W. 441.
[44] See the *Supreme Court Practice 1991*, Vol.1, para 72/A2 *et seq.*
[45] Guide to Commercial Court Practice, para. 15.2 (*Supreme Court Practice 1991*, Vol.1, para. 72/A19).
[46] Para. 15.3

Without prejudice meetings may be ordered in some cases. Where supplementary reports are necessary, these should be exchanged or served not later than three weeks before trial, preferably by agreement, but parties should endeavour to exchange before the lodging of pre-trial checklists.[47] Paginated and legible bundles of all authoritative sources should be prepared (if necessary with translations) in good time, so that they can be given to counsel and lodged with the court with the other trial documents.[48] Parties are encouraged to consider the appointment of assessors or a court expert.[49]

At trial it is usual for the evidence of expert witnesses, or the experts on a particular topic, to be heard together at the same time and after the factual evidence has been given. Parties should agree as to this before trial if possible, but it should at the latest be raised at the pre-trial review or, if one does not take place, at the beginning of the trial.[50] Experts need not give lengthy evidence in chief, and in most cases can, subject to new matters which may arise, simply adopt their reports and be cross-examined, and re-examined in chief, upon them.[51] Any party adopting a different course must be prepared to justify it.[52] Experts' reports will usually in any event have been read by the judge in advance.[53]

---

[47] Para. 15.5
[48] *Ibid.*
[49] Para. 15.6. Despite this encouragement a court expert is very infrequently appointed: see Chap. 3, pp. 64–65.
[50] Para. 15.4. See too *Bayerrische Ruckversicherung Aktien-Gesellschaft* v. *Clarkson Puckle Overseas Ltd, The Times*, January 29, 1989.
[51] Para. 19.4 (*Supreme Court Practice 1991*, vol.1, para. 72/A24).
[52] *Ibid.*
[53] Para. 14.7 (*Supreme Court Practice 1991*, Vol.1, para 72/A18).

Part F: FIELDS OF LITIGATION

CHAPTER 19

Medical Reports in Personal Injury Cases

A. DISCLOSURE OF REPORTS

Because of the similar form in which expert medical evidence tends to be prepared and adduced in personal injuries cases, in the majority of such cases the necessary directions are likely to be more or less identical. R.S.C. Order 25, rule 8 provides a mechanism for automatic directions where the parties agree that these are appropriate.[1] There is however no compulsion to use this procedure, and if the directions which it lays down are insufficient a party may elect to pursue the general procedure under R.S.C. Order 38, Part IV, by seeking directions from the court. Although medical negligence actions are now treated no differently from other personal injuries cases under R.S.C. Order 38, rule 36,[2] they cannot be pursued by the use of automatic directions.[3]

Rule changes introduced in 1990 however now provide that, in all personal injuries cases, whether or not involving allegations of medical negligence, and whether or not pursued under the automatic directions procedure, the statement or particulars of claim must when served be accompanied by a medical report and a statement of pecuniary loss, unless directions are sought to the contrary.[4]

1 Service of medical report by the plaintiff

R.S.C. Order 18, rule 12 (1A) provides as follows:

> "Subject to paragraph (1B), a plaintiff in an action for personal injuries shall serve with his statement of claim–
> (a) a medical report, and
> (b) a statement of the special damages claimed."

There is thus a clear duty upon the plaintiff not to serve the statement of claim without these two additional documents unless, as is discussed

---

[1] See below, pp. 336–338.
[2] See below, pp. 338–339.
[3] R.S.C. Ord. 25, r.8(5).
[4] R.S.C. (Amendment No.4) 1989 (S.I. 1989 No. 2427); County Court (Amendment No.4) Rules 1989 (S.I. 1989 No. 2426).

below, he immediately seeks directions from the court. The same applies where the automatic directions procedure is adopted, and in the county courts.[5] The requisite content of the two documents to be served with the statement of claim is defined in R.S.C. Order 18, rule 12 (1C) as follows:

> " 'medical report' means a report substantiating all the personal injuries alleged in the statement of claim which the plaintiff proposes to adduce in evidence as part of his case at the trial;
> 'a statement of the special damages claimed' means a statement giving full particulars of the special damages claimed for expenses and losses (including loss of earnings and of pension rights)."

The medical report must thus cover each separate medical fact upon which the case will rest, in so far as this can be ascertained at the time. Subsequent amendments to it will have to be justified on the normal principles of amendments to pleadings. Clearly any actual changes in the medical position, or matters not identified initially, would justify subsequent amendment so long as no substantial prejudice was caused to the defendant, and that any apparent disadvantage could be properly reflected in a special order as to costs.

The "statement of special damages claimed" is something of a misnomer, because it includes not only a schedule of special damages proper, but also an estimate of future expenses and losses including loss of earnings and of pension rights, both up to and after trial. The estimate must thus include a calculation, albeit tentative, as to all aspects of quantum save the award for pain, suffering and loss of amenity. It is perhaps more accurately described as a statement of pecuniary loss.

A plaintiff may, if he asserts some reason for not complying with these duties, issue a summons for directions, and R.S.C. Order 18, rule 12(1B) provides that:

> "Where the documents to which paragraph (1A) applies are not served with the statement of claim, the Court may–
> (a) specify the period of time within which they are to be provided, or
> (b) make such other order as it thinks fit (including an order dispensing with the requirements of paragraph (1A) or staying the proceedings)."

This provision gives the master or registrar a discretion to make an order in accordance with the general rules relating to expert evidence. The particular circumstances which it contemplates are those where a medical report will be forthcoming, but there is a good practical reason for the

---

[5] C.C.R. Ord. 20, rr. 27 and 28.

delay, or where the plaintiff asserts "special reasons" (under R.S.C. Order 38, rule 37(1)) why no disclosure should take place.[6]

Clearly, given that the principle of simultaneous mutual exchange has in effect been abandoned in personal injuries cases, arguments based upon that principle alone are unlikely to succeed. A possible difficulty is one of rapidly changing medical symptoms and prognosis, but this would usually be effectively dealt with by service of an interim medical report with the statement of claim, to be updated subsequently.

The rule changes do not affect the right of parties to call such evidence as they choose, and to disclose only that evidence which they propose to adduce at trial. Compliance with R.S.C. Order 18, rule 12 (1A) and (1B) satisfies the general duty to disclose or seek directions as to disclosure of expert's reports. A plaintiff may adduce further medical reports, but these must also be accompanied by a further statement of pecuniary loss, though only presumably if the further medical report has any material effect upon the pecuniary loss, or if there is some other reason for amendment. This applies both generally[7] and where the automatic directions procedure is adopted.[8] These provisions also make it clear that the plaintiff's disclosure obligations are satisfied by compliance with R.S.C. Order 18, rule 12 if the disclosed report is the only one to be relied upon at trial. The new rules do not alter the fact, confirmed in *Turner* v. *Carlisle City Council*,[9] that a defendant is not obliged by the rules to adduce medical evidence at all. A party may of course adduce the disclosed report of the other.[10]

Documents in the nature of pleadings Although they do not have that formal status, the medical report and statement of pecuniary loss are now in effect schedules to the statement of claim. The explanatory notes in the *Supreme Court Practice* express what is not apparent from the amended rules themselves, namely that amendments to these documents will require leave if it is necessary to depart from them at trial. Apart from the strict procedural requirements, it is clear that especially close attention must be paid to the content both of the statement of claim and of the supporting documents now required. In particular there will require to be clear correspondence between the facts and opinions expressed in the medical report and the pleaded case. It will certainly be necessary to achieve as close a correspondence as possible between the history and complaints described in the report, and the evidence which the plaintiff himself will give as to these matters, bearing in mind the

---

[6] See chap. 2, pp. 41–43.
[7] R.S.C. Ord. 38, r. 37(2).
[8] R.S.C. Ord. 25, r. 8(1A).
[9] (1989) 8 C.L. 259.
[10] R.S.C. Ord. 38, r. 42.

principle that the expert may only give evidence as to observed fact or his opinion upon it, so that his recording of the history given by the plaintiff (or others) in the report is not admissible evidence of those facts.[11]

Where the first medical report arises out of events and treatment before solicitors were instructed, as often happens in more serious cases where extensive hospital attendance is necessary after an accident, it is difficult for solicitors to exercise any control over how complaints and symptoms are recorded. Where control can be asserted, however, it is important to ensure that the plaintiff (or proposed plaintiff) does not omit to explain all complaints and symptoms, both as experienced at the time and outside the examination room, and that these are fully recorded in the report before it is served with the statement of claim. A full proof should be taken from the client before service to ensure that no substantial dichotomy arises, or if it does that it is unavoidable.

Changes in the medical position Although the provisions as to early disclosure of medical evidence will mean that in many instances the case will need to be in a more advanced state of evidential preparedness than was usual hitherto, they need not entail undue delay in service of the statement of claim. The medical position is seldom stable by the time proceedings are issued, and there is no reason why a medical report should not be clearly preliminary in nature, so long as it records in full the position at that time. The supporting notes in the *Supreme Court Practice* make the requirement that medical reports be amended, not simply updated, if the personal injuries alleged in the statement of claim and the medical report served with it are subject to change over time. It is unclear how rigorously this proposition, which does not appear in the rules themselves, will be enforced, but it is conceivable that it may in some instances entail substantial amendment to the pleadings and initial medical report before trial. In addition to the considerations already discussed, this reinforces the need for accurate drafting of the initial medical report.

2 Automatic directions in personal injury actions

R.S.C., Order 25, rule 8, in so far as it relates to the adducing of expert evidence under the automatic procedure, provides that:

> "(1) When the pleadings in any action to which this rule applies are deemed to be closed the following directions shall take effect automatically:"
>
> "(b) subject to paragraph (2) where any party intends to place

---

[11] R. v. *Turner* [1975] Q.B. 834.

reliance at the trial on expert evidence, he shall, within 10 weeks, disclose the substance of that evidence to the other parties in the form of a written report, which shall be agreed if possible;

(c) unless such reports are agreed, the parties shall be at liberty to call as expert witnesses those witnesses the substance of whose evidence has been disclosed in accordance with the preceding sub-paragraph, except that the number of expert witnesses shall be limited in any case to two medical experts and one expert of any other kind;"

"(1A) Nothing in paragraph(1) shall require a party to produce a further medical report if he proposes to rely at the trial only on the report provided pursuant to Order 18, rule 12 (1A) or (1B) but, where a party claiming damages for personal injuries discloses a further report, that report shall be accompanied by a statement of the special damages claimed and, in this paragraph, 'statement of the special damages claimed' has the same meaning as in Order 18, rule 12 (1C)."

"(2) Where paragraph 1(b) applies to more than one party the reports shall be disclosed by mutual exchange, medical for medical and non-medical for non-medical, within the time provided or as soon thereafter as the reports on each side are available.

(3) Nothing in paragraph (1) shall prevent any party to an action to which this rule applies from applying to the Court for such further or different directions or orders as may, in the circumstances, be appropriate or prevent the making of an order for the transfer of the proceedings to a county court."

"(5) This rule applies to any action for personal injuries except—
(a) any Admiralty action; and
(b) any action where the pleadings contain an allegation of a negligent act or omission in the course of medical treatment."

These provisions are appropriate, and saving of time and costs, in many straightforward personal injuries cases. They are inappropriate in, *inter alia*, the following cases:

(i) Admiralty actions and medical negligence actions,[12] for the latter of which two medical witnesses will seldom be adequate if liability is contested;
(ii) cases in which a party wishes to call more than two medical witnesses and/or one other expert witness[13];
(iii) road accident claims, and other claims where there has been

---

[12] R.S.C., Ord. 25, r. 8(5).
[13] R.S.C., Ord. 25, r. 8(1)(b).

an admission of liability, if discovery is sought of documents relating to issues other than special damages alone[14];

(iv) cases in which further directions are sought which, though consistent with R.S.C. Order 25, rule 8, are more specific in some particular.

A party may, for these or any other reasons, elect to adopt the general procedure of obtaining directions pursuant to R.S.C. Order 38, rule 36. There is nothing to prevent the parties from complying with the automatic directions, and then seeking further directions relating to expert evidence on summons, such as a 'without prejudice meeting' of experts under R.S.C. Order 38, rule 38. Indeed a further order of this or another kind would be considerably facilitated by such compliance as the master or registrar, and the parties, would be fully aware of which issues of an expert nature arose, and whether the evidence in its present form was conducive to fair hearing of the action, without undue prolixity.

County courts There is no automatic directions procedure in the county courts, or any broad equivalent of R.S.C. Order 25, rule 8. Save for this, however, the procedure for adducing expert medical evidence, as with expert evidence generally, is almost identical.[15] There is nothing to prevent parties from adopting the automatic procedure by consent.

3 Medical negligence actions

Medical negligence actions were, until 1987, in a class of their own in respect of the adducing of expert evidence.[16] Now they are treated under the rules like any other action save that unlike other personal injuries actions, they are not subject to the automatic directions procedure under R.S.C. Order 25, rule 8. It is unlikely in any event that the two medical witnesses provided for under the automatic directions procedure would be adequate in a medical negligence action in which liability was contested.

Expert evidence in medical negligence cases is now, as in other actions, subject to disclosure unless there are "special reasons" for not disclosing.[17] Although no doubt there are instances in cases of medical negligence, as with other forms of action, where pre-trial disclosure is not merited, the logic of treating them as *sui generis* for disclosure purposes has always been somewhat elusive. Indeed it might be thought that, if

---

[14] R.S.C. Ord. 25, r. 8(1)(a).
[15] C.C.R. Ord. 20, rr. 27 and 28.
[16] See *e.g. Rahman* v. *Kirklees Area Health Authority (Practice Note)* [1980] 1 W.L.R. 1244, now of little importance.
[17] R.S.C. Ord. 38, r. 37. See Chap. 2, pp. 41–43 above.

anything, the reverse should be the case if, as Lord Donaldson M.R. suggested in *Naylor* v. *Preston Area Health Authority*:[18]

> "in professional negligence cases, and in particular in medical negligence cases, there is a duty of candour resting upon the professional man."[19]

The illogicality of the former approach was recognised, shortly before the 1987 changes in the rules, both in *Naylor* and in *Wilsher* v. *Essex Area Health Authority*,[20] in which this game of "forensic blind man's buff"[21] was subjected to trenchant criticism by Mustill L.J. One justification was said to be founded upon the possibility that early disclosure of expert evidence might be of reduced value where it was based upon hypothetical facts which were not yet verifiable by the expert,[22] although doubtless this was equally capable of arising in cases other than those concerning medical negligence.

B. PREPARATION OF MEDICAL REPORTS

Medical reports in personal injuries cases, whether going to the issue of liability or, as is more usual, that of quantum of damages, entail in their preparation some distinctive features which can give rise to difficulty. In particular they usually involve the need for the plaintiff to attend for examinations by doctors nominated by both parties, in itself a small restriction on personal liberty, but they may also involve what amount to assaults by the expert, albeit often of a very mild and technical kind, though on occasion more serious. Often a doctor acting as expert witness for a plaintiff is also treating the plaintiff for the condition, and problems of consent are, though not impossible, much less likely to occur where this is the case.

1 Enforcing the co-operation of the party to be medically examined

The court will grant a stay of proceedings where the plaintiff will not co-operate with reasonable requirements of a medical expert witness:[23]

> "whenever it is just and reasonable to do so [and] the conduct of the

---

[18] [1987] 1 W.L.R. 958 C.A.
[19] *Ibid.*, at 967.
[20] [1987] 2 W.L.R. 425.
[21] *Ibid.*, at 461.
[22] *Naylor* v. *Preston Area Health Authority*, above n. 18, at 968.
[23] Each party is required to provide such information as the court requires on the summons for directions; R.S.C., Ord. 25, r. 6.

plaintiff in refusing a reasonable request is such as to prevent the just determination of the cause."[24]

The Court of Appeal in *Edmeades* v. *Thames Board Mills*[25] held that this is the only remedy available: there is no power positively to order a plaintiff to undergo a medical examination and to enforce the order by committal to prison for contempt of court. The burden of proof rests upon the party applying for the examination to demonstrate that it is reasonable, both that the examination be required, and in its form.[26] The same applies in relation to the number of examinations sought.[27]

The position where a plaintiff seeks to have a defendant examined, for instance where an allegedly negligent driver suffered a heart-attack while driving,[28] is less clear. The Court of Appeal has ordered such a defendant to undergo a medical examination,[29] though this seems to be contrary to the dictum of Lord Widgery in *Edmeades*.[30] It has been suggested that, because the rules make no provision for it, to strike out the defence would be a more draconian step than staying a plaintiff's action,[31] although there appears to be no practical alternative.

2 Conditional agreement to examination: ousting rules of court

The examinee may agree to be medically examined, but on some condition, whether arising out of an objection of a personal nature, or on advice from his legal advisers as to how best to obtain an advantage in the litigation. Any attempt to oust the effect of the procedural rules relating to expert evidence by such a condition will however be regarded as an unreasonable refusal to submit to examination, if it is in other respects reasonable so to submit. The scope for such attempts by plaintiffs is now somewhat reduced by the 1990 rule changes requiring early disclosure of medical evidence.

A different test applies where the defendant seeks facilities for a medical examination of a plaintiff widow in a fatal accident case. In *Baugh* v. *Delta Water Fittings*[32] Lawson J. held that, in the ordinary case, a request for such facilities would not be regarded as reasonable, and that it was only if the defendants already had evidence that the widow had

---

[24] *Edmeades* v. *Thames Board Mills* [1969] 2 Q.B. 67 at 71.
[25] *Ibid.*
[26] *Lane* v. *Willis* [1972] 1 All E.R. 430 at 436.
[27] *Ibid.*, at 435.
[28] *Cosgrove* v. *Baker* 1979 C.A., No. 744, December 14, 1979 (Roskill and Templeman L.JJ.); see Kemp and Kemp, *The Quantum of Damages*, Vol. 1, para. 15–038.
[29] *Ibid.*.
[30] Above n. 24 at 72.
[31] Kemp and Kemp, *The Quantum of Damages*, Vol. 1, para. 15–014.
[32] [1971] 1 W.L.R. 1295.

other than a normal life expectancy that they might be permitted to confirm this by medical examination. Lawson J. reluctantly accepted that the court did have power to grant a stay in such circumstances,[33] though he appeared to confine such an order to cases in which there were "genuine and substantial grounds"[34] for so doing. He added *per curiam* that, in an appropriate case, where an examination was properly requested but refused, the trial judge might draw such inferences as he wished from the plaintiff's failure so to submit.[35]

In *Megarity v. Ryan*[36] it was held that Order 38 Part IV is a "complete code"[37] dealing with the adducing of expert evidence at trial, and that conditions purportedly ousting their effect "cannot have been the intention of those rules."[38] The most frequently imposed condition is one requiring service of the report resulting from the examination, either with or without mutual disclosure of the examinee's own report, and this practice was accepted by the courts prior to the introduction of new rules in 1974.[39] It was held thereafter, however, that if no examination took place there could be no request to consider under the old rule 37, and that the rules therefore make the assumption of unconditional submission to examination.[40] This rationale equally applies to the rules currently in force.[41]

3 Conditional agreement to examination: own doctor to be present

The examinee may, for a variety of reasons, which may be psychologically based even in a case of entirely physical disability, seek to insist that his or her own doctor be present when being examined by another party's expert witness. It has however been held that the onus is upon the examinee to show "good or substantial reasons"[42] for such a condition. In *Hall v. Avon Area Health Authority*[43] it was held that a conditional submission of this kind is to be treated, in effect, as a refusal to submit, unless such reasons are shown.[44] The reasons advanced in this case as justifying such a condition were that the plaintiff was a 52 year old

---

[33] *Ibid.* at 1298.
[34] *Ibid.*, at 1301, adopting the words of the Winn Committee on Personal Injuries Litigation (1968 Cmnd. 3691), para. 313.
[35] *Ibid.*, at 1297.
[36] [1980] 1 W.L.R. 1237, C.A.
[37] *Ibid.*, at 1240. See also *Rover International v. Cannon Film Sales* [1981] 1 W.L.R. 1597.
[38] *Megarity v. Ryan*, above n. 36, at 1240.
[39] See *Clarke v. Martlew* [1973] 1 Q.B. 58; *McGinley v. Burke* [1973] 1 W.L.R. 990.
[40] *Cluer v. Chiltern* (1975) 119 S.J. 85.
[41] Introduced by R.S.C. (Amendment) 1987 (S.I. 1987 No. 1473).
[42] *Hall v. Avon Area Health Authority* [1980] 1 W.L.R. 481 at 491.
[43] *Ibid.*
[44] *Ibid.*, at 491.

woman, that her expert would have been able to testify to the inaccuracy of the defendant's expert's report, and that plaintiffs had suffered injury to their feelings by such examinations in the past (though not by this particular doctor). These were not regarded by Stephenson L.J. as sufficient reasons.[45] The court did suggest limited circumstances which might amount to good reason, for instance where the examinee was in a nervous state, confused by a serious head injury, or where the doctor in question had a reputation for a fierce examining manner. However the solution to this in most cases would be, not the attendance of their own doctor, but to take a relative or friend, or "in some (perhaps rare) cases"[46] a member of staff of the plaintiff's solicitors' firm.

If however the purpose of such an examination is, as it must be, to permit the examining party full access to the facts upon which its expert may express his opinion, it is difficult to see why such condition, in many cases, should be objectionable, except where costs issues are concerned. Logically, it should be for the examining party to show good reasons why such a medical representative should not attend. This would be consistent with the cases on other aspects of medical examinations, such as *Starr v. National Coal Board*[47] in which it has been held that the onus is on the party seeking the stay to show that it should be granted. The main concern of the Court of Appeal in *Hall v. Avon Area Health Authority*[48] appears to be the policy consideration that to permit such a condition as a general rule would be:

> "a serious addition to the costs of the litigation and also an inexcusable requirement, on the part of the processes of litigation and justice, of the precious time of highly qualified consultants."[49]

Three points emerge. First, such a condition will usually be regarded as unreasonable. Secondly, there are limited circumstances in which such a condition might potentially be reasonable, but the examinee's objection will usually be met by the attendance of a relative, friend, or in some cases a legal representative. Thirdly, if this is not regarded as sufficient, the examinee must show good or substantial reasons for such a condition in the particular case, as to which he bears the burden of proof. It was suggested in *Hall v. Avon Health Authority*[50] that the same principles apply here as in a case of outright refusal to be examined. There is some doubt as to the exact position as to burden of proof in the latter case.[51] It is submitted however that the only realistic manner in which an examinee

---

[45] *Hall v. Avon Area Health Authority* [1980] 1 W.L.R. 481 at 491.
[46] *Ibid.*, at 494, *per* Cumming-Bruce L.J.
[47] [1977] 1 W.L.R. 63.
[48] Above n. 42.
[49] *Ibid.*, at 494, *per* Cumming-Bruce L.J.
[50] Above n. 42 *per* Stephenson L.J., 491.
[51] See *e.g. Starr v. National Coal Board* [1977] 1 W.L.R. 63, and below, pp. 343–344.

can show "good or substantial reasons" is if he bears the burden on that issue, albeit the defendant may first have been required to shift the burden by showing his objections to be, on general principles, reasonable.

4 Conditional agreement to examination: different doctor

There is a number of possible objections to a particular doctor, ranging from fear of the manner in which the examination will allegedly be conducted, either physically or psychologically, to fear of its results, either because the doctor is said to be a 'defendant's witness' through frequent appointments by defendants in personal injury actions, or because of alleged bias against a particular plaintiff, or for a particular defendant. In *Starr* v. *National Coal Board*,[52] the plaintiff agreed to be examined by any doctor, of similar qualifications and experience, but not the individual selected by the defendant. No reason was offered for this insistence. The Court of Appeal held that although the onus was on the party seeking a stay, namely the defendant, to show why it should be granted, both parties had a duty to put evidence before the court as to their reasons for contending and acting as they did:

> "the particular facts of the case upon which the discretion has to be exercised are all-important. The discretion cannot be exercised unless each party discloses the reasons for his action ... I do not regard this as a question of onus of proof. There is, in my judgment, a duty upon each party in such a situation to provide the court with the necessary material known to him ... [but] ... at the end of the day it must be for him who seeks the stay to show that, in the discretion of the court, it should be imposed."[53]

This dictum of Scarman L.J., containing as it does a degree of internal contradiction, seems to have the result that the burden is on the defendant, but that he will inevitably have discharged it if the plaintiff fails to bring evidence of good reason for not granting a stay. The discretion will be exercised by reference to "the interests of justice."[54]

It is suggested that the most logical and practical way of expressing the rule as to onus as it emerges from the various and somewhat inconsistent dicta of the courts is as follows. The burden of proof lies on the party seeking a stay, namely the defendant.[55] If however the defendant discharges this burden by demonstrating upon evidence that the doctor is prima facie appropriate, the burden shifts to the plaintiff to show, by evi-

---

[52] [1977] 1 W.L.R. 63.
[53] *Ibid.*, at 71.
[54] *Ibid.*, at 71.
[55] *Lane* v. *Willis* [1972] 1 All E.R. 430 at 436.

dence not mere assertion,[56] that his objections are good ones in the circumstances of the particular case.

The difficulties in relation to onus arise in part out of the essential equality of the two competing claims in such a case:

> "First . . . there is the plaintiff's right to personal liberty. But on the other side there is an equally fundamental right—the defendant's right to defend himself in the litigation as he and his advisers think fit; and this is a right which includes the freedom to choose the witnesses that he will call. It is particularly important that a defendant should be able to choose his own expert witnesses, if the case be one in which expert testimony is significant."[57]

It is clear that the individual circumstances are all-important, and the courts will not attempt to make general rules as to which circumstances will invariably persuade the courts of the reasonableness of the objection. Scarman L.J. however gave two examples of objections which might potentially attract the protection of the courts, namely the woman plaintiff who preferred a female doctor to perform the examination, and cases where the objection was "of a very personal character, in no way reflecting on the competence or character of the doctor."[58] It seems clear that allegations of bias will require strong evidence to be persuasive, and that usually they will not justify a refusal to be examined. Such matters should be elicited in cross-examination of the doctor at trial. An objection that a doctor only ever acts for insurers (*i.e.* defendants) has been held not, *per se*, to be a reasonable ground for refusal.[59]

5 Medical tests during examination

Almost all forensic medical examinations, though performed not for treatment purposes but to facilitate the expression of an opinion, necessarily entail, or can only effectively be performed with the assistance of, physical tests, many of which will involve what is in law an assault if not consented to, albeit sometimes of the most technical kind. Some such tests will result in some physical discomfort or pain for the examinee, and a very small minority may carry a small risk of further injury. The courts have, principally in the decisions of Hodgson J. in *Aspinall* v. *Sterling Mansell*[60] and Webster J. in *Prescott* v. *Bulldog Tools Ltd.*,[61] laid down

---
[56] *Starr* v. *N.C.B.*, above n. 47, at 71. This is broadly consistent with some observations of Edmund-Davies L.J., *per curiam*, in *Murphy* v. *Ford Motor Co.* (1970) 114 S.J. 886, C.A.
[57] *Ibid.*, at 71, *per* Scarman L.J.
[58] *Ibid.*, at 72.
[59] *Murphy* v. *Ford Motor Co.* (1970) 114 S.J. 886, C.A.
[60] [1981] 3 All E.R. 866.
[61] [1981] 3 All E.R. 869.

guidelines as to how such conflicts should be resolved, although the two judges do part company in some respects. It is suggested that the following broad principles can be stated on the basis of these two decisions:

(i) the test is one of reasonableness, to be decided on the facts of the particular case;

(ii) the issue is the reasonableness of the plaintiff's refusal, not of the defendant's request.[62] The two judges differed as to whether any *a priori* assumptions could be made about the competing claims. It was Hodgson J.'s view that "the plaintiff's right to personal liberty must prevail,"[63] whereas Webster J. stated that the court must "balance the one against the other,"[64] and that he could see

> "no reason in principle why one right should be regarded as more important than another"[65];

(iii) onus: neither decision contains a clear statement as to this, but both appear to assume that the general approach in *Starr* v. *National Coal Board*[66] should prevail.[67] It is submitted that the rule in *Starr* v. *National Coal Board*, itself an unclear decision, should be employed in such cases as follows. The onus lies on the party seeking a stay (*i.e.* the defendant). However there is a duty on both parties to adduce evidence in support of their positions. In most cases, given that the defendant's request is prima facie reasonable if the expert is to be fully informed, the burden effectively shifts, and the plaintiff who fails to support his case with clear evidence will probably fail to resist the defendant's application[68];

(iv) the reasonableness of the plaintiff's refusal is to be judged by reference to an objective test, though in the light of the advice which the plaintiff actually received from legal and medical advisers.[69] Thus the question is whether a reasonable man, though with the plaintiff's disability and in receipt of the advice proffered to the plaintiff, would have refused to submit to the particular test in issue;

(v) where the only consequence of the proposed test is either an

---

[62] *Aspinall* v. *Sterling Mansell*, above n. 60, at 868.
[63] *Ibid.*
[64] *Prescott* v. *Bulldog Tools Ltd.*, above n. 61, at 875.
[65] *Ibid.*
[66] [1977] 1 W.L.R. 63.
[67] *Aspinall* v. *Sterling Mansell*, above n. 60, at 868, *Prescott* v. *Bulldog Tools Ltd;* above n. 61, at 874.
[68] See too pp. 343–344 above.
[69] *Prescott* v. *Bulldog Tools Ltd.*, above n. 61, at 874. The headnote in the All England Reports (at page 869) is not perhaps entirely representative of the *ratio decidendi* of Webster J.'s judgment in this respect.

assault of a technical kind, or some immediate but short-lived pain or discomfort, the matter is to be resolved upon the principles enunciated above;

(vi) where there is a risk, albeit possibly a small one, of injury in addition to that already sustained by the plaintiff, the position is less clear. Hodgson J., in *Aspinall*, took the view that the existence of a risk of serious injury, however small, concluded the matter in the plaintiff's favour:

> "I do not think it can ever be unreasonable for a plaintiff to refuse to undergo a procedure which carries with it a risk, however minimal, so long as it can be called real, of serious injury."[70]

Webster J., in *Prescott*, expressly disagreed with this view, and suggested that any such circumstances should be judged by reference to the reasonableness test.[71] There was no category of medical test which *per se*, as a matter of law, entitled the plaintiff to refuse to submit to it without the possibility of a stay of proceedings. Webster J. did though list five categories of possible tests,[72] and indicated what is perhaps obvious, that as a matter of fact the plaintiff's reasons for refusal will require to be most cogent in respect of the least irksome or risk-bearing tests.

In so far as the two decisions are inconsistent on this point, it is submitted that the views of Webster J. in *Prescott* are to be preferred. First, despite the suggestion in *Aspinall* to the contrary[73] it is almost impossible to place particular procedures or tests in fixed categories which determine whether they are reasonable or not,[74] in particular when the plaintiff's circumstances must be considered. Secondly, the view of Hodgson J.[75] that personal liberty must prevail is not consistent with Court of Appeal authorities on other aspects of medical examination,[76] which recognise that the two competing claims, of the plaintiff to personal liberty, and of the defendant to call such relevant evidence as it wishes, are of equal importance, and that the test of primacy is the circumstances of the particular case. However, what Hodgson J. purported to state as a rule of law was accepted by Webster J. as, in practical terms, more or less inevitable, namely that few judges would insist on the plaintiff submitting to

---

[70] *Aspinall* v. *Sterling Mansell*, above n. 60, at 868.
[71] *Prescott* v. *Bulldog Tools Ltd.*, above n. 61, at 874.
[72] *Ibid*, at 874–875.
[73] Above n. 60, at 868.
[74] Indeed Hodgson J. appeared to suggest that the use of a hypodermic syringe (discomfort but no risk) was in the same category as patch-testing for dermatitis (risk of recrudescence).
[75] *Aspinall* v. *Sterling Mansell*, above n. 60, at 868.
[76] *Starr* v. *N.C.B.* [1977] 1 W.L.R. 63 at 70–71, *per* Scarman L.J. It is perhaps surprising that Hodgson J. purported to rely upon *Starr* v. *N.C.B.* as authority for his own decision.

the possibility of further serious injury,[77] even though the risk might be small.

It may be supposed that the court will also be concerned as to whether the information to be obtained by the use of the proposed test goes to the root of the medical matters in issue, or relates only to a minor aspect of them. In the latter case the court could presumably debar a plaintiff, by way of partial stay, from seeking damages in relation to that limited aspect of his pleaded injuries.

6 Joint examinations

It has been suggested that in some cases a joint examination may be an appropriate way of allaying the plaintiff's fears (whether reasonable or not).[78] If both doctors are satisfied that their task can properly be performed thus, there can be little objection to such a course.[79]

7 Ethical duty of the examining doctor

The doctor asked to prepare a report, who is not involved in the substantive treatment of the plaintiff, is in a somewhat anomalous position as far as professional ethics are concerned. It is possible that matters may come to light, during an examination, which though unrelated to the litigation, are of medical significance for the plaintiff. Ormrod L.J. has expressed the view, *obiter*, that where the doctor discovers another, more serious medical condition, he is nevertheless under no duty to inform the plaintiff,[80] presumably because he is not his patient. Certainly no liability can arise from a contractual retainer where the defendant's expert examines the plaintiff. The appropriate course is probably to inform the plaintiff's own doctors, who can then act, in accordance with their professional duty, in such manner as they see fit.

C. CONTENTS OF MEDICAL REPORTS

The content of experts' reports generally is discussed in Chapter 4. Medical reports prepared for personal injuries litigation are likely to contain both fact and opinion, though much of the factual evidence may presuppose expert knowledge. They will also include, in the usual case, a summary of the plaintiff's history, and of his present suffering and disability,

---

[77] *Prescott* v. *Bulldog Tools Ltd.*, above n. 61 at 875.
[78] *Hall* v. *Avon A.H.A.* [1980] 1 W.L.R. 481 at 492.
[79] As to difficulties which could arise, however, see *Nokes* v. *Davies*, (unreported), May 5, 1970; Kemp and Kemp, vol. 1, para. 15–018.
[80] *Megarity* v. *Ryan* [1980] 1 W.L.R. 1237 at 1243.

some of which may have been gained from hospital or general practitioner notes, but other parts of which may simply have been given by the plaintiff in response to questions. Of course it is open to the defendant, if relevant aspects of such evidence are challenged, to cross examine the plaintiff and call original evidence in rebuttal, both in order to discredit the plaintiff, and to attempt to show that the expert's opinion is founded upon erroneous premises. Hearsay evidence of this kind, however, is not proved when recorded in a medical report unless either the plaintiff gives evidence of these matters, or the parties agree them,[81] as they should be encouraged to do. The mere fact that such material is solemnly recorded by the expert in his report invests it with no weight unless it is independently proved or agreed.[82]

As with experts' reports generally, medical reports must confine themselves to the kinds of oral evidence which the witness may give (including stating the assumed facts upon which opinions are based). They must not extend to matters which are for argument between counsel as to the merits of the respective parties' cases.[83]

Despite some judicial disapproval of the practice, experts' reports may be settled by counsel, though in many personal injuries proceedings this will be neither necessary nor cost effective. [84] Once the expert has prepared the report, the solicitors should not obscure particular passages which are unhelpful to their case,[85] or ask the expert to alter the report to favour the plaintiff's case.[86] Where legal advisers wish, with no improper motive, to ensure that the expert does not include prejudicial or irrelevant material in his report, this should probably be achieved by a full and precise letter of instruction to the expert concerned[87] rather than by excision after the event.

D. AGREEING MEDICAL REPORTS

1 Procedure

Where reports have been agreed, there will often be a saving of time and expense if the trial judge has sight of the reports before trial. A practice

---

[81] *Henthorn* v. *Fisk*, (unreported), 1980 C.A. No. 776 (Kemp and Kemp, 15–006).
[82] See *R.* v. *Turner* [1975] Q.B. 834.
[83] *Hinds* v. *London Transport Executive* [1979] R.T.R. 103.
[84] Bar Code of Conduct, para 607 and Annexe H para 5.8; but *cf. Whitehouse* v. *Jordan* [1981] 1 W.L.R. 246 at 256, *per* Lord Wilberforce.
[85] *Kelly* v. *L.T.E.* [1982] 1 W.L.R. 1055 at 1061.
[86] *Ibid.*, at 1064–1065.
[87] See *Noble* v. *Robert Thompson* (1979) 76 L.S.Gaz. 1060; Kemp and Kemp, vol. 1, para. 15–020 I.

direction provides that copies should be lodged with the court in the usual case[88].

2 Agreed reports must agree

The Court of Appeal has set out the appropriate procedure to be followed to ensure that "agreed" medical reports do in fact agree, and what should be done when they appear to conflict in some material respect[89]:

> "Agreed medical reports should be in agreement. This is particularly important in the field of prognosis. It is therefore, in my judgment, essential that those preparing for trial should scrutinize the reports with care in order to ensure that no conflict has emerged. If it has, the medical advisers should confer and, if agreement is reached, they should sign a joint report for presentation to the court. The reason for this is obvious. It is thoroughly undesirable, and indeed irregular, for the court to be called upon to make its own choice between so-called agreed medical reports which are in fact in conflict. Not seeing and hearing those responsible for preparing the reports, the court is faced with the impossible task of choosing between them."[90]

3 Oral evidence by the expert

One of the principal purposes of agreeing evidence is the saving of time and costs, both for the benefit of the parties and of the court. The courts have however made it clear that there is a number of circumstances in which, albeit there are agreed medical reports, some or all of the medical experts should nevertheless attend at trial to give oral evidence. First, the court will usually require oral expert evidence in very serious cases of personal injury:

> "an obligation lies upon the judge to insist in serious cases that he has oral evidence before he makes an assessment."[91]

In such cases the level of costs will usually not be significant by comparison with the damages in issue. Secondly, the agreed reports must be capable of being interpreted without expert medical assistance. Expert evidence is frequently required, in all areas of practice, not only for the purpose of expressing opinions, but in order to assist the court in a technically difficult field with which the judge may not be familiar.[92] The sig-

---

[88] Practice Direction (Q.B.D.) (Personal Injuries Actions: Experts' Reports), November 29, 1989 [1990] 2 C.L. 295, [1990] 1 W.L.R. 93. See too p. 353.
[89] *Hambridge* v. *Harrison* (C.A.), *The Times*, March 6, 1973.
[90] *Ibid.*, per Edmund-Davies, L.J., and see Kemp and Kemp, Vol. 1, para. 15–023. And *cf.* R.S.C. Ord. 38, r. 38, introduced since this decision.
[91] *Mullard* v. *Ben Line Steamers* [1970] 1 W.L.R. 1414 at 1419.
[92] See *Proctor* v. *Peebles* [1941 2 All E.R. 80.

nificance of this problem where medical reports are concerned was explained in *Jones* v. *Griffith*[93] by Widgery L.J.:

> "the 'agreed medical report' has only one virtue—namely, that it saves the time and expense of calling the doctors. But this is not the kind of case where that is an economy. Where a medical report is agreed, the effect is that the words of the report are treated as though they had been given in evidence, and it is not open to counsel to embellish them beyond, perhaps, some necessary reference to dictionaries to indicate the meaning of some of the terms. All too often in cases of this kind the argument becomes an argument as to the proper construction of the words used by the doctor, when if the court is properly to be assisted, it should have the opportunity of itself examining the doctors."[94]

Harman L.J. expressed the following view:

> "Reports couched in terms of jargon are, I think, of no use to the court at all: they are merely the raw material on which the medical evidence should be based; and when, as in the present case, that material is of a highly technical and very difficult nature it seems to me quite wrong that the chief witness on the neurological side should not have been put into the box in order that he might help the judge out of this morass of difficulties."[95]

The third situation in which oral expert evidence may need to be called is that where the plaintiff proposes to give evidence contrary in some material respects to the agreed reports. Unfortunate though this is, and unusual though it should be, where the conflict is serious the experts should be called and if necessary an adjournment should be granted.[96]

4 Oral evidence by the plaintiff

In the great majority of cases, whether the medical reports are agreed or not, the plaintiff will give oral evidence. Where reports are agreed it may be necessary to adduce oral evidence from the plaintiff as to matters contained in the reports, particularly where the personal injuries are of such a nature that the kind and degree of suffering and disability is better and more graphically explained by the plaintiff than in the somewhat

---

[93] [1969] 1 W.L.R. 795.
[94] *Ibid.*, at 801.
[95] *Ibid.*, at 802.
[96] *Gilson* v. *Howe* (unreported) 1970 C.A. No. 46; Kemp and Kemp, vol. 1, para. 15–025. It has however been suggested that the courts should not allow evidence to be adduced to show that an expert has changed his mind since reports were agreed: See *Pursell* v. *Railway Executive* [1951] 1 All E.R. 536

dispassionate terms of an expert's report. Such conditions as headaches, depression, anxiety and any injury involving substantial pain will often be better explained thus.[97] Furthermore, much in a medical report is likely to be based upon what the plaintiff told the doctor, and thus technically hearsay. It will usually be appropriate for this to be confirmed by the plaintiff in evidence,[98] though the parties may have agreed the facts as well as the opinions contained in the reports.

5 Plaintiff's condition or prognosis changes before trial

In many personal injuries cases it will be impossible for medical reports prepared sometime before trial, whether agreed or not, to constitute a conclusive opinion on the plaintiff's injuries. This will often be because the injuries undergo changes in the period immediately before trial. Many injuries, however, are uncertain in their prognosis after trial, and likely future developments can be very significant for the level of damages, as the relevant post-trial period may be much longer than that pre-trial. Furthermore it may simply be that the best estimate of prognosis can be made at the latest possible moment, namely at the time of the hearing. This problem can sometimes be met by the preparation of final reports immediately pre-trial. However, as medical experts freely accept, expressing the prognosis in the apparently certain terms required by the forensic process is in many cases a very speculative business, and it may well be of assistance to the judge to see and hear the expert in court in order to explore the question in such detail as is possible.[99]

Where the injury is one such as epilepsy, in which the risk of its developing on some future occasion diminishes with time, the court must at least have updated reports available, if they are agreed.[1] It will usually be clear to both parties that, where an injury has not resolved or settled finally, the plaintiff's condition or prognosis may change. Where however unusual developments have occurred before trial, the party alleging them should notify the other party of its allegation.[2] It might be thought that where the judge proposed to find against the prognosis given in agreed reports he should hear evidence from the experts in order to put the alternative view, but the Court of Appeal has said this is not always necessary.[3] In circumstances of uncertain prognosis an application for

---

[97] *Hope and Ward* v. *Hope*, (unreported), 1981, C.A. No. 415; Kemp and Kemp, vol. 1, para. 15–004.
[98] *Henthorn* v. *Fisk*, (unreported), 1980 C.A. No. 776; Kemp and Kemp, vol. 1, para. 15–003.
[99] See, *e.g., Burk* v. *Wooley*, (unreported), 1980 C.A. 774; Kemp and Kemp, vol. 2, para. 3–463.
[1] *Kaiser* v. *Carlswood Glassworks Ltd.* (1965) 109 S.J. 537 C.A.
[2] *Wooding* v. *Dowty Rotol*, (unreported), 1968 C.A. No. 184.
[3] *Eachus* v. *Leonard* (1968) 106 S.J. 918, *per* Ormrod L.J.

6 Judge departs from agreed medical reports

The decision in the case is for the court, not for the witness.[4] Therefore it must always be open to the judge to make findings contrary to the opinions of experts, even where the reports are agreed. It is clear that, having heard evidence from the plaintiff, the court can draw conclusions directly contrary to those of experts in agreed reports, whether as to the causation of particular symptoms,[5] or as to the issue of prognosis.[6] It appears further that there is no obligation to hear evidence from the experts whose agreed reports are being thus disregarded. Ormrod L.J. has taken the view that the prognosis, if it is not specially agreed as a fact, is "no more than an intelligent estimate by experienced doctors of a plaintiff's future condition,"[7] for which reason the judge may form his own view as to prognosis. It is not clear whether Ormrod L.J. is, in adopting this course, drawing a distinction between the prognosis and other medical evidence, with the result that prognosis evidence is, because more speculative, therefore more suitable for the imposition of a lay opinion. It is submitted that, unless the damages in relation to this issue are small, the appropriate course will often be to hear oral evidence from the medical experts if their agreed reports are to be departed from.[8]

7 Number of agreed reports

Despite old dicta to the effect that agreed reports should be in the form of a single document signed by both parties,[9] the regular practice of the courts is to accept reports separately prepared by each party's medical expert. A joint report will be appropriate where "agreed" reports do not in fact agree, and the medical experts are asked to prepare a statement resolving or clarifying the conflicts.[10] It should be noted that the procedure under R.S.C. Order 38, rule 38 is also available, pursuant to which the experts may meet without prejudice and prepare a joint statement. There is no objection to medical experts so doing in the appropriate case. The practice and procedure for without prejudice meetings of experts are discussed in Chapter 4.

---

[4] See Ch. 10, pp. 205–211. Though *cf. McLean* v. *Weir* (1977) 3 C.C.L.T. 87 at 101.
[5] *Stevens* v. *Simons*, *The Times*, November 20, 1987.
[6] *Eachus* v. *Leonard* (1962) 106 S.J. 918.
[7] *Ibid.*
[8] *Cf. Gilson* v. *Howe*, above note 88.
[9] *Harrison* v. *Liverpool Corporation* [1948] 2 All E.R. 449.
[10] *Hambridge* v. *Harrison*, *The Times*, March 6, 1973, C.A.

8 Adducing the other party's expert's report in evidence

Quite apart from the above mentioned circumstances in which reports may be agreed, where one party discloses a report by court order (but not where disclosure is voluntary), the other party may if it wishes adduce that report in evidence.[11] Presumably the law as to when oral evidence should in any event be called at trial[12] applies where a party does so.

E. DISCLOSURE OF MEDICAL RECORDS

It will in some cases be necessary, both for general evidential purposes and in particular in order that experts may properly advise, for copies of medical records, and especially hospital records, already in existence, to be obtained. There are statutory provisions under which application may be made to the court for discovery of such records,[13] both pre-action against a prospective party,[14] and after the issue of proceedings against a person or body not party to the proceedings.[15] In neither case may the litigant himself obtain such discovery, which is for the sole use of his legal and/or medical advisers.[16] No such order will be made if it is "likely to be injurious to the public interest."[17]

F. LODGING OF REPORTS

As soon after setting down as is practicable experts' reports, whether medical or otherwise, should in personal injuries cases be lodged with the court, to give the judge an opportunity to read them before trial.[18] On the face of each report there should be stated the name of the party for whom the report was prepared, the date when it was given, and whether or not it is an agreed report.[19] Reports should be lodged even though a party proposes to object to the admissibility of all or part of their contents at trial.[20]

---

[11] R.S.C. Ord. 38, r. 42.
[12] See sections 3, 4 and 5 above.
[13] The relevant procedural provisions are R.S.C. Ord. 24, r. 7A and C.C.R. Ord. 13, r. 7(1)(g); Supreme Court Act 1981, s.33(2); County Courts Act 1984, s.52(2).
[14] Supreme Court Act 1981, s.33(2): County Courts Act 1984, s.52(2).
[15] Supreme Court Act 1981, s.34(2); County Courts Act 1984, s.53(2).
[16] Supreme Court Act 1981, s.33(2)(b) and s.34(2)(b): County Courts Act 1984, s.52(2)(a) and s.53(2)(b).
[17] Supreme Court Act 1987, s.35(1); County Courts Act 1984, s.54(1).
[18] *Practice Direction (Q.B.D.) (Expert Evidence – Lodgement of Reports in Personal Injury Actions)*, November 29, 1989 [1990] 2 C.L. 295.
[19] *Ibid*, at para. 4.
[20] *Prest v. West Cumbria Health Authority* [1990] 3 C.L.Y. 339.

CHAPTER 20

Construction Claims

Construction claims, a term used generically to include all disputes arising out of building, engineering or other construction work, have in recent years developed a substantial body of law. In the vast majority of such claims, the questions of law are those which the courts in general are well acquainted with: contractual disputes, negligence allegations and issues as to the quantum of damages. Two factors set construction cases apart, however. These are the very particular nature of the standard forms of contract which now govern most large, and many of the smaller, construction works and the fact that the evidence in such disputes, whether of fact or of opinion,[1] is largely expert in nature. Thus many of the participants in the factual events are likely, quite apart from any opinions they may be asked to express in the proceedings, to be experts. This, as with patents disputes, in relation to which similar considerations apply, justifies the existence of separate courts, the Official Referees' courts, for the hearing of civil actions. Many construction disputes, however, either pursuant to the contract or by subsequent agreement, are heard by arbitrators, who are themselves usually possessed of some expert knowledge in the relevant field. The Official Referees' courts are in fact designated as the appropriate forum for any proceedings raising issues of substantial scientific or technical complexity, though in practice their workload is very largely comprised of construction cases.

A. OFFICIAL REFEREES' BUSINESS

The procedure in relation to expert evidence before Official Referees is that contained in R.S.C. Order 38, Part IV, namely that which applies generally. This is discussed at length in Chapter 2, and the general principles relating thereto are no less applicable in Official Referees' cases. However some special considerations do arise procedurally in construction cases, and indeed the Official Referees have been more progressive in recent years than other judges in encouraging the parties to do by consent what recent changes to R.S.C. Order 38, Part IV now enable the courts to require by order. The mutual incentive driving these trends has been the fact that construction disputes by their nature tend to raise complex

---

[1] As to expert evidence of fact, see Chap. 6, pp. 119–121.

matters which can only be resolved at some length and at considerable cost. Any means of narrowing issues and reducing the need for lengthy and sometimes repetitive oral evidence is therefore generally welcomed. Unlike the position with most Queen's Bench actions, Official Referees themselves conduct pre-trial matters, and often at an earlier stage after the issue of proceedings than is general. The system of giving cases fixed dates at a relatively early stage concentrates minds and assists in keeping the parties to timetables as to such matters as exchange of experts' reports. Although there is a heavy burden on a party not to serve pleadings making allegations as to professional negligence without clear expert evidence to support them,[2] only in an exceptional case will this be accepted as a reason for not complying with a limitation period.[3] A party must show that the expert evidence will be forthcoming, but could not be obtained within the relevant limitation period.[4] Consideration must also be given to the ability of other parties' experts to examine the building in the dispute. A party may be debarred from pursuing third party proceedings if delay in their prosecution prevents a party's expert from examining defective works.[5]

Directions hearings before the Official Referee will not usually occur until some pleadings have been exchanged, although the application for directions must under R.S.C. Order 36, rule 6 be made within 14 days of notice of intention to defend. The parties may already have served schedules to the pleadings in Scott Schedule form, or the judge may order that this be done, and possibly give directions as to the appropriate column headings. Particularly in smaller cases the importance of costs considerations may lead to an expert other than a lawyer settling the relevant particulars. This practice is one which should be rigorously controlled by a party's lawyers, particularly counsel who has signed the body of the pleading. One particular danger is the linguistically appropriate, but legally misleading, use of descriptive words relating to defects and poor workmanship, such as "inadequate" and "defective."

1 Directions as to disclosure of reports

Any party seeking to call expert evidence in civil proceedings must make application for directions relating to disclosure of reports etc.,[6] under R.S.C. Order 38, rule 36.[7] The duty, sometimes misunderstood, is to

---

[2] See *Worboys* v. *Acme Investments* (1969) 4 B.L.R. 133.
[3] *Portico Housing Association Ltd.* v. *Brian Moorehead and Ptnrs.* (1985) 6 Constr. L.R. 1 at 89. See too though the decision of the House of Lords in *Kleinwort Benson Ltd.* v. *Barbrak Ltd.* [1987] 2 W.L.R. 1053.
[4] *Portico Housing Association Ltd.* v. *Brian Moorehead and Partners*, above n. 3.
[5] *Courtenay-Evans* v. *Stuart Passey & Associates* [1986] 1 All E.R. 932.
[6] Discussed at length in Chap. 2.
[7] Unless one of the less common methods under that rule is justified. See Chap. 2, pp. 52–55.

apply for directions, not actually to obtain them.[8] Thus if the court takes the view that expert evidence is unnecessary, a party has performed all pre-trial requirements relating to experts, and may simply call the expert at trial if he can persuade the trial judge that the evidence is relevant, as to which a fairly broad view is usually taken at the admissibility stage, and that the expert is suitably qualified. Difficulties of this kind are not common in practice. They are reduced still further in Official Referees' cases, because the judge who is to try the case is, in so far as listing permits it, the one who hears applications for directions, and can therefore rule as to admissibility at an early stage. This is particularly useful where questions arise as to how many experts of different disciplines should be called. The same considerations apply to the number of expert witnesses.[9] All these matters may be and often are agreed by the parties,[10] though usually for confirmation at a directions hearing.

It has for some time been the almost invariable practice in construction cases in the Official Referees' courts for mutual disclosure of experts' reports to take place,[11] and R.S.C. Order 38, rule 37 now provides that this should occur in all cases save where "special reasons" for doing otherwise arise. Similarly the procedure for advance disclosure of lay witness statements[12] has for a number of years been adopted in many Official Referees' cases for some items. These may of course sometimes be proofs of evidence of proposed witnesses who, though they give evidence only of fact, are in fact experts, merely because the participants in the relevant events in construction cases are often possessed of expertise. Expert evidence, for the purposes of the rules, is given a broad interpretation which may include matters which can be philosophically analysed as factual,[13] and care should be taken as to this. Whenever there is doubt as to whether a proposed witness, for example a surveyor who observed the performance of works now alleged to have been performed negligently or in breach of contract, is an expert, directions should be sought as to the necessity for disclosure as expert evidence, rather than subsequent exchange pursuant to R.S.C. Order 38, rule 2A.[14] An "in house" expert is no less an expert for his lack of independence.[15]

[8] *Sullivan* v. *West Yorkshire Passenger Transport Executive* [1985] 2 All E.R. 134. See Chap. 2, pp. 35–36.
[9] R.S.C. Ord. 38, r. 4.
[10] R.S.C. Ord. 38, r. 36.
[11] See *Practice Direction* [1968] 1 W.L.R 1425, which in cases of conflict must now be superseded by R.S.C. Order 38, Part IV.
[12] R.S.C. Ord. 38, r. 2A.
[13] *The Torenia* [1988] 2 Lloyd's Rep. 210 at 232–234. For discussion of this case see Chap. 6, pp. 119–121.
[14] Orders under rule 2A are now common in civil proceedings (see *Richard Saunders and Partners* v. *Eastglen Ltd.*, *The Times*, July 28, 1989) and almost universal in construction cases.
[15] *Shell Pensions Trust* v. *Pell Frischmann & Partners* [1986] 2 All E.R. 911, *per* H.H.J. Newey Q.C.

In the vast majority of cases mutual exchange of reports will be ordered of the "substance" of the evidence. This does not mean a précis or summary, but such material as is necessary for the other parties to agree or rebut the evidence. In a defects case, each defect needs to be specifically canvassed, at least by way of schedule. In construction cases, any plans or other technical drawings, and if appropriate photographs, upon which the expert will rely or which are necessary for comprehension of his opinion, must be disclosed with the report.[16] In most cases the expert will not cite literature of a professional nature of which he is merely aware. If it is relevant however, and to be relied upon specifically, it should be disclosed with the report.[17] One area in which this necessity is liable to arise is that of negligence, where there is a dispute as to whether a respected body of professionals would have adopted the course taken by the alleged tortfeasor.[18] Professional literature is also highly material where issues arise as to the "state of the art," for example within a particular branch of engineering practice, at a particular time. It is unnecessary to refer to literature, such as standard text books in the field, merely because it has contributed to the formation of the witness's opinion.[19]

In construction cases a very substantial amount of time and money can be saved by recording matters in a systematic manner, often by way of schedule. This follows from the relatively complex sequence of relevant events in even apparently straightforward contractual claims. Thus claims as to delay can be much simplified by schedules of agreed events, with reference to certificates issued by the architect, surveyor or engineer at the chronologically appropriate points. Schedules of defects, if not in Scott Schedule form then at least systematically presented, can likewise save time, and litigators should also endeavour to encourage experts to employ where possible the same numbering and cross-referencing system, preferably from the earliest stages of the action. In a surprisingly large number of cases what appeared to be issues in dispute disappear when it is recognised, for example, that a particular item of cost covers more than one defect or item of expenditure. If the system of numbering and scheduling is agreed these time consuming misunderstandings need not arise. It is often, paradoxically, cost effective to hold more than one without prejudice meeting, or at least for an exchange of correspondence or telephone calls to occur at the outset.

---

[16] *The Planter* [1955] 1 Lloyd's Rep. 279.
[17] *Naylor v. Preston A.H.A.* [1987] 1 W.L.R. 958 at 970, *per* Sir John Donaldson M.R.
[18] See Chap. 7, pp. 141–145.
[19] See further Chap. 8, pp. 173–176.

2 Without prejudice meetings of experts

The rules now provide for the person conducting the summons for directions (whether Master, Registrar or Official Referee) to consider the necessity for,[20] and if proper order,[21] a "without prejudice" meeting of experts. The Official Referees have, despite the relatively recent introduction of this rule, long given directions as to without prejudice meetings, and for experts to prepare a written statement outlining areas of agreement and disagreement. The first line of cases arising out of rule 38 has emanated from the Official Referees' Courts. These and other aspects of its use are discussed fully in Chapter 4, in particular the problems of privilege which such meetings can raise.

3 Further procedural considerations

Parties should consider the need for a view of the relevant land or structure, and the question whether formal provision should be made for the judge and expert witnesses to attend.[22-25] There may, particularly in complex disputes as to questions of engineering, be a need to consider provision for expert inspection or experiments, and possibly for preservation of the subject matter of the action.[26] Consideration may also need to be given at the outset of the hearing to whether experts should give their entire evidence sequentially (as is usual) or alternately point by point. The latter course may be justified by the nature of the issue, though it has been said to be in decline as a practice.[27] Proper pre-trial disclosure and business-like without prejudice meetings of experts may well dispose of many of the advantages which such a course might otherwise have offered.

B. ARBITRATION

A very large number of construction claims are subject to arbitration proceedings,[28] usually pursuant to an arbitration clause in the contract, but also by election of the parties in other circumstances. The advantages are a reduction in the waiting time as compared with court listing and a perception by construction professionals that they are being heard by fellow practitioners who readily understand most technical aspects of the dis-

---

[20] R.S.C. Ord. 25, r. 4; *Practice Direction* [1974] 1 W.L.R. 904.
[21] R.S.C. Ord. 38, r. 38.
[22-25] See R.S.C. Ord. 38, r. 8(1).
[26] See Chap. 4, pp. 79–82 and R.S.C. Ord. 29, rr.2 and 3.
[27] E. Fay, *Official Referees' Business*, (2nd ed. 1988), para. 13–07.
[28] As to arbitration proceedings generally, see Chap. 17, pp. 322–324.

pute, and the context, both commercial and professional, in which it arose. It may well reduce the need for lengthy oral explanation of expert evidence to be heard by an arbitrator, and may in some cases dispense with the need to engage independent expert evidence at all. Many construction contracts, particularly those in standard form issued under the auspices of bodies such as the Joint Contracts Tribunal, provide for the architect, surveyor or engineer to act in a quasi-judicial capacity during the performance and at the completion of the works, deciding upon such matters as the issue of interim and final certificates, and assessing the cause of any delay and consequent lengthening of the contract period. Such persons do not in general however act as arbitrators proper in this capacity.[29] Although they are under a duty to act fairly, they are unlike arbitrators liable to an action in negligence at the suit of the building owners.[30]

The general principles of admissibility of expert evidence do not differ as between the courts and arbitrations, albeit the arbitrator is himself probably expert in an allied field. Parties may call such expert witnesses as they wish, subject to a possibly adverse costs ruling where the evidence is unnecessary. Arbitrators are not, save perhaps in the most straightforward matters, there to replace expert witnesses, but to facilitate their best employment:

> "one reason for having an arbitrator is so that he should be able to understand the expert evidence, not so that he should have to do without it."[31]

The arbitrator may of course rely upon his general knowledge, experience and expertise, but only as to general questions which arise, not so as to supply items of evidence specific to the case which the parties' witnesses have not provided.[32]

Most arbitrators in the construction field are governed by the court rules as to adducing expert evidence.[33] They may also however be governed by the particular rules of the body responsible for the particular standard form of contract. These are incorporated either because a term of the parties' agreement so provides, or by consent. Thus the Institute of Civil Engineers (I.C.E.) Arbitration Procedure permits the arbitrator, if experts' reports have been exchanged,[34] to examine the experts himself at the hearing, the parties or their representatives only being permitted to

---

[29] *Sutcliffe* v. *Thackrah* [1974] A.C. 727.
[30] *Ibid.* See too *Arenson* v. *Arenson* [1977] A.C. 405.
[31] *J. Longley & Co. Ltd.* v. *South West Regional Health Authority* (1983) 25 B.L.R. 56 at 63, *per* Lloyd J.
[32] *Fox* v. *Wellfair Ltd.* [1981] 2 Lloyd's Rep. 514. See further Chap. 17, pp. 322–324.
[33] Civil Evidence Act 1972, s.5(2). As to these rules, see further Chap. 2. See also Civil Evidence Act 1968, s.10(3) and (4).
[34] See I.C.E. Arbitration Procedure, r. 16.2.

cross-examine or re-examine, having first given notice of the nature of the proposed questions.[35] This is only a power, and the arbitrator may in his discretion conduct matters in a more conventional manner. It may however speed up the hearing considerably, particularly if the parties have been diligent in agreeing such facts and figures as they can.[36] The I.C.E. also provides for a "special procedure" for experts which the parties may adopt if they choose.[37] It is only suitable in straightforward cases in which the matters in dispute are confined largely to questions of expert judgment. It would not be appropriate where substantial questions of fact must be resolved, and is intended to permit the experts to act in effect as advocates for the parties, although they should attempt to adopt an impartial stance when expressing matters of expert opinion. Arbitrators should not in general refuse to permit proper representation and cross-examination unless the arbitration clause so provides or the parties agree, even where apparently transient issues such as interim certificates are in dispute.[38] The Joint Contracts Tribunal Arbitration Rules (1988 edition), by contrast, make no specific provision for expert evidence, although arbitrations pursuant to its provisions are of course covered by the rules relating to evidence generally.

C. COSTS AND EXPERTS' FEES

Solicitors instructing experts must be aware, at an early stage, of which costs are likely to be recovered, and whether as damages or costs. Costs in both court proceedings and arbitrations usually follow the event, though a broad discretion exists as to this, and specific orders may be made disallowing items of cost which were unnecessarily or wrongly incurred. Such specific orders are perhaps not made as frequently as they profitably could be at the hearing, although the taxing master may take a view as to the reasonableness or necessity of individual items of cost. The reasonable fees of expert witnesses should be recoverable in general in respect of pre-trial preparation and reporting, and in relation to appearance at the hearing.[39]

A difficulty which can occur, and is particularly likely in construction cases, is that an expert's advice or other assistance is employed not only for forensic purposes, but also in relation to remedying defects in the building or other structure itself. Logically the former is an item of costs, whereas the latter, if recoverable from the party liable at all, should be an

---

[35] See I.C.E. Arbitration Procedure, r. 13(1)(c).
[36] Ibid., r. 13(1)(a).
[37] Ibid., r. 22.
[38] See *Town and City Properties Ltd.* v. *Wiltshier Southern Ltd.* (1988) 44 B.L.R. 109.
[39] The general principles are discussed at greater length in Chap. 11, above.

item of damages and claimed as such. In fact the taxing master has a discretion to award any costs "incidental to" the claim,[40] so that expert assistance with the claim could properly be an item of costs even if some of the relevant work was performed before the issue of proceedings.[41] However a party cannot obtain, under the guise of damages, items disallowed as costs by the taxing master.[42]

Where remedial works are recommended by an engineer in a construction case, his fees are clearly allowable as damages if "incurred as a natural consequence of the defendant's breach."[43] This will be clearly demonstrable where the parties agree upon an independent engineer and upon the necessity for the works advised by him.[44] The position where an expert is employed in both the substantive and the forensic context is less clear. The fees of a construction claims consultant (whom the judge decided was an expert) were allowed as costs in relation to his work preparing a case for arbitration, but disallowed in relation to his preparation of a final account for submission to the architect, and also for work in the course of the hearing of the arbitration, not as an expert witness, but as an adviser.[45] The fact that an item could be claimed as damages does not preclude its recovery as costs, for example where a surveyor prepares plans and specifications necessary both for remedying the defects and for the prosecution of the claim.[46] However an architect's fee which is properly an item of costs cannot be claimed as damages (which might presumably result in a higher award, together with interest) merely because it is possible to analyse it as flowing in some remote sense from the original breach of contract:

> "All the costs of litigation which arise out of a breach of contract are, in a sense, the result of that breach, but not all such costs are recoverable as damages."[47]

The position where work is attributable both to remedying defects and to the forensic role is not the subject of clear authority,[48] though Stephenson L.J. expressed the view *obiter* that a damages claim might possibly be founded upon a report prepared partially with the purpose of remedying defects.[49]

---

[40] R.S.C. Ord. 62, r. 2(4).
[41] *Ross v. Caunters* [1980] Ch. 297 at 323–324; *Société Anonyme Pêcheries Ostendaises v. Merchants' Marine Ins. Co.* [1928] 1 K.B. 750.
[42] *Cockburn v. Edwards* (1881) 18 Ch. D. 449; see also *Ross v. Caunters*, above n. 41.
[43] *Peak Construction (Liverpool) Ltd. v. Mackinney Foundations* (1970) 69 L.G.R. 1 at 10.
[44] *Ibid.*
[45] *J. Longley & Co. Ltd. v. S.W.R.H.A.*, above n. 31.
[46] *Manakee v. Brattle* [1970] 1 W.L.R. 1607.
[47] *Hutchinson v. Harris* (1978) 10 B.L.R. 19 at 39. See too *Bolton v. Mahadeva* [1972] 1 W.L.R. 1009 at 1014.
[48] The judgment in *Manakee v. Brattle*, above n. 46, does not analyse this question at length.
[49] *Hutchinson v. Harris* above n. 47, at 38–39.

It must always be in the discretion of the judge, arbitrator or taxing master to take a pragmatic view upon the merits. It is suggested however that where readily identifiable and separable parts of the expert's fees relate to work clearly of a forensic or non–forensic nature, the order should be divided accordingly, and if no substantive damages claim has been made, compensation only made in respect of the items specifically attributable to costs. If a report and its preparation is principally for the purposes of the claim, but is also incidentally of some use in remedying defects, it should properly be allowable in full in costs. Stephenson L.J. speaks of the "main purpose"[50] of a report. Medical reports in personal injuries cases, principally forensic in purpose, are properly allowed in costs even though they may include diagnostic and prescriptive comment which is of considerable medical, as well as forensic, assistance to the plaintiff. There is no reason to differ in construction and other cases where this combination of functions occurs.

Where cases are settled, it may be difficult to argue that experts' fees should be recovered as costs if they have been pleaded as part of the substantive claim, and this should be considered when loss and damage schedules are pleaded. Otherwise, the terms of the settlement should make express provision.

D. ADMISSIBILITY AND WEIGHT

1 Admissibility

The evidence in construction cases is frequently given almost entirely by experts, although some of it will be of a commonplace factual kind. Witnesses who have expertise may be called simply because they were involved as professionals in the subject matter of the dispute, or as independent experts able to express an opinion as to the technical issues, or often both. The question of whether a proposed witness has the necessary expertise is one to be resolved on the facts, and this is discussed further in Chapters 1 and 6. There are of course many specialisms within the profession of civil engineer, or surveyor, but the fact that a witness has no direct experience of a particular specialism does not disqualify him from being an expert. His evidence will be of probative value if his expertise renders him better able than the tribunal of fact to draw inferences as to the technical subject matter. An arbitrator who has a similar expertise, however, may legitimately take the view that a generalist professional cannot add anything to that expertise which the arbitrator can and is expected to bring to bear upon the dispute. If he does so, he should make

---

[50] *Hutchinson v. Harris* above n. 47, at 39.

this clear to the parties.[51] Although the usual course is to admit such evidence, but to attribute little evidential weight to it at the adjudication stage, there is nothing to prevent an arbitrator taking an early view of the potential merit of such evidence, particularly given the assumption that arbitrations are intended to be a swifter and less costly means of dispute resolution than recourse to the courts.

The question of expertise is a matter for the tribunal, and even in a field such as construction, in which many specialists are involved with numerous qualifications, rigorously controlled by the professional institutions, it is only the expertise itself which must be demonstrated, not the path by which it was achieved,[52] subject to its relevance to matters in issue. Thus in *J. Longley and Co. Ltd. v. South-West Regional Health Authority*,[53] Lloyd J. held that a construction industry claims consultant could properly be regarded as an expert, despite the fact that he had no qualifications as an architect or quantity surveyor of a kind relevant to the matters in issue, namely the causes of delay in the completion of building works:

> "an expert may be qualified by skill and experience, as well as by professional qualifications."[54]

The tribunal must simply decide whether the expert evidence is necessary "in order to reach an informed judgment on the facts."[55] The same general principle applies to which questions the expert may answer, and the prohibition upon evidence given in relation to the very point which the judge or arbitrator must decide is one in relation to which no all-embracing rule can be framed[56]:

> "the dividing line between what an expert witness can and cannot be asked is often very narrow."[57]

In *Longley v. S.W.R.H.A.* the claims consultant was permitted to give evidence in relation to delay, but probably only because the causes were many. Evidence was admissible as to the:

> "interrelations of various alleged causes of delay. If there had been but a single cause of delay, and if the question had been how much delay resulted from that cause, then expert evidence might well have been excluded. But here there was a multitude of causes, all reacting

---

[51] See *Fox v. Wellfair* [1981] 2 Lloyd's Rep. 514.
[52] See Chap. 1, pp. 10–14, and Chap. 6, pp. 127–131.
[53] Above n. 31.
[54] *Ibid.*, at 62. The editors of the Building Law Reports caution, correctly, that not all judges and arbitrators would share Lloyd J.'s view of a claims consultant's expertise.
[55] *Longley* v. *S.W.R.H.A.*, above n. 31, at 62.
[56] The Civil Evidence Act 1972, s.3(3), removes any general exclusion as to this. See above Chap. 7, pp. 150–154.
[57] *Longley* v. *S.W.R.H.A.*, above n. 31, at 62.

on each other to a greater or lesser extent. In those circumstances the assessment of delay resulting from any individual cause called for a high degree of skill, as well as experience of how building operations are in fact carried on."[58]

2 Weight

There is no hierarchy as between expert witnesses save the merits of their evidence. It will often be decisive that a number of respected professionals take a particular view, but the evidence of a single expert may be preferred if this is more persuasive or if his field is the more particularly relevant to matters in issue. Thus an architect's evidence may be accepted, even though it was contradicted by that of three engineers, because they were expressing opinions in "a profession other than their own."[59] The architect's evidence was the only opinion which was "directly relevant,"[60] albeit the engineers were practising in a related field. Likewise, where two experts have overlapping but not coterminous expertise the court may well, though not obliged to, prefer the evidence of the witness whose expertise is greater in respect of matters in issue before the courts.[61]

There is similarly no hierarchy as between real evidence and evidence of expert opinion, and the tribunal of fact can use its own observation, particularly a view in construction cases, to confirm or dismiss the evidence of experts, especially where the dispute can be partly resolved upon non-specialist material:

> "where the matter for decision is one of ordinary common sense, the judge of fact is entitled to form his own judgment on the real evidence of a view, just as much as on the oral evidence of witnesses."[62]

3 Expert evidence as to negligence

Although there is no rule of law that expert evidence must be adduced in support of an allegation of professional negligence, it is in almost all cases practically essential. This follows from the fact that the subject matter is likely to be of a technical nature. It is also the case that the courts will be slow to find that a professional has been negligent without clear evidence demonstrating that the alleged act or omission caused the

---

[58] *Ibid.*, at 63.
[59] *Investors in Industry Commercial Properties Ltd.* v. *South Bedfordshire District Council* (1985) 5 Con. L.R. 1 at 32.
[60] *Ibid.*
[61] *Kaliszewska* v. *John Clague and Ptnrs.* (1984) 5 Con. L.R. 62.
[62] *Buckingham* v. *Daily News Ltd.* [1956] 2 Q.B. 534 at 531, *per* Denning L.J.

loss, and that an appropriate professional standard was not reached.[63] Certainly in a construction case it is almost inconceivable that a party would prove such an allegation in the absence of expert evidence in the courts, though an arbitrator might on occasion consider himself able so to find unassisted. Thus in an action in negligence against architects, evidence of what the architects "could reasonably have been expected to know and do in their position at the relevant time"[64] is not only admissible, but there would be "no question"[65] of a finding of professional negligence unless there was:

> "appropriate expert evidence to support the allegation that their conduct fell below the standard which might reasonably be expected of an ordinarily competent architect."[66]

There may be cases in which expert opinion is unnecessary because of the obvious nature of the act or omission, such as an ordinary dwelling without a front door.[67] Such cases, no doubt in any event fairly infrequent, are unlikely to be defended as to liability, so that the issue is not live at trial save as to quantum. The vast majority of cases have features which are in some respect unconventional, so that conventional and well known standards alone are insufficient. It would be "grossly unfair"[68] to architects if in cases relating to a special type of dwelling "the courts could without the normal evidence condemn a professional man."[69] Although again there is no rule of law or evidence which so provides, many tribunals would be unimpressed, by logical extension of the general practice, with evidence from a witness of lesser status or seniority in the relevant profession than the alleged tortfeasor, and it would be a difficult task to establish negligence upon the evidence of a generalist expert without specialist knowledge of the particular discipline concerned.

The courts will try each case upon the evidence as to professional standards, and not purport to lay down rules to be followed in future cases. Experts, and *a fortiori* the courts, cannot compose an unvarying list of factors to be taken into account in a particular expert operation or calculation, and the most that can usually be done is to list a number of relevant ones.[70] There may however be a generally accepted margin for error where numerical calculations are concerned.[71]

---

[63] For further discussion of this see Chap. 7, pp. 141–145.
[64] *Investors in Industry Commercial Properties* v. *South Beds. District Council* above n. 59, at 31.
[65] *Ibid.*
[66] *Ibid.*, at 32.
[67] *Worboys* v. *Acme Investments* (1969) 4 B.L.R. 133 at 139.
[68] *Ibid.*
[69] *Ibid.*
[70] See *Singer and Friedlander* v. *John D. Wood & Co.* (1977) 243 E.G. 212 at 213.
[71] *Ibid.*

There may be codes of practice published under the auspices of the government or one of the professional institutions. Breach by a professional of a relevant code establishes a strong prima facie case of negligence in most instances:

> "bearing in mind the function of codes, a design which departs substantially from them is prima facie a faulty design, unless it can be demonstrated that it conforms to an accepted engineering practice by rational analysis."[72]

The effect of a departure from a code would usually be that the burden of proof shifts, in practical evidential terms though not as a matter of law, to the defendant, who then, in the case of engineering design:

> "must show that the design is capable of rational analysis and is adequate and safe."[73]

This could only in practice be achieved with clear and persuasive expert evidence. Codes of practice may also be employed evidentially, not as setting an entire standard, but as demonstrating factors which should always be taken into account in particular circumstances. Thus it was held that a British Standard Code of Practice[74] should have put designers on notice that there would be problems of vibration in buildings of a particular kind.[75] It is however for the court (or arbitrator) to decide whether negligence is proven in the individual case:

> "other designers might have fallen short, too. It is for the judge to set the standard of what a competent designer could do."[76]

and this is particularly so, in relation to codes and other general standards, where a new method of construction is concerned.[77] The court will also be concerned not to rely too closely upon codes as indicators of negligence given the rapidly changing techniques in some fields of engineering. In negligence proceedings concerning the design of television masts, engineers had relied closely upon a Code of Practice relating to the "lattice" form of mast.[78] It was held inappropriate however in relation to the new "cylindrical" design of mast and this constituted a simple matter of negligence:

> "the error arose not from difficulty of calculation but from the omis-

---

[72] *Bevan Investments Ltd.* v. *Blackhall and Struthers* [1973] 2 N.Z.L.R. 45 at 66.
[73] *Ibid.*
[74] C.P. 117; Pt. 1, (1965).
[75] *Greaves and Co. Ltd.* v. *Baynham Meikle and Partners* [1975] 1 W.L.R. 1095.
[76] *Ibid.*, at 1102, *per* Lord Denning M.R.
[77] See *Ibid.*
[78] *I.B.A.* v. *E.M.I and B.I.C.C.* (1980) 14 B.L.R. 1.

sion of what seems to me to have been a simple piece of reasoning about known facts."[79]

While the court will be guided by, and usually must hear, evidence as to general professional practice, it is always for the court to set the standard itself. It:

> "is not necessarily bound by such evidence for the Court must retain its own freedom to conclude that the general practice of a particular profession falls below the standard required by the law."[80]

The court is placed in considerable difficulty where it takes the view that the general standard in the field, as demonstrated by the evidence, is too low, for the court must reach its decision upon the evidence. Ultimately, however, the court must decide.

Where evidence was adduced as to the general practice of architects if an obligation for periodic inspection or supervision is accepted, it was described as "useful and persuasive . . . [but] not of course decisive of the legal obligations which such a retainer as an architect imports."[81] In such a case:

> "evidence as to the ordinary practice of architects may materially assist a court in deciding what in a particular case should have been done to meet the requirement of due care in supervision. It is for the court to decide whether in the circumstances there was a lack of reasonable care."[82]

4 Expert evidence as to contractual obligations

Questions of contractual construction are of course, given the contract's status as a legal document, questions of law for the court. However the construction of the document may need to be considered in the light of the "factual matrix"[83] inhabited by the draftsmen or signatories, and expert evidence may be relevant as to this. It would be wrong in such circumstances to hear the question of contractual construction as a preliminary, and separate, issue, before the expert evidence in the case has been heard, as the exercise may then become "very nearly hypothetical."[84] Complex contracts with many non-legal technical terms may justify the adducing of expert evidence as to the meaning of such terms. Such meanings can usually be agreed.

---

[79] *Ibid.*, at 36.
[80] *McLaren Maycroft* v. *Fletcher* [1973] 2 N.Z.L.R. 100 at 108.
[81] *Florida Hotels Pty. Ltd.* v. *Mayo* [1965] 113 C.L.R. 588 at 593.
[82] *Ibid.*, at 601.
[83] *Reardon Smith Line* v. *Yngvar Hansen Tangen* [1976] 1 W.L.R. 989 at 997. See further Chap. 7, pp. 160–161.
[84] *Holland Dredging* v. *Dredging and Construction Co.* (1987) 37 B.L.R. 1 at 29.

E. QUANTUM OF DAMAGES

The need for expert evidence in support of a claim for damages in construction cases is dictated by the issues. In some breach of contract cases it may be possible to define the loss by virtue of the contractual terms, as with a liquidated damages clause for delay. More often however it is a matter of assessing evidentially the financial consequences of a particular breach of contract, or of duty in tort, and these require expert assessment by reference to the cost of rectification or some other measure of loss. The current law as to damages for negligent valuation makes it almost inevitable that expert evidence will be required as to loss in such cases.[85] Most claims for a *quantum meruit* or *quantum valebat* will require expert evidence, as the court will not know what rates are usual or reasonable, though an arbitrator might. Even though damages often cannot be accurately assessed, in that the court may be indulging in a fairly imprecise estimating exercise, in so far as expert evidence is adduced it must be strictly proved and shown to be admissible. Where damages based upon the likely revenue of a sports complex were in issue, it was wrong to admit hearsay evidence as to this.[86] Expert evidence may logically be admissible as to only part of the calculation exercise. Thus in a negligent surveyor's valuation case, it may be necessary to hear expert evidence as to the cost of repairs, but it would be for the judge, having heard this evidence, to go a stage further and consider whether a buyer would have reduced his offer for the house by exactly the cost of the repairs (*i.e.* the sum arrived at by the experts) or by some other amount which did not precisely reflect these costs.[87]

Delay A recurrent problem in the assessment of damages in construction cases is the appropriate method by which to assess the loss to a contractor occasioned by delay keeping him on site, or with his labour and plant tied up and unable to do other work, for a period longer than that stipulated by the contract. The usual method employed is the 'Hudson' formula, judicially approved in an English[88] and a Canadian decision.[89] It has long been recognised to be, though difficult to suggest a replacement for, incomplete in some respects. In particular it provides no method of determining the contribution to fixed overheads to be taken as

---

[85] See *e.g. Philips v. Ward* [1956] 1 W.L.R. 471; *Perry v. Sidney Phillips & Sons* [1982] 1 W.L.R. 1297.
[86] *Bevan v. Blackhall and Struthers (No. 2)* [1978] 2 N.Z.L.R. 97.
[87] *Fryer v. Bunney* (1982) 263 E.G. 158.
[88] *J. F. Finnegan Ltd. v. Sheffield City Council* (1988) 43 B.L.R. 124 at 134–136.
[89] *Ellis Don v. Parking Authority of Toronto* [1978] 21 B.L.R. 7.

the crucial figure in the otherwise arithmetical formula. Wallace[90] has suggested that the 'Eichleay' formula, used in the United States, may provide part of the solution, by incorporating a calculation to show the expenditure on fixed overheads during the original contract period. The percentage contribution of the contract in question is then calculated by setting it against the total of all the company's invoices over that period. This percentage could also be calculated by reference to contract prices (the contract in question set against all contract prices current during the original contract period).

Whichever arithmetical calculation is employed, expert evidence will usually be necessary to support the background assumptions upon which it is based, although an arbitrator may well have the knowledge to dispense with the need for it. In particular, unless the contractor can show by direct evidence that he had contracts available which he had to decline, evidence of the state of the market at the time is logically essential. It may also be advisable to have expert assistance as to what can properly be inferred from the contractor's accounts about its fixed overheads during the relevant period. Similar evidence may be necessary as to loss of profit, though this may be more of an accountancy exercise. Although the purpose of such formulas might be thought to be to provide a reasonably accurate method of calculation in circumstances where direct evidence is unavailable or scanty, in fact they raise as many evidential (and often expert evidential) questions as they dispense with. It may be that this cannot be avoided where parties proceed with construction works in good faith, on the premise that delay warranting compensation, other than liquidated damages,[91] will probably not occur, and therefore do not gather evidence as they proceed. The importance, however, of good site records, and committing as much as possible contemporaneously to writing, can never be over emphasised.

---

[90] I. N. Duncan Wallace, *Construction Contracts: Principles and Policies in Tort and Contract* (1986), pp. 128–130.

[91] Liquidated damages, unless the contract provides otherwise, are usually an exhaustive remedy for delay: see *Temloc Ltd.* v. *Errill Properties Ltd.* (1987) 39 B.L.R. 30.

CHAPTER 21

Patents

Patents proceedings require specific discussion for two principal reasons: first, because the pre-trial procedure in relation to the adducing of expert evidence and allied matters is subject to special rules, and secondly because many of the substantive questions are decided by reference to expert standards and knowledge, so that issues of admissibility are particular and of some importance. The main procedural provisions are contained in R.S.C. Order 104.

A. PRE-TRIAL PROCEDURE

1 Inspection

In many patents proceedings the need to be able to carry out inspections of items or processes in issue, and in some cases to carry out experiments upon them, is central to the evidence, both as a method of adducing matters of fact which one party would otherwise not have access to, and as a basis for the opinions of experts. Much of the evidence will be in the nature of expert evidence of fact: matters of pure observation which nevertheless require expertise for their comprehension.[1] Before the summons for directions is heard, application may be made under R.S.C. Order 29, rule 3,[2] but thereafter pursuant to R.S.C. Order 104,[3] for inspection. Inspection may be ordered as to anything which may be relevant to the proceedings, including such things as models if a party seeks to adduce them in evidence.[4] Where inspection is to be of an industrial or other process, the defendant may be required to operate the process by running machines or otherwise operating the process to facilitate proper observation.[5]

Secrecy A party will frequently be concerned to maintain secrecy in respect of an inspection, either in relation to the subject-matter in issue,

---

[1] See Chap. 1, p. 9
[2] See Chap. 4, pp. 80–81.
[3] R.S.C., Ord. 104, r. 14(2)(*h*); see also r. 11 and the notes thereto in the *Supreme Court Practice*.
[4] *British Celanese* v. *Courtaulds* (1933) 50 R.P.C. 63 at 80.
[5] *British Xylenite Co. Ltd.* v. *Fibrenyle Ltd.* [1959] R.P.C. 252.

or as to other items or processes present in the building where inspection takes place. The court often in such circumstances makes an order limiting the inspection to named individuals or classes of individuals. The fact that a process is likely to receive publicity in any event, possibly through the auspices of the Patent Office, may be relevant.[6] The judicial view has been expressed that the parties themselves should see the processes with their "own eyes,"[7] but where secrecy is a genuine concern this may only be justified if the party himself, or for example the managing director of a plaintiff company, can only properly give evidence with direct knowledge of the secret matter.[8] The correct approach is to balance the strict need for secrecy against the general principle of openness in litigation and the needs of the parties to adduce and challenge such evidence as they wish. The courts should thus:

> "direct disclosure to selected individuals upon terms aimed at securing that there will not be either use or further disclosure of the information in ways which might prejudice the Defendant."[9]

The aim must be to grant:

> "as full a degree of appropriate disclosure as will be consistent with adequate protection of any trade secret of the respondent."[10]

The court may be influenced by the possibility of enforcement, so that where it was proposed that a French scientist should perform experiments upon secret chemical materials, the court in refusing leave was influenced by the difficulties of enforcement abroad,[11] particularly as the party asserting the need for secrecy was satisfied that any named scientist in England should be employed.[12] An appropriate order for directions would be that inspection be carried out by one or two experts, possibly with the plaintiff and his lawyers,[13] with liberty to take samples, with an order that no disclosure be made of any part of the secret process, save that the plaintiff may be informed, without details being provided, of whether in the opinion of the experts there has been an infringement.[14] The court may decide to defer inspection until after trial of a preliminary issue if this may obviate the need for inspection, or affect its nature or

---

[6] *British Syphon Co. Ltd. v. Homewood* [1956] R.P.C. 225 at 227.
[7] *Flower v. Lloyd* [1876] W.N. 230.
[8] See *British Syphon v. Homewood*, above n. 6, at 227. See too *Swain v. Edlin-Sinclair Tyre Co.* (1903) 20 R.P.C. 435.
[9] *Warner-Lambert Co. v. Glaxo Laboratories Ltd* [1975] R.P.C. 354 at 356; affirmed in *Roussel Uclaf v. I.C.I. plc* [1989] R.P.C. 59.
[10] *Warner-Lambert v. Glaxo*, above n. 9, at 358.
[11] *Roussel Uclaf v. I.C.I.*, above n. 9.
[12] *Ibid.*
[13] See *e.g. Edler v. Victoria Press Manufacturing Co.* (1910) 27 R.P.C. 114.
[14] See *British Thomson-Houston v. Duram* (1920) 37 R.P.C. 121; *Coloured Asphalte Co. Ltd. v. British Asphalt and Bitumen Ltd* (1935) 53 R.P.C. 89.

extent.[15] If necessary the inspectors may be directed not to disclose trade secrets in relation to processes other that those in issue but situated at the relevant premises.[16]

It is in the nature of secret processes that a party suspecting a patent infringement may do so without direct evidence or full knowledge of the manner of its occurrence. Only inspection may confirm or undermine these suspicions. The court will order inspection where there appears to be a prima facie case of infringement, though the plaintiff has no particulars.[17] Mere belief or suspicion of infringement is not sufficient: there must be some prima facie evidence.[18] However the plaintiff may not have to assemble a full prima facie case in law, and the court may order inspection where it could bring a swift end to the action.[19] Presumably in many such cases, subject to secrecy limitations, the defendant would not object to the order. The court may also order the taking of samples.[20]

2 Experiments

R.S.C. Order 104, rule 12 provides that:

> "(1) Where a party desires to establish any fact by experimental proof he shall within 21 days after service of the lists of documents under rule 11 serve on the other party a notice stating the facts which he desires to establish and giving full particulars of the experiments proposed to establish them.
> (2) A party upon whom a notice under paragraph (1) is served shall, within 21 days after service thereof, serve upon the other party a notice stating in respect of each fact whether or not he admits it.
> (3) Where any fact which a party desires to establish by experimental proof is not admitted he may at the hearing of the summons for directions apply for directions in respect of such experiments."

It is important that the notice makes as precise a scientific statement of the proposed experiment as is possible,[21] though an application to amend may be sympathetically received if experiments bring further facts to light.[22] Otherwise there is seldom good reason for not including all relevant matters in the notice.[23] A party may be permitted to serve out of time if no application is swiftly made to enforce time limits.[24]

---

[15] *Mc Dougall* v. *Partington* (1890) 7 R.P.C. 351.
[16] *British Celanese Ltd.* v. *Courtaulds Ltd.* (1933) 50 R.P.C. 63 at 80.
[17] *Edler* v. *Victoria Press Manufacturing Co.*, above n. 13.
[18] *Wahl* v. *Buhler-Miag (England) Ltd.* [1979] F.S.R. 183.
[19] *British Xylenite Co. Ltd.* v. *Fibrenyle Ltd.*, above n. 5, at 263.
[20] R.S.C. Ord. 29, r. 3.
[21] *Van der Lely* v. *Watveare Overseas Ltd.* [1982] F.S.R. 122.
[22] *Ibid.*
[23] See *Oak Manufacturing Co.* v. *Plessey Co. Ltd.* (1950) 67 R.P.C. 71.
[24] *Reeve Bros* v. *Lewis Reed and Co.* [1968] R.P.C. 452.

There is no definition in the rules of the term "experiment". It has been said to be:

> "a test or trial of something brought into existence while the action is in progress and relating to some issue in the action,"[25]

and the notion that it must have been produced for the purposes of the action has received judicial support elsewhere.[26] However it appears to denote more than a straightforward scientific analysis, so that while the making of a pipe for the action would be an experiment, mere analysis of the chemical content of the pipe would not.[27]

Although one purpose of the rules as to inspection and experiments is to save time and costs, they can sometimes have the opposite effect,[28] and the court will be vigilant to limit the number and type of experiments adducible in evidence to those of which notice has been given.[29] The particular order may reflect factors such as the oppression caused to the defendant by the existence of an interlocutory injunction.[30] The taxing master, in addition to having a discretion as to the costs of experiments conducted before proceedings were commenced, may make adverse orders in relation to superfluous or inadmissible experiments conducted during the proceedings.[31]

3 Directions as to expert evidence

The general provisions of R.S.C. Order 38, Part IV in relation to expert evidence do not apply to patents proceedings.[32] R.S.C. Order 104, rule 13 provides that:

> "Where a party intends to adduce oral expert evidence he shall not later than 14 days before the hearing of the summons for directions under rule 14 give notice to every other party and to the Court of the name of each expert he intends to call as witness.
> This rule is without prejudice to the power of the Court to restrict the number of expert witnesses."

Furthermore by R.S.C. Order 104, rule 14(2) directions may be given, *inter alia*:

> " . . . (e) for the taking by affidavit of evidence relating to matters

---

[25] *International de Lavaud* v. *Stanton Ironworks Co. Ltd.* (1941) 58 R.P.C. 177 at 198.
[26] *British Celanese* v. *Courtaulds Ltd.*, above n. 16, at 84.
[27] *International de Lavaud* v. *Stanton*, above n. 25, at 198–199.
[28] *Ibid.*, at 197.
[29] *British Thomson-Houston Co. Ltd.* v. *Tungstalite Ltd.* (1938) 55 R.P.C. 280 at 285. See also *Re White's Patent* [1957] R.P.C. 405 at 407 for form of order.
[30] *American Cyanamid Co.* v. *Ethicon Ltd.* [1978] R.P.C. 667.
[31] *Re Nossen's Letter Patent* [1969] 1 W.L.R. 638.
[32] R.S.C. Ord. 104, r. 14(4).

requiring expert knowledge, and for the filing of such affidavits and the service of copies thereof on the other parties;

(f) for the holding of a meeting of such experts as the judge may specify, for the purpose of producing a joint report on the state of the relevant art;

(g) for the exchanging of experts' reports, in respect of those matters on which they are not agreed . . . ".

While the provisions as to expert evidence are not therefore identical to those in Order 38, they are broad enough to permit a similar range of orders. There is nothing to prevent experts agreeing at a meeting under rule 14(2)(f) a wider range of matters than those relevant to 'the state of the relevant art." It appears to be recognised in patent actions, as it is now formally recognised by R.S.C. Order 38, Part IV, that mutual disclosure of experts' reports will often be in the general interest,[33] subject to the need for confidentiality in relation to secret processes. There is little reason why there should not in most cases, where there is agreement, be an agreed statement as to the scientific background, as contemplated by rule 14(2)(f),[34] and, if this is of assistance, as to background technical matters in dispute.[35] A specimen order for directions incorporating all questions of expert evidence, inspection and experiments has been promulgated,[36] though it is to be used only as a guide.

4 Court Experts

There is provision under R.S.C. Order 104, rule 15[37] for the appointment of a "scientific adviser" to assist the judge as to technical matters, either by sitting with him at trial, or:

"by inquiring and reporting on any question of fact or of opinion not involving a question of law or construction."[38]

Where this latter course is taken the appropriate rules as to court experts under R.S.C. Order 40[39] apply. There is no provision excluding the appointment of a Court Expert proper under R.S.C. Order 40 in patent cases, so that the appointment may be under either Order.

---

[33] *Hughes* v. *Ingersoll-Rand Co. Ltd.* [1977] F.S.R. 406. In some patent matters however exchange is unnecessary because the witnesses will form their opinions, quite properly, during the hearing of the case.
[34] See also *Olin Matheson Chemical Corp.* v. *Biorex Laboratories Ltd.* [1970] R.P.C. 157.
[35] *Valensi* v. *British Radio Corp. Ltd.* [1972] R.P.C. 373. The parties here agreed that it should be referred to though not agreed.
[36] *Practice Direction* [1973] 1 W.L.R. 1425.
[37] Pursuant to the Supreme Court Act 1981, s.70(3).
[38] R.S.C. Ord. 104, 15(1)(b).
[39] R.S.C. Ord. 40, rr. 2, 3, 4 and 6.

Such appointments are not frequently made, but perhaps more often in patent than in other proceedings, and the court must in patent actions consider the necessity or otherwise of making such an appointment.[40] In those isolated reported examples of such an appointment it has been seen as a beneficial measure,[41] and it has been emphasised that the court should obtain "the man best qualified to assist."[42] There is little sense in appointing as an adviser to the judge someone who is not as eminent and specialised an expert as the witnesses or the representatives of the parties themselves. The court may make the appointment at an early stage, well before trial, if it is clear even without seeing all the documents that it will be a complex matter warranting such advice.

The judge may make an appointment of his own motion, unlike the position under R.S.C. Order 40, which provides only for the parties to make application. The court would be unlikely act contrary to the wishes of the parties where the legal and factual issues were clear,[43] and may well if an adviser is appointed confine his task to that of advising at trial, rather than reporting and thus perhaps duplicating the work of the expert witnesses.[44] If the report is prepared, the judge must read it, even if its conclusions are rejected.[45] There is also provision for the appointment of assessors,[46] and this has been done in patent actions,[47] though it seldom is. Section 70(3) of the Supreme Court Act 1981 does not preclude the possibility of appointment of an "assessor" rather than a "scientific adviser," but it appears to be assumed that it is the latter, if any, who would be appointed in modern patents matters.

B. ADMISSIBILITY

The Patent Court is in the nature of an expert tribunal and questions of admissibility and evaluation of expert evidence must be treated in that context. The Court of Appeal, usually constituted of judges with little or no experience of patents matters, will hesitate even longer than in other cases before overturning the trial judge's findings on "jury-questions,"

---

[40] R.S.C. Ord. 104, r. 14(3)(b).
[41] *Valensi* v. *British Radio Corp. Ltd* [1971] F.S.R. 403.
[42] *Ibid.*
[43] See *General Tire and Rubber Co. Ltd.* v. *Firestone Tyre and Rubber Co. Ltd.* [1972] R.P.C. 457 at 471.
[44] *Valensi* v. *B.R.C.*, above n. 41.
[45] *Non-Drip Measure Co. Ltd.* v. *Strangers Ltd.* (1941) 59 R.P.C. 1 at 24.
[46] Supreme Court Act 1981, s.70.
[47] See *Marconi* v. *Helsby Wireless Telegraph Co. Ltd.* (1914) 31 R.P.C. 121; *Mullard* v. *Philco* (1935) 52 R.P.C. 261.

and would need very convincing evidence to do so.[48] Furthermore the Court of Appeal is at a considerable disadvantage where the trial judge himself observed tests and experiments being conducted.[49]

It is not possible to make a definitive list of those issues upon which expert evidence is or is not admissible, as judicial views in some areas have been somewhat inconsistent or, more often, have developed over time. The courts in previous eras did not hesitate to make the attempt. Thus in *Brooks v. Steele and Currie*,[50] Lindley L.J. expressed the view that:

> "The nature of the invention must be obtained from the Specification, the interpretation of which is for the Judge, and not for any expert. The Judge may, and indeed generally must be assisted by expert evidence to explain technical terms, to show the practical working of machinery described or drawn, and to point out what is old and what is new in the Specification. Expert evidence is also admissible, and is often required to show the particulars in which an alleged invention has been used by an alleged infringer, and the real importance of whatever differences there may be between the Plaintiff's inventions and whatever is done by the Defendant."[51]

Despite this, Lindley L.J. was concerned that the reality was different,[52] and that experts were often permitted to trespass into the forbidden areas in theory preserved for the judge alone. *Terrell*[53] expresses the general view that expert evidence is admissible as to the intelligibility and sufficiency of the specification to a competent technician, novelty, utility, the state of common knowledge in the art and the meaning of technical terms. It is though inadmissible on questions relating to the degree of any of these issues, obviousness and whether there has in fact been an infringement. This is satisfactory as a general statement, but requires specific analysis as to the questions of construction of the specification and the relationship between the concept of obviousness and the state of common general knowledge.

1 Meaning of the specification

The early cases generally support the views of Lindley L.J. cited above, in attempting to confine the use of expert evidence quite rigorously, where the language of the specification is concerned, to the meaning of individ-

---

[48] *Johns-Manville* [1967] R.P.C. 479 at 496.
[49] *A.A.A.S. fur A.A.S. v. London Aluminium Co. Ltd.* (1922) 39 R.P.C. 296 at 309.
[50] (1897) 14 R.P.C. 46.
[51] *Ibid.*, at 73.
[52] *Ibid.*, at 73.
[53] *Terrell on Patents* (1979) at para. 14.138.

ual technical terms.[54] This is because the meaning of the specification, both in its intention and objectively, is an ultimate issue which the judge must decide. This task of explaining technical terms was expanded upon by Neville J., in *Crosfield* v. *Techno-Chemical Laboratories*,[55] thus:

> "expert evidence ... is required for the purpose of explaining words, or terms of science or art, appearing in the documents which have to be construed by the Court, or to inform the Court in case the import of a word or phrase differs from its popular meaning."[56]

The expert should not therefore answer the question "what is the invention the patentee claims by his specification?"[57] Neville J. took the view that expert evidence on this question added nothing to the factual evidence because an expert would answer the question in the same way as would any other person "who possessed his knowledge of the technical meaning of the words employed,"[58] so that once the judge was armed with that limited information he was in an equally good position to construe the document, provided that any necessary scientific background material was imparted to him.[59]

Perhaps the definitive early statement of the position was that of Lord Tomlin in *British Celanese* v. *Courtaulds Ltd.*,[60] who repeated the fears expressed by Lindley L.J. some 38 years earlier that despite the authorities experts were regularly being permitted by judges to express views as to the more general sense of the specification. He reinforced the restrictive approach:

> "The area of territory in which in cases of this kind an expert witness may legitimately move is not doubtful. He is entitled to give evidence as to the state of the art at any given time. He is entitled to explain the meaning of any technical terms used in the art. He is entitled to say whether in his opinion that which is described in the specification on a given hypothesis as to its meaning is capable of being carried into effect by a skilled worker. He is entitled to say what at a given time to him as skilled in the art a given piece of apparatus or a given sentence on any given hypothesis as to its meaning would have taught or suggested to him. He is entitled to say whether in his opinion a particular operation in connection with the art could be carried out and generally to give any explanation required as to facts of a scientific kind.

---

[54] *Gadd* v. *Mayor of Manchester* (1892) 67 L.T. 569 at 582.
[55] (1913) 29 T.L.R. 378.
[56] *Ibid.*, at 379.
[57] *Badische* v. *Levinstein* (1887) 12 App.Cas. 710 at 717–718.
[58] *Crosfield*, above n. 55, at 379.
[59] *Ibid.*
[60] (1935) 152 L.T. 537.

> He is not entitled to say nor is counsel entitled to ask him what the specification means, nor does the question become any more admissible if it takes the form of asking him as an engineer or as a chemist. Nor is he entitled to say whether any given step or alteration is obvious, that being a question for the court."[61]

Whether pursuant to principle, or by way of reluctant but resigned concession to actual practice, more recent decisions appear to have relaxed the rigorous approach of the early authorities. Graham J. has assumed that a technical statement in the specification may extend to phrases, sentences and even paragraphs,[62] and it might in some cases be a somewhat casuistic exercise to distinguish between permitting expert evidence upon the meaning of a number of such phrases, sentences of paragraphs in the specification and simply expressing an opinion as to its entire technical meaning. Such a view might be reinforced by reference to Lord Diplock's explanation that the construction of a specification requires a purposive, rather than a purely literal, interpretation.[63] The trend, if such it be, away from the early restrictive approach has been regretted,[64] but it is perhaps too early to say that the dicta of Lindley L.J. and Lord Tomlin no longer represent the true position, although European developments may tend to hasten change.[65]

Expert evidence is necessary however, where two specifications appear to refer to the same chemical compound, though their meanings have changed over time:[66]

> "in all cases . . . where the two documents profess to describe an external thing, the identity of signification between the two documents containing the same description, must belong to the province of evidence and not to the province of construction."[67]

Further by contrast with written documents such as specifications, a photograph, or presumably any pictorial representation of a technical nature, may be explained by experts.[68] Lawyers are not experts in the reading or interpretation of photographs, and:

> "the question is what the eye of the man with appropriate engineering skill and experience would see in the photograph."[69]

---

[61] *Ibid.*, at 543.
[62] *American Cyanamid v. Ethicon* [1979] R.P.C. 215 at 252.
[63] *Catnic Components Ltd. v. Hill and Smith Ltd.* [1982] R.P.C. 183 at 243.
[64] See e.g. *Encyclopedia of U.K. and European Patent Law*, para. 3–311.
[65] See European Patent Convention, art. 69; Patents Act 1977, s.125(3).
[66] *Bett v. Menzies* [1862] 10 H.L.C. 117.
[67] *Ibid.*, at 153–154.
[68] *Van Der Lely N.V. v. Bamford's Ltd.* [1963] R.P.C. 61.
[69] *Ibid.*, at 71, *per* Lord Reid.

2 Obviousness and the question of common general knowledge

It is clear in principle that the questions of obviousness and of common general knowledge, though inextricably linked, are to be distinguished by the fact that the former is a legal term for the court, while the latter is a concept to be decided upon evidence which may very well need to be of an expert nature. The court will consider obviousness in the round, not submitting to the "step-by-step" approach which argues that if each of a number of stages of the "invention" process was a straightforward and obvious one to a practitioner in the field, then the entire process must also have been so.[70]

Experts may clearly give evidence as to the state of common general knowledge in the art at the relevant time, either by reference to their own knowledge, or usually more persuasively by reference to what was known by others, given that the "skilled craftsman" test is the one generally applied, so that a highly qualified specialist witness could not be said to be typical. The general liberty of a party to adduce such evidence is not restricted by a limited order as to disclosure of documents.[71]

Any evidence of a group or general opinion will be particularly persuasive as to common general knowledge. Evidence that scientific opinion at the time, to the effect that it was not possible to achieve the result in question by the means in question, will tend strongly to show an inventive step.[72] However opinion, and opinion as to opinion, is, however apparently universal, not as satisfactory as clear fact. Thus the court may place more reliance upon the actual practice at the material time than on the expert opinion adduced before it, for example as to the temperature at which a process should be conducted.[73] This too conforms more closely to the skilled craftsman standard, and for the same reason the court may prefer evidence as to what students of science know by contrast with the knowledge of distinguished scientists.[74]

In addition to evidence of practice at the time, a party has been permitted to procure a workman of skill in the field through the labour exchange and ask him to weld according to the specification, as evidence of the sufficiency of the instructions contained in it.[75] Such a method of adducing evidence might also be indicative of knowledge. The behaviour

---

[70] *Technograph Printed Circuits Ltd. v. Mills and Rockley Electronics Ltd.* [1972] R.P.C. 346 at 372.
[71] *Aluma Systems Inc. v. Hunnebeck GmbH* [1982] F.S.R. 239.
[72] *Douglas Packing Co. v. W. Evans & Co. Ltd.* (1929) 46 R.P.C. 493 at 507–508.
[73] *British Thomson-Houston v. Helsby* (1924) 41 R.P.C. 345 at 407.
[74] *Automatic Coil Winder Co. Ltd. v. Taylor Electrical Instruments Ltd.* (1943) 60 R.P.C. 111 at 119. See also *John Wright v. General Gas Appliances Ltd.* (1928) 46 R.P.C. 169 at 177–178.
[75] *A.A.A.S. v. London Aluminium Co.* (1920) 37 R.P.C. 153.

of the parties, themselves skilled in the field, is admissible and on occasion of great weight, as where employees of the patentor who denied an inventive step were found to have claimed at an earlier stage that they had themselves invented the alleged invention.[76] Simplicity is not of particular weight *per se*: many new combinations of old components appear simple in retrospect.[77]

Expert witnesses or others may adduce publications as evidence of common general knowledge. Other patent specifications may be adduced as part of such knowledge,[78] though they would not be relevant if not widely circulated.[79] Foreign patent specifications are relevant if shown to be generally known.[80] Professional and technical journals and papers are admissible, but not if:

> "in ordinary probability they would not be known to competent members of [the relevant] trade or profession."[81]

Litigation on this issue tends to reveal documents which are the outcome of a lengthy search or within the knowledge of a particular expert witness, but they are often misleading as to common general knowledge at the relevant time.[82]

3 Scientific background material

Whatever the issue, so long as matters of scientific or technical difficulty are involved, an expert may always assist the court by explaining the scientific background, thus permitting compehension of the technical issues in the case.[83] The background may be agreed or not.

---

[76] *Vickers* v. *Siddell* (1890) 7 R.P.C. 293 at 304.
[77] *Ibid.*, at 305.
[78] *Sutcliffe* v. *Abbott* (1902) 20 R.P.C. 50 at 55.
[79] *Campbell* v. *Hopkins* (1933) 50 R.P.C. 213.
[80] *Clark* v. *Adie* (1877) 2 App.Cas. 423.
[81] *British Ore Concentration Syndicate Ltd.* v. *Minerals Separation Ltd.* (1909) 26 R.P.C. 124 at 138.
[82] *Ibid.*
[83] See the dicta of Lindley L.J. and Lord Tomlin cited at pp. 376 and 377 above.

CHAPTER 22

Matrimonial and Other Proceedings Involving Children

A. WELFARE REPORTS

1 Ordering the report

The ordering by the court of welfare reports will be seriously considered where any substantial long-term decision is to be made in relation to children, and sometimes in relation to interim access or other short-term decisions. Although the parties may make representations as to such reports, and may frequently concur in supporting their preparation pursuant to an order, the court may act of its own motion. The High Court in wardship matters acts pursuant to its inherent paternal jurisdiction. The High Court and county courts in divorce proceedings may order welfare reports by rule 95(1) of the Matrimonial Causes Rules 1977:

> "A judge or the registrar may at any time refer to a court welfare officer for investigation and report any matter arising in matrimonial proceedings which concerns the welfare of a child."

There is also provision in certain circumstances for a registrar to order such a report upon application, before the substantive matter comes on for hearing, where all parties agree.[1] As to custody proceedings under the Guardianship of Minors Act 1971 and the Guardianship Act 1973 it is provided by section 6(1) of the latter Act that:

> "If the court dealing with an application under section 5 or 9 of the Guardianship of Minors Act 1971 or section 1(3) or 3(3) of this Act requests a local authority to arrange for an officer of the authority to make to the court a report, orally or in writing, with respect to any specified matter, (being a matter appearing to the court to be relevant to the application), or requests a probation officer to make such a report to the court, it shall be the duty of the local authority or probation officer to comply with the request."

There is also provision for a single justice in magistrates' court proceedings under the Acts of 1971 and 1973 to request a report before the hearing of the substantive application.[2] Where proceedings are in a

[1] Matrimonial Causes Rules 1977 (S.I. 1977 No. 344), r. 95(2).
[2] Guardianship Act 1973, s.6(6).

magistrates' court under the Domestic Proceedings and Magistrates' Courts Act 1978 the court, or a single justice before the substantive hearing,[3] may request reports as follows, by section 12(3) of that Act:

> "Where the court on such an application is of the opinion that it has not sufficient information to decide whether to exercise its powers under . . . sections 8 to 10 and, if so, in what manner, the court may, at any stage of the proceedings on that application, request a local authority to arrange for an officer of the authority to make to the court a report, orally or in writing, with respect to any such matter as the court may specify (being a matter appearing to the court to be relevant to the decision) or may request a probation officer to make such a report to the court; and it shall be the duty of the local authority or probation officer to comply with the request."

Although the powers are broadly to the same effect, it can be seen that the Matrimonial Causes Rules grant a very general discretion, while the Guardianship Act 1973 and the Domestic Proceedings and Magistrates' Courts Act 1978 both require the information requested to be "relevant." The latter Act also requires the court to take the view that it "has not sufficient information" upon which to make the substantive orders sought. This clearly entails the court, having considered the question, making a specific finding as to the inadequacy of available information without such a report.[4]

It will of course seldom be the case that a party will seek to prevent the obtaining of a report, save where the delay involved is clearly detrimental, either to children involved, or to the prospects of success of the party which seeks to upset the status quo. Parties are usually aware that an unwillingness fully to co-operate with the gathering of such evidence for the court will not assist their case. It has been said by the Court of Appeal that it is desirable to have such a report in "almost all" custody cases.[5] The practice, however, of almost invariably ordering updated reports in cases being appealed has been criticised, and the Court of Appeal will only order such reports where they are clearly necessary and the decision of the court at first instance is plainly wrong.[6]

2 Preparation of the report

The court should attempt to specify the matters upon which reports are to be made, though the welfare officer is at liberty to bring such matters

---

[3] Domestic Proceedings and Magistrates' Courts Act 1978, s.12(9).
[4] Such requests have become almost automatic in some courts.
[5] *Southgate* v. *Southgate* (1978) 8 Fam.Law 246.
[6] *M. v. M.* (1989) Fam.Law 393.

as the court should have in mind to its attention.[7] The parties should of course be co-operative with the welfare officer, who will need access to all relevant information. In divorce proceedings there is express provision for the court file to be made available if necessary,[8] while in other proceedings the court will exercise its discretion. The reporter should make as full an investigation of the relevant facts as is possible in the circumstances, and reports confined to what the welfare officer was told by the parties are "useless."[9] The investigation should not be confined to interviews and meetings in the reporter's office, but should include visits to the parties in their homes,[10] where possible with the relevant children present. The reporter should always attempt to see the children with each of the parents in custody applications.[11] The reporter must:

> "investigate the circumstances of the child or children concerned and all the important figures in their lives so as to provide the court with reliable factual observations and factual details which will be the basis on which the judge can form his opinion."[12]

The report must take a balanced view of the facts, and consider them from the point of view of both parents.[13] This implies the need to do more than merely state the facts and then a conclusion, but to set out the reporter's reasoning, looking at matters from both sides. In preparing the report, the officer should confine himself to steps necessary for the proper preparation of his report. It is wrong for the court, for instance, to instruct a welfare officer to advise the natural father to accept his responsibilities to his children.[14] Likewise he should not generally take it upon himself to engage in such extraneous advice or assistance, other than in an incidental manner, though he may be asked for example to supervise access if no-one else is available.[15]

A particular problem which has arisen is the difficulty of preparing an investigative report for the court while simultaneously engaging in conciliation between the parties. In proceedings under the Domestic Proceedings and Magistrates' Courts Act 1978 there are specific provisions as to the admissibility in evidence of statements made by the parties during meetings with a probation officer "with a view to the reconciliation" of the parties.[16] The higher courts have however disapproved of the practice

---

[7] *Practice Direction* [1981] 1 W.L.R. 1162.
[8] Matrimonial Causes Rules 1977, rule 95(3)(a).
[9] *Re H. (Conciliation: Welfare Reports)* [1986] 1 F.L.R. 476.
[10] *Ibid.*, and see *Merriman* v. *Hardy* (1987) 151 J.P.N. 526; *Clarkson* v. *Winkley* (1987) 151 J.P.N. 526.
[11] *Edwards* v. *Edwards* [1986] 1 F.L.R. 187.
[12] *Scott* v. *Scott* [1986] 2 F.L.R. 320 at 322, *per* Dillon L.J.
[13] *H.* v. *H. (Child Custody)* (1984) Fam.Law 112.
[14] *Re A. (A Minor)* (1979) 10 Fam.Law 114.
[15] See *Practice Direction* [1980] 1 W.L.R. 334.
[16] Domestic Proceedings and Magistrates' Courts Act 1978, s.12(7).

of combining the two functions in one person, and have taken the view that an officer who has been or becomes involved in conciliation between the parties must not prepare the report for the court.[17] A court welfare department which ignores this has "misconceived its function."[18] If conciliation is attempted and fails, the conciliator must assign the task of preparing the report to another welfare officer.[19] A *Practice Direction* has been issued in relation to this question,[20] and it has since been held to apply equally in the magistrates' courts.[21] It provides that:

> "A Judge or Registrar, before ordering an inquiry and report by a Court Welfare Officer, should, where local conciliation facilities exist, consider whether the case is a suitable one for attempts to be made to settle any of the issues by the conciliation process, and if so, a direction to this effect should be included in the order. If conciliation fails, any report which is ordered must be made by an officer who did not act as a conciliator.
>
> Where the court directs an enquiry and report by a Welfare Officer, it is the function of the Welfare Officer to assist the court by investigating the circumstances of the child, or children, concerned and the important figures in their lives, to report what he sees and hears, to offer the court his assessment of the situation and, where appropriate to make a recommendation. In such circumstances, it is not the role of the Welfare Officer to attempt conciliation although he may encourage the parties to settle their differences if the likelihood of a settlement arises during the course of his enquiries."

It is clearly therefore the duty of the welfare officer to confine himself to the particular task in hand, whichever it be, and not to attempt to combine the two. It is also wrong for the court to place in the hands of the welfare officer decisions as to access[22] or arrangements for the children's daily care.[23] The principles as to the inclusion of hearsay in welfare reports are discussed below.

Delay The preparation of a welfare report, if it is to be thoroughly performed, will involve delay in the court proceedings. Apart from the workload of individual welfare officers, appointments may have to be made with third parties, and the welfare officer may have to time his visits to coincide with access periods. Delays of a few months may have a very real effect on the merits of the case. Despite this however, it is

---

[17] *Re H.*, above n. 9.
[18] *Scott v. Scott*, above n. 12, at 322.
[19] *Clarkson v. Winkley*, above n. 10; *cf. Merriman v. Hardy*, above n. 10.
[20] [1986] 2 F.L.R. 171. See also *Practice Direction* [1983] 1 W.L.R. 1420.
[21] *Clarkson v. Winkley*, above n. 10.
[22] *Orford v. Orford* (1979) 10 Fam.Law 14.
[23] *Kirkham-Woodcraft v. Kirkham-Woodcraft* (1984) Fam.Law 57.

important to avoid if at all possible the need for reports by different welfare officers, which is usually less satisfactory than a report by one officer,[24] albeit delayed.

It may be appropriate to request a short interim report, if necessary adjourning briefly for its preparation,[25] where it is clear that the main report and hearing will not be concluded for some time. Where the delay is likely to be very substantial, for instance of the order of 10 or 11 months, it "may well" be better to hear the case without a report,[26] and where a delay of nine months was experienced it was stated that the court should either have arranged for quicker preparation of the report or proceeded in its absence.[27] The test where the court must choose between adjourning a fixed hearing or proceeding without a delayed welfare report is always the welfare of the children, and the court should if necessary start the case without one, but be prepared to adjourn in mid-hearing if it was not possible to proceed without the report.[28]

Disclosure of reports The entire report should be disclosed to the parties.[29] In divorce proceedings, the welfare officer must file his report on completion of the investigation, whereupon the registrar sends a copy to the parties.[30] The officer can apply for directions at any time[31] and should be notified of the date of the hearing by the registrar.[32] In magistrates' court proceedings under the Guardianship of Minors Act 1971 and the Guardianship Act 1973 the officer either reports orally to the court, or supplies written copies before or during a hearing of the application.[33] It is usual for the reports to be made available to the parties in wardship and custody matters in the High Court and county courts. The rules here described clearly provide no guarantee that a party has notice of the contents of the report before the substantive hearing, and indeed it remains the fact that in many courts the report does not become available until the morning of the full hearing. Where it contains controversial matters this is regrettable, for a number of reasons. A party may not have a proper opportunity to give detailed instructions to legal advisers on matters which are not accepted. Witnesses may need to be called to rebut allegations made.

It is always open to a party to request an adjournment, and in appropriate circumstances he should of course do so. In reality there is con-

---

[24] *Practice Note* (1973) 117 S. J. 88.
[25] *Re W; Re L (Minors: Interim Custody)* [1987] 2 F.L.R. 67.
[26] *Cafell* v. *Cafell* [1984] F.L.R. 169 at 171.
[27] *Plant* v. *Plant* (1983) 4 F.L.R. 305.
[28] *Re H. (Minors) (Welfare Reports)* [1990] 2 F.L.R. 172 at 178.
[29] *Webb* v. *Webb* [1986] 1 F.L.R. 462, C.A.
[30] Matrimonial Causes Rules 1977, r. 95(3)(*b*).
[31] *Ibid.*, r. 95(3)(*c*).
[32] *Ibid.*, r. 95(3)(*d*).
[33] Guardianship Act 1973, s.6(2)(*a*).

siderable pressure not to adjourn, both in order to avoid further uncertainty for the children, and because the status quo may become more difficult to upset the longer it continues. The pressure on court lists also often makes it impossible to adjourn for a short period only. The practice of disclosing reports on the day of the hearing has been described as "unfortunate . . . amounting to unfairness."[34] Copies of reports should be supplied by the court to a party requiring them for the purposes of an appeal.[35] Save in respect of the parties and the court reports are confidential and should be marked as such.[36]

3 Welfare officer attending the hearing to give evidence

In magistrates' court proceedings a party may require the welfare officer to attend the hearing and give evidence, if the court does not exercise its discretion to do so. The parties may adduce evidence upon matters thus raised.[37] In the High Court and county courts a party who wishes to hear evidence from the welfare officer should make application to the registrar for an order to this effect, or if little time is available inform the officer himself that the judge will be asked to secure his attendance at court, and in lengthy cases a convenient date and time for his attendance should be agreed.[38] The welfare officer is an officer of the court, not a witness, but if he is required to give evidence he can expect no special treatment,[39] and may be cross-examined as may any expert witness. The right to question the welfare officer is "an important right in adversarial proceedings."[40] Furthermore the court should be particularly concerned to elucidate the welfare officer's views in evidence where it is minded to depart from his recommendations.[41] As an officer of the court a welfare officer cannot, it has been held, be compelled to give evidence by a party in High Court and county court proceedings,[42] in which there is no statutory right to require this, and:

> "they may or may not give evidence and submit themselves to cross-examination."[43]

It is wholly a matter for the judge's discretion, though this would only exceptionally be exercised so as to prevent all cross-examination. It is

---

[34] *Edwards v. Edwards* [1986] 1 F.L.R. 187 at 196.
[35] C. v. C (1982) 126 S.J. 243; *Clode v. Clode* (1982) 3 F.L.R. 360.
[36] *Practice Direction* [1984] 1 W.L.R. 446.
[37] Guardianship Act 1973, s.6(3); Domestic Proceedings and Magistrates' Courts Act 1978, s.12(5) and (6).
[38] *Practice Direction* [1981] 1 W.L.R. 1162.
[39] *Edwards v. Edwards*, above n. 34.
[40] W. v. W. [1988] 2 F.L.R. 505 at 514.
[41] *Ibid.*, at 514.
[42] *Cadman v. Cadman* (1982) 3 F.L.R. 275.
[43] *Ibid.*, at 277.

wrong to permit the appearance of injustice by the judge conducting a private conversation with the welfare officer, and this will usually invalidate the court's decision, though there might be exceptional circumstances in which it was necessary.[44]

4 Departing from the welfare officer's recommendation

The decision in proceedings concerning children is always one for the court. However the recommendations of welfare officers do carry particular weight, and should not lightly be rejected. If the judge does depart from such recommendations, he should always give his reasons for doing so, as should justices.[45] There may be a number of reasons why the judge (or justices) chooses not to adopt the recommendations:

> "He may assess the facts differently; he may have reached a professional view of the impact of these facts upon the welfare of the child; he may have been given evidence of matters not available to the welfare officers; he may even have observed attitudes and behaviour of the parties when they appeared before him which would lead him to differ. But, whatever the reasons are, it is desirable that they should be given."[46]

Matters may emerge in cross-examination of the parties which the welfare officer was not able to uncover in his own investigation, and this would justify the court in coming to a different view.[47] It is particularly important that the court should examine the welfare officer in court where it proposes to reject his recommendations.[48] His views must not simply be ignored. The court may reject but it must consider his views.[49] If the case is appealed the Court of Appeal will not interfere with the findings of a judge who has rejected the welfare officer's recommendation, if he has given sound reasons based upon evidence adduced before him in court.[50]

5 Independent social workers

It is open to parties to legal proceedings to call such witnesses as they wish to in support of their case, so long as the evidence that is adduced is relevant, and if the witness is an expert, he has the appropriate expertise.

---

[44] *H. v. H.* (1983) 3 F.L.R. 119; *Re B. (A Minor)* [1990] 1 F.L.R. 300 at 303.
[45] *Stephenson v. Stephenson* [1985] F.L.R. 1140. See too *Clark v. Clark* (1970) 114 S.J. 381 and *Dickinson v. Dickinson* (1982) 13 Fam.Law 174; *Foxon v. Foxon* [1981] C.L.Y. 1778.
[46] *W. v. W.*, above n. 40, at 511.
[47] *J. v. J.* (1978) 9 Fam.Law 91.
[48] *Foxon v. Foxon*, above n. 46. See also *W. v. W.*, above n. 40, at 514.
[49] *Hutchinson v. Hutchinson* (1981) 2 F.L.R. 167 at 170.
[50] *Leete v. Leete and Stevens* [1984] Fam.Law. 21, C.A.

In cases concerning children however the policy of the legislation, and of the courts in so far as their procedures are self-imposed, is that the court's primary means of access to expert advice on the generality of the case is to request a welfare officer to report to the court having conducted an investigation.

Frequently the only convincing way in which the opinion of a welfare officer can be challenged is by adducing the expert evidence of an independent social worker to rebut it. However the courts have discouraged the calling of such witnesses, and the party seeking to do so will experience considerable difficulty in getting persuasive evidence of this kind before the court, especially because an independent social worker will seldom have the opportunity to see the children, in particular in the presence of the parties, and will therefore be at a considerable disadvantage when giving evidence, if indeed it is deemed admissible at all. The philosophy underlying the principle of confining the expert evidence as to the case generally to a welfare officer has been described by Hollings J. in relation to wardship proceedings:

> "the whole object, in my judgment, of a court welfare service, is to provide one service, one man or one woman, who will carry out the investigations which involve parties and their relationships and the conditions for the ward concerned and the relationship of the ward with his parents."[51]

Four principal reasons have been offered for the higher courts' marked absence of enthusiasm for social workers called by a party:—delay, avoiding the need for the child to undergo a number of interviews, the limited utility of an opinion where the expert has not seen the child and the need for confidential information to be kept within the smallest possible group of people.[52] The *Practice Direction* issued in relation to such evidence indicates the handicaps under which an independent social worker operates:

> "The Family Division of the High Court in matrimonial wardship or guardianship proceedings or any divorce county court in matrimonial proceedings may entertain the evidence of an 'independent' reporter but the following points should be noted.
>   1. No person (other than the party who instructs the 'independent' reporter) is under any obligation to discuss the case with or to be interviewed by the 'independent' reporter.
>   2. Where the child is a ward of court, the 'independent' reporter should not interview the child without leave of the court.

---

[51] *Re P. (A Minor)* [1989] 2 F.L.R. 43 at 49.
[52] *R. v. Sunderland Juvenile Court, ex p. G.* [1988] 2 F.L.R. 40. See also *Re C. (A Minor)* [1984] F.L.R. 419.

3. The 'independent' reporter may not see a report by the court welfare officer. This is confidential to the parties and the court.
4. The court welfare officer may not discuss the case with the 'independent' reporter unless authorised by the court.
5. Where the court has ordered an inquiry and report from a court welfare officer the court should not depart from the usual practice of relying on that report or of ordering a further report by a different court welfare officer.

Practitioners will bear in mind that the party wishing to obtain the services of an 'independent' reporter may if legally aided, need the authority of the area committee."[53]

Despite the lack of encouragement provided by the practice direction and the courts there is no doubt that a party may adduce expert evidence of a social worker without prior leave of the court, save in wardship proceedings,[54] though the court will nevertheless need to be persuaded that the evidence is relevant, and that there are no other reasons for refusing to admit it.[55] The evidence of a social worker has been held to be inadmissible where the proposed witness had a very limited knowledge of the facts, because the evidence would have to be confined to general observations about rehabilitation and access.[56] This illustrates a major difficulty with such evidence, which is that the proposed witness will almost certainly not have the extensive access to parties, children and other persons of which the court-appointed welfare officer has the benefit. The court must authorise for him to see confidential documents.[57] This may permit the court to refuse to receive any evidence of opinion other than from the court appointed reporter.

Because the court has available to it the court welfare service,[58] it should not itself appoint an 'independent' social worker.[59] It has been said to be doubtful whether in any event it has the power to do so in the absence of both parties' consent,[60] and on general principles this is probably so.[61] Where a party does engage a social worker to prepare a report and appear as a witness care should be exercised as to terminology. The courts have objected to the expression "welfare report" other than when the court welfare officer has prepared it,[62] and to the appellation "inde-

---

[53] See also *Re C. (A Minor)* [1984] F.L.R. 419.
[54] *Re C. (Wardship: Independent Social Worker)* [1985] F.L.R. 56.
[55] *R. v. Sunderland Juvenile Court, ex p. G.*, above n. 52.
[56] *Re C (Wardship: Independent Social Worker)*, above n. 54.
[57] *Ibid.*
[58] And such other persons as can be requested to investigate and report.
[59] *Cadman v. Cadman* (1982) 3 F.L.R. 275.
[60] *Ibid.*
[61] See Chap. 3, pp. 65–68.
[62] *Re El-G. (Minors)* (1983) 4 F.L.R. 421.

pendent," because this suggests that they are of equal status to the guardian *ad litem* or court welfare officer, whose independence is thereby somehow in question.[63] A party should also ensure that it has made prior application to the Legal Aid Area Committee for the cost of engaging a social worker, otherwise it may have to show that it was an unusual case.[64] An adverse order as to costs or the Legal Aid taxation may be considered by the court where a social worker is employed by a party after the court has refused to admit such evidence.[65]

B. OTHER EXPERTS' REPORTS

It is always open to a party to adduce any expert evidence it wishes, so long as it can be demonstrated to be relevant and of sufficient probative value. Where children are concerned, however, parties and their advisers should exercise great care before obtaining reports and calling witnesses for which the prerequisite is a medical, whether physiological or psychiatric, examination of the child. It is wrong for a mother to arrange on an access visit for the child to see a child psychiatrist without consulting the father or his solicitors.[66] In any event the weight of the evidence may be low if the professional has only heard one party's account of matters.[67] Likewise professionals should take care not to advise or encourage parties to take steps which are improper. A father should not on an access visit, advised by a doctor, have tape recorded the child's words for evidential use: it was a gross abuse of such a visit.[68] There is further discussion below as to the position where a guardian *ad litem* has been appointed.

The provisions of R.S.C. Order 38, Part IV apply in family cases unless the Matrimonial Causes Rules provide otherwise. R.S.C. Order 38, rule 36 does not apply to undefended divorces.[69] It may be advantageous for experts to meet without prejudice under R.S.C. Order 38, rule 38.[70] Such meetings are discussed in detail in Chapter 4. Experts in children cases

---

[63] *R. v. Sunderland Juvenile Court, ex p. G.*, above n. 52, at 51.
[64] *Bishop v. Wiltshire County Council* (1984) Fam.Law 118.
[65] *Re C. (Wardship: Independent Social Worker)* above n. 54.
[66] *Re A-W (Minors)* (1977) 5 Fam.Law 95. As to the necessity of obtaining leave before having a child examined psychiatrically in wardship cases, see *Practice Direction* [1985] 1 W.L.R. 360 and 1289. Leave for medical examination of a child allegedly sexually abused is by *inter partes* application to the Family Division, save in exceptional circumstances: *K.S.M. v. C.G.* (1988) 18 Fam.Law 173.
[67] *Ibid.* See also *B. (M.) v. B. (R.)* [1968] 3 All E.R. 170 at 174.
[68] *Re C. (An Infant)*, *The Times*, November 10, 1986.
[69] Matrimonial Causes Rules 1977 (S.I. 1977 No. 344), r. 42. As to county courts see C.C.R. Ord. 20, Pt. IV.
[70] See *Re J. (A Minor) (Expert Evidence)*, *The Times*, July 31, 1990, *per* Cazalet J.

should recognise their duty to give an independent opinion without bias to the party calling them, and should not mislead by omission.[71]

C. GUARDIAN AD LITEM

1 Introduction

Almost all proceedings concerning children permit the appointment of a guardian *ad litem* to represent the child's interests other than for the purpose of bringing proceedings. The guardian *ad litem* may take a number of forms, ranging from a relative or other person who simply attempts to act in the child's best interests in a decision-making capacity, perhaps also relaying the child's wishes to the courts, through to social work or other professionals whose task is, in addition to fulfilling this first function, to investigate the child's circumstances and act in effect as an expert witness in reporting facts and opinions to the court. It is the second category with which this section is principally concerned. Specific provisions cover the procedure for the guardian *ad litem*'s appointment and conduct in particular forms of legal proceedings.[72] Guardians *ad litem* are also much used in wardship proceedings, often in the guise of the Official Solicitor.[73] Where professional guardians *ad litem* are concerned panels of approved persons provide the courts with a statutorily monitored system of selection.[74]

Where the relevant statute or rules provide a discretion as to appointment, the Divisional Court (and Court of Appeal) will not interfere with a decision not to appoint a guardian *ad litem* unless no reasonable court could have come to that decision.[75] A guardian *ad litem* continues to act, in the absence of a contrary intention, for the appeal proceedings.[76] The duties of a guardian *ad litem* for a wife may be expressly extended to the ancillary relief part of divorce proceedings.[77] However, although a guardian *ad litem* has statutory status in the Juvenile Court, he has no inherent status or authority beyond that court, and has no *locus standi*

---

[71] See *Re J. (A Minor)*, above n. 70.
[72] See Adoption Act 1976, s.65(1)(*a*); Adoption Rules 1984 (S.I. 1984 No. 265), rr. 6 and 18; Magistrates' Courts (Adoption) Rules 1984 (S.I. 1984 No. 611), rr. 6 and 18; Children and Young Persons Act 1969, ss. 32A and 32B; Justices Clerks Rules 1970 (S.I. 1970 No. 231), r. 3 and Sched.; Matrimonial Causes Rules 1977 (S.I. 1977 No. 344), rr. 72, 112 and 115; R.S.C. Ord. 80; Magistrates' Courts (Young Persons) Rules 1988 (S.I. 1988 No. 913), rr. 31, 32 and 34.
[73] As to which, see below, pp. 393–395.
[74] Guardians Ad Litem and Reporting Officers (Panels) Regulations 1983 (S.I. 1983 No. 1908).
[75] *R. v. Plymouth Juvenile Court, ex p. F. and F.* [1987] 1 F.L.R. 169.
[76] *Re S.* [1959] 1 W.L.R. 921.
[77] *Bone v. Bone* [1953] 2 All E.R. 879.

greater than that of any other interested person to initiate wardship proceedings.[78]

2 Role in the proceedings

In adoption matters, the duties of the guardian *ad litem* are to investigate all the circumstances, including any reports, to advise as to the child's presence at the hearing, and to report.[79] He may also "perform such other duties as appear to him to be necessary or as the court may direct."[80] A reporting officer has duties to investigate and report in addition to his specific responsibility for ensuring full consent and witnessing the signature of the parent or guardian.[81] Where a report contains substantial criticism of a party, it should be disclosed so as to provide an opportunity for rebuttal, or the court should accede to a request for an adjournment.[82] Reports should not be delivered on the day of the hearing.[83] If the judge is to take into account any of the matters raised in the report, he must give any party affected the opportunity to answer any criticism in evidence.[84] It is a matter for the judge's discretion how best to achieve this, particularly where confidential matters are concerned.[85] Although a guardian *ad litem* has a status different from that of an expert witness, it is wrong for him to retire with justices (or the judge) for a "cosy chat," and this would justify a rehearing of the matter.[86]

Where, as is often the position in cases concerning children, a local authority is involved, the guardian *ad litem's* relationship with the authority is of considerable importance. Where there is a conflict arising out of their respective legal duties, they should seek directions from the court.[87] The guardian *ad litem* has duties to investigate all the circumstances. The local authority has a:

> "corresponding and reciprocal duty . . . to disclose to the guardian *ad litem* any major changes in the circumstances of the child which are proposed,"[88]

and a further duty:

---

[78] *A. v. Berkshire County Council* [1989] 1 F.L.R. 273; *Re T. (Minors) (Wardship: Jurisdiction)* [1989] 2 W.L.R. 954.
[79] See rr. 6 and 18 of both the Adoption Rules 1984 (S.I. 1984 No. 265) and the Magistrates' Courts (Adoption) Rules 1984 (S.I. 1984 No. 611).
[80] *Ibid.*
[81] *Ibid.*, r. 17.
[82] *R. v. West Malling Juvenile Court, ex p. K.* [1986] 2 F.L.R. 405.
[83] *Ibid.*
[84] *Re B., The Times*, October 21, 1983.
[85] *Ibid.* See also pp. 395–396.
[86] *Re B.* [1975] Fam. 127.
[87] *R. v. Waltham Forest London Borough, ex p. G.* [1989] 2 F.L.R. 138.
[88] *R. v. North Yorkshire County Council, ex p. M.* [1988] 3 W.L.R. 1344 at 1348.

"to listen to the views of the guardian *ad litem* . . . while a case is in train, the local authority ought not to make any major decisions without informing the guardian *ad litem* before the decision is made of the proposal and listening to her views."[89]

The local authority has a "grave responsibility" in this area which will only be fulfilled if "full consultation" is maintained throughout the court proceedings.[90] It was wrong to withdraw care proceedings without such consultation.[91]

3 Official Solicitor

Any dispute between parties about the appointment of the Official Solicitor, or another guardian *ad litem* in his place, is to be resolved by the court, for example where the Official Solicitor declines to act, but a party seeks a guardian *ad litem*, or where the Official Solicitor will act, but is not acceptable to a party.[92] Where a person of unsound mind is concerned, the Official Solicitor may act although no judicial inquiry has pronounced on the soundness of that party's mind, however some prima facie evidence should be forthcoming as to this.[93] In wardship proceedings, where a minor is joined as a party, the Official Solicitor should always be the first person to be invited to act as guardian *ad litem*.[94] The court should consider a number of matters with care before appointing a person other than the Official Solicitor in such circumstances, including:

> "whether there is some compelling reason why he or she should be preferred to the Official Solicitor; whether the alternative candidate possesses the necessary expertise and experience to undertake the work; and whether he possesses corresponding facilities to those available to the Official Solicitor of obtaining any psychiatric, paediatric or other expert evidence that might be required particularly at short notice. Further questions that should be considered, not only by the court but also by any prospective guardian, are as to his ability to obtain the legal representation necessary in the High Court and to obtain remuneration, not only for such representation, but also for himself: as I understand the position, the first is likely to be covered by legal aid, but not the second."[95]

The court should also have in mind the likelihood in wardship cases that

---

[89] R. v. *North Yorkshire County Council*, above, n. 88 at 1349.
[90] R. v. *Birmingham Juvenile Court, ex p. G. and R.* [1988] 1 W.L.R. 950 at 957.
[91] *Ibid.*
[92] *Re J. D. (Wardship)* [1984] 5 F.L.R. 359.
[93] *Wickens* v. *Wickens* [1952] 2 All E.R. 98.
[94] *Re J. D. (Wardship)*, above n. 92; *Re C. (A Minor)* [1984] 5 F.L.R. 419; *Re A., B., C. and D. (Minors)* [1988] 2 F.L.R. 500.
[95] *Re A., B., C. and D. (Minors)* above n. 94, at 503.

continuity of representation may be needed over a number of years.[96] Where in wardship two parties, perhaps a child and a minor or incapable parent, need a guardian *ad litem*, the court will consider inviting the Official Solicitor to act for the child, unless he has already acted for the parent in the present or other proceedings.[97] The court should then consider appointing a near relative, or a welfare officer.[98] Futhermore where parties disagree as to whether or not there should be a medical examination of and report upon the ward, the Official Solicitor should be appointed as guardian *ad litem*.[99] He may then, subject to any views the judge may have, decide whether an examination is necessary. It is wholly wrong for a party to arrange for such a medical examination without the Official Solicitor's consent where he already acts.[1] The view has been expressed, albeit *obiter*, that there is the added advantage that an expert instructed by the Official Solicitor is more likely to avoid the perils of being influenced in his views by the interests of the party for whom he acts.[2]

The Official Solicitor only acts for persons the subject of existing proceedings, and cannot institute proceedings, for instance on behalf of a child,[3] though where he is appointed as next friend he may take any measures on the child's behalf which will benefit the child in the litigation.[4] The Official Solicitor is ultimately responsible to the court, and subject to its authority. If the court decides that a medical examination or blood test of a child should take place, although it will always take account of their views, the Official Solicitor or other guardian *ad litem* cannot prevent this occurring.[5] There is no distinction between therapeutic and forensic examinations or tests where this principle is concerned.[6] In wardship proceedings no important step in the child's life should be taken without the court's consent, and this would extend to the medical examination of the ward.[7] The Official Solicitor's report to the court will be given considerable weight, and it will often be advantageous for this to be made with the benefit of having heard the other evidence in the case.[8] He may also be encouraged to continue to act after particular proceedings, both as to any subsequent proceedings and in the practical imple-

---

[96] *Re A., B., C. and D.* (Minors) above, n. 94, at 503.
[97] *Practice Direction* [1984] 1 W.L.R. 34.
[98] *Ibid.*
[99] *Re R. (P.M.)* [1968] 1 All E.R. 691 at 693. See also *Re S. (Infants)* [1967] 1 All E.R. 202 at 209.
[1] *Re R. (P.M.)*, above n. 99, at 692. See also *Re C., The Times*, November 10, 1986.
[2] *Re S.*, above n. 99, at 209.
[3] *Re D. (A Minor)* [1976] F. 185.
[4] *Ibid.* See also *Re Taylor* [1972] 2 Q.B. 369 at 381.
[5] *Re L.* [1968] P. 119.
[6] *Ibid.*, at 168. See also *Re S.*, above n. 99.
[7] *Re S.*, above n. 99; *Re L.*, above n. 5, at 168.
[8] *Re J. D.*, above, n. 92.

mentation of any order of the court.[9] Where relations between the parties are strained or otherwise difficult, he may be a useful channel of communication.[10]

4 Confidentiality of the guardian ad litem's report

In many proceedings the guardian *ad litem*, in addition to representing a child or other person's interests, is asked by the court to report, usually in writing. This report is in the nature of an expert's report containing both fact and opinion, although guardians adopt the practice in care proceedings of reporting only facts and preliminary opinions, reserving an overall view of the merits of the case until hearing the evidence of the other parties, or indeed of writing the entire report only after hearing the evidence. The fact that the guardian *ad litem* is appointed by the court, but acts nevertheless for a person interested in the proceedings, can place him in a somewhat ambivalent position, and this is particularly manifest in relation to the questions of confidentiality and disclosure of the contents of the report.[11] Similar difficulties may arise where the Official Solicitor acts as guardian *ad litem*.

The rules governing the appointment and conduct of a guardian *ad litem* may make specific provision for disclosure,[12] and where this is required before the hearing it must be provided to a party who requests it, and this should be done as early as possible, and preferably before the day of the hearing.[13] In other forms of proceedings, such as adoption, the report is entirely confidential, though the court has a discretion to disclose necessary material:

> "the parties have no right to see the reports except in so far as the justices or the judges think fit to disclose their contents at the hearing."[14]

Unnecessary secrecy should always be avoided if possible,[15] though in adoption matters there are often likely to be areas of necessary confidentiality such as the identity of prospective adopters.[16] A common problem is that the report may contain material which is critical of a party to the case, often a parent who is not regarded by the guardian *ad litem* as suitable to care for the child. In such cases the court must consider whether

---

[9] *Re J.D.*, above n. 92.
[10] *Ibid.*
[11] See also, pp. 399–401, below as to confidentiality in family proceedings generally, and above Chap. 9, pp. 195–202.
[12] Magistrates' Courts (Children and Young Persons) (Amendment) Rules 1984 (1984 S.I. No. 567), r. 20.
[13] *R. v. Epsom Juvenile Court, ex p. G.* [1988] 1 W.L.R. 145 at 149.
[14] *Re J. S.* [1959] 1 W.L.R. 1218 at 1221. See also *Re P. A.* [1971] 1 W.L.R. 1530.
[15] See, as to the Official Solicitor, *Re K.* [1965] A.C. 201.
[16] *Re M* [1973] 1 Q.B. 108 at 126.

the party should be informed of the critical material and be given an opportunity to rebut it.[17] It has been said to be a proper exercise of the judicial discretion to disclose to a party in adoption proceedings any allegation made against him, contained in confidential welfare report, which is relevant to the issue of adoption, particularly where the allegations:

> "have a direct bearing on whether he or she should be allowed to adopt the child or resist its adoption,"[18]

and there seems little reason why the same should not apply in relation to the report of a guardian *ad litem*, although the court must always exercise its discretion on the facts of the individual case.

The courts will always entertain suggestions as to a practical compromise. In *Re K.*,[19] Upjohn L.J. approved the "common-sense and excellent"[20] practice of showing the confidential material only to the legal representatives of the parties where allegations need to be met by the parties for whom they act.[21] This advantage should not in general however be extended to an independent social worker acting as expert witness for one of the parties.[22] A new trial may be ordered where the court has failed to provide a party with adequate information to launch a proper rebuttal, and has relied upon undisclosed material:

> "it is of prime importance that a party should not be sent away from the court with any justifiable grievance that he has not had the fullest opportunity of putting his case to the court and meeting any objection which the other side have succeeded in bringing to the attention of the judge."[23]

Reports should be forwarded to the judge's clerk where a party appeals.[24] The appeal court may then take its own view as to disclosure to the parties.

D. OTHER EVIDENTIAL CONSIDERATIONS

1 Hearsay

The question of the admissibility of hearsay evidence in family cases, particularly those involving children, has for some time been a vexed one.

---

[17] *Re C.* (1982) 3 F.L.R. 95.
[18] *Re G. (T.J.)(An Infant)* [1963] 2 Q.B. 73 at 97–98.
[19] [1963] Ch. 381.
[20] *Ibid.*, at 397; affirmed in the House of Lords: [1965] A.C. 201.
[21] See also *Re M.* [1973] 1 Q.B. 108.
[22] *R. v. Sunderland Juvenile Court, ex p. G.* [1988] 2 F.L.R. 40.
[23] *Re T.* (1982) 3 F.L.R. 183.
[24] *Re J. S.*, above n. 14.

The courts, and particularly those in which magistrates sit, have been subject to widely varying practice, arising in part out of the conceptual difficulties of the rule as it is usually applied, and in part out of a concern that the relative informality of family hearings should not be threatened by an unduly legalistic approach to the rules of evidence, particularly where the welfare of children is involved. In fact the proper evidential rules as to hearsay admit without difficulty a wider range of evidence than is often fully appreciated by magistrates. Courts often wrongly exclude evidence, for example of what children have said on a particular occasion, when it could properly be admitted as evidence of a state of mind, rather than of the truth of the statement itself. The opposite tendency, of admitting almost any statement by a child, particularly where it is reported by an apparently trustworthy professional witness (whether giving expert evidence or otherwise) is not unusual either.

Welfare reports in general may contain statements which offend against the hearsay rule,[25] although courts should be very wary of relying, in deciding a material issue, upon evidence which would otherwise be inadmissible. The recent attitude of the higher courts had been to restrict any trend towards the general admissibility of hearsay in children's cases where not specifically authorised by statute,[26] though the special nature of the wardship jurisdiction has been confirmed by the Court of Appeal to justify a more flexible approach, subject to the exercise of caution in the attribution of weight.[27] Even where a social worker gave evidence which consisted of 'double' and 'treble' hearsay the courts took the view that:

> "the court should not exclude hearsay ... but should carefully assess the weight to be attached to such indirect evidence."[28]

The matter has now been regularised, for proceedings in all courts in which issues concerning the welfare of children may arise save the Domestic Court, by the Children (Admissibility of Hearsay Evidence) Order 1990,[29] which came into force, both for existing and new proceedings, on March 10, 1990. Article 2 provides as follows:

> "(1) In civil proceedings before the High Court or a county court, evidence given in connection with the upbringing, maintenance or welfare of a child, shall be admissible notwithstanding any rule of law relating to hearsay.

---

[25] See Domestic Proceedings and Magistrates' Courts Act 1978, s.12(6); Guardianship Act 1973, s.6(3A).
[26] See *e.g. Bradford City Metropolitan Council* v. *K (Minors)* [1989] 2 F.L.R. 507.
[27] *Re W. (Minors) The Times*, November 10, 1989. See also *Re K. (Infants)* [1965] A.C. 201 at 245.
[28] *Re N. (Minors)* [1987] 1 F.L.R. 65.
[29] S.I. 1990 No. 143, introduced pursuant to the Children Act 1989, s.96(3) and s. 104(1).

(2) In civil proceedings before a juvenile court:—
    (*a*) a statement made by a child,
    (*b*) a statement made by a person concerned with or having control of a child, that he has assaulted, neglected or ill-treated the child,
    (*c*) a statement included in any report made by a guardian *ad litem* under rule 25(3)(*a*) of the Magistrates' Courts (Children and Young Persons) Rules 1988 or by a local authority under section 9(1) of the Children and Young Persons Act 1969,
shall be admissible as evidence in connection with the upbringing, maintenance or welfare of a child notwithstanding any rule of law relating to hearsay."

The High Court and county courts therefore have the widest possible capacity to hear evidence of a hearsay nature, whether from lay or expert witnesses, in any cases concerning the upbringing, maintenance or welfare of a child. Juvenile courts have a more restrictive role, though it is to be noted that nothing included in the report of a guardian *ad litem* will be excluded on hearsay grounds.

It is not entirely clear how the higher courts will interpret these new rules, though they undoubtedly render unauthoritative some of the more recent judicial pronouncements on the admissibility of hearsay evidence.[30] Welfare reports have been regarded as somewhat exceptional, in that much of the information gathered by a welfare officer is inevitably hearsay in form. Despite the new rules it is likely that the courts will continue to encourage welfare officers to attempt to confirm as much of this hearsay matter with direct observation, though it is always preferable for such hearsay information as is relied upon by the welfare officer to be recorded in his report, so that the court can test it by reference to other admissible evidence in the case.[31]

Regardless of the increased admissibility of hearsay evidence under the new rules, the courts will undoubtedly continue to be wary of attributing substantial weight to evidence which cannot be directly tested by cross-examination, and may decline to rely upon it where, for example, it relates to serious allegations against parents,[32] or where a local authority has been concerned with a case over a long period and can therefore only adduce documentary evidence as to the early part of that period.[33] If the

---

[30] Such as the cases cited in notes 26 and 27 above, *Re H.; Re K.* [1989] 2 F.L.R. 313 and *Bradford City Metropolitan Council* v. *K. and K.* [1990] Fam.Law 140.

[31] The use of hearsay material in welfare reports has been discussed in a number of decisions: *Thompson* v. *Thompson* [1986] 1 F.L.R. 212; *Malsom* v. *Malsom* (1982) 12 Fam. Law 91; *Webb* v. *Webb* [1986] 1 F.L.R. 462.

[32] See *Re N. (Minors)* [1987] 1 F.L.R. 65.

[33] See *Re P. (Minors)* [1987] 2 F.L.R. 421.

evidence is admissible, however, it cannot then be excluded on grounds of prejudice,[34] though this will be highly material to the attribution of weight.

Proceedings in juvenile courts, which may under the 1990 rules only admit certain classes of hearsay evidence, are civil proceedings, but ones to which the Civil Evidence Acts of 1968 and 1972 do not apply, so that these statutes may not be employed to adduce hearsay evidence inadmissible under the 1990 rules.[35] However the Evidence Act 1938 probably does apply to civil proceedings in magistrates' courts,[36] so that some statements in writing may be admissible under section 1 if the maker is not a "person interested in the case."[37] The section is probably limited to fact however, not extending to the opinions of experts.[38]

2 Privilege and confidentiality

Questions of confidentiality may arise in relation to reports prepared by welfare officers[39] and guardians *ad litem*,[40] whether because their contents should by their nature not be published generally, because they contain specific matters as to which questions of confidence and privilege arise, or because they contain facts or expressions of opinion which it is not in the child's interest that a party, usually a parent, should know. A welfare officer's report is confidential to the parties and the court for which it was prepared. It may be used in subsequent proceedings in a different court, but leave of the original court would be required.[41] A judge in subsequent proceedings cannot himself order its use, though he may impose an injunction preventing such use until the original court's leave has been obtained.[42] Issues of privilege and confidence may also however arise out of evidence given by experts simply as witnesses, whether in an independent capacity, or as a representative of a local authority or adoption agency. The general principles are discussed in Chapter 9.

While recognising that there is a small number of instances in which such considerations are paramount, the courts will proceed on the assumption that it is important that as much relevant evidence as possible should be available to them when making important decisions on issues such as the adoption, care and custody of children. They will therefore encourage any steps which may be taken to avoid the need for an exclu-

---

[34] *Bradford City Metropolitan Council* v. *K. (Minors)*, above n. 26.
[35] *Ibid.*
[36] *R.* v. *Wood Green Crown Court, ex p. P.* (1983) 4 F.L.R. 206.
[37] *Ibid.*
[38] *Ibid.*, at 216; *cf. Dass* v. *Masih* [1968] 1 W.L.R. 756 at 767.
[39] See above, pp. 381–387.
[40] See above, pp. 391–396.
[41] *Brown* v. *Matthews* [1990] 2 W.L.R. 879.
[42] *Ibid.*

sory decision, such as allowing a probation officer simply to refresh his memory from the confidential documents,[43] or encouraging psychiatrists to base their opinions upon material not subject to privilege, so that the parties were not frustrated by their inability to challenge their views.[44] Applications for disclosure of records and notes to which privilege may attach should be made at least a week before the hearing,[45] so that there is time to take such steps as best preserve the proper balance between confidence and openness. There is no material which is of such a nature that it will never be the subject of a disclosure order, at least to a limited extent. Thus disclosure may be ordered in adoption proceedings when the interests of justice require that information be passed to the Attorney-General.[46] In wardship proceedings the judge has a complete discretion, flowing from the paternal nature of the jurisdiction, as to whether disclosure should be ordered in the interests of the child's welfare.[47] The Official Solicitor should not submit confidential reports as a matter of routine, but only in exceptional circumstances where harm may otherwise be caused to the child.[48]

The court can always exercise control over the degree to which disclosure occurs, even where a subpoena is issued to a witness. In *Re M. (Minors),*[49] a wardship case, the parents of the ward issued a *subpoena duces tecum* requiring a probation officer to produce some records. The probation service asserted privilege based upon the fact that the records were kept pursuant to statutory rules, the Probation Rules 1965. Booth J. held that the subpoena itself only required the witness to attend court and produce, but not to disclose, the documents. Having produced them, the witness could then request a ruling from the court as to whether they were, in whole or in part, protected by privilege. There is no general power to order discovery in family proceedings involving children, so that the witness must be required to attend court, and each document considered individually as to relevance and privilege.[50] The issue of a *subpoena duces tecum* is a strong step to take, and parties should attempt to obtain voluntary disclosure before resorting to it, for example where medical records are concerned.[51]

The nature and extent of privilege in the public interest is discussed at length in Chapter 9, as is the authoritative decision of the House of Lords

---

[43] *Re M. (Minors)* [1987] 1 F.L.R. 46.
[44] *Re S. and W. (1982)* 12 Fam.Law 151.
[45] *Re P. (Minors) (Child Abuse)* [1988] 1 F.L.R. 328.
[46] *Ex p. Originating Summons in an Adoption Application, The Times,* June 4, 1990.
[47] *Re K.* [1965] A.C. 201.
[48] *Ibid.*
[49] [1987] 1 F.L.R. 46.
[50] *R. v. Greenwich Juvenile Court, ex p. London Borough of Greenwich* (1977) 7 Fam.Law 171.
[51] *Re S.L. (A Minor)* [1987] 2 F.L.R. 412.

in *D.* v. *N.S.P.C.C.*[52] In family as in other proceedings there is no fixed rule in any class of case. Even adoption agencies may be required to disclose their 'confidential' records if they cannot persuade the court that natural fathers will by such disclosure be dissuaded from coming forward to assist the agency in planning adoptions.[53] Furthermore it is misguided for parties or witnesses to attempt to place a blanket of confidentiality over a set or category of documents: each one must be considered on its merits, and a local authority in care proceedings should consider how much it can safely reveal, not how much it is entitled to conceal.[54] Local authorities concerned with care proceedings must approach the question of disclosure of documents, for example to parents who have allegedly sexually abused their child, on the basis that the child's welfare demands that the parents be given the fullest opportunity to test the evidence against them. This means that all relevant documents not subject to public immunity should be disclosed, a principle which is particularly important in the juvenile courts where there are no formal rules as to discovery.[55]

Any privilege is grounded not in the confidential nature of the documents, or evidence, but in the public interest.[56] Local authority records kept pursuant to a statutory duty may however have a good claim to privilege, and may indeed be regarded as prima facie privileged, only to be disclosed in the clear public interest.[57] They are probably in a special category of immunity, but the court must nonetheless exercise its discretion in relation to each document on its merits, and not simply refuse disclosure on principle. If necessary it should look at the document in order to decide, but only if there are definite grounds for so doing.[57a] The issue in the case is highly material, and may indicate where the public interest lies. Thus child care records may be protected against a "fishing expedition" in a damages claim.[58]

3 Weight

The weight to be attributed to the different aspects of the evidence is a matter entirely for the court. It must of course be guided by statutory

---

[52] [1978] A.C. 171.
[53] *R.* v. *Bournemouth Justices, ex p Gray, and ex p. Rodd* [1987] 1 F.L.R. 36. See also, as to the disclosure of adoption records, *Re An Adoption Application* [1990] 1 F.L.R. 412 and *Practice Note* [1990] 1 F.L.R. 414.
[54] *R.* v. *Greenwich Juvenile Court, ex p. London Borough of Greenwich*, above n. 50, at 172.
[55] *R.* v. *Hampshire County Council, ex p. K.* [1990] 1 F.L.R. 330 at 336.
[56] *Re M. (Minors)* above n. 43.
[57] *Re D. (Infants)* [1970] 1 W.L.R. 599.
[57a] *Re M.* [1990] 2 F.L.R. 36.
[58] *Gaskin* v. *Liverpool City Council* [1980] 1 W.L.R. 1549. This decision may however be of doubtful authority: see *Re M.* [1990] 2 F.L.R. 36.

words, for example where these require the welfare of a child to be accorded "first consideration"[59] or regarded as the "first and paramount consideration."[60] Where the interests of the child are the court's only statutory concern, it is wrong to balance them against some notional "rights" of the parents.[61] Where psychological or psychiatric evidence has been admitted, the court may properly be inclined to rely on its own inferences rather than the expert evidence where a child is happy and normal.[62] The psycho-analytical approach is not generally favoured by the judiciary in such circumstances,[63] assuming in any event that such evidence is admissible at all.[64] The court should be wary too of relying on documentary and hearsay sources, however admissible and however unimpeachable the source, where it may be unreliable for some reason. Thus the court was wrong to place great reliance upon a letter from a social worker which was not expected to be taken into account judicially.[65] Where evidence is convincing and weighty, it need not be corroborated. It is usually not necessary to call a number of members of the same care team, save in rare and exceptional cases.[66] Solicitors may be penalised in costs for unnecessary duplication of evidence.[67] However the probative value of expert evidence may be low if a child has seen a professional who has only been told the facts of the case by one of two parents in dispute.[68]

E. CHILD SEXUAL ABUSE

There is considerable dispute as to the reasons for the dramatic rise in the number of cases concerning child sexual abuse coming before the courts. It has been variously suggested that it is explained by an actual increase in its incidence, more awareness among social workers and other professionals of its prevalence, or the development of medical diagnosis techniques. It now appears unlikely that the first is a complete explanation, though it has also been suggested that social work and medical professionals in the field have overestimated the general level of such abuse, and have been on occasion too hasty to reach a positive finding or diag-

---

[59] Matrimonial Causes Act 1973, s.25(1) (as amended).
[60] Guardianship of Minors Act 1971, s.1.
[61] *Re P. (A Minor)* [1987] 2 F.L.R. 467 at 470.
[62] *J. v. C.* [1970] 726.
[63] *S. v. W.* (1980) 11 Fam.Law 81.
[64] See *R. v. Turner* [1975] Q.B. 834.
[65] *B. v. W* [1979] 1 W.L.R. 1041.
[66] *Re Yeomans (Minors)* (1985) 15 Fam.Law 121.
[67] *Ibid.*
[68] *Re A-W (Minors)* (1974) 5 Fam.Law 95. See too *B.(M.) v. B.(R.)* [1968] 3 All E.R. 170 at 174.

nosis.[69] What is certain is that the courts have been required very quickly to come to terms with the evidential difficulties presented by the range of family proceedings which may arise out of allegations of child sexual abuse. The principal difficulty in this field lies in the divergent requirements of evidence gathering for therapeutic or other medical purposes, and those for forensic purposes.

When the first substantial wave of such cases came before the higher courts, in the mid to late 1980s, there was undoubtedly a divergence of judicial view as to the appropriate response of the courts to the conduct of professionals in the child abuse field. This difference of approach has been expressly recognised in a least one case.[70] One strand of judicial opinion has adopted a somewhat sceptical approach to professional practice in the field, particularly in so far as children who may have been abused are interviewed, often with the aid of anatomically correct dolls, and positive findings of sexual abuse are made on the basis of answers to questions which may have been framed in a suggestive or presumptuous form.[71] Another approach, which may be said latterly to have gained in support in the higher courts, accepts that the predominant purpose of such interviews is not the gathering of evidence for forensic purposes. Thus, the courts must either make such evidential use as they properly can of the material gathered by the medical and other non-legal professionals, or at the most make suggestions as to the conduct of such interviews which do not undermine their medical purposes.[72] In particular it has been suggested that a video recording should where possible be arranged of any disclosure interviews, so that the court can itself see the exact circumstances in which particular allegations or suggestions were made, and so that other experts instructed by parties to the case can make their own observations as to the soundness of the procedures adopted and of the inferences to be drawn from the child's words and conduct.[73]

It has been emphasised however that such techniques are not helpfully viewed as themselves being on trial when such matters come before the court.[74] Furthermore medical interviews of this kind are "a pioneering technique undergoing a constant process of modification in the light of experience,"[75] to which the courts must continually adapt. One of the

---

[69] See Report of the Inquiry into Child Abuse in Cleveland 1987 (1988, Cmnd. 412).
[70] C. v. C. [1987] 1 F.L.R. 321 at 330, *per* Hollis J.
[71] See *e.g.* C. v. C., *ibid.*; *Re G. (Minors)* [1987] 1 F.L.R. 310; *Re E. (A Minor)* [1987] 1 F.L.R. 269.
[72] See *e.g. Re H. (Minors)* [1987] 1 F.L.R. 332; *Re W. (Minors)* [1987] 1 F.L.R. 297; *Re M. (A Minor)* [1987] 1 F.L.R. 293; *Re N. (Minors)* [1987] 1 F.L.R. 280; C. v. C. [1988] 1 F.L.R. 462.
[73] *Re M. (A Minor)*, above n. 72; *Re N. (Minors)* above n. 72; *Re Z. (Minors)* [1989] 2 F.L.R. 3.
[74] *Re H. (Minors)*, above n. 72, at 337.
[75] *Ibid.*, at 337–338.

most difficult aspects is the suggestion that it may be necessary for therapeutic or other medical reasons for the interview to be built upon the preconception, uneasy for courts which see themselves as the fact-finding forum, that abuse has in fact taken place. As Ewbank J. has observed:

> "may be this is necessary. It is not of course a very satisfactory preconception when the matter comes to court."[76]

There are two particular aspects of professional involvement in cases of alleged child sexual abuse. The first is the medical examination of children for physical signs of sexual abuse. There is considerable conflict of opinion within medical circles as to the appropriate procedures, and what inferences can properly be drawn from particular physical symptoms. These principal difficulties were analysed at some length during the Cleveland Inquiry.[77] Evidence as to such matters given in court presents no particular problems unfamiliar to the legal system, contentious and complex though the medical issues may be. The second aspect is the kind of technique developed at the Great Ormond Street Hospital, centred upon disclosure interviews with the child. These techniques, themselves still very much in the early stages of development, present a considerable challenge to traditional evidential principles, springing substantially from the fact that their purpose, form and frequently their assumptions are not those to which conventional evidential rules are easily applied.[78]

1 Interviews: forensic utility

Notwithstanding the reservations which have been judicially expressed about the manner in which interviews of children have been conducted, the courts now in general accept that, properly controlled, they can form a central and beneficial part of the medical investigation of child sexual abuse, and also have a therapeutic role. It is important however that, while the non-legal professionals may not be principally concerned with forensic needs, they are constantly aware of the possibility that such interviews may need to be analysed in the courts. In particular it must be recognised that the parties to any court proceedings may be entitled to call their own expert witnesses, who should be able to form their own judgments as to the conduct of the interview and the appropriate conclusions to be drawn from it. Where it does not materially interfere with the conduct of the interview, a video-recording should be made, as this is the only way to obtain a record which makes it possible to re-examine it

---

[76] *Re G. (Minors)*, above n. 71, at 315.
[77] Above n. 69.
[78] See generally, *ibid.*, Chap. 12.

from every aspect.[79] The demeanour of the interviewer and child, the tone of voice and manner of delivery of questions and answers are all of significance. It has been said that the evidential standing of such a video recording is doubtful,[80] but they are generally received in evidence in practice, if only because they are the 'best evidence' of what in fact occurred. Where it is not possible to make a video or other recording, an effort should be made to ensure the presence throughout of an independent psychiatrist or psychologist as observer.[81] Ultimately however a social worker, police officer or other participant or observer may give oral evidence as to what occurred, if this is the best evidence available.[82] The Cleveland Inquiry broadly supported the use of video recordings,[83] particularly because of the opportunity thus provided to other experts to observe and comment upon the interview thereafter.[84]

It has been suggested judicially that in some instances an interview may, quite apart from evidential considerations, be unhelpful to a family in which allegations of child sexual abuse have been made, whether because it may confirm in a mother's mind that her husband was guilty of abuse even though the court was not so satisfied,[85] or because a psychological social worker's unwarrantedly firm conclusion from such an interview may lead to a series of events seriously prejudicing the child and the father.[86] The courts appear generally however to have accepted that such interviews will continue to form an important element in the non-legal professionals' investigation and treatment of child sexual abuse, and that the role of the courts is limited to drawing such conclusions from them as can be evidentially justified, and making tentative suggestions as to how such interviews may be conducted and presented so as to be forensically useful. Their forensic utility may however be much reduced where it is judged clinically necessary to build into the interview the assumption that child abuse has taken place.[87] The suggestion that such interviews may only be in the child's best interests if such an assumption can justifiably be made,[88] which would mean that if the fact of sexual abuse was in issue in court the interview would be of little or no assistance, has not received general assent in the courts. Even where such an assumption has been clearly made, however, the interview may

---

[79] As to questions of disclosure to parties, and the likely attitude of hospitals to applications for disclosure, see R. Crewdson and C. Martin, "The Great Ormond Street Policy on Video Recordings," (1989) 19 Fam.Law 161.
[80] *Re E. (A Minor)*, above n. 71.
[81] *Re Z. (Minors)*, above n. 73.
[82] *R. v. Hove Juvenile Court, ex p. W* [1989] 2 F.L.R. 145.
[83] See, above n. 69, para. 12.53.
[84] *Ibid.*, para. 12.46.
[85] *C. v. C.* [1987] 1 F.L.R. 321.
[86] *Re E. (A Minor)* above n. 71.
[87] *Ibid.*
[88] *C. v. C.*, above n. 85.

retain some value as to issues such as access, which may remain an open question even after a positive finding of abuse by the court.

Latey J. has made some observations on the general approach to such interviews by those who organise and conduct them[89] which, though *obiter*, have since been approved elsewhere,[90] and provide helpful guidance to professionals in the field as to how, without undermining their clinical purpose and techniques, interviews may also assist in the forensic process.[91] Latey J. emphasised that he did not purport to be giving clinical advice, merely an indication of the usual evidential needs of the court. There were, said the judge, based upon the experience of the Great Ormond Street Hospital, two particular categories of case to be distinguished. The first was where there was already in existence clear evidence of abuse, possibly even supported by a conviction. In such a case the forensic aspect of the interview could generally be ignored. The second category contained a minority of cases, in which there was at the outset no more than a combination of alerting symptoms. Here, though the therapeutic purpose of the interview was the dominant one, the court may well need evidential assistance too. The medical team should make an appraisal before an interview as to which category the case fell into. If it was the second category, a number of points should be observed.

The interview should always be recorded on video as it is in the interests of justice between the parties that a full and independent record should be made. The court should be able to draw its own conclusions as to such matters as the precise questions put to the child, the intonation used in speech, and the gestures displayed. Furthermore it may well be that an expert not initially involved in the case will later be called upon to express an opinion on the interview, and he should not be placed at a disadvantage in so doing. Clinicians should attempt where possible to reconcile the needs of therapy with the evidential needs of the court. Where there has been an initial diagnosis that abuse has occurred, the interview should set out to "disconfirm" the diagnosis, because a positive diagnosis which survived this process would be the more valid. Those conducting and recording the interview should record and interpret indications of innocent as well as sinister events.

It can be envisaged that the guidance of Latey J. may be reluctantly followed in some instances in so far as it is suggested that interviews be conducted so as to disconfirm an initial diagnosis. Although no doubt this may yield forensically significant evidence, it must necessarily in some cases conflict with the primary, therapeutic, purpose of the interview.

---

[89] *Re M. (A Minor)*, above n. 72. These observations have been approved by the Court of Appeal in *Re W. (Minors)* [1990] 1 F.L.R. 203 at 214.
[90] *Re Z. (Minors)* above n. 73.
[91] These views were supported by Bush J. in *Re Z.*, above n. 90.

2 Conduct of interviews

The form of questions put to children during interviews is dictated by the purposes of the interview so far as the professionals conducting and organising it are concerned. There may be good reason in their experience to put questions in a form which would be either wholly inadmissible, or admissible only in limited circumstances, if the questions were put in court. There are three particular methods or forms of questioning which may raise difficulties: first, hypothetical questions, secondly, leading questions (suggesting, directly or by implication, the answer expected), and thirdly pressing the child to give answers which he or she is reluctant to give (treating as 'hostile' someone whose cause you are pursuing, in effect conducting a cross-examination of your own witness). It is clear, however, that the child's welfare may be best served in part by the successful pursuit of litigation resulting in protective orders for care, or custody and access. The interview may thus be counter-productive if, though the medical team satisfies itself as to diagnosis and therapeutic treatment, the form of the interview precludes the possibility of court protection for the child.

The courts will always however, and necessarily so, look at the individual circumstances of the case and the interview when deciding whether it should be admitted and what issues it, or a particular answer or behaviour elicited or demonstrated during its course, is probative of. The hypothetical question, for instance, is in general prohibited in court when put to a lay witness, who must describe only what he perceived through his senses, save where what he would have done in particular given circumstances is itself an issue in the case. A hypothetical question put to a child, however, may be highly probative. A young child asked, in the context of alleged sexual abuse, "if he did that, how would it feel?" may give an answer which a child could only give if he or she had knowledge outside the normal experience of his or her contemporaries.

If questions which would normally be forbidden when put in the course of court proceedings are to be admissible by way of medical interview it is clear that there must be some objective means for the court to assess their probative value. Thus, as already discussed, there should be a record, if possible by way of video recording, enabling independent persons, both experts within the field and the court, to assess the answers given in the light of all the circumstances of intonation and demeanour. The courts will be swift to disregard answers which, perhaps because they are negative, vague or unclear, do not permit an independent person to make a positive inference of abuse.[92] There has been something of a divergence of judicial view as to the correct approach to hypothetical and

---

[92] *Re E. (A Minor)*, above n. 71.

leading questions. Although the courts have emphasised their dangers, in some instances suggesting that they should be avoided,[93] it seems clear that the courts will consider the evidence of interviews containing such questions if they appear justified by the circumstances, and if they are put in a way which minimises the risks inherent in such forms of inquiry. Latey J. has said of an interview forming part of the evidence before him:

> "certainly there were some leading questions. Certainly there was some questioning on an hypothetical basis. But has anyone, in this country or elsewhere, yet found a way of leading a child along without use of these methods? It is how it is done that matters, and then the interpretation to be put on the answers and reactions of the child. The fact is in this case that a good deal of what was elicited from [the child] was spontaneous."[94]

It has been acknowledged by the courts that it may sometimes be justified to put pressure on a child who is unwilling to answer questions put neutrally or sympathetically, particularly where it is necessary to "match" the trauma of what has happened to the child[95] (if the allegations are correct). The court will however be wary that there may follow "a very real risk that the child will say that something has occurred which has not."[96] It is common practice for interviews to be conducted with the assistance of anatomically correct dolls. Such techniques are still in their experimental stage, and there remains considerable doubt as to whether they assist in eliciting the truth.[97] The courts have not however generally excluded such evidence, but accorded to it the weight which is appropriate in the circumstances given the professional controversy as to its utility, particularly in the light of the other evidence in the case. The Cleveland Report made the recommendation that such dolls should be used only by those "particularly qualified"[98] to do so, and not as a "routine prop"[99] in such interviews.

3 Weight

In so far as there has been a division of judicial opinion as to the reception of evidence in child sex abuse cases, this appears in general to have been resolved in favour at least of permitting almost all evidence, includ-

---

[93] C. v. C. [1987] 1 F.L.R. 321, *per* Hollis J.
[94] C. v. C. [1988] 1 F.L.R. 462 at 465.
[95] *Re N. (Minors)*, above n. 72, at 286.
[96] *Ibid.*
[97] *Ibid.*
[98] Report of the Inquiry into Child Abuse in Cleveland 1987 (1988, Cmnd. 412), para. 12.64. See also C. v. C. [1987] 1 F.L.R. 321 at 330.
[99] *Ibid.* It is clear that despite the clear views of the Cleveland Report and the higher courts, interviews employing such dolls continue to be conducted in an inappropriate manner: see *Re E., The Times*, April 2, 1990.

ing that of interviews with children, to be adduced before the court. Given this inclusive approach, however, there is obviously a need for some rigour in the attribution of weight to the various kinds of material before the court. Many of the reported decisions demonstrate a liberal approach to the question of admissibility, followed by a result in the particular case which demonstrates that the decision rests substantially upon those parts of the case which consist of evidence traditionally admissible and of clear probative value in any event. It has been said that diagnostic and therapeutic interviews form "a significant, but never an exclusive,"[1] part of the evidence. Evidence unrelated to the inferences to be drawn from an interview, such as the action of an alleged abuser in going openly and directly to the police and his doctor once an allegation had been made,[2] may be less equivocal and more reliable. Whether or not the court accepts the need for leading questions to have been put to a child in interview, answers which are given "unprompted" will be given more weight.[3]

Although the admissibility in evidence of an interview recorded on video is now not in doubt, presumably because this is preferable to other methods of relating the events recorded, its evidential value has been said nevertheless to be doubtful.[4] Waite J. has said that he has found a video recording:

> "helpful, but only in so far as it assists me to test the general probative value of the medical evidence. I do not see it as my function to draw any independent inferences of my own from what I have observed by viewing it. Like the evidence of the doctors themselves, it is part of the evidential fabric and no more than that."[5]

The video recording is, Waite J. has observed in another case, just a means of assessing the probative value of the interview.[6] It is however of central importance if the interview is to be adduced before the court, to the extent that the interview may be accorded no weight whatsoever if a video recording has been made but erased from the tape.[7] This must depend however on what other 'best' evidence is available.

It has become clear, in particular in the course of the Cleveland Inquiry, that apparently abnormal medical symptoms, though they may tend to show that sexual abuse has occurred, are not reliably regarded as themselves conclusive of abuse. This view has since found support in the

---

[1] *Re H. (Minors)* [1987] 1 F.L.R. 332 at 337.
[2] C. v. C., above n. 98.
[3] *Re X. (A Minor)* [1989] 1 F.L.R. 30.
[4] *Re E. (A Minor)* [1987] 1 F.L.R. 269. See also C v. C [1987] 1 F.L.R. 321, in which a similar view was expressed.
[5] *Re H. (Minor)* [1987] 1 F.L.R. 332 at 338.
[6] *Re W. (Minors)* [1987] 1 F.L.R. 297.
[7] C. v. C. [1987] 1 F.L.R. 321.

courts.⁸ Where such physiological evidence is concerned, consistency of technical language is essential.⁹

The courts will draw forensic inferences from diagnostic and therapeutic interviews, and are particularly assisted by the ability of professionals not originally involved in treatment of the child to comment upon their conduct with the assistance of a video recording. They should not do so, however, without having either been present at the interview or having seen and heard a full visual and sound record.¹⁰ Furthermore it has been said that social workers without expertise in psychology or psychiatry are not qualified to draw conclusions from disclosures allegedly made by children.¹¹ The fact that it is obviously of benefit for independent professionals to see video recordings does not mean that they are necessarily to be disclosed to lay parties in the case. Particular medical teams may take a strict view of the confidentiality of their relationship with the child as patient,¹² and the courts may need to adopt a pragmatic approach to evidential disclosure which serves the needs of justice without unnecessarily undermining professional confidences.¹³

The courts should in general have the benefit of expert assistance when considering the probative value of interview evidence recorded on video, especially where lay justices are concerned, being people:

> "exposed by the newspapers and by television to a host of 'expert' opinions on matters of this kind. If justices are likely to benefit from guidance, it is better that they should have it from an expert witness who can be cross-examined before them and whose views can be tested in that way rather than that they should act upon the half-remembered and untested opinions of others expressed in a wider context."¹⁴

Even judges may need to be wary of considering the particular issues before them as part of a wider controversy or campaign.¹⁵

Whatever expert evidence is before the court, however, the court must finally assess the issues, and must rest its decision upon "some evidence of significance,"¹⁶ not expert opinion which merely advises caution in

---

⁸ *Re Z. (Minors)* [1989] 2 F.L.R. 3.
⁹ Cleveland Report, above n. 98, para. 11.6.
¹⁰ *Ibid.*
¹¹ *Ibid.*
¹² See R Crewdson and C. Martin, "The Great Ormond Street Policy on Video Recordings" (1989) 19 Fam.Law 161.
¹³ See *e.g. Re H.* (1987) 17 Fam.Law 155, a county court decision in which the judge permitted a mother's legal and medical adviser to see the video recording, but the mother herself only a transcript of it, an approach broadly consistent with the decision in *Re K.* [1963] Ch. 381.
¹⁴ *R. v. Hove Juvenile Court, ex p. W.* [1989] 2 F.L.R. 145 at 155.
¹⁵ *Re F. (Minors)* [1988] 2 F.L.R. 123 at 130.
¹⁶ *Ibid.*, at 129.

general terms.[17] Indeed it may be, though it is a matter of some difficulty to establish a precise rule, that where serious allegations are made, against for instance the father of an allegedly abused child, the standard of proof should be higher than is necessary simply to make a finding that abuse of some kind has occurred.[18] Conversely, the court may be justified in finding that a child should not be left in his present environment, even though specific allegations of abuse are "incapable of formal proof."[19] It is perhaps the case that this latter approach is more easily justified within the paternal wardship jurisdiction than in other forms of proceedings where specific applications must be made and formally proved.

F. BLOOD AND OTHER SCIENTIFIC TESTS OF PATERNITY

In a number of proceedings concerning children the question of paternity may arise either as the principal issue in the case, or as a prerequisite to other questions, such as maintenance. The legal rules governing the scientific tests which may be ordered by the courts are discussed in Chapter 14.[20]

---

[17] *Re F. (Minors)* [1988] 2 F.L.R. 123.
[18] *Re G.* [1987] 1 W.L.R. 1461 at 1466.
[19] *Ibid.*
[20] At pp. 270–278.

CHAPTER 23

Criminal Sentencing

A. PROBATION OFFICERS

Probation officers have two principal functions in the court process. They may be asked to provide a report to the court upon an offender, either for general sentencing purposes or for a particular reason such as assessing suitability for a community service order, and they are also involved in the supervision and monitoring of the offender after sentence, in particular and most frequently in the case of probation orders, community service orders and supervision orders. Probation officers additionally provide a valuable informal function in acting as advisers to those who have come into contact with the courts in the past. The first of these functions is that which chiefly raises issues of expert evidence. The function of probation officers in relation to offenders under 13 is performed by local authority social workers, but there are regional variations as to responsibility for offenders aged 13 to 16.[1]

A Home Office Circular in 1986[2] set out guidelines as to the correct general approach of probation officers to the task of preparing and presenting social inquiry reports. Their task is to:

> "set the offending behaviour into the individual's social context, examine the offender's view of that behaviour, and assess the likely effect of the range of measures available to the court on the offender and any dependants."[3]

It is not a plea in mitigation on behalf of the offender but:

> "an impartial professional consideration of the circumstances which led to the commission of the offence and of the scope for minimising the risk of future offending."[4]

1 Obtaining a social inquiry report

Social inquiry reports are prepared either because the court has indicated that it requires one, or because the case falls into a category in which the local policy of the probation service is to prepare reports in advance of

---

[1] See Children and Young Persons Act 1969, s. 9 and s. 34(3).
[2] Circular 92/1986.
[3] *Ibid.*, para. 5.
[4] *Ibid.*, para. 6.

the main hearing where there is a likelihood that it will be of assistance.[5] A defendant, or his legal representative, has no right to commission a report from a probation officer without reference to the court.[6] Specific statutory provisions govern the circumstances in which the court must, or usually should, order a report. The court should not in acting pursuant to these be influenced by considerations such as the difficulty of obtaining a report or the seriousness of the offence if a report would be of assistance in sentencing.[7]

The court must before making a community service order consider a report from a probation officer or local authority social worker, and hear evidence from him if necessary.[8] Although the court must be satisfied that the offender is suitable for such an order, it is not bound by the assessment, although it would be very unlikely to depart from it, if it thought that order to be appropriate. The court must obtain a report on an offender under 21 before imposing detention in a young offender's institution or a sentence of custody for life,[9] unless it is of the opinion that it is unnecessary.[10] If in circumstances where justices decline to obtain a report they impose a sentence of over four months in a young offenders' institution, their reasons for so declining must be given in open court.[11] Where the offender is over 21 and has not been imprisoned before, but the court is considering imprisonment, they must obtain reports to determine whether there is any other way of dealing with him,[12] unless of the opinion that it is unnecessary.[13] A magistrates' court must express its reasons for not obtaining a report in such circumstances in open court.[14]

2 Content of the social inquiry report

The 1986 Home Office Circular gives detailed guidance as to the proper approach to the preparation and presentation of information and recommendations in the report. There is no objection to hearsay being included, or to the drawing of inferences from the facts. It should however make a clear distinction between fact and opinion, and between verified and unverified information.[15] Where important information is not direct evidence, its source should be stated, particularly where it concerns the facts surrounding the commission of the offence, and if the reporter

---

[5] Circular 92/1986, para. 17.
[6] R. v. *Adams* (1970) Crim.L.R. 693.
[7] R. v. *Massheder* (1983) 5 Cr.App.R.(S.) 442.
[8] Powers of Criminal Courts Act 1973, s.14(3).
[9] Criminal Justice Act 1982, s.2(2).
[10] *Ibid.*, s.2(3).
[11] *Ibid.*, s.2(6) and s.1(4).
[12] Powers of Criminals Courts Act 1973, s.20A. See also s.20.
[13] *Ibid.*, s.20A(2).
[14] *Ibid.*, s.20A(4).
[15] Circular 92/1986, para. 8.

has doubts about the truth or reliability of the information, he should express them.[16] He should provide details of the offender's criminal history, and ensure that he obtains the principal information from the police.[17] He may well however have had previous dealings with the offender, and therefore be able to provide such details from his own knowledge. It is not infrequently the case that the court thus becomes aware of convictions which the prosecution through administrative error is unable to provide. Reports should be expressed in language free from professional jargon or technical terms unfamiliar to the offender and the court.[18] The report may make an assessment of how far and by which means the offender might be encouraged and assisted not to repeat his offending behaviour, and review the sentencing options, the probation officers' function being to stop him reoffending.[19] He may make a specific sentencing recommendation if he feels able to, though if this includes supervision a plan should be outlined.[20] If a financial penalty is possible, the offender's means and commitments should be assessed.[21]

The courts have not sought generally to impose restrictions upon the manner in which recommendations are made in the report, and have reinforced the requirement that they focus on the needs of the offender, leaving to the court the question of the wider public interest.[22] Certain judges in the higher courts have though felt it necessary on occasion to criticise probation officers for taking an "unrealistic" approach, usually where non-custodial options have been extensively reviewed in the report in a case which could only justify a custodial sentence. Lawton L.J. has adopted this view in a number of cases,[23] his particular concern being that while a recommendation which was clearly inappropriate would carry no weight with an experienced judge, a recorder or bench of magistrates may not be so impervious to the report's influence. It may also place defence counsel in a difficult position if he feels he must, against his better judgment, attempt to support the recommendation in the report, and raise false hopes in the defendant of the prospect of success on appeal if the court does not follow the recommendation.[24] Perhaps an equally forceful reason for caution in this field is that if the court takes the view that a probation officer's recommendation as to sentence is completely

---

[16] Circular 92/1986, para. 8.
[17] *Ibid*, para. 8
[18] *Ibid*., para. 10.
[19] *Ibid*., paras. 12 and 13.
[20] *Ibid*., para. 14.
[21] *Ibid*., para. 15.
[22] See *R. v. Mulcahy*, March 29, 1977, C.A., reported in Thomas, *Current Sentencing Practice*, at L5.3(a).
[23] *R. v. Smith and Woolard* (1978) 67 Cr.App.R. 21; *R. v. Blowers* [1977] Crim.L.R. 51; *R. v. James* (1981) 3 Cr.App.R.(S.) 233.
[24] *R. v. Blowers* above n. 23.

misconceived, it could also doubt the worth of the remainder of the report, which may nonetheless contain useful information and observations as to the offender's circumstances which are relevant whatever the appropriate tariff may suggest. The danger of the probation officer recommending altogether too lenient a course is substantially reduced in the magistrates' courts, where because of the limits to custodial sentences which may be imposed the court will seldom wholly exclude consideration of non-custodial options.

However the probation officer's duty is to consider, from the offender's point of view, how to prevent him re-offending,[25] and if he is of opinion that this is best achieved by a particular, apparently lenient, course he would be evading his duty if he did not say so in his report. When taking an ostensibly unconventional approach however he should clearly set out the reasons for it,[26] so it is not assumed that he is simply giving the offender the benefit of his doubt.

3   Use of the report

The court has a complete discretion as to whether to follow or depart from recommendations in the social inquiry report. The court in adjourning for a report makes no implied promise that a non-custodial sentence will be imposed.[27] A copy of the report should be given by the court to the offender, or his counsel or solicitor, though if he is under 17 and unrepresented a copy need not be given to him, unless a parent or guardian is present in which case they should receive a copy.[28] The report should not be read aloud in court, unless the particular circumstances justify it.[29] The circumstances may justify reading aloud a small part of the report, although most proper functions of the court can be achieved by referring to particular paragraphs or lines by identification rather than verbatim repetition. The report should always be produced before mitigation, so that reference can be made to its contents.[30] Furthermore the offender's representative may wish to cross-examine the probation officer, and this he must be permitted to do.[31] If the officer who prepared the report is not, as frequently occurs, in court, an adjournment may be justified to secure his attendance for cross-examination. On no account should justices (or the judge) retire privately with the probation officer,

---

[25] See Home Office Circular, 92/1986.
[26] See the discussion in E. Stockdale and K. Devlin, *Sentencing*, (1987) paras. 4.24 to 4.26. See also the commentary on *R. v. Blowers* (1977) Crim.L.R. 51 at 51–52.
[27] Though see *R. v. Ward* (1982) 4 Cr.App.R.(S.) 103.
[28] Powers of Criminals Courts Act 1973, s.46(1) and (2).
[29] *R. v. Smith*, October 23, 1967, reported in Thomas, above n. 22, at L5.4(a).
[30] *R. v. Kirkham*, February 9, 1968, reported in Thomas, above n. 22, at L5.4(b).
[31] *Ibid.*

even where the purpose of such a course is to explore options more lenient than those which the court was initially considering.[32]

Probation orders The court will pay particular attention to a recommendation that a probation order be imposed[33] because the officer would not suggest it, having interviewed and investigated the circumstances of the offender, unless he felt that there was positive benefit to be gained from it, given that he or a colleague would be responsible for its supervision. The court may attach requirements to a probation order,[34] but before doing so it must obtain a report from the probation officer as to the offender's circumstances and the feasibility of securing compliance with the requirements which are being considered.[35] A day centre requirement must similarly be preceded by a report as to the availability of a place.[36] A requirement as to psychiatric treatment may only be imposed upon the report of a qualified medical practitioner,[37] and the court must be satisfied that arrangements have been made for his treatment,[38] although he may subsequently be transferred to a place providing more suitable medical treatment.[39] Where during the conduct of the treatment, or at its conclusion, the responsible medical practitioner takes the view that a variation of the requirement is justified, he must report to the supervising probation officer, who then applies for the variation at the supervising court.[40]

B. MEDICAL REPORTS

It is always open to the prosecution or the defence to adduce medical and, in particular psychiatric, evidence before the court on any sentencing issue to which it is relevant. In addition there are three particular circumstances in which such evidence is either mandatory, or almost so. First, where a requirement of medical treatment is proposed to be attached to a probation or supervision order, as discussed above. Secondly, where the defendant is or may be suffering from a relevant mental disorder, the Mental Health Act 1983 makes provision for certain orders and for the expert evidence which is prerequisite to their impo-

---

[32] *R. v. Aberdare Justices, ex p. Jones* [1973] Crim.L.R. 45.
[33] Under of the Powers of Criminal Courts Act 1973, s.2.
[34] As to requirements attached to a supervision order, see the Children and Young Persons Act 1969, s.12A(6) and s.12C.
[35] Powers of Criminal Courts Act 1973, s.2(3) and s.4A(1). Home Office Circular (28/1971) advises that a report should be obtained although not statutorily required for an order without conditions.
[36] *Ibid.*, s.4B(1).
[37] As to supervision orders, see the Children and Young Persons Act 1969, s.12B.
[38] *Ibid.*, s.3.
[39] *Ibid.*, s.3(5) and (6).
[40] *Ibid.*, Sched. 1, para. 4.

sition. Thirdly, where the court is considering imposing a sentence of life imprisonment and it has a discretion to do so. The last two circumstances are discussed below. The principles of admissibility and weight applicable to psychiatric and psychological evidence generally are discussed at length in Chapter 12.

1 The Mental Health Act 1983

The courts may make a number of orders under this Act where the defendant clearly or possibly suffers from a mental disorder as defined by the material sections of the Act, which all stipulate the medical evidence required before an order may be made. Three forms of order may be made before sentence for imprisonable offences,[41] each requiring expert medical evidence[42] to be obtained as a prerequisite.

First, under section 35 of the Act a person can be remanded to hospital for a report on his mental condition, when awaiting trial or sentence in the Crown Court or in a magistrates' court when awaiting sentence, or by consent, or where the court is satisfied that he did the act or made the omission charged.[43] The court must be satisfied on the written or oral evidence of a registered medical practitioner that the accused is suffering from a relevant mental disorder,[44] and that the report could not practicably be made if he was given bail.[45] The court must also be satisfied by report that proper arrangements have been made at the hospital.[46] Further such remands may be made upon further medical reports, if the making of the substantive report renders this necessary.[47] The accused may obtain his own medical report during such a remand if he seeks termination of the order.[48]

Secondly, the Crown Court may, under section 36 of the Mental Health Act 1983 remand the accused to hospital for medical treatment instead of remanding him in custody. The court must be satisfied as to the necessity for this upon the written or oral evidence of two registered medical practitioners. Similar provisions exist as for section 35 orders in respect of arrangements at the hospital,[49] further remands,[50] and the

---

[41] Other than those carrying a mandatory life sentence.
[42] See the Mental Health Act 1983, s.54(1) as to the qualifications required of the witnesses.
[43] Ibid., s.35(2)(b).
[44] Ibid., s.35(3)(a).
[45] Ibid., s.35(3)(b).
[46] Ibid., s.35(4).
[47] Ibid., s.35(5).
[48] Ibid., s.35(8).
[49] Ibid., s.36(3).
[50] Ibid., s.36(4).

liberty of the accused to obtain his own medical report to challenge the order.[51]

Thirdly, a magistrates' court or the Crown Court may after conviction and before sentence make an interim hospital order under section 38. Such an order may be made where the court considers that a full hospital order under section 37 may be appropriate, because of the nature of the offender's mental disorder.[52] The court may only act on the written or oral evidence of two medical practitioners,[53] and must be satisfied as to arrangements at the hospital.[54]

The chief substantive order in lieu of sentence which may be made pursuant to the 1983 Act is a hospital order under section 37. Both the Crown Court and a magistrates' court[55] may impose it. The court may only act upon the evidence, oral or written, of two registered medical practitioners.[56] It must be satisfied as to arrangements at the hospital.[57] The Crown Court, but not a magistrates' court, may additionally impose, upon a person subject to a hospital order under section 37, a restriction order. Section 41 provides for this in circumstances requiring the protection of the public. One of the registered medical practitioners whose evidence was adduced for the making of the hospital order must attend court and give oral evidence,[58] though no provision is made as to the nature of the evidence to be given.

2 Discretionary life imprisonment

Where the court is considering a sentence of life imprisonment, in circumstances in which its imposition is not mandatory, the court should order medical reports of a psychiatric nature unless exceptional circumstances indicate that they are unnecessary.[59] The circumstances in which a court does consider this sentence are likely to be those where the offender will potentially be a danger to the public over a long period, and this will almost certainly be founded upon mental instability of some kind.[60] Psychiatric evidence is almost invariably the only appropriate way of assessing this risk.[61] The court may exceptionally take a different

---

[51] *Ibid.*, s.36(7).
[52] Mental Health Act 1983, s.38(1)(*b*).
[53] *Ibid.*, s.38(1).
[54] *Ibid.*, s.38(4).
[55] The Magistrates' Court need not convict, but may merely be satisfied that the accused did the act or made the omission charged: Mental Health Act, s.37(3).
[56] *Ibid.*, s.37(2).
[57] *Ibid.*, s.37(4).
[58] *Ibid.*, s.41(2).
[59] R. v. *Virgo* (1988) 10 Cr. App. R(S.) 427.
[60] R. v. *De Havilland* (1983) 5 Cr. App. R(S.) 109.
[61] *Ibid.*

view if, in a case involving violence, "the very nature of the violence is such as to demonstrate the unstable character of an accused person,"[62] and that therefore the risk to the public of a determinate sentence is in any event too great.[63]

---

[62] R. v. *Virgo*, above, n. 59, at 431.
[63] R. v. *Virgo*, above, n. 59.

CHAPTER 24

Drink/Driving Offences

A. EXPERT EVIDENCE

Prosecutions for drink/driving offences have been challenged principally in two ways, as to both of which a substantial body of case law has emerged. First, the correctness of the procedures employed by the police, both at the roadside and thereafter, have been questioned, and secondly scientific analyses of blood alcohol levels have been attacked, both as to whether the correct results have been obtained, and as to what factual inferences can properly be drawn from them. The law however has been substantially revised.[1] One of the chief effects of these revisions has been the removal of the majority of defences based upon the former, procedural category of failures,[2] so that the courts may become substantially concerned with defences in the latter category, in which evidential considerations of a largely expert nature play a considerable part. The two principal statutory provisions out of which such questions arise are sections 5 and 6 of the Road Traffic Act 1972,[3] which are concerned with driving, attempting to drive or being in charge of a motor vehicle while unfit through drink or drugs (section 5), and when the proportion of alcohol in the breath, blood or urine exceeds the prescribed limit (section 6).

It may additionally, however, be necessary for a defendant to raise and prove issues of expert evidence, upon the balance of probabilities, in three particular circumstances. First, he may show that, though in charge of a vehicle while unfit or over the prescribed limit, there was no likelihood of his driving while in that condition.[4] Secondly he may, though having committed an offence of this kind, seek to avoid disqualification by showing the "special reason" that he was not aware how much alcohol he had drunk through no fault of his own, for example because his beer was "laced" with spirits.[5] Thirdly, section 10(2) of the Road Traffic Act 1972 provides that where a test has been performed as to the alcohol content in the breath, blood or urine of the accused in connection with non-drugs related offences under sections 5 and 6, "it shall be assumed" that the specimen given represented the alcohol level at the time of the

---

[1] In particular by the Transport Acts of 1981 and 1982.
[2] See the Road Traffic Act 1972 s.8(1), and *Fox* v. *Chief Constable of Gwent* [1985] R.T.R. 337, H.L.
[3] As amended.
[4] Road Traffic Act 1972, s.5(3) and s.6(2).
[5] *Pugsley* v. *Hunter* [1973] R.T.R. 284.

alleged offence. This assumption can be upset, however, if the accused shows, again on the balance of probabilities, that he drank such a quantity of alcohol, between the time of the alleged offence and the time the specimen was given, that if he had not done so he would prior to this drink have been under the prescribed limit or fit to drive.

1 The need for expert evidence and its admissibility

The prosecution can only prove that the accused exceeded the prescribed limit by adducing expert evidence, or by means of the print-out from a breath testing machine operated by a police officer trained in its use, who is probably an expert for that limited purpose if called. Likewise the accused cannot prove a particular alcohol level without expert evidence. In *D.P.P.* v. *Frost*[6] the accused was found in his car at night, stationary, and a breath test proved positive. His defence, which the justices accepted, was that he did not in fact intend to drive until some hours later, after 9 a.m. He was charged with being in charge of a vehicle while unfit and while over the prescribed limit. It was held that the justices could not properly find that he would have been under the limit by 9 a.m., on the balance of probabilities, without expert evidence as to the likely expulsion of alcohol from his body up to that time. By contrast it was open to them to decide, upon lay evidence alone, that he would by that time have been fit to drive, thus affording a defence to the section 5 charge.

Although the lay bench may draw the inference of unfitness from facts adduced from lay witnesses, such witnesses may not express the view that a person was unfit to drive. They may however say that a person was drunk, if they state the facts upon which that view is based.[7] Describing his general demeanour as "drunk" is a "compendious mode" of conveying a set of facts.[8] Medical opinion is however clearly admissible as to unfitness to drive, and of particular weight. A police surgeon may well examine the accused, and may express an opinion about fitness some time after arrest.[9] The fact that the accused drove normally for a time raises no presumption of fitness, and medical evidence is always admissible as to fitness notwithstanding that the accused's observed driving was safe.[10]

The admissibility of expert evidence is of course always dependent upon the nature of the issue and the wording of the statute. The assumption, contained in section 10(2) of the Road Traffic Act 1972, that the

---

[6] [1989] R.T.R. 11.
[7] R. v. *Davies (No. 2)* [1962] 1 W.L.R. 1111; *Sherrard* v. *Jacob* [1965] N.I. 151.
[8] See Chap. 1, pp. 20–21, where this exception to the rule as to lay opinion evidence is discussed.
[9] *Dryden* v. *Johnson* [1961] Crim. L.R. 551.
[10] *Murray* v. *Muir* (1940) S.C. (J.) 127.

level of alcohol in the accused's body is not less than that in the specimen, and that evidence of this level, if available, must always be taken into account was, until the decision of the House of Lords in *Cracknell* v. *Willis*,[11] thought to exclude, by the wording of the section, expert evidence as to the accuracy of the Lion Intoximeter 3000, a breath test device. It is now clear that its reliability may be challenged with any evidence, including that of experts. In the unlikely event that the prosecution calls totally unnecessary expert evidence, it has been held that the defence should in the interests of natural justice have the opportunity to cross-examine the expert.[12] This approach appears to be a doubtful one on general principles. If the evidence is unnecessary, it is irrelevant, and therefore inadmissible. The proper course would be for it to be ruled inadmissible, and for the court to make it clear, if the evidence has already been given, that it will not be taken into account.

2 Analysis of bodily samples

Evidence of the analysis of samples, whether of breath by an approved breath testing device, or of blood or urine by an analyst, may be given in documentary form. A breath testing machine print-out may be adduced if accompanied by a certificate signed by a constable[13] and if other rules as to service are complied with.[14] The defence may however require the constable's attendance.[15]

An authorised[16] analyst's laboratory result may likewise be adduced by certificate.[17] The accused may not require his attendance, as he should have been given part of the specimen which he may have analysed. If he elects to call his own analyst as an expert witness, the prosecution may well then call the authorised analyst in rebuttal. The authorised analyst may permit staff in his laboratory to do the analysis under his supervision[18]:

> "it is not incumbent on an analyst to perform every stage and step in the process of analysis himself or herself so long as the analyst is able to say that the analysis was overall under his or her supervision."[19]

Although the words "a laboratory test," which previously made it clear that the authorised analyst need not himself perform the actual analysis

---

[11] [1988] R.T.R. 1.
[12] *Young* v. *Flint* [1987] R.T.R. 300.
[13] Road Traffic Act 1972, s.10(3)(*a*).
[14] *Ibid.*, s.10(5) and 10(8).
[15] *Ibid.*, s.10(5) and 10(8).
[16] *Ibid.*, s.10(9).
[17] *Ibid.*, s.10(3)(*b*) and 10(8).
[18] *R.* v. *Kershberg* [1976] R.T.R. 526.
[19] *Ibid.*, at 532. See also *R.* v. *Rutter* [1977] R.T.R. 105.

no longer appear, the current statutory words do not alter matters. On general principles an expert may give evidence of results obtained not by him but by staff under his supervision,[20] and the Act does not exclude this.

Breath testing devices A number of machines have been approved for breath tests at a police station, when operated by a trained police officer. Such a trained officer may if necessary give oral evidence of the meaning of the symbols used on the print-out,[21] though in the great majority of cases the print-out, which is real evidence,[22] is simply adduced accompanied by a signed certificate as discussed above. The officer may also give oral evidence of the reading given by the machine where for some reason the print-out is not available.[23] There is a presumption, consistent with general evidential principles,[24] that the machine is operating reliably unless the contrary is proved.[25] A trained officer may give evidence that the accused's efforts resulted in a failure to deliver sufficient breath into the machine for a result to be obtained.[26] In all the circumstances, it is submitted that the trained officer acts as expert witness though police officers in general are not necessarily so.[27]

3 Weight

In drink/driving proceedings, as with all others, the degree of weight to be accorded to the expert evidence is a matter for the court, which must never allow "trial by expert" to occur.[28] A particular form of argument put on behalf of the defence in drink/driving cases arises where two analysts achieve results which diverge substantially. This is usually put in one of two ways: either that there is such a wide divergence between the two analyses that the court cannot be sure of either of them, or that the analyses diverge somewhat, and because the lower one is fairly close to, though in excess of, the legal limit, there must therefore be doubt as to whether the proper figure may not be slightly below the limit.

There is certainly no rule of law, or presumption, that because two analyses are wide apart there must be a doubt, and to suggest otherwise, the court held in *R. v. Sodo*,[29] would be "heresy". The two analyses in

---

[20] See *R. v. Kershberg*, above n. 18.
[21] *Gaimster v. Marlow* [1984] R.T.R. 49
[22] *Castle v. Cross* [1985] R.T.R. 62 at 68. See also *The Statue of Liberty* [1968] 1 W.L.R. 739.
[23] *D.P.P. v. Parkin* [1989] Crim. L.R. 379.
[24] *Tingle Jacobs & Co. v. Kennedy* [1964] 1 W.L.R. 638.
[25] *D.P.P. v. Parkin*, above n. 23, and see *Burditt v. Roberts* [1986] R.T.R. 391.
[26] *Castle v. Cross*, above n. 22, at 68.
[27] *R. v. Oakley* [1980] 70 Cr.App.R. 7.
[28] See the discussion of the 'ultimate issue', Chap. 7, pp. 150–154.
[29] [1975] R.T.R. 357.

that case were 86mg./100ml. and 48mg./100ml. There is no reason why the court should not attempt, if it is safe to do so, to choose between the two expert views.[30] Even if the two analysts' results are fairly close, for example one being 77mg./100ml. and the other being 83mg./100ml. (the legal limit is 80mg/100ml), the higher courts will not upset a finding of guilt, though such a result may be "surprising."[31] It is common for the prosecution analyst to make a deduction from his average reading to represent a margin for error in the accused's favour. There is no objection to the court applying the same margin to the defence analyst's result, thus indicating a level below the legal limit.[32] It should be noted that such a margin is reasonable because the analyst will usually discount any results which appear obviously erratic, and then take an average of the remaining figures. This is by contrast with the breath test, where the reading used is that relating to the lower of the two samples of breath given. Where analysts have used different equipment and methods of analysis, the court may elect to adopt the results obtained by the more modern and theoretically accurate equipment, though there is no other ground on which to fault the other analyst's results.[33] As with all evidence, there is no precedence of expert over lay witness evidence, or vice-versa. The court may prefer the factual evidence of the accused, or another lay witness, as to what he actually drank, to the expert evidence of analysts.[34]

The court must assess the reliability of analyses, whether by human analysts or by a breath testing machine, as it thinks fit. Grounds for doubting its reliability may be of a purely factual or of an expert nature. Even where, however, there is good reason to doubt the reliability of the results of a breath test upon expert opinion, the court must convict if the experts both agree that the accused must have exceeded the legal limit in any event.[35] Indeed it is necessary for an acquittal in such circumstances for the court to have before it expert evidence that the lower of the two readings may be inaccurate to such an extent that the sample of breath could have been below the limit.[36]

B. BLOOD SAMPLES

Where, for the reasons set out in section 8(3) of the Road Traffic Act 1972, a breath sample is not given, a blood or urine sample is taken.

---

[30] *R. v. Kershberg*, above n. 18, at 531–532.
[31] *R. v. Elliott* [1976] R.T.R. 308 at 313.
[32] *Walker v. Hodgins* [1983] Crim. L.R. 555.
[33] *Stephenson v. Clift* [1988] R.T.R. 171.
[34] *R. v. Marr* [1977] R.T.R. 168.
[35] *Gordon v. Thorpe* [1986] Crim. L.R. 61.
[36] *Newton v. Woods* [1987] R.T.R. 41.

Blood samples must be taken by a medical practitioner, who may prove that it was taken, and by consent, by certificate.[37] The specimen must if the accused requests it be divided into two parts, one of which is given to him for his own analysis should he seek one.[38] In taking a sample of blood from the accused the doctor does not act as agent of the police, and if he advises the accused as to how to act he does not offer an inducement or in any other respect make representations on behalf of the police or prosecution.[39] It appears however that if the accused submits to a medical examination having been told that the results would not be used in evidence they will be inadmissible.[40]

The doctor may decide how a blood sample is to be taken, and it constitutes a refusal under section 8(7) for the accused to insist on a particular method, unless the doctor's opinion is that there are good medical reasons for such a condition. A requirement that the blood be taken only from a finger was therefore a refusal.[41] Although the doctor has a discretion as to how the blood is taken, the procedure must comply with section 10(6). Thus, where a doctor took some blood from the accused's right arm, putting some into each of two bottles, then topped one bottle up with blood from a second specimen from the left arm, the statutory procedure had not been followed and the analysis results were inadmissible.[42]

Quality of the sample The sample which the accused receives, to be used for his own analysis if he wishes, must be capable of analysis by the use of ordinary equipment and ordinary skill by a reasonably competent analyst.[43] The burden of proof as to this is upon the prosecution.[44] In the days when gas chromatography equipment was not widely available it was held to be open to the court to rule a sample inadequate if it was too small for analysis by a pathology laboratory without such equipment.[45] Shortly afterwards, however, a sample was held adequate which because it had clotted could only be analysed on the more advanced gas chromatography equipment, because a wider range of analysts now had such equipment.[46] There is no rule of law, however, about what equipment should be available to analysts selected by the accused, it is a question of fact in the particular case. Equipment which is ordinary in London or

---

[37] Road Traffic Act 1972, s.10(4) and 10(5).
[38] *Ibid.*, s.10(6).
[39] See *R. v. Nowell* (1948) 32 Cr.App.R. 173; *R. v. Lanfear* [1968] 2 Q.B. 77.
[40] *R. v. Payne* [1963] 1 W.L.R. 637.
[41] *Rushton v. Higgins* [1972] R.T.R. 456.
[42] *Dear v. D.P.P.* [1988] Crim.L.R. 316.
[43] *R. v. Nixon* [1969] 1 W.L.R. 1055; *Smith v. Cole* [1970] R.T.R. 459.
[44] *Cronkshaw v. Rydeheard* (1969) 113 S.J. 673.
[45] *Ibid.*
[46] *Smith v. Cole* [1970] R.T.R. 459. In any event both analysts agreed that the accused must have been over the limit.

Manchester is not necessarily so in Bodmin or Inverness.[47] The fact that the prosecution's specimen was chosen at random is persuasive evidence, if it is capable of analysis to the appropriate standard, that the accused's specimen was also so capable.[48]

Longevity The sample must remain capable of analysis for a reasonable time, and this is a question of fact. The higher courts have declined to lay down guidelines, though it has been observed that it would certainly be unreasonable if it became unsusceptible to proper analysis after one hour, but unobjectionable if it became so after a year.[49] Within these parameters widely varying findings by justices have been supported on appeal, the matter being one of fact for them. Justices were entitled to find that the accused's sample was reasonable even though they accepted that it had deteriorated after one day, when the prosecution sample had not. The accused's sample was reasonable when handed to him, and this is when it must have the quality of suitability.[50] It must, however, when handed to him, be in "a condition which will enable it to remain suitable ... for a reasonable period of time."[51] The courts should however pay proper attention to doubts thrown upon the quality of blood samples by expert witnesses, in looking at the evidence as a whole, and must be satisfied that the totality of the evidence demonstrates to the criminal standard that the prescribed limit was exceeded by the accused.[52]

C. BACK-CALCULATION

Back-calculation, or back-tracking,[53] is a method by which an analyst may estimate the level of alcohol in an individual at a time some hours previous to that when a sample was taken. By the use of tables recording the rate at which alcohol levels rise and fall in persons of different size, weight, etc., a range can be estimated within which the individual's level is likely to have stood at the material time, usually when driving a motor vehicle. There is some controversy, both among analysts and in the medical profession, as to whether such a procedure is one which scientists should engage in, and in particular as to whether the calculation in a particular case can be performed with the degree of certainty appropriate to the forensic context, especially in criminal courts with the high standard

---

[47] *Nugent* v. *Hobday* [1972] Crim.L.R. 569.
[48] *Kierman* v. *Willcock* [1972] R.T.R. 270.
[49] *Thompson* v. *Charlwood* (1969) 113 S.J. 1004.
[50] *Ward* v. *Keene* [1970] R.T.R. 177.
[51] *R.* v. *Wright* [1975] R.T.R. 193, in which the accused's sample had deteriorated when analysed, three days after the prosecution's sample was successfully analysed. The accused's was held to be a reasonable sample.
[52] *Nicholson* v. *Watts* [1973] R.T.R. 208.
[53] *Gumbley* v. *Cunningham* [1989] 2 W.L.R. 1 at 6.

of proof which prosecution evidence must satisfy. The decision of the House of Lords in *Gumbley* v. *Cunningham*[54] has however confirmed that it is open not only to defendants seeking to prove issues on the balance of probabilities, but also to the prosecution to employ such evidence in support of its case, though it has purported to limit these circumstances somewhat. The House of Lords took the view that the words of section 10(2) of the Road Traffic Act 1972 clearly did not exclude such a procedure and that so long as certain safeguards were observed, courts could properly admit evidence in relation to it.

1 Admissibility

It has long been unequivocally open to the accused to adduce back-calculation evidence in support of the 'hip-flask' defence, where he asserts that he has drunk alcohol between driving and being tested, thus affording a complete defence,[55] and where, though guilty of an offence of drink/driving, he raised as a "special reason" why he should not be disqualified the fact that he had no way of knowing that some or all of what he drank contained alcohol.[56] In both cases the accused must establish on the balance of probabilities not only these facts, but that it is the particular drink consumed in these special circumstances which itself accounts for his being in excess of the prescribed limit.

In *Pugsley* v. *Hunter*,[57] a "special reasons" case, it was held by Lord Widgery that unless there is non-expert factual evidence upon which a layman can reliably and confidently say that the excess is explained by the circumstances in which the accused came to drink alcohol unknowingly (often, as here, by alleged 'lacing' of a drink containing little or no alcohol with a strongly alcoholic drink), the only way to discharge the onus is with medical evidence. It has subsequently, and it is submitted correctly, been observed that Lord Widgery probably did not intend, by use of the word "medical," specifically to exclude other scientific evidence, for example from a chemical analyst,[58] and indeed Cusack J., who sat with Lord Widgery, used the term "scientific."[59]

This decision has been confirmed as equally applicable in cases raising the 'hip-flask' defence. Thus unless the accused can show upon clear factual evidence that he drank only a very small quantity of alcohol before driving, but a much larger quantity after doing so and before being tested, he must adduce scientific evidence, which inevitably must

---

[54] *Gumbley* v. *Cunningham*, above n. 53.
[55] Road Traffic Act 1972, s.10(2).
[56] *Pugsley* v. *Hunter* [1973] R.T.R. 284.
[57] *Ibid*.
[58] *Dawson* v. *Lunn* [1986] R.T.R. 234 at 239, *per* Goff L.J.
[59] Above n. 56, at 292.

include a back-calculation. In *Smith* v. *Geraghty*,[60] a 'lacing' case, the logic of these decisions was not departed from, but Glidewell L.J. did attempt to restrict the circumstances in which such expert evidence was heard to those where there was "reasonably clear, straightforward and relatively simple evidence" available.[61]

It is now clear, as has been observed, that such evidence is also available to the prosecution to prove an offence of exceeding the prescribed limit under section 6 of the Road Traffic Act 1972,[62] and it should thus also be available in cases under section 5, both for the prosecution and for the defence. Defendants who wish to adduce such evidence would be well advised to avoid expensive adjournments by giving notice of intention to do so an adequate time before the hearing date so that the prosecution can obtain any rebuttal evidence it may wish to adduce.[63]

Reference to specialist published sources The expert witness will need to make reference, in performing and explaining a back-calculation, to tables of destruction rates which are based upon tests of different individuals of varying body-weight and other physical characteristics, with test results for a range of levels of alcohol intake. These may simply have been published by individual scientists, or they may have been produced as a result of the deliberations of a specialist committee under the auspices of a government department or professional body, such as the British Medical Association.

The expert may rely upon these sources even though they are hearsay in form, and despite the fact that he may have had neither any part in their preparation, nor any experience of the truth of the results in other circumstances.[64] The expert may also refer to general texts describing the effect of such things as eating food at the time of drinking alcohol. Under no circumstances however should the court attempt a back-calculation without proper expert assistance. *Dawson* v. *Lunn*[65] was described by Goff L.J. as demonstrating the:

> "dangers of laymen, in other words those who are not scientifically qualified, dabbling as amateurs in science."[66]

The defence had placed before justices an article from the *British Medical Journal* concerning the destruction rate of alcohol from the blood, a course to which the prosecution raised no objection. Such evidence is,

---

[60] [1986] R.T.R. 222.
[61] *Ibid.*, at 232. See further below, pp. 429-430.
[62] See *Gumbley* v. *Cunningham*, above n. 53.
[63] See *Pugsley* v. *Hunter*, above n. 56, at 292.
[64] *R.* v. *Somers* [1963] 1 W.L.R. 1306. See also *R.* v. *Abadom* [1983] 1 W.L.R. 126, discussed fully in Chap. 8, pp. 177–180.
[65] Above n. 58.
[66] *Ibid.*, at 238.

both as to back-calculation and generally, inadmissible unless adopted by an expert witness as part of his oral evidence.[67]

2 Limits to reliance upon back-calculation

While the technique of back-calculation has been ruled to be evidentially admissible in the circumstances already discussed, the higher courts have been concerned not to encourage justices to rely upon it uncritically when it is adduced by the parties. In cases where the accused seeks to raise a defence or special reason, even though the standard of proof to be achieved is the balance of probabilities, justices must exercise considerable care in their approach to such evidence. In *Smith* v. *Geraghty*,[68] a 'lacing' case, Glidewell L.J. said:

> "as a generality, it is in my view most undesirable that justices should be drawn into or allow themselves to be drawn into considering detailed calculations with all the variations which necessarily have to be built into such calculations, with the margins of error which there are."[69]

He described the circumstances in which justices should consider relying upon such evidence:

> "going back to the level of alcohol in the blood at the time of driving is clearly permissible but only practicable . . . provided that there is reasonably clear, straightforward and relatively simple evidence to show it."[70]

In *Gumbley* v. *Cunningham*, this approach was endorsed both in the Divisional Court and the House of Lords, as applicable to cases in which the prosecution seeks to prove an excess alcohol prosecution by back-calculation. Mann J. expressed the view that:

> "the prosecution should not seek to rely on evidence of back-calculation save where that evidence is easily understood and clearly persuasive of the presence of excess alcohol at the time when a defendant was driving. Moreover, justices must be very careful especially where there is conflicting evidence not to convict unless, upon the scientific and other evidence which they find it safe to rely on, they are sure an excess of alcohol was in the defendant's body when he was actually driving as charged."[71]

This approach was expressly approved in the House of Lords, though the

[67] *R.* v. *Abadom*, above n. 64.
[68] [1986] R.T.R. 222.
[69] *Ibid.*, at 232.
[70] *Ibid.*, at 232.
[71] [1987] 3 W.L.R. 1072 at 1080.

appeal did not concern this aspect of the case.[72] The courts appear therefore to be inviting justices to apply the burden and standard of proof rigorously at both stages of the process: first, in deciding whether the expert evidence is safe to rely on, and secondly, if it is, in drawing factual inferences from it as to guilt.[73] If in performing the first stage of this operation they demand that the evidence fulfils Glidewell L.J.'s requirement that it be "reasonably clear, straightforward and relatively simple," it may be suggested that evidence of back-calculation could never be admissible, certainly to support a prosecution, because it is an inherently complicated calculation. There are at least four variables to be accounted for:—

(i) rates of alcohol elimination vary widely as between individuals;
(ii) rates of elimination vary in the same individual on different occasions;
(iii) the concentration of alcohol in the body rises for a period, itself variable, before it begins to fall;
(iv) once elimination begins it does not occur at a steady rate.

It can be seen thus that any back-calculation is a very speculative exercise, before any account is taken of other relevant factors such as how much food has been consumed and when. As well as being inherently complicated, the evidence cannot easily be given in the "clear" terms that the criminal standard requires, because the most the expert can do, however precisely he has calculated, is to cite a wide range of possible alcohol levels inside or outside which he believes the accused must have been at the material time.[74] It is however a matter for the justices to decide whether these difficulties render the evidence so speculative as to be unreliable.

---

[72] [1989] 2 W.L.R. 1 at 6.
[73] See also *R. v. Platt* [1981] Crim. L.R. 332, C.A.
[74] See *e.g.* J. A. Dossett, (1987) 84 L.S.Gaz. 2925.

CHAPTER 25

Obscenity

A. GENERAL

A publication is obscene under the Obscene Publications Act 1959, section 1(1) if its effect is:

> "such as to deprave and corrupt persons who are likely . . . to read, see or hear the matter"

contained in the publication. The question whether a particular publication has this effect is one for the court, and expert evidence is not relevant or admissible, because a witness is in no better position to assess such moral or ethical questions than the court. However, by section 4(1) of the Act, the publisher may have a defence of "public good" if he can show that the publication is:

> "in the interests of science, literature, art or learning, or of other objects of general concern."

It is provided by section 4(2) that, where this defence is raised, expert evidence is admissible as to one specific issue of the defence:

> "the opinion of experts as to the literary, artistic, scientific or other merits of an article may be admitted in any proceedings under this Act either to establish or to negative the said ground."

The equivalent defence is available in respect of theatre productions under section 3(1) of the Theatres Act 1961, to which the same test of obscenity applies, when a production is held to be:

> "in the interests of drama, opera, ballet or any other act, or of literature or learning."

It will seen from the cases that it is important, from the point of view of expert evidence, to distinguish between the prior question whether something is in the interests of art, science, drama, opera, etc., upon which such evidence is admissible, and the secondary question whether it is, having surmounted that hurdle, and though "obscene," justified as being to the public good, which as with obscenity itself is a question for the courts alone, not for witnesses, lay or expert.

B. ADMISSIBILITY

1 Expert evidence inadmissible as to obscenity

Expert evidence may be adduced in relation to the issues in section 4(1) of the Obscene Publications Act 1959. Having adduced expert evidence upon these issues, its results may not be employed to negate a finding of obscenity under section 1.[1] This is because the "public good" defence only arises once it is established that an article is in fact obscene.[2] In *Att.-Gen.'s Reference (No. 3 of 1977)*[3] it was argued that the word "learning" in section 4(1) could include the "education" or "teaching" of individuals, and that publications might not be "obscene" for this reason. The court held however, adopting the expressions used in *D.P.P. v. Jordan*,[4] that section 1 was directed to something having "an immediate and direct effect on people's conduct or character,"[5] whereas section 4(1) was concerned with "inherent impersonal values of a less transient character."[6] As expert evidence could only be adduced as to the latter, the experts could not give evidence which tended to demonstrate the former. Therefore, "learning" was to be construed in its more limited sense of "the product of scholarship."[7] Any contention that the publication is in the public interest, because being obscene it is attractive to a number of people, if put, would have to be so put without expert evidence in support.[8] Such a contention is unlikely to succeed in any event because it tends to defeat the entire object of the Act.[9] Although it has been questioned whether the best results are achieved by excluding such evidence,[10] there is no doubt that the question of obscenity must be assessed by the jury alone unassisted by "expert, that is psychological or sociological or medical, advice."[11]

2 Expert evidence on factual issues prior to issue of obscenity

Although expert evidence is clearly inadmissible on the issue of whether something "tends to deprave and corrupt" and is therefore "obscene" within section 1, it may be admissible on subsidiary factual issues which

---

[1] *D.P.P. v. Jordan* [1977] A.C. 699 H.L. See also *Calder v. Powell* [1965] 1 Q.B. 539.
[2] *Att.-Gen.'s Reference (No. 3 of 1977)* (1978) 67 Cr.App.R. 393 at 396.
[3] *Ibid.*
[4] Above n. 1, at 718–719.
[5] *Att.-Gen.'s Reference (No. 3 of 1977)*, above n. 2, at 397.
[6] *Ibid.*, at 397.
[7] *Ibid.*, at 397.
[8] See *R. v. Summer* [1977] Crim.L.R. 362.
[9] *Ibid.*
[10] See *e.g. R. v. Anderson* [1972] 1 Q.B. 304 at 313.
[11] *D.P.P. v. Whyte* [1972] A.C. 849 at 862, *per* Lord Wilberforce.

relate to it, if these are beyond the knowledge and experience of the jury. In *D.P.P. v. A. and B.C. Chewing Gum*[12] the defendants were prosecuted for selling packets of bubblegum containing cards which were allegedly obscene. The prosecution called evidence of child psychiatrists as to the likely effect of reading the cards on the minds of children, who were clearly the major market for the bubblegum. The Court of Appeal stated that such evidence was admissible on this limited question, though not on the issue of obscenity itself:

> "it would be perfectly proper to call a psychiatrist and ask him in the first instance what his experience, if any, with children was, and to say what the effect on the minds of children of different groups would be if certain types of photographs or pictures were put before them, and indeed, having got his general evidence, to put one or more of the cards in question to him and say what would their effect be upon the child. . . . it would be wrong to ask the direct question as to whether any particular cards tended to corrupt or deprave, because that final stage was a matter which was entirely for the justices."[13]

It has been suggested in other cases that *D.P.P. v. A. and B.C. Chewing Gum* was "highly exceptional and confined to its own circumstances,"[14] and decided in "very special circumstances,"[15] although a judge in one of these cases appeared to be under the misapprehension that the expert psychiatric evidence had been said to be admissible upon the issue of whether the articles were obscene or not,[16] which the words of Lord Parker C.J. make it clear it had not.

There is however no need to treat the decision as exceptional, whether to the case of publications directed at children, or the particular type of publication, namely cards in bubblegum packets. For the particular effect of unusual material upon young minds, and the consequences this may have for the long-term psychological development of children, is not something which all or even most members of a jury can be expected to appreciate. It is therefore expert evidence admissible on ordinary principles. It is merely a more contentious example of kinds of circumstance in which expert evidence has in other cases been admitted on factual questions prior to the question of obscenity, but separate from the ultimate issue of whether the publication in fact tends to deprave and corrupt. Thus in *Shaw v. D.P.P.*[17] Ashworth J., at first instance, held that

---

[12] [1968] 1 Q.B. 159, C.A.
[13] *Ibid.*, at 164, *per* Lord Parker C.J.
[14] *R. v. Anderson*, above n. 10, at 313.
[15] *R. v. Calder and Boyars* [1969] 1 Q.B. 151. See also *R. v. Stamford* [1972] 2 Q.B. 391.
[16] *R. v. Anderson*, above n. 10, at 313, *per* Lord Widgery C.J.
[17] [1962] A.C. 220.

expert evidence (of prostitutes practising sadism) was admissible to assist the court with the meaning of an abbreviation allegedly used by a prostitute, namely "corr." Moreover in *R. v. Grossman and Skirving*,[18] a prosecution concerning a pamphlet describing methods of taking certain drugs, expert evidence was admissible as to the effects of cocaine, and in particular the consequences of persons ingesting it in the manner suggested in the pamphlet. The position, entirely consistent with *D.P.P. v. A. and B.C. Chewing Gum*, was stated to be as follows:

> "it is, of course, not possible to lay down rules which will be applicable to all types of potentially corrupting material. The effects of some will be within the experience of the ordinary man or woman and that is apparent from cases such as *D.P.P. v. Jordan*... In other cases matters will not be within the experience of the ordinary man or woman. On which side of the line any particular matter lies will be a question for the judge to decide. It may not be a decision which is easy to make but it is one he will have to make."[19]

3 Expert evidence on the "public good" defence

Section 4(2) provides that expert evidence may be given on the specific question of the "literary, artistic, scientific or other merits" of a publication,[20] but as has been seen this evidence may not extend to the question whether such merits as it may be found to contain in fact demonstrate publication to be to the "public good." Where such evidence is to be heard, the judge has a discretion as to whether the experts for the prosecution or defence are heard first.[21]

The expert may illustrate the literary or other merits of a book by means of a comparison with other books, but the comparison ceases to be legitimate when it extends to a discussion of the degree of obscenity of other publications which have not been prosecuted but are much read.[22] The issue of obscenity, indeed, apart from the question of expert evidence, must be related only to the publication in question, and not extend to comparisons.[23] Expert evidence may not be given to show that persons may be encouraged to read by the material, though it is obscene,[24] and the word "learning" in section 4(1) does not permit of evidence of edu-

---

[18] (1985) 81 Cr.App.R. 9.
[19] *Ibid.* at 16.
[20] Theatres Act 1968, s.3(2) likewise, permits expert evidence on the question of whether the performance is "in the interests of drama, opera, ballet or of any other act, or of literature or learning."
[21] *R. v. Calder and Boyars* [1969] 1 Q.B. 151.
[22] *R. v. Penguin Books* [1961] Crim.L.R. 176. Though *quaere R. v. Summer*, above n. 8.
[23] *R. v. Reiter* [1964] 2 Q.B. 16.
[24] *R. v. Summer*, above n. 8.

cation of this kind.[25] The public good defence however is ultimately a question for the trier of fact, whether or not expert evidence is heard. If therefore the court, having read the publication, disagrees with the expert evidence adduced by the defence, it may reject it.[26] This is particularly so because the onus of proof as to public good is, on the balance of probabilities, upon the defence.

---

[25] *Att.-Gen.'s Reference (No. 3 of 1977)*, above n. 2, at 397.
[26] *Calder v. Powell* [1965] 1 Q.B. 509 at 516.

Index

ABNORMALITY, MENTAL,
  rule as to, 229–232
ACCOUNTANCY EVIDENCE,
  auditing, as to, 288–289
  categories of, 286
  codes of practice as, 288
  generally, 286–287
  professional negligence, in cases of, 287–288
ACTUARIAL EVIDENCE,
  admissibility of, 280–283
  calculations, 279–280
  failure of courts to comprehend, 281, 283
  future loss issues, in, 281–282, 283–284, 285
  generally, 279
  hearsay, as, 283
  imprecision of, 281, 284
  limitations of, 282–283
  limited purposes, use of for, 280–281
ADMIRALTY PROCEEDINGS, 328–329
ADMISSIBILITY OF EVIDENCE,
  actuarial evidence, of, 280–283
  arbitration of construction claims, in, 362–364
  British Pharmacopœia, of, 181
  confessions, of, 232
  contract, in actions of, 158–161
  Coroner's Court proceedings, in, 320–321
  credibility of witnesses, of evidence as to, 154
  death certificate, of, 182
  determined by issue, 126–127
  dictionaries, of, 181–182
  drink/driving cases, in, 421–422, 427–429
  facts extrinsic to proceedings, of, 169–172
  forensic evidence, of, 260–262, 263–264
  generally, 10, 103, 121–124
  human nature, of evidence concerning, 153–154
  Lands Tribunal cases, in, 258–259
  lay standards, of, 154
  maps, of, 182
  market research surveys, of, 289
  meaning of words, of evidence as to, 155–158
  obscenity cases, in, 431, 432

ADMISSIBILITY OF EVIDENCE—*cont.*
  Official Referees' business, in, 356
  patents cases, in. *See* PATENTS CASES.
  photofit pictures, of, 182
  planning inquiries, in, 317–319
  pre-trial directions, when seeking, 35–36
  prior report of another expert, of, 167–169
  probative value, on account of, 4–5, 121–124
  psychiatric evidence, of, 232–235
  psychological studies of normal witnesses, of, 242
  records, of, 54–55
  relevance, on account of, 4
  sexual abuse cases, child, in, 408–409
  society of individuals, of research as to, 167
  statistical tables, of, 180–181
  statute, by,
    reports normally hearsay, of, 182–183
    statutory powers, of report of expert acting pursuant to, 169
  survey evidence, of, 165–167, 289
  textbooks, of, 174–176
  tracking dogs, of evidence relating to, 263
  ultimate issues, of questions on, 150–154
  valuation evidence, of, 248–252
  weight and, 205–206
AFFIDAVIT EVIDENCE,
  foreign law, in proof of, 303–304
  generally, 53–54
ANTON PILLER ORDER, 81–82
ARBITRATION PROCEEDINGS,
  construction claims, in,
    adducing expert evidence in, 359–360
    advantages of, 358–359
    admissibility of evidence in, 359
    arbitrator as expert, 359
    expert's fees as costs or damages, 360–362
    Institute of Civil Engineers Arbitration Procedure, 359, 360
    Joint Contracts Tribunal Arbitration Rules 1988, 360
    weight of evidence in, 364
  costs in, 224
  strict rules of evidence not applicable to, 322–324

INDEX

ARBITRATION PROCEEDINGS—cont.
  valuation, as to. *See* VALUATION OF LAND AND BUILDINGS.
ASSESSORS,
  Admiralty proceedings, in, 328–329
  advice given by, 71
  advisory role of, 72
  costs and, 224
  Court of Appeal and, 73
  expert evidence and, 72
  function of, 70–71
  industrial tribunal, right of to appoint, 311, 312
  nature of, 70–71
  nautical, 328–329
  planning inquiries, in, 315
  power of court to appoint,
    county court, in, 69–70
    High Court, in, 68–69
  remuneration of, 70
AUDITING EVIDENCE, 288–289
AUTOMATIC DIRECTIONS. *See* MEDICAL REPORTS: personal injuries cases, in.
AUTOMATISM,
  psychiatric evidence as to, 236

BACK-CALCULATION. *See* DRINK/DRIVING OFFENCES.
BIAS,
  expert witness, of, 114, 213–214
BLOOD TESTS,
  drink/driving cases, in. *See* DRINK/DRIVING OFFENCES.
  parentage, as to. *See* PARENTAGE, EVIDENCE OF.
BOOKS. *See* TEXTBOOKS.
BRITISH PHARMACOPŒIA,
  admissibility of, 181
BUILDING CLAIMS. *See* CONSTRUCTION CLAIMS.
BURDEN OF PROOF. *See* PROOF.

CATEGORIES OF EXPERT EVIDENCE, 9, 119
CHILDREN, PROCEEDINGS INVOLVING,
  confidentiality and, 200–202, 399–401
  disclosure and, 400
  guardian *ad litem* in,
    appointment of, 391
    duties of, 392
    generally, 391–392
    local authority, relationship of with, 392–393
    Official Solicitor as, 391, 393–395
    professional, 391
    report of, 395–396
    role of in proceedings, 392–393
    who may be, 391
  hearsay evidence in, 183, 396–399

CHILDREN, PROCEEDINGS INVOLVING—cont.
  improper advice as to, professionals giving, 390
  independent opinion, experts to give, 390–391
  medical examination of children in, 394
  medical reports in, 390
  paternity and. *See* PARENTAGE, EVIDENCE OF.
  privilege and, 200–202, 399–401
  sexual abuse cases,
    admissibility of evidence in, 408–409
    evidential difficulties presented by, 403–404
    incidence of, 402
    interviews in,
      beneficial to medical investigation, 404
      conduct of, 407–408
      forensic utility of, 404–406
      harmful to family, 405
      video recordings in, 404–405, 406, 409, 410
    weight of evidence in, 408–410
  weight of evidence in, 401–402
  welfare reports in,
    appeal cases, in, 382
    balanced view of facts necessary, 383
    conciliation concurrent with preparation of, 383–384
    confidentiality of, 399
    contents of, 382–383
    delay in preparation of, 384–385
    disclosure of, 385–386
    hearing case without, 385
    hearsay in, 397
    independent social worker challenging, 387–390
    interim reports, 385
    recommendations of, court departing from, 387
    "relevant" information, to contain, 382
    statutory provisions as to, 381–382
    welfare officer,
      duties of in preparing, 383
      evidence at hearing, giving, 386–387
      when ordered, 381
    without prejudice meetings in, 390
CLOSE OF CASES, EVIDENCE AFTER,
  civil proceedings, in, 114–115
  criminal proceedings, in,
CO-DEFENDANTS,
  psychiatric evidence as to disposition of, 238–240
COMMERCIAL COURT, PROCEEDINGS IN, 329–330
COMPARABLES. *See* VALUATION OF LAND AND BUILDINGS.

COMPELLABILITY OF WITNESS, 104–105
"COMPENDIOUS MODE" PRINCIPLE, 18, 20–21
COMPETENCE OF WITNESS, 104
COMPUTER EVIDENCE, 54–55
CONFESSIONS,
  admissibility of, 232
CONFIDENTIALITY,
  children, in proceedings involving, 200–202, 399–401
  exceptions to principal rule,
    court's discretion, 197–199
    statutory or other necessity, 196–197
  principal rule, 195–196
  public interest as matter of law, 199–202
CONFLICTING EXPERT EVIDENCE, 206–207
CONSTRUCTION CLAIMS,
  admissibility in, 362–364
  arbitration of. See ARBITRATION PROCEEDINGS.
  contractual obligations, expert evidence as to, 367
  damages, claims for in,
    quantum,
      delay, as to, 368–369
      generally, 368
    expert's fees as costs or damages, 360–362
    generally, 354
  negligence, expert evidence as to,
    case to be tried on own facts, 365
    codes of practice, relating to breaches of, 366–367
    need for, 364
    standard of proof required, 364–365
    unconventional nature of most cases requiring, 365
  Official Referees deciding. See OFFICIAL REFEREES' BUSINESS.
  weight of evidence in, 364
CONTRACT,
  claims in as to breach of professional standards,
    expert opinion as issue, 141–142
  construction of, evidence as to,
    customary meaning, 159
    factual matrix of parties and, 160–161
    generally, 158–159
CONTRADICTION WITHIN EXPERT EVIDENCE, 14–15
COPYRIGHT CASES,
  expert opinion in, 145
  surveys, evidence from in, 165–167, 289
CORONER'S COURT PROCEEDINGS,
  admissible expert evidence, 320–321
  inquisitorial nature of, 320
  procedure and practice in, 321–322
COSTS,
  adviser only, of expert as, 222

COSTS—cont.
  appeal hearings, of experts at, 222
  arbitrations, in, 224
  assessors and, 224
  cancellation fees, of, 223
  court experts and, 224
  criminal proceedings, in 225–226
  damages and, 218–221
  disclosure affecting, 221–222
  experts' fees and, 223–224
  generally, 216
  in-house experts and, 51, 216–217
  interpreters, of, 217
  Lands Tribunal, in, 258
  legal aid cases, in, 222
  limbs of claim which fail, of, 222
  necessity for expert evidence and, 216–218
  non-expert gathering evidence, of, 217–218
  number of experts and, 218
  partially allowable, 217
  pre-trial considerations, 221–222
  separation of, 217
  solicitor liable personally for, 222
  trial, considerations at, 222–223
  witness not called, when, 222, 223
COUNSEL,
  duties of when speaking to expert, 92
  report drafted by, 87–88
COURT APPOINTED EXPERTS,
  assessors. See ASSESSORS.
  Chancery Chambers, hearings in, 73
  costs and, 224
  county court, in, 64
  definition of "expert", 61, 62
  expert witnesses. See witnesses called by court, below.
  generally, 60
  infrequency of appointment of, reasons for, 64–65
  interpreters, 74–76
  patents cases, in, 374–375
  power to appoint, 61–62
  procedure following appointment of, 62–64
  referees, 73
  shorthand writers, 76–78
  witnesses called by court,
    expert witnesses, 67–68
    generally, 66
CREDIBILITY OF LAY WITNESSES,
  evidence as to, 154
CREDIT,
  cross-examination as to, 113–114
CROSS-EXAMINATION OF EXPERT WITNESSES, 112–114

439

DEATH CERTIFICATE,
   admissibility of, 182
DICTIONARIES,
   admissibility of, 181–182
   judicial notice of, 181–182
DIRECTIONS, AUTOMATIC. *See* MEDICAL
   REPORTS: personal injuries cases, in.
DIRECTIONS, PRE-TRIAL. *See* PRE-TRIAL
   DIRECTIONS.
DISCLOSURE,
   See generally REPORTS, EXPERTS':
      disclosure of,
   children, in proceedings involving, 400
   costs affected by, 221–222
   experts' reports, of. *See* REPORTS,
      EXPERTS'.
   guardian *ad litem*'s report, of, 395–396
   medical negligence actions, in, 38,
      338–339
   medical records, of, 353
   non-disclosure, when permitted, 85
   Official Referees' business, in, 355–357
   only issue when seeking directions, as,
      35–36
   order not made for, when,
      right of party to call evidence, 35–36
   personal injuries cases, in. *See* MEDICAL
      REPORTS: personal injuries cases, in.
   pre-trial rules, as rationale for, 32–33
   public interest and, 199–202
   rules not complied with, when,
      leave to adduce expert evidence, 103,
         110
   welfare report, of, 385–386
DISPOSITION, EVIDENCE OF CO-
   DEFENDANTS', 238–240
DISPUTED EVIDENCE,
   challenge of, 112
DNA TESTING. *See* PARENTAGE, EVIDENCE
   OF.
DOCTORS,
   hearsay evidence of, 164–165
DOCUMENTS,
   inspection of, 81–82, 83
   legal,
      construction of,
         foreign, 157–158
         generally, 156–157
   non-legal,
      meaning of, 158
   privilege and, 188
DOGS, TRACKING, 262–263
DRINK/DRIVING OFFENCES,
   admissibility of evidence in, 421–422
   analysis of bodily samples, evidence as to,
      422–423
   back-calculation,
      admissibility of evidence as to,
         427–429

DRINK/DRIVING OFFENCES—*cont.*
   back calculation—*cont.*
      controversy surrounding, 426–427
      "hip flask" defence, 427
      nature of, 426
      need for expert evidence in, 428
      reliance on, limits to, 429–430
      tables of destruction rates, reference to,
         428–429
   blood samples,
      longevity of, 426
      quality of, 425–426
      taking of, 424–425
   breath testing devices, 423
   challenging prosecutions for,
      420–421
   lay witness evidence, 421
   need for expert evidence in, 421
   police officer as expert witness, 423
   weight of evidence in, 423–424

EVIDENCE WRONGFULLY OBTAINED, 124
EXPERIMENTS UPON PROPERTY,
   civil proceedings, in, 79, 80–81
   criminal proceedings, in, 83
   death, in actions relating to, 82
   patents cases, in, 372–373
   personal injuries cases, in, 82
EXPERT, COURT APPOINTED. *See* COURT
   APPOINTED EXPERT.
EXPERTISE,
   assessing, 13
   degree of, 13
   field of,
      admissible, 125–127
      appropriate to case, 127–131
      novel sciences, 131–134
      scientific method, not subject strictly to,
         12
   imprecision of test of, 13
   possession of, 11–12
   weight attached to, 5, 12–13
EXPERT OPINION. *See* OPINION, EXPERT.
EXPERTS' REPORTS. *See* REPORTS, EXPERTS'.
EXPERT WITNESS. *See* WITNESS, EXPERT.
EXTRINSIC MATERIAL. *See* HEARSAY.

FACT AND OPINION,
   distinction between, 17–22
FACT, EVIDENCE OF,
   competence of witness and, 104
   expert witness giving, 170–171
   lay witness giving,
      general rule, 16–17
   patents cases, in, 370
   weight attached to. *See* WEIGHT OF
      EVIDENCE.
FEES,
   expert's, 223–224

FINGERPRINTS,
  evidence, as, 261–262
  taking of, 84
FOOTMARKS, 264
FOREIGN LAW, PROOF OF,
  affidavit evidence and, 303–304
  certificate of ambassador as, 304
  competence of expert witness in,
    academic study providing, 298–299
    counsel disbarred as witness, 302
    issue determining, 301
    legal qualifications in relevant country, 298
    non-lawyers, 299–300
    office, holding of as, 300–301
    practical considerations relevant, 301–302
    weight attached to evidence and, 302–303
  effect of law to be ascertained, 304–305
  expert evidence not required as to,
    precedent, provided by, 294–298
    statute, provided by, 294
  generally, 294
  interrogatories as evidence, 304
  judicial notice and, 294, 295
  judicial reliance on expert evidence, 306–309
  no expert evidence, when, 309
  oral evidence, requirement for, 303
  precedent, foreign,
    doubtful, when, 305–306
    when no, 305
  sovereign capacity, acts done in and, 309
  texts of foreign laws as evidence, 304
FOREIGN PROCEEDINGS,
  compellability of witness as to, 106
FORENSIC SCIENTIFIC EVIDENCE,
  analysis of substances, 263–264
  dogs, tracking, 262–263
  fingerprints, 261–262
  footmarks, 264
  generally, 260–261
  handwriting. See HANDWRITING, ANALYSIS OF.
  hypnosis, 264
  linguistic analysis, 264–265
  new forensic sciences, 264–265
  odontology, 264
  parentage, as to. See PARENTAGE, EVIDENCE OF.
  photofits, 265
  polygraphs, 264
  truth drugs, 264
  visual images of suspects, 265

GROUP REACTIONS. See OPINION, EXPERT.
GUARDIANS AD LITEM. See CHILDREN, PROCEEDINGS INVOLVING.

HANDWRITING, ANALYSIS OF,
  civil proceedings, in,
    generally, 269
    issues which may be canvassed, 269–270
    wills, relating to, 270
  criminal proceedings, in,
    expert, what constitutes, 266, 268
    expert witness, need for, 266–268
    ex improviso, 269
    genuineness of sample, proof of necessary, 266
    jury, warning to be given to, 268
    lay witnesses and, 266–268
    statutory provisions as to, 266
HEARSAY EVIDENCE,
  actuarial evidence as, 283
  admissible without expert evidence, 181–182
  children, in proceedings involving, 183, 396–399
  common law, exceptions to rule at, 184–185
  Civil Evidence Acts, under, 53–55
  comparables, in evidence of, 251–252
  doctors, of, 164–165
  extrinsic material and,
    adoption of, 181
    generally, 172–173
    influence on expert's opinion, as, 173–176
    specifically cited, 176, 181
  facts extrinsic to proceedings, comparison with as, 169–172
  generally, 162–163
  Lands Tribunal proceedings, in, 258–259
  market research surveys as, 289
  planning inquiries, in, 318
  prior report of another expert, relying on, 167–169
  psychiatric evidence and, 233
  Restrictive Practices Court, in, 325–326
  scientific teamwork, evidence gathered from and, 163–164
  social inquiry report, in, 413
  society of individuals, research into as, 167
  statute, admissible by, 182–183
  statutory powers, report of expert acting pursuant to as, 169
  surveys, evidence gathered from as, 165–167, 289
  tracking dogs, as to, 263
  written evidence, fo, 53–55
HIERARCHY OF EVIDENCE,
  no, 209–210
HISTORICAL DEVELOPMENT OF EXPERT EVIDENCE, 6–9

441

HOSTILE WITNESS,
   expert as, 111–112
HUMAN NATURE, ASSESSMENT OF,
   inadmissibility of questions of, 153–154
HYPNOSIS,
   forensic scientific evidence, as, 264
   use of, 242–243
HYPOTHETICAL QUESTIONS, 147–151

INDUSTRIAL TRIBUNALS, 311–313
IN-HOUSE EXPERTS,
   taxation of costs and, 51–216–217
INQUIRIES. See STATUTORY TRIBUNALS AND
      INQUIRIES; PLANNING INQUIRIES.
INSPECTION OF PROPERTY,
   civil proceedings, in, 80
   criminal proceedings, in, 83
   death, in actions relating to, 82
   patents cases, in. See PATENTS CASES.
   personal injuries cases, in, 82
INTELLIGENCE QUOTIENT (IQ),
   relevance of to criminal proceedings,
      231–232
INTERPRETERS,
   costs of, 217
   court appointed expert, as, 74–76
   privilege and, 190

JOINT WRITTEN STATEMENT. See WITHOUT
      PREJUDICE MEETINGS.
JUDICIAL NOTICE,
   custom, of, 25
   dictionaries and, 181–182
   facts in general, of, 23–24
   foreign law, proof of and, 294–295
   judges with personal knowledge, by, 27
   paradox inherent in, 23
   public policy, for reasons of, 22–23
   sovereignty, of, 26
   statute, stipulated by, 24–25
   technical term or phrase, of, 24
   territory, of, 25–26
   textbook, of, 174

KNOWLEDGE, SPECIALIST. See SPECIALIST
      KNOWLEDGE.

LANDS TRIBUNAL. See VALUATION OF LAND
      AND BUILDINGS.
LAY WITNESSES. See WITNESSES, LAY.
LEAVE TO ADDUCE EXPERT EVIDENCE,
   court's discretion to give, 53
   disclosure rules not complied with, when,
      103, 110
LEGAL AID,
   costs and, 222
LEGAL METHOD, 15–16
LEGITIMACY OF CHILD. See PARENTAGE,
      EVIDENCE OF.

LIE-DETECTORS. See POLYGRAPHS.
LINGUISTIC ANALYSIS, FORENSIC, 264–265

MARKET RESEARCH SURVEYS, EVIDENCE
      FROM,
   admissibility of, 289
   conduct of survey, stipulations as to,
      290–292
   disclosure of survey, 290, 292
   expert evidence, as, 289–290
   hearsay, as, 167, 289
   researcher as expert, 289–290
MEANING OF WORDS,
   legal documents, in, 156–158
   non-legal statements, of, 158
   statute, in, 155–156
MEDICAL EXAMINATIONS,
   children, of, 394
   civil proceedings, in, 81
   criminal proceedings, in, 84
   personal injuries cases, in. See MEDICAL
      REPORTS.
MEDICAL REPORTS,
   personal injuries cases, in,
      agreed reports,
         judge departing from, 352
         must agree, 349
         number of, 352
      oral evidence and,
         expert giving, 349–350
         plaintiff giving, 350–351
         plaintiff's condition changes before
            trial, when, 351–352
         procedure as to, 348–349
      amendments to, 334, 335, 336
      automatic directions,
         county court, in, 338
         inappropriate, when, 337–338
         medical negligence actions and, 338
         statutory provisions as to, 336–337
      changes in medical position and, 336
      contents of, 334, 347–348
      definition of, 334
      disclosure of medical records, 353
      documents in nature of pleadings,
         334–335
      further medical reports, 335
      interim report, 335
      lodging of, 353
      medical examinations,
         conditional agreement to undergo,
            party giving,
         different doctor to make
            examination, 343–344
         ousting rules of court, 340–341
         own doctor to be present, 341–343
         ethical duty of examining doctor,
            347
         joint examinations, 347

MEDICAL REPORTS—*cont.*
  personal injuries cases—*cont.*
    medical examinations—*cont.*
      party unwilling to undergo, when, 339–340
      tests during, 344–347
    medical negligence actions, 338–339
    other party's reports, adducing, 353
    preparation of,
      generally, 339
    service of by plaintiff,
      statutory provisions as to, 333
    statement of pecuniary loss, 334, 335
    statement of special damages claimed, 334
    summons for directions, 334–335
    without prejudice meetings, 352
  sentencing, issues relating to,
    life imprisonment discretionary, when, 418–419
    Mental Health Act 1983, under, 417–418
    when mandatory, 416–417
METHODS OF ADDUCING EXPERT EVIDENCE, 34–35, 135 *et seq.*

NATURE OF EXPERT EVIDENCE, 9, 119–121
NEGLIGENCE, CASES OF,
  expert opinion in, 141–145
NON-PROFESSIONAL STANDARDS. *See* OPINION, EXPERT.
NORMAL WITNESSES,
  psychological studies of, 242
NOVEL SCIENCES, 131–134, 264
NUMBER OF EXPERTS,
  costs and, 218
  directions as to, 36, 50–51

OBSCENITY,
  definition of obscene, 431
  expert evidence inadmissible as to, 431, 432
  factual issues prior to issue of, 432–434
  "public good" defence, 431, 434–435
OBSERVATION OF PROPERTY,
  civil proceedings, in, 80–81
  criminal proceedings, in, 82–83
  death, in actions relating to, 82
  personal injuries cases, in, 82
ODONTOLOGY, FORENSIC, 264
OFFICIAL REFEREES' BUSINESS,
  admissibility of evidence in, 356
  directions, duty to apply for in, 355–356
  disclosure, directions as to, 355–357
  generally, 354–355
  procedural considerations, 358
  schedules, use of in, 357
  "substance of evidence" in, 357
  without prejudice meetings in, 358

OFFICIAL SOLICITOR. *See* CHILDREN, PROCEEDINGS INVOLVING: guardian *ad litem*.
OPINION AND FACT,
  distinction between, 17–22
OPINION, EVIDENCE OF,
  competence of witness and, 104
  expert evidence not required to be, 120
OPINION, EVIDENCE OF,
  "facts" as, 17
  lay witness giving, 17–22
  special character of, 17
  weight attached to. *See* WEIGHT OF EVIDENCE.
OPINION, EXPERT,
  applying expertise to facts, 140–141
  factual comparisons as, 138–140
  factual foundations for, laying, 136–138
  generalisations as, 138
  group reactions, concerning, 145–146
  hypothetical questions and, 147–151
  non-professional standards, on, 146–147
  precision of, 136
  professional standards, on,
    court to set standard of care, 144–145
    opinion an issue, 141–142
    opinion not an issue, 142–144
ORAL EVIDENCE,
  admission of, 53

PARENTAGE, EVIDENCE OF,
  blood tests,
    children, on, 274–275
    court's discretion as to ordering, 274–276
    performance of, 274
    procedural rules of court, 274
    reluctance of party to undergo, 275–276
    statutory provisions as to, 270–273
  DNA testing, 273–274
  failure to undergo tests,
    adverse inferences drawn from, 275, 278
  probalistic nature of, 276–278
  standards of proof of, 276–278
PASSING-OFF CASES,
  expert opinion in, 145
  surveys, evidence from in, 165–167, 289
  ultimate issue, questions on in, 153
PATENTS CASES,
  admissibility in,
    common general knowledge, 379–380
    generally, 375–376
    obviousness, 379
    scientific background material, of, 380
    specification, meaning of and, 376–378
  court experts in, 374–375

443

INDEX

PATENTS CASES—cont.
  directions as to expert evidence in, 373–374
  experiments in, 372–373
  fact, evidence of,
    expert evidence usually, 370
  generally, 370
  inspections in,
    need for, 370
    secrecy and, 370–372
    statutory provisions providing, 370
    when ordered, 370
  meaning of words in, evidence as to, 157
  prima facie evidence in infringement, need for, 372
  surveys, evidence gathered from in, 165–167, 289
PERJURY, 214–215
PERSONAL INJURIES CASES,
  See generally MEDICAL REPORTS.
  adducing expert evidence in, 34n, 13, 35
  automatic directions in. See MEDICAL REPORTS: personal injuries cases, in.
  guidelines to principle of disclosure, as, 38
PHOTOFIT PICTURES,
  admissibility of, 182
  forensic evidence, as, 265
PLANNING INQUIRIES,
  admissibility of evidence in, 317–319
  assessor, appointment of in, 315
  hearsay evidence in, 318
  natural justice, need to observe in, 318
  procedure in,
    generally, 315–317
    pre-inquiry, 314–315
  rules governing, 313–314
  weight of evidence in, 319–320
  written statements for, 314–315
  written summaries for, 314–316
PLANS,
  accompanying report,
    disclosure of, 45
  preparation of by police, 84
POLICE OFFICER,
  expert witness, as, 131, 268, 423
POLYGRAPHS, 244–245, 264
PRE-TRIAL DIRECTIONS,
  admissibility of evidence and, 35–36
  agreement not to seek, 49–50
  all expert witnesses included in, 35
  application for made by one party only, 36
  court giving of own motion, 36
  disclosure only issue in, 35
  enforcement of, 49
  number of experts, as to, 50–51
  procedure, 36–37
  revocation of, 49
  time for applying for, 37

PRE-TRIAL DIRECTIONS—cont.
  variation of, 49
  without prejudice meetings, as to, 51–52
  See also REPORTS, EXPERTS': disclosure of.
PRE-TRIAL PROCEDURE,
  civil proceedings, in,
    court experts, appointment of, 55
    number of experts, directions as to, 50–51
    oral evidence, adducing, 53
    other party's report, adducing, 55–56
    statutory rules,
      complete code, constituting, 33–34
      county court, in, 31–32
      generally, 31, 34
      rationale for, 32–33
  criminal proceedings, in, 56–59
  See also PRE-TRIAL DIRECTIONS; REPORTS, EXPERTS': disclosure of.
PRIMARY EVIDENCE,
  definition of, 21
PRIVILEGE,
  disclosure and, 39
  documents, of, 188
  expert evidence not attracting, 193–194
  generally, 186–188
  legal adviser, of communications with, 188
  litigant, enforceable by, 186, 187
  party-party communications, of, 194–195
  self-incrimination, against, 187
  spouse, of, 187
  third parties, of communications with,
    "dominant purpose" rule, 190–192
    generally, 188–190
    interpreters, 190
    previous litigation and, 190
    several prospective defendants, where, 192–193
  waiver of, 187
  witness, attaching to, 187–188
PROBATION OFFICER. See SOCIAL INQUIRY REPORT.
PROBATIVE VALUE OF EVIDENCE,
  admissibility and, 121–124
  concept of, 4–5
  experts' and lay witnesses' evidence contrasted, 5
PROFESSIONAL STANDARDS. See OPINION, EXPERT.
PROOF,
  burden of, 203–204
  legal and scientific distinguished, 204
  standard of, 204–205
PROPERTY IN EXPERT EVIDENCE, 55–56
PROPERTY, PRESERVATION OF,
  civil proceedings, in, 80

PROPERTY, PRESERVATION OF—cont.
  criminal proceedings, in, 82–83
  death, in actions relating to, 82
  personal injuries cases, in, 82
PSYCHIATRIC EVIDENCE,
  abnormality rule, 229–232
  admissibility of, 232–235
  assessment of, 236–238
  automatism, as to, 236
  civil proceedings, in,
    sanity of individual, as to, 245–246
  co-defendants, as to, 238–240
  confessions and, 232
  defendant's choice as to whether given, 236
  diminished responsibility, as to, 235, 236, 237–238
  disposition, as to, 238–240
  generally, 229
  hypnosis and, 242–243
  intelligence quotient (IQ) as, 231–232
  jury's freedom to accept or reject, 236–237
  necessity for expert evidence, 236
  polygraphs and, 224–245
  truth drugs and, 243–244
  ultimate issue and, 233–235
  witness's mental abnormality, as to, 240–241
PSYCHOLOGICAL EVIDENCE,
  generally, 229
  normal witnesses, studies of, 242
PUBLIC INTEREST,
  confidentiality and, 199–202

RECORDS,
  admissibility of, 54–55
RELEVANCE OF EVIDENCE,
  admissibility and, 121
  concept of, 4
RELIABILITY OF WITNESSES,
  lay witnesses, 261
  mental abnormality and, 240–241
  psychological studies on, 242
RENT ASSESSMENT COMMITTEES. See
    VALUATION OF LAND AND BUILDINGS.
REPORTS, EXPERTS',
  adducing, 109–110
  agreeing, 88–89
  disclosure of,
    duty of expert, 41, 91–92
    enforcement of order for, 49
    entire report, of,
      advantages of, 40
    matters detrimental to case, of, 41
    medical negligence actions, in, 38, 338–339
    mutuality, principle of, 33, 43–44
    non-mutual, 48

REPORTS, EXPERTS'—cont.
  disclosure of—cont.
    partial disclosure, 39, 44–45
    personal injuries cases as guidelines to, 38
    personal injuries cases, medical reports in, 333–339
    plans accompanying report, 45
    privilege and, 39
    professional literature and, 45–46
    revocation of order for, 49
    sequential, 33, 46–48. See also
        MEDICAL REPORTS: personal injuries cases, in.
    simultaneous,
      personal injuries cases, not applying to, 335
    presumption of in rules, 33
    "special reasons" for not ordering, 37, 38, 39, 41–43
    statutory provisions as to, 37–38
    "substance of the evidence" to be disclosed, 40–41
    time for, 46–48
    variation of order for, 49
  drafting of,
    counsel, by, 87–88
    generally, 85–87
  form of, 84, 86
  non-disclosure,
    when permitted, 85
  other party's, adducing, 110
RESTRICTIVE PRACTICES COURT,
  adducing expert evidence in, 325–327
  hearsay evidence in, 325–327
  special nature of evidence in, 325
  trade witnesses in, 327–328
  unchallenged evidence in, 327
RULES OF EXPERT EVIDENCE,
  positive nature of, 3–4

SAMPLES OF PROPERTY,
  civil proceedings, in, 79, 80–81
  criminal proceedings, in, 83
  death, in actions relating to, 82
  personal injuries cases, in, 82
SANITY,
  evidence as to in civil proceedings, 245–246
SCIENTIFIC METHOD, 15–16
SCIENTIFIC TEAMWORK,
  evidence gathered from, 163–164
SECONDARY EVIDENCE,
  definition of, 21–22
SEXUAL ABUSE OF CHILDREN. See
    CHILDREN, PROCEEDINGS INVOLVING.
SHORTHAND WRITERS, 76–78
SKETCH OF SUSPECT,
  forensic evidence, as, 265

INDEX

SOCIAL INQUIRY REPORT,
  contents of, 413–414
  discretion of court to disregard, 415
  hearsay in, 413
  nature of, 412
  probation officer,
    approach of in preparing, 412
  probation order,
    recommendation for in, 416
  reasons for preparing, 412–413
  use of, 415–416
  when ordered, 413
SOCIETY OF INDIVIDUALS,
  research as to, 167
SOLICITOR,
  costs, personally liable for, 222
  professional, not expert, witness, as, 217
SPECIALIST KNOWLEDGE,
  tribunals possessing,
    lay tribunals, 26–27
    specialist tribunals,
      generally, 27
      judge as specialist, 28
STATISTICAL TABLES,
  admissibility of, 180–181
STANDARD OF PROOF. *See* PROOF.
STATUTES,
  meaning of words of, 155–156
STATUTORY TRIBUNALS AND INQUIRIES,
  generally, 310–311
  See also INDIVIDUAL TRIBUNALS.
SURVEYS,
  evidence gathered from, 167–167

TAPE-RECORDINGS,
  accuracy of, 83–84
TESTS ON PROPERTY. *See* EXPERIMENTS
  UPON PROPERTY.
TEXTBOOKS,
  admissibility of, 174–176
THEORETICAL KNOWLEDGE,
  expert possessing only, 129–130
TRADEMARKS CASES,
  expert opinion in, 145–146
  ultimate issue, questions on in, 153
TRIAL, EVIDENCE AFTER,
  civil proceedings, in, 116–117
  criminal proceedings, in, 117–118
TRIBUNALS. *See* STATUTORY TRIBUNALS
  AND INQUIRIES *and* Individual
  Tribunals.
TRUTH DRUGS, 243–244, 264

ULTIMATE ISSUE, QUESTIONS ON,
  credibility of witnesses and, 154
  civil proceedings, in, 150–151
  criminal proceedings, in, 151–153
  generally, 150
  human nature and, 153–154

ULTIMATE ISSUE, QUESTIONS ON—*cont.*
  lay standards and, 154
  psychiatric evidence and, 233–235

VALUATION OF LAND AND BUILDINGS,
  admissibility of evidence as to, 248–252
  arbitration normally used to settle
    disputes of, 247
  arbitrator, by,
    decision of contrasted with
      independent expert's, 254
    exclusion of from case, 256
    expertise, employing own, 254–255
    obligations of, 254–255
  art, not science, as, 253
  business accounts of tenant,
    irrelevance of to, 248
  comparables,
    generally, 248, 249–251
    hearsay and, 251–252
    Lands Tribunal cases, in, 257–258, 259
  expert evidence normally required in, 247
  higher courts,
    reluctance of to interfere in, 248
  information, need for fullest possible in,
    249
  joint instruction of independent expert,
    247
  Lands Tribunal, in,
    admissibility of evidence in, 258–259
    costs in, 258
    pre-trial procedure, 256–258
    statutory provisions as to, 256–258
    weight of evidence in, 258–259
  local knowledge, tribunal's, and, 255
  methods of, 252–254
  negligence of valuer, 247–248
  "non-speaking", 247
  open mind, need for expert to maintain,
    253–254
  practice and statutory requirements,
    relationship between, 248
  precise figures and, 254
  profits as basis for, 248
  rateable values,
    relevance of to, 249
  Rent Assessment Committee, by,
    general approach of, 253
    rules pursuant to statute, 254
    statutory powers of, 256
  rent for business purposes,
    main area of dispute in, as, 247
  review date,
    matters occurring after consideration
      of, 248–249
  "speaking", 247
  surveyor as expert, 247
  tenant's rights and, 249
  takings as basis for, 248

446

VALUATION OF LAND AND BUILDINGS—*cont.*
 trading figures and, 248
 tribunal's own expertise and, 254–256
 weight of evidence and, 252–256
 zoning, 250–251, 259
VISUAL IMAGES OF SUSPECTS, 265
VOICE-PRINTING, 264

WEIGHT OF EVIDENCE,
 admissibility and, 205–206
 appeal, on, 211–212
 children, in proceedings involving, 401–402
 conflicting expert evidence, of, 206–207
 foreign law, proof of and, 302–303
 Lands Tribunal, in, 258–259
 opinion and fact, of,
  court considering evidence of both, 208–209
  expert evidence alone, case tried on, 208
  generally, 207–208
  jury, directions to, 211
  preferring lay evidence, 209–211
 planning inquiries, at, 319–320
 valuation evidence, attaching to, 252–256
WELFARE REPORTS. *See* CHILDREN, PROCEEDINGS INVOLVING.
WILLS,
 handwriting analysis in, 270
WITHOUT PREJUDICE MEETINGS,
 children, in proceedings involving, 390
 conduct of, 98–99
 duty of experts to meet and, 90
 expert's evidence in court following, 97–98
 joint written statement,
  cannot be ordered, 52
  parties agreeing to be bound by, 97
  status of, 95–97
 medical reports and, 352
 Official Referees' business, in, 358
 pre-trial, 94–95
 statutory provisions as to, 51–52, 92–93

WITHOUT PREJUDICE MEETINGS—*cont.*
 when taking place,
  before or after exchange of reports, 93
  during trial, 93–94
WITNESS, EXPERT,
 bias of, 114, 213–214
 calling of, 106–108
 compellability of, 104–106
 compensation, rights of to, 223
 competence of, 104
 court calling, 67–68
 cross-examination of,
  credit, as to, 113–114
  disputed evidence, when, 112
  tribunal, by, 112–113
 definition of expert, 10–11
 duty of,
  evidence contrary to case and, 90–92
  generally, 5, 89–90, 135–136
 examination in chief of, 108–112
 generalist as, 127–128
 hostile witness, as, 111–112
 limited practical issue and, 130
 no property in, 105–106
 police officer as, 131, 268, 423
 qualifications of, establishing, 108–109
 qualifying due to particular circumstances, 130
 refreshing memory, 110–111
 secondary occupation and, 130–131
 theoretical knowledge only, possessing, 128–130
WITNESS, LAY,
 evidence of fact, generally confined to giving, 16–17
 evidence of opinion, giving, 17–22
 inability of to give expert evidence, 5
WITNESS OF FACT,
 expert as, 12–13
WORDS, MEANING OF. *See* MEANING OF WORDS.
WRITTEN EVIDENCE,
 admission of, 53–55

ZONING, 250–251, 259

447